HISTORY
OF THE
CHRISTIAN CHURCH

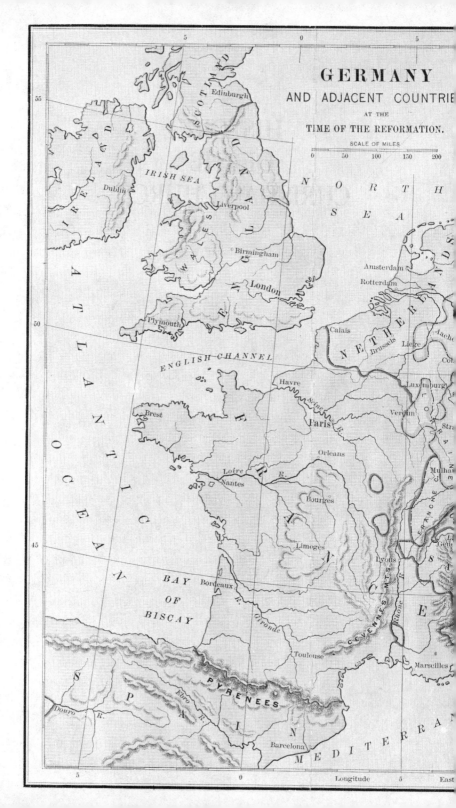

GERMANY
AND ADJACENT COUNTRIES
AT THE
TIME OF THE REFORMATION.

SCALE OF MILES

0   50   100   150   200

NORTH SEA

IRISH SEA

Edinburgh

SCOTLAND

IRELAND

Dublin

Liverpool

WALES

Birmingham

London

ENGLAND

Plymouth

ENGLISH CHANNEL

ATLANTIC OCEAN

Amsterdam

Rotterdam

NETHERLAND

Calais

Brussels   Liège   Aache

Luxemburg

Havre

Seine R.

Verdun

Paris

Str

Brest

Orleans

RAI

Loire R.

Nantes

Mulha

Bourges

FRANCE

Limoges

Lyons

BAY OF BISCAY

Bordeaux

Gironde

CEVENNES MTS.

Rhone

S

E

Toulouse

Marseilles

SPAIN

Ebro R.

PYRENEES

Douro R.

Barcelona

MEDITERRAN

Longitude   5   East

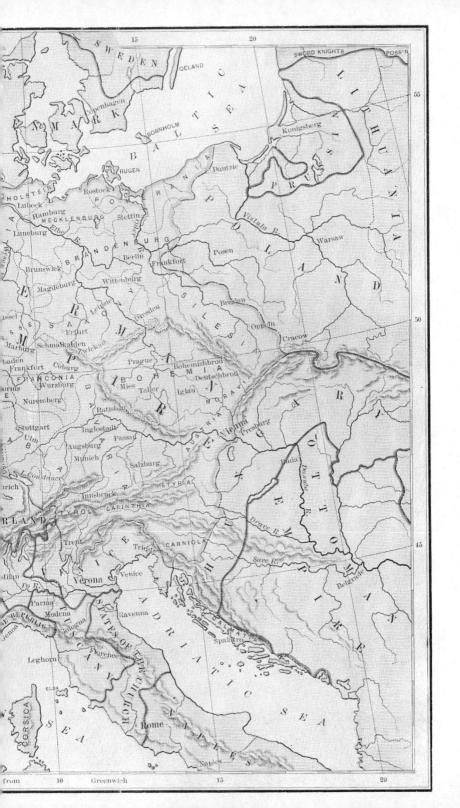

HISTORY OF THE CHRISTIAN CHURCH

Philip Schaff

Christianus sum. Christiani nihil a me alienum puto

VOLUME 7

THE GERMAN REFORMATION

The Beginning of the Protestant Reformation up to the
Diet of Augsburg
1517–1530

HENDRICKSON
PUBLISHERS

Hendrickson Publishers, Inc.
P. O. Box 3473
Peabody, Massachusetts 01961-3473

HISTORY OF THE CHRISTIAN CHURCH, 8 vols.
by Philip Schaff

Volume 1, originally published 1858; this printing, third edition, revised
Volume 2, originally published 1858; this printing, fifth edition
Volume 3, originally published 1867; this printing, fifth edition, revised
Volume 4, originally published 1885(?); this printing, first edition
Volume 5, by David S. Schaff, originally published 1907(?); this printing,
    first edition
Volume 6, by David S. Schaff, originally published 1910(?); this printing,
    first edition
Volume 7, originally published 1888; this printing, second edition, revised
Volume 8, originally published 1892; this printing, third edition, revised

Volumes 1 and 2 were originally published as a one-volume work. In the
original seven-volume series, published by Charles Scribner's Sons,
1882–1910, the current volumes 7 and 8 were combined into one volume,
in two fronts.

Second printing — January 2002

Printed in the United States of America

ISBN 1-56563-196-X

PREFACE.

I PUBLISH the history of the Reformation in advance of the concluding volume on the Middle Ages, which will follow in due time.

The Reformation was a republication of primitive Christianity, and the inauguration of modern Christianity. This makes it, next to the Apostolic age, the most important and interesting portion of church history. The Luther and Zwingli celebrations of 1883 and 1884 have revived its memories, and largely increased its literature; while scholars of the Roman Church have attempted, with great ability, an ultramontane reconstruction of the history of Germany and Europe during the period of the Reformation. The *Cultur-Kampf* is still going on. The theological battles of the sixteenth century are being fought over again in modern thought, with a slow but steady approach to a better understanding and final settlement. Protestantism with its freedom can afford to be fair and just to Romanism, which is chained to its traditions. The dogma of papal infallibility is fatal to freedom of investigation. Facts must control dogmas, and not dogmas facts. Truth, the whole truth, and nothing but the truth, is the aim of the historian; but truth should be told in love (Eph. 4 : 15).

The signs of the times point to a new era in the ever onward march of Christ's kingdom. God alone foreknows the future, and sees the end from the beginning. We poor mortals know only "in part," and see "in a mirror, darkly." But, as the plans of Providence unfold themselves, the prospect widens, old prejudices melt away, and hope and charity expand with our vision. The historian must be impartial, without being neutral or indifferent. He must follow the footsteps of Divine Providence, which shapes our ends, and guides all human events in the interest of truth, righteousness, and peace.

I have collected much material for a comprehensive history of the Reformation, in the libraries of Europe, during several summer visits (thirteen in all), and digested it at home. I have studied the Luther literature in Berlin, the Zwingli literature in Zürich, the Calvinistic literature in Geneva and Paris, the English and Scotch Reformation in London, Oxford, and Edinburgh. Two years ago I revisited, with great satisfaction, the classical localities made memorable by the Reformation, — Wittenberg, Eisleben, Eisenach, the Wartburg, Halle, Leipzig, Jena, Weimar, Erfurt, Gotha, Heidelberg, Zürich, Geneva, — and found kind friends and Christian brethren everywhere. At Marburg, Coburg, Augsburg, I had been before. By way of contrast I made in the same year an interesting tour through Roman-Catholic Spain, the land of Ferdinand and Isabel, Charles V., Philip II., and Ignatius Loyola, and compared her former and present state with the Protestant North. In Italy I have been three times, including a three-months sojourn in Rome. A visit to the places of events brings one nearer to the actors, and puts one almost into the position of a witness.

This volume embraces, besides a general introduction to modern church history, the productive period of the German Reformation, from its beginning to the Diet of Augsburg (1530), and the death of Luther (1546), with a concluding estimate of the character and services of this extraordinary man. I have used the new Weimar edition of his works as far as published; for the other parts, Walch and the Erlangen edition. Of modern Protestant historians I have chiefly consulted Ranke (my teacher), and Köstlin (my friend), with whose views on Luther and the Reformation I am in essential harmony. I have also constantly compared the learned Roman-Catholic works of Döllinger, and Janssen, besides numerous monographs. The reader will find classified lists of the sources and literature in all leading sections (e.g., pp. 94, 99, 183, 272, 340, 399, 421, 494, 579, 612, 629, 695, 706), and occasional excursions into the field of the philosophy of church history (as in the introductory chapter, and in §§ 49, 56, 63, 79, 87, 99, etc.). In these I have endeavored to interpret the past in the light of the present, and to make the movements of the sixteenth century more intelligible through their results in the nineteenth. For we must judge the tree by its fruits. "God's mills grind slowly, but wonderfully fine."

I am conscious of the defects of this new attempt to reproduce the history of the Reformation, which has so often been told by friend and foe, but too often in a partisan spirit. I have done the best I could. God expects no more from his servants than faithfulness in the use of their abilities and opportunities.

THE AUTHOR.

NEW YORK, September, 1888.

CONTENTS

HISTORY OF THE REFORMATION.

CHAPTER I.

ORIENTATION.

MEDIÆVAL AND MODERN CHRISTIANITY.

		PAGE
§ 1.	THE TURNING POINT OF MODERN HISTORY	1
§ 2.	PROTESTANTISM AND ROMANISM	3
§ 3.	NECESSITY OF A REFORMATION	8
§ 4.	PREPARATIONS FOR THE REFORMATION	12
§ 5.	THE GENIUS AND AIM OF THE REFORMATION	14
§ 6.	THE AUTHORITY OF THE SCRIPTURES	16
§ 7.	JUSTIFICATION BY FAITH	20
§ 8.	THE PRIESTHOOD OF THE LAITY	24
§ 9.	THE REFORMATION AND RATIONALISM	26
§ 10.	PROTESTANTISM AND DENOMINATIONALISM	43
§ 11.	PROTESTANTISM AND RELIGIOUS LIBERTY	50
§ 12.	INTOLERANCE AND LIBERTY IN ENGLAND AND AMERICA	71
§ 13.	CHRONOLOGICAL LIMITS	86
§ 14.	GENERAL LITERATURE ON THE REFORMATION	89

FIRST BOOK.

THE GERMAN REFORMATION, TILL THE DIET OF AUGSBURG.

1517–1530.

CHAPTER II.

LUTHER'S TRAINING FOR THE REFORMATION (1483–1517).

		PAGE
§ 15.	LITERATURE ON THE GERMAN REFORMATION	94
§ 16.	GERMANY AND THE REFORMATION	97
§ 17.	THE LUTHER LITERATURE	99
§ 18.	LUTHER'S YOUTH AND TRAINING (with Luther's portrait)	105

PAGE

§ 19. LUTHER IN THE UNIVERSITY OF ERFURT 109
§ 20. LUTHER'S CONVERSION 112
§ 21. LUTHER AS A MONK 113
§ 22. LUTHER AND STAUPITZ (with portrait of Staupitz) . . 117
§ 23. LUTHER'S EXPERIENCE OF JUSTIFICATION 122
§ 24. LUTHER ORDAINED TO THE PRIESTHOOD 125
§ 25. LUTHER IN ROME (with portrait of Luther by Giorgione) . . 126
§ 26. THE UNIVERSITY OF WITTENBERG (with illustration) . . 132
§ 27. LUTHER AS ACADEMIC TEACHER TILL 1517. HIS EXEGETI-
      CAL LECTURES 135
§ 28. LUTHER AND MYSTICISM. THE THEOLOGIA GERMANICA . 141
§ 29. THE PENITENTIAL PSALMS. THE EVE OF THE REFORMATION. 143

CHAPTER III.

THE REFORMATION FROM THE PUBLICATION OF LUTHER'S THESES TO THE DIET OF WORMS (1517-1521).

§ 30. THE SALE OF INDULGENCES 146
§ 31. LUTHER AND TETZEL 148
§ 32. THE NINETY-FIVE THESES (Oct. 31, 1517) 155
      NOTES. — TEXT OF THE THESES. 160
§ 33. THE THESES CONTROVERSY 167
§ 34. ROME'S INTERPOSITION: LUTHER AND PRIERIAS (1518) . . 170
§ 35. LUTHER AND CAJETAN (October, 1518) 172
§ 36. LUTHER AND MILTITZ (January, 1519) 175
§ 37. THE LEIPZIG DISPUTATION (June and July, 1519) . . . 178
§ 38. PHILIP MELANCHTHON, LITERATURE (with portrait) . 183
§ 39. MELANCHTHON'S TRAINING 185
§ 40. MELANCHTHON'S EARLY LABORS 189
§ 41. LUTHER AND MELANCHTHON 191
§ 42. ULRICH VON HUTTEN AND LUTHER 196
§ 43. LUTHER'S CRUSADE AGAINST POPERY (1520) . . . 203
§ 44. THE ADDRESS TO THE GERMAN NOBILITY (July, 1520) . . 206
§ 45. THE BABYLONIAN CAPTIVITY OF THE CHURCH (October, 1520) 213
§ 46. CHRISTIAN FREEDOM. LUTHER'S THIRD AND LAST LETTER
      TO THE POPE (October, 1520) 220
§ 47. THE BULL OF EXCOMMUNICATION (June 15, 1520) . . . 227
      NOTES. — TEXT OF THE PAPAL BULL (with fac-simile) . . . 233
§ 48. LUTHER BURNS THE POPE'S BULL, AND FOREVER BREAKS
      WITH ROME (Dec. 10, 1520) 247
§ 49. THE REFORMATION AND THE PAPACY 252
§ 50. EMPEROR CHARLES V. (with portrait) 262
§ 51. THE ECCLESIASTICAL POLICY OF CHARLES V. . . . 272
§ 52. THE ABDICATION OF CHARLES, AND HIS CLOISTER-LIFE . 276
§ 53. THE DIET OF WORMS (1521) 287
§ 54. LUTHER'S JOURNEY TO WORMS 294

PAGE

§ 55. LUTHER'S TESTIMONY BEFORE THE DIET OF WORMS (April 17 and 18, 1521) 300
§ 56. REFLECTIONS ON LUTHER'S TESTIMONY 311
§ 57. PRIVATE CONFERENCES. CONDUCT OF THE EMPEROR . . 314
§ 58. THE BAN OF THE EMPIRE (May 8 (26), 1521) . . . 318
§ 59. STATE OF PUBLIC OPINION. POPULAR LITERATURE . . 321

CHAPTER IV.

THE REFORMATION FROM THE DIET OF WORMS TO THE PEASANTS' WAR (1521-1525).

§ 60. A NEW PHASE IN THE HISTORY OF THE REFORMATION . 329
§ 61. LUTHER AT THE WARTBURG (April, 1521, to March, 1522) . 330
§ 62. LUTHER'S TRANSLATION OF THE BIBLE 340
    NOTES. — THE PRE-LUTHERAN GERMAN BIBLE 351
§ 63. A CRITICAL ESTIMATE OF LUTHER'S VERSION . . . 354
    NOTES. — THE REVISION OF LUTHER'S VERSION, AND THE ANGLO-AMERI-
    CAN REVISION OF KING JAMES'S VERSION 366
§ 64. MELANCHTHON'S THEOLOGY. LOCI THEOLOGICI . . 368
§ 65. PROTESTANT RADICALISM. DISTURBANCES AT ERFURT . 375
§ 66. THE REVOLUTION AT WITTENBERG. CARLSTADT AND THE
    NEW PROPHETS 378
§ 67. LUTHER RETURNS TO WITTENBERG (March, 1522) . . . 382
§ 68. LUTHER RESTORES ORDER IN WITTENBERG. THE END OF
    CARLSTADT 387
§ 69. THE DIETS OF NÜRNBERG (1522-1524). POPE ADRIAN VI. . 392
§ 70. LUTHER AND HENRY VIII. (1522) 396
§ 71. DESIDERIUS ERASMUS (with portrait) 399
§ 72. ERASMUS AND THE REFORMATION (with portrait) . . 421
§ 73. THE FREE-WILL CONTROVERSY (1524-1527) 428
§ 74. WILIBALD PIRKHEIMER 434
§ 75. THE PEASANTS' WAR (1523-1525) 440

CHAPTER V.

THE INNER DEVELOPMENT OF THE REFORMATION, FROM THE PEASANTS' WAR TO THE DIET OF AUGSBURG (1525-1530).

§ 76. THE THREE ELECTORS (with three portraits) . . . 450
§ 77. LUTHER'S MARRIAGE (with portraits of Luther and Catharine
    von Bora) 454
§ 78. LUTHER'S HOME-LIFE AND PRIVATE CHARACTER . . 460
§ 79. REFLECTIONS ON CLERICAL FAMILY LIFE 473
§ 80. REFORMATION OF PUBLIC WORSHIP 484
§ 81. PROMINENT FEATURES OF EVANGELICAL WORSHIP . . 490
§ 82. BEGINNINGS OF EVANGELICAL HYMNODY 494

PAGE

§ 83. LUTHER AND COMMON SCHOOLS 512
§ 84. RECONSTRUCTION OF CHURCH GOVERNMENT AND DISCIPLINE, 515
§ 85. ENLARGED CONCEPTION OF THE CHURCH. AUGUSTIN, WICLIF,
HUS, LUTHER 520
NOTES. — LUTHER'S VIEWS ON THE CHURCH FATHERS . . . 534
§ 86. CHANGES IN THE VIEWS OF THE MINISTRY. DEPARTURE
FROM THE EPISCOPAL SUCCESSION. LUTHER ORDAINS A
DEACON AND CONSECRATES A BISHOP 536
§ 87. RELATION OF CHURCH AND STATE 542
§ 88. CHURCH VISITATION IN SAXONY 546
§ 89. LUTHER'S CATECHISMS (1529) 550
§ 90. THE TYPICAL CATECHISMS OF PROTESTANTISM . . . 555

CHAPTER VI.

PROPAGATION AND PERSECUTION OF PROTESTANTISM.

§ 91. CAUSES AND MEANS OF PROGRESS 558
§ 92. THE PRINTING-PRESS AND THE REFORMATION . . . 560
§ 93. PROTESTANTISM IN SAXONY 567
§ 94. THE REFORMATION IN NÜRNBERG 569
§ 95. THE REFORMATION IN STRASSBURG 570
§ 96. PROTESTANTISM IN NORTH GERMANY 573
§ 97. PROTESTANTISM IN AUGSBURG AND SOUTH GERMANY . 577
§ 98. THE REFORMATION IN HESSE 579
§ 99. THE REFORMATION IN PRUSSIA 588
§ 100. PROTESTANT MARTYRS 600

CHAPTER VII.

THE SACRAMENTARIAN CONTROVERSIES.

§ 101. SACERDOTALISM AND SACRAMENTALISM 603
§ 102. THE ANABAPTIST CONTROVERSY. LUTHER AND HÜBMAIER, 606
§ 103. THE EUCHARISTIC CONTROVERSY 612
§ 104. LUTHER'S THEORY BEFORE THE CONTROVERSY . . . 615
§ 105. LUTHER AND CARLSTADT 617
§ 106. LUTHER AND ZWINGLI 620
§ 107. THE MARBURG CONFERENCE (with facsimile of signatures) 629
§ 108. THE MARBURG CONFERENCE (continued). DISCUSSION AND
RESULT. 637
NOTE. — ON THE ORIGIN OF THE SENTENCE: In necessariis unitas, etc. 650
§ 109. LUTHER'S LAST ATTACK ON THE SACRAMENTARIANS. HIS
RELATION TO CALVIN 654
§ 110. REFLECTIONS ON THE ETHICS OF THE EUCHARISTIC CON-
TROVERSY 662
§ 111. THE EUCHARISTIC THEORIES COMPARED. LUTHER, ZWINGLI,
CALVIN 669

CHAPTER VIII.

THE POLITICAL SITUATION BETWEEN 1526 AND 1529.

§ 112. The First Diet of Speier, and the beginning of the
  Territorial System (1526) 683
§ 113. The Emperor and the Pope. The Sacking of Rome
  (1527) 687
§ 114. A War Panic (1528) 689
§ 115. The Second Diet of Speier, and the Protest (1529), 690
§ 116. The Reconciliation of the Emperor and the Pope.
  The Crowning of the Emperor (1529) . . . 693

CHAPTER IX.

THE DIET AND CONFESSION OF AUGSBURG (1530).

§ 117. The Diet of Augsburg 695
§ 118. The Negotiations, the Recess of Augsburg, and the
  Peace of Nürnberg 701
§ 119. The Confession of Augsburg 706
§ 120. The Confutation and the Apology 715
§ 121. The Tetrapolitan Confession 718
§ 122. Zwingli's Confession 721
§ 123. Luther at the Coburg 723
§ 124. Luther's Public Character, and Place in History, 730
§ 125. Ein feste Burg ist unser Gott 742

ILLUSTRATIONS.

	PAGE
LUTHER. By Cranach	107
STAUPITZ. From a Portrait in St. Peter's Convent in Salzburg	117
LUTHER AT FLORENCE. By Giorgione	131
WITTENBERG IN 1546	133
THE LUTHER-HOUSE	135
LUTHER'S STUDY	136
MELANCHTHON. By Dürer	183
LEO X. By Raphael	226
FACSIMILE OF THE POPE'S BULL OF EXCOMMUNICATION	233, 234
CHARLES V. By Beham	263
ERASMUS. By Dürer	400
ERASMUS. By Holbein	422
THE THREE SAXON ELECTORS. By Cranach	451
LUTHER AND CATHARINE VON BORA. By Cranach	457
FACSIMILE OF SIGNATURES TO THE MARBURG CONFERENCE.	631
FACSIMILE OF A LETTER OF LUTHER	745

Several of the Luther pictures are taken (by arrangement with my friends, the author and publishers) from the American edition of Dr. Köstlin's smaller biography of Luther (New York, Charles Scribner's Sons, 1883). Others appear here for the first time, and were expressly prepared for this work; as the Florentine Luther, and the fac-simile of Leo's Bull of Excommunication.

HISTORY

OF

THE REFORMATION

FROM A. D. 1517 TO 1605.

CHAPTER I.

ORIENTATION.

Now the Lord is the Spirit: and where the Spirit of the Lord is, there is liberty.— 2 Cor. 3: 17.

§ 1. *The Turning Point of Modern History.*

THE Reformation of the sixteenth century is, next to the introduction of Christianity, the greatest event in history. It marks the end of the Middle Ages and the beginning of modern times. Starting from religion, it gave, directly or indirectly, a mighty impulse to every forward movement, and made Protestantism the chief propelling force in the history of modern civilization.

The age of the Reformation bears a strong resemblance to the first century. Both are rich beyond any other period in great and good men, important facts, and permanent results. Both contain the ripe fruits of preceding, and the fruitful germs of succeeding ages. They are turning points in the history of mankind. They are felt in their effects to this day, and will be felt to the end of time. They refashioned the world from the innermost depths of the human soul in its contact with the infinite

1

Being. They were ushered in by a providential concurrence of events and tendencies of thought. The way for Christianity was prepared by Moses and the Prophets, the dispersion of the Jews, the conquests of Alexander the Great, the language and literature of Greece, the arms and laws of Rome, the decay of idolatry, the spread of skepticism, the aspirations after a new revelation, the hopes of a coming Messiah. The Reformation was preceded and necessitated by the corruptions of the papacy, the decline of monasticism and scholastic theology, the growth of mysticism, the revival of letters, the resurrection of the Greek and Roman classics, the invention of the printing press, the discovery of a new world, the publication of the Greek Testament, the general spirit of enquiry, the striving after national independence and personal freedom. In both centuries we hear the creative voice of the Almighty calling light out of darkness.

The sixteenth century is the age of the renaissance in religion, literature, and art. The air was stirred by the spirit of progress and freedom. The snows of a long winter were fast melting before the rays of the vernal sun. The world seemed to be renewing its youth; old things were passing away, all things were becoming new. Pessimists and timid conservatives took alarm at the threatened overthrow of cherished notions and institutions, and were complaining, fault-finding and desponding. A very useless business. Intelligent observers of the signs of the times looked hopefully and cheerfully to the future. "O century!" exclaimed Ulrich von Hutten, "the studies flourish, the spirits are awake, it is a luxury to live." And Luther wrote in 1522: "If you read all the annals of the past, you will find no century like this since the birth of Christ. Such building and planting, such good living and dressing, such enterprise in commerce, such a stir in all the arts, has not been since Christ came into the world. And how numerous are the sharp and intelligent people who leave nothing hidden and unturned: even a boy of twenty years knows more nowadays than was known formerly by twenty doctors of divinity."

The same may be said with even greater force of the nineteenth century, which is eminently an age of discovery and invention, of enquiry and progress. And both then as now the enthusiasm for light and liberty takes two opposite directions, either towards skepticism and infidelity, or towards a revival of true religion from its primitive sources. But Christianity triumphed then, and will again regenerate the world.

The Protestant Reformation assumed the helm of the liberal tendencies and movements of the renaissance, directed them into the channel of Christian life, and saved the world from a disastrous revolution. For the Reformation was neither a revolution nor a restoration, though including elements of both. It was negative and destructive towards error, positive and constructive towards truth ; it was conservative as well as progressive ; it built up new institutions in the place of those which it pulled down ; and for this reason and to this extent it has succeeded.

Under the motherly care of the Latin Church, Europe had been Christianized and civilized, and united into a family of nations under the spiritual government of the Pope and the secular government of the Emperor, with one creed, one ritual, one discipline, and one sacred language. The state of heathenism and barbarism at the beginning of the sixth century contrasts with the state of Christian Europe at the beginning of the sixteenth century as midnight darkness compared with the dawn of the morning. But the sun of the day had not yet arisen.

All honor to the Catholic Church and her inestimable services to humanity. But Christianity is far broader and deeper than any ecclesiastical organization. It burst the shell of mediæval forms, struck out new paths, and elevated Europe to a higher plane of intellectual, moral and spiritual culture than it had ever attained before.

§ 2. *Protestantism and Romanism.*

Protestantism represents the most enlightened and active part of modern church history, but not the whole of it.

Since the sixteenth century Western Christendom is divided and runs in two distinct channels. The separation may be compared to the Eastern schism of the ninth century, which is not healed to this day ; both parties being as firm and unyielding as ever on the doctrinal question of the *Filioque*, and the more important practical question of Popery. But Protestantism differs much more widely from the Roman church than the Roman church differs from the Greek, and the Protestant schism has become the fruitful mother of minor divisions, which exist in separate ecclesiastical organizations.

We must distinguish between Catholicism and Romanism. The former embraces the ancient Oriental church, the mediæval church, and we may say, in a wider sense, all the modern evangelical churches. Romanism is the Latin church turned against the Reformation, consolidated by the Council of Trent and completed by the Vatican Council of 1870 with its dogma of papal absolutism and papal infallibility. Mediæval Catholicism is preevangelical, looking to the Reformation ; modern Romanism is anti-evangelical, condemning the Reformation, yet holding with unyielding tenacity the œcumenical doctrines once sanctioned, and doing this all the more by virtue of its claim to infallibility.

The distinction between pre-Reformation Catholicism and post-Reformation Romanism, in their attitude towards Protestantism, has its historical antecedent and parallel in the distinction between pre-Christian Israel which prepared the way for Christianity, and post-Christian Judaism which opposed it as an apostasy.

Catholicism and Protestantism represent two distinct types of Christianity which sprang from the same root, but differ in the branches.

Catholicism is legal Christianity which served to the barbarian nations of the Middle Ages as a necessary school of discipline ; Protestantism is evangelical Christianity which answers the age of independent manhood. Catholicism is traditional, hierarchical, ritualistic, conservative; Protestantism is biblical, democratic, spiritual, progressive. The former is ruled by the principle of authority, the latter by the principle of freedom. But the law, by awakening a sense of sin and exciting a desire for redemption, leads to the gospel; parental authority is a school of freedom; filial obedience looks to manly self-government.

The characteristic features of mediæval Catholicism are intensified by Romanism, yet without destroying the underlying unity.

Romanism and orthodox Protestantism believe in one God, Father, Son, and Holy Spirit, and in one divine-human Lord and Saviour of the race. They accept in common the Holy Scriptures and the œcumenical faith. They agree in every article of the Apostles' Creed. What unites them is far deeper, stronger and more important than what divides them.

But Romanism holds also a large number of "traditions of the elders," which Protestantism rejects as extra-scriptural or anti-scriptural; such are the papacy, the worship of saints and relics, transubstantiation, the sacrifice of the mass, prayers and masses for the dead, works of supererogation, purgatory, indulgences, the system of monasticism with its perpetual vows and ascetic practices, besides many superstitious rites and ceremonies.

Protestantism, on the other hand, revived and developed the Augustinian doctrines of sin and grace; it proclaimed the sovereignty of divine mercy in man's salvation, the sufficiency of the Scriptures as a rule of faith, and the sufficiency of Christ's merit as a source of justification; it asserted the right of direct access to the Word of God and the throne of grace, without human mediators; it secured Christian freedom from bondage; it substituted social morality for monkish asceticism, and a simple, spiritual worship for an imposing ceremonialism that addresses the senses and imagination rather than the intellect and the heart.

The difference between the Catholic and Protestant churches was typically foreshadowed by the difference between Jewish and Gentile Christianity in the apostolic age, which anticipated, as it

were, the whole future course of church history. The question
of circumcision or the keeping of the Mosaic law, as a condition
of church membership, threatened a split at the Council of Jerusalem, but was solved by the wisdom and charity of the apostles,
who agreed that Jews and Gentiles alike are "saved through the
grace of the Lord Jesus" (Acts 15 : 11). Yet even after the
settlement of the controversy by the Jerusalem compromise Paul
got into a sharp conflict with Peter at Antioch on the same question, and protested against his older colleague for denying by his
timid conduct his better conviction, and disowning the Gentile
brethren. It is not accidental that the Roman Church professes to
be built on Peter and regards him as the first pope ; while the
Reformers appealed chiefly to Paul and found in his epistles to
the Galatians and Romans the bulwark of their anthropology
and soteriology, and their doctrine of Christian freedom. The
collision between Paul and Peter was only temporary; and so
the war between Protestantism and Romanism will ultimately
pass away in God's own good time.

The Reformation began simultaneously in Germany and Switzerland, and swept with astonishing rapidity over France, Holland, Scandinavia, Bohemia, Hungary, England and Scotland ;
since the seventeenth century it has spread by emigration to North
America, and by commercial and missionary enterprises to every
Dutch and English colony, and every heathen land. It carried
away the majority of the Teutonic and a part of the Latin nations, and for a while threatened to overthrow the papal
church.

But towards the close of the sixteenth century the triumphant
march of the Reformation was suddenly arrested. Romanism
rose like a wounded giant, and made the most vigorous efforts to
reconquer the lost territory in Europe, and to extend its dominion
in Asia and South America. Since that time the numerical relation of the two churches has undergone little change. But the
progress of secular and ecclesiastical history has run chiefly in
Protestant channels.

In many respects the Roman Church of to-day is a great improvement upon the Mediæval Church. She has been much benefited by the Protestant Reformation, and is far less corrupt and far more prosperous in Protestant than in Papal countries. She was driven to a counter-reform which abolished some of the most crying abuses and infused new life and zeal into her clergy and laity. No papal schism has disgraced her history since the sixteenth century. No pope of the character of Alexander VI. or even Leo X. could be elected any more. She lives chiefly of the past, but uses for her defence all the weapons of modern warfare. She has a much larger membership than either the Greek or the Protestant communion; she still holds under her sway the Latin races of both hemispheres; she satisfies the religious wants of millions of human beings in all countries and climes; she extends her educational, benevolent and missionary operations all over the globe; she advances in proportion as Protestantism degenerates and neglects its duty; and by her venerable antiquity, historical continuity, visible unity, centralized organization, imposing ritual, sacred art, and ascetic piety she attracts intelligent and cultured minds; while the common people are kept in ignorance and in superstitious awe of her mysterious authority with its claim to open the gates of heaven and hell and to shorten the purgatorial sufferings of the departed. For good and evil she is the strongest conservative force in modern society, and there is every reason to believe that she will last to the end of time.

Thus the two branches of Western Christendom seem to hold each other in check, and ought to stimulate each other to a noble rivalry in good works.

The unhappy divisions of Christendom, while they are the source of many evils, have also the good effect of multiplying the agencies for the conversion of the world and facilitating the free growth of every phase of religious life. The evil lies not so much in the multiplicity of denominations, which have a mission to fulfil, as in the spirit of sectarianism and exclusivism, which denies the rights and virtues of others. The Reformation of the sixteenth century is not a finale, but a movement still in progress. We may look hopefully forward to a higher, deeper and broader Reformation, when God in His overruling wisdom and mercy, by a pentecostal effusion of His Holy Spirit upon all the churches, will reunite what the sin and folly of men have divided. There must and will be, in the fullest sense of Christ's prophecy, "one flock, one Shepherd" (John 10 : 16).[1]

§ 3. *Necessity of a Reformation.*

The corruption and abuses of the Latin church had long been the complaint of the best men, and even of general councils. A reformation of the head and the members was the watchword at Pisa, Constance, and Basel, but remained a *pium desiderium* for a whole century.

Let us briefly review the dark side in the condition of the church at the beginning of the sixteenth century.

The papacy was secularized, and changed into a selfish tyranny whose yoke became more and more unbearable. The scandal of the papal schism had indeed been removed, but papal morals, after a temporary improvement, became worse than ever during the years 1492 to 1521. Alexander VI. was a monster of iniquity; Julius II. was a politician and warrior rather than a chief shepherd of souls; and Leo X. took far more interest in the revival of heathen literature and art than in religion, and is said to have even doubted the truth of the gospel history.

No wonder that many cardinals and priests followed the scan-

---

[1] We say "one *flock*" (μία ποίμνη), not "one *fold*" (which would require μία αὐλή). The latter is a strange mistranslation which has passed from the Latin version (*ovile*) into King James's version, and has often been abused as an argument for the papacy and ecclesiastical uniformity. It is corrected in the Revision. The two flocks, Jews and Gentiles, became one flock in the one Shepherd (ποιμήν), not by entrance into the αὐλή of the Jews. There may be one flock in many folds or ecclesiastical organizations. The prophecy was no doubt already fulfilled in the Apostolic Church (Eph. 2: 11–22), but awaits a higher fulfillment when "the fullness of the Gentiles shall come in, and all Israel shall be saved." Rom. 11: 25, 26.

dalous example of the popes, and weakened the respect of the laity for the clergy. The writings of contemporary scholars, preachers and satirists are full of complaints and exposures of the ignorance, vulgarity and immorality of priests and monks. Simony and nepotism were shamefully practiced. Celibacy was a foul fountain of unchastity and uncleanness. The bishoprics were monopolized by the youngest sons of princes and nobles without regard to qualification. Geiler of Kaisersberg, a stern preacher of moral reform at Strassburg (d. 1510), charges all Germany with promoting ignorant and worldly men to the chief dignities, simply on account of their high connections. Thomas Murner complains that the devil had introduced the nobility into the clergy, and monopolized for them the bishoprics.[1] Plurality of office and absence from the diocese were common. Archbishop Albrecht of Mainz was at the same time archbishop of Magdeburg and bishop of Halberstadt. Cardinal Wolsey was archbishop of York while chancellor of England, received stipends from the kings of France and Spain and the doge of Venice, and had a train of five hundred servants. James V. of Scotland (1528–1542) provided for his illegitimate children by making them abbots of Holyrood House, Kelso, Melrose, Coldingham and St. Andrews, and intrusted royal favorites with bishoprics.

Discipline was nearly ruined. Whole monastic establishments and orders had become nurseries of ignorance and superstition, idleness and dissipation, and were the objects of contempt and ridicule, as may be seen from the controversy of Reuchlin with the Dominicans, the writings of Erasmus, and the *Epistolæ Virorum Obscurorum.*

Theology was a maze of scholastic subtleties, Aristotelian dia-

---

[1] In his *Narrenbeschwörung* (1512):

> "*Aber seit der Teufel hat*
> *Den Adel bracht in Kirchenstat,*
> *Seit man kein' Bischof mehr will han*
> *Er sei denn ganz ein Edelmann,*" etc.

lectics and idle speculations, but ignored the great doctrines of the gospel. Carlstadt, the older colleague of Luther, confessed that he had been doctor of divinity before he had seen a complete copy of the Bible. Education was confined to priests and nobles. The mass of the laity could neither read nor write, and had no access to the word of God except the Scripture lessons from the pulpit.

The priest's chief duty was to perform, by his magic words, the miracle of transubstantiation, and to offer the sacrifice of the mass for the living and the dead in a foreign tongue. Many did it mechanically, or with a skeptical reservation, especially in Italy. Preaching was neglected, and had reference, mostly, to indulgences, alms, pilgrimages and processions. The churches were overloaded with good and bad pictures, with real and ficti-tious relics. Saint-worship and image-worship, superstitious rites and ceremonies obstructed the direct worship of God in spirit and in truth.

Piety which should proceed from a living union of the soul with Christ and a consecration of character, was turned outward and reduced to a round of mechanical performances such as the recital of Paternosters and Avemarias, fasting, alms-giving, con-fession to the priest, and pilgrimage to a holy shrine. Good works were measured by the quantity rather than the quality, and vitiated by the principle of meritoriousness which appealed to the selfish motive of reward. Remission of sin could be bought with money; a shameful traffic in indulgences was carried on under the Pope's sanction for filthy lucre as well as for the building of St. Peter's Dome, and caused that outburst of moral indignation which was the beginning of the Reformation and of the fearful judgment on the Church of Rome.

This is a one-sided, but not an exaggerated description. It is true as far as it goes, and needs only to be supplemented by the bright side which we shall present in the next section.

Honest Roman Catholic scholars, while maintaining the infal-libility and consequent doctrinal irreformability of their church, admit in strong terms the decay of discipline and the necessity of a moral reform in the sixteenth century.[1]

The best proof is furnished by a pope of exceptional integrity, Adrian VI., who made an extraordinary confession of the papal and clerical corruption to the Diet of Nürnberg in 1522, and tried earnestly, though in vain, to reform his court. The Council of Trent was called not only for the extirpation of heresy, but in part also "for the reformation of the clergy and Christian people;"[2] and Pope Pius IV., in the bull of confirmation, likewise declares that one of the objects of the Council was "the correction of morals and the restoration of ecclesiastical discipline."[3]

On the other hand, it must be admitted that the church was more than once in a far worse condition, during the papal schism in the fourteenth, and especially in the tenth and eleventh centuries; and yet she was reformed by Pope Hildebrand and his successors without a split and without an alteration of the Catholic Creed.

Why could not the same be done in the sixteenth century? Because the Roman church in the critical moment resisted reform with all her might, and forced the issue: either no reformation at all, or a reformation in opposition to Rome.

The guilt of the western schism is divided between the two parties, as the guilt of the eastern schism is; although no human

---

[1] So Bellarmine and Bossuet. Möhler also (in his *Kirchengesch.* III. 99) says: "We do not believe that the period before the Reformation was a flourishing period of church history, for we hear from it a thousand voices for a reformation in the head and members (*wir hören aus derselben den tausendstimmigen Ruf nach einer Verbesserung an Haupt und Gliedern uns entgegentönen*)." Even Janssen, the eulogist of mediæval Germany, devotes the concluding section of the first volume of his *Geschichte des deutschen Volkes* (p. 594–613) to a consideration of some of the crying evils of those times.

[2] Sess. I. (held Dec. 13, 1545): "*ad extirpationem hæresium, ad pacem et unionem ecclesiæ, ad reformationem cleri et populi Christiani.*" See Smets, *Concilii Trident. Canones et Decreta*, p. 10.

[3] "*Ad plurimas et perniciosissimas hæreses extirpandas, ad corrigendos mores, et restituendam ecclesiasticam disciplinam,*" etc. See Smets, *l. c.* 209.

tribunal can measure the share of responsibility. Much is due, no doubt, to the violence and extravagance of the Protestant opposition, but still more to the intolerance and stubbornness of the Roman resistance. The papal court used against the Reformation for a long time only the carnal weapons of political influence, diplomatic intrigue, secular wealth, haughty pride, scholastic philosophy, crushing authority, and bloody persecution. It repeated the course of the Jewish hierarchy, which crucified the Messiah and cast the apostles out of the synagogue.

But we must look beyond this partial justification, and view the matter in the light of the results of the Reformation.

It was evidently the design of Providence to develop a new type of Christianity outside of the restraints of the papacy, and the history of three centuries is the best explanation and vindication of that design. Every movement in history must be judged by its fruits.

The elements of such an advance movement were all at work before Luther and Zwingli protested against papal indulgences.

§ 4. *The Preparations for the Reformation.*

C. ULLMANN: *Reformatoren vor der Reformation.* Hamburg, 1841, 2d ed. 1866, 2 vols. (Engl. trans. by R. Menzies, Edinb. 1855, 2 vols.). C. DE BONNE-CHOSE: *Réformateurs avant la réforme du xvi. siècle.* Par. 1853, 2 vols. A good résumé by GEO. P. FISHER: *The Reformation.* New York, 1873, ch. III. 52-84; and in the first two lectures of CHARLES BEARD: The *Reformation,* London, 1883, p. 1–75. Comp., also the numerous monographs of various scholars on the Renaissance, on Wiclif, Hus, Savonarola, Hutten, Reuchlin, Erasmus, etc. A full account of the preparation for the Reformation belongs to the last chapters of the History of Mediæval Christianity (see vol. V.). We here merely recapitulate the chief points.

Judaism before Christ was sadly degenerated, and those who sat in Moses' seat had become blind leaders of the blind. Yet "salvation is of the Jews;" and out of this people arose John the Baptist, the Virgin Mary, the Messiah, and the Apostles. Jerusalem, which stoned the prophets and crucified the Lord, witnessed also the pentecostal miracle and became the mother church of Christendom. So the Catholic church in the sixteenth century, though corrupt in its head and its members, was still the church of the living God and gave birth to the Reformation, which removed the rubbish of human traditions and reopened the pure fountain of the gospel of Christ.

The Reformers, it should not be forgotten, were all born, baptized, confirmed, and educated in the Roman Catholic Church, and most of them had served as priests at her altars with the solemn vow of obedience to the pope on their conscience. They stood as closely related to the papal church, as the Apostles and Evangelists to the Synagogue and the Temple ; and for reasons of similar urgency, they were justified to leave the communion of their fathers; or rather, they did not leave it, but were cast out by the ruling hierarchy.

The Reformation went back to first principles in order to go forward. It struck its roots deep in the past and bore rich fruits for the future. It sprang forth almost simultaneously from different parts of Europe and was enthusiastically hailed by the leading minds of the age in church and state. No great movement in history—except Christianity itself—was so widely and thoroughly prepared as the Protestant Reformation.

The reformatory councils of Pisa, Constance, and Basel; the conflict of the Emperors with the Popes; the contemplative piety of the mystics with their thirst after direct communion with God; the revival of classical literature; the general intellectual awakening; the biblical studies of Reuchlin, and Erasmus; the rising spirit of national independence; Wiclif, and the Lollards in England; Hus, and the Hussites in Bohemia; John von Goch, John von Wesel, and Johann Wessel in Germany and the Netherlands; Savonarola in Italy; the Brethren of the Common Life, the Waldenses, the Friends of God,—contributed their share towards the great change and paved the way for a new era of Christianity. The innermost life of the church was pressing forward to a new era. There is scarcely a principle or doctrine of the Reformation which was not anticipated and advocated in the fourteenth and fifteenth centuries. Luther made the remark, that his opponents might charge him with having borrowed everything from John Wessel if he had known his writings earlier. The fuel was abundant all over Europe, but it required the spark which would set it ablaze.

Violent passions, political intrigues, the ambition and avarice of princes, and all sorts of selfish and worldly motives were mixed up with the war against the papacy. But they were at work likewise in the introduction of Christianity among the heathen barbarians. "Wherever God builds a church, the devil builds a chapel close by." Human nature is terribly corrupt and leaves its stains on the noblest movements in history.

But, after all, the religious leaders of the Reformation, while not free from faults, were men of the purest motives and highest aims, and there is no nation which has not been benefited by the change they introduced.

§ 5. *The Genius and Aim of the Reformation.*

Is. AUG. DORNER: On the *formal*, and the *material Principle of the Reformation.* Two essays, first published in 1841 and 1857, and reprinted in his *Gesammelte Schriften*, Berlin, 1883, p. 48–187. Also his *History of Protestant Theology*, Engl. trans. 1871, 2 vols.

PHIL. SCHAFF: *The Principle of Protestantism*, Chambersburg, Penn., 1845 (German and English); *Protestantism and Romanism*, and the *Principles of the Reformation*, two essays in his "Christ and Christianity," N. York, 1885. p. 124–134. Also *Creeds of Christendom*, Vol. I. 203-219.

DAN. SCHENKEL: *Das Princip des Protestantismus.* Schaffhausen, 1852 (92 pages). This is the concluding section of his larger work, *Das Wesen des Protestantismus*, in 3 vols.

K. F. A. KAHNIS: *Ueber die Principien des Protestantismus.* Leipzig, 1865. Also his *Zeugniss von den Grundwahrheiten des Protestantismus gegen Dr. Hengstenberg.* Leipzig, 1862.

CHARLES BEARD: *The Reformation of the Sixteenth Century in its relation to Modern Thought and Knowledge.* Hibbert Lectures for 1883. London, 1883. A Unitarian view, written with ample learning and in excellent spirit.

HENRY WACE and C. A. BUCHHEIM: *First Principles of the Reformation, or the 95 Theses and three Primary Works of Dr. M. Luther.* London, 1885.

The literature on the difference between Lutheran and Reformed or Calvinistic Protestantism is given in SCHAFF'S *Creeds of Christendom*, I. 211.

The spirit and aim of evangelical Protestantism is best expressed by Paul in his anti-Judaistic Epistle to the Galatians: "For freedom did Christ set us free; stand fast, therefore, and be not entangled again in a yoke of bondage." Christian freedom is so inestimable a blessing that no amount of abuse can justify a relapse into a state of spiritual despotism and slavery. But only those who have enjoyed it, can properly appreciate it.

The Reformation was at first a purely religious movement, and furnishes a striking illustration of the all-pervading power of religion in history. It started from the question : What must a man do to be saved? How shall a sinner be justified before God, and attain peace of his troubled conscience? The Reformers were supremely concerned for the salvation of the soul, for the glory of Christ and the triumph of his gospel. They thought much more of the future world than of the present, and made all political, national, and literary interests subordinate and subservient to religion.[1]

Yet they were not monks, but live men in a live age, not pessimists, but optimists, men of action as well as of thought, earnest, vigorous, hopeful men, free from selfish motives and aims, full of faith and the Holy Ghost, equal to any who had preceded them since the days of the Apostles. From the centre of religion they have influenced every department of human life and activity, and given a powerful impulse to political and civil liberty, to progress in theology, philosophy, science, and literature.

The Reformation removed the obstructions which the papal church had interposed between Christ and the believer. It opened

---

[1] What Dr. Baur, the critical Tübingen historian, says of Luther, is equally applicable to all the other Reformers: "*Dass für Luther die Reformation zur eigensten Sache seines Herzens geworden war, dass er sie in ihrem reinsten religiösen Interesse auffasste, getrennt von allen ihr fremdartigen blos äusserlichen Motiven, dass es ihm um nichts anderes zu thun war, als um die Sache des Evangeliums und seiner seligmachenden Kraft, wie er sie an sich selbst in seinem innern Kampf um die Gewissheit der Sündenvergebung erfahren hatte, diess ist es, was ihn zum Reformator machte.*" *Gesch. der Christl. Kirche*, vol. IV. 5 (ed. by his son, 1863). Froude says of Luther: "He revived and maintained the spirit of piety and reverence in which, and by which alone, real progress is possible." *Luther*, Preface, p. vi.

the door to direct union with him, as the only Mediator between God and man, and made his gospel accessible to every reader without the permission of a priest. It was a return to first principles, and for this very reason also a great advance. It was a revival of primitive Christianity, and at the same time a deeper apprehension and application of it than had been known before.

There are three fundamental principles of the Reformation: the supremacy of the *Scriptures* over tradition, the supremacy of *faith* over works, and the supremacy of the Christian *people* over an exclusive priesthood. The first may be called the objective, the second the subjective, the third the social or ecclesiastical principle.[1]

They resolve themselves into the one principle of *evangelical freedom,* or *freedom in Christ.* The ultimate aim of evangelical Protestantism is to bring every man into living union with Christ as the only and all-sufficient Lord and Saviour from sin and death.

§ 6. *The Authority of the Scriptures.*

The objective principle of Protestantism maintains that the Bible, as the inspired record of revelation, is the only infallible rule of faith and practice; in opposition to the Roman Catholic coördination of Scripture and ecclesiastical *tradition,* as the joint rules of faith.

The teaching of the living church is by no means rejected, but

---

[1] German writers distinguish usually two principles of the Reformation, the authority of the Scriptures, and justification by faith, and call the first the *formal* principle (or *Erkenntnissprincip, principium cognoscendi*), the second the *material* principle (*principium essendi*); the third they omit, except Kahnis, who finds a third principle in the idea of the invisible church, and calls this the *Kirchenprincip.* The Lutheran Church gives to the doctrine of justification by faith the first place; and the Formula of Concord calls it "*articulus præcipuus in tota doctrina Christiana.*" But the Reformed confessions give the first place to the doctrine of the normative authority of Scripture, from which alone all articles of faith are to be derived, and they substitute for the doctrine of justification by faith the ulterior and wider doctrine of election and salvation by free grace through faith. The difference is characteristic, but does not affect the essential agreement.

subordinated to the Word of God; while the opposite theory virtually subordinates the Bible to tradition by making the latter the sole interpreter of the former and confining interpretation within the limits of an imaginary *consensus patrum*. In the application of the Bible principle there was considerable difference between the more conservative Lutheran and Anglican Reformation, and the more radical Zwinglian and Calvinistic Reformation; the former contained many post-scriptural and extra-scriptural traditions, usages and institutions, which the latter, in its zeal for primitive purity and simplicity, rejected as useless or dangerous; but all Reformers opposed what they regarded as anti-scriptural doctrines; and all agreed in the principle that the church has no right to impose upon the conscience articles of faith without clear warrant in the Word of God.

Every true progress in church history is conditioned by a new and deeper study of the Scriptures, which has "first, second, third, infinite draughts." While the Humanists went back to the ancient classics and revived the spirit of Greek and Roman paganism, the Reformers went back to the sacred Scriptures in the original languages and revived the spirit of apostolic Christianity. They were fired by an enthusiasm for the gospel, such as had never been known since the days of Paul. Christ rose from the tomb of human traditions and preached again his words of life and power. The Bible, heretofore a book of priests only, was now translated anew and better than ever into the vernacular tongues of Europe, and made a book of the people. Every Christian man could henceforth go to the fountain-head of inspiration, and sit at the feet of the Divine Teacher, without priestly permission and intervention. This achievement of the Reformation was a source of incalculable blessings for all time to come. In a few years Luther's version had more readers among the laity than ever the Latin Vulgate had among priests; and the Protestant Bible societies circulate more Bibles in one year than were copied during the fifteen centuries before the Reformation.

We must remember, however, that this wonderful progress was only made possible by the previous invention of the art of printing and by the subsequent education of the people. The Catholic Church had preserved the sacred Scriptures through ages of ignorance and barbarism; the Latin Bible was the first gift of the printing press to the world; fourteen or more editions of a German version were printed before 1518; the first two editions of the Greek Testament we owe to the liberality of a Spanish cardinal (Ximenes), and the enterprise of a Dutch scholar in Basel (Erasmus); and the latter furnished the text from which, with the aid of Jerome's Vulgate, the translations of Luther and Tyndale were made.

The Roman church, while recognizing the divine inspiration and authority of the Bible, prefers to control the laity by the teaching priesthood, and allows the reading of the Scriptures in the popular tongues only under certain restrictions and precautions, from fear of abuse and profanation. Pope Innocent III. was of the opinion that the Scriptures were too deep for the common people, as they surpassed even the understanding of the wise and learned. Several synods in Gaul, during the thirteenth century, prohibited the reading of the Romanic translation, and ordered the copies to be burnt. Archbishop Berthold, of Mainz, in an edict of January 4th, 1486, threatened with excommunication all who ventured to translate and to circulate translations of sacred books, especially the Bible, without his permission. The Council of Constance (1415), which burnt John Hus and Jerome of Prague, condemned also the writings and the bones of Wiclif, the first translator of the whole Bible into the English tongue, to the flames; and Arundel, archbishop of Canterbury and chancellor of England, denounced him as that "pestilent wretch of damnable heresy who, as a complement of his wickedness, invented a new translation of the Scriptures into his mother tongue." Pope Pius IV. (1564), in the conviction that the indiscriminate reading of Bible versions did more harm than good (*plus detrimenti quam utilitiatis*), would not allow laymen to read the sacred book except by special permission of a bishop or an inquisitor. Clement VIII. (1598) reserved the right to grant this permission to the Congregation of the Index. Gregory XV. (1622), and Clement XI. (in the Bull *Unigenitus*, 1713), repeated the conditional prohibition. Benedict XIV., one of the liberal popes, extended the permission to read the Word of God in the vernacular to all the faithful, yet with the proviso that the translation be approved in Rome and guarded by explanatory notes from the writings of the fathers and Catholic scholars (1757). This excludes, of course, all Protestant versions, even the very best. They are regarded as corrupt and heretical and have often been committed to the flames in Roman Catholic countries, especially in connection with the counter-Reformation of the Jesuits in Bohemia and elsewhere. The first edition of Tyndale's New Testament had to be smuggled into England and was publicly burnt by order of Tunstall, bishop of London, in St. Paul's church-yard near the spot from which Bibles are now sent to all parts of the globe. The Bible societies have been denounced and condemned by modern popes as a "pestilence which perverts the gospel of Christ into a gospel of the devil." The Papal Syllabus of Pius IX. (1864), classes "*Societates Biblicæ*" with Socialism, Communism, and Secret Societies, calls them "pests frequently rebuked in the severest terms," and refers for proof, to several Encyclicals from November 9th, 1846, to August 10th, 1863.[1]

Such fulminations against Protestant Bible societies might be in some measure excused if the popes favored Catholic Bible societies, which would be the best proof of zeal for the spread of

---

[1] Schaff, *Creeds of Christendom*, II. 218 ; Köllner, *Symbolik* II. 351, sqq.; Hase, *Handbuch der Protestant. Polemik*, fourth ed., 1878, p. 68 sqq. There were indeed vernacular translations of the Bible long before the Reformation; but it is a most astounding exaggeration when Perrone, as quoted by Hase, asserts (*Prae-lect. Theol.* III. § 317): "*Per idem tempus* 800 *plus minus editiones Bibliorum aut N. T. ante Reformationem prodierant, ac per universam Europam catholicam circumferebantur, antequam vel protestantis nomen agnosceretur. Et ex his* 200 *versiones in linguis vernaculis diversarum gentium omnium manibus libere versabantur.*"

the Scriptures. But such institutions do not exist. Fortunately papal bulls have little effect in modern times, and in spite of official prohibitions and discouragements, there are zealous advocates of Bible reading among modern Catholics, as there were among the Greek and Latin fathers. [1] Nor have the restrictions of the Council of Trent been able to prevent the progress of Biblical scholarship and exegesis even in the Roman church. *E pur si muove.* The Bible, as well as the earth, moves for all that.

Modern Protestant theology is much more just to ecclesiastical tradition than the Reformers could be in their hot indignation against the prevailing corruptions and against the papal tyranny of their day. The deeper study of ecclesiastical and secular history has dispelled the former ignorance on the "dark ages," so called, and brought out the merits of the fathers, missionaries, schoolmen, and popes, in the progress of Christian civilization.

But these results do not diminish the supreme value of the sacred Scripture as an ultimate tribunal of appeal in matters of faith, nor the importance of its widest circulation. It is by far the best guide of instruction in holy living and dying. No matter what theory of the mode and extent of inspiration we may hold, the fact of inspiration is plain and attested by the universal consent of Christendom. The Bible is a book of holy men, but just as much a book of God, who made those men witnesses of truth and sure teachers of the way of salvation.

§ 7. *Justification by Faith.*

The subjective principle of Protestantism is the doctrine of justification and salvation by faith in Christ; as distinct from the doctrine of justification by faith and *works* or salvation by grace and *human merit.* Luther's formula is *sola fide.* Calvin goes further back to God's *eternal election,* as the ultimate

---

[1] See L. Van Ess, *Auszüge über das nothwendige und nützliche Bibellesen aus den Kirchenvätern und anderen kathol. Schriften,* second ed., 1816; also the preface to his translation of the New Testament.

ground of salvation and comfort in life and in death.   But Luther and Calvin meant substantially the same thing, and agree in the more general proposition of *salvation by free grace through living faith in Christ* (Acts 4: 12), in opposition to any Pelagian or Semipelagian compromise which divides the work and merit between God and man.   And this is the very soul of evangelical Protestantism.[1]

Luther assigned to his solifidian doctrine of justification the central position in the Christian system, declared it to be the article of the standing or falling (Lutheran) church, and was unwilling to yield an inch from it, though heaven and earth should collapse.[2] This exaggeration is due to his personal experience during his convent life.   The central article of the Christian faith on which the church is built, is not any specific dogma of the Protestant, or Roman, or Greek church, but the broader and deeper truth held by all, namely, the divine-human personality and atoning work of Christ, the Lord and Saviour.   This was the confession of Peter, the first creed of Christendom.

The Protestant doctrine of justification differs from the Roman Catholic, as defined (very circumspectly) by the Council of Trent, chiefly in two points.   Justification is conceived as a declaratory and judicial act of God, in distinction from sanctification, which is a gradual growth ; and faith is conceived as a fiducial act of the heart and will, in distinction from theoretical belief and blind

---

[1] Only in this sense can it be called Augustinian; for otherwise Augustin's conception of *justificatio* is catholic, and he identifies it with *sanctificatio*.   Moreover he widely differs from the Protestant conception of the church and its authority.   Luther felt the difference in his later years.

[2] *Articuli Smalcaldici*, p. 305 (ed. Rechenb., or 310 ed. Müller): " *De hoc articulo* [*solam fidem nos justificare*] *cedere or aliquid contra illum largiri aut permittere nemo piorum potest etiamsi cœlum et terra et omnia corruant.*   (Acts 4: 12; Isa. 53: 3). *Et in hoc articulo sita sunt et consistunt omnia, quæ contra papam, diabolum et universum mundum in vita nostra docemus, testamur et agimus.   Quare opportet nos de hac doctrina esse certos, et minime dubitare, alioquin actum est prorsus, et papa et diabolus et omnia adversa jus et victoriam contra nos obtinent.*"   Luther inserted in his translation of Rom. 3: 28, the word *allein* (*sola fide*, hence the term *solifidianism*), and the revised *Probebibel* of 1883 retained it.   On the exegetical questions involved, see my annotations to Lange on Romans 3: 28.

submission to the church. The Reformers derived their idea from Paul, the Romanists appealed chiefly to James (2: 17–26); but Paul suggests the solution of the apparent contradiction by his sentence, that "in Christ Jesus neither circumcision availeth anything nor uncircumcision, but *faith working through love.*"

Faith, in the biblical and evangelical sense, is a vital force which engages all the powers of man and apprehends and appropriates the very life of Christ and all his benefits. It is the child of grace and the mother of good works. It is the pioneer of all great thoughts and deeds. By faith Abraham became the father of nations; by faith Moses became the liberator and legislator of Israel; by faith the Galilean fishermen became fishers of men; and by faith the noble army of martyrs endured tortures and triumphed in death; without faith in the risen Saviour the church could not have been founded. Faith is a saving power. It unites us to Christ. Whosoever believeth in Christ "hath eternal life." "We believe," said Peter at the Council of Jerusalem, "that we shall be saved through the grace of God," like the Gentiles who come to Christ by faith without the works and ceremonies of the law. "Believe in the Lord Jesus, and thou shalt be saved," was Paul's answer to the question of the jailor: "What must I do to be saved?"

Protestantism does by no means despise or neglect good works or favor antinomian license; it only subordinates them to faith, and measures their value by quality rather than quantity. They are not the condition, but the necessary evidence of justification; they are not the root, but the fruits of the tree. The same faith which justifies, does also sanctify. It is ever "working through love" (Gal. 5: 6). Luther is often charged with indifference to good works, but very unjustly. His occasional unguarded utterances must be understood in connection with his whole teaching and character. "Faith," in his own forcible language which expresses his true view, "faith is a living, busy, active, mighty thing, and it is impossible that it should not do good without ceasing; it does not ask whether good works are to be done, but before the question is put, it has done them already, and is always engaged in doing them; you may as well separate burning and shining from fire, as works from faith."

The Lutheran doctrine of Christian freedom and justification by faith alone, like that of St. Paul on which it was based, was made the cloak of excesses by carnal men who wickedly reasoned, "Let us continue in sin that grace may abound" (Rom. 6: 1), and who abused their "freedom for an occasion to the flesh" (Gal. 5: 13). All such consequences the apostle cut off at the outset by an indignant "God forbid."

The fact is undeniable, that the Reformation in Germany was accompanied and followed by antinomian tendencies and a degeneracy of public morals. It rests not only on the hostile testimonies of Romanists and separatists, but Luther and Melanchthon themselves often bitterly complained in their later years of the abuse of the liberty of the gospel and the sad state of morals in Wittenberg and throughout Saxony.[1]

But we should remember, first, that the degeneracy of morals, especially the increase of extravagance, and luxury with its attending vices, had begun in Catholic times in consequence of discoveries and inventions, the enlargement of commerce and wealth.[2] Nor was it near as bad as the state of things which Luther had witnessed at Rome in 1510, under Pope Julius II., not to speak

---

[1] The weight of Döllinger's three volumes on the *Reformation* (1848) consists in the collection of such unfavorable testimonies from the writings of Erasmus, Wizel, Haner, Wildenauer, Crotus Rubeanus, Biblicanus, Staupitz, Amerpach, Pirkheimer, Zasius, Frank, Denk, Hetzer, Schwenkfeld, Luther, Melanchthon, Spalatin, Bugenhagen, and others. They give, indeed, a very gloomy, but a very one-sided picture of the times. Janssen makes good use of these testimonies. But both these Catholic historians, whose eminent learning is undeniable, wrote with a polemic aim, and make the very truth lie by omitting the bright side of the Reformation. Comp. on this subject the controversial writings of Köstlin and Ebrard against Janssen, and Janssen's replies, *An meine Kritiker*, Freiburg i. B. 1883 (Zehntes Tausend, 227 pages), and *Ein zweites Wort an meine Kritiker*, Freib. 1883 (Zwölftes Tausend, 144 pages).

[2] Even Janssen admits this, but is silent about the greater corruption in Rome. See his *Geschichte des Deutschen Volkes* I. 375 sqq. Comp. his *Ein zweites Wort an meine Kritiker*, p. 82.

of the more wicked reign of Pope Alexander VI. Secondly, the degeneracy was not due so much to a particular doctrine, as to the confusion which necessarily followed the overthrow of the ecclesiastical order and discipline, and to the fact that the Lutheran Reformers allowed the government of the church too easily to pass from the bishops into the hands of secular rulers. Thirdly, the degeneracy was only temporary during the transition from the abolition of the old to the establishment of the new order of things. Fourthly, the disorder was confined to Germany. The Swiss Reformers, from the start, laid greater stress on discipline than the Lutheran Reformers, and organized the new church on a more solid basis. Calvin introduced a state of moral purity and rigorism in Geneva such as had never been known before in the Christian church. The Huguenots of France, the Calvinists of Holland, the Puritans of England and New England, and the Presbyterians of Scotland are distinguished for their strict principles and habits. An impartial comparison of Protestant countries and nations with Roman Catholic, in regard to the present state of public and private morals and general culture, is eminently favorable to the Reformation.

§ 8.   *The Priesthood of the Laity.*

The social or ecclesiastical principle of Protestantism is the general priesthood of believers, in distinction from the special priesthood which stands mediating between Christ and the laity.

The Roman church is an exclusive hierarchy, and assigns to the laity the position of passive obedience. The bishops are the teaching and ruling church ; they alone constitute a council or synod, and have the exclusive power of legislation and administration. Laymen have no voice in spiritual matters, they can not even read the Bible without the permission of the priest, who holds the keys of heaven and hell.

In the New Testament every believer is called a saint, a priest, and a king. "All Christians," says Luther, " are truly of the spiritual estate, and there is no difference among them, save of office alone.   As St. Paul says, we are all one body, though each member does its own work, to serve the others.   This is because we have one baptism, one gospel, one faith, and are all Christians alike; for baptism, gospel and faith, these alone make spiritual and Christian people."   And again: "It is faith that makes men priests, faith that unites them to Christ, and gives them the indwelling of the Holy Spirit, whereby they become filled with all holy grace and heavenly power.   The inward anointing—this oil, better than any that ever came from the horn of bishop or pope—gives them not the name only, but the nature, the purity, the power of priests; and this anointing have all they received who are believers in Christ."

This principle, consistently carried out, raises the laity to active co-operation in the government and administration of the church; it gives them a voice and vote in the election of the pastor; it makes every member of the congregation useful, according to his peculiar gift, for the general good.   This principle is the source of religious and civil liberty which flourishes most in Protestant countries.   Religious liberty is the mother of civil liberty.   The universal priesthood of Christians leads legitimately to the universal kingship of free, self-governing citizens, whether under a monarchy or under a republic.

The good effect of this principle showed itself in the spread of Bible knowledge among the laity, in popular hymnody and congregational singing, in the institution of lay-eldership, and in the pious zeal of the magistrates for moral reform and general education.

But it was also shamefully perverted and abused by the secular rulers who seized the control of religion, made themselves bishops and popes in their dominion, robbed the churches and convents, and often defied all discipline by their own immoral conduct.   Philip of Hesse, and Henry VIII. of England, are conspicuous examples of Protestant popes who disgraced the cause of the Reformation.   Erastianism and Territorialism whose motto is: *cujus regio, ejus religio*, are perversions rather than legitimate developments of lay-priesthood. The true development lies in the direction of general education, in congregational self-support and self-government, and in the intelligent co-operation of the laity with the ministry in all good works, at home and abroad. In this respect the Protestants of England, Scotland, and North America, are ahead of the Protestants on the Continent of Europe. The Roman church is a church of priests and has the grandest temples of worship; the Lutheran church is a church of theologians and has most learning and the finest hymns; the Reformed church is a church of the Christian people and has the best preachers and congregations.

§ 9. *The Reformation and Rationalism.*

G. FRANK: *De Luthero rationalismi præcursore.* Lips., 1857.

S. BERGER: *La Bible au seizième siècle; étude sur les origines de la critique.* Paris, 1879.

CHARLES BEARD: *The Reformation of the Sixteenth Century in relation to Modern Thought and Knowledge* (Hibbert Lectures). London, 1883. Lect. V.

Comp. also LECKY: *History of Rationalism in Europe.* London, 4th ed. 1870, 2 vols. GEORGE P. FISHER: *Faith and Rationalism.* New York, 1879, revised 1885 (191 pages).

The Roman Catholic Church makes Scripture and tradition the supreme rule of faith, laying the chief stress on tradition, that is, the teaching of an infallible church headed by an infallible Pope, as the judge of the meaning of both.[1]

Evangelical Protestantism makes the Scripture alone the supreme rule, but uses tradition and reason as means in ascertaining its true sense.

Rationalism raises human reason above Scripture and tradition, and accepts them only as far as they come within the limits of its comprehension. It makes rationality or intelligibility the measure of credibility. We take the word Rationalism here in the

---

[1] "I am the tradition" (*la tradizione son io*), said Pope Pius IX., during the Vatican Council which substituted an infallible papacy for an infallible council, in conflict both with œcumenical councils and popes who officially denounced Pope Honorius III. as a Monotheletic heretic. See vol. IV. 500 sqq.

technical sense of a theological system and tendency, in distinction from rational theology. The legitimate use of reason in religion is allowed by the Catholic and still more by the Protestant church, and both have produced scholastic systems in full harmony with orthodoxy. Christianity is above reason, but not against reason.

The Reformation is represented as the mother of Rationalism both by Rationalistic and by Roman Catholic historians and controversialists, but from an opposite point of view, by the former to the credit, by the latter to the disparagement of both.

The Reformation, it is said, took the first step in the emancipation of reason: it freed us from the tyranny of the church. Rationalism took the second step: it freed us from the tyranny of the Bible. "Luther," says Lessing, the champion of criticism against Lutheran orthodoxy, "thou great, misjudged man! Thou hast redeemed us from the yoke of tradition: who will redeem us from the unbearable yoke of the letter! Who will at last bring us a Christianity such as thou would teach us now, such as Christ himself would teach!"

Roman Catholics go still further and hold Protestantism responsible for all modern revolutions and for infidelity itself, and predict its ultimate dismemberment and dissolution.[1] But this charge is sufficiently set aside by the undeniable fact that modern infidelity and revolution in their worst forms have appeared chiefly in Roman Catholic countries, as desperate reactions against

[1] This charge is sanctioned by several papal Encyclicals; it is implied, negatively, in the Syllabus of Pius IX. (1864), and, positively, though cautiously, in the Encyclical of Leo XIII *Immortale Dei* (Nov. 1, 1885), which characterizes the Reformation movements (without naming them) as "those pernicious and deplorable revolutionary tendencies which were aroused in the sixteenth century, and which, after introducing confusion into Christendom, soon, by a natural course, entered the domain of philosophy, and from philosophy into all the lines of civil society." Hasak, in his book—*Dr. M. Luther* (Regensburg, 1881), takes as his motto: "Be reconciled to the Church of God, the old mother church, which, for these eighteen hundred years, has been the preserver of the eternal truth, before the bloody flood of atheism and the socialistic republic breaks upon us as a true judgment of the world."

hierarchical and political despotism.   The violent suppression of the Reformation in France ended at last in a radical overthrow of the social order of the church.   In Roman Catholic countries, like Spain and Mexico, revolution has become a chronic disease. Romanism provokes infidelity among cultivated minds by its excessive supernaturalism.

The Reformation checked the skepticism of the renaissance, and the anarchical tendencies of the Peasants' War in Germany and of the Libertines in Geneva.   An intelligent faith is the best protection against infidelity; and a liberal government is a safe-guard against revolution.

The connection of the Reformation with Rationalism is a his-torical fact, but they are related to each other as the rightful use of intellectual freedom to the excess and abuse of it.   Rationalism asserts reason against revelation, and freedom against divine as well as human authority.   It is a one-sided development of the negative, protesting, antipapal and antitraditional factor of the Reformation to the exclusion of its positive, evangelical faith in the revealed will and word of God.   It denies the supernatural and miraculous.   It has a superficial sense of sin and guilt, and is essentially Pelagian; while the Reformation took the opposite Augustinian ground and proceeded from the deepest conviction of sin and the necessity of redeeming grace.   The two systems are thus theoretically and practically opposed to each other.   And yet there is an intellectual and critical affinity between them, and Rationalism is inseparable from the history of Protestantism.   It is in the modern era of Christianity what Gnosticism was in the ancient church—a revolt of private judgment against the popular faith and church orthodoxy, an overestimate of theoretic knowl-edge, but also a wholesome stimulus to inquiry and progress. It is not a church or sect (unless we choose to include Socinian-ism and Unitarianism), but a school in the church, or rather a number of schools which differ very considerably from each other.

Rationalism appeared first in the seventeenth century in the Church of England, though without much effect upon the people, as Deism, which asserted natural religion versus revealed religion; it was matured in its various phases after the middle of the eighteenth century on the Continent, especially in Protestant Germany since Lessing (d. 1781) and Semler (d. 1791), and gradually obtained the mastery of the chairs and pulpits of Lutheran and Reformed churches, till about 1817, when a revival of the positive faith of the Reformation spread over Germany and a serious conflict began between positive and negative Protestantism, which continues to this day.

1. Let us first consider the relation of the Reformation to the use of reason as a general principle.

The Reformation was a protest against human authority, asserted the right of private conscience and judgment, and roused a spirit of criticism and free inquiry in all departments of knowledge. It allows, therefore, a much wider scope for the exercise of reason in religion than the Roman church, which requires unconditional submission to her infallible authority. It marks a real progress, but this progress is perfectly consistent with a belief in revelation on subjects which lie beyond the boundary of time and sense. What do we know of the creation, and the world of the future, except what God has chosen to reveal to us? Human reason can prove the possibility and probability of the existence of God and the immortality of the soul, but not the certainty and necessity. It is reasonable, therefore, to believe in the supernatural on divine testimony, and it is unreasonable to reject it.

The Reformers used their reason and judgment very freely in their contest with church authority. Luther refused to recant in the crisis at Worms, unless convinced by testimonies of the Scriptures and "cogent arguments." [1] For a while he was disposed to avail himself of the humanistic movement which was

---

[1] "*Scripturæ sacræ testimoniis vel evidenti ratione*," or "*evidentissimis rationibus;*" in the German form, as repeated by him on the occasion, "*durch Zeugnisse der heil. Schrift und durch helle Gründe.*" See Köstlin II. 452 sq. and 800. The words seem to assign to reason an independent position by the side of the Scriptures, but in case of conflict Luther always allowed the decision to the Scriptures.

skeptical and rationalistic in its tendency, but his strong religious nature always retained the mastery. He felt as keenly as any modern Rationalist, the conflict between natural reason and the transcending mysteries of revelation. He was often tormented by doubts and even temptations to blasphemy, especially when suffering from physical infirmity. A comforter of others, he needed comfort himself and asked the prayers of friends to fortify him against the assaults of the evil spirit, with whom he had, as he thought, many a personal encounter. He confessed, in 1524, how glad he would have been five years before in his war with papal superstition, if Carlstadt could have convinced him that the Eucharist was nothing but bread and wine, and how strongly he was then inclined to that rationalistic view which would have given a death blow to transubstantiation and the mass. He felt that every article of his creed—the trinity in unity, the incarnation, the transmission of Adam's sin, the atonement by the blood of Christ, baptismal regeneration, the real presence, the renewal of the Holy Spirit, the resurrection of the body—transcended human comprehension. In Aug. 2, 1527, during the raging of the pestilence at Wittenberg, he wrote to Melanchthon, who was absent at Jena: "For more than a week I have been tossed about in death and hell; so that, hurt in all my body, I still tremble in every limb. For having almost wholly lost Christ, I was driven about by storms and tempests of despair and blasphemy against God. But God, moved by the prayers of the saints, begins to have pity upon me, and has drawn my soul out of the lowest hell. Do not cease to pray for me, as I do for you. I believe that this agony of mine pertains to others also." [1]

In such trials and temptations he clung all the more mightily to the Scriptures and to faith which believes against reason and hopes against hope. "It is a quality of faith," he says in the explanation of his favorite Epistle to the Galatians, "that it

---

[1] *Briefe*, ed. de Wette, III. 189: "*Ego sane . . . plus tota hebdomada in morte et inferno jactatus, ita ut toto corpore læsus adhuc tremam membris*," etc. Comp. Luther's letters to Spalatin, July 10th and Aug. 19th, 1527, *l. c.* III. 187, 191.

wrings the neck of reason and strangles the beast, which else the whole world, with all creatures, could not strangle. But how? It holds to God's Word, and lets it be right and true, no matter how foolish and impossible it sounds. So did Abraham take his reason captive and slay it, inasmuch as he believed God's Word, wherein was promised him that from his unfruitful and as it were dead wife, Sarah, God would give him seed."

This and many similar passages clearly show the bent of Luther's mind. He knew the enemy, but overcame it; his faith triumphed over doubt. In his later years he became more and more a conservative churchman. He repudiated the mystic doctrine of the inner word and spirit, insisted on submission to the written letter of the Scriptures, even when it flatly contradicted reason. He traced the errors of the Zwickau prophets, the rebellious peasants, the Anabaptists, and the radical views of Carlstadt and Zwingli, without proper discrimination, to presumptuous inroads of the human reason into the domain of faith, and feared from them the overthrow of religion. He so far forgot his obligations to Erasmus as to call him an Epicurus, a Lucian, a doubter, and an atheist. Much as he valued reason as a precious gift of God in matters of this world, he abused it with unreasonable violence, when it dared to sit in judgment over matters of faith.[1]

---

[1] He called reason "the mistress of the devil," "the ugly devil's bride," "a poisonous beast with many dragons' heads," "God's bitterest enemy." The coarsest invective against this gift of God is found in the last sermon he preached at Wittenberg, in the year of his death (1546), on Rom. 12: 3. He here represents reason as the fountain of gross and subtle idolatry, and says: " *Wucherei, Säuferei, Ehebruch, Mord, Todtschlag, etc., die kann man merken, und verstehet auch die Welt, dass sie Sünde sein; aber des Tuefels Braut, Ratio, die schöne Metze, fähret herein, und will klug sein, und was sie saget, meinet sie, es sei der heilige Geist; wer will da helfen? Weder Jurist, Medicus, noch König oder Kaiser. Denn es ist die höchste Hure die der Teufel hat.*" And again: " *Derohalben wie ein junger Gesell muss der bösen Lust wehren, ein Alter dem Geiz: also ist die Vernunft von Art und Natur eine schädliche Hure.*" . . . " *Die Vernunft ist und soll in der Taufe ersänft sein.*" " *Höre auf, du verfluchte Hure; willst du Meisterin sein über den Glauben, welcher sagt, dass im Abendmahl des Herrn sei der wahre Leib und das wahre Blut; item dass die Taufe nicht schlecht Wasser ist . . . Diesem Glauben muss die Vernunft unterthan und gehorsam sein.*" And much of the same sort,

Certainly, Luther must first be utterly divested of his faith, and the authorship of his sermons, catechisms and hymns must be called in question, before he can be appealed to as the father of Rationalism. He would have sacrificed his reason ten times rather than his faith.

Zwingli was the most clear-headed and rationalizing among the Reformers.[1] He did not pass through the discipline of monasticism and mysticism, like Luther, but through the liberal culture of Erasmus. He had no mystic vein, but sound, sober, practical common sense. He always preferred the plainest sense of the Bible. He rejected the Catholic views on original sin, infant damnation and the corporeal presence in the eucharist, and held advanced opinions which shocked Luther and even Calvin. But he nevertheless reverently bowed before the divine authority of the inspired Word of God, and had no idea of setting reason over it. His dispute with Luther was simply a question of interpretation, and he had strong arguments for his exegesis, as even the best Lutheran commentators must confess.

Calvin was the best theologian and exegete among the Reformers. He never abused reason, like Luther, but assigned it the office of an indispensable handmaid of revelation. He constructed with his logical genius the severest system of Protestant orthodoxy which shaped French, Dutch, English and American theology, and fortified it against Rationalism as well as against Romanism. His orthodoxy and discipline could not keep his own church in Geneva from becoming Socinian in the eighteenth century, but he is no more responsible for that than Luther for the Rationalism of Germany, or Rome for the infidelity of Voltaire. Upon the whole, the Reformed churches in England,

with vehement denunciations of the *Schwärmergeister* and *Sacramentirer* (the sectaries and Zwinglians). See *Werke*, ed. Walch XII. col. 1530 sqq. It is noteworthy that Luther first abused reason in his book on the Slavery of the Human Will against the semi-Pelagianism of Erasmus. But his assaults on Aristotle and the scholastic theology began several years earlier, before 1517.

[1] Luther felt this when he told him at Marburg: "You have a different spirit."

Scotland and North America, have been far less invaded by Rationalism than Germany.

2. Let us now consider the application of the principle of free inquiry to the Bible.[1]

The Bible, its origin, genuineness, integrity, aim, and all its circumstances and surroundings are proper subjects of investigation; for it is a human as well as a divine book, and has a history, like other literary productions. The extent of the Bible, moreover, or the canon, is not determined by the Bible itself or by inspiration, but by church authority or tradition, and was not fully agreed upon till the close of the fourth century, and even then only by provincial synods, not by any of the seven œcumenical councils. It was therefore justly open to reinvestigation.

The Church of Rome, at the Council of Trent, settled the canon, including the Apocrypha, but without any critical inquiry or definite theological principle; it simply confirmed the traditional usage, and pronounced an anathema on every one who does not receive all the books contained in the Latin Vulgate.[2] She also checked the freedom of investigation by requiring conformity to a defective version and a unanimous consensus of the fathers, although such an exegetical consensus does not exist except in certain fundamental doctrines.

The Reformers re-opened the question of the extent of the canon, as they had a right to do, but without any idea of sweep-

---

[1] Comp. here the Critical Introductions to the Bible, and especially Reuss, *Histoire du Canon des Saintes Écritures*, Strasbourg, 1863. Ch. XVI. p. 308 sqq.; Hunter's Engl. transl. (1884) p. 290 sqq.

[2] Sess. IV. (April 8th, 1546): "*Si quis autem libros ipsos integros cum omnibus suis partibus, prout in ecclesia catholica legi consueverunt, et in veteri Vulgata Latina editione habentur, pro sacris et canonicis non susceperit et traditiones prœdictas sciens et prudens contempserit, anathema sit.*" Schaff, *Creeds* II. 82. There were, however, protesting voices in the council: some desired to recognize the old distinction between *Homologumena* and *Antilegomena;* others simply an enumeration of the sacred books used in the Catholic church, without a dogmatic definition. Sarpi censures the council for its decision, and there are Catholic divines (as Sixtus Senensis, Du Pin, Jahn), who, in spite of the decision, make a distinction between protocanonical and deuterocanonical books.

ing away the traditional belief or undermining the authority of
the Word of God. On the contrary, from the fulness of their
faith in the inspired Word, as contained in the Scriptures, they
questioned the canonicity of a few books which seem to be lacking in sufficient evidence to entitle them to a place in the Bible.
They simply revived, in a new shape and on doctrinal rather
than historical grounds, the distinction made by the Hebrews and
the ancient fathers between the canonical and apocryphal books
of the Old Testament, and the Eusebian distinction between the
Homologumena and *Antilegomena* of the New Testament, and
claimed in both respects the freedom of the ante-Nicene church.

They added, moreover, to the external evidence, the more
important internal evidence on the intrinsic excellency of the
Scripture, as the true ground on which its authority and claim to
obedience rests; and they established a firm criterion of canonicity, namely, the purity and force of teaching Christ and his
gospel of salvation. They did not reject the testimonies of the
fathers, but they placed over them what Paul calls the "demonstration of the Spirit and of power" (1 Cor. 2: 4).

Luther was the bold pioneer of a higher criticism, which was
indeed subjective and arbitrary, but, after all, a criticism of faith.
He made his central doctrine of justification by faith the criterion
of canonicity.[1] He thus placed the material or subjective principle of Protestantism above the formal or objective principle, the
truth above the witness of the truth, the doctrine of the gospel
above the written Gospel, Christ above the Bible. Romanism,
on the contrary, places the church above the Bible. But we must
remember that Luther first learnt Christ from the Bible, and

---

[1] "This," he says in the Preface to the Epistle of James, "is the true touch-
stone (*der rechte Prüfstein*) of all books, whether they make Christ their sole
topic and aim" [literally "drive Christ," *Christum treiben*], "or not; since all
Scripture shows Christ (Rom. 3), and St. Paul wishes to know nothing but
Christ (1 Cor. 2). That which does not teach Christ is not apostolic, though
St. Peter and Paul should teach it; again, that which preaches Christ is
apostolic, though Judas, Annas, Pilate and Herod should say it." The devil
himself can quote Scripture.

especially from the Epistles of Paul, which furnished him the key for the understanding of the scheme of salvation.

He made a distinction, moreover, between the more important and the less important books of the New Testament, according to the extent of their evangelic purity and force, and put Hebrews, James, Jude, and Revelation at the end of the German Bible.[1]

He states his reason in the Preface to the Hebrews as follows: "Hitherto we have had the right and genuine books of the New Testament. The four that follow have been differently esteemed in olden times." He therefore appeals to the ante-Nicene tradition, but his chief objection was to the contents.

He disliked, most of all, the Epistle of James because he could not harmonize it with Paul's teaching on justification by faith *without* works,[2] and he called it an epistle of straw as compared with the genuine apostolic writings.[3]

---

[1] In this distinction Carlstadt had preceded him in his book, *De Canon. Scripturis* (Wittenb. 1520, reprinted in Credner's *Zur Gesch. des Kanons*, 1847, p. 291–412). Carlstadt divided the books of the canon into three *ordines:* (1) *libri summae dignitatis* (the Pentateuch, though not written by Moses, and the Gospels); (2) *secundae dignitatis* (the Prophets and 15 Epistles); (3) *tertiae dignitatis* (the Jewish Hagiographa and the seven Antilegomena of the New Testament).

[2] He rejects the epistle first of all, "because it gives righteousness to works in flat contradiction to Paul and all other Scriptures;" secondly, "because, while undertaking to teach Christian people, it does not once mention the passion, the resurrection, the Spirit of Christ; it names Christ twice, but teaches nothing about him; it calls the law a law of liberty, while Paul calls it a law of bondage, of wrath, of death and of sin." He offered his doctor's cap to any who could harmonize James and Paul on the subject of justification, and jests about the trouble Melanchthon took to do it. He made the contradiction unnecessarily stronger by inserting his *allein* (*sola*) before *durch den Glauben* in Rom. 3: 28. He first attacked the Epistle of James in his book *De Captivitate Babylonica*, in 1520, where he calls it an epistle unworthy of the apostolical spirit. Carlstadt seems to have fallen out with Luther in the same year on this question; for he defended the Epistle against the *frivola argumenta* of a *bonus sacerdos amicitiæ nostræ* (who can be no other than Luther), in his book *De canonicis Scripturis*, Wittenbergæ, 1520.

[3] The comparison must not be overlooked. He says: *gegen sie, i. e.* as compared with the Epistles of Paul, Peter and John, previously mentioned. See the passage in full below. He could not be blind to the merits of James as a fresh, vigorous teacher of practical Christianity.

He objected to the Epistle to the Hebrews because it seems to deny (in chs. 6, 10 and 12) the possibility of repentance after baptism, contrary to the Gospels and to Paul, and betrays in ch. 2: 3, a post-apostolic origin. He ascribed the authorship to Apollos by an ingenious guess, which, though not supported by ancient tradition, has found great favor with modern commentators and critics,[1] chiefly because the authorship of any other possible writer (Paul, Barnabas, Luke, Clement) seems to offer insuperable difficulties, while the description of Apollos in Acts 18. 24–28, compared with the allusions in 1 Cor. 1: 12; 3 : 6; 4: 6; 16: 12, seems to fit exactly the author of this anonymous Epistle.

He called the Epistle of Jude an "unnecessary epistle," a mere extract from Second Peter and post-apostolic, filled with apocryphal matter, and hence rejected by the ancient fathers.

He could at first find no sense in the mysteries of the Apocalypse and declared it to be "neither apostolic nor prophetic," because it deals only with images and visions, and yet, notwithstanding its obscurity, it adds threats and promises, "though nobody knows what it means"; but afterwards he modified his judgment when the Lutheran divines found in it welcome weapons against the church of Rome.

The clearest utterance on this subject is found at the close of his preface to the first edition of his German version of the New Testament (1522), but it was suppressed in later editions.[2]

Luther's view of inspiration was both strong and free. With the profoundest conviction of the divine contents of the Bible, he distinguished between the revealed truth itself and the human wording and reasoning of the writers. He says of one of the

---

[1] Bleek, de Wette, Tholuck, Lünemann, Kendrick (in Lange), Hilgenfeld, de Pressensé, Davidson, Alford, Farrar, and others.

[2] See note at the end of this section. His *Table Talk* contains bold and original utterances on Esther, Ecclesiastes and other books of the Old Testament; see Reuss on the *Canon*, p. 330 sqq. While Luther on the one hand limited the canon, he seemed disposed on the other hand to extend it, when he declared Melanchthon's *Loci Theologici* to be worthy of a place in the canon. But this was merely an extravagant compliment.

rabbinical arguments of his favorite apostle : " My dear brother Paul, this argument won't stick." [1]

Luther was, however, fully aware of the subjective and con-jectural character of these opinions, and had no intention of obtruding them on the church : hence he modified his prefaces in later editions. He judged the Scriptures from an exclusively dogmatic, and one-sidedly Pauline standpoint, and did not con-sider their gradual historical growth.

A few Lutheran divines followed him in assigning a subordi-nate position to the seven Antilegomena of the New Testament; [2] but the Lutheran church, with a sound instinct, accepted for popular use the traditional catholic canon (not even expressly excluding the Jewish Apocrypha), yet retained his arrangement of the books of the New Testament.[3] The Rationalists, of course, revived, intensified, and carried to excess the bold opinions of Luther, but in a spirit against which he would himself raise the strongest protest.

The Reformed divines were more conservative than Luther in accepting the canonical books, but more decided in rejecting the Apocrypha of the Old Testament. The Reformed Confessions usually enumerate the canonical books.

Zwingli objected only to the Apocalypse and made no doctrinal use of it, because he did not deem it an inspired book, written by the same John who wrote the fourth Gospel.[4] In this view he has many followers, but the severest critical school of our days (that of Tübingen) assigns it to the Apostle John. Wolfgang

Comp. his comments on the allegory of Sarah and Hagar in his Latin Com. on Gal. 3 : 25 (Erl. ed. II. 252).

[2] Brentius, Flacius, Urbanus Regius, the authors of the Magdeburg Centuries, and Chemnitz.

[3] None of the symbolical books of the Lutheran church gives a list of the canon, but the Formula of Concord (p. 570) declares that the "*prophetica et apostolica scripta V. et N. T.*" are the "*unica regula et norma secundum quam om-nia dogmata omnesque doctores aestimari et judicari opporteat.*"

[4] " *Us Apocalypsi nehmend wir kein Kundschafft an, denn es nit ein biblisch Buch ist.*"   *Werke*, ed. Schuler and Schulthess, II. 1. p. 169.   In another place he says: "*Apocal. liber non sapit os et ingenium Joannis.*"   *De clar. Verbi Dei*, p. 310.

Musculus mentions the seven Antilegomena, but includes them in the general catalogue of the New Testament; and Oecolampadius speaks of six Antilegomena (omitting the Hebrews), as holding an inferior rank, but nevertheless appeals to their testimony.[1]

Calvin had no fault to find with James and Jude, and often quotes Hebrews and Revelation as canonical books, though he wrote no commentary on Revelation, probably because he felt himself incompetent for the task. He is silent about Second and Third John. He denies, decidedly, the Pauline authorship, but not the canonicity, of Hebrews.[2] He is disposed to assign Second Peter to a pupil of Peter, who wrote under the auspices and by direction of the Apostle; but he guards in this case, also, against unfavorable inferences from the uncertainty of origin.[3]

Calvin clearly saw the inconsistency of giving the Church the right of determining the canon after denying her right of making an article of faith. He therefore placed the canon on the authority of God who bears testimony to it through the voice of the Spirit in the hearts of the believer. The eternal and inviolable truth of God, he says, is not founded on the pleasure and judgment of men, and can be as easily distinguished as light from darkness, and white from black. In the same line, Peter Vermilius denies that "the Scriptures take their authority from the Church. Their certitude is derived from God. The Word is older than the Church. The Spirit of God wrought in the hearts of the hearers and readers of the Word so that they recognized it to be truly divine." This view is clearly set forth in several

---

[1] See Reuss, p. 315 sq. Eng. ed.

[2] In the introduction to his Com. on Hebrews: "*Ego ut Paulum auctorem agnoscam adduci nequeo.*" His reasons are, the difference of style and of the *docendi ratio,* and because the writer counts himself with the disciples of the Apostles (2: 3); but nevertheless he accepts the book as inspired and canonical, because it more clearly than any other book treats of the priesthood and sacrifice of Christ.

[3] In *Argum. Ep. Sec. Petri,* he notes "*manifestum discrimen*" between the first and second Epistle, and adds: "*Sunt et aliæ probabiles conjecturæ ex quibus colligere licet alterius esse potius quam Petri,*" but he sees in it "*nihil Petro indignum*"

Calvinistic Confessions.[1] In its exclusive form it is diametrically opposed to the maxim of Augustin, otherwise so highly esteemed by the Reformers: "I should not believe the gospel except as moved by the authority of the Church."[2] But the two kinds of evidence supplement each other. The human authority of tradition though not the final ground of belief, is indispensable as an historical witness of the genuineness and canonicity, and is of great weight in conflict with Rationalism. There is no essential antagonism between the Bible and the Church in the proper sense of the term. They are inseparable. The Church was founded by Christ and the apostles through the preaching of the *living* Word of God, and the founders of the Church are also the authors of the *written* Word, which continues to be the shining and guiding light of the Church; while the Church in turn is the guardian, preserver, translator, propagator, and expounder of the Bible.

3. The liberal views of the Reformers on inspiration and the canon were abandoned after the middle of the sixteenth century, and were succeeded by compact and consolidated systems of theology. The evangelical scholasticism of the seventeenth century strongly resembles, both in its virtues and defects, the catho-

---

[1] The Second Helvetic Confession, c. 1 and 2, and the Belgic Confession, art. 5, combine the testimony of tradition and that of the Holy Spirit, but lay chief stress upon the latter. So the Gallican Conf., art. 4: "We know these books to be canonical and the sure rule of our faith, *not so much* by the common accord and consent of the church (*non tant par le commun accord et consentement de l'eglise*), as by the testimony and inward illumination of the Holy Spirit, which enables us to distinguish them from other ecclesiastical books, upon which, however useful, we cannot found any articles of faith." The Westminster Confession, ch. I. 4, sets aside the testimony of tradition, saying: "The authority of the Holy Scripture, for which it ought to be believed and obeyed, dependeth *not* upon the testimony of any man or church, but *wholly* upon God (who is truth itself), the Author thereof; and therefore it is to be received, because it is the Word of God." The Scripture proofs given are, 2 Pet. 1: 19, 21; 2 Tim. 3: 16; 1 John 5: 9; 1 Thess. 2: 13; but they have no bearing upon the question of canonicity.

[2] "*Ego evangelio non crederem, nisi me moveret ecclesiae auctoritas,*" *Contra Ep. Fundam.*, c. 5. A thoroughly Roman catholic principle in opposition to the Manichæan heresy. But the testimony of the church is indispensable only in the history of the origin of the several books, and the formation of the *canon*.

lic scholasticism of the Middle Ages which systematized and contracted the patristic theology, except that the former was based on the Bible, the latter on church tradition. In the conflict with Romanism the Lutheran and Calvinistic scholastics elaborated a stiff, mechanical theory of inspiration in order to set an infallible book against an infallible pope. The Bible was identified with the Word of God, dictated to the sacred writers as the penmen of the Holy Ghost. Even the classical purity of style and the integrity of the traditional text, including the Massoretic punctuation, were asserted in the face of stubborn facts, which came to light as the study of the origin and history of the text advanced. The divine side of the Scriptures was exclusively dwelled upon, and the human and literary side was ignored or virtually denied. Hence the exegetical poverty of the period of Protestant scholasticism. The Bible was used as a repository of proof texts for previously conceived dogmas, without regard to the context, the difference between the Old and New Testaments, and the gradual development of the divine revelation in accordance with the needs and capacities of men.

4. It was against this Protestant bibliolatry and symbololatry that Rationalism arose as a legitimate protest. It pulled down one dogma after another, and subjected the Bible and the canon to a searching criticism. It denies the divine inspiration of the Scriptures, except in a wider sense which applies to all works of genius, and treats them simply as a gradual evolution of the religious spirit of Israel and the primitive Christian Church. It charges them with errors of fact and errors of doctrine, and resolves the miracles into legends and myths. It questions the Mosaic origin of the Pentateuch, the genuineness of the Davidic Psalms, the Solomonic writings, the prophecies of Deutero-Isaiah and Daniel, and other books of the Old Testament. It assigns not only the Eusebian Antilegomena, but even the Gospels, Acts, the Catholic Epistles, and several Pauline Epistles to the post-apostolic age, from A. D. 70 to 150.

In its later developments, however, Rationalism has been

obliged to retreat and make several concessions to orthodoxy. The canonical Gospels and Acts have gained by further investigation and discovery;[1] and the apostolic authorship of the four great Epistles of Paul to the Romans, Corinthians, and Galatians and the Apocalypse of John is fully admitted by the severest school of criticism (that of Tübingen). A most important admission: for these five books teach or imply all the leading facts and truths of the gospel, and overthrow the very foundations of Rationalism. With the Christ of the Gospels, and the Apostle Paul of his acknowledged Epistles, Christianity is safe.

Rationalism was a radical revolution which swept like a flood over the Continent of Europe. But it is not negative and destructive only. It has made and is still making valuable contributions to biblical philology, textual criticism, and grammatico-historical exegesis. It enlarges the knowledge of the conditions and environments of the Bible, and of all that belongs to the human and temporal side of Christ and Christianity. It cultivates with special zeal and learning the sciences of Critical Introduction, Biblical Theology, the Life of Christ, the Apostolic and post-Apostolic Ages.

5. These acquisitions to exegetical and historical theology are a permanent gain, and are incorporated in the new evangelical theology, which arose in conflict with Rationalism and in defense of the positive Christian faith in the divine facts of revelation and the doctrines of salvation. The conflict is still going on with increasing strength, but with the sure prospect of

---

[1] Thus Mark is regarded by many Rationalists as the primitive Gospel based on Peter's sermons. Matthew has received valuable testimonies from the discovery of the Greek Barnabas who quotes him twice, and from the discovery of the Didache of the Apostles, which contains about twenty reminiscences from the first Gospel. On the Johannean question the Tübingen critics have been forced to retreat from 170 to 140, 120, 110, almost to the lifetime of John. The Acts have received new confirmation of their historical credibility from the excavations in Cyprus and Ephesus, and the minute test of the nautical vocabulary of chapter 27 by an experienced seaman. On all these points see the respective sections in the first volume of this *History*, ch. XII. p. 569 sqq.; 715 sqq.; 731 sqq ; and 853 sqq.

the triumph of truth. Christianity is independent of all critical
questions on the canon, and of human theories of inspiration;
else Christ would himself have written the Gospels, or commanded
the Apostles to do so, and provided for the miraculous preservation and inspired translation of the text. His "words are spirit,
and are life." "The flesh profiteth nothing." Criticism and
speculation may for a while wander away from Christ, but will
ultimately return to Him who furnishes the only key for the solution of the problems of history and human life. "No matter,"
says the world-poet Goethe in one of his last utterances, "how
much the human mind may progress in intellectual culture, in
the science of nature, in ever-expanding breadth and depth : it
will never be able to rise above the elevation and moral culture
which shines in the Gospels."

NOTES.

The famous close of the Preface of Luther's edition of the German New
Testament was omitted in later editions, but is reprinted in Walch's ed. XIV.
104 sqq., and in the Erlangen Frankf. ed. LXIII. (or eleventh vol. of the
Vermischte Deutsche Schriften), p. 114 sq.   It is verbatim as follows:

"*Aus diesem allen kannst du nu recht urtheilen unter allen Büchern, und Unter-
schied nehmen, welchs die besten sind.   Denn, nämlich, ist Johannis Evangelion, und
St. Pauli Episteln, sonderlich die zu den Römern, und Sanct Peters erste Epistel der
rechte Kern und Mark unter allen Büchern; welche auch billig die ersten sein
sollten, und einem jeglichen Christen zu rathen wäre, dass er dieselben am ersten und
allermeisten läse, und ihm durch täglich Lesen so gemein mächte, als das täglich Brod.*

"*Denn in diesen findist [findest] du nicht viel Werk und Wunderthaten Christi
beschrieben; du findist aber gar meisterlich ausgestrichen, wie der Glaube an Christum
Sünd, Tod und Hölle überwindet, und das Leben, Gerechtigkeit und Seligkeit gibt.
Welchs die rechte Art ist des Evangelii, wie du gehöret hast.*

"*Denn wo ich je der eins mangeln sollt, der Werke oder der Predigt Christi, so
wollt ich lieber der Werke. denn seiner Predigt mangeln.   Denn die Werke helfen
mir nichts; aber seine Worte, die geben das Leben, wie er selbst sagt (Joh. 5. V. 51).
Weil nu Johannes gar wenig Werke von Christo, aber gar viel seiner Predigt schreibt;
wiederumb die andern drei Evangelisten viel seiner Werke, wenig seiner Worte
beschreiben: ist Johannis Evangelion das einige zarte, recht(e) Hauptevangelion, und
den andern dreien weit fürzuziehen und höher zu heben. Also auch Sanct Paulus und
Petrus Episteln weit über die drei Evangelia, Matthäi, Marci und Lucä vorgehen.*

"*Summa, Sanct Johannis Evangel. und seine erste Epistel, Sanct Paulus Epis-
tel(n), sonderlich die zu den Römern, Galatern, Ephesern, und Sanct Peters erste
Epistel. das sind die Bücher, die dir Christum zeigen, und alles lehren, das dir zu
wissen noth und selig ist ob du sohon kein ander Buch noch Lehre nummer [nimmer-*

mehr] *sehest and horist [hörest].   Darumb ist Sanct Jakobs Epistel ein recht stroh-
ern(e) Epistel, gegen sie, denn sie doch kein(e) evangelisch(e) Art an ihr hat.   Doch
davon weiter in andern Vorreden."*

§ 10. *Protestantism and Denominationalism.*[1]

The Greek Church exists as a patriarchal hierarchy based on
the first seven œcumenical councils with four ancient local centres:
Jerusalem, Antioch, Alexandria, Constantinople; to which must
be added, since 1725, St. Petersburg where the Holy Synod of
orthodox Russia resides.   The patriarch of Constantinople claims
a primacy of honor, but no supremacy of jurisdiction over his fel-
low-patriarchs.

The Roman Church is an absolute monarchy, headed by an infallible pope who claims to be vicar of Christ over all Christendom
and unchurches the Greek and the Protestant churches as schismatical and heretical.

The Reformation came out of the bosom of the Latin Church
and broke up the *visible* unity of Western Christendom, but prepared the way for a higher spiritual unity on the basis of freedom
and the full development of every phase of truth.

Instead of one organization, we have in Protestantism a number
of distinct national churches and confessions or denominations.
Rome, the local centre of unity, was replaced by Wittenberg,
Zurich, Geneva, Oxford, Cambridge, Edinburgh.   The one great
pope had to surrender to many little popes of smaller pre-
tensions, yet each claiming and exercising sovereign power in
his domain.   The hierarchical rule gave way to the cæsaropapal
or Erastian principle, that the owner of the territory is also the
owner of its religion (*cujus regio, ejus religio*), a principle first

---

[1] *Denominationalism* is, I believe, an American term of recent origin, but useful and necessary to express the fact, without praise or blame, that Protestant
Christianity exists in various ecclesiastical organizations, some of which are
large, others small, some differing in doctrine, others only in polity and worship,
some liberal and catholic, others contracted and exclusive.   I use it in this
neutral sense, in preference to *Confessionalism* which implies confessional or
doctrinal difference, and *Sectarianism* which implies bigotry and is a term of
reproach.

maintained by the Byzantine Emperors, and held also by the Czar of Russia, but in subjection to the supreme authority of the œcumenical councils. Every king, prince, and magistrate, who adopted the Reformation, assumed the ecclesiastical supremacy or summepiscopate, and established a national church to the exclusion of Dissenters or Nonconformists who were either expelled, or simply tolerated under various restrictions and disabilities.

Hence there are as many national or state churches as there are independent Protestant governments; but all acknowledge the supremacy of the Scriptures as a rule of faith and practice, and most of them also the evangelical confessions as a correct summary of Scripture doctrines. Every little principality in monarchical Germany and every canton in republican Switzerland has its own church establishment, and claims sovereign power to regulate its creed, worship, and discipline. And this power culminates not in the clergy, but in the secular ruler who appoints the ministers of religion and the professors of theology. The property of the church which had accumulated by the pious foundations of the Middle Ages, was secularized during the Reformation period and placed under the control of the state, which in turn assumed the temporal support of the church.

This is the state of things in Europe to this day, except in the independent or free churches of more recent growth, which manage their own affairs on the voluntary principle.

The transfer of the episcopal and papal power to the head of the state was not contemplated by the Reformers, but was the inevitable consequence of the determined opposition of the whole Roman hierarchy to the Reformation. The many and crying abuses which followed this change in the hands of selfish and rapacious princes, were deeply deplored by Melanchthon, who would have consented to the restoration of the episcopal hierarchy on condition of the freedom of gospel preaching and gospel teaching.

The Reformed church in Switzerland secured at first a greater degree of independence than the Lutheran; for Zwingli controlled the magistrate of Zurich, and Calvin ruled supreme in Geneva under institutions of his own founding; but both closely united the civil and ecclesiastical power, and the former gradually assumed the supremacy.

Scandinavia and England adopted, together with the Reformation, a Protestant episcopate which divides the ecclesiastical supremacy with the head of the state; yet even there the civil ruler is legally the supreme governor of the church.

The greatest Protestant church-establishments or national churches are the Church of England, much weakened by dissent, but still the richest and most powerful of all; the United Evangelical Church of Prussia which, since 1817, includes the formerly separated Lutheran and Reformed confessions; the Lutheran Church of Saxony (with a Roman Catholic king); the Lutheran Churches of Denmark, Sweden, and Norway; the Reformed Churches of Switzerland, and Holland; and the Reformed or Presbyterian Church of Scotland.

Originally, all evangelical Protestant churches were embraced under two confessions or denominations, the Lutheran which prevailed and still prevails in Germany and Scandinavia, and the Reformed which took root in Switzerland, France, Holland, England and Scotland, and to a limited extent also in Germany, Bohemia and Hungary. The Lutheran church follows the larger portion of German and Scandinavian emigrants to America and other countries, the Reformed church in its various branches is found in all the Dutch and British colonies, and in the United States.

From these two confessions should be distinguished the Anglican Church, which the continental historians from defective information usually count with the Reformed Church, but which stands midway between evangelical Protestantism and Roman Catholicism, and may therefore be called Anglo-Catholic. She is indeed moderately Reformed in her doctrinal articles,[1] but in

---

[1] The Thirty-nine Articles of Religion, as revised under Elizabeth (1563 and 1571), are borrowed in part, verbatim, from the Augsburg Confession of 1530 and the Würtemberg Confession of 1552, but are moderately Calvinistic in the

polity and ritual she is much more conservative than the Calvinistic and even the Lutheran confession, pays greater deference to the testimony of the ancient fathers, and lays stress upon her unbroken episcopal succession.

The confessional division in the Protestant camp arose very early. It was at first confined to a difference of opinion on the eucharistic presence, which the Marburg Conference of 1529 could not remove, although Luther and Zwingli agreed in fourteen and a half out of fifteen articles of faith. Luther refused any compromise. Other differences gradually developed themselves, on the ubiquity of Christ's body, predestination, and baptismal regeneration, which tended to widen and perpetuate the split. The union of the two Confessions in Prussia and other German states, since 1817, has not really healed it, but added a third Church, the United Evangelical, to the two older Confessions which still continue separate in other countries.

The controversies among the Protestants in the sixteenth century roused all the religious and political passions and cast a gloom over the bright picture of the Reformation. Melanchthon declared that with tears as abundant as the waters of the river Elbe he could not express his grief over the distractions of Christendom and the "fury of theologians." Calvin also, when invited, with Melanchthon, Bullinger and Buzer, in 1552, by Archbishop Cranmer to Lambeth Palace for the purpose of framing a concensus-creed of the Reformed churches, was willing to cross ten seas for the cause of Christian union.[1] But the noble scheme was frustrated by the stormy times, and still remains a *pium desiderium.*

doctrine of the Lord's Supper, and on predestination; the five Lambeth Articles of 1595, and the Irish Articles of Archbishop Ussher (1615) are strongly Calvinistic, and the latter furnished the basis of the Westminster Confession. But the Lambeth Articles and the Irish Articles were gradually forgotten, and the Book of Common Prayer which is based on the office of Sarum, has practically much greater influence than even the Thirty-nine Articles. See Schaff, *Creeds of Christendom,* vol. I. 624 sqq., 630 sqq., 658 sqq., 662 sqq.

[1] See the correspondence in Cranmer's *Works,* publ. by the Parker Society, vol. II. 430–433.

Much as we must deplore and condemn sectarian strife and bitterness, it would be as unjust to charge them on Protestantism, as to charge upon Catholicism the violent passions of the trinitarian, christological and other controversies of the Nicene age, or the fierce animosity between the Greek and Latin Churches, or the envy and jealousy of the monastic orders of the Middle Ages, or the unholy rivalries between Jansenists and Jesuits, Gallicans and Ultramontanists in modern Romanism. The religious passions grow out of the selfishness of depraved human nature in spite of Christianity, whether Greek, Roman, or Protestant, and may arise in any denomination or in any congregation. Paul had to rebuke the party spirit in the church at Corinth. The rancor of theological schools and parties under one and the same government is as great and often greater than among separate rival denominations. Providence overrules these human weaknesses for the clearer development of doctrine and discipline, and thus brings good out of evil.

The tendency of Protestantism towards individualism did not stop with the three Reformation Churches, but produced other divisions wherever it was left free to formulate and organize the differences of theological parties and schools. This was the case in England, in consequence of what may be called a second Reformation, which agitated that country during the seventeenth century, while Germany was passing through the horrors of the Thirty Years' War.

The Toleration Act of 1689, after the final overthrow of the semi-popish and treacherous dynasty of the Stuarts, gave the Dissenters who were formerly included in the Church of England, the liberty to organize themselves into independent denominations under the names of Presbyterians, Independents or Congregationalists, Baptists, Quakers; all professing the principles of the Reformation, but differing in minor points of doctrine, and especially in discipline, and the mode of worship.

The Methodist revival of religion which shook England and the American colonies during the eighteenth century, gave rise to a new denomination which spread with the enthusiasm of an army of conquest and grew into one of the largest and most influential communions in English-speaking Christendom.

In Scotland, the original unity of the Reformed Kirk was likewise broken up, mostly on the question of patronage and the sole headship of Christ, so that the Scotch population is now divided chiefly into three branches, the Established Church, the United Presbyterian Church, and the Free Church of Scotland; ail holding, however, to the Westminster standards.

In Germany, the Moravian brotherhood acquired a legal existence, and fully earned it by its missionary zeal among the heathen, its educational institutions, its pure discipline and stimulating influence upon the older churches.

All these Churches of Great Britain and the Continent were transplanted by emigration to the virgin soil of North America, where they mingle on a basis of equality before the law and in the enjoyment of perfect religious freedom. But few communions are of native growth. In America, the distinction between church and sect, churchmen and dissenters, has lost its legal meaning. And even in Europe it is weakened in the same proportion in which under the influence of modern ideas of toleration and freedom the bond of union of church and state is relaxed, and the sects or theological parties are allowed to organize themselves into distinct communities.

Thus Protestantism in the nineteenth century is divided into half a dozen or more large denominations, without counting the minor divisions which are even far more numerous. The Episcopalians, the Lutherans, the Presbyterians, the Congregationalists, the Methodists, and the Baptists, are distinct and separate families. Nor is the centrifugal tendency of Protestantism exhausted, and may produce new denominations, especially in America, where no political power can check its progress.

To an outside spectator, especially to a Romanist and to an infidel, Protestantism presents the aspect of a religious chaos or anarchy which must end in dissolution.

But a calm review of the history of the last three centuries and the present condition of Christendom leads to a very different conclusion. It is an undeniable fact that Christianity has the strongest hold upon the people and displays the greatest vitality and energy at home and abroad, in English-speaking countries, where it is most divided into denominations and sects. A comparison of England with Spain, or Scotland with Portugal, or the United States with Mexico and Peru or Brazil, proves the advantages of living variety over dead uniformity. Division is an element of weakness in attacking a consolidated foe, but it also multiplies the missionary, educational, and converting agencies. Every Protestant denomination has its own field of usefulness, and the cause of Christianity itself would be seriously weakened and contracted by the extinction of any one of them.

Nor should we overlook the important fact, that the differences which divide the various Protestant denominations are not fundamental, and that the articles of faith in which they agree are more numerous than those in which they disagree. All accept the inspired Scriptures as the supreme rule of faith and practice, salvation by grace, and we may say every article of the Apostles' Creed; while in their views of practical Christianity they unanimously teach that our duties are comprehended in the royal law of love to God and to our fellow-men, and that true piety and virtue consist in the imitation of the example of Christ, the Lord and Saviour of all.

There is then unity in diversity as well as diversity in unity.

And the tendency to separation and division is counteracted by the opposite tendency to Christian union and denominational intercommunion which manifests itself in a rising degree and in various forms among Protestants of the present day, especially in England and America, and on missionary fields, and which is sure to triumph in the end. The spirit of narrowness, bigotry and exclusiveness must give way at last to a spirit of evangelical catholicity, which leaves each denomination free to work out its own mission according to its special charisma, and equally free to co-operate in a noble rivalry with all other denominations for the glory of the common Master and the building up of His Kingdom.

The great problem of Christian union cannot be solved by returning to a uniformity of belief and outward organization. Diversity in unity and unity in diversity is the law of God in history as well as in nature. Every aspect of truth must be allowed room for free development. Every possibility of Christian life must be realized. The past cannot be undone; history moves zig-zag, like a sailing vessel, but never backwards. The work of church history, whether Greek, Roman, or Protestant, cannot be in vain. Every denomination and sect has to furnish some stones for the building of the temple of God.

And out of the greatest human discord God will bring the richest concord.

§ 11. *Protestantism and Religious Liberty.*

Comp. Ph. Schaff: *The Progress of Religious Freedom as shown in the History of Toleration Acts,* N. York, 1889. (126 pages.)

The Reformation was a grand act of emancipation from spiritual tyranny, and a vindication of the sacred rights of conscience in matters of religious belief. Luther's bold stand at the Diet of Worms, in the face of the pope and the emperor, is one of the sublimest events in the history of liberty, and the eloquence of his testimony rings through the centuries.[1] To break the force of the pope, who called himself and was believed to be, the visible vicar of God on earth, and who held in his hands the keys of the kingdom of heaven, required more moral courage than to fight a hundred battles, and it was done by an humble monk in the might of faith.

If liberty, both civil and religious, has since made progress, it is due in large measure to the inspiration of that heroic act. But

[1] Froude says (*Luther,* p. 38): "The appearance of Luther before the Diet on this occasion, is one of the finest, perhaps it is the very finest, scene in human history."

the progress was slow and passed through many obstructions and reactions. "The mills of God grind slowly, but wonderfully fine."

It seems one of the strangest inconsistencies that the very men who claimed and exercised the right of protest in essentials, should have denied the same right to others, who differed from them in nonessentials. After having secured liberty from the yoke of popery, they acted on the persecuting principles in which they had been brought up. They had no idea of toleration or liberty in our modern sense. They fought for liberty *in* Christ, not *from* Christ, for liberty to preach and teach the gospel, not to oppose or pervert it. They were as intensely convinced of their views as their Roman opponents of theirs. They abhorred popery and heresy as dangerous errors which should not be tolerated in a Christian society. John Knox feared one Romish mass in Scotland more than an army of ten thousand French invaders. The Protestant divines and princes of the sixteenth century felt it to be their duty to God and to themselves to suppress and punish heresy as well as civil crimes. They confounded the law with the gospel. In many cases they acted in retaliation, and in self-defense. They were surrounded by a swarm of sects and errorists who claimed to be the legitimate children of the Reformation, exposed it to the reproach of the enemies and threatened to turn it into confusion and anarchy. The world and the church were not ripe for a universal reign of liberty, nor are they even now.

Religious persecution arises not only from bigotry and fanaticism, and the base passions of malice, hatred and uncharitableness, but also from mistaken zeal for truth and orthodoxy, from the intensity of religious conviction, and from the alliance of religion with politics or the union of church and state, whereby an offence against the one becomes an offence against the other. Persecution is found in all religions, churches and sects which had the power; while on the other hand all persecuted religions, sects, and parties are advocates of toleration and freedom, at least for themselves. Some of the best as well as the worst men have been persecutors, believing that they served the cause of God by fighting his enemies. Saul of Tarsus, and Marcus Aurelius, the Stoic saint and philosopher on the throne of the Cæsars, have in ignorance persecuted Christianity, the one from zeal for the law of Moses, the other from devotion to the laws and gods of Rome. Charlemagne thought he could best promote Christianity among the heathen Saxons by chasing them through the river for wholesale baptism. St. Augustin, Thomas Aquinas, and Calvin were equally convinced of the right and duty of the civil magistrate to punish heresy. A religion or church established by law must be protected by law against its enemies. The only sure guarantee against persecution is to put all churches on an equal footing before the law, and either to support all or none.

Church history is lurid with the infernal fires of persecutions, not only of Christians by heathens and Mohammedans, but of Christians by Christians.

But there is a silver lining to every cloud, and an overruling Providence in all human wickedness. The persecutions test character, develop moral heroism, bring out the glories of martyrdom, and sow the bloody seed of religious liberty. They fail of their object when the persecuted party has the truth on its side, and ultimately result in its victory. This was the case with Christianity in the Roman empire, and to a large extent with Protestantism. They suffered the cross, and reaped the crown.

Let us now briefly survey the chief stages in the history of persecution, which is at the same time a history of religious liberty.

1. The New Testament furnishes not a single passage in favor of persecution. The teaching and example of Christ and the Apostles are against it. He came to save the world, not to destroy it. He declared that His kingdom is not of this world. He rebuked the hasty Peter for drawing the sword, though it was in defense of his Master; and he preferred to suffer and to die rather than to call the angels of God to aid against his enemies. The Apostles spread the gospel by spiritual means and condemned the use of carnal weapons.

For three hundred years the church followed their example and advocated freedom of conscience. She suffered persecution from Jews and Gentiles, but never retaliated, and made her way to triumph through the power of truth and a holy life sealed by a heroic death.[1]

2. The change began with the union of church and state under Constantine the Great, in the East, and Charles the Great, in the West. Both these emperors represent the continuation of the old Roman empire under the dominion of the sword and the cross.

The mediæval theory of the Catholic Church assumes a close alliance of Cæsar and Pope, or the civil and ecclesiastical power, in Christian countries, and the exclusiveness of the Catholic communion out of which there can be no salvation. The Athanasian Creed has no less than three damning clauses against all who dissent from the orthodox doctrine of the Trinity and the Incarnation. From this point of view every heresy, i. e., every departure from catholic orthodoxy, is a sin and a crime against society, and punishable both by the church and the state, though in different ways. "The church does not thirst for blood," [2] but excommunicates the obstinate heretic and hands him over to the civil magistrate to be dealt with according to law. And the laws of pagan Rome and Christian Rome were alike severe against every open dissent from the state religion. The Mosaic legislation against idolatry and blasphemy, which were punished by death, as a crime against the theocracy and as treason against Jehovah,[3] seemed to afford divine authority for similar enactments under

---

[1] Justin Martyr, Tertullian, and Lactantius made some of the strongest pleas in favor of religious liberty. See vol. II. 35 and 825.

[2] "Ecclesia non sitit sanguinem," a maxim held by the Catholic church even in the darkest days of persecution. When the first blood of heretics was shed by order of the Emperor Maximus who punished some Priscillianists in Spain by the sword in 388, St. Ambrose of Milan and St. Martin of Tours loudly protested against the cruelty and broke off communion with the bishops who had approved it.

[3] Ex. 22: 20; Num. 25: 2–8; Deut. 13: 1–14; 17: 2–5; Lev. 24: 14–16; comp. 1 Kings 21: 10, 13. The law was executed against Stephen, the protomartyr, Acts 6· 11, 13; 7: 58.

the Christian dispensation, in spite of the teaching and example
of Christ and his Apostles. The Christian emperors after Constantine persecuted the heathen religion and heretical sects, as
their heathen predecessors had persecuted the Christians as enemies of the national gods. The Justinian code, which extended its
influence over the whole Continent of Europe, declares Christian
heretics and schismatics, as well as Pagans and Jews, incapable
of holding civil or military offices, forbids their public assemblies
and ecclesiastical acts, and orders their books to be burned.

The leading divines of the church gave sanction to this theory.
St. Augustin, who had himself been a heretic for nine years, was
at first in favor of toleration.[1] But during the Donatist controversy, he came to the conclusion that the correction and coërcion
of heretics and schismatics was in some cases necessary and wholesome. His tract on the *Correction of the Donatists* was written
about 417, to show that the schismatical and fanatical Donatists
should be subjected to the punishment of the imperial laws. He
admits that it is better that men should be led to worship God
by teaching than be driven to it by fear of punishment or pain;
but he reasons that more men are corrected by fear. He derives
the proof from the Old Testament. The only passages from the
New Testament which he is able to quote, would teach a com-

---

[1] He begins his anti-Manichæan work, *Adv. Epistolam Manichœi quam
vocant fundamenti*, written in 397, with these noble Christian sentiments: "My
prayer to the one true, almighty God, of whom and by whom and in whom
are all things, has been and is now, that in opposing and refuting the heresy
of you Manichæans, as you may after all be heretics more from thoughtless-
ness than from malice, He would give me a calm and composed mind, aiming
at your recovery rather than your discomfiture. For, while the Lord by his
servants overthrows the kingdoms of error, his will concerning erring men, as
far as they are men, is that they should be restored rather than destroyed. And
in every case where, previous to the final judgment, God inflicts punishment
. . . we must believe that the designed effect is the recovery of men, and not
their ruin; while there is a preparation for the final doom in the case of those
who reject the means of recovery." And in ch. 3 he says to the Manichæans,
remembering his own former connection with them: "I can on no account treat
you angrily; for I must bear with you now as formerly I had to bear with myself, and I must be as patient with you as my associates were with me, when I
went madly and blindly astray in your beliefs."

pulsory salvation rather than punishment, but are really not to the point. He refers to Paul's conversion as a case of compulsion by Christ himself, and misapplies the word of our Lord in the parable of the Supper: "Constrain them to come in." [1] Yet he professed, on the other hand, the correct principle that "no man can believe against his will." [2] And he expressly discouraged the infliction of the death-penalty on heretics. [3]

Thomas Aquinas, next to Augustin, the highest authority among the canonized doctors of the Latin church, went a step further. He proved, to the satisfaction of the Middle Ages, that the rites of idolaters, Jews, and infidels ought not to be tolerated, [4] and that heretics or corruptors of the Christian faith, being worse criminals than debasers of money, ought (after due admonition) not only to be excommunicated by the church, but also be put to death by the state. [5] He does not quote a Bible passage in favor of the

---

[1] *De Correct. Donatist*, c. 6, § 24: "The Lord himself (Luke 14: 23) bids the guests in the first instance to be invited to His great supper, and afterwards to be compelled." He understands the highways and hedges of the parable to mean heresies and schisms, and the Supper of the Lord to mean the unity of the body of Christ in the sacrament of the altar and the bond of peace. He says (ch. 7, § 25) that when the imperial laws against heresy first were sent to Africa, he with certain brethren opposed their execution, but afterwards justified them as a measure of catholic self-defense against the fanatical violence of the Donatists. The result was, that both Catholics and Donatists were overwhelmed in ruin by the Vandal conquerors, who were Arian heretics.

[2] "*Credere non potest homo nisi volens.*" See his *Tract. XXVI. in Joan.* c. 2, where he says: "A man can come to church unwillingly, can approach the altar unwillingly, partake of the sacrament unwillingly; but he can not believe unless he is willing. If we believed with the body, men might be made to believe against their will. But believing is not a thing done with the body." I am pleased to find an approving reference to this sentence in the Encyclical of Pope Leo XIII. of Nov. 1, 1885.

[3] In a letter to Proconsul Donatus (Ep. C.) he adjured him by Jesus Christ, not to repay the Donatists in kind, and says: "*Corrigi eos cupimus, non necari.*"

[4] *Summa Theol. Secunda Secundæ*, Quæst. x., Art. 11.

[5] *Ibid.* Quæst. xi., Art. 3, where he says of heretics: "*Meruerunt non solum ab ecclesia per excommunicationem seperari, sed etiam per mortem a mundo excludi . . . Si falsarii pecuniæ vel alii malefactores statim per sæculares principes juste morti traduntur, multo magis hæretici statim ex quo de hærisi convincuntur, possunt non solum excommunicari, sed et juste occidi.*"

death-penalty of heretics; on the contrary he mentions three
passages which favor toleration of heretics, 2 Tim. 2: 24; 1 Cor.
11: 19; Matt. 13: 29, 30, and then tries to deprive them of
their force by his argument drawn from the guilt of heresy.

The persecution of heretics reached its height in the papal
crusades against the Albigenses under Innocent III., one of the
best of popes; in the dark deeds of the Spanish Inquisition; and in
the unspeakable atrocities of the Duke of Alva against the Protestants in the Netherlands during his short reign (1567–1573).[1]

The horrible massacre of St. Bartholomew (Aug. 24, 1572)
was sanctioned by Pope Gregory XIII., who celebrated it by
public thanksgivings, and with a medal bearing his image, an
avenging angel and the inscription, *Ugonottorum strages*.[2]

---

[1] Gibbon asserts that "the number of Protestants who were executed [by the
Spaniards] in a single province and a single reign, far exceeded that of the
primitive martyrs in the space of three centuries, and in the Roman empire."
Decline and Fall, Ch. xvi., towards the close. Grotius, to whom he refers, states
that the number of Dutch martyrs exceeded 100,000; Sarpi reduces the number
to 50,000. Alva himself boasted that during his six years' rule as the agent
of Philip II., he had caused 18,000 persons to be executed, but this does not
include the much larger number of those who perished by siege, battle, and in
prisons. At the sack of Haarlem, 300 citizens, tied two and two and back to
back, were thrown into the lake, and at Zutphen 500 more, in the same manner, were drowned in the Yssel. See Motley, *Rise of the Dutch Republic*, vol.
II. 504: "The barbarities committed amid the sack and ruin of those blazing
and starving cities are almost beyond belief; unborn infants were torn from
the living bodies of their mothers; women and children were violated by the
thousands; and whole populations burned and hacked to pieces by soldiers in
every mode which cruelty, in its wanton ingenuity, could devise."

[2] See De Thou, *Hist.* lib. LXIII.; Gieseler, IV. 304 (Am. ed.); Wachler,
Die Pariser Bluthochzeit, 2d ed., Leipzig, 1828; Henry White, *Massacre of St.
Bartholomew*, N. Y., 1868; Henry M. Baird, *History of the Rise of the Huguenots*,
New York, 1879; Henri Bordier, *La Saint-Barthélemy et la Critique moderne*,
Paris, 1879; H. Baumgarten, *Vor der Bartholomæusnacht*, Strassburg, 1882.
The number of victims of that massacre in Paris and throughout France, is
variously stated from 10,000 to 100,000; De Thou and Ranke give 20,000 as
the most moderate estimate (2,000 in Paris). Roman Catholic writers defend
the pope on the ground of ignorance; but he had abundant time to secure
full information from his nuncio and others before the medals were struck.
It is said that Philip II. of Spain, for the first time in his life, laughed aloud
when he heard of the massacre.

The infamous dragonnades of Louis XIV. were a continuation of the same politico-ecclesiastical policy on a larger scale, aiming at the complete destruction of Protestantism in France, in violation of the solemn edict of his grandfather (1598, revoked 1685), and met the full approval of the Roman clergy, including Bishop Bossuet, the advocate of Gallican liberties.[1]

The most cruel of the many persecutions of the innocent Waldenses in the valleys of Piedmont took place in 1655, and shocked by its boundless violence the whole Protestant world, calling forth the vigorous protest of Cromwell and inspiring the famous sonnet of Milton, his foreign secretary:

> "Avenge, O Lord, thy slaughtered saints, whose bones
> Lie scattered on the Alpine mountains cold,
> Even them who kept thy truth so pure of old,
> When all our fathers worshiped stocks and stones."

These persecutions form the darkest, we may say, the satanic chapters in church history, and are a greater crime against humanity and Christianity than all the heresies which they in vain tried to eradicate.

The Roman church has never repented of her complicity with these unchristian acts. On the contrary, she still holds the *principle* of persecution in connection with her doctrine that there is no salvation outside of her bosom. The papal Syllabus of 1864 expressly condemns, among the errors of modern times, the doctrine of religious toleration.[2] Leo XIII., a great admirer of

---

[1] See the French histories of Martin, Benoit, Michelet, De Félice, Ranke, Soldan, Von Polenz, and other works quoted by H. M. Baird in Schaff-Herzog II., 1037. The number of French refugees is estimated as high as 800,000; Baird reduces it to 400,000. Martin thinks, that taking all in all, "France lost the activity of more than a million of men, and of the men that produced most." Many of the descendants of the refugees whom the Elector Frederic William of Prussia so hospitably invited to Berlin, fought against France in the Napoleonic wars, and aided in the terrible retribution of 1870.

[2] Among the errors condemned are these, ? X., 78 and 79: "In the present day it is no longer expedient that the Catholic religion shall be held as *the only religion of the state, to the exclusion of all other modes of worship.*" " Whence it has been wisely provided by law, that persons coming to reside therein shall enjoy the public exercise of their own worship." The condemnation of tolera-

the theology of St. Thomas Aquinas, in his Encyclical of Nov. 1, 1885, "concerning the Christian constitution of states," wisely moderates, but reaffirms, in substance, the political principles of his predecessor.[1] A revocation would be fatal to the Vatican dogma of papal infallibility. The *practice* of persecution is a question of power and expediency; and although isolated cases still occur from time to time,[2] the revival of mediæval intolerance

tion implies the approval of intolerance. See Schaff, *Creeds of Christendom*, II., 232. Janssen, while he condemns the Protestant persecutions of Catholics, approves the Catholic persecutions of Protestants in the time of the Reformation. He says: "*Für die katholische Geistlichkeit, die katholischen Fürsten und Magistrate und das katholische Volk war es ein Kampf der Sebsterhaltung, wenn sie Alles aufboten, um dem Protestantismus den Eingang in ihre Gebiete zu wehren und ihn, wenn er eingedrungen war, daraus wieder zu entfernen.*"—*Geschichte des deutschen Volkes*, III., 193.

[1] After glorifying the Middle Ages and the hierarchical rule of the church over the state, Leo XIII. in that Encyclical proceeds to say: "No doubt the same excellent state of things would have continued, if the agreement of the two powers had continued, and greater things might rightfully have been expected, if men had obeyed the authority, the teaching office, and the counsels of the church with more fidelity and perseverance. For that is to be regarded as a perpetual law which Ivo, of Chartres, wrote to Pope Paschal II.: 'When kingship and priesthood are agreed, the world is well ruled, the church flourishes and bears fruit. But when they are at variance, not only do little things not grow, but even great things fall into miserable ruin and decay.'" Then the pope rejects among the evil consequences of the "revolution" of the sixteenth century (meaning, of course, the Reformation) the erroneous opinion that "no religion should be publicly professed [by the state]; nor ought one to be preferred to the rest; nor ought there to be any inquiry which of many is alone true; nor ought one to be specially favored, but to each alike equal rights ought to be assigned, provided only, that the social order incurs no injury from them." This is probably aimed at Italy and France, but implies also a condemnation of the separation of church and state as it exists in the United States. Further on, the pope approvingly refers to the Encyclical *Mirari Vos* of Gregory XVI. (Aug. 15, 1832), which condemns the separation of church and state, and to the Syllabus of Pius IX., who "noted many false opinions and ordered them to be collected together in order that in so great a conflux of errors Catholics might have something which they might follow without stumbling."

[2] Thus, in 1852, the Madiai family were imprisoned in Florence for holding prayer meetings and reading the Bible, and in 1853, Matamoras, Carrasco and their friends were imprisoned and condemned to the galleys at Madrid for the same offense, and were only released after a powerful protest of an international deputation of the Evangelical Alliance. No *public* worship except the Roman Catholic was tolerated in the city of Rome before 1870.

is an impossibility, and would be condemned by intelligent and liberal Roman Catholics as a folly and a crime.

3. The Protestant theory and practice of persecution and toleration.

(a) The Lutheran Reformers and Churches.

Luther was the most advanced among the Reformers in the ideas of toleration and liberty. He clearly saw the far-reaching effect of his own protest against Rome, and during his storm- and pressure-period, from 1517 to 1521, he was a fearless champion of liberty. He has left some of the noblest utterances against coërcion in matters of conscience, which contain almost every essential feature of the modern theory on the subject. He draws a sharp line between the temporal power which is confined to the body and worldly goods, and the spiritual government which belongs to God. He says that "no one can command or ought to command the soul, except God, who alone can show it the way to heaven;" that "the thoughts and mind of man are known only to God;" that "it is futile and impossible to command, or by force to compel any man's belief;" that "heresy is a spiritual thing which no iron can hew down, no fire burn, no water drown;" that "belief is a free thing which cannot be enforced."[1] He opposed the doctrine of the Anabaptists with every argument at his command, but disapproved the cruel persecution to which they were subjected in Protestant as well as Catholic countries. "It is not right," he said in a book against them (1528), "and I deeply regret that such wretched people should be so miserably murdered, burned, and cruelly put to

---

[1] See his tract, written in 1523, *Von weltlicher Obrigkeit, wie weit man ihr Gehorsam schuldig sei?* In Walch X. 426–479, especially the second part, col. 451 sqq. "*Der Seelen kann und soll niemand gebieten, er wisse denn ihr den Weg zu weisen gen Himmel. Das kann aber kein Mensch thun, sondern Gott allein. Darum in den Sachen, die der Seelen Seligkeit betreffen, soll nichts denn Gottes Wort gelehret und angenommen werden*" (453). *Es ist ein frei Werk um den Glauben, dazu man niemand kann zwingen . . . Zum Glauben kann und soll man niemand zwingen*" (455 sq.). He justly confines the duty of obedience taught in Rom. 13: 1, and 1 Pet. 2: 13, to secular matters, and qualifies them by Matt. 22: 21.

death; every one should be allowed to believe what he pleases. If he believes wrongly, he will have punishment enough in the eternal fire of hell. Why should they be tortured in this life also?" [1] If heretics were to be punished by death, the hangman would be the best (the most orthodox) theologian. "I can in no way admit," he wrote to his friend Link in 1528, "that false teachers should be put to death: it is enough that they should be banished." [2]

To this extent, then, he favored punishment of heretics, but no further. He wanted them to be silenced or banished by the government. He spent his violence in *words*, in which he far outstripped friends and foes, and spared neither papists, nor Zwinglians, nor Anabaptists, nor even temporal princes like Henry VIII., Duke George of Saxony, and Duke Henry of Brunswick.[3] But his *acts* of intolerance are few. He refused

---

[1] *Von der Wiedertaufe, an zwei Pfarrherrn,* written in Dec., 1527 or Jan., 1528, and addressed to two pastors in a Roman Catholic country (probably under the rule of Duke George of Saxony). See Walch XVII., 2644, and the Erl. Frankf. ed. xxvi., or of the *Reformations-historische Schriften* III. (2d ed. 1885), p. 283, from which I quote the whole passage: "*Doch ist's nicht recht, und ist mir wahrlich leid, dass man solche elende Leute so jämmerlich ermordet, verbrennet und greulich umbringt; man sollte ja einen jeglichen lassen gläuben, was er wollt. Gläubet er unrecht, so hat er gnug Strafen an dem ewigen Feur in der Höllen. Warumb will man sie denn auch noch zeitlich martern, soferne sie allein im Glauben irren, und nicht auch daneben aufruhrisch oder sonst der Oeberkeit widerstreben? Lieber Gott, wie bald ists geschehen, dass einer irre wird und dem Teufel in Strick fället! Mit der Schrift und Gottes Wort sollt man ihn wehren und widerstehen; mit Feuer wird man wenig ausrichten.*'

[2] *Briefe,* de Wette III., 347 sq.: "*Quod quaeris, an liceat magistratui occidere pseudoprophetas? Ego ad judicium sanguinis tardus sum, etiam ubi meritum abundat . . . . Nullo modo possum admittere, falsos doctores occidi: satis est eos relegari.*" He gives as a reason that the law of the death penalty among the Jews and Papists was made a pretext for killing true prophets and saints.

[3] His coarse attack on Henry VIII., "by God's disfavor (or, disgrace, *Ungnade*) king of England," is well known. In his book, *Von weltlicher Obrigkeit,* which is dedicated to his own prince, Duke John, he ventures the opinion that wise and pious rulers have from the beginning of the world been rare birds, and that princes are usually the greatest fools or worst boobies on earth (*sie sind gemeiniglich die grössten Narren oder die ärgsten Buben auf Erden*). Walch X., 460 and 464. "*Es sind gar wenig Fürsten, die man nicht für Narren und Buben hält. Das macht, sie beweisen sich auch also, und der gemeine Mann wird verständig.*" *Ibid.,* 464.

the hand of fellowship to Zwingli, and would not have tolerated him at Wittenberg. He begged the elector, John, to prevent a certain Hans Mohr from spreading Zwinglian opinions in Coburg. He regretted the toleration of the Zwinglians in Switzerland after their defeat, which he uncharitably interpreted as a righteous judgment of God.[1]

A few words on his views concerning the toleration of the Jews who had to suffer every indignity from Christians, as if they were personally responsible for the crime of the crucifixion. Luther was at first in advance of public opinion. In 1523 he protested against the cruel treatment of the Jews, as if they were dogs, and not human beings, and counseled kindness and charity as the best means of converting them. If the apostles, he says, who were Jews, had dealt with the heathen, as we heathen Christians deal with the Jews, no heathen would ever have been converted, and I myself, if I were a Jew, would rather become anything else than a Christian.[2] But in 1543 he wrote two violent books against the Jews.[3] His intercourse with several Rabbis filled him with disgust and indignation against their pride, obstinacy, and blasphemies. He came to the conclusion that it was useless to dispute with them and impossible to convert them. Moses could do nothing with Pharaoh by warnings, plagues and miracles, but had to let him drown in the Red Sea. The Jews would crucify their expected Messiah, if he ever should come, even worse than

---

[1] In a letter to Albrecht of Brandenburg, a. 1532, after he heard of Zwingli's death. De Wette IV., 349–355. In the same letter he speaks of Zwingli's salvation only problematically, as having possibly occurred in the last moment! He lays there the greatest stress on the real presence as a fundamental article of faith.

[2] See his tract entitled *Dass Jesus Christus ein geborner Jude sei*, in the Erl. Frkf. ed. Bd. XIX., p. 45–75. He says that if I were a Jew and suffered what the Jews had to suffer from popes, bishops and monks, "*so wäre ich eher eine Sau worden denn ein Christ. Denn sie haben mit den Jüden gehandelt, als wären es Hunde, und nicht Menschen*" (p. 47).

[3] *Von den Jüden und ihren Lügen*, Wittenb., 1543, and *Vom Schem Hamphoras und vom Geschlecht Christi*, Wittenb., 1543. In the Erl. Frkf. ed. Bd. XXXII., 99–274, and 275–358.

they crucified the Christian Messiah. They are a blind, hard, incorrigible race.[1] He went so far as to advise their expulsion from Christian lands, the prohibition of their books, and the burning of their synagogues and even their houses in which they blaspheme our Saviour and the Holy Virgin. In the last of his sermons, preached shortly before his death at Eisleben, where many Jews were allowed to trade, he concluded with a severe warning against the Jews as dangerous public enemies who ought not to be tolerated, but left the alternative of conversion or expulsion.[2]

Melanchthon, the mildest of the Reformers, went—strange to say—a step further than Luther, not during his lifetime, but eight years after his death, and expressly sanctioned the execution of Servetus for blasphemy in the following astounding letter to Calvin, dated Oct. 14, 1554 : " Reverend sir and dearest brother: I have read your work in which you have lucidly refuted the horrible blasphemies of Servetus, and I thank the Son of God, who has been the arbiter ($\beta\rho\alpha\beta\varepsilon\upsilon\tau\acute{\eta}s$) of this your contest. The church, both now and in all generations, owes and will owe you a debt of gratitude. I entirely assent to your judgment. (*Tuo judicio prorsus adsentior.*) And I say, too, that your magistrates did right in that, after solemn trial, they put the blasphemer (*hominem blasphemum*) to death." [3] He expressed here his deliberate conviction to which he adhered. Three years later, in

---

[1] "*Ein Jüde oder jüdisch Herz ist so stock-stein-eisen-teufel-hart, dass es mit keiner Weise zu bewegen ist. . . . Summa, es sind junge Teufel, zur Höllen verdammt*" (*l. c.* p. 276). He had no hope of the future conversion of the Jews, which some justly derived from Rom. 11, but "*St. Paulus meinet gar viel ein Anderes*" (277).

[2] "*Vermahnung wider die Jüden,*" 1546, Erl. ed. LXV., 186–188. He concludes: "*Wollen sich die Jüden zu uns bekehren und von ihrer Lästerung und was sie uns sonst gethan haben, aufhören, so wollen wir es ihnen gerne vergeben: wo aber nicht, so sollen wir sie auch bei uns nicht dulden noch leiden.*" This reminds one of the way in which Prince Bismarck in the year 1886 proposed to deal with the Poles in Posen as enemies of Prussia and Germany: to buy them out, and expel them from the land of their birth. In several other respects, both favorable and unfavorable, that great statesman may be called the political Luther of the nineteenth century.

[3] *Corpus Reform. Opera Mel.* VIII., 362. Comp. H. Tollin, *Ph. Melanchthon*

a warning against the errors of Theobald Thammer, he called the execution of Servetus "a pious and memorable example to all posterity."[1] We cannot tell what Luther might have said in this case had he lived at that time. It is good for his reputation that he was spared the trial.[2]

The other Lutheran Reformers agreed essentially with the leaders. They conceded to the civil ruler the control over the religious as well as political opinions of their subjects. Martin Bucer went furthest in this direction and taught in his "Dialogues" (1535) the right and the duty of Christian magistrates to reform the church, to forbid and punish popish idolatry, and all false religions, according to the full rigor of the Mosaic law.[3]

In accordance with these views of the Lutheran Reformers the Roman Catholics in Lutheran countries were persecuted, not, indeed, by shedding their blood as the blood of Protestants was shed in Roman Catholic countries, but by the confiscation of their church property, the prohibition of their worship, and, if it seemed necessary, by exile. In the reorganization of the church in Electoral Saxony in 1528, under the direction of the Wittenberg Reformers, the popish priests were deprived of their benefices, and even obstinate laymen were forced to sell their property and to leave their country. "For," said the Elector, "although it is not our intention to bind any one to what he is to believe and hold, yet will we, for the prevention of mischievous tumult and other inconveniences, suffer neither sect nor separation in our territory."[4]

---

und M. Servet. Eine Quellen-Studie. Berlin, 1876 (198 pages). Tollin wrote several monographs on Servetus in his various relations.

[1] *Ibid.*, IX., 133: "*Dedit vero et Genevensis Reipubl. Magistratus ante annos quatuor punitæ insanabilis blasphemiæ adversus Filium Dei, sublato Serveto Arragone, pium et memorabile ad omnem posteritatem exemplum.*"

[2] Luther knew only the Servetus of 1531, and once refers to him in his *Table-Talk*, as a fanatic who mastered theology by false philosophy. See Tollin, *Luther und Servet*, Berlin, 1875 (61 pages).

[3] See Tollin, *Butzer's Confutatio der Libri VII. De Trinitatis Erroribus*, in the "Studien und Kritiken" for 1875; and *Michael Servet und Martin Butzer*, Berlin, 1880; Baum, *Capito und Butzer* (1860), pp. 489 sq., 478, and 495 sq.; also Janssen, *Gesch. des deutschen Volkes*, vol. III., 194.

[4] "*Denn wiewohl unsere Meinung nicht ist, jemand zu verbinden, was er glauben*

The Protestant dissenters fared no better in Lutheran Saxony. The Philippists (Melanchthonians) or Crypto-Calvinists were outlawed, and all clergymen, professors and school teachers who would not subscribe the Formula of Concord, were deposed (1580). Dr. Caspar Peucer, Melanchthon's son-in-law, professor of medicine at Wittenberg and physician to the Elector Augustus of Saxony, was imprisoned for ten years (1576–1586) for no other crime than "Philippism" (*i. e.* Melanchthonianism), and Nicolas Crell, the chancellor of Saxony, was, after ten years' confinement, beheaded at Dresden for favoring Crypto-Calvinism at home and supporting the Huguenots abroad, which was construed as high treason (1601).[1] Since that time the name of Calvin was as much hated in Saxony as the name of the Pope and the Turk.[2]

In other Lutheran countries, Zwinglians and Calvinists fared no better. John a Lasco, the Reformer of Poland and minister of a Protestant congregation in London, when fleeing with his followers, including many women and children, from the persecution of the bloody Mary, was not allowed a resting place at Copenhagen, or Rostock, or Lübeck, or Hamburg, because he could not accept the Lutheran doctrine of the real presence, and the poor fugitives were driven from port to port in cold winter, till at last they found a temporary home at Emden (1553).[3]

---

und halten soll, so wollen wir doch zur Verhütung schädlicher Aufruhre und anderer Unrichtigkeiten keine Sekten noch Trennung in unseren Landen dulden." Köstlin II., 29. What a difference between this restriction and the declaration of Frederick the Great, that in his dominions every body may be saved after his own fashion (*nach seiner eigenen Façon*).

[1] Fr. Koch, *De Vita Caspar. Peuceri* Marburg, 1856. Richard, *Der churfürstl. sächs. Kanzler Dr. Nic. Krell*, Dresden, 1859, 2 vols. Henke, *Kaspar Peucer und Nik. Krell*, Marburg, 1865. Calinich, *Kampf und Untergang des Melanchthonismus in Kursachsen*, Leipzig, 1866; *Zwei sächsische Kanzler*, Chemnitz, 1868.

[2] The following lines were familiar during the seventeenth century:

"*Gottes Wort und Lutheri Schrift*
Sind des Papst's und Calvini Gift."

[3] Hermann Dalton (of St. Petersburg), in his *Johannes a Lasco* (Gotha, 1881), pp. 427–438, gives a graphic description of what he calls Laski's "martyrdom in

In Scandinavia every religion except the Lutheran was forbidden on pain of confiscation and exile, and these laws were in force till the middle of the nineteenth century. Queen Christina lost her Swedish crown by her apostasy from Lutheranism, which her father had so heroically defended in the Thirty Years' War.

(b) The Swiss Reformers, though republicans, were not behind the Germans in intolerance against Romanists and heretics.

Zwingli extended the hand of brotherhood to Luther, and hoped to meet even the nobler heathen in heaven, but had no mercy on the Anabaptists, who threatened to overthrow his work in Zürich. After trying in vain to convince them by successive disputations, the magistrate under his control resorted to the cruel irony of drowning their leaders (six in all) in the Limmat near the lake of Zürich (between 1527 and 1532).[1]

Zwingli counselled, at the risk of his own life, the forcible introduction of the Reformed religion into the territory of the Catholic Forest Cantons (1531); forgetting the warning of Christ to Peter, that they who take the sword shall perish by the sword.[2]

Calvin has the misfortune rather than the guilt of pre-eminence for intolerance among the Reformers. He and Servetus are the best abused men of the sixteenth century; and the depreciation of the good name of the one and the exculpation of the bad name of the other have been carried far beyond the limits of historic truth and justice. Both must be judged from the standpoint of the sixteenth, not of the nineteenth, century.

Denmark and North Germany." Calvin raised his indignant protest against this cruel treatment of his brethren, but in the same year Servetus was made to suffer death for heresy and blasphemy under Calvin's eye!

[1] Bullinger, *Reformationsgeschichte*, I., 382. Comp. his *Von der Wiedertäufer Ursprung*, etc., 1560. Hagenbach, *Kirchengesh.*, III., 350 sqq. Emil Egli, *Die Züricher Wiedertäufer zur Reformationszeit*, Zürich, 1884. Nitsche, *Gesch. der Wiedertäufer in der Schweiz*, Einsiedeln, 1885.

[2] The statue erected to his memory at Zürich, August 25th, 1885, represents him as holding the Bible in his right hand and the sword with his left. Dr. Alex. Schweizer protested (as he informed me) against the sword, and took no part in the festivities of the dedication of the monument.

The fatal encounter of the champion of orthodoxy and the champion of heresy, men of equal age, rare genius, and fervent zeal for the restoration of Christianity, but direct antipodes in doctrine, spirit and aim, forms the most thrilling tragedy in the history of the Reformation. The contrast between the two is almost as great as that between Simon Peter and Simon Magus.[1] Their contest will never lose its interest. The fires of the funeral pile which were kindled at Champel on the 27th of October, 1553, are still burning and cast their lurid sparks into the nineteenth century.

Leaving the historical details and the doctrinal aspect for another chapter,[2] we confine ourselves here to the bearing of the case on the question of toleration.

Impartial history must condemn alike the intolerance of the victor and the error of the victim, but honor in both the strength of conviction. Calvin should have contented himself with banishing his fugitive rival from the territory of Geneva, or allowing him quietly to proceed on his contemplated journey to Italy, where he might have resumed his practice of medicine in which he excelled. But he sacrificed his future reputation to a mistaken sense of duty to the truth and the cause of the Reformation in Switzerland and his beloved France, where his followers were denounced and persecuted as heretics. He is responsible, on his own frank confession, for the arrest and trial of Servetus, and he fully assented to his condemnation and death "for heresy and blasphemy," except that he counselled the magistrate, though in vain, to mitigate the legal penalty by substituting the sword for the fire.[3]

---

[1] Servetus probably imagined himself to represent the Apostle when he called Calvin "Simon Magus." He did identify himself with the archangel Michael fighting against the dragon, i.e. the Pope of Rome, Apoc. 12 : 7.

[2] Together with the extensive literature.

[3] Servetus appeared on a Sunday morning, August 13th, 1553, in one of the churches at Geneva and was recognized by one of the worshippers, who at once informed Calvin of the fact, whereupon he was thrown into prison. "*Nec sane dissimulo*," says Calvin (*Opera*, vol. VIII., col. 461, ed. Baum, Reuss, etc.), "*mea opera consilioque jure in carcerem fuisse conjectum.*" Beza, in his *Vita Calv.*, reports

But the punishment was in accordance with the mediæval laws and wellnigh universal sentiment of Catholic and Protestant Christendom; it was unconditionally counselled by four Swiss magistrates which had been consulted before the execution (Zurich, Berne, Basel, and Schaffhausen), and was expressly approved by all the surviving reformers : Bullinger, Farel, Beza, Peter Martyr, and (as we have already seen) even by the mild and gentle Melanchthon. And strange to say, Servetus himself held, in part at least, the theory under which he suffered : for he admitted that incorrigible obstinacy and malice deserved death,[1] referring to the case of Ananias and Sapphira; while schism and heresy should be punished only by excommunication and exile.

Nor should we overlook the peculiar aggravation of the case. We may now put a more favorable construction on Servetus' mystic and pantheistic or panchristic Unitarianism than his contemporaries, who seemed to have misunderstood him, friends as well as foes; but he was certainly a furious fanatic and radical heretic, and in the opinion of all the churches of his age a reckless blasphemer, aiming at the destruction of historic Christianity. He was thus judged from his first book (1531),[2] as well as his

the fact as providential that Servetus, "*a quodam agnitus, Calvino Magistratum admonente*," was arrested. Servetus had previously applied for a safe-conduct from Vienne to Geneva, but Calvin refused it, and wrote to Farel, February 13th, 1546 : "*Si venerit, modo valeat mea auctoritas, vivum exire numquam patiar.*" During the process, he expressed the hope, in a letter to Farel (August 20th, 1553), that Servetus might be condemned to death, but that the sentence be executed in a milder form (*Opera* XIV., col. 590) : "*Spero capitale saltem fore judicium, pœnae vero atrocitatem [ignem] remitti cupio.*" In the same letter he gives a sketch of the system of Servetus as teaching a pantheistic diffusion of the deity in wood, stone, and even in devils.

[1] "*Hoc crimen*," he says in the 27th of his letters to Calvin (*Opera* VIII., 708), "*est morte simpliciter dignum.*" Calvin refers to this admission of Servetus (VIII., 462) and charges him with inconsistency.

[2] *De Trinitatis Erroribus Libri septem. Per Michaelem Serveto, aliàs Reves ab Aragonia Hispanum. Anno M.D.XXXI.* No place of publication is given in the copy before me, but it was printed at Hagenau in the Alsace, as appears from the trial at Geneva. The book excited the greatest indignation in Oecolampadius and Bucer. Luther called it an awfully wicked book (*ein gräulich bös Buch*). Bucer thought the author ought to be torn to pieces.

last (1553),[1] and escaped earlier death only by concealment, practicing medicine under a fictitious name and the protection of a Catholic archbishop. He had abused all trinitarian Christians, as tritheists and atheists; he had denounced the orthodox doctrine of the Holy Trinity, as a dream of St. Augustin, a fiction of popery, an invention of the devil, and a three-headed Cerberus.[2] He had attacked with equal fury infant-baptism, as a detestable abomination, a killing of the Holy Spirit, an abolition of regeneration, and overthrow of the entire kingdom of Christ, and pronounced a woe on all baptizers of infancy who close the kingdom of heaven against mankind. He had been previously condemned to the stake by the Roman Catholic tribunal of the inquisition, after a regular trial, in the archiepiscopal city of Vienne in France, partly on the ground of his letters to Calvin procured from Geneva, and burned in effigy with his last book after his escape. He then rushed blindly into the hands of Calvin, whom he denounced, during the trial, as a liar, a hypocrite, and a Simon Magus, with a view, apparently, to overthrow his power, in league with his enemies, the party of the Libertines, which had then the majority in the council of Geneva.[3]

Considering all these circumstances Calvin's conduct is not only explained, but even justified in part. He acted in harmony with

---

[1] *Christianismi Restitutio* .... MDLIII., secretly printed at Vienne in France, with his initials on the last page, M. S. V. (*i. e.: Villanovanus*).

[2] Such blasphemy of the Trinity appeared to be blasphemy of the Deity itself. Hence Beza calls Servetus "*ille sacræ Triadis, id est omnis veræ Deitatis hostis, adeoque monstrum ex omnibus quantumvis rancidis et portentosis hæresibus conflatum.*" *Calv. Vita,* ad a. 1553. He charges his book with being "full of blasphemies." Servetus called Jesus "the Son of the eternal God," but obstinately refused to call him "the eternal Son of God," in other words, to admit his eternal divinity.

[3] "The year 1553," says Beza in *Calvini Vita,* ad a. 1553, "by the impatience and malice of the factious [the Libertines] was a year so full of trouble that not only the church, but the republic of Geneva, came within a hair's breadth of ruin. .... All power had fallen into their hands, that nothing seemed to hinder them from attaining the ends for which they had so long been striving." Then he mentions the trial of Servetus as the other danger, which was aggravated by the first.

the public law and orthodox sentiment of his age, and should therefore not be condemned more than his contemporaries, who would have done the same in his position.[1]

But all the humane sentiments are shocked again by the atrocity of the execution; while sympathy is roused for the unfortunate sufferer who died true to his conviction, reconciled to his enemies, and with the repeated prayer in the midst of the flames : " Jesus, thou Son of the eternal God, have mercy upon me ! "

---

[1] H. Tollin, a Reformed clergyman of Magdeburg, the most enthusiastic and voluminous advocate of Servetus and his system, admits this, saying (*Charakterbild M. Servet's*, Berlin, 1876, p. 6): "*Nicht Calvin ist schuldig der That, sondern der Protestantismus seiner Zeit.*" Another apologist, Dardier (in Lichtenberger's "Encyclopédie" XI. 581), says the same: *C'est la Réforme tout entière qui est coupable.*" The famous Christian philosopher, Samuel Taylor Coleridge, went further. In one of his last utterances, in his *Table-Talk*, sub Jan. 3, 1834 (to which a friend directed my attention), he expressed his views as follows : " I have known books written on tolerance, the proper title of which would be—intolerant or intolerable books on tolerance. Should not a man who writes a book expressly to inculcate tolerance learn to treat with respect, or at least with indulgence, articles of faith which tens of thousands ten times told of his fellow-subjects or his fellow-creatures believe with all their souls, and upon the truth of which they rest their tranquillity in this world, and their hopes of salvation in the next,—those articles being at least maintainable against his arguments, and most certainly innocent in themselves ?—Is it fitting to run Jesus Christ in a silly parallel with Socrates—the Being whom thousand millions of intellectual creatures, of whom I am an humble unit, take to be their Redeemer, with an Athenian philosopher, of whom we should know nothing except through his glorification in Plato and Xenophon?—And then to hitch LATIMER and SERVETUS together! To be sure, there was a stake and a fire in each case, but where the rest of the resemblance is I cannot see. What ground is there for throwing the odium of Servetus's death upon Calvin alone?—Why, the mild Melanchthon wrote to Calvin, expressly to testify his concurrence in the act, and no doubt he spoke the sense of the German Reformers ; the Swiss churches *advised* the punishment in formal letters, and I rather think there are letters from the English divines, approving Calvin's conduct !—Before a man deals out the slang of the day about the great leaders of the Reformation, he should learn to throw himself back to the age of the Reformation, when the two great parties in the church were eagerly on the watch to fasten a charge of heresy on the other. Besides, if ever a poor fanatic thrust himself into the fire, it was Michael Servetus. He was a rabid enthusiast, and did everything he could in the way of insult and ribaldry to provoke the feeling of the Christian church. He called the Trinity *triceps monstrum et Cerberum quemdam tri-partitum*, and so on."

The enemies of Calvin raised, in anonymous and pseudonymous pamphlets, a loud protest against the new tribunal of popery and inquisition in Geneva, which had boasted to be an asylum of all the persecuted. The execution of Servetus was condemned by his anti-trinitarian sympathizers, especially the Italian refugees in Switzerland, and also by some orthodox Christians in Basel and elsewhere, who feared that it would afford a powerful argument to the Romanists for their persecution of Protestants.

Calvin felt it necessary, therefore, to come out with a public defense of the death-penalty for heresy, in the spring of 1554.[1] He appealed to the Mosaic law against idolatry and blasphemy, to the expulsion of the profane traffickers from the temple-court (Matt. 21 : 12), and he tries to refute the arguments for toleration which were derived from the wise counsel of Gamaliel (Acts 5 : 34), the parable of the tares among the wheat (Matt. 13 : 29), and Christ's rebuke of Peter for drawing the sword (Matt. 26 : 52). The last argument he disposes of by making a distinction between private vengeance and public punishment.

Beza also defended, with his usual ability, in a special treatise, the punishment of heretics, chiefly as a measure of self-defense of the state which had a right to give laws and a duty to protect religion. He derived the doctrine of toleration from scepticism and infidelity and called it a diabolical dogma.[2]

The burning of the body of Servetus did not destroy his soul. His blood was the fruitful seed of the doctrine of toleration and the Unitarian heresy, which assumed an organized form in the Socinian sect, and afterward spread in many orthodox churches, including Geneva.

---

[1] *Defensio orthodoxæ fidei de sacra trinitate contra prodigiosos errores Michaelis Serveti Hispani ubi ostenditur hæreticos jure gladii coërcendos esse.* In Calvin's *Opera,* ed. Reuss, etc., vol. VIII. 483–644. Bullinger urged him to the task in a letter of December 12th, 1553 (*Opera,* XIV. 698): "*Vide, me Calvine, ut diligenter et pie omnibus piis describas Servetum cum suo exitu, ut omnes abhorreant a bestia.*"

[2] *De hæreticis a civili magistratu puniendis, adversus Martini Bellii* (an unknown person) *farraginem et novorum academicorum sectam.* Geneva (Oliva Rob. Stephani), 1554; second ed. 1592; French translation by Nic. Colladon, 1560. See Heppe's *Beza,* p. 38 sq.

Fortunately the tragedy of 1553 was the last spectacle of burning a heretic in Switzerland, though several years later the Antitrinitarian, Valentine Gentile, was beheaded in Berne (1566).

(c) In France the Reformed church, being in the minority, was violently and systematically persecuted by the civil rulers in league with the Roman church, and it is well for her that she never had a chance to retaliate. She is emphatically a church of martyrs.

(d) The Reformed church in Holland, after passing through terrible trials and persecutions under Spanish rule, showed its intolerance toward the Protestant Arminians who were defeated by the Synod of Dort (1619). Their pastors and teachers were deposed and banished. The Arminian controversy was, however, mixed up with politics ; the Calvinists were the national and popular party under the military lead of Prince Maurice ; while the political leaders of Arminianism, John van Olden Barneveldt and Hugo Grotius, were suspected of disloyalty for concluding a truce with Spain (1609), and condemned, the one to death, the other to perpetual banishment. With a change of administration the Arminians were allowed to return (1625), and disseminated, with a liberal theology, principles of religious toleration.

§ 12. Religious Intolerance and Liberty in England and America.

THE history of the Reformation in England and Scotland is even more disfigured by acts of intolerance and persecution than that of the Continent, but resulted at last in greater gain for religious freedom. The modern ideas of well regulated, constitutional liberty, both civil and religious, have grown chiefly on English soil.

At first it was a battle between persecution and mere toleration, but toleration once legally secured prepared the way for full religious liberty.

All parties when persecuted, advocated liberty of conscience, and all parties when in power, exercised intolerance, but in different degrees. The Episcopalians before 1689 were less intolerant than the Romanists under Queen Mary; the Presbyterians before 1660 were less intolerant than the Episcopalians; the Independents less intolerant (in England) than the Presbyterians (but more intolerant in New England); the Baptists, Quakers, Socinians and Unitarians consistently taught freedom of conscience, and were never tempted to exercise intolerance. Finally all became tolerant in consequence of a legal settlement in 1689, but even that was restricted by disabling clauses. The Romanists used fire and sword; the Episcopalians fines, prisons, pillories, nose-slittings, ear-croppings, and cheek-burnings; the Presbyterians tried depositions and disabilities; the Independents in New England exiled Roger Williams, the Baptist (1636), and hanged four Quakers (two men and two women, 1659, 1660 and 1661) in Boston, and nineteen witches in Salem (1692). But all these measures of repression proved as many failures and made persecution more hateful and at last impossible.

1. The first act of the English Reformation, under Henry VIII., was simply the substitution of a domestic for a foreign popery and tyranny; and it was a change for the worse. No one was safe who dared to dissent from the creed of the despotic monarch who proclaimed himself "the supreme head of the Church of England." At his death (1547), the six bloody articles were still in force; but they contained some of the chief dogmas of Romanism which he held in spite of his revolt against the pope.

2. Under the brief reign of Edward VI. (1547–1553), the Reformation made decided progress, but Anabaptists were not tolerated; two of them, who held some curious views on the incarnation, were burnt as obstinate heretics, Joan Bocher, commonly called Joan of Kent, May 2, 1550, and George van Pare, a Dutchman, April 6, 1551. The young king refused at first to sign the death-warrant of the woman, correctly thinking that the sentence was " a piece of cruelty too like that which they had condemned in papists ; " at last he yielded to Cranmer's authority.

who argued with him from the law of Moses against blasphemy, but he put his hand to the warrant with tears in his eyes and charged the archbishop with the responsibility for the act if it should be wrong.

3. The reign of the bloody Queen Mary (1553–1558) was a fearful retaliation, but sealed the doom of popery by the blood of Protestant martyrs, including the Reformers, Cranmer, Latimer, and Ridley, who were burnt in the market place at Oxford.

4. Queen Elizabeth (1558–1603), by virtue of her office, as " Defender of the Faith, and supreme governor of the Church " in her dominions, permanently established the Reformed religion, but to the exclusion of all dissent. Her penal code may have been a political necessity, as a protection against domestic treason and foreign invasion, but it aimed systematically at the annihilation of both Popery and Puritanism. It acted most severely upon Roman Catholic priests, who could only save their lives by concealment or exile. Conformity to the Thirty-nine Articles and the Book of Common Prayer was rigidly enforced; attendance upon the Episcopal service was commanded, while the mass and every other kind of public worship were forbidden under severe penalties. The rack in the tower was freely employed against noblemen suspected of disloyalty to the queen-pope. The statute *de haereticis comburendis* from the reign of Henry IV. (1401) remained in force, and two Anabaptists were burnt alive under Elizabeth, and two Arians under her successor. The statute was not formally abolished till 1677. Ireland was treated ecclesiastically as well as politically as a conquered province, and England is still suffering from that cruel polity, which nursed a hereditary hatred of the Catholic people against their Protestant rulers, and made the removal of the Irish grievances the most difficult problem of English statesmanship.

Popery disappeared for a while from British soil, and the Spanish Armada was utterly defeated. But Puritanism, which fought in the front rank against the big pope at Rome, could not

be defeated by the little popes at home. It broke out at last in
open revolt against the tyranny of the Stuarts, and the cruelties
of the Star Chamber and High-Commission Court, which were
not far behind the Spanish Inquisition, and punished freedom
of speech and of the press as a crime against society.

5. Puritanism ruled England for about twenty years (1640 to
1660), which form the most intensely earnest and excited period
in her history. It saved the rights of the people against the
oppression of their rulers, but it punished intolerance with intolerance, and fell into the opposite error of enforcing Puritan, in
the place of Episcopal, uniformity, though with far less severity.
The Long Parliament abolished the Episcopal hierarchy and
liturgy (Sept. 10, 1642), expelled about two thousand royalist
clergymen from their benefices, and executed on the block Archbishop Laud (1644) and King Charles I. (1649), as traitors; thus
crowning them with the glory of martyrdom and preparing the
way for the Restoration. Episcopalians now became champions
of toleration, and Jeremy Taylor, the Shakespeare of the English
pulpit, raised his eloquent voice for the *Liberty of Prophesying*
(1647), which, however, he afterward recalled in part when he
was made a bishop by Charles II. (1661).[1]

The Westminster Assembly of Divines (1643–1652), which
numbered one hundred and twenty-one divines and several lay-
deputies and is one of the most important ecclesiastical meetings
ever held, was intrusted by Parliament with the impossible task
of framing a uniform creed, discipline and ritual for three kingdoms. The extraordinary religious commotion of the times gave
rise to all sorts of religious opinions from the most rigid orthodoxy to deism and atheism, and called forth a lively pamphlet
war on the subject of toleration, which became an apple of discord in the Assembly. Thomas Edwards, in his *Gangræna*
(1645), enumerated, with uncritical exaggeration, no less than
sixteen sects and one hundred and seventy-six miscellaneous

---

[1] Coleridge regards this revocation as the only blot on Taylor's character.
His second wife was a natural daughter of Charles I.

" errors, heresies and blasphemies," exclusive of popery and deism.[1]

There were three theories on toleration, which may be best stated in the words of George Gillespie, one of the Scottish commissioners of the Assembly.[2]

(a) The theory of the " Papists who hold it to be not only no sin, but good service to God to extirpate by fire and sword all that are adversaries to, or opposers of, the Church and Catholic religion." Under this theory John Hus and Jerome of Prague were burnt at the Council of Constance. Gillespie calls it, in the Preface, " the *black* devil of idolatry and tyranny."

(b) " The second opinion doth fall short as far as the former doth exceed : that is, that the magistrate ought not to inflict any punishment, nor put forth any coërcive power upon heretics and sectaries, but on the contrary grant them liberty and toleration." This theory is called " the *white* devil of heresy and schism," and ascribed to the Donatists (?), Socinians, Arminians and Independents. But the chief advocate was Roger Williams, the Baptist, who became the founder of Rhode Island.[3] He went to the root

---

[1] For the extensive literature on the subject see the list of Dr. Dexter, *The Congregationalism of the last three hundred years as seen in its Literature* (N. York, 1880), Appendix, pp. 49–82. The Hansard Knollys (Baptist) Society has published, in 1846 at London, a series of *Tracts on Liberty of Conscience and Persecution*, written from 1614–1661. I mention only those which I have myself examined in the rich McAlpin Collection of the Union Theol. Seminary, N. York.

[2] *Wholesome Severity reconciled with Christian Liberty, or the true Resolution of a present Controversie concerning Liberty of Conscience. Here you have the question stated, the middle way between Popish tyrannie and Schismatizing Liberty approved, and also confirmed from Scripture, and the testimonies of Divines, yea, of whole churches* . . . . *And in conclusion a Parænetick to the five Apologists for choosing Accommodation rather than Toleration.* London, 1645 (40 pages). Dexter (p. 56) assigns the pamphlet, which is anonymous, to Gillespie, and its sentiments agree with those he expressed in a sermon he preached before the House of Lords, August 27, 1645.

[3] He wrote " *The Bloody Tenent of Persecution,*" etc., 1644 (248 pp.), and " *The Bloody Tenent yet more Bloody,*" etc., 1652 (373 pp.). Among the anonymous pamphlets on the same side, we mention *The Compassionate Samaritane, Unbinding the Conscience, and pouring oyle into the wounds which have been made upon the Separation,* etc., 1644 (84 pp.).

of the question, and demanded complete separation of politics from religion. Long before him, the Puritan Bishop Hooper, and Robert Browne, the renegade founder of Congregationalism, had taught the primitive Christian principle that the magistrates had no authority over the church and the conscience, but only over civil matters. Luther expressed the same view in 1523.[1]

(c) "The third opinion is that the magistrate may and ought to exercise his coërcive power in suppressing and punishing heretics and sectaries less or more, according as the nature and degree of the error, schism, obstinacy, and danger of seducing others may require." For this theory Gillespie quotes Moses, St. Augustin, Calvin, Beza, Bullinger, Voëtius, John Gerhard, and other Calvinistic and Lutheran divines. It was held by the Presbyterians in England and Scotland, including the Scottish commissioners in the Assembly, and vigorously advocated by Dr. Samuel Rutherford, Professor of Divinity in St. Andrews,[2] and

---

[1] Dr. Dexter asserts (p. 101) that "Robert Browne is entitled to the proud pre-eminence of having been the first writer clearly to state and defend in the English tongue the true and now accepted doctrine of the relation of the magistrate to the church," in his *Treatise of Reformation*, published in 1582. Comp. Dexter, p. 703 sq., and Append. p. 8. But this is an error. Bishop John Hooper of Gloucester, who suffered martyrdom under Queen Mary (1555), says in one of his earliest treatises: "As touching the superior powers of the earth, it is well known to all that have readen and marked the Scripture that it appertaineth nothing unto their office to make any law to govern the conscience of their subjects in religion." *Early Writings of Bishop Hooper*, p. 280, quoted by Dr. Mitchell, *The Westminster Assembly*, p. 16, where may be found a still stronger passage in Latin to the same effect: "*Profecto Christus non ignem, non carceres, non vincula, non violentiam, non bonorum confiscationem, non regineæ majestatis terrorem media organa constituit quibus veritas verbi sui mundo promulgaretur ; sed miti ac diligenti prædicatione evangelii sui mundum ab errore et idololatria converti præcepit.*" *Later Writings of Bp. Hooper*, p. 386. The same principle found expression among Mennonites and Anabaptists of the Reformation period, and may be traced back to the Apostolic and the Ante-Nicene period, when Christianity had no connection whatever with politics and secular government.

[2] He wrote *A Free Disputation against pretended Liberty of Conscience tending to resolve Doubts moved by Mr. John Goodwin, John Baptist, Dr. Jer. Taylor, the Belgick Arminians, Socinians, and other authors contending for lawlesse Liberty, or licentious Toleration of Sects and Heresies.* London, 1649. 410 pages. He calls the advocates of toleration "Libertines."

most zealously by Thomas Edwards, a Presbyterian minister in London.[1] It had a strong basis in the national endorsement of the Solemn League and Covenant, and triumphed in the Westminster Assembly. It may therefore be called the Presbyterian theory of the seventeenth century. But it was never put into practice by Presbyterians, at least not to the extent of physical violence, against heretics and schismatics either in England or Scotland.[2]

The Westminster Confession of Faith, in its original shape, declares, on the one hand, the great principle of religious liberty, that "God alone is Lord of the conscience," but also, on the other hand, that dangerous heretics "may lawfully be called to account, and proceeded against by the censures of the church, *and by the power of the civil magistrate.*"[3] And it assigns to the civil magistrate the power and duty to preserve "unity and peace in the church," to suppress "all blasphemies and heresies," to pre-

---

[1] The author of *Reasons against Independent Government of Particular Congregations: as also against the Toleration of such churches to be erected in this kingdom. Presented to the House of Commons.* London, 1641 (56 pp.). *Antapologia; or, a Full Answer to the Apologeticall Narration of Mr. Goodwin, Mr. Nye, Mr. Sympson, Mr. Burroughs, Mr. Bridge, Members of the Assembly of Divines. Wherein many of the controversies of these times are handled.* London, 1646 (259 pp.). *The First and Second Part of Gangræna; or, A Catalogue and Discovery of many of the Errors, Heresies, Blasphemies and pernicious Practices of the Sectaries of this time, vented and acted in England in these four last years,* etc. London, 1646. The first part has 116, the second part 178 pages. They were followed by *The Third Part of Gangræna; or, A New and Higher Discovery of Errors,* etc. London, 1646 (295 pp.), and by *The Casting down of the last and strongest hold of Satan; or, A Treatise against Toleration and pretended Liberty of Conscience.* London, 1647 (218 pp.).—"The ministers of Christ within the province of London," December 14, 1647, sent out a *Testimony of the Truth of Jesus Christ, and to our Solemn League and Covenant; as also Against the Errors, Heresies and Blasphemies of these times, and the Toleration of them.* London, 1648 (38 pp.).

[2] Dr. M'Crie, in his *Annals of English Presbytery* (pp. 190, 191), says: "It admits of being shown that even the hypothetical intolerance of our Presbyterian fathers differed essentially from Romish and Prelatic tyranny. . . . In point of fact it never led them to persecute, it never applied the rack to the flesh, or slaked its vengeance in blood or the maiming of the body."

[3] Chapter XX., 2, 4. The clause "and by the power of the civil magistrate," is omitted in the American recension of the Westminster Confession.

vent or reform "all corruptions and abuses in worship and discipline," and for this purpose "to call synods and be present at them." [1]

6. The five Independent members of the Assembly under the lead of Dr. Goodwin protested against the power given to the civil magistrate and to synods.[2] The obnoxious clauses of the Confession were therefore omitted or changed in the Congregational recension called "the Savoy Declaration" (1658).[3]

But the toleration of the Independents, especially after they obtained the ascendancy under Cromwell's protectorate, differed very little from that of the Presbyterians. They were spoiled by success.[4] They excluded from their program Popery, Prelacy,

---

[1] Ch. XXIII., 3; comp. Ch. XXXI., 1, 2. These sections were changed and adapted to the separation of Church and State by the united Synod of Philadelphia and New York which met at Philadelphia, May 28, 1787. See the comparative statement in Schaff, *Creeds of Christendom*, vol. I., 807 sq. and III., 607, 653 sq., 668 sq. The Presbyterian churches in Scotland, England and Ireland adhere to the original Confession, but with an express disavowal of persecuting sentiments. Schaff, I., 799 sq.

[2] Goodwin wrote several pamphlets in favor of toleration: *An Apologeticall Narration, Humbly submitted to the Hon. Houses of Parliament* (by Goodwin, Nye, Bridge, Simpson, and Burroughes). London, 1643 (32 pp.). Θεομαχία; *or, the grand imprudence of men running the hazard of fighting against God in suppressing any way, doctrine or practice concerning which they know not certainly whether it be from God or no*, 1644 (52 pp.). *Innocencie's Triumph*, 1644 (64 pp.). *Cretensis; or, a brief Answer to Mr. T. Edwards, his Gangræna*, 1646. *Anapologesiates Antapologias; or, the Inexcusableness of that grand Accusation of the Brethren, called Antapologia . . . . proving the utter insufficiency of the Antapologist for his great undertaking in behalf of the Presbyterian cause: with answers to his arguments or reasons (so call'd) for the support thereof . . . . especially in the point of Non-toleration . . . . Publ. by Authoritie.* London, 1646 (253 pp.); with a long Preface, dated "From my studie in *Coleman street*, July 17, 1646;" chiefly directed against Edwards. *Hagiomastix; or, the Scourge of the Saints displayed in his colours of Ignorance and Blood*, etc. London, 1646 (134 pp.). *A Postscript or Appendix to a treatise intituled, Hagiomastix.* London, 1646 (28 pp.). *The Apologist condemned; or, a Vindication of the Thirty Queries (with their author) concerning the power of the Civil Magistrate in Matters of Religion.* London, 1653 (32 pp.). *Peace Protected and Discontent Disarmed*, etc. London, 1654 (78 pp.). Συγκρητισμος; *or, Dis-Satisfaction Satisfied.* London, 1654 (24 pp.).

[3] See Schaff, vol. I., 829 sq. and III., 718–723.

[4] Dexter (p. 660) says: "During the short protectorate of that wonderful man, these lowly Independents came into relations so close with the ruling

and Socinianism. Dr. Owen, their most distinguished divine, who preached by command a sermon before Parliament on the day after the execution of Charles I., entitled " Righteous Zeal encouraged by Divine Protection" (Jer. 15: 19, 20), and accepted the appointment as Dean of Christ Church and Vice-Chancellor of the University at Oxford, laid down no less than sixteen fundamentals as conditions of toleration.[1] He and Dr. Goodwin served on the Commission of the forty-three Triers which, under Cromwell's protectorate, took the place of the Westminster Assembly. Cromwell himself, though the most liberal among the English rulers and the boldest protector of Protestantism abroad, limited toleration to Presbyterians, Independents, Baptists and Quakers, all of whom recognized the sacred Scriptures and the fundamental articles of Christianity; but he had no toleration for Romanists and Episcopal Royalists, who endangered his reign and who were suspected of tolerating none but themselves. His great foreign secretary, John Milton, the most eloquent advocate of liberty in the English language, defended the execution of the king, and was intolerant to popery and prelacy.

Had Cromwell reigned longer, the Triers and the Savoy Conference which he reluctantly appointed, would probably have repeated the vain attempt of the Westminster Assembly to impose a uniform creed upon the nation, only with a little more liberal "accommodation" for orthodox dissenters (except "papists" and "prelatists"). Their brethren in New England where they had full sway, established a Congregational theocracy which had no room even for Baptists and Quakers.

7. Cromwell's reign was a brief experiment. His son was

religious power, that—in order to fill important places—some of them were led to do violence to their noblest fundamentals." Several leading Baptists were guilty of the same inconsistency.

[1] See Alex. F. Mitchell, *The Westminster Assembly, its History and Standards.* London, 1883, pp. 203 and 493. "Owen, Goodwin, Simpson, and Nye were chiefly concerned in drawing up a list of fundamentals which the Parliament of 1654 wished to impose on all who claimed toleration. Neal gives sixteen of them. The Journal of the House of Commons speaks of twenty."

incompetent to continue it. Puritanism had not won the heart
of England, but prepared its own tomb by its excesses and
blunders. Royalty and Episcopacy, which struck their roots deep
in the past, were restored with the powerful aid of the Presbyterians. And now followed a reaction in favor of political and
ecclesiastical despotism, and public and private immorality, which
for a time ruined all the good which Puritanism had done.

Charles II., who "never said a foolish thing and never did a
wise one," broke his solemn pledges and took the lead in intolerance and licentiousness. The Act of Uniformity was re-enacted
May 19, 1662, and went into operation on St. Bartholomew's
Day, August 24, 1662, made hideous by the St. Bartholomew Massacre, nearly a hundred years before. "And now came in," says
Baxter, one of the most moderate as well as most learned and
pious of the Nonconformists, " the great inundation of calamities,
which in many streams overwhelmed thousands of godly Christians, together with their pastors." All Puritan ministers were
expelled from their livings and exposed to starvation, their
assemblies forbidden, and absolute obedience to the king and
conformity to episcopacy were enforced, even in Scotland.
The faithful Presbyterians in that country (the Covenanters)
were subjected by the royal dragonnades to all manner of indignities and atrocities. "They were hunted"—says an English
historian [1]—" like criminals over the mountains ; their ears were
torn from their roots ; they were branded with hot irons ; their
fingers were wrenched asunder by the thumbkins ; the bones of
their legs were shattered in the boots ; women were scourged
publicly through the streets ; multitudes were transported to the
Barbadoes ; an infuriated soldiery was let loose upon them, and
encouraged to exercise all their ingenuity in torturing them."

The period of the Restoration is, perhaps, the most immoral
and disgraceful in English history. But it led at last to the final
overthrow of the treacherous and semi-popish dynasty of the
Stuarts, and inaugurated a new era in the history of religious

[1] Lecky, *History of Rationalism in Europe*, II., 48 (N. Y. ed.).

liberty. Puritanism was not dead, but produced some of its best and most lasting works—Milton's *Paradise Lost*, and Bunyan's *Pilgrim's Progress*—in this period of its deepest humiliation and suffering.

8. The act of TOLERATION under the reign of William and Mary, 1689, made an end to violent persecutions in England. And yet it is far from what we now understand by religious liberty. Toleration is negative, liberty positive; toleration is a favor, liberty a right; toleration may be withdrawn by the power which grants it, liberty is as inalienable as conscience itself; toleration is extended to what cannot be helped and what may be in itself objectionable, liberty is a priceless gift of the Creator.

The Toleration of 1689 was an accommodation to a limited number of Dissenters—Presbyterians, Independents, Baptists and Quakers, who were allowed liberty of separate organization and public worship on condition of subscribing thirty-six out of the Thirty-Nine Articles of the Church of England. Roman Catholics and Unitarians were excluded, and did not acquire toleration in England till the nineteenth century, the former by the Act of Emancipation passed April 13, 1829. Even now the Dissenters in England labor under minor disabilities and social disadvantages, which will continue as long as the government patronizes an established church. They have to support the establishment, in addition to their own denomination. Practically, however, there is more religious liberty in England than anywhere on the Continent, and as much as in the United States.

9. The last and most important step in the progress of religious liberty was taken by the UNITED STATES of America in the provision of the Federal Constitution of 1787, which excludes all religious tests from the qualifications to any office or public trust. The first amendment to the Constitution (1789) enacts that "Congress shall make no law respecting an establishment of religion, or prohibiting the free exercise thereof."[1]

[1] Ph. Schaff, *Church and State in the United States*, New York, 1888.

Thus the United States government is by its own free act prevented from ever establishing a state-church, and on the other hand it is bound to protect freedom of religion, not only as a matter of opinion, but also in its public exercise, as one of the inalienable rights of an American citizen, like the freedom of speech and of the press. History had taught the framers of the Constitution that persecution is useless as well as hateful, and that it has its root in the unholy alliance of religion with politics. Providence had made America a hospitable home for all fugitives from persecution,—Puritans, Presbyterians, Huguenots, Baptists, Quakers, Reformed, Lutherans, Roman Catholics, etc.—and foreordained it for the largest development of civil and religious freedom consistent with order and the well-being of society. When the colonies, after a successful struggle for independence, coalesced into one nation they could not grant liberty to one church or sect without granting it to all. They were thus naturally driven to this result. It was the inevitable destiny of America. And it involved no injustice or injury to any church or sect.

The modern German empire forms in some measure a parallel. When it was formed in 1870 by the free action of the twenty or more German sovereignties, it had to take them in with their religion, and abstain from all religious and ecclesiastical legislation which might interfere with the religion of any separate state.

The constitutional provision of the United States in regard to religion is the last outcome of the Reformation in its effect upon toleration and freedom, not foreseen or dreamed of by the Reformers, but inevitably resulting from their revolt against papal tyranny. It has grown on Protestant soil with the hearty support of all sects and parties. It cuts the chief root of papal and any other persecution, and makes it legally impossible. It separates church and state, and thus prevents the civil punishment of heresy as a crime against the state. It renders to Cæsar the things that are Cæsar's, and renders to God the things that are God's. It marks a new epoch in the history of legislation and civilization. It is the American contribution to church history. No part of the federal constitution is so generally accepted and so heartily approved as that which guarantees religious liberty, the most sacred and most important of all liberties. It is regarded almost as an axiom which needs no argument.

Religious liberty has thus far been fully justified by its effects. It has stimulated the fullest development of the voluntary principle. The various Christian churches can live in peace and harmony together, and are fully able to support and to govern themselves without the aid of the secular power. This has been proven by the experience of a century, and this experience is the strongest argument in favor of the separation of church and state. Christianity flourishes best without a state-church.

The separation, however, is peaceful, not hostile, as it was in the Ante-Nicene age, when the pagan state persecuted the church. Nor is it a separation of the nation from Christianity. The government is bound to protect all forms of Christianity with its day of rest, its churches, its educational and charitable institutions.[1] Even irreligion and infidelity are tolerated within the limits of the law of self-preservation. Religious liberty may, of course, be abused like any other liberty. It has its necessary boundary in the liberty of others and the essential interests of society. The United States government would not tolerate, much less protect, a religion which requires human sacrifices, or sanctions licentious rites, or polygamy, or any other institution inconsistent with the laws and customs of the land, and subversive of the foundation of the state and the order of Christian civilization. Hence the recent prohibition of polygamy in the Territories, and the unwillingness of Congress to admit Utah into the family of States unless polygamy is abolished by the Mormons. The majority of the population decides the religion of a country, and, judged by this test, the American people are as Christian as any other on earth, only in a broader sense which recognizes all forms

---

[1] The government even indirectly supports it in part by exempting church buildings, hospitals, colleges and theological seminaries from public taxation, and by appointing chaplains for the army and navy and for Congress, in deference to the Christian sentiment of the people.

of Christianity. While Jews and infidels are not excluded from the enjoyment of any civil or political right on account of their religion or irreligion, they cannot alter the essentially Christian character of the sentiments, habits and institutions of the nation.

There are three important institutions in which church and state touch each other even in the United States, and where a collision of interests may take place: education in the public schools, marriage, and Sunday as a day of civil and sacred rest. The Roman Catholics are opposed to public schools unless they can teach in them *their* religion which allows no compromise with any other; the Mormons are opposed to monogamy, which is the law of the land and the basis of the Christian family; the Jews may demand the protection of their Sabbath on Saturday, while infidels want no Sabbath at all except perhaps for amusement and dissipation. But all these questions admit of a peaceful settlement and equitable adjustment, without a relapse into the barbarous measures of persecution.

The law of the United States is supreme in the Territories and the District of Columbia, but does not forbid any of the States to establish a particular church, or to continue a previous establishment. The Colonies began with the European system of state-churchism, only in a milder form, and varying according to the preferences of the first settlers. In the New England Colonies— except Rhode Island founded by the Baptist Roger Williams —orthodox Congregationalism was the established church which all citizens were required to support; in Virginia and the Southern States, as also in New York, the Episcopal Church was legally established and supported by the government.[1] Even those

---

[1] A Presbyterian minister, Francis Makemie, was arrested on a warrant of the Episcopal Governor Cornby of New York, Jan. 20, 1707, for preaching in a private house, without permission, and although he was ably defended in a public trial and acquitted on the ground that he had been licensed to preach under the Act of Toleration, he had to pay the costs of the prosecution as well as the defence to the large amount of £83 7s. 6d. See Briggs, *American Presbyterianism*, New York, 1885, pp. 152–154.

Colonies which were professedly founded on the basis of religious toleration, as Maryland and Pennsylvania, enacted afterwards disabling clauses against Roman Catholics, Unitarians, Jews and infidels. In Pennsylvania, the Quaker Colony of William Penn, no one could hold office, from 1693 to 1775, without subscribing a solemn declaration of belief in the orthodox doctrine of the Holy Trinity and condemning the Roman Catholic doctrine of transubstantiation and the mass as idolatrous.[1]

The great revolution of legislation began in the Colony of Virginia in 1776, when Episcopacy was disestablished, and all other churches freed from their disabilities.[2] The change was brought about by the combined efforts of Thomas Jefferson (the leading statesman of Virginia, and a firm believer in absolute religious freedom on the ground of philosophic neutrality), and of all dissenting denominations, especially the Presbyterians, Baptists and Quakers. The other Colonies or States gradually followed the example, and now there is no State in which religious freedom is not fully recognized and protected.

The example of the United States exerts a silent, but steady and mighty influence upon Europe in raising the idea of mere toleration to the higher plane of freedom, in emancipating religion from the control of civil government, and in proving the advan-

---

[1] Comp. Dr. Charles J. Stillé, *Religious Tests in Provincial Pennsylvania. A paper read before the Hist. Soc. of Penna.*, Nov. 9, 1885. Philada., 1886. 58 pp. "It is hard to believe," he says, p. 57, "that a man like Franklin, for instance, would at any time have approved of religious tests for office; yet Franklin's name is attached over and over again in the Qualification Books to the Declaration of Faith, which he was forced to make when he entered upon the duties of the various offices which he held. He must have been literally forced to take such a test; for we find him on the first opportunity, when the people of this commonwealth determined to declare their independence alike of the Penn family and of the Crown of Great Britain, raising his voice against the imposition of such tests as had been taken during the Provincial period. Franklin was the president and the ruling spirit of the convention which framed the State Constitution of 1776, and to his influence has generally been ascribed the very mild form of test which by that instrument was substituted for the old one."

[2] The act of 1776 was completed by an act of October, 1785. See Hening, *Collection of the Laws of Virginia*, vol. XII. 84.

tages of the primitive practice of ecclesiastical self-support and self-government.

The best legal remedy against persecution and the best guarantee of religious freedom is a peaceful separation of church and state; the best moral remedy and guarantee is a liberal culture, a comprehensive view of the many-sidedness of truth, a profound regard for the sacredness of conscientious conviction, and a broad and deep Christian love as described by the Apostle Paul.

§ 13. *Chronological Limits.*

The Reformation period begins with Luther's Theses, A. D. 1517, and ends with the Peace of Westphalia, A. D. 1648. The last event brought to a close the terrible Thirty Years' War and secured a legal existence to the Protestant faith (the Lutheran and Reformed Confession) throughout Germany.

The year 1648 marks also an important epoch in the history of English and Scotch Protestantism, namely, the ratification by the Long Parliament of the doctrinal standards of the Westminster Assembly of Divines (1643 to 1652), which are still in use among the Presbyterian Churches in England, Scotland, Ireland and the United States.

Within this period of one hundred and thirty-one years there are several minor epochs, and the dates vary in different countries.

The German Reformation, which is essentially Lutheran, divides itself naturally into four sub-periods: 1. From 1517 to the Augsburg Diet and Augsburg Confession, 1530. 2. From 1530 to the so-called "Peace of Augsburg," 1555. 3. From 1555 to the "Formula of Concord," 1577, which completed the Lutheran system of doctrine, or 1580 (when the "*Book* of Concord" was published and enforced). 4. From 1580 to the conclusion of the Thirty Years' War, 1648.

The Scandinavian Reformation followed closely in the path of the Lutheran Reformation of Germany, and extends, likewise, to the Thirty Years' War, in which Gustavus Adolphus, of

Sweden, took a leading part as defender of Protestantism. The Reformation triumphed in Sweden in 1527, in Denmark and Norway in 1537.

The Swiss Reformation was begun by Zwingli and completed by Calvin, and is accordingly divided into two acts: 1. The Reformation of German Switzerland to the death of Zwingli, 1517 to 1531. 2. The Reformation of French Switzerland to the death of Calvin, 1564, or we may say, to the death of Beza, 1605.

The introduction of the Reformed church into Germany, especially the Palatinate, falls within the second period.

In the stormy history of French Protestantism, the years 1559, 1598 and 1685, mark as many epochs. In 1559, the first national synod was held in Paris and gave the Reformed congregations a compact organization by the adoption of the Gallican Confession and the Presbyterian form of government. In 1598, the Reformed church secured a legal existence and a limited measure of freedom by the Edict of Nantes, which King Henry IV. gave to his former fellow-religionists. But his bigoted grandson, Louis XIV., revoked the edict in 1685. Since that time the French Reformed church continued like a burning bush in the desert; while thousands of her sons reluctantly left their native land, and contributed, by their skill, industry and piety, to the prosperity of Switzerland, Holland, Germany, England, and North America.

The Reformation in Holland includes the heroic war of emancipation from the Spanish yoke and passed through the bloody bath of martyrdom, until after unspeakable sufferings under Charles V. and Philip II., the Utrecht Union of the seven Northern Provinces (formed in 1579), was reluctantly acknowledged by Spain in 1609. Then followed the internal theological war between Arminianism and Calvinism, which ended in the victory of the latter at the National Synod of Dort, 1619.

The progressive stages of the English Reformation, which followed a course of its own, were influenced by the changing policy of the rulers, and are marked by the reigns of Henry VIII.,

1527–1547; of Edward VI., 1547–1553; the papal reaction
and period of Protestant martyrdom under Queen Mary, 1553–
1558; the re-establishment of Protestantism under Queen Elizabeth, 1558–1603. Then began the second Reformation, which
was carried on by the people against their rulers. It was the
struggle between Puritanism and the semi-popery of the Stuart
dynasty. Puritanism achieved a temporary triumph, deposed
and executed Charles I. and Archbishop Laud; but Puritanism
as a national political power died with Cromwell, and in 1660
Episcopacy and the Prayer Book were restored under Charles
II., till another revolution under William and Mary in 1688
made an end to the treacherous rule of the Stuarts and gave
toleration to the Dissenters, who hereafter organized themselves
in separate denominations, and represent the left wing of English
Protestantism.

The Reformation in Scotland, under the lead of John Knox
(1505–1572), the Luther of the North, completed its first act in
1567 with the legal recognition and establishment by the Scotch
Parliament. The second act was a struggle with the papal
reaction under Queen Mary of Scots, till 1590. The third act
may be called the period of anti-Prelacy and union with English
Puritanism, and ended in the final triumph of Presbyterianism
in 1690. Since that time, the question of patronage and the
relation of church and state have been the chief topics of agitation and irritation in the Church of Scotland and gave rise to a
number of secessions; while the Westminster standards of faith
and discipline have not undergone any essential alteration.

The Reformed faith secured a partial success and toleration in
Poland, Hungary, Transylvania, Bohemia and Moravia, but
suffered severely by the Jesuitical reaction, especially in Bohemia.
In Italy and Spain the Reformation was completely suppressed;
and it is only since the overthrow of the temporal rule of the
Pope in 1871, that Protestants are allowed to hold public worship
in Rome and to build churches or chapels.

§ 14.   *General Literature on the Reformation.*

SOURCES.

I. On the Protestant side: (1) The works of the REFORMERS, especially LUTHER, MELANCHTHON, ZWINGLI, CALVIN, CRANMER, KNOX. They will be quoted in the chapters relating to their history.

(2) Contemporary Historians: JOH. SLEIDAN (Prof. of law in Strassburg, d. 1556): *De Statu Religionis et Reipublicæ Carolo V. Cæsare commentarii.* Libri XXVI. Argentor. 1555 fol., best ed. by Am Ende, Francof. ad M. 1785-86, 3 vols. Engl. transl. by Bohun, London, 1689, 3 vols. fol. French transl. with the notes of Le Courayer, 1767. Embraces the German and Swiss Reformation.

The *Annales Reformationis* of SPALATIN, and the *Historia Reformationis* of FR. MYCONIUS, refer only to the Lutheran Reformation. So, also, LÖSCHER'S valuable collection of documents, 3 vols. See below § 15.

II. Roman Catholic: (1) Official documents. *Leonis X. P. M. Regesta*, ed. by Cardinal HERGENRÖTHER under the auspices of Pope Leo XIII., from the Vatican archives. Freiburg i. B. 1884 sqq., 12 fascic. The first three parts contain 384 pages to A. D. 1514. — *Monumenta Reformationis Lutheranæ ex tabulariis secretioribus S. Sedis*, 1521-'25, ed. by PETRUS BALAN, Ratisbonæ, 1884 (589 pages). Contains the acts relating to the Diet of Worms, with the reports of Aleander, the papal legate, and the letters of Clement VII. from 1523-'25. It includes a document of 1513, heretofore unknown, which disproves the illegitimate birth of Clement VII. and represents him as the son of Giuliano de Medici and his wife, Floreta. *Monumenta Sæculi XVI. Historiam illustrantia*, ed. by BALAN, vol. I. Oeniponte, 1885 (489 pages).

(2) Controversial writings: JOH. ECK (d. 1563): *Contra Ludderum*, 1530. 2 Parts fol. Polemical treatises on the Primacy, Penance, the Mass, Purgatory, etc. JO. COCHLÆUS (canon of Breslau, d. 1552): *Commentaria de Actis et Scriptis Lutheri ab Anno Dom. 1517 ad A. 1547 fideliter conscripta.* Mogunt. 1549 fol.; Par. 1565; Colon. 1568.—LAUR. SURIUS (a learned Carthusian, d. at Cologne, 1578): *Commentarius rerum in orbe gestarum ab a. 1500-1564.* Colon. 1567. Against Sleidan.

HISTORICAL REPRESENTATIONS.

I. Protestant works.

(1) The respective sections in the General Church Histories of SCHRÖCKH (*Kirchengesch. seit der Reformation*, Leipzig, 1804-'12, 10 vols.), MOSHEIM, GIESELER (Bd. III. Abth. I. and II., 1840 and 1852; Engl. transl. N. Y. vols. IV. and V., 1862 and 1880), BAUR (Bd. IV. 1863), HAGENBACH (vol. III., also separately publ. 4th ed. 1870; Engl. transl. by Miss Eveline Moore, Edinburgh, 1878, 2 vols.; especially good on the Zwinglian Reformation). More briefly treated in the compends of GUERICKE, NIEDNER, HASE (11th ed. 1886), EBRARD, HERZOG (vol. IIIrd), KURTZ (10th ed. 1887, vol. IInd).

All these works pay special attention to the Continental Reformation, but very little to that of England and Scotland.

Neander comes down only to 1430; his lectures on modern church history (which I heard in 1840) were never published. Gieseler's work is most valuable for its literature down to 1852, and extracts from the sources, but needs an entire reconstruction, which is contemplated by Prof. Brieger at Leipzig.

(2) JEAN HENRI MERLE D'AUBIGNÉ (usually miscalled *D'Aubigné*, which is simply an addition indicating the place of his ancestors, d. 1872): *Histoire de la réformation du 16. siècle,* Paris, 1835–'53, 5 vols., 4th ed. 1861 sqq.; and *Histoire de la réformation en Europe au temps du Calvin,* Par., 1863–'78, 8 vols. (including a posthumous vol.). Also in German by Runkel (Stuttgart, 1848 sqq.), and especially in English (in several editions, some of them mutilated). Best Engl. ed. by Longman, Green & Co., London, 1865 sqq.; best Am. ed. by Carter, New York, 1870–'79, the first work in 5, the second in 8 vols. Merle's *History,* owing to its evangelical fervor, intense Protestantism and dramatic eloquence, has had an enormous circulation in England and America through means of the Tract Societies and private publishers.

H. STEBBING: *History of the Reformation.* London, 1836, 2 vols.

G. WADDINGTON (Anglican, d. 1869): *A History of the Reformation on the Continent.* London, 1841, 3 vols. (Only to the death of Luther, 1546.)

F. A. HOLZHAUZEN: *Der Protestantismus nach seiner geschichtl. Entstehung, Begründung und Fortbildung.* Leipzig, 1846–'59, 3 vols. Comes down to the Westphalian Treaty. The author expresses his standpoint thus (III. XV.): *"Die christliche Kirche ist ihrer Natur nach wesentlich Eine, und der kirchliche Auflösungs-process, welcher durch die Reformation herbeigeführt worden ist, kann keinen anderen Zweck haben, als ein neues höheres positives Kirchenthum herzustellen."*

B. TER HAAR (of Utrecht): *Die Reformationsgeschichte in Schilderungen.* Transl. from the Dutch by *C. Gross.* Gotha, 5th ed. 1856, 2 vols.

DAN. SCHENKEL (d. 1885): *Die Reformatoren und die Reformation.* Wiesbaden, 1856. *Das Wesen des Protestantismus aus den Quellen des Ref. zeitalters.* Schaffhausen, 1862, 3 vols.

CHARLES HARDWICK (Anglican, d. 1859): *A History of the Christian Church during the Reformation.* Cambridge and London, 1856. Third ed. revised by W. Stubbs (bishop of Chester), 1873.

J. TULLOCH (Scotch Presbyt., d. 1886): *Leaders of the Reformation: Luther, Calvin, Latimer, Knox.* Edinb., 1859; 3d ed. 1883.

L. HÄUSSER (d. 1867): *Geschichte des Zeitalters der Reformation,* 1517–1648. Ed. by Oncken, Berlin, 1868 (867 pages). Abridged Engl. transl. by Mrs. Sturge, N. Y., 1874.

E. L. TH. HENKE (d. 1872): *Neuere Kirchengesch.* Ed. by Dr. Gass, Halle, 1874, 2 vols. The first vol. treats of the Reformation.

FR. SEEBOHM: *The Era of the Protestant Revolution.* London and N. York, 1874.

J. A. WYLIE: *History of Protestantism.* London, 1875-77, 3 vols.

GEORGE P. FISHER (Prof. of Church History in Yale College): *The Reformation.* New York, 1873. A comprehensive work, clear, calm, judicial, with a useful bibliographical Appendix (p. 567-591).

J. M. LINDSAY (Presbyt.): *The Reformation.* Edinb., 1882. (A mere sketch.)

CHARLES BEARD (Unitarian): *The Reformation in its relation to Modern Thought and Knowledge.* Hibbert Lectures. London, 1883; 2d ed., 1885. Very able. German translation by F. Halverscheid. Berlin, 1884.

JOHN F. HURST (Method. Bishop): *Short History of the Reformation.* New York, 1884 (125 pages).

LUDWIG KELLER: *Die Reformation und die älteren Reformparteien.* Leipz., 1885 (516 pages). In sympathy with the Waldenses and Anabaptists.

Two series of biographies of the REFORMERS, by a number of German scholars, the Lutheran series in 8 vols., Elberfeld, 1861-'75, and the Reformed (Calvinistic) series in 10 vols., Elberfeld, 1857-'63. The Lutheran series was introduced by Nitzsch, the Reformed by Hagenbach. The several biographies will be mentioned in the proper places.

(3) For the *general* history of the world and the church during and after the period of the Reformation, the works of LEOPOLD VON RANKE (d. 1886) are of great importance, namely : *Fürsten und Völker von Südeuropa im 16. und 17. Jahrh.* (Berlin 1827, 4th ed. enlarged 1877); *Geschichten der romanischen und germanischen Völker von 1494-1514* (3d ed. 1885); *Die römischen Päpste, ihre Kirche und ihr Staat im 16. und 17. Jahrh.* (Berlin, 8th ed. 1885, 3 vols. Engl. trans. by Sarah Austin, Lond. 4th ed. 1867, 3 vols.) ; *Französische Geschichte im 16. und 17. Jahrh.* (Stuttgart, 1852, 4th ed. 1877, 6 vols.) ; *Englische Geschichte vornehmlich im 16. u. 17. Jahrh.* (4th ed. 1877, 6 vols.; Engl. transl. publ. by the Clarendon Press); and especially his classical *Deutsche Geschichte im Zeitalter der Reformation* (Berlin, 1839-'43, 6th ed. 1880-'82, in 6 vols.; transl. in part by S. Austin, 1845-'47, 3 vols.). Ranke is a master of objective historiography from the sources in artistic grouping of the salient points, and is in religious and patriotic sympathy with the German Reformation ; while yet he does full justice to the Catholic church and the papacy as a great power in the history of religion and civilization. In his 85th year he began to dictate in manly vigor a Universal History down to the time of Emperor Henry IV. and Pope Gregory VII., 1881-86; to which were added 2 posthumous vols. by Dove and Winter, 1888, 9 vols. in all. His library was bought for the University in Syracuse, N.Y.

For the general literature see HENRY HALLAM: *Introduction to the Literature of Europe in the 15th, 16th, and 17th Centuries.* London, 1842, etc. N. York ed., 1880, in 4 vols.

II. Roman Catholic works.

(1) The respective sections in the General Church Histories of MÖHLER (d. 1838, ed. from lectures by Gams, Regensburg, 1867-1868, 3 vols.; the third vol. treats of the Reformation), ALZOG (10th ed. 1882, 2 vols.; Engl. transl. by Pabish and Byrne, Cincinnati, 1874 sqq., 3 vols.), KRAUS (2d ed. 1882), and Cardinal HERGENRÖTHER (third ed. 1885). Comp. also, in part, the Histories of the Council of Trent by SARPI (d. 1623), and PALLAVICINI (d. 1667).

(2) THUANUS (DE THOU, a moderate Catholic, d. 1617): *Historiarum sui Temporis libri* 138. Orleans (Geneva), 1620 sqq., 5 vols. fol. and London, 1733, 7 vols. fol.; French transl. London, 1734, 16 vols. 4to. Goes from 1546 to 1607.

LOUIS MAIMBOURG (Jesuit, d. at Paris, 1686): *Histoire du Lutheranisme*, Paris, 1680; *Histoire du Calvinisme*, 1682. Controversial, and inspired by partisan zeal; severely handled by R. Bayle in his *Critique générale de l'histoire du Calvinisme de M.*, Amsterd., 1684.

Bp. BOSSUET (d. 1704): *Histoire des variations des églises protestantes.* Paris, 1688, 2 vols. and later edd., also in his collected works, 1819 sqq. and 1836 sqq. English transl., Dublin, 1829, 2 vols. German ed. by Mayer, Munich, 1825, 4 vols. A work of great ability, but likewise polemical rather than historical. It converted Gibbon to Romanism, but left him at last a skeptic, like Bayle, who was, also, first a Protestant, then a Romanist for a short season.

KASPAR RIFFEL: *Kirchengesch. der neusten Zeit.* Mainz, 1844–'47, 3 vols.

MARTIN JOHN SPALDING (since 1864 Archbishop of Baltimore, d. 1872): *History of the Protest. Reformation in Germany and Switzerland, and in England, Ireland, Scotland, the Netherlands, France, and Northern Europe.* Louisville, 1860; 8th ed., revised and enlarged. Baltimore, 1875, 2 vols. No Index. Against Merle d'Aubigné. The Archbishop charges D'Aubigné (as he calls him) with being a "bitter partisan, wholly unreliable as an historian," and says of his work that it is "little better than a romance," as he "omits more than half the facts, and either perverts or draws on his imagination for the remainder." His own impartiality and reliableness as an historian may be estimated from the following judgments of the Reformers: "Luther, while under the influence of the Catholic Church, was probably a moderately good man; he was certainly a very bad one after he left its communion" (I. 72). "*Heu! quantum mutatus ab illo!*" (77). "His violence often drove him to the very verge of insanity. . . . He occasionally inflicted on Melanchthon personal chastisement" (87). Spalding quotes from Audin, his chief authority (being apparently quite ignorant of German): "Luther was possessed not by one, but by a whole troop of devils" (89). Zwingli (or Zuingle, as he calls him) he charges with "downright paganism" (I. 175), and makes fun of his marriage and the marriages of the other Reformers, especially Bucer, who "became the husband of no less than three ladies in succession: and one of them had been already married three times—all too, by a singular run of good luck, in the reformation line" (176). And this is all that we learn of the Reformer of Strassburg. For Calvin the author seems to draw chiefly on the calumnies of Audin, as Audin drew on those of Bolsec. He describes him as "all head and no heart"; "he crushed the liberties of the people in the name of liberty;" "he combined the cruelty of Danton and Robespierre with the eloquence of Murat and Mirabeau, though he was much cooler, and therefore more successful than any one of them all;" "he was a very

Nero." Spalding gives credit to Bolsec's absurd stories of the monstrous crimes and horrible death of Calvin, so fully contradicted by his whole life and writings, and the testimonies of his nearest friends, as Beza, Knox, etc. (I. 375, 384, 386, 388, 391). And such a work by a prelate of high character and position seems to be the principal source from which American Roman Catholics draw their information of the Reformation and of Protestantism!

The historico-polemical works of DÖLLINGER and JANSSEN belong to the history of the *German* Reformation and will be noticed in the next section.

BOOK I.

THE GERMAN REFORMATION TILL THE DIET OF AUGSBURG, A.D. 1530.

CHAPTER II.

LUTHER'S TRAINING FOR THE REFORMATION, A.D. 1483–1517.

§ 15. *Literature of the German Reformation.*

SOURCES.

I. PROTESTANT SOURCES:

(1) The Works of the REFORMERS, especially LUTHER and MELANCHTHON. See §§ 17, 32. The reformatory writings of Luther, from 1517–1524, are in vol. XV. of Walch's ed., those from 1525–1537 in vol. XVI., those from 1538–1546 in vol. XVII. See also the Erlangen ed., vols. 24–32 (issued separately in a second ed. 1883 sqq.), and the Weimar ed., vol. I. sqq.

(2) Contemporary writers:

G. SPALATIN (Chaplain of Frederick the Wise and Superintendent in Altenburg, d. 1545): *Annales Reformationis oder Jahrbücher von der Reform. Lutheri* (to 1543). Ed. by *Cyprian*, Leipz., 1718.

FRID. MYCONIUS (or Mekum, Superintendent at Gotha, d. 1546): *Historia Reformationis vom Jahr Christi* 1518–1542. Ed. by *Cyprian*, Leipzig, 1718.

M. RATZEBERGER (a physician, and friend of Luther, d. 1559): *Luther und seine Zeit*. Ed. from MS. in Gotha by *Neudecker*, Jena, 1850 (284 pp.).

(3) Documentary collections:

V. E. LÖSCHER (d. 1749): *Vollständige Reformations=Acta und Documenta* (for the years 1517–'19). Leipzig, 1720–'29, 3 vols.

CH. G. NEUDECKER: *Urkunden aus der Reformationszeit*, Cassel, 1836; *Actenstücke aus der Zeit der Reform.*, Nürnberg, 1838; *Neue Beiträge*, Leipzig, 1841.

C. E. FÖRSTEMANN: *Archiv. f. d. Gesch. der Reform.*, Halle, 1831 sqq.; *Neues Urkundenbuch*, Hamburg, 1842.

TH. BRIEGER: *Quellen und Forschungen zur Geschichte der Reformation*. Gotha, 1884 sqq. (Part I. *Aleander und Luther*, 1521.)

II. ROMAN CATHOLIC SOURCES. See § 14, p. 89.

HISTORIES.

I. Protestant historians:

LUD. A SECKENDORF (a statesman of thorough education and exemplary integrity, d. 1692): *Commentarius historicus et apologeticus de Lutheranismo.* Francof. et Lips., 1688; Lipsiæ, 1694, fol. Against the Jesuit Maimbourg.

CHR. A. SALIG (d. 1738): *Vollständige Historie der Augsburger Confession* (from 1517–1562). Halle, 1730–'35. 3 vols.

G. J. PLANCK (d. 1833): *Geschichte der Entstehung, der Veränderungen und der Bildung unseres protest. Lehrbegriffs bis zur Einführung der Concordienformel.* Leipzig, 2d ed., 1791–1800, 6 vols. Important for the doctrinal controversies in the Luth. Church. Followed by the *Geschichte der protest. Theologie von der Konkordienformel an bis in die Mitte des achtzehnten Jahrh.* Göttingen, 1831, 1 vol.

H. G. KREUSSLER: *D. Mart. Luthers Andenken in Münzen nebst Lebensbeschreibungen merkwürdiger Zeitgenossen desselben. Mit 47 Kupfern und der Ansicht Wittenbergs und Eisenachs zu Luthers Zeit.* Leipzig, 1818. Chiefly interesting for the numerous illustrations.

PHIL. MARHEINECKE (d. 1846): *Geschichte der teutschen Reformation.* Berlin, 2d ed., 1831, 4 vols. One of the best books, written in Lutherlike popularity of style.

K. HAGEN: *Deutschlands literar. und relig. Verhältnisse im Reformationszeitalter.* Erlangen, 1841–'44, sqq., 3 vols.

CH. G. NEUDECKER: *Gesch. des evang. Protestantismus in Deutschland.* Leipzig, 1844, sq., 2 vols.

C. HUNDESHAGEN (d. 1873): *Der deutsche Protestantismus.* Frankfurt, 1846, 3d ed. 1850. Discusses the genius of the Reformation as well as modern church questions.

H. HEPPE (German Reformed, d. 1879): *Gesch. des deutschen Protestantismus in den Jahren 1555–'85.* Marburg, 1852 sqq., 4 vols., 2d ed., 1865 sq. He wrote, also, a number of other books on the Reformation, especially in Hesse.

MERLE D'AUBIGNÉ'S *History of the Reformation,* see § 14. The first division treats of the German Reformation and is translated into German by *Runkel,* Stuttgart, 1848–1854, 5 vols., republ. by the American Tract Society. Several English editions, London and New York.

WILH. GASS: *Geschichte der protestantischen Dogmatik.* Berlin, 1854–'67, 4 vols.

G. PLITT: *Geschichte der evang. Kirche bis 1530.* Erlangen, 1867.

IS. A. DORNER (d. 1884): *Geschichte der protestantischen Theologie, besonders in Deutschland.* München, 1867. The first Book, pp. 1–420, treats of the Reformation period of Germany and Switzerland. English translation, Edinburgh, 1871, 2 vols.

CH. P. KRAUTH (d. 1882): *The Conservative Reformation.* Philadelphia, 1872. A dogmatico-historical vindication of Lutheranism.

K. F. A. KAHNIS (d. 1888) : *Die deutsche Reformation.* Leipzig, vol. I. 1872 (till 1520, unfinished).

G. WEBER : *Zur Geschichte des Reformationszeitalters.* Leipzig, 1874.

FR. V. BEZOLD : *Gesch. der deutschen Reformation.* Berlin, 1886.

The Elberfeld series of biographies of the Lutheran Reformers, with extracts from their writings, 1861–1875. It begins with C. SCHMIDT's *Melanchthon,* and ends with KÖSTLIN's *Luther* (the large work in 2 vols., revised 1883).

Schriften des Vereins für Reformationsgeschichte. Halle, 1883 sqq. A series of monographs on special topics in the Reformation history, especially that of Germany, published by a Society formed in the year of the Luther celebration for the literary defence of Protestantism against Romanism. Kolde, Benrath, Holdewey, Bossert, Walther, are among the contributors. The series includes also an essay on *Wiclif* by Buddensieg (1885), one on the Revocation of the Edict of Nantes by Theod. Schott (1885), and one on Ignatius of Loyola by E. Gothein (1885).

Of secular histories of Germany during the Reformation period, comp. especially, LEOPOLD VON RANKE: *Deutsche Gesch. im Zeitalter der Reformation* (6th ed., 1881, 6 vols.), a most important work, see § 14. Also, KARL AD. MENZEL (d. 1855): *Neuere Geschichte der Deutschen seit der Reformation.* Berlin, 2d ed., 1854 sq., 6 vols. WOLFGANG MENZEL (d. 1873): *Geschichte der Deutschen,* 6th ed., 1872 sq., 3 vols. L. STACKE: *Deutsche Geschichte.* Bielefeld u. Leipzig, 1881, 2 vols. (Vol. II. by W. BOEHM, pp. 37–182.) GOTTLOB EGELHAAF (Dr. Phil., Prof. in the Karls-Gymnasium at Heilbronn): *Deutsche Geschichte im Zeitalter der Reformation. Gekrönte Preisschrift des Allgemeinen Vereins für Deutsche Literatur.* Berlin, 1885. In the spirit of Ranke's great work on the same topic, with polemic reference to Janssen. It extends from 1517 to the Peace of Augsburg, 1555. (450 pages.)

II. Roman Catholic historians. See the Lit. in § 14.

IGNATIUS DOELLINGER (Prof. of Ch. Hist. in Munich, since 1870 *Old* Catholic): *Die Reformation, ihre innere Entwicklung und ihre Wirkung im Umfange des Luther. Bekenntnisses.* Regensburg, 1846–'48, 3 vols.; 2d ed., 1853. A learned collection of testimonies against the Reformation and its effects from contemporary apostates, humanists, and the Reformers themselves (Luther and Melanchthon), and those of their followers who complain bitterly of the decay of morals and the dissensions in the Lutheran church. The author has, nevertheless, after he seceded from the Roman communion, passed a striking judgment in favor of Luther's greatness.

KARL WERNER: *Geschichte der kathol. Theologie in Deutschland.* München, 1866.

JOH. JANSSEN: *Geschichte des deutschen Volkes seit dem Ausgang des Mittelalters.* Freiburg, i. B. 1876–'88, 6 vols. (down to 1618). This masterpiece of Ultramontane historiography is written with great learning and ability from a variety of sources (especially the archives of Frankfurt, Mainz, Trier, Zürich, and the Vatican), and soon passed through twelve editions. It called out able defences of the Reformation by Kawerau (five articles in

Luthardt's "Zeitschrift für kirchliche Wissenschaft und kirchl. Leben," 1882 and 1883), Köstlin, Lenz, Schweizer, Ebrard, Baumgarten, and others, to whom Janssen calmly replied in *An meine Kritiker*, Freiburg, i. B., tenth thousand, 1883 (227 pp.), and *Ein zweites Wort an meine Kritiker*, Freib. i. B., twelfth thousand, 1883 (144 pp.). He disclaims all "tendency," and professes to aim only at the historical truth. Admitted, but his *standpoint* is false, because he views the main current of modern history as an apostasy and failure; while it is an onward and progressive movement of Christianity under the guidance of Divine providence and the ever present spirit of its Founder. He reads history through the mirror of Vatican Romanism, and we need not wonder that Pope Leo XIII. has praised Janssen as "a light of historic science and a man of profound learning."

Janssen gives in each volume, in alphabetical order, very full lists of books and pamphlets, Catholic and Protestant, on the different departments of the history of Germany from the close of the fifteenth to the close of the sixteenth century. See vol. I. xxvii.-xliv.; vol. II. xvii.-xxviii.; vol. III. xxv.-xxxix.; vol. IV. xviii.-xxxi.; vol. V. xxv.-xliii.

For political history: FR. v. BUCHHOLZ: *Ferdinand I.* Wien, 1832 sqq., 9 vols. HURTER: *Ferdinand II.* Schaffhausen, 1850 sqq.

§ 16. *Germany and the Reformation.*

GERMANY invented the art of printing and produced the Reformation. These are the two greatest levers of modern civilization. While other nations sent expeditions in quest of empires beyond the sea, the Germans, true to their genius of inwardness, descended into the depths of the human soul and brought to light new ideas and principles. Providence, it has been said, gave to France the dominion of the land, to England the dominion of the sea, to Germany the dominion of the air. The air is the region of speculation, but also the necessary condition of life on the land and the sea.

The characteristic traits which Tacitus ascribes to the heathen Germans, contain already the germ of Protestantism. The love of personal freedom was as strong in them as the love of authority was in the Roman race. They considered it unworthy of the gods to confine them within walls, or to represent them by images; they preferred an inward spiritual worship which communes directly with the Deity, to an outward worship which appeals to the senses through forms and ceremonies, and throws visible

media between the finite and the infinite mind. They resisted
the aggression of heathen Rome, and they refused to submit to
Christian Rome when it was forced upon them by Charlemagne.

But Christianity as a religion was congenial to their instincts.
They were finally Christianized, and even thoroughly Romanized
by Boniface and his disciples. Yet they never felt quite at home
under the rule of the papacy. The mediæval conflict of the
emperor with the pope kept up a political antagonism against
foreign rule; the mysticism of the thirteenth and fourteenth
centuries nursed the love for a piety of less form and more heart,
and undermined the prevailing mechanical legalism; dissatisfaction with the pope increased with his exactions and abuses, until
at last, under the lead of a Saxon monk and priest, all the national
forces combined against the anti-christian tyranny and shook it
off forever. He carried with him the heart of Germany. No
less than one hundred grievances against Roman misrule were
brought before the Diet of Nürnberg in 1522.[1] Erasmus says
that when Luther published his Theses all the world applauded
him.[2] It is not impossible that all Germany would have embraced the Reformation if its force had not been weakened and
its progress arrested by excesses and internal dissensions, which
gave mighty aid to the Romanist reaction.

Next to Germany, little Switzerland, Holland, Scandinavia,
England and Scotland, inhabited by kindred races, were most
active in completing that great act of emancipation from popery
and inaugurating an era of freedom and independence.

Nationality has much to do with the type of Christianity. The
Oriental church is identified with the Greek and Slavonic races,
and was not affected by the Reformation of the sixteenth century;
hence she is not directly committed for or against it, and is less
hostile to evangelical Protestantism than to Romanism, although

---

[1] The famous "*centum gravamina adversus sedem Romanam totumque ecclesiasti-
cum ordinem.*"

[2] "*Totus mundus illi magno consensu applausit.*" In a letter of Dec. 12, 1524,
to Duke George of Saxony who was opposed to the Reformation.

she agrees, in doctrine, discipline and worship, far more with the latter. The Roman Catholic Church retained her hold upon the Latin races, which were at first superficially touched by the Reformation, but reacted, and have ever since been vacillating between popery and infidelity, or between despotism and revolution. Even the French, who under Henry IV. were on the very verge of becoming Protestant, are as a nation more inclined to swing from Bossuet to Voltaire than to Calvin; although they will always have a respectable minority of intelligent Protestants. The Celtic races are divided; the Welsh and Scotch became intensely Protestant, the Irish as intensely Romanist. The Teutonic or Germanic nations produced the Reformation chiefly, but not exclusively; for the French Calvin was the greatest theologian among the Reformers, and has exerted a stronger influence in shaping the doctrine and discipline of Protestantism outside of Germany than any of them.

§ 17. *The Luther Literature.*

The Luther literature is immense and has received large additions since 1883. The richest collections are in the Royal Library at Berlin (including Dr. Knaake's); in the public libraries of Dresden, Weimar, Wittenberg, Wolfenbüttel, München; in America, in the Theol. Seminary at Hartford (Congregationalist), which purchased the Beck collection of over 1,200 works, and in the Union Theol. Sem., New York, which has the oldest editions.

For the Luther literature comp. J. A. FABRICIUS: *Centifolium Lutheranum*, Hamburg, 1728 and 1730, 2 Parts; VOGEL: *Bibliotheca biographica Lutherana*, Halle, 1851, 145 pages; JOHN EDMANDS: *Reading Notes on Luther*, Philada., 1883; BECK (publisher): *Bibliotheca Lutherana*, Nördlingen, 1883 (185 pages, with titles of 1236 books, now at Hartford), 1884: *Bibliographie der Luther-Literatur des J. 1883*, Frankf. a. M. 1884, enlarged ed. 1887 (52 and 24 pages, incomplete).

LUTHER'S WORKS.

Oldest editions: Wittenberg, 12 German vols., 1539-'59, and 7 Latin, 1545-'58; Jena, 8 German and 4 Latin vols., 1555-'58, with 2 supplements by Aurifaber, 1564-'65; Altenburg, 10 vols., 1661-'64; Leipzig, 22 vols., 1729-'40, fol. — The three best editions are:

(1) The Halle edition by JOHANN GEORG WALCH, Halle, 1740-1750, in 24 vols., 4to. Republished with corrections and additions by DR. WALTHER, STÖCKHARDT, KÄHLER, etc., Concordia College, St. Louis, 1880 sqq., 25 vols.

(2) The Erlangen-Frankfurt ed. by PLOCHMANN, IRMISCHER, and ENDERS, etc., Erlangen, and Frankfurt a. M., 1827 sqq., 2d ed., 1862-1883, 101 vols.

8vo. (not yet finished). German writings, 67 vols.; *Opera Latina,* 25 vols.; *Com. in Ep. and Gal.,* 3 vols.; *Opera Latina varii argumenti ad reformationis hist. pertinentia,* 7 vols. The most important for our purpose are the *Reformations-historische Schriften* (9 vols., second ed., 1883–'85), and the *Briefwechsel* (of which the first vol. appeared in 1884; 6 vols. are promised).

(3) The Weimar edition (the fourth centennial memorial ed., patronized by the Emperor of Germany), by Drs. KNAAKE, KAWERAU, BERTHEAU, and other Luther scholars, Weimar, 1883 sqq. This, when completed, will be the critical standard edition, It gives the works in chronological order and strict reproduction of the first prints, with the variations of later edd., even the antiquated and inconsistent spelling, which greatly embarrasses the reader not thoroughly familiar with German. The first volume contains Luther's writings from 1512–1518; the second (1884), the writings from 1518–1519; vols. III. and IV. (1885–'6), the Commentaries on the Psalms; vol. VI. (1888), the continuation of the reformatory writings till 1520; several other vols. are in press.

I have usually indicated, from which of these three editions the quotations are made. The last was used most as far as it goes, and is quoted as the " Weimar ed."

The first collected ed. of Luther's German works appeared in 1539 with a preface, in which he expresses a wish that all his books might be forgotten and perish, and the Bible read more instead. (See Erl. Frkf. ed. I., pp. 1–6.)

Selections of Luther's *Works* by PFIZER (Frankf., 1837, sqq.); ZIMMERMANN (Frankf., 1846 sq.); OTTO VON GERLACH (Berlin, 1848, 10 vols., containing the *Reformatorische Schriften*).

The *Letters* of LUTHER were separately edited by DE WETTE, Berlin, 1825, sqq., 5 vols.; vol. VI. by J. C. SEIDEMANN, 1856 (716 pp., with an addition of *Lutherbriefe,* 1859); supplemented by C. A. H. BURKHARDT, Leipz., 1866 (524 pp.); a revised ed. with comments by Dr. E. L. ENDERS (pastor at Oberrad near Frankfurt a. M.), 1884 sqq. (in the Erl. Frankf. ed.). The first volume contains the letters from 1507 to March, 1519. For selection see C. ALFRED HASE: *Lutherbriefe in Auswahl und Uebersetzung,* Leipzig, 1867 (420 pages). TH. KOLDE: *Analecta Lutherana, Briefe und Actenstücke zur Geschichte Luther's.* Gotha, 1883. Contains letters of Luther and to Luther, gathered with great industry from German and Swiss archives and libraries.

Additional Works of Luther:

The *Table Talk* of Luther is best edited by AURIFABER, 1566, etc. (reprinted in Walch's ed. vol. xxii.); by FÖRSTEMANN and BINDSEIL, Leipzig, 1844–'48, 4 vols. (the German Table Talk); by BINDSEIL: *Martini Lutheri Colloquia, Latina, etc.,* Lemgoviæ et Detmoldæ, 1863–'66, 3 vols.; and in the Frankf. Erl. ed., vols. 57–62. Dr. CONR. CORDATUS: *Tagebuch über Dr. Luther geführt,* 1537, first edited by Dr. Wrampelmeyer, Halle, 1885, 521 pages. Last and best edition by HOPPE, St. Louis, 1887 (vol. xxii. of Am. ed. of Walch).

GEORG BUCHWALD: *Andreas Poach's handschriftl. Sammlung ungedruckter Predigten D. Martin Luthers aus den Jahren 1528 bis 1546. Aus dem Originale zum ersten Mal herausgegeben.* Leipzig, 1884, to embrace 3 vols. (Only the

first half of the first vol., published 1884, and the first half of the third
vol., 1885; very few copies sold.)   The MS. collection of Andreas Poach
in the public library at Zwickau embraces nine volumes of Luther's sermons from 1528–1546. They are based on stenographic reports of Dia-
conus Georg Rörer of Wittenberg (ordained by Luther 1525, d. at Halle,
1557), who took full Latin notes of Luther's German sermons, retaining,
however, in strange medley a number of German words and phrases.
P. TSCHACKERT: *Unbekannte Predigten u. Scholien Luthers*, Berlin, 1888. MSS.
of sermons from Oct. 23, 1519, to April 2, 1521, discovered in the University Library at Königsberg. They will be publ. in the Weimar edition.

II. BIOGRAPHIES OF LUTHER:

(1) By contemporaries, who may be included in the sources.

MELANCHTHON wrote *Vita Lutheri*, a brief but weighty sketch, 1546, often
reprinted, translated into German by Matthias Ritter, 1555, with Melanchthon's account of Luther's death to the students in the lecture room, the
funeral orations of Bugenhagen and Cruciger (157 pages); a new transl.
by Zimmermann, with preface by G. J. Planck, Göttingen, 1813; ed. of the
original in *Vitæ quatuor Reformatorum, Lutheri a Melanchthone, Melanchthonis
a Camerario, Zwinglii a Myconio, Calvini a Beza*, prefaced by Neander, Berlin, 1841. JUSTUS JONAS gives an account of Luther's last sickness
and death as an eye-witness, 1546. MATHESIUS (Luther's pupil and
friend, d. 1561) preached seventeen sermons on Luther's life, first published 1565, and very often since, though mostly abridged, *e. g.*, an illustrated popular ed. with preface by G. H. v. Schubert, Stuttgart, 1846;
jubilee edition, St. Louis and Dresden, 1883. JOH. COCHLÆUS, a Roman
Cath. antagonist of Luther, wrote *Commentaria de actis et scriptis Martini Lutheri Saxonis, chronographica, ex ordine ab anno Dom. 1517 usque
ad annum 1546 (inclusive), fideliter conscripta*. Mayence, 1549 fol.

(2) Later Biographies till 1875 (the best marked *) by

*WALCH (in his ed. of L.'s Works, vol. XXIV. pp. 3–875); KEIL (4 parts in
1 vol., Leipz., 1764); SCHRŒCKH (Leipz., 1778); UKERT (Gotha, 2 vols.,
1817); PFIZER (Stuttgart, 1836); STANG (with illustrations, Stuttg.,
1836); JÆKEL (Leipz., 1841, new ed. Elberfeld, 1871); *MEURER (Dresden, 1843–'46, 3 vols. with illustrations, abridged in 1 vol., 1850, 3d ed.,
1870, mostly in Luther's own words); *JUERGENS (Leipz., 1846–'47,
3 vols., reaching to 1517, very thorough, but unfinished); J. M. AUDIN
(Rom. Cath., *Hist. de la vie, des ouvrages et des doctrines de M. Luth.*, Paris,
1839, 7th ed., *revue et corrigée*, 1856, 3 vols.—a storehouse of calumnies,
also in German and English);[1] * M. MICHELET (*Mémoirs de L.*, écrits par

---

[1] Audin wrote also the Lives of Calvin, of Henry VIII., and of Leo X. (published between
1839 and 1847), with the same French vivacity and Roman Catholic hostility; yet, while
he does not understand Luther as a Protestant Christian and a reformer, he tries to
do justice to him as a man and a genius. He says (III., 380): "*Luther est le grand prédi-*

lui-même, traduits et mis en ordre, Paris, 1835, also Brussels, 1845, 2 vols.; the best biography in French; Eng. transl. by HAZLITT, London, 1846, and by G. H. SMITH, London and N. Y., 1846);[1] LEDDERHOSE (Karlsruh, 3d ed., 1883; French transl. of the first ed., Strassburg, 1837); GENTHE (Leipz., 1842, with seventeen steel engravings); WESTERMANN (Halle, 1845); WEYDMANN (*Luther, ein Charakter—und Spiegelbild für unsere Zeit*, Hamburg, 1850); B. SEARS (English, publ. by the Am. Sunday School Union, Philada., 1850, with special reference to the youth of L.); JGN. DŒLLINGER (R. C., *Luther, eine Skizze*, Freiburg i. B., 1851); KŒNIG and GELZER (with 48 fine illustrations, Hamb. u. Gotha, 1851; Engl. ed. with transl. of the text by Archdeacon HARE and CATH. WINKWORTH, Lond. and N. Y., 1856); *JUL. HARE (*Vindication of Luther against his English Assailants*, first publ. as a note in his *The Mission of the Comforter*, London, 1846, vol. II., 656–878, then separately, 2d ed., 1855, the best English appreciation of L.); H. WŒRSLEY (*Life of Luther*, London, 1856, 2 vols.); WILDENHAHN (Leipz., 1861); MUELLER (Nürnberg, 1867); HENKE (*Luther u. Melanchthon*, Marburg, 1867); H. W. J. THIERSCH (*Luther, Gustav Adolf und Maximilian I. von Bayern*, Nördlingen, 1869, pp. 3–66); VILMAR (*Luther, Melanchthon und Zwingli*, Frankf. a. M., 1869); H. LANG (Berlin, 1870, rationalistic); ACKERMANN (Jena, 1871); GASPARIN (*Luther et la réforme au XVIe. siècle*, Paris, 1873); SCHAFF (a sketch in Appleton's "Cyclopædia," 1858, revised 1874); RIETSCHEL (*Martin Luther und Ignatius Loyola*, Wittenberg, 1879).

(3) Recent Biographies, published since 1875, by

* JUL. KŒSTLIN (Elberfeld, 1875, 2 vols., 2d ed. revised 1883; 3d ed. unchanged; upon the whole the best German biography; also an abridged ed. for popular use with 64 illustrations, 3d ed., 1883. English transl. of the small ed. by an anonymous writer with the author's sanction,

---

cateur de la réforme. Il eut presque tous les dons de l'orateur : une inépuisable fécondité de pensées, une imagination aussi prompte à recevoir qu'à produire ses impressions, une abondance et une suplesse de style inexprimables. Sa voix était claire et retentissante, son oeil brillant de flamme, sa tête antique, sa poitrine large, ses mains d'une rare beauté, son geste ample et rich. . . . C'était à la fois Rabelais et Montaigne : Rabelais avec sa verve drolatique de style, Montaigne avec ses tournures qui burinent et cisèlent." The editor of the 7th ed., in his introductory notice (p. xviii.), says that those biographies of Audin have given to the Reformation " le coup de grace," and thus finished the work of Bossuet's *Variations ;* but Protestantism still lives, even in Catholic and infidel France.

[1] Michelet lets Luther tell his own story as far as possible, and compares this story with the *Confessions* of Augustin and of Rousseau, which it unites. " *Dans saint Augustin* " (he says, I., 6), " *la passion, la nature, l'individualité humaine, n'apparaissent que pour être immolées à la grâce divine. C'est l'histoire d'une crise de l'âme, d'une renaissance, d'une Vita nuova ; le saint eût rougi de nous faire mieux connaître l'autre vie qu'il avait quitté. Dans Rousseau, c'est tous le contraire ; il ne s'agit plus de la grace ; la nature règne sans partage, elle triomphe, elle s'étale ; cela va quelquefois jusqu'au dégout. Luther a présenté, non pas l'équilibre de la grâce et de la nature, mais leur plus douloureux combat. Les luttes de la sensibilité, les tentations plus hautes du doute, bien d'autres hommes en eut suffert ; Pascal les cut évidemment, il les étouffa et il en mourat. Luther n'a rien caché, il ne s'est pu contenir. Il a donné à voir en lui à sonder, la plaie profonde de notre nature. C'est le seul homme peut-être où l'on puisse étudier à plaisir cette terrible anatomie."*

Lond. and N. Y., 1883; another by Morris, Philad., 1883; comp. also Köstlin's art. *Luther* in Herzog, 2d ed., vol. IX.; his *Festschrift*, 1883, in several edd., transl. by Eliz. P.Weir: *Martin Luther the Reformer*, London, 1883; and his polemic tract: *Luther und Janssen, der Deutsche Reformator und ein ultramontaner Historiker*, Halle, 3d ed., 1883); V. HASAK (R. Cath., Regensb., 1881); REIN (Leipz., 1883, English transl. by Behringer, N. Y., 1883); ROGGE (Leipz., 1883); *PLITT and PETERSEN (Leipzig, 1883); *MAX LENZ (2d ed. Berlin, 1883); F. KUHN (*Luther, sa vie et son œuvre*, Paris, 1883, 3 vols.); C. BURK (4th ed., Stuttg., 1884); *TH. KOLDE (*M. Luther*, Gotha, 1884, 2 vols.); J. A. FROUDE (*Luther, a Short Biography*, Lond. and N. Y., 1883); JOHN RAE (*M. Luth.*: Lond., 1884); PAUL MARTIN, *i. e.*, M. RADE of Schönbach (*Dr. M. Luther's Leben*, etc., Neusalza, 1885–87, 3 vols.); PETER BAYNE (*M. Luth.*: *his Life and Times*, Lond. and N. Y., 1887, 2 vols.).

On Luther's wife and his domestic life: W. BESTE: *Die Gesch. Catherina's von Bora.* Halle, 1843 (131 pp.). G. HOFMANN: *Katharina von Bora, oder M. L. als Gatte und Vater.* Leipzig, 1846. JOHN G. MORRIS: *Life of Cath. von Bora*, Baltimore, 1856. MOR. MEURER: *Katherina Luther geborne von Bora.* Dresden, 1854; 2d ed., Leipzig, 1873.

III. LUTHER'S THEOLOGY.

W. BESTE: *Dr. M. Luther's Glaubenslehre.* Halle, 1845 (286 pp.). THEODOS. HARNACK (senior): *L.'s Theologie*, Bd I. Erlang., 1862, Bd. II., 1886. *JUL. KŒSTLIN: *L.'s Theologie.* Stuttg., 1863, 2d ed., 1883, 2 vols. By the same: *Luther's Lehre von der Kirche*, 1853, new ed., Gotha, 1868. CH. H. WEISSE; *Die Christologie Luthers*, Leipz., 1852 (253 pp.). LUTHARDT: *Die Ethik Luthers*, Leipz., 1867, 2d ed., 1875. LOMMATZSCH: *Luther's Lehre vom ethisch-relig. Standpunkt aus*, Berlin, 1879. H. C. MŒNCKEBERG: *Luther's Lehre von der Kirche.* Hamburg, 1876. HERING: *Die Mystik Luther's.* Leipz., 1879. KATTENBUSCH: *Luther's Stellung z. den ökumenischen Symbolen.* Giessen, 1883.

IV. LUTHER AS BIBLE TRANSLATOR.

G. W. PANZER: *Entwurf einer vollständigen Gesch. der deutschen Bibelübers. Dr. M. Luther's von 1517–1581.* Nürnberg, 1783. H. SCHOTT: *Gesch. der teutschen Bibelübers. Dr. M. Luther's.* Leipz., 1835. BINDSEIL: *Verzeichniss der Original-Ausgaben der Luther. Uebersetzung der Bibel.* Halle, 1841. MŒNCKEBERG and FROMMANN: *Vorschläge zur Revision von M. L.'s Bibelübers.* Halle, 1861-62. THEOD. SCHOTT: *Martin Luther und die deutsche Bibel.* Stuttgart, 1883. E. RIEHM (Prof. in Halle and one of the Revisers of the Luther-Bible): *Luther als Bibelübersetzer.* Gotta. 1884. Comp. the *Probebibel* of 1883 (an official revision of Luther's version), and the numerous pamphlets for and against it.

V. LUTHER AS A PREACHER.

E. JONAS: *Die Kanzelberedtsamkeit Luther's.* Berlin, 1852 (515 pp.). Best ed. of his sermons by G. SCHLOSSER: *Dr. Martin Luther's Evangelien-Predigten auf alle Sonn—und Festage des Kirchenjahres aus seiner Haus-und Kirchenpostille*, Frankfurt a. M., 1883; 4th ed., 1885.

VI. LUTHER AS POET AND MUSICIAN.

A. J. RAMBACH : *Luther's Verdienst um den Kirchengesang.* Hamburg, 1813
AUG. GEBAUER : *Martin Luther und seine Zeitgenossen als Kirchenlieder-
dichter.* Leipzig, 1828 (212 pp.). C. VON WINTERFELD : *Dr. M. Luth.
deutsche geistliche Lieder nebst den wahrend seines Lebens dazu gebraüchlichen
Stimmweisen.* Leipzig, 1840 (132 pp., 4to). B. PICK : *Luther as a
Hymnist,* Philad., 1875; *Ein feste Burg* (in 21 languages), Chicago, 1883.
BACON and ALLEN : *The Hymns of Martin Luther with his original
Tunes.* Germ. and Eng., N. Y., 1883. Dr. DANNEIL : *Luther's Geistliche
Lieder nach seinen drei Gesangbüchern von 1524, 1529, 1545.* Frank-
furt a. M., 1883. E. ACHELIS : *Die Entstehungszeit v. Luther's geistl.
Liedern.* Marburg, 1884.

VII. SPECIAL POINTS IN LUTHER'S LIFE AND WORK.

JOHN G. MORRIS : *Quaint Sayings and Doings concerning Luther.* Philadelphia,
1857. TUZSCHMANN : *Luther in Worms.* Darmstadt, 1860. KŒHLER :
Luther's Reisen. Eisenach, 1872. W. J. MANN and C. P. KRAUTH : *The
Great Reformation and the Ninety-five Theses.* Philad., 1873. ZITZLAFF : *L.
auf der Koburg.* Wittenberg, 1882. KOLDE . *L. auf dem Reichstag zu Worms.*
Halle, 1883. GLOCK : *Grundriss der Pädagogik Luther's.* Karlsruh, 1883.

VIII. COMMEMORATIVE ADDRESSES OF 1883 AND 1884.

*Festschriften zur 400 jährigen Jubelfeier der Geburt Dr. Martin Luther's, herausgege-
ben vom königl. Prediger-Seminar in Wittenberg.* Wittenberg, 1883. (Addresses by Drs. SCHMIEDER, RIETSCHEL, and others.) P. KLEINERT : *L.
im Verhältniss zur Wissenschaft* (Academic oration). Berlin, 1883 (35 pp.).
ED. REUSS : *Akad. Festrede zur Lutherfeier.* Strassburg, 1883. TH. BRIE-
GER : *Neue Mittheilungen über Luther in Worms.* Marburg, 1883, and *Luther
und sein Werk.* Marb., 1883. AD. HARNACK : *M. Luther in seiner Bedeutung
für die Gesch. der Wissenschaft und der Bildung.* Giessen, 1883 (30 pp.).
Vid Upsala Universitets Luthersfest, den 10 Nov., 1883, with an oration of
K. H. GEZ. VON SCHEELE (Prof. of Theol. at Upsala, appointed Bishop
of Visby in Gothland, 1885). Upsala, 1883. G. N. BONWETSCH : *Unser
Reformator Martin Luther.* Dorpat, 1883. APPENZELLER, RŒTSCHI, OET-
TLI, and others : *Die Lutherfeier in Bern.* Bern, 1883. Prof. SALMOND
(of Aberdeen) : *Martin Luther.* Edinburgh, 1883. J. M. LINDSAY : *M.
Luther,* in the 9th ed. of "Encyclop. Brit.," vol. XV. (1883), 71-84. JEAN
MONOD : *Luther j'usqu'en 1520.* Montauban, 1883. J. B. BITTINGER : *M.
Luth.* Cleveland, 1883. E. J. WOLF, and others : *Addresses on the Reforma-
tion.* Gettysburg, 1884. The *Luther Document* (No. XVII.) of the Ameri-
can Evang. Alliance, with addresses of Rev. Drs. WM. M. TAYLOR and
PHILLIPS BROOKS. N. Y., 1883. *Symposiac on Luther,* seven addresses of
the seven Professors of the Union Theol. Seminary in New York, held
Nov. 19, 1883. JOS. A. SEISS : *Luther and the Reformation* (an eloquent
commemorative oration delivered in Philad. and New York). Philad. 1884.
S. M. DEUTSCH : *Luther's These vom Jahr 1519 über die päpstliche Gewalt*
Berlin, 1884. H. CREMER : *Reformation und Wissenschaft.* Gotha, 1883

IX. ROMAN CATHOLIC ATTACKS.

The Luther-celebration gave rise not only to innumerable Protestant glorifications, but also to many Roman Catholic defamations of Luther and the Reformation. The ablest works of this kind are by JANSSEN (tracts in defence of his famous History of Germany, noticed in § 15), G. G. EVERS, formerly a Lutheran pastor (*Katholisch oder protestantisch?* Hildesheim, 4th ed., 1883; *Martin Luther's Anfänge*, Osnabrück, 3d ed., 1884; *Martin Luther*, Mainz, 1883 sqq., in several vols.), WESTERMAYER (*Luther's Werk im Jahr* 1883), GER-MANUS, HERRMANN, RŒTTSCHER, DASBACH, RŒM, LEOGAST, etc. See the "Historisch-politische Blätter" of Munich, and the "Germania" of Berlin, for 1883 and 1884 (the chief organs of Romanism in Germany), and the Protestant review of these writings by WILH. WALTHER: *Luther im neusten römischen Gericht.* Halle, 1884 (166 pages).

§ 18. *Luther's Youth and Training.*

In order to understand the genius and history of the German Reformation we must trace its origin in the personal experience of the monk who shook the world from his lonely study in Wittenberg, and made pope and emperor tremble at the power of his word.

All the Reformers, like the Apostles and Evangelists, were men of humble origin, and gave proof that God's Spirit working through his chosen instruments is mightier than armies and navies. But they were endowed with extraordinary talents and energy, and providentially prepared for their work. They were also aided by a combination of favorable circumstances without which they could not have accomplished their work. They made the Reformation, and the Reformation made them.

Of all the Reformers Luther is the first. He is so closely identified with the German Reformation that the one would have no meaning without the other. His own history is the formative history of the church which is justly called by his name, and which is the incarnation and perpetuation of his genius. No other Reformer has given his name to the church he reformed, and exercised the same controlling influence over its history. We need not discuss here the advantages and disadvantages of this characteristic difference; we are only concerned with the fact.

Martin Luther was born Nov. 10. 1483, an hour before midnight, at Eisleben in Prussian Saxony, where he died, Feb. 18, 1546.[1]

On the day following he was baptized and received the name of the saint of the day.

His parents had recently removed to that town[2] from their original home at Möhra near Eisenach in Thuringia, where Boniface had first preached the gospel to the Germans. Six months after Luther's birth they settled at Mansfeld, the capital of a rich mining district in the Harz mountains, which thus shares with the Thuringian forest the honor of being the home of the Luther family. They were very poor, but honest, industrious and pious people from the lower and uncultivated ranks.

Luther was never ashamed of his humble, rustic origin. "I am," he said with pride to Melanchthon, "a peasant's son; my father, grandfather, all my ancestors were genuine peasants."[3] His mother had to carry the wood from the forest on her back, and father and mother, as he said, "worked their flesh off their bones," to bring up seven children (he had three younger brothers and three sisters). Afterward his father, as a miner, acquired some property, and left at his death 1250 guilders;

---

[1] His name is differently spelled: *Luder, Ludher, Lutter, Luttherr, Luther.* The Reformer himself varied. In his first book, on the Penitential Psalms, 1517, he signed his name after the preface *Martinus Luder,* but soon afterward he adopted the spelling *Luther.* In the University records of Erfurt he was inscribed as *Ludher,* in the Wittenberg records, first as *Luder* and *Lüder.* He derived his name from *lauter, clear,* afterward from *Lothar,* which means *laut (klut), renowned,* according to others *Leutherr, i. e.: Herr der Leute, lord of the people.* See *Erfurter Matrikel; Album Acad. Viteberg.,* and *Lib. Decanorum facultatis theol. Acad. Viteb.* ed. Förstemann; Walch, *L.'s Werke* I., 46 sqq.; Jürgens I., 11–13: Knaake, in "Zeitschr, f. hist. Theol.," 1872, p. 465; Köstlin, *Mart. Luther,* I. 21 (2d ed. 1883). The year of Luther's birth rests on the testimony of his brother James; his mother distinctly remembered the day and the hour, but not the year. Melanchthon's *Vita Luth.* 2; Köstlin, I. 25 and 776.

[2] The story that they went to the fair at Eisenach cannot be proven.

[3] "*Ich bin eines Bauern Sohn; mein Vater, Grossvater, Ahnherr sind rechte Bauern gewest. Darauf ist mein Vater gen Mansfeld gezogen und ein Berghauer worden: daher bin ich.*" Mathesius wisely remarks with reference to the small beginnings of Luther: "*Wass gross soll werden, muss klein angehen; und wenn die Kinder zärtlich und herrlich erzogen werden, schadet es ihnen ihr Leben lang.*"

LUTHER.
(From a Portrait by Cranach in the Town Church at Weimar.)

a guilder being worth at that time about sixteen marks, or four dollars.[1]

Luther had a hard youth, without sunny memories, and was brought up under stern discipline. His mother chastised him, for stealing a paltry nut, till the blood came; and his father once flogged him so severely that he fled away and bore him a temporary grudge;[2] but Luther recognized their good intentions, and cherished filial affection, although they knew not, as he said, to distinguish the *ingenia* to which education should be adapted. He was taught at home to pray to God and the saints, to revere the church and the priests, and was told frightful stories about the devil and witches which haunted his imagination all his life.

In the school the discipline was equally severe, and the rod took the place of kindly admonition. He remembered to have been chastised no less than fifteen times in one single morning. But he had also better things to say. He learned the Catechism, *i. e.*: the Creed, the Lord's Prayer, and the Ten Commandments, and several Latin and German hymns. He treasured in his memory the proverbial wisdom of the people and the legendary lore of Dietrich von Bern, of Eulenspiegel and Markolf.

He received his elementary education in the schools of Mansfeld, Magdeburg, and Eisenach. Already in his fourteenth year he had to support himself by singing in the street.

Frau Ursula Cotta, the wife of the wealthiest merchant at

---

[1] Köstlin, I., 26; II., 498. In his small biography, pp. 6 and 7 (Engl. ed.), Köstlin gives the pictures of Hans and Margaret Luther. There is a striking resemblance between Luther and his mother, whom Melanchthon describes as a modest, God-fearing, and devout woman. Her maiden name was Ziegler (not Lindemann, as usually given). Luther's father is said to have escaped by flight trial for murdering a peasant at Möhra in a fit of anger; but this tradition rests only on the testimony of J. Wicel (*Epist. libri quatuor*, Lips., 1537), who fell away from Protestantism. It is discredited by Köstlin (I., 24). Janssen (II. 66) leaves it in doubt.

[2] *Table Talk* (Erl. Frkf. ed. LXI. 213): "*Man soll die Kinder nicht zu hart stäupen; denn mein Vater stäupet mich einmal so sehr, dass ich ihn flohe und ward ihm gram, bis er mich wieder zu ihm gewöhnete.*"

Eisenach, immortalized herself by the benevolent interest she took in the poor student. She invited him to her table "on account of his hearty singing and praying," and gave him the first impression of a lady of some education and refinement. She died, 1511, but he kept up an acquaintance with her sons and entertained one of them who studied at Wittenberg. From her he learned the word : "There is nothing dearer in this world than the love of woman."[1]

The hardships of Luther's youth and the want of refined breeding show their effects in his writings and actions. They limited his influence among the higher and cultivated classes, but increased his power over the middle and lower classes. He was a man of the people and for the people. He was of the earth earthy, but with his bold face lifted to heaven. He was not a polished diamond, but a rough block cut out from a granite mountain and well fitted for a solid base of a mighty structure. He laid the foundation, and others finished the upper stories.

§ 19. *Luther in the University of Erfurt.*

At the age of eighteen, in the year 1501, he entered, as "Martinus Ludher ex Mansfeld," the University of Erfurt, which had been founded a hundred years before (1392) and was then one of the best in Germany.[2] By that time his father was able to assist him so that he was free of care and could acquire a little library.

---

[1] He says in his *Table-Talk* : "*Darumb sagte meine Wirthin zu Eisenach recht, als ich daselbst in die Schule ging :*

> ' *Es ist kein lieber Ding auf Erden*
> *Als Frauenlieb', wem sie mag werden.*' "

See *Works*, Erl. Frkf. ed. LXI., 212; Jürgens, I., 281 sqq.; Kolde, I., 36; Janssen, II., 67. The relation of Luther to this excellent lady has been made the subject of a useful religious novel by Mrs. Eliz. Charles, under the title: *Chronicles of the Schönberg-Cotta Family. By two of themselves.* London and New York (M. W. Dodd), 1864. The diary is fictitious.

[2] See the description by Jürgens, I., 351 sqq.; and Kampschulte, *Die Universität Erfurt in ihrem Verh. z. Humanismus u. Reformation*, Trier, 1358. Two parts. The University was abolished in 1816.

He studied chiefly scholastic philosophy, namely : logic, rhetoric, physics and metaphysics.   His favorite teacher was Truttvetter, called " Doctor Erfordiensis." [1]   The palmy days of scholasticism which reared those venerable cathedrals of thought in support of the traditional faith of the church in the thirteenth century, had passed away, and were succeeded by the times of barren disputes about Realism and Nominalism or the question whether the general ideas (the *universalia*) had an objective reality, or a merely nominal, subjective existence in the mind.   Nominalism was then the prevailing system.

On the other hand the humanistic studies were reviving all over Europe and opened a new avenue of intellectual culture and free thought.   The first Greek book in Greek letters (a grammar) which was published in Germany, appeared in Erfurt.   John Crotus Rubeanus (Jäger) who studied there since 1498 and became rector of the University in 1520 and 1521, was one of the leaders of humanism and the principal author of the first part of the famous anti-monkish *Epistolæ obscurorum virorum* (1515) ; he was at first an intimate friend of Hutten and Luther, and greeted the latter on his way to Worms (1521) as the man who " first after so many centuries dared to strangle the Roman license with the sword of the Scripture," but afterward he fell away from the Reformation (1531) and assailed it bitterly.[2]

Luther did not neglect the study of the ancient classics, especially Cicero, Vergil, Plautus, and Livy.[3]   He acquired sufficient mastery of Latin to write it with clearness and vigor, though not with elegance and refinement.   The knowledge of Greek he acquired afterward as professor at Wittenberg.   In classical culture he never attained the height of Erasmus and Melanchthon, of Calvin and Beza ; but in original thought and in the mastery of his own mother tongue he was unrivalled.   He always regarded the languages as the sheath for the sword of the Spirit.

[1] See Kampschulte, *l. c.* I., 43 sqq., and G. PLITT, *Jodocus Truttvetter, der Lehrer Luthers,* 1876.

[2] Jürgens, I., 449; Kampschulte, *De Johanne Croto Rubiano,* 1862.

[3] O. G. Schmidt, *Luther's Bekanntschaft mit den alten Classikern,* 1883.

Beside his literary studies he cultivated his early love for music. He sang, and played the lute right merrily. He was a poet and musician as well as a theologian. He prized music as a noble gift of God, as a remedy against sadness and evil thoughts, and an effective weapon against the assaults of the devil. His poetic gift shines in his classical hymns. He had a rich font of mother wit and quaint humor.

His moral conduct was unblemished; and the mouth of slander did not dare to blacken his reputation till after the theological passions were roused by the Reformation. He went regularly to mass and observed the daily devotions of a sincere Catholic. He chose for his motto: to pray well is half the study. He was a devout worshipper of the Virgin Mary.

In his twentieth year he first saw a complete (Latin) Bible in the University Library, and was surprised and rejoiced to find that it contained so much more than was ever read or explained in the churches.[1] His eye fell upon the story of Samuel and his mother, and he read it with delight. But he did not begin a systematic study of the Bible till he entered the convent ; nor did he find in it the God of love and mercy, but rather the God of righteousness and wrath. He was much concerned about his personal salvation and given to gloomy reflections over his sinful condition. Once he fell dangerously ill, and was seized with a fit of despair, but an old priest comforted him, saying : "My dear Baccalaureus, be of good cheer ; you will not die in this sickness : God will yet make a great man out of you for the comfort of many."

In 1502 he was graduated as Bachelor of Arts, in 1505 as Master of Arts. This degree, which corresponds to the modern Doctor of Philosophy in Germany, was bestowed with great solemnity. "What a moment of majesty and splendor," says

---

[1] " *Da ich zwanzig Jahre alt war, hatte ich noch keine Bibel gesehen; ich meinte, es wären keine Evangelien und Episteln mehr, denn die in den Postillen sind.*" *Werke,* Erl. ed., LX., 255. This was partly his own fault, for several editions of the Latin Vulgate and the German Bible were printed before 1500.

Luther, "was that when one took the degree of Master, and torches were carried before him. I consider that no temporal or worldly joy can equal it." His talents and attainments were the wonder of the University.

According to his father's ambitious wish, Luther began to prepare himself for the profession of law, and was presented by him with a copy of the *Corpus juris*. But he inclined to theology, when a remarkable providential occurrence opened a new path for his life.

§ 20. *Luther's Conversion.*

In the summer of 1505 Luther entered the Augustinian convent at Erfurt and became a monk, as he thought, for his life time. The circumstances which led to this sudden step we gather from his fragmentary utterances which have been embellished by legendary tradition.

He was shocked by the sudden death of a friend (afterward called Alexius), who was either killed in a duel,[1] or struck dead by lightning at Luther's side. Shortly afterward, on the second of July, 1505, two weeks before his momentous decision, he was overtaken by a violent thunderstorm near Erfurt, on his return from a visit to his parents, and was so frightened that he fell to the earth and tremblingly exclaimed: "Help, beloved Saint Anna! I will become a monk." His friend Crotus (who afterward became an enemy of the Reformation) inaptly compared this event to the conversion of St. Paul at the gates of Damascus.[2] But Luther was a Christian before he became a monk.

On the sixteenth of July he assembled his friends who in vain tried to change his resolution, indulged once more in social song, and bade them farewell. On the next day they accompanied

---

[1] Mathesius: "*da ihm ein guter Gesell erstochen ward.*"

[2] In a letter which Crotus wrote to Luther from Bologna, Nov., 1519: "*Perge, ut cœpisti, relinque exemplum posteris. Nam ista facis non sine numine divum. Ad hæc respexit divina providentia, cum te redeuntem a parentibus cœleste fulmen veluti alterum Paulum ante oppidum Erfurdianum in terram prostravit, atque inter Augustiana septa compulit e nostro consortio.*" Döllinger I. 139.

him, with tears, to the gates of the convent. The only books he took with him were the Latin poets Vergil and Plautus.

His father almost went mad, when he heard the news. Luther himself declared in later years, that his monastic vow was forced from him by terror and the fear of death and the judgment to come; yet he never doubted that God's hand was in it. "I never thought of leaving the convent: I was entirely dead to the world, until God thought that the time had come."

This great change has nothing to do with Luther's Protestantism. It was simply a transition from secular to religious life— such as St. Bernard and thousands of Catholic monks before and since passed through. He was never an infidel, nor a wicked man, but a pious Catholic from early youth; but he now became overwhelmed with a sense of the vanity of this world and the absorbing importance of saving his soul, which, according to the prevailing notion of his age, he could best secure in the quiet retreat of a cloister.

He afterward underwent as it were a second conversion, from the monastic and legalistic piety of mediæval Catholicism to the free evangelical piety of Protestantism, when he awoke to an experimental knowledge of justification by free grace through faith alone.

§ 21. *Luther as a Monk.*

The Augustinian convent at Erfurt became the cradle of the Lutheran Reformation. All honor to monasticism: it was, like the law of Israel, a wholesome school of discipline and a preparation for gospel freedom. Erasmus spent five years reluctantly in a convent, and after his release ridiculed monkery with the weapons of irony and sarcasm; Luther was a monk from choice and conviction, and therefore all the better qualified to refute it afterward from deep experience. He followed in the steps of St. Paul, who from a Pharisee of the Pharisees became the strongest opponent of Jewish legalism.

If there ever was a sincere, earnest, conscientious monk, it was Martin Luther. His sole motive was concern for his salvation.

To this supreme object he sacrificed the fairest prospects of life. He was dead to the world and was willing to be buried out of the sight of men that he might win eternal life. His latter opponents who knew him in convent, have no charge to bring against his moral character except a certain pride and combativeness, and he himself complained of his temptations to anger and envy.[1]

It was not without significance that the order which he joined, bore the honored name of the greatest Latin father who, next to St. Paul, was to be Luther's chief teacher of theology and religion; but it is an error to suppose that this order represented the anti-Pelagian or evangelical views of the North African father; on the contrary it was intensely catholic in doctrine, and given to excessive worship of the Virgin Mary, and obedience to the papal see which conferred upon it many special privileges.

St. Augustin, after his conversion, spent several weeks with some friends in quiet seclusion on a country-seat near Tagaste, and after his election to the priesthood, at Hippo in 391, he established in a garden a sort of convent where with like-minded brethren and students he led an ascetic life of prayer, meditation and earnest study of the Scriptures, yet engaged at the same time in all the public duties of a preacher, pastor and leader in the theological controversies and ecclesiastical affairs of his age.

His example served as an inspiration and furnished a sort of authority to several monastic associations which arose in the thirteenth century. Pope Alexander IV. (1256) gave them the so-called rule of St. Augustin. They belonged to the mendicant monks, like the Dominicans, Franciscans and Carmelites. They laid great stress on preaching. In other respects they differed little from other monastic orders. In the beginning of the sixteenth century they numbered more than a hundred settlements in Germany.

The Augustinian congregation in Saxony was founded in 1493, and presided over since 1503 by John von Staupitz, the Vicar-

[1] Köstlin, I., 88 sq., 780.

General for Germany, and Luther's friend. The convent at Erfurt was the largest and most important next to that at Nürnberg. The monks were respected for their zeal in preaching, pastoral care, and theological study. They lived on alms, which they collected themselves in the town and surrounding country. Applicants were received as novices for a year of probation, during which they could reconsider their resolution ; afterward they were bound by perpetual vows of celibacy, poverty and obedience to their superiors.

Luther was welcomed by his brethren with hymns of joy and prayer. He was clothed with a white woollen shirt, in honor of the pure Virgin, a black cowl and frock, tied by a leathern girdle. He assumed the most menial offices to subdue his pride : he swept the floor, begged bread through the streets, and submitted without a murmur to the ascetic severities. He said twenty-five Paternosters with the Ave Maria in each of the seven appointed hours of prayer. He was devoted to the Holy Virgin and even believed, with the Augustinians and Franciscans, in her immaculate conception, or freedom from hereditary sin—a doctrine denied by the Dominicans and not made an article of faith till the year 1854. He regularly confessed his sins to the priest at least once a week. At the same time a complete copy of the Latin Bible was put into his hands for study, as was enjoined by the new code of statutes drawn up by Staupitz.

At the end of the year of probation Luther solemnly promised to live until death in poverty and chastity according to the rules of the holy father Augustin, to render obedience to Almighty God, to the Virgin Mary, and to the prior of the monastery. He was sprinkled with holy water, as he lay prostrate on the ground in the form of a cross. He was greeted as an innocent child fresh from baptism, and assigned to a separate cell with table, bedstead, and chair.[1]

The two years which followed, he divided between pious exer-

[1] The cell and furniture were destroyed by fire, March 7, 1872. The cell was reconstructed, and the convent is now an orphan-asylum (*Martinsstift*).

cises and theological studies. He read diligently the Scriptures, and the later schoolmen,—especially Gabriel Biel, whom he knew by heart, and William Occam, whom he esteemed on account of his subtle acuteness even above St. Thomas and Duns Scotus, without being affected by his sceptical tendency. He acknowledged the authority of Aristotle, whom he afterward denounced and disowned as "a damned heathen."[1] He excited the admiration of his brethren by his ability in disputation on scholastic questions.

His heart was not satisfied with brain work. His chief concern was to become a saint and to earn a place in heaven. "If ever," he said afterward, "a monk got to heaven by monkery, I would have gotten there." He observed the minutest details of discipline. No one surpassed him in prayer, fasting, night watches, self-mortification. He was already held up as a model of sanctity.

But he was sadly disappointed in his hope to escape sin and temptation behind the walls of the cloister. He found no peace and rest in all his pious exercises. The more he seemed to advance externally, the more he felt the burden of sin within. He had to contend with temptations of anger, envy, hatred and pride. He saw sin everywhere, even in the smallest trifles. The Scriptures impressed upon him the terrors of divine justice. He could not trust in God as a reconciled Father, as a God of love and mercy, but trembled before him, as a God of wrath, as a consuming fire. He could not get over the words: "I, the Lord thy God, am a jealous God." His confessor once told him: "Thou art a fool, God is not angry with thee, but thou art angry with God." He remembered this afterward as "a great and glorious word," but at that time it made no impression on him.

---

[1] "*Der vermaladeite Heide Aristoteles.*" Luther's attitude to scholasticism and the great Greek philosopher changed again when, in support of the eucharistic presence, he had to resort to the scholastic distinctions between various kinds of presence. Comp. Fr. Aug. Berthold Nitzsch, *Luther und Aristoteles.* Kiel, 1883.

He could not point to any particular transgression ; it was sin as an all-pervading power and vitiating principle, sin as a corruption of nature, sin as a state of alienation from God and hostility to God, that weighed on his mind like an incubus and brought him at times to the brink of despair.

He passed through that conflict between the law of God and the law of sin which is described by Paul (Rom. vii.), and which ends with the cry : "O wretched man that I am ! who shall deliver me out of the body of this death ? " He had not yet learned to add : "I thank God through Jesus Christ our Lord. There is now no condemnation to them that are in Christ Jesus. For the law of the Spirit of life in Christ Jesus made me free from the law of sin and of death."

§ 22. *Luther and Staupitz.*

JOHN VON STAUPITZ.
(From the portrait in St. Peter's Convent at Salzburg.)

I. The mystic writings of Staupitz have been republished in part by KNAAKE in *Johannis Staupitii Opera.* Potsdam, 1867, vol. I. His *"Nachfolge Christi"* was first published in 1515 ; his book *"Von der Liebe Gottes"* (especially esteemed by Luther) in 1518, and passed through several editions ; republ. by Liesching, Stuttgart, 1862. His last work *" Von dem heiligen rechten christlichen Glauben,"* appeared after his death, 1525, and is directed against Luther's doctrine of justification by faith without works. His twenty-four letters have been published by KOLDE: *Die Deutsche Augustiner Congregation und Johann von Staupitz.* Gotha, 1879, p. 435 sqq.

II. On Luther and Staupitz: GRIMM: *De Joh. Staupitio ejusque in sacr. instaur. meritis,* in Illgen's "Zeitschrift für hist. Theol.," 1837 (VII., 74–79). ULLMANN: *Die Reformatoren vor der Reformation,* vol. II., 256–284 (very good, see there the older literature). DŒLLINGER: *Die Reformation,* I., 153–155. KAHNIS: *Deutsche Reformat.,* I., 150 sqq. ALBR. RITSCHL: *Die Lehre v. der Rechtfertigung und Versöhnung,* 2d ed., I., 124–129 (on Staupitz's theology). MALLET: in Herzog,[2] XIV., 648–653. PAUL ZELLER: *Staupitz. Seine relig.- dogmat. Anschauungen und dogmengesch. Stellung,* in the "Theol. Studien und Kritiken," 1879. LUDWIG KELLER: *Johann von Staupitz, und das Waldenserthum,* in the "Historische Taschenbuch," ed. by W. Maurenbrecher, Leipzig, 1885, p. 117–167; also his *Johann von Staupitz und die Anfänge der Reformation,* Leipzig, 1888. Dr. Keller connects Staupitz with the Waldenses and Anabaptists, but without proof. KOLDE: *Joh. von Staup. ein Waldenser und Wiedertäufer,* in Brieger's "Zeitschrift für Kirchengesch." Gotha, 1885, p. 426–447. DIECKHOFF: *Die Theol. des Joh. v. Staup.,* Leipz., 1887.

In this state of mental and moral agony, Luther was comforted by an old monk of the convent (the teacher of the novices) who reminded him of the article on the forgiveness of sins in the Apostles' Creed, of Paul's word that the sinner is justified by grace through faith, and of an incidental remark of St. Bernard (in a Sermon on the Canticles) to the same effect.

His best friend and wisest counsellor was Johann von Staupitz, Doctor of Divinity and Vicar-General of the Augustinian convents in Germany. Staupitz was a Saxon nobleman, of fine mind, generous heart, considerable biblical and scholastic learning, and deep piety, highly esteemed wherever known, and used in important missions by the Elector Frederick of Saxony. He belonged to the school of practical mysticism or Catholic pietism, which is best represented by Tauler and Thomas a Kempis. He cared more for the inner spiritual life than outward forms and observances, and trusted in the merits of Christ rather than in good works of his own, as the solid ground of comfort and peace. The love of God and the imitation of Christ were the ruling ideas of his theology and piety. In his most popular book, *On the Love of God,*[1]

---

[1] It passed through three editions between 1518 and 1520. See Knaake, I.,

he describes that love as the inmost being of God, which makes everything lovely, and should make us love Him above all things; but this love man cannot learn from man, nor from the law which only brings us to a knowledge of sin, nor from the letter of the Scripture which kills, but from the Holy Spirit who reveals God's love in Christ to our hearts and fills it with the holy flame of gratitude and consecration. " The law," he says in substance, " makes known the disease, but cannot heal. But the spirit is hid beneath the letter; the old law is pregnant with Christ who gives us grace to love God above all things. To those who find the spirit and are led to Christ by the law, the Scriptures become a source of edification and comfort. The Jews saw and heard and handled Christ, but they had him not in their heart, and therefore they were doubly guilty. And so are those who carry Christ only on their lips. The chief thing is to have him in our heart. The knowledge of the Christian faith and the love to God are gifts of pure grace beyond our art and ability, and beyond our works and merits."

Staupitz was Luther's spiritual father, and " first caused the light of the gospel to shine in the darkness of his heart." [1] He directed him from his sins to the merits of Christ, from the law to the cross, from works to faith, from scholasticism to the study of the Scriptures, of St. Augustin, and Tauler. He taught him that true repentance consists not in self-imposed penances and punishments, but in a change of heart and must proceed from the contemplation of Christ's sacrifice, in which the secret of God's eternal will was revealed. He also prophetically assured him that God would overrule these trials and temptations for his future usefulness in the church. [2]

---

86 sq. Keller says that it was often republished by the Anabaptists, whom he regards as the successors of the mediæval Waldenses, or " Brethren."

[1] " *Per quem primum cœpit Evangelii lux de tenebris splendescere in cordibus nostris.*" So Luther says in his letter to Staupitz, Sept. 17, 1518 (DeWette II., 408 sq.), where he addresses him as " *reverendus in Christo pater,*" and signs himself " *filius tuus Martinus Lutherus.*"

[2] In a letter of comfort to Hieronymus Weller, Nov. 6, 1530 (DeWette, IV.,

He encouraged Luther to enter the priesthood (1507), and brought him to Wittenberg ; he induced him to take the degree of Doctor of Divinity, and to preach. He stirred him up against popery,[1] and protected him in the transactions with Cardinal Cajetan. He was greeted by Scheurl in 1518 as the one who would lead the people of Israel out of captivity.

But when Luther broke with Rome, and Rome with Luther, the friendship cooled down. Staupitz held fast to the unity of the Catholic Church and was intimidated and repelled by the excesses of the Reformation. In a letter of April 1, 1524,[2] he begs Luther's pardon for his long silence and significantly says in conclusion : " May Christ help us to *live* according to his gospel which now resounds in our ears and which many carry on their lips ; for I see that countless persons abuse the gospel for the freedom of the flesh.[3] Having been the precursor of the holy evangelical doctrine, I trust that my entreaties may have some effect upon thee." The sermons which he preached at Salzburg since 1522 breathe the same spirit and urge Catholic orthodoxy and obedience.[4] His last book, published after his death (1525) under the title, " Of the holy *true* Christian Faith," is a virtual protest against Luther's doctrine of justification by faith *alone* and a plea for a practical Christianity which shows itself in good works. He contrasts the two doctrines in these words : " The fools say, he who believes in Christ, needs no works ; the Truth says, whosoever will be my disciple, let him follow Me ; and whosoever will follow Me, let him deny himself

---

187), Luther says, that in his sadness and distress in the convent he consulted Staupitz and opened to him his " *horrendas et terrificas cogitationes*," and that he was told by him : " *Nescis Martine, quam tibi illa tentatio sit utilis et necessaria. Non enim temere te sic exercet Deus, videbis, quod ad res magnas gerendas te ministro utetur.*"

[1] Luther : " *D. Staupitius me incitabat contra papam (al. papatum)*." In *Colloquia*, ed. Bindseil, III., 188.

[2] First published by K. Krafft, in " *Briefe und Documente aus der Zeit der Reformation*," Elberfeld (1876), p. 54 sq.

[3] " *Ad libertatem carnis video innumeros abuti evangelio*."

[4] Extracts from these sermons were first published by Kolde.

and carry my cross day by day; and whosoever loves Me, keeps my commandments. . . . The evil spirit suggests to carnal Christians the doctrine that man is justified without works, and appeals to Paul. But Paul only excluded works of the law which proceed from fear and selfishness, while in all his epistles he commends as necessary to salvation such works as are done in obedience to God's commandments, in faith and love. Christ fulfilled the law, the fools would abolish the law; Paul praises the law as holy and good, the fools scold and abuse it as evil because they walk according to the flesh and have not the mind of the Spirit."[1]

Staupitz withdrew from the conflict, resigned his position, 1520, left his order by papal dispensation, became abbot of the Benedictine Convent of St. Peter in Salzburg and died Dec. 28, 1524, in the bosom of the Catholic church which he never intended to leave.[2] He was evangelical, without being a Protestant.[3] He cared little for Romanism, less for Lutheranism, all for practical Christianity. His relation to the Reformation resembles that of Erasmus with this difference, that he helped to prepare the way for it in the sphere of discipline and piety, Erasmus in the

---

[1] Knaake, *l. c.*, I., 130 sqq.; Keller, *Reform.*, 346 sq. It must have been this book which Link sent to Luther in the year 1525, and which Luther returned with a very unfavorable judgment. Döllinger (*l. c.*, I., 155) thinks that Luther looked upon the death of Staupitz as a sort of divine judgment, as he looked afterward upon the death of Zwingli.

[2] Neverthless his books were put in the Index by the Council of Trent, 1563, and were burnt as heretical with all his correspondence by order of his successor, Abbot Martin of St. Peter, in the court of the convent at Salzburg in 1584. See Fr. Hein. Reusch (Old Cath.), *Der Index der verbotenen Bücher*, Bd. I. (Bonn, 1883), p. 279: "*Staupitius ist in den Index gekommen, weil Cochlœus bei dem Jahre 1517 ihn neben Luther als Gegner Tetzels erwähnt. Er ist in der 1. Classe geblieben bis auf diesen Tag, obschon man in Rom oder wenigstens in Trient, jedenfalls Benedict XIV. wohl hätte wissen können, dass er als guter Katholik, als Abt von St. Peter zu Salzburg gestorben.*" This is only one of several hundred errors in this papal catalogue of heretical books.

[3] Or, as Luther expressed it in his letter to Staupitz of Feb. 9, 1521, he wavered between Christ and the Pope: "*Ich fürchte, ihr möchtet zwischen Christo und dem Papste in der Mitte schweben, die ihr doch in heftigem Streit sehet.*" He told him in the same letter that he was no more that preacher of grace and of the cross (*ein solcher Gnaden-und Kreuzprediger*) as formerly.

sphere of scholarship and illumination. Both were men of mediation and transition ; they beheld from afar the land of promise,
but did not enter it.

§ 23. *The Victory of Justifying Faith.*

(Comp. § 7.)

The secret of Luther's power and influence lies in his heroic
faith. It delivered him from the chaos and torment of ascetic
self-mortification and self-condemnation, gave him rest and peace,
and made him a lordly freeman in Christ, and yet an obedient
servant of Christ. This faith breathes through all his writings,
dominated his acts, sustained him in his conflicts and remained
his shield and anchor till the hour of death. This faith was born
in the convent at Erfurt, called into public action at Wittenberg,
and made him a Reformer of the Church.

By the aid of Staupitz and the old monk, but especially by the
continued study of Paul's Epistles, he was gradually brought to
the conviction that the sinner is justified by faith alone, without works of law. He experienced this truth in his heart
long before he understood it in all its bearings. He found in it
that peace of conscience which he had sought in vain by his
monkish exercises. He pondered day and night over the meaning of " the righteousness of God " (Rom. 1 : 17), and thought
that it is the righteous punishment of sinners ; but toward the
close of his convent life he came to the conclusion that it is the
righteousness which God freely gives in Christ to those who
believe in him. Righteousness is not to be acquired by man
through his own exertions and merits ; it is complete and perfect
in Christ, and all the sinner has to do is to accept it from Him
as a free gift. Justification is that judicial act of God whereby
he acquits the sinner of guilt and clothes him with the righteousness of Christ on the sole condition of personal faith which
apprehends and appropriates Christ and shows its life and power
by good works, as a good tree bringing forth good fruits. For
faith in Luther's system is far more than a mere assent of the

mind to the authority of the church: it is a hearty trust and full surrender of the whole man to Christ; it lives and moves in Christ as its element, and is constantly obeying his will and following his example. It is only in connection with this deeper conception of faith that his doctrine of justification can be appreciated. Disconnected from it, it is a pernicious error.

The Pauline doctrine of justification as set forth in the Epistles to the Romans and Galatians, had never before been clearly and fully understood, not even by Augustin and Bernard, who confound justification with sanctification.[1] Herein lies the difference between the Catholic and the Protestant conception. In the Catholic system justification (δικαίωσις) is a gradual process conditioned by faith and good works; in the Protestant system it is a single act of God, followed by sanctification. It is based upon the merits of Christ, conditioned by faith, and manifested by good works.[2]

This experience acted like a new revelation on Luther. It shed light upon the whole Bible and made it to him a book of life and comfort. He felt relieved of the terrible load of guilt by an act of free grace. He was led out of the dark prison house of self-inflicted penance into the daylight and fresh air of God's redeeming love. Justification broke the fetters of legalistic slavery, and

---

[1] Luther himself felt how widely he differed in this doctrine from his favorite Augustin. He said afterward in his *Table Talk*: "*Principio Augustinum vorabam, non legebam; aber da mir in Paulo die Thür aufging, dass ich wusste was justificatio fidei wär, ward es aus mit ihm.*" Köstlin, I., 780. Yet if we reduce the doctrine of justification by faith to the more general term of salvation by free grace, it was held as clearly and strongly by Augustin and, we may say, is held by all true Christians. Janssen (II., 71) says: "Of all the books recognized and used by the (Catholic) Church, whether learned or popular, there is not one which does not contain the doctrine of justification by *Christ alone* (*die Lehre von der Rechtfertigung durch Christus allein*)." But the question between the Roman church and Luther turned on the *subjective appropriation* of the righteousness of Christ which is the *objective ground* of justification and salvation; while faith is the *subjective condition*.

[2] Modern exegesis has justified this view of δικαιόω and δικαίωσις, according to Hellenistic usage, although etymologically the verb may mean *to make just,* i. e., to sanctify, in accordance with verbs in όω (*e. g.* δηλόω, φανερόω, τυφλόω, *to make* manifest, etc.). See the Commentaries on Romans and Galatians.

filled him with the joy and peace of the state of adoption; it opened to him the very gates of heaven.

Henceforth the doctrine of justification by faith alone was for him to the end of life the sum and substance of the gospel, the heart of theology, the central truth of Christianity, the article of the standing or falling church. By this standard he measured every other doctrine and the value of every book of the Bible. Hence his enthusiasm for Paul, and his dislike of James, whom he could not reconcile with his favorite apostle. He gave disproportion to solifidianism and presented it sometimes in most unguarded language, which seemed to justify antinomian conclusions; but he corrected himself, he expressly condemned antinomianism, and insisted on good works and a holy life as a necessary manifestation of faith.[1] And it must not be forgotten that the same charge of favoring antinomianism was made against Paul, who rejects it with pious horror: "Let it never be!"

Thus the monastic and ascetic life of Luther was a preparatory school for his evangelical faith. It served the office of the Mosaic law which, by bringing the knowledge of sin and guilt, leads as a tutor to Christ (Rom. 3: 20; Gal. 3: 24). The law convicted, condemned, and killed him; the gospel comforted, justified, and made him alive. The law enslaved him, the gospel set him free. He had trembled like a slave; now he rejoiced as a son in his father's house. Through the discipline of the law he died to the law, that he might live unto God (Gal. 2: 19).

---

[1] The boldest and wildest utterance of Luther on justification occurs in a letter to Melanchthon (De Wette's ed. II. 37), dated Aug. 1, 1521, where he gives his opinion on the vow of celibacy and says: "*Esto peccator et pecca fortiter, sed fortius fide (crede) et gaude in Christo, qui victor est peccati, mortis et mundi.*" But it loses all its force as an argument against him and his doctrine, first by being addressed to Melanchthon, who was not likely to abuse it, and secondly by implying an impossibility; for the *fortius crede* and the concluding *ora fortiter* neutralize the *fortiter pecca*. Paul, of course, could never have written such a passage. He puts the antinomian inference: "Let us continue in sin that grace may abound" into the form of a question, and answers it by an indignant μὴ γένοιτο. Rom. 6: 1. This is the difference between the wisdom of an apostle and the zeal of a reformer.

In one word, Luther passed through the experience of Paul. He understood him better than any mediæval schoolman or ancient father. His commentary on the Epistle to the Galatians is still one of the best, for its sympathetic grasp of the contrast between law and gospel, between spiritual slavery and spiritual freedom.

Luther held this conviction without dreaming that it conflicted with the traditional creed and piety of the church. He was brought to it step by step. The old views and practices ran along side with it, and for several years he continued to be a sincere and devout Catholic. It was only the war with Tetzel and its consequences that forced him into the position of a Reformer and emancipated him from his old connections.

§ 24. *Luther Ordained to the Priesthood.*

In the second year of his monastic life and when he was still in a state of perplexity, Luther was ordained to the priesthood, and on May 2, 1507, he said his first mass. This was a great event in the life of a priest. He was so overwhelmed by the solemnity of offering the tremendous sacrifice for the living and the dead that he nearly fainted at the altar.

His father had come with several friends to witness the solemnity and brought him a present of twenty guilders. He was not yet satisfied with the monastic vows. "Have you not read in Holy Writ," he said to the brethren at the entertainment given to the young priest, "that a man must honor father and mother?" And when he was reminded, that his son was called to the convent by a voice from heaven, he answered: "Would to God, it were no spirit of the devil." He was not fully reconciled to his son till after he had acquired fame and entered the married state.

Luther performed the duties of the new dignity with conscientious fidelity. He read mass every morning, and invoked during the week twenty-one particular saints whom he had chosen as his helpers, three on each day.

But he was soon to be called to a larger field of influence.

§ 25. *Luther in Rome.*[1]

"*Roma qua nihil possis visere majus.*"—(Horace.)

" *Vivere qui sancte vultis, discedite Roma.*
  Omnia hic ecce licent, non licet esse probum."
" *Wer christlich leben will und rein,*
  Der zieh aus Rom und bleib daheim.
  Hie mag man thun was man nur will,
  Allein fromm sein gilt hier nicht viel."

(Old poetry quoted by Luther, in Walch, XXII., 2372.)

" *Prächtiger, als wir in unserm Norden,*
  Wohnt der Bettler an der Engelspforten,
  Denn er sieht das ewig einz'ge Rom :
  Ihn umgibt der Schönheit Glanzgewimmel,
  Und ein zweiter Himmel in den Himmel
  Steigt Sanct Peter's wundersamer Dom.
  Aber Rom in allem seinem Glanze
  Ist ein Grab nur der Vergangenheit,
  Leben duftet nur die frische Pflanze,
  Die die grüne Stunde streut."—(Schiller.)

An interesting episode in the history of Luther's training for the Reformation was his visit to Rome. It made a deep impression on his mind, and became effective, not immediately, but several years afterward through the recollection of what he had seen and heard, as a good Catholic, in the metropolis of Christendom.

In the autumn of the year 1510,[2] after his removal to Wittenberg, but before his graduation as doctor of divinity, Luther was sent to Rome in the interest of his order and at the suggestion

---

[1] Luther's dicta about Rome and his Roman journey are collected in Walch's ed., vol. XXII., 2372–2379; KŒHLER: *Luther's Reisen* (1872), p. 2–20; JÜRGENS, II., 266–358; KŒSTLIN, I., 100–107 ; LENZ, 45–47 ; KOLDE, I., 73–79 ; and in Brieger's "Zeitschrift für Kirchengesch," II., 460 sqq. Comp. also, on the R. Cath. side, the brief account of *Janssen*, II., 72. AUDIN devotes his third chapter to the Roman journey (I., 52–65).

[2] The chronology is not quite certain. The date 1511 is adopted by Köstlin and Kolde. Others date the Rome journey back to 1510 (Mathesius, Seckendorf, Jürgens, and Luther himself, in his tract *Against Popery invented by the Devil*, Erl. ed. XXVI., 125, though once he names the year 1511).

of Staupitz, who wished to bring about a disciplinary reform and closer union of the Augustinian convents in Germany, but met with factious opposition.

In company with another monk and a lay brother, as the custom was, he traveled on foot, from convent to convent, spent four weeks in Rome in the Augustinian convent of Maria del popolo, and returned to Wittenberg in the following spring. The whole journey must have occupied several months. It was the longest journey he ever made, and at the same time, his pilgrimage to the shrines of the holy apostles where he wished to make a general confession of all his sins and to secure the most efficient absolution.

We do not know whether he accomplished the object of his mission.[1] He left no information about his route, whether he passed through Switzerland or through the Tyrol, nor about the sublime scenery of the Alps and the lovely scenery of Italy.[2] The beauties of nature made little or no impression upon the Reformers, and were not properly appreciated before the close of the eighteenth century.[3] Zwingli and Calvin lived on the

[1] Kolde (I., 81) conjectures that the decision of Rome in the controversy among the Augustinians went against Staupitz, who soon after 1512 left Wittenberg.

[2] He passed through Suabia and Bavaria, as we may judge from his description of the people (Walch, XXII., 2359): " *Wenn ich viel reisen sollte, wollte ich nirgends lieber, denn durch Schwaben und Baierland ziehen ; denn sie sind freundlich und gutwillig, herbergen gerne, gehen Freunden und Wandersleuten entgegen, und thun den Leuten gütlich, und gute Ausrichtung um ihr Geld.*" He seems to have seen Switzerland also, of which he says (*ib.*, p. 2360): "*Schweiz ist ein dürr und bergig Land, darum sind sie endelich und hurtig, müssen ihre Nahrung underswo suchen.*"

[3] We seek in vain for descriptions of natural scenery among the ancient classics, but several Hebrew Psalms celebrate the glory of the Creator in his works. The Parables of our Lord imply that nature is full of spiritual lessons. The first descriptions of the beauties of nature in Christian literature are found in the Epistles of St. Basil, Gregory of Nazianzum and Gregory of Nyssa. See this *Ch. Hist.*, vol. III., 896 sqq. The incomparable beauties of Switzerland were first duly appreciated and made known to the world by Albrecht von Haller of Bern (in his poem, "*Die Alpen*"), Gœthe (*Schweizerreise*), and Schiller (in *Wilhelm Tell*, where he gives the most charming picture of the Lake of the Four Cantons, though he never was there).

banks of Swiss lakes and in view of the Swiss Alps, but never allude to them; they were absorbed in theology and religion.

In his later writings and Table-Talk, Luther left some interesting reminiscences of his journey. He spoke of the fine climate and fertility of Italy, the temperance of the Italians contrasted with the intemperate Germans, also of their shrewdness, craftiness, and of the pride with which they looked down upon the "stupid Germans" and "German beasts," as semi-barbarians; he praised the hospitals and charitable institutions in Florence; but he was greatly disappointed with the state of religion in Rome, which he found just the reverse of what he had expected.

Rome was at that time filled with enthusiasm for the renaissance of classical literature and art, but indifferent to religion. Julius II., who sat in Peter's chair from 1503 to 1513, bent his energies on the aggrandizement of the secular dominion of the papacy by means of an unscrupulous diplomacy and bloody wars, founded the Vatican Museum, and liberally encouraged the great architects and painters of his age in their immortal works of art. The building of the new church of St. Peter with its colossal cupola had begun under the direction of Bramante; the pencil of Michael Angelo was adorning the Sixtine chapel in the adjoining Vatican Palace with the pictures of the Prophets, Sibyls, and the last judgment; and the youthful genius of Raphael conceived his inimitable Madonna, with the Christ-child in her arms, and was transforming the chambers of the Vatican into galleries of undying beauty. These were the wonders of the new Italian art; but they had as little interest for the German monk as the temples and statues of classical Athens had for the Apostle Paul.

When Luther came in sight of the eternal city, he fell upon the earth, raised his hands and exclaimed, "Hail to thee, holy Rome![1] Thrice holy for the blood of martyrs shed here." He passed the colossal ruins of heathen Rome and the gorgeous palaces of Christian Rome. But he ran, "like a crazy saint," through all the churches and crypts and catacombs with an

[1] "Salve! Sancta Roma."

unquestioning faith in the legendary traditions about the relics and miracles of martyrs.[1] He wished that his parents were dead that he might help them out of purgatory by reading mass in the most holy place, according to the saying: "Blessed is the mother whose son celebrates mass on Saturday in St. John of the Lateran." He ascended on bended knees the twenty-eight steps of the famous Scala Santa (said to have been transported from the Judgment Hall of Pontius Pilate in Jerusalem), that he might secure the indulgence attached to this ascetic performance since the days of Pope Leo IV. in 850, but at every step the word of the Scripture sounded as a significant protest in his ear: "The just shall live by faith" (Rom. 1 : 17).[2]

Thus at the very height of his mediæval devotion he doubted its efficacy in giving peace to the troubled conscience. This doubt was strengthened by what he saw around him. He was favorably struck, indeed, with the business administration and police regulations of the papal court, but shocked by the unbelief, levity and immorality of the clergy. Money and luxurious living seemed to have replaced apostolic poverty and self-denial. He saw nothing but worldly splendor at the court of Pope Julius II., who had just returned from the sanguinary siege of a town conducted by him in person. He afterward thundered against him as a man of blood. He heard of the fearful crimes of Pope Alexander VI. and his family, which were hardly known and believed in Germany, but freely spoken of as undoubted facts in the fresh remembrance of all Romans. While he was reading one mass, a Roman priest would finish seven. He was urged to hurry up (*passa, passa!*), and to "send her Son home to our Lady." He heard priests, when consecrating the elements, repeat in Latin the words: "Bread thou art, and bread thou shalt

---

[1] "*Auch ich war ein so toller Heiliger,*" he said, "*lief durch alle Kirchen und Klüften, glaubte alles, was daselbst erlogen und erstunken ist.*"

[2] This interesting incident rests on the authority of his son Paul, who heard it from the lips of his father in 1544. Modern Popes, Pius VII. and Pius IX., have granted additional indulgences to those who climb up the Scala Santa.

remain; wine thou art, and wine thou shalt remain." The term "a good Christian" (*buon Christiano*) meant "a fool." He was told that "if there was a hell, Rome was built on it," and that this state of things must soon end in a collapse.

He received the impression that "Rome, once the holiest city, was now the worst." He compared it to Jerusalem as described by the prophets.[1] All these sad experiences did not shake his faith in the Roman church and hierarchy, so unworthily represented, as the Jewish hierarchy was at the time of Christ; but they returned to his mind afterward with double force and gave ease and comfort to his conscience when he attacked and abused popery as "an institution of the devil."[2]

Hence he often declared that he would not have missed "seeing Rome for a hundred thousand florins; for I might have felt some apprehension that I had done injustice to the Pope; but as we see, so we speak."

Six years after his visit the building of St. Peter's Dome by means of the proceeds from papal indulgences furnished the occasion for the outbreak of that war which ended with an irrevocable separation from Rome.

In the Pitti Gallery of Florence there is a famous picture of Giorgione which represents an unknown monk with strongly Teutonic features and brilliant eyes, seated between two Italians, playing on a small organ and looking dreamily to one side. This central figure has recently been identified by some connoisseurs as a portrait of Luther taken at Florence a few months before the death of Giorgione in 1511. The identity is open to doubt, but the resemblance is striking.[3]

---

[1] "*Es gehet uns wie den Propheten, die klagen auch über Jerusalem, und sagen: Die feine gläubige Stadt is zur Hure geworden. Denn aus dem Besten kommt allezeit das Aergste, wie die Exempel zeigen zu allen Zeiten.*" Walch, XXII., 2378.

[2] This was the topic of one of his last and most abusive works: "*Wider das Papstthum zu Rom vom Teufel gestiftet.*" March, 1545.

[3] Comp. "Revista Christiana," Firenze, 1883, p. 422. The picture on the opposite page is from a photograph made in Florence.

GIORGIONE'S PORTRAIT OF LUTHER IN FLORENCE, 1510.
From the Pitti Gallery in Florence.

131

§ 26. *The University of Wittenberg.*

GROHMANN: *Annalen der Universität zu Wittenberg*, 1802, 2 vols. MUTHER: *Die Wittenberger Universitäts und Facultatstätsstudien v. Jahr* 1508. Halle, 1867. K. SCHMIDT: *Wittenberg unter Kurfürst Friedrich dem Weisen.* Erlangen, 1877. JUERGENS: II., 151 sqq. and 182 sqq. (very thorough). KŒSTLIN, I., 90 sqq. KOLDE: *Friedrich der Weise und die Anfänge der Reformation*, Erlangen, 1881; and his *Leben Luther's*, 1884, I., 67 sqq.

In the year 1502 Frederick III., surnamed the Wise, Elector of Saxony (b. 1463, d. 1525), distinguished among the princes of the sixteenth century for his intelligence, wisdom, piety, and cautious protection of the Reformation, founded from his limited means a new University at Wittenberg, under the patronage of the Virgin Mary and St. Augustin. The theological faculty was dedicated to the Apostle Paul, and on the anniversary of his conversion at Damascus a mass was to be celebrated and a sermon preached in the presence of the rector and the senate.

Frederick was a devout Catholic, a zealous collector of relics, a believer in papal indulgences, a pilgrim to the holy land; but at the same time a friend of liberal learning, a protector of the person of Luther and of the new theology of the University of Wittenberg, which he called his daughter, and which he favored to the extent of his power. Shortly before his death he signified the acceptance of the evangelical faith by taking the communion in both kinds from Spalatin, his chaplain, counsellor and biographer, and mediator between him and Luther. He was unmarried and left no legitimate heir. His brother, John the Constant (1525–1532), and his nephew, John Frederick the Magnanimous (1532–1547), both firm Protestants, succeeded him; but the latter was deprived of the electoral dignity and part of his possessions by his victorious cousin Moritz, Duke of Saxony, after the battle of Mühlberg (1547). The successors of Moritz were the chief defenders of Lutheranism in Germany till Augustus I. (1694–1733) sold the faith of his ancestors for the royal crown of Poland and became a Roman Catholic.

Wittenberg an der Elbe die Haupstatt in Chur Sachsen. 1546

Elb Flus.

WITTENBERG. From an old engraving.

133

Wittenberg[1] was a poor and badly built town of about three thousand inhabitants in a dull, sandy, sterile plain on the banks of the Elbe, and owes its fame entirely to the fact that it became the nursery of the Reformation theology. Luther says that it lay at the extreme boundary of civilization,[2] a few steps from barbarism, and speaks of its citizens as wanting in culture, courtesy and kindness. He felt at times strongly tempted to leave it. Melanchthon who came from the fertile Palatinate, complained that he could get nothing fit to eat at Wittenberg. Myconius, Luther's friend, describes the houses as "small, old, ugly, low, wooden." Even the electoral castle is a very unsightly structure. The Elector laughed when Dr. Pollich first proposed the town as the seat of the new university. But Wittenberg was one of his two residences (the other being Torgau), had a new castle-church with considerable endowments and provision for ten thousand masses per annum, and an Augustinian convent which could furnish a part of the teaching force, and thus cheapen the expenses of the institution.

The university was opened October 18, 1502. The organization was intrusted to Dr. Pollich, the first rector, who on account of his extensive learning was called "lux mundi," and who had accompanied the Elector on a pilgrimage to Jerusalem (1493), and to Staupitz, the first dean of the theological faculty, who fixed his eye at once upon his friend Luther as a suitable professor of theology.

Wittenberg had powerful rivals in the neighboring, older and better endowed Universities of Erfurt and Leipzig, but soon overshadowed them by the new theology. The principal professors were members of the Augustinian order, most of them from Tübingen and Erfurt. The number of students was four hundred and sixteen in the first semester, then declined to fifty-

---

[1] Probably, Weissenberg, from the white sand-hills on the Elbe. So Jürgens II., 190. The original inhabitants of the region were Slavs (Wends), but expelled or absorbed by the Saxons. The town dates from the twelfth century.

[2] "In termino civilitatis."

five in 1505, partly in consequence of the pestilence, began to rise again in 1507, and when Luther and Melanchthon stood on the summit of their fame, they attracted thousands of pupils from all countries of Europe.   Melanchthon heard at times eleven languages spoken at his hospitable table.

§ 27. *Luther as Professor till* 1517.

Luther was suddenly called by Staupitz from the Augustinian Convent of Erfurt to that of Wittenberg with the expectation of becoming at the same time a lecturer in the university. He arrived there in October, 1508, was called back to Erfurt in

THE "LUTHER-HOUSE" (previously the Augustinian Convent), before its recent restoration. It contains the Luther-Museum.

autumn, 1509, was sent to Rome in behalf of his order, 1510, returned to Wittenberg, 1511, and continued there till a few days before his death, 1546.

He lived in the convent, even after his marriage. His plain study, bed-room and lecture-hall are still shown in the "Luther-haus." The lowliness of his work-shop forms a sublime contrast to the grandeur of his work. From their humble dwellings

Luther and Melanchthon exerted a mightier influence than the contemporary popes and kings from their gorgeous palaces.

Luther combined the threefold office of sub-prior, preacher and professor. He preached both in his convent and in the town-church, sometimes daily for a week, sometimes thrice in one day, during Lent in 1517 twice every day. He was supported by the convent. As professor he took no fees from the students, and received only a salary of one hundred guilders, which after his marriage was raised by the Elector John to two hundred guilders.[1]

LUTHER'S ROOM IN WITTENBERG. From a photograph.

He first lectured on scholastic philosophy and explained the Aristotelian dialectics and physics. But he soon passed through the three grades of bachelor, licentiate, and doctor of divinity (October 18th and 19th, 1512), and henceforth devoted himself exclusively to the sacred science which was much more congenial to

---

[1] " *Wäre es nicht geschehen,*" says Luther, " *so hatte ich nach meiner Verheira-thung mir vorgenommen, für Honorar zu lesen. Aber da mir Gott zuvorkam, so habe ich mein Leben lang kein Exemplar* [he means, of his writings] *verkauft, noch gelesen um Lohn, will auch den Ruhm, will's Gott, mit mir ins Grab nehmen.*" Jürgens, II., 248 sq.

his taste. Staupitz urged him into these academic dignities,[1] and the Elector who had been favorably impressed with one of his sermons, offered to pay the expenses (fifty guilders) for the acquisition of the doctorate.[2] Afterward in seasons of trouble Luther often took comfort from the title and office of his doctorate of divinity and his solemn oath to defend with all his might the Holy Scriptures against all errors.[3] He justified the burning of the Pope's bull in the same way. But the oath of ordination and of the doctor of theology implied also obedience to the Roman church (*ecclesiæ Romanæ obedientiam*) and her defence against all heresies condemned by her.[4]

With the year 1512 his academic teaching began in earnest, and continued till 1546, at first in outward harmony with the Roman church, but afterward in open opposition to it.

He was well equipped for his position, according to the advantages of his age, but very poorly, according to modern requirements, as far as technical knowledge is concerned.

[1] Luther remembered the pear tree under which Staupitz overcame his objections to the labors and responsibilities of the doctorate. He thought himself unable to endure them with his frail body, but Staupitz replied playfully and in prophetic anticipation of the great work in store for him: "*In Gottes Namen! Unser Herr Gott hat grosse Geschäfte; Er bedarf droben auch kluger Leute; wenn Ihr nun sterbet, so müsset Ihr dort sein Rathgeber sein.*"

[2] See K. F. Th. Schneider, *Luther's Promotion zum Doctor und Melanchthon's zum Baccalaureus der Theologie*, Neuwied, 1860 (38 pp.). He gives Luther's Latin oration which he delivered in honor of theology on the text: "I will give you a mouth and wisdom" (Luke 21: 15). The expenses of the promotion to the degree of the baccalaureate, Luther never paid. The records of the dean note this fact: "*Adhuc non satisfecit facultati,*" and Luther afterward wrote on the margin: "*Nec faciet, quia tunc pauper et sub obedientia nihil habuit.*" Schneider, p. 6.

[3] See his utterances on the importance of his doctorate in Mathesius (*Sermons* I. and XV.) and Jürgens (II., 405–408). Jürgens points out and explains (p. 424 sqq.) the inconsistency of Luther in his appeal to human authority and overestimate of the official title. Every step in his public career was accompanied by scruples of conscience which he had to solve the best way he could.

[4] Köstlin says (Engl. transl. of the short biography, p. 65): "Obedience to the Pope was not required at Wittenberg, as it was at other universities." But it is implied in obedience to the Roman church. The university was chartered by the Emperor Maximilian, but the Elector had not neglected to secure the papal sanction. See Jürgens, II. 207.

Although a doctor of divinity, he relied for several years almost exclusively on the Latin version of the Scriptures. Very few professors knew Greek, and still less, Hebrew. Luther had acquired a superficial idea of Hebrew at Erfurt from Reuchlin's *Rudimenta Hebraica.*[1] The Greek he learned at Wittenberg, we do not know exactly when, mostly from books and from his colleagues, Johann Lange and Melanchthon. As late as Feb. 18th, 1518, he asked Lange, "the Greek," a question about the difference between ἀνάθημα and ἀνάθεμα, and confessed that he could not draw the Greek letters.[2] His herculean labor in translating the Bible forced him into a closer familiarity with the original languages, though he never attained to mastery. As a scholar he remained inferior to Reuchlin or Erasmus or Melanchthon, but as a genius he was their superior, and as a master of his native German he had no equal in all Germany. Moreover, he turned his knowledge to the best advantage, and always seized the strong point in controversy. He studied with all his might and often neglected eating and sleeping.

Luther opened his theological teaching with David and Paul, who became the pillars of his theology. The Psalms and the Epistles to the Romans and Galatians remained his favorite books. His academic labors as a commentator extended over thirty-three years, from 1513 to 1546, his labors as a reformer embraced only twenty-nine years, from 1517 to 1546. Beginning with the Psalms, 1513, he ended with Genesis, November 17th, 1545, three months before his death.

His first lectures on the Psalms are still extant and have

---

[1] This book, published at Pforzheim, 1506, at the author's expense, is the first Hebrew grammar written by a Christian, and broke the path for Hebrew learning in Germany. So far Reuchlin was right in calling it a *monumentum ære perennius.*

[2] DeWette, I. 34 : " *Petimus a te, Græce, ut controversiam nostram dissolvas, quæ sit distantia inter anathema per epsilon, et anathema per η . . . . Nescio figuras literarum pingere.*" In his *Table Talk* he says : " *Ich kann weder griechisch noch hebräisch ; ich will aber dennoch einem Griechen und Hebräer ziemlich begegnen.*" Comp. on his linguistic studies and accomplishments, Jürgens, I. 470 sqq.; II. 428 sqq.

recently been published from the manuscript in Wolfenbüttel.[1] They are exegetically worthless, but theologically important as his first attempt to extract a deeper spiritual meaning from the Psalms. He took Jerome's Psalter as the textual basis;[2] the few Hebrew etymologies are all derived from Jerome, Augustin (who knew no Hebrew), and Reuchlin's Lexicon. He followed closely the mediæval method of interpretation which distinguished four different senses, and neglected the grammatical and historical interpretation. Thus Jerusalem means literally or historically the city in Palestine, allegorically the good, tropologically virtue, anagogically reward; Babylon means literally the city or empire of Babylon, allegorically the evil, tropologically vice, anagogically punishment. Then again one word may have four bad and four good senses, according as it is understood literally or figuratively.[3] Sometimes he distinguished six senses. He emphasized the prophetic character of the Psalms, and found Christ and his work everywhere.[4] He had no sympathy with the method of

[1] He had the Latin text of the Psalms printed, and wrote between the lines and on the margin his notes in very small and almost illegible letters. Köstlin gives a fac-simile page in *Luther's Leben*, p. 72 (Engl. ed. p. 64). The whole was published with painstaking accuracy by Kawerau in the third volume of the Weimar ed. (1885).

[2] The innumerable references to the *Hebræus* are never intended for the original, but for Jerome's *Psalterium juxta Hebræos*. Paul de Lagarde has published an edition, Lips., 1874.

[3] Luther illustrates this double four-fold scheme of exegesis by the following table (Weimar ed. III. 11):

LITERA OCCIDENS	SPIRITUS VIVIFICANS *de corpore*
MONS ZION { *hystorice terra Canaan* / *Allegorice Synagoga vel persona eminens in eadem* / *tropologice Justitia pharisaica et legalis* / *anagogice Gloria futura secundum carnem*	MONS ZION { *hystorice populus in Zion existens Babylonico Ecclesiastico* { *doctor / Episcopus / eminens* / *Allegorice Ecclesia vel quilibit* / *Tropologice Justitia fidei vel alia excellen . . .* / *Anagogice gloria eterna in celis.*

Econtra VALLIS CEDRON *per oppositum.*

[4] This fanciful allegorizing and spiritualizing method of interpreting the Psalms by which they are made to teach almost anything that is pious and edifying, is still popular even in some Protestant churches, especially the

Nicolaus Lyra to understand the Psalter from the times of the writer. Afterward he learned to appreciate him.[1] He followed Augustin, the *Glossa ordinaria*, and especially the *Quincuplex Psalterium* of Faber Stapulensis (Paris, 1508 and 1513). He far surpassed himself in his later comments on the Psalms.[2] It was only by degrees that he emancipated himself from the traditional exegesis, and approached the only sound and safe method of grammatico-historical interpretation of Scripture from the natural meaning of the words, the situation of the writer and the analogy of his teaching, viewed in the light of the Scriptures as a whole. He never gave up altogether the scholalistic and allegorizing method of utilizing exegesis for dogmatic and devotional purposes, but he assigned it a subordinate place. "Allegories," he said, "may be used to teach the ignorant common people, who need to have the same thing impressed in various forms." He measured the Scriptures by his favorite doctrine of justification by faith, and hence depreciated important books, especially the Epistle of James and the Apocalypse. But when his dogmatic conviction required it, he laid too much stress on the letter, as in the eucharistic controversy.

From the Psalms he proceeded to the Epistles of Paul. Here he had an opportunity to expound his ideas of sin and grace, the difference between the letter and the spirit, between the law and the gospel, and to answer the great practical question, how a sinner may be justified before a holy God and obtain pardon and peace. He first lectured on Romans and explained the difference between the righteousness of faith and the righteousness of works. He never published a work on Romans except a preface which contains a masterly description of faith. His lectures on

Church of England. Comp. *e. g.* Dr. Neale and Dr. Littledale's *Commentary on the Psalms from primitive and mediæval writers*. London, fourth ed., 1884, 4 vols. The celebrated Baptist preacher, Spurgeon, has written a commentary on the Psalms, in seven volumes, which is likewise full of allegorizing interpretation, but mostly derived from older Protestant and Puritan sources.

[1] Hence the saying: "*Si Lyra non lyrasset, Lutherus non saltasset.*"

[2] Ed. by Dr. Bertheau in the fourth vol. of the Weimar ed. (1886).

Galatians he began October 27th, 1516, and resumed them repeatedly.. They appeared first in Latin, September, 1519, and in a revised edition, 1523, with a preface of Melanchthon.[1] They are the most popular and effective of his commentaries, and were often published in different languages. John Bunyan was greatly benefited by them. Their chief value is that they bring us into living contact with the central idea of the epistle, namely, evangelical freedom in Christ, which he reproduced and adapted in the very spirit of Paul. Luther always had a special preference for this anti-Judaic Epistle and called it his sweetheart or his wife.[2]

These exegetical lectures made a deep impression. They were thoroughly evangelical, without being anti-catholic. They reached the heart and conscience as well as the head. They substituted a living theology clothed with flesh and blood for the skeleton theology of scholasticism. They were delivered with the energy of intense conviction and the freshness of personal experience. The genius of the lecturer flashed from his deep dark eyes which seem to have struck every observer. "This monk," said Dr. Pollich, "will revolutionize the whole scholastic teaching." Christopher Scheurl commended Luther to the friendship of Dr. Eck (his later opponent) in January, 1517, as "a divine who explained the epistles of the man of Tarsus with wonderful genius." Melanchthon afterward expressed a general judgment when he said that Christ and the Apostles were brought out again as from the darkness and filth of prison.

§ 28. *Luther and Mysticism. The Theologia Germanica.*

In 1516 Luther read the sermons of Tauler, the mystic revival preacher of Strassburg (who died in 1361), and discovered the

---

[1] See the first ed. in the Weimar ed. of his works, vol. II. 436–618. This commentary of 1519 must be distinguished from the larger work of 1535 which has the same title, but rests on different lectures.

[2] In December, 1531: "*Epistola ad Galatas ist meine Epistola, der ich mich vertraut habe, meine Kethe von Bora.*" Weimar ed. II. 437. Melanchthon called Luther's commentary the thread of Theseus in the labyrinth of N. T. exegesis.

remarkable book called "German Theology," which he ascribed to Tauler, but which is of a little later date from a priest and custos of the *Deutsch-Herrn Haus* of Frankfort, and a member of the association called "Friends of God." It resembles the famous work of Thomas a Kempis in exhibiting Christian piety as an humble imitation of the life of Christ on earth, but goes beyond it, almost to the very verge of pantheism, by teaching in the strongest terms the annihilation of self-will and the absorption of the soul in God. Without being polemical, it represents by its intense inwardness a striking contrast to the then prevailing practice of religion as a mechanical and monotonous round of outward acts and observances.

Luther published a part of this book from an imperfect manuscript, December, 1516, and from a complete copy, in 1518, with a brief preface of his own.[1] He praises it as rich and over-precious in divine wisdom, though poor and unadorned in words and human wisdom. He places it next to the Bible and St. Augustin in its teaching about God, Christ, man, and all things, and says in conclusion that "the German divines are doubtless the best divines."

There are various types of mysticism, orthodox and heretical, speculative and practical.[2] Luther came in contact with the practical and catholic type through Staupitz and the writings of St. Augustin, St. Bernard, and Tauler. It deepened and spiritualized his piety and left permanent traces on his theology. The Lutheran church, like the Catholic, always had room for mystic tendencies. But mysticism alone could not satisfy him, especially

[1] Both prefaces are printed in the Weimar ed. of his works I. 153 and 378 sq. The book itself has gone through many editions; the best is by Franz Pfeiffer, *Theologia deutsch*, Stuttgart, 1851, third ed. 1855. There is a good English translation by Susanna Winkworth, *Theologia Germanica*, with additions by Canon Kingsley and Chevalier Bunsen, (London, 1854, new ed. 1874; reprinted at Andover, 1846). Several characteristic mystic terms, as *Entwerdung, Gelassenheit, Vergottung*, are hardly translatable.

[2] Ed. von Hartmann, the pessimist, says (*Die Philos. des Unbewussten*, Berlin, 1869, p. 276): "*Die Mystik ist eine Schlingpflanze, die an jedem Stabe emporwuchert und sich mit den extremsten Gegensätzen gleichgut abzufinden weiss.*"

after the Reformation began in earnest. It was too passive and sentimental and shrunk from conflict. It was a theology of feeling rather than of action. Luther was a born fighter, and waxed stronger and stronger in battle. His theology is biblical, with such mystic elements as the Bible itself contains.[1]

§ 29. *The Penitential Psalms. The Eve of the Reformation.*

The first original work which Luther published was a German exposition of the seven Penitential Psalms, 1517.[2] It was a fit introduction to the reformatory Theses which enjoin the true evangelical repentance. In this exposition he sets forth the doctrines of sin and grace and the comfort of the gospel for the understanding of the common people. It shows him first in the light of a popular author, and had a wide circulation.

Luther was now approaching the prime of manhood. He was the shining light of the young university, and his fame began to spread through Germany. But he stood not alone. He had valuable friends and co-workers such as Dr. Wenzeslaus Link, the prior of the convent, and John Lange, who had a rare knowledge of Greek. Carlstadt also, his senior colleague, was at that time in full sympathy with him. Nicolaus von Amsdorf, of the same age with Luther, was one of his most faithful adherents, but more influential in the pulpit than in the chair. Christoph Scheurl, Professor of jurisprudence, was likewise intimate with Luther.

---

[1] See Hermann Hering, *Die Mystik Luthers im Zusammenhange seiner Theologie und in ihrem Verh. zur älteren Mystik.* Leipzig, 1879. He distinguishes three periods in Luther's relation to mysticism: (1) *Romanisch-mystische Periode;* (2) *Germanisch-mystische Periode;* (3) Conflict with the false mysticism of Münzer, Carlstadt, the Zwickau Prophets, and Schwenkfeldt.

[2] Weimar ed., vol. I. 154–220. A Latin copy had appeared already in 1513 and is preserved in the library at Wolfenbüttel, from which Prof. E. Riehm of Halle published it: *Initium theologiæ Lutheri. S. exempla scholiorum quibus D. Lutherus Psalterium interpretari cœpit. Part. I. Septem Psalmi pœnitentiales. Textum originalem nunc primum de Lutheri autographo exprimendum curavit.* Halle, 1874. Luther's closing lectures of 1516 exist likewise in MS. at Dresden, from which they were published by J. C. Seidemann in: *Doctoris M. Lutheri scholæ ineditæ de Psalmis annis* 1513–1516. Dresden, 1876, in 2 vols.

Nor must we forget Georg Spalatin, who did not belong to the university, but had great influence upon it as chaplain and secretary of the Elector Frederick, and acted as friendly mediator between him and Luther. The most effective aid the Reformer received, in 1518, in the person of Melanchthon.[1]

The working forces of the Reformation were thus fully prepared and ready for action. The scholastic philosophy and theology were undermined, and a biblical, evangelical theology ruled in Wittenberg. It was a significant coincidence, that the first edition of the Greek Testament was published by Erasmus in 1516, just a year before the Reformation.[2]

Luther had as yet no idea of reforming the Catholic church, and still less of separating from it. All the roots of his life and piety were in the historic church, and he considered himself a good Catholic even in 1517, and was so in fact. He still devoutly prayed to the Virgin Mary from the pulpit; he did not doubt the intercession of saints in heaven for the sinners on earth; he celebrated mass with full belief in the repetition of the sacrifice on the cross and the miracle of transubstantiation; he regarded the Hussites as " sinful heretics " for breaking away from the unity of the church and the papacy which offered a bulwark against sectarian division.

But by the leading of Providence he became innocently and reluctantly a Reformer. A series of events carried him irresistibly from step to step, and forced him far beyond

---

[1] On the early colleagues of Luther, see Jürgens, II. 217–235.

[2] Luther made good use of it for his translation, but was not pleased with the writings of Erasmus. As early as March 1, 1517, he wrote to John Lange: " I now read our Erasmus, but he pleases me less every day. It is well enough that he should constantly and learnedly refute the monks and priests, and charge them with a deep-rooted and sleepy ignorance. But I fear he does not sufficiently promote Christ and the grace of God, of which he knows very little. He thinks more of the human than the divine. . . . Not every one who is a good Greek and Hebrew, is also for this reason a good Christian. The blessed Jerome with his five tongues did not equal the one-tongued Augustin, although Erasmus thinks differently." — *Briefe*, ed. De Wette, I. 52.

his original intentions.   Had he foreseen the separation, he would have shrunk from it in horror.   He was as much the child of his age as its father, and the times molded him before he molded the times.   This is the case with all men of Providence: they are led by a divine hand while they are leading their fellow-men.

NOTES.

The works of Luther written before the 95 Theses (reprinted in the Weimar ed., I. 1–238, III., IV.) are as follows: Commentary on the Psalms; a number of sermons; *Tractatus de his, qui ad ecclesias confugiunt* (an investigation of the right of asylum; first printed 1517, anonymously, then under Luther's name, 1520, at Landshut; but of doubtful genuineness); *Sermo præscriptus præposito in Litzka*, 1512 (a Latin sermon prepared for his friend, the Provost Georg Mascov of Leitzkau in Brandenburg); several *Latin Sermons* from 1514–1517; *Quæstio de viribus et voluntate hominis sine gratia disputata*, 1516; Preface to his first edition of " German Theology," 1516; *The seven Penitential Psalms*, 1517; *Disputatio contra scholasticam theologiam*, 1517. The last are 97 theses against the philosophy of Aristotle, of whom he said, that he would hold him to be a devil if he had not had flesh.   These theses were published in September, 1517, and were followed in October by the 95 Theses against the traffic in Indulgences.

The earliest letters of Luther, from April 22, 1507, to Oct. 31, 1517, are addressed to Braun (vicar at Eisenach), Spalatin (chaplain of the Elector Frederick), Lohr (prior of the Augustinian Convent at Erfurt), John Lange, Scheurl, and others.   They are printed in Latin in Löscher's *Reformations-Acta*, vol. I. 795–846; in De Wette's edition of *Luther's Briefe*, I. 1–64; German translation in Walch, vol. XXI.   The last of these ante-Reformation letters is directed to Archbishop Albrecht of Mainz, and dated from the day of the publication of the Theses, Oct. 31, 1517 (DeWette I. 67–70).   The letters begin with the name of " Jesus."

CHAPTER III.

THE GERMAN REFORMATION FROM THE PUBLICATION OF
LUTHER'S THESES TO THE DIET OF WORMS, A.D. 1517–1521.

§ 30.   The Sale of Indulgences.

ST. PETER'S DOME is at once the glory and the shame of
papal Rome. It was built over the bones of the Galilæan
fisherman, with the proceeds from the sale of indulgences
which broke up the unity of Western Christendom. The
magnificent structure was begun in 1506 under Pope Julius
II., and completed in 1626 at a cost of forty-six millions
scudi, and is kept up at an annual expense of thirty thousand scudi (dollars).[1]

Jesus began his public ministry with the expulsion of the
profane traffickers from the court of the temple. The Reformation began with a protest against the traffic in indulgences which profaned and degraded the Christian religion.

The difficult and complicated doctrine of indulgences is
peculiar to the Roman Church. It was unknown to the Greek
and Latin fathers. It was developed by the mediæval schoolmen, and sanctioned by the Council of Trent (Dec. 4, 1563),
yet without a definition and with an express warning against
abuses and evil gains.[2]

---

[1] On St. Peter's church, see the archæological and historical works on
Rome, and especially Heinr. von Geymüller, *Die Entwürfe für Sanct Peter
in Rom*, Wien (German and French); and Charles de Lorbac, *Saint-Pierre
de Rome, illustré de plus de 130 gravures sur bois*, Rome, 1879 (pp. 310).

[2] The Council incidentally admits that these evil gains have been the most
prolific source of abuses, — "*unde plurima in Christiano populo abusuum
causa fluxit*," — and hence it ordained that they are to be wholly abolished:
"*omnino abolendos esse.*" (Schaff, *Creeds of Christendom*, II. 205 sq.)   A
strong proof of the effect of the Reformation upon the Church of Rome.

146

In the legal language of Rome, *indulgentia* is a term for amnesty or remission of punishment. In ecclesiastical Latin, an *indulgence* means the remission of the temporal (not the eternal) punishment of sin (not of sin itself), on condition of penitence and the payment of money to the church or to some charitable object. It may be granted by a bishop or archbishop within his diocese, while the Pope has the power to grant it to all Catholics. The practice of indulgences grew out of a custom of the Northern and Western barbarians to substitute pecuniary compensation for punishment of an offense. The church favored this custom in order to avoid bloodshed, but did wrong in applying it to *religious* offenses. Who touches money touches dirt; and the less religion has to do with it, the better. The first instances of such pecuniary compensations occurred in England under Archbishop Theodore of Canterbury (d. 690). The practice rapidly spread on the Continent, and was used by the Popes during and after the crusades as a means of increasing their power. It was justified and reduced to a theory by the schoolmen, especially by Thomas Aquinas, in close connection with the doctrine of the sacrament of penance and priestly absolution.[1]

The sacrament of penance includes three elements, — contrition of the heart, confession by the mouth (to the priest), and satisfaction by good works, such as prayer, fasting, almsgiving, pilgrimages, all of which are supposed to have an atoning efficacy. God forgives only the eternal punishment of sin, and he alone can do that; but the sinner has to bear the temporal punishments, either in this life or in purgatory; and these punishments are under the control of the church or the priesthood, especially the Pope as its legitimate head. There are also works of supererogation, performed by Christ

[1] Thomas Aquinas, *Summa Theol.*, Pars III. Quæst. LXXXIV., *De Sacramento Pœnitentiæ;* and in the supplement to the Third Part, Quæst. XXV.-XXVII., *De Indulgentia.* Comp. literature in vol. IV. 381.

and by the saints, with corresponding extra-merits and extra-rewards; and these constitute a rich treasury from which the Pope, as the treasurer, can dispense indulgences for money. This papal power of dispensation extends even to the departed souls in purgatory, whose sufferings may thereby be abridged. This is the scholastic doctrine.

The granting of indulgences degenerated, after the time of the crusades, into a regular traffic, and became a source of ecclesiastical and monastic wealth. A good portion of the profits went into the papal treasury. Boniface VIII. issued the first bull of the jubilee indulgence to all visitors of St. Peter's in Rome (1300). It was to be confined to Rome, and to be repeated only once in a hundred years, but it was afterwards extended and multiplied as to place and time.

The idea of selling and buying by money the remission of punishment and release from purgatory was acceptable to ignorant and superstitious people, but revolting to sound moral feeling. It roused, long before Luther, the indignant protest of earnest minds, such as Wiclif in England, Hus in Bohemia, John von Wesel in Germany, John Wessel in Holland, Thomas Wyttenbach in Switzerland, but without much effect.

The Lateran Council of 1517 allowed the Pope to collect one-tenth of all the ecclesiastical property of Christendom, ostensibly for a war against the Turks; but the measure was carried only by a small majority of two or three votes, and the minority objected that there was no immediate prospect of such a war. The extortions of the Roman curia became an intolerable burden to Christendom, and produced at last a successful protest which cost the papacy the loss of its fairest possessions.

§ 31. *Luther and Tetzel.*

I. On the Indulgence controversy: LUTHER's *Works*, WALCH's ed., XV. 3–462; Weim. ed. I. 229–324. LÖSCHER: *Reformations-Acta.* Leipzig, 1720. Vol. I. 355–539. J. KAPP: *Schauplatz des Tetzelschen Ablasskrams.* Leipzig, 1720. JÜRGENS: *Luther*, Bd. III. 460–580. KAHNIS:

Die d. Ref., I.18 1 sqq. KÖSTLIN, I. 153 sqq. KOLDE, I. 126 sqq. On the Roman-Catholic side, JANSSEN: *Geschichte*, etc., II. 64 sqq.; 77 sqq.; and *An meine Kritiker*, Freiburg-i.-B., 1883, pp. 66–81. — On the editions of the Theses, compare KNAAKE, in the Weimar ed. I. 229 sqq.

EDW. BRATKE: *Luther's 95 Thesen und ihre dogmengesch. Voraussetzungen.* Göttingen, 1884 (pp. 333). Gives an account of the scholastic doctrine of indulgences from Bonaventura and Thomas Aquinas down to Prierias and Cajetan, an exposition of Luther's Theses, and a list of books on the subject. A. W. DIECKHOFF (of Rostock): *Der Ablassstreit. Dogmengeschichtlich dargestellt.* Gotha, 1886 (pp. 260).

II. On Tetzel in particular: (1) Protestant biographies and tracts, all very unfavorable. (*a*) Older works by G. HECHT: *Vita Joh. Tetzeli.* Wittenberg, 1717. JAC. VOGEL: *Leben des päpstlichen Gnadenpredigers und Ablasskrämers Tetzel.* Leipzig, 1717, 2d ed., 1727. (*b*) Modern works: F. G. HOFMANN: *Lebensbeschreibung des Ablasspredigers Tetzel.* Leipzig, 1844. Dr. KAYSER: *Geschichtsquellen über den Ablasspred. Tetzel kritisch beleuchtet.* Annaberg, 1877 (pp. 20). Dr. FERD. KÖRNER: *Tetzel, der Ablassprediger*, etc. Frankenberg-i.-S. 1880 (pp. 153; chiefly against Gröne). Compare also BRATKE and DIECKHOFF, quoted above.

(2) Roman-Catholic vindications of Tetzel by VAL. GRÖNE (Dr. Th.): *Tetzel und Luther, oder Lebensgesch. und Rechtfertigung des Ablasspredigers und Inquisitors Dr. Joh. Tetzel aus dem Predigerorden.* Soest und Olpe, 1853, 2d ed. 1860 (pp. 237). E. KOLBE: *P. Joh. Tetzel. Ein Lebensbild dem kathol. Volke gewidmet.* Steyl, 1882 (pp. 98, based on Gröne). K. W. HERMANN: *Joh. Tetzel, der päpstl. Ablassprediger.* Frankf.-a.-M., 2te Aufl. 1883 (pp. 152). JANSSEN: *An meine Kritiker*, p. 73 sq. G. A. MEIJER, Ord. Præd. (Dominican): *Johann Tetzel, Aflaatprediker en inquisiteur. Eene geschiedkundige studie.* Utrecht, 1885 (pp. 150). A calm and moderate vindication of Tetzel, with the admission (p. 137) that the last word on the question has not yet been spoken, and that we must wait for the completion of the *Regesta* of Leo X. and other authentic publications now issuing from the Vatican archives by direction of Leo XIII. But the main facts are well established.

The rebuilding of St. Peter's Church in Rome furnished an occasion for the periodical exercise of the papal power of granting indulgences. Julius II. and Leo X., two of the most worldly, avaricious, and extravagant Popes, had no scruple to raise funds for that object, and incidentally for their own aggrandizement, from the traffic in indulgences. Both issued several bulls to that effect.[1]

Spain, England, and France ignored or resisted these bulls for financial reasons, refusing to be taxed for the benefit of Rome. But Germany, under the weak rule of Maximilian, yielded to the papal domination.

Leo divided Germany into three districts, and committed in 1515 the sale for one district to Albrecht, Archbishop of Mainz and Magdeburg, and brother of the Elector of Brandenburg.[2]

This prelate (born June 28, 1490, died Sept. 24, 1545), though at that time only twenty-five years of age, stood at the head of the German clergy, and was chancellor of the German Empire. He received also the cardinal's hat in 1518. He was, like his Roman master, a friend of liberal learning and courtly splendor, worldly-minded, and ill fitted for the care of souls. He had the ambition to be the Mæcenas of Germany. He was himself destitute of theological education, but called scholars, artists, poets, free-thinkers, to his court, and honored Erasmus and Ulrich von Hutten with presents and pensions. "He had a passionate love for music," says an Ultramontane historian, "and imported musicians from Italy to give luster to his feasts, in which ladies often participated. Finely wrought carpets, splendid mirrors adorned his halls and chambers; costly dishes and wines covered his table. He appeared in public with great pomp; he kept a body-guard of one hundred and fifty armed knights; numerous courtiers in splendid attire followed him when he rode out; he was surrounded by pages who were to learn in his presence the refinement of cavaliers." The same Roman-Catholic historian censures the extravagant court of

---

[1] See the papal documents in Pallavicini, in Löscher (I. 369–383), and Walch, *L.'s Werke*, XV. 313 sqq. Compare Gieseler, IV. 21 sq. (New York ed.); Hergenröther's *Regesta Leonis X.* (1884 sqq.).

[2] J. May: *Der Kurfürst Albrecht II. von Mainz*, München, 1875, 2 vols.

Pope Leo X., which set the example for the secularization
and luxury of the prelates in Germany.[1]

Albrecht was largely indebted to the rich banking-house
of Fugger in Augsburg, from whom he had borrowed thirty
thousand florins in gold to pay for the papal pallium. By
an agreement with the Pope, he had permission to keep
half of the proceeds arising from the sale of indulgences.
The agents of that commercial house stood behind the preachers of indulgence, and collected their share for the repayment
of the loan.

The Archbishop appointed Johann Tetzel (Diez) of the
Dominican order, his commissioner, who again employed his
sub-agents.

Tetzel was born between 1450 and 1460, at Leipzig, and
began his career as a preacher of indulgences in 1501. He
became famous as a popular orator and successful hawker of
indulgences. He was prior of a Dominican convent, doctor
of philosophy, and papal inquisitor (*hæreticæ pravitatis inquisitor*). At the end of 1517 he acquired in the University of
Frankfurt-on-the-Oder the degree of Licentiate of Theology,
and in January, 1518, the degree of Doctor of Theology, by
defending, in two disputations, the doctrine of indulgences
against Luther.[2] He died at Leipzig during the public debate

---

[1] Janssen, II. 60, 64: "*Das Hofwesen so mancher geistlichen Fürsten
Deutschlands, insbesondere das des Erzbischofs Albrecht von Mainz, stand in
schreiendem Widerspruch mit dem eines kirchlichen Würdeträgers, aber der
Hof Leo's X., mit seinem Aufwand für Spiel und Theater und allerlei
weltliche Feste entsprach noch weniger der Bestimmung eines Oberhauptes
der Kirche. Der Verweltlichung und Ueppigkeit geistlicher Fürstenhöfe in
Deutschland ging die des römischen Hofes voraus, und erstere wäre ohne diese
kaum möglich gewesen.*" He quotes (II. 76) Emser and Cardinal Sadolet
against the abuses of indulgences in the reign of Leo X. Cardinal Hergenröther, in the dedicatory preface to the *Regesta Leonis X.* (Fasc. I. p.
ix), while defending this Pope against the charge of religious indifference,
censures the accumulation of ecclesiastical benefices by the same persons, as
Albrecht, and the many abuses resulting therefrom.

[2] Löscher (I. 505–523) gives both dissertations, the first consisting of 106,
the second of 50 theses, and calls them "*Proben von den stinkenden*

between Eck and Luther, July, 1519. He is represented by
Protestant writers as an ignorant, noisy, impudent, and immoral charlatan, who was not ashamed to boast that he saved
more souls from purgatory by his letters of indulgence than
St. Peter by his preaching.[1] On the other hand, Roman-
Catholic historians defend him as a learned and zealous servant of the church. He has only an incidental notoriety, and
our estimate of his character need not affect our views on the
merits of the Reformation. We must judge him from his published sermons and anti-theses against Luther. They teach
neither more nor less than the usual scholastic doctrine of
indulgences based on an extravagant theory of papal authority. He does not ignore, as is often asserted, the necessity
of repentance as a condition of absolution.[2] But he probably did not emphasize it in practice, and gave rise by
unguarded expressions to damaging stories. His private
character was certainly tainted, if we are to credit such
a witness as the papal nuncio, Carl von Miltitz, who had the

Schäden des Papstthums." He ascribes, however, the authorship to Conrad
Wimpina, professor of theology at Frankfort-on-the-Oder, who afterwards
published them as his own, without mentioning Tetzel, in his *Anacepha-
laiosis Sectarum errorum*, etc., 1528 (Löscher, I. 506, II. 7). Gieseler, Köstlin, and Knaake are of the same opinion. Gröne and Hergenröther assign
them to Tetzel.

[1] Mathesius, Myconius, and Luther (*Wider Hans Wurst*, 1541, in the
Erl. ed. XXVI. 51) ascribe to him also the blasphemous boast that he had
the power by letters of indulgence to forgive even a carnal sin against the
Mother of God ("*wenn einer gleich die heil. Jungfrau Maria, Gottes Mutter,
hätte geschwächt und geschwängert*"). Luther alludes to such a monstrous
saying in Thes. 75, and calls it insane. But Tetzel denied and disproved the
charge as a slander, in his *Disp.* I. 99–101 ("*Subcommissariis ac prædica-
toribus veniarum* IMPONERE, *ut si quis per impossibile Dei genetricem semper
virginem violasset* . . . ODIO AGITARI AC FRATRUM SUORUM SANGUINEM
SITIRE*"), and in his letter to Miltitz, Jan. 31, 1518. See Köstlin, I. 160 and
785, *versus* Körner and Kahnis. Kayser also (*l.c.* p. 15) gives it up, although
he comes to the conclusion that Tetzel was "*ein unverschämter und sitten-
loser Ablassprediger*" (p. 20).

[2] In Theses 55 and 56 of his first Disputation (1517), he says that the soul,
after it is *purified* (*anima purgata, ist eine Seele gereinigt*), flies from purgatory to the vision of God without hinderance, and that it is an *error* to suppose
that this cannot be done before the payment of money into the indulgence
box. See the Latin text in Löscher, I. 509.

best means of information, and charged him with avarice, dishonesty, and sexual immorality.[1]

Tetzel traveled with great pomp and circumstance through Germany, and recommended with unscrupulous effrontery and declamatory eloquence the indulgences of the Pope to the large crowds who gathered from every quarter around him. He was received like a messenger from heaven. Priests, monks, and magistrates, men and women, old and young, marched in solemn procession with songs, flags, and candles, under the ringing of bells, to meet him and his fellow-monks, and followed them to the church; the papal bull on a velvet cushion was placed on the high altar, a red cross with a silken banner bearing the papal arms was erected before it, and a large iron chest was put beneath the cross for the indulgence money. Such chests are still preserved in many places. The preachers, by daily sermons, hymns, and processions, urged the people, with extravagant laudations of the Pope's bull, to purchase letters of indulgence for their own benefit, and at the same time played upon their sympathies for departed relatives and friends whom they might release from their sufferings in purgatory "as soon as the penny tinkles in the box."[2]

---

[1] "*Auch hatte er zwei Kinder.*" The letter of Miltitz is printed in Löscher, III. 20; in Walch, XV. 862; and in Kayser, *l.c.* 4 and 5. Tetzel's champions try to invalidate the testimony of the papal delegate by charging him with intemperance. But drunkards, like children and fools, usually tell the truth; and when he wrote that letter, he was sober. Besides, we have the independent testimony of Luther, who says in his book against Duke Henry of Brunswick (*Wider Hans Wurst*, p. 50), that in 1517 Tetzel was condemned by the Emperor Maximilian to be drowned in the Inn at Innsbruck ("for his great virtue's sake, you may well believe"), but saved by the Duke Frederick, and reminded of it afterwards in the Theses-controversy, and that he confessed the fact.

[2] " *Sobald der Pfennig im Kasten klingt,*
       Die Seel' aus dem Fegfeuer springt."

Mathesius and Johann Hess, two contemporary witnesses, ascribe this sentence (with slight verbal modifications) to Tetzel himself. Luther mentions it in Theses 27 and 28, and in his book *Wider Hans Wurst* (Erl. ed. XXVI. 51).

The common people eagerly embraced this rare offer of salvation from punishment, and made no clear distinction between the guilt and punishment of sin; after the sermon they approached with burning candles the chest, confessed their sins, paid the money, and received the letter of indulgence which they cherished as a passport to heaven. But intelligent and pious men were shocked at such scandal. The question was asked, whether God loved money more than justice, and why the Pope, with his command over the boundless treasury of extra-merits, did not at once empty the whole purgatory for the rebuilding of St. Peter's, or build it with his own money.

Tetzel approached the dominions of the Elector of Saxony, who was himself a devout worshiper of relics, and had great confidence in indulgences, but would not let him enter his territory from fear that he might take too much money from his subjects. So Tetzel set up his trade on the border of Saxony, at Jüterbog, a few hours from Wittenberg.[1]

There he provoked the protest of the Reformer, who had already in the summer of 1516 preached a sermon of warning against trust in indulgences, and had incurred the Elector's displeasure by his aversion to the whole system, although he himself had doubts about some important questions connected with it.

Luther had experienced the remission of sin as a free gift of grace to be apprehended by a living faith. This experience was diametrically opposed to a system of relief by means of payments in money. It was an irrepressible conflict of principle. He could not be silent when that barter was carried to the very threshold of his sphere of labor. As a preacher, a pastor, and a professor, he felt it to be his duty

---

[1] Jüterbog is now a Prussian town of about seven thousand inhabitants, on the railroad between Berlin and Wittenberg. In the Nicolai church, Tetzel's chest of indulgences is preserved.

to protest against such measures: to be silent was to betray his theology and his conscience.

The jealousy between the Augustinian order to which he belonged, and the Dominican order to which Tetzel belonged, may have exerted some influence, but it was certainly very subordinate. A laboring mountain may produce a ridiculous mouse, but no mouse can give birth to a mountain. The controversy with Tetzel (who is not even mentioned in Luther's Theses) was merely the occasion, but not the cause, of the Reformation: it was the spark which exploded the mine. The Reformation would have come to pass sooner or later, if no Tetzel had ever lived; and it actually did break out in different countries without any connection with the trade in indulgences, except in German Switzerland, where Bernhardin Samson acted the part of Tetzel, but after Zwingli had already begun his reforms.

§ 32. *The Ninety-five Theses. Oct. 31, 1517.*

Lit. in § 31.

After serious deliberation, without consulting any of his colleagues or friends, but following an irresistible impulse, Luther resolved upon a public act of unforeseen consequences. It may be compared to the stroke of the axe with which St. Boniface, seven hundred years before, had cut down the sacred oak, and decided the downfall of German heathenism. He wished to elicit the truth about the burning question of indulgences, which he himself professed not fully to understand at the time, and which yet was closely connected with the peace of conscience and eternal salvation. He chose the orderly and usual way of a learned academic disputation.

Accordingly, on the memorable thirty-first day of October, 1517, which has ever since been celebrated in Protestant Germany as the birthday of the Reformation, at twelve o'clock he affixed (either himself or through another) to the doors of the castle-church at Wittenberg, ninety-five Latin Theses on the subject of indulgences, and invited a public discussion. At the same time he sent notice of the fact to Archbishop Albrecht of Mainz, and to Bishop Hieronymus Scultetus, to whose diocese Wittenberg belonged. He chose the eve of All Saints' Day (Nov. 1), because this was one of the most frequented feasts, and attracted professors, students, and people from all directions to the church, which was filled with precious relics.[1]

No one accepted the challenge, and no discussion took place. The professors and students of Wittenberg were of one mind on the subject. But history itself undertook the disputation and defence. The Theses were copied, translated, printed, and spread as on angels' wings throughout Germany and Europe in a few weeks.[2]

The rapid circulation of the Reformation literature was promoted by the perfect freedom of the press. There was, as yet, no censorship, no copyright, no ordinary book-trade in the modern sense, and no newspapers; but colportors, students, and friends carried the books and tracts from house to house. The mass of the people could not read, but they listened attentively to readers. The questions of the Reformation were eminently practical, and interested all

---

[1] The wooden doors of the *Schlosskirche* were burnt in 1760, and replaced in 1858 by metal doors, bearing the original Latin text of the Theses. The new doors are the gift of King Frederick William IV., who fully sympathized with the evangelical Reformation. Above the doors, on a golden ground, is the Crucified, with Luther and Melanchthon at his feet, the work of Professor von Klöber. In the interior of the church are the graves of Luther and Melanchthon, and of the Electors Frederick the Wise and John the Constant. The *Schlosskirche* was in a very dilapidated condition, and undergoing thorough repair, when I last visited it in July, 1886. It must not be confounded with the *Stadtkirche* of Wittenberg, where Luther preached so often, and where, in 1522, the communion was, for the first time, administered in both kinds.

[2] Knaake (Weim. ed. I. 230) conjectures that the Theses, as affixed, were *written* either by Luther himself or some other hand, and that he had soon afterwards a few copies printed for his own use (for Agricola, who was in Wittenberg at that time, speaks of a copy *printed* on a half-sheet of paper):

classes ; and Luther handled the highest themes in the most popular style.

The Theses bear the title, " Disputation to explain the Virtue of Indulgences." They sound very strange to a modern ear, and are more Catholic than Protestant. They are no protest against the Pope and the Roman Church, or any of her doctrines, not even against indulgences, but only against their abuse. They expressly condemn those who speak against indulgences (Th. 71), and assume that the Pope himself would rather see St. Peter's Church in ashes than have it built with the flesh and blood of his sheep (Th. 50). They imply belief in purgatory. They nowhere mention Tetzel. They are silent about faith and justification, which already formed the marrow of Luther's theology and piety. He wished to be moderate, and had not the most distant idea of a separation from the mother church. When the Theses were republished in his collected works (1545), he wrote in the preface : " I allow them to stand, that by them it may appear how weak I was, and in what a fluctuating state of mind, when I began this business. I was then a monk and a mad papist (*papista insanissimus*), and so submersed in the dogmas of the Pope that I would have readily murdered any person who denied obedience to the Pope."

but that irresponsible publishers soon seized and multiplied them against his will. Jürgens says (III. 480) that two editions were printed in Wittenberg in 1517, on four quarto leaves, and that the Berlin Library possesses two copies of the second edition. The Theses were written on two columns, in four divisions; the first three divisions consisted of twenty-five theses each, the fourth of twenty. The German translation is from Justus Jonas. The Latin text is printed in all the editions of Luther's works, in Löscher's Acts, and in Ranke's *Deutsche Geschichte* (6th ed., vol. VI. 83–89, literally copied from an original preserved in the Royal Library in Berlin). The semi-authoritative German translation by Justus Jonas is given in Löscher, Walch (vol. XVIII.), and O. v. Gerlach (vol. I.), and with a commentary by Jürgens (*Luther*, III. 484 sqq.). An English translation in Wace and Buchheim, *Principles of the Reformation*, London, 1883, p. 6 sqq. I have compared this translation with the Latin original as given by Ranke, and in the Weimar edition, and added it at the end of this section with some alterations, insertions, and notes.

But after all, they contain the living germs of a new theology. The form only is Romish, the spirit and aim are Protestant. We must read between the lines, and supply the negations of the Theses by the affirmations from his preceding and succeeding books, especially his *Resolutiones*, in which he answers objections, and has much to say about faith and justification. The Theses represent a state of transition from twilight to daylight. They reveal the mighty working of an earnest mind and conscience intensely occupied with the problem of sin, repentance, and forgiveness, and struggling for emancipation from the fetters of tradition. They might more properly be called " a disputation *to diminish the virtue* of papal indulgences, and to magnify the full and free grace of the gospel of Christ." They bring the personal experience of justification by faith, and direct intercourse with Christ and the gospel, in opposition to an external system of churchly and priestly mediation and human merit. The papal opponents felt the logical drift of the Theses much better than Luther, and saw in them an attempt to undermine the whole fabric of popery. The irresistible progress of the Reformation soon swept the indulgences away as an unscriptural, mediæval tradition of men.[1]

The first Thesis strikes the keynote: " Our Lord and Master when he says, ' Repent,'[2] desires that the whole life of

---

[1] Jürgens (III. 481) compares the Theses to flashes of lightning, which suddenly issued from the thunder-clouds. Hundeshagen (in Piper's " Evangel. Kalender" for 1859, p. 157), says: "Notwithstanding the limits within which Luther kept himself at that time, the Theses express in many respects the whole Luther of later times: the frankness and honesty of his soul, his earnest zeal for practical Christianity, the sincere devotion to the truths of the Scriptures, the open sense for the religious wants of the people, the sound insight into the abuses and corruptions of the church, the profound yet liberal piety." Ranke's judgment of the Theses is brief, but pointed and weighty: "*Wenn man diese Sätze liest, sieht man, welch ein kühner, grossartiger und fester Geist in Luther arbeitet. Die Gedanken sprühen ihm hervor, wie unter dem Hammerschlag die Funken.*" — *Deutsche Gesch.*, vol. I. p. 210.

[2] Luther gives the Vulgate rendering of μετανοεῖτε, *pœnitentiam agite, do penance*, which favors the Roman Catholic conception that repentance con-

believers should be a repentance."[1] The corresponding Greek noun means change of mind (μετάνοια), and implies both a turning away from sin in sincere sorrow and grief, and a turning to God in hearty faith. Luther distinguishes, in the second Thesis, true repentance from the sacramental penance (i.e., the confession and satisfaction required by the priest), and understands it to be an internal state and exercise of the mind rather than isolated external acts; although he expressly affirms, in the third Thesis, that it must manifest itself in various mortifications of the flesh. Repentance is a continual conflict of the believing spirit with the sinful flesh, a daily renewal of the heart. As long as sin lasts, there is need of repentance. The Pope can not remit any sin except by declaring the remission of God; and he can not remit punishments except those which he or the canons impose (Thes. 5 and 6). Forgiveness presupposes true repentance, and can only be found in the merits of Christ. Here comes in the other fundamental Thesis (62): "The true treasury of the church is the holy gospel of the glory and the grace of God." This sets aside the mediæval notion about the overflowing treasury of extra-merits and rewards at the disposal of the Pope for the benefit of the living and the dead.

We have thus set before us in this manifesto, on the one hand, human depravity which requires lifelong repentance, and on the other the full and free grace of God in Christ, which can only be appropriated by a living faith. This is, in substance, the evangelical doctrine of justification by

sists in certain outward acts. He first learned the true meaning of the Greek μετάνοια a year later from Melanchthon, and it was to him like a revelation.

[1] "*Dominus et magister noster Jesus Christus dicendo 'Pœnitentiam agite,' etc.* [Matt. 4: 17], *omnem vitam fidelium pœnitentiam esse voluit.*" In characteristic contrast, Tetzel begins his fifty counter Theses with a glorification of the Pope as the supreme power in the church: "*Docendi sunt Christiani, ex quo in Ecclesia potestas Papæ est suprema et a solo Deo instituta, quod a nullo puro homine, nec a toto simul mundo potest restringi aut ampliari, sed a solo Deo.*"

faith (although not expressed in terms), and virtually destroys the whole scholastic theory and practice of indulgences. By attacking the abuses of indulgences, Luther unwittingly cut a vein of mediæval Catholicism ; and by a deeper conception of repentance which implies faith, and by referring the sinner to the grace of Christ as the true and only source of remission, he proclaimed the undeveloped principles of evangelical Protestantism, and kindled a flame which soon extended far beyond his original intentions.

NOTES.

THE NINETY-FIVE THESES.

DISPUTATION OF DR. MARTIN LUTHER CONCERNING PENITENCE AND INDULGENCES.

In the desire and with the purpose of elucidating the truth, a disputation will be held on the underwritten propositions at Wittenberg, under the presidency of the Reverend Father Martin Luther, Monk of the Order of St. Augustin, Master of Arts and of Sacred Theology, and ordinary Reader of the same in that place.[1] He therefore asks those who cannot be present, and discuss the subject with us orally, to do so by letter in their absence. In the name of our Lord Jesus Christ. Amen.

1. Our Lord and Master Jesus Christ in saying: "Repent ye" [lit.: Do penance, *pœnitentiam agite*], etc., intended that the whole life of believers should be penitence [*pœnitentiam*].[2]

2. This word *pœnitentia* cannot be understood of sacramental penance, that is, of the confession and satisfaction which are performed under the ministry of priests.

3. It does not, however, refer solely to inward penitence; nay, such inward penitence is naught, unless it outwardly produces various mortifications of the flesh [*varias carnis mortificationes*].

4. The penalty [*pœna*] thus continues as long as the hatred of self — that is, true inward penitence [*pœnitentia vera intus*] — continues; namely, till our entrance into the kingdom of heaven.

---

[1] The German translation inserts here the name of Tetzel (*wider Bruder Johann Tetzel, Prediger Ordens*), which does not occur in the Latin text.

[2] The first four theses are directed against the scholastic view of sacramental penitence, which emphasized isolated, outward acts ; while Luther put the stress on the *inward* change which should extend *through life*. As long as there is sin, so long is there need of repentance. St. Augustin and St. Bernard spent their last days in deep repentance and meditation over the penitential Psalms. Luther retained the Vulgate rendering, and did not know yet the true meaning of the Greek original (μετάνοια, change of mind, conversion). The Theses vacillate between the Romish and the Evangelical view of repentance.

5. The Pope has neither the will nor the power to remit any penalties, except those which he has imposed by his own authority, or by that of the canons.[1]

6. The Pope has no power to remit any guilt, except by declaring and warranting it to have been remitted by God; or at most by remitting cases reserved for himself: in which cases, if his power were despised, guilt would certainly remain.

7. God never remits any man's guilt, without at the same time subjecting him, humbled in all things, to the authority of his representative the priest [*sacerdoti suo vicario*].

8. The penitential canons are imposed only on the living, and no burden ought to be imposed on the dying, according to them.

9. Hence the Holy Spirit acting in the Pope does well for us in that, in his decrees, he always makes exception of the article of death and of necessity.

10. Those priests act unlearnedly and wrongly, who, in the case of the dying, reserve the canonical penances for purgatory.

11. Those tares about changing of the canonical penalty into the penalty of purgatory seem surely to have been sown while the bishops were asleep.

12. Formerly the canonical penalties were imposed not after, but before absolution, as tests of true contrition.

13. The dying pay all penalties by death, and are already dead to the canon laws, and are by right relieved from them.

14. The imperfect soundness or charity of a dying person necessarily brings with it great fear, and the less it is, the greater the fear it brings.

15. This fear and horror is sufficient by itself, to say nothing of other things, to constitute the pains of purgatory, since it is very near to the horror of despair.

16. Hell, purgatory, and heaven appear to differ as despair, almost despair, and peace of mind [*securitas*] differ.

17. With souls in purgatory it seems that it must needs be that, as horror diminishes, so charity increases.

18. Nor does it seem to be proved by any reasoning or any scriptures, that they are outside of the state of merit or the increase of charity.

19. Nor does this appear to be proved, that they are sure and confident of their own blessedness, at least all of them, though we may be very sure of it.

20. Therefore the Pope, when he speaks of the plenary remission of all penalties, does not mean simply of all, but only of those imposed by himself.

21. Thus those preachers of indulgences are in error who say that, by the indulgences of the Pope, a man is loosed and saved from all punishment.

22. For, in fact, he remits to souls in purgatory no penalty which they would have had to pay in this life according to the canons.

---

[1] This thesis reduces the indulgence to a mere remission of the ecclesiastical punishments which refer only to this life. It destroys the effect on purgatory. Compare Thesis 8.

23. If any entire remission of all the penalties can be granted to any one, it is certain that it is granted to none but the most perfect, that is, to very few.

24. Hence the greater part of the people must needs be deceived by this indiscriminate and high-sounding promise of release from penalties.

25. Such power as the Pope has over purgatory in general, such has every bishop in his own diocese, and every curate in his own parish, in particular.

26. [In the Latin text, I.] The Pope acts most rightly in granting remission to souls, not by the power of the keys (which is of no avail in this case), but by the way of suffrage [*per modum suffragii*].

27. They preach man, who say that the soul flies out of purgatory as soon as the money thrown into the chest rattles [*ut jactus nummus in cistam tinnierit*].

28. It is certain, that, when the money rattles in the chest, avarice and gain may be increased, but the suffrage of the Church depends on the will of God alone.

29. Who knows whether all the souls in purgatory desire to be redeemed from it, according to the story told of Saints Severinus and Paschal? [1]

30. No man is sure of the reality of his own contrition, much less of the attainment of plenary remission.

31. Rare as is a true penitent, so rare is one who truly buys indulgences — that is to say, most rare.

32. Those who believe that, through letters of pardon, they are made sure of their own salvation, will be eternally damned along with their teachers.

33. We must especially beware of those who say that these pardons from the Pope are that inestimable gift of God by which man is reconciled to God.

34. For the grace conveyed by these pardons has respect only to the penalties of sacramental satisfaction, which are of human appointment.

35. They preach no Christian doctrine, who teach that contrition is not necessary for those who buy souls out of purgatory, or buy confessional licenses.

36. Every Christian who feels true compunction has of right plenary remission of pain and guilt, even without letters of pardon.

37. Every true Christian, whether living or dead, has a share in all the benefits of Christ and of the Church, given him by God, even without letters of pardon.

38. The remission, however, imparted by the Pope, is by no means to be despised, since it is, as I have said, a declaration of the Divine remission.

39. It is a most difficult thing, even for the most learned theologians, to exalt at the same time in the eyes of the people the ample effect of pardons, and the necessity of true contrition.

---

[1] These saints were reported to have preferred to suffer longer in purgatory than was necessary for their salvation, in order that they might attain to the highest glory of the vision of God.

40. True contrition seeks and loves punishment; while the ampleness of pardons relaxes it, and causes men to hate it, or at least gives occasion for them to do so.

41. Apostolical pardons ought to be proclaimed with caution, lest the people should falsely suppose that they are placed before other good works of charity.

42. Christians should be taught that it is not the mind of the Pope, that the buying of pardons is to be in any way compared to works of mercy.

43. Christians should be taught, that he who gives to a poor man, or lends to a needy man, does better than if he bought pardons.

44. Because, by a work of charity, charity increases, and the man becomes better; while, by means of pardons, he does not become better, but only freer from punishment.

45. Christians should be taught that he who sees any one in need, and, passing him by, gives money for pardons, is not purchasing for himself the indulgence of the Pope, but the anger of God.

46. Christians should be taught, that, unless they have superfluous wealth, they are bound to keep what is necessary for the use of their own households, and by no means to lavish it on pardons.

47. Christians should be taught, that, while they are free to buy pardons, they are not commanded to do so.

48. Christians should be taught that the Pope, in granting pardons, has both more need and more desire that devout prayer should be made for him, than that money should be readily paid.

49. Christians should be taught that the Pope's pardons are useful if they do not put their trust in them, but most hurtful if through them they lose the fear of God.

50. [Lat. text XXV.] Christians should be taught, that, if the Pope were acquainted with the exactions of the preachers of pardons, he would prefer that the Basilica of St. Peter should be burnt to ashes, than that it should be built up with the skin, flesh, and bones of his sheep.

51. [I.] Christians should be taught, that as it would be the wish of the Pope, even to sell, if necessary, the Basilica of St. Peter, and to give of his own to very many of those from whom the preachers of pardons extract money.

52. Vain is the hope of salvation through letters of pardon, even if a commissary — nay, the Pope himself — were to pledge his own soul for them.

53. They are enemies of Christ and of the Pope, who, in order that pardons may be preached, condemn the word of God to utter silence in other churches.

54. Wrong is done to the Word of God when, in the same sermon, an equal or longer time is spent on pardons than on the words of the gospel [*verbis evangelicis*].

55. The mind of the Pope necessarily is that if pardons, which are a

very small matter [*quod minimum est*], are celebrated with single bells, single processions, and single ceremonies, the gospel, which is a very great matter [*quod maximum est*], should be preached with a hundred ceremonies.

56. The treasures of the Church, whence the Pope grants indulgences, are neither sufficiently named nor known among the people of Christ.[1]

57. It is clear that they are at least not temporal treasures; for these are not so readily lavished, but only accumulated, by many of the preachers.

58. Nor are they the merits of Christ and of the saints; for these, independently of the Pope, are always working grace to the inner man, and the cross, death, and hell to the outer man.

59. St. Lawrence said that the treasures of the Church are the poor of the Church, but he spoke according to the use of the word in his time.

60. We are not speaking rashly when we say that the keys of the Church, bestowed through the merits of Christ, are that treasure.

61. For it is clear that the power of the Pope is alone sufficient for the remission of penalties and of reserved cases.

62. The true treasure of the Church is the holy gospel of the glory and the grace of God [*Verus thesaurus ecclesiœ est sacrosanctum Evangelium gloriœ et gratiœ Dei*].

63. This treasure, however, is deservedly most hateful [*merito odiosissimus; der allerfeindseligste und verhassteste*], because it makes the first to be last.

64. While the treasure of indulgences is deservedly most acceptable, because it makes the last to be first.

65. Hence the treasures of the gospel are nets, wherewith of old they fished for the men of riches.

66. The treasures of indulgences are nets, wherewith they now fish for the riches of men.

67. Those indulgences, which the preachers loudly proclaim to be the greatest graces, are seen to be truly such as regards the promotion of gain [*denn es grossen Gewinnst und Geniess trägt*].

68. Yet they are in reality the smallest graces when compared with the grace of God and the piety of the cross.

69. Bishops and curates are bound to receive the commissaries of apostolical pardons with all reverence.

70. But they are still more bound to see to it with all their eyes, and take heed with all their ears, that these men do not preach their own dreams in place of the Pope's commission.

71. He who speaks against the truth of apostolical pardons, let him be the anathema and accursed [*sit anathema et maledictus; der sei ein Fluch und vermaladeiet*].

---

[1] This and the following theses destroy the theoretical foundation of indulgences, namely, the scholastic fiction of a treasury of supererogatory merits of saints at the disposal of the Pope.

72. But he, on the other hand, who exerts himself against the wantonness and license of speech of the preachers of pardons, let him be blessed.

73. As the Pope justly thunders [Lat., *fulminat*; G. trs., *mit Ungnade und dem Bann schlägt*] against those who use any kind of contrivance to the injury of the traffic in pardons;

74. Much more is it his intention to thunder against those who, under the pretext of pardons, use contrivances to the injury of holy charity and of truth.

75. [XXV.] To think that papal pardons have such power that they could absolve a man even if — by an impossibility — he had violated the Mother of God, is madness.

76. [I.] We affirm, on the contrary, that papal pardons [*veniœ papales*] can not take away even the least venial sins, as regards the guilt [*quoad culpam*].

77. The saying that, even if St. Peter were now Pope, he could grant no greater graces, is blasphemy against St. Peter and the Pope.

78. We affirm, on the contrary, that both he and any other Pope has greater graces to grant; namely, the gospel, powers, gifts of healing, etc. (1 Cor. xii. 9).

69. To say that the cross set up among the insignia of the papal arms is of equal power with the cross of Christ, is blasphemy.

80. Those bishops, curates, and theologians who allow such discourses to have currency among the people, will have to render an account.

81. This license in the preaching of pardons makes it no easy thing, even for learned men, to protect the reverence due to the Pope against the calumnies, or, at all events, the keen questionings, of the laity;

82. As, for instance: Why does not the Pope empty purgatory for the sake of most holy charity and of the supreme necessity of souls, — this being the most just of all reasons, — if he redeems an infinite number of souls for the sake of that most fatal thing, money, to be spent on building a basilica — this being a slight reason?

83. Again: Why do funeral masses and anniversary masses for deceased continue, and why does not the Pope return, or permit the withdrawal of, the funds bequeathed for this purpose, since it is a wrong to pray for those who are already redeemed?

84. Again: What is this new kindness of God and the Pope, in that, for money's sake, they permit an impious man and an enemy of God to redeem a pious soul which loves God, and yet do not redeem that same pious and beloved soul, out of free charity, on account of its own need?

85. Again: Why is it that the penitential canons, long since abrogated and dead in themselves in very fact, and not only by usage, are yet still redeemed with money, through the granting of indulgences, as if they were full of life?

86. Again: Why does not the Pope, whose riches are at this day more

ample than those of the wealthiest of the wealthy, build the one Basilica of St. Peter with his own money, rather than with that of poor believers?

87. Again: Why does the Pope remit or impart to those who, through perfect contrition, have a right to plenary remission and participation?

88. Again: What greater good would the Church receive if the Pope, instead of once as he does now, were to bestow these remissions and participations a hundred times a day on any one of the faithful?

89. Since it is the salvation of souls, rather than money, that the Pope seeks by his pardons, why does he annul the letters and pardons granted long ago, since they are equally efficacious?

90. To repress these scruples and arguments of the laity by force alone, and not to solve them by giving reasons, is to expose the Church and the Pope to the ridicule of their enemies, and to make Christian men unhappy.

91. If, then, pardons were preached according to the spirit and mind of the Pope, all these questions would be resolved with ease; nay, would not exist.

92. Away then with all those prophets who say to the people of Christ, "Peace, peace," and there is no peace.

93. Blessed be all those prophets, who say to the people of Christ, "The cross, the cross," and there is no cross.

94. Christians should be exhorted to strive to follow Christ their head through pains, deaths, and hells;

95. [Lat. Text, XX.] And thus trust to enter heaven through many tribulations, rather than in the security of peace [per securitatem pacis].

PROTESTATION.

I, Martin Luther, Doctor, of the Order of Monks at Wittenberg, desire to testify publicly that certain propositions against pontifical indulgences, as they call them, have been put forth by me. Now although, up to the present time, neither this most celebrated and renowned school of ours nor any civil or ecclesiastical power has condemned me, yet there are, as I hear, some men of headlong and audacious spirit, who dare to pronounce me a heretic, as though the matter had been thoroughly looked into and studied. But on my part, as I have often done before, so now too I implore all men, by the faith of Christ, either to point out to me a better way, if such a way has been divinely revealed to any, or at least to submit their opinion to the judgment of God and of the Church. For I am neither so rash as to wish that my sole opinion should be preferred to that of all other men, nor so senseless as to be willing that the word of God should be made to give place to fables devised by human reason.

§ 33.   *The Theses-Controversy.*   *1518.*

LUTHER'S *Sermon vom Ablass und Gnade*, printed in February, 1518 (Weimar ed. I. 239–246; and in Latin, 317–324); *Kurze Erklärung der Zehn Gebote*, 1518 (I. 248–256, in Latin under the title *Instructio pro Confessione peccatorum*, p. 257–265); *Asterisci adversus Obeliscos Eckii*, March, 1518 (I. 278–316); *Freiheit des Sermons päpstlichen Ablass und Gnade belangend*, June, 1518, against Tetzel (I. 380–393); *Resolutiones disputationum de indulgentiarum virtute*, August, 1518, dedicated to the Pope (I. 522–628). Letters of LUTHER to Archbishop Albrecht, Spalatin, and others, in De Wette, I. 67 sqq.

TETZEL'S *Anti-Theses*, 2 series, one of 106, the other of 50 sentences, are printed in LÖSCHER'S *Ref. Acta*, I. 505–514, and 518–523. ECK'S *Obelisci*, *ibid*. III. 333.

On the details of the controversy, see JÜRGENS (III. 479 sqq.), KÖSTLIN (I. 175 sqq.), KOLDE (I. 126 sqq.), BRATKE, and DIECKHOFF, as quoted in § 31.

The Theses of Luther were a tract for the times. They sounded the trumpet of the Reformation. They found a hearty response with liberal scholars and enemies of monastic obscurantism, with German patriots longing for emancipation from Italian control, and with thousands of plain Christians waiting for the man of Providence who should give utterance to their feelings of indignation against existing abuses, and to their desire for a pure, scriptural, and spiritual religion. " Ho, ho !" exclaimed Dr. Fleck, " the man has come who will do the thing." Reuchlin thanked God that " the monks have now found a man who will give them such full employment that they will be glad to let me spend my old age in peace." [1]

---

[1] The prophetic dream of the Elector, so often told, is a poetic fiction. Köstlin discredits it, I. 786 sq. The Elector Frederick dreamed, in the night before Luther affixed the Theses, that God sent him a monk, a true son of the Apostle Paul, and that this monk wrote something on the door of the castle church at Wittenberg with a pen which reached even to Rome, pierced the head and ears of a lion (Leo), and shook the triple crown of the Pope. Merle d'Aubigné relates the dream at great length as being, " beyond reasonable doubt, true in the essential parts." He appeals to an original MS., written from the dictation of Spalatin, in the archives of Weimar, which was published in 1817. But that MS., according to the testimony of Dr. Burkhardt, the librarian, is only a copy of the eighteenth century. No trace of such a dream can be found before 1591. Spalatin, in his own writings and his letters to Luther and Melanchthon, nowhere refers to it.

But, on the other hand, the Theses were strongly assailed and condemned by the episcopal and clerical hierarchy, the monastic orders, especially the Dominicans, and the universities, in fact, by all the champions of scholastic theology and traditional orthodoxy. Luther himself, then a poor, emaciated monk, was at first frightened by the unexpected effect, and many of his friends trembled. One of them told him, "You tell the truth, good brother, but you will accomplish nothing; go to your cell, and say, God have mercy upon me." [1]

The chief writers against Luther were Tetzel of Leipzig, Conrad Wimpina of Frankfurt-on-the-Oder, and the more learned and formidable John Eck of Ingolstadt, who was at first a friend of Luther, but now became his irreconcilable enemy. These opponents represented three universities and the ruling scholastic theology of the Angelic Doctor St. Thomas Aquinas. But they injured their cause in public estimation by the weakness of their defence. They could produce no arguments for the doctrine and practice of indulgences from the Word of God, or even from the Greek and Latin fathers, and had to resort to extravagant views on the authority of the Pope. They even advocated papal infallibility, although this was as yet an open question in the Roman Church, and remained so till the Vatican decree of 1870.

Luther mustered courage. In all his weakness he was strong. He felt that he had begun this business in the name and for the glory of God, and was ready to sacrifice life itself for his honest conviction. He took comfort from the counsel of Gamaliel. In several letters of this period he subscribed himself *Martinus Eleutherios* (Freeman), but added, *vielmehr Knecht* (rather, Servant): he felt free of men, but bound in Christ. When his friend Schurf told him, "They will not bear it;" he replied, "But what, if they have to bear it?" He answered all his opponents, directly and indirectly,

---

[1] Albert Krantz of Hamburg, who died Dec. 7, 1517. Köstlin, I. 177.

in Latin and German, from the pulpit and the chair, and
through the press. He began now to develop his formidable
polemical power, especially in his German writings. He had
full command over the vocabulary of common sense, wit,
irony, vituperation, and abuse. Unfortunately, he often
resorted to coarse and vulgar expressions which, even in
that semi-barbarous age, offended men of culture and taste,
and which set a bad example for his admirers in the fierce
theological wars within the Lutheran Church.[1]

The discussion forced him into a conflict with the papal
authority, on which the theory and traffic of indulgences were
ultimately made to rest. The controversy resolved itself
into the question whether that authority was infallible and
final, or subject to correction by the Scriptures and a general
Council. Luther defended the latter view; yet he protested
that he was no heretic, and that he taught nothing contrary
to the Scriptures, the ancient fathers, the œcumenical councils, and the decrees of the Popes. He still hoped for a favorable hearing from Leo X., whom he personally respected.
He even ventured to dedicate to him his *Resolutiones*, a defence of the Theses (May 30, 1518), with a letter of abject
humility, promising to obey his voice as the very voice of
Christ.[2]

---

[1] He said of Tetzel, that he dealt with the Bible "*wie die Sau mit dem Ha-
bersack*" (as the hog with the meal-bag); of the learned Cardinal Cajetan,
that he knew as little of spiritual theology as "the donkey of the harp;" he
called Alveld, professor of theology at Leipzig, "a most asinine ass," and
Dr. Eck "*Dreck:*" for which he was in turn styled *luteus, lutra*, etc. Such
vulgarities were common in that age, but Luther was the roughest of the rough,
as he was the strongest of the strong. His bark, however, was much worse
than his bite, and beneath his abusive tongue and temper dwelt a kind and
generous heart. His most violent writings are those against Emser (*An den
Emserschen Steinbock*), King Henry VIII., Duke Henry of Brunswick
(*Wider Hans Wurst*), and his last attack upon popery as "instituted by the
Devil" (1545), of which Döllinger says (*Luther*, p. 48), that it must have been
written "*im Zustande der Erhitzung durch berauschende Getränke.*"

[2] "*Beatissime Pater,*" he says in the dedication, "*prostratum me pedibus
tuæ Beatitudinis offero cum omnibus, quæ sum et habeo. Vivifica, occide,
voca, revoca, approba, reproba, ut placuerit: vocem tuam vocem Christi in*

Such an anomalous and contradictory position could not last long.

In the midst of this controversy, in April, 1518, Luther was sent as a delegate to a meeting of the Augustinian monks at Heidelberg, and had an opportunity to defend, in public debate, forty conclusions, or "theological paradoxes," drawn from St. Paul and St. Augustin, concerning natural depravity, the slavery of the will, regenerating grace, faith, and good works. He advocates the *theologia crucis* against the *theologia gloriæ*, and contrasts the law and the gospel. "The law says, 'Do this,' and never does it: the gospel says, 'Believe in Christ,' and all is done." The last twelve theses are directed against the Aristotelian philosophy.[1]

He found considerable response, and sowed the seed of the Reformation in the Palatinate. Among his youthful hearers were Bucer (Butzer) and Brentz, who afterwards became distinguished reformers, the one in Strassburg and England, the other in the duchy (now kingdom) of Würtemberg.

§ 34. *Rome's Interposition. Luther and Prierias. 1518.*

R. P. *Silvestri Prieratis ordinis prædicatorum et s. theol. professoris celeber-rimi, s. palatii apostolici magistri, in præsumptuosas Martini Lutheri conclusiones de potestate papæ dialogus.* In Löscher, II. 13–39. Knaake (*Werke*, I. 644) assigns the first edition to the second half of June, 1518, which is more likely than the earlier date of December, 1517, given by Löscher (II. 12) and the Erlangen ed. He mentions five separate editions, two of which were published by Luther without notes; afterwards he published an edition with his refutation.

Ad Dialogum Silvestri Prierati de potestate papæ responsio. In LÖSCHER, II. 390–434; Weim. ed. I., 647–686, II. 48–56. German translation in WALCH, XVIII. 120–200.

Pope Leo X. was disposed to ignore the Wittenberg movement as a contemptible monkish quarrel; but when it

---

te præsidentis et loquentis agnoscam. Si mortem merui, mori non recusabo. Domini enim est terra et plenitudo ejus, qui est benedictus in sæcula, Amen, qui et te servet in æternum, Amen. Anno MDXVIII." Works (Weimar ed.), I. 529; also in De Wette, *Briefe*, I. 119–122.

[1] Weim. ed., I. 350–376. Comp. Köstlin, I. 185 sqq.

threatened to become dangerous, he tried to make the German monk harmless by the exercise of his power. He is reported to have said first, " Brother Martin is a man of fine genius, and this outbreak is a mere squabble of envious monks ; " but afterwards, " It is a drunken German who wrote the Theses ; when sober he will change his mind."

Three months after the appearance of the Theses, he directed the vicar-general of the Augustinian Order to quiet down the restless monk. In March, 1518, he found it necessary to appoint a commission of inquiry under the direction of the learned Dominican Silvester Mazzolini, called from his birthplace Prierio or Prierias (also Prieras), who was master of the sacred palace and professor of theology.

Prierias came to the conclusion that Luther was an ignorant and blasphemous arch-heretic, and hastily wrote a Latin dialogue against his Theses, hoping to crush him by subtile scholastic distinctions, and the weight of papal authority (June, 1518). He identified the Pope with the Church of Rome, and the Church of Rome with the Church universal, and denounced every departure from it as a heresy. He said of Luther's Theses, that they bite like a cur.

Luther republished the Dialogue with a reply, in which he called it " sufficiently supercilious, and thoroughly Italian and Thomistic " (August, 1518).

Prierias answered with a *Replica* (November, 1518). Luther republished it likewise, with a brief preface, and sent it to Prierias with the advice not to make himself any more ridiculous by writing books.

The effect of this controversy was to widen the breach.

In the mean time Luther's fate had already been decided. The Roman hierarchy could no more tolerate such a dangerous man than the Jewish hierarchy could tolerate Christ and the apostles. On the 7th of August, 1518, he was cited to appear in Rome within sixty days to recant his heresies. On the 23d of the same month, the Pope demanded of the

Elector Frederick the Wise, that he should deliver up this "child of the Devil" to the papal legate.

But the Elector, who was one of the most powerful and esteemed princes of Germany, felt unwilling to sacrifice the shining light of his beloved university, and arranged a peaceful interview with the papal legate at the Diet of Augsburg on promise of kind treatment and safe return.

§ 35. *Luther and Cajetan. October, 1518.*

The transactions at Augsburg were published by Luther in December, 1518, and are printed in LÖSCHER, II. 435–492 ; 527-551; in WALCH, XV. 636 sqq.; in the Weim. ed., II. 1–40. Luther's Letters in DE WETTE, I. 147–167. Comp. KAHNIS, I. 215-235; KÖSTLIN, I. 204-238 (and his shorter biogr., Eng. trans., p. 108).

Luther accordingly proceeded to Augsburg in humble garb, and on foot, till illness forced him within a short distance from the city to take a carriage. He was accompanied by a young monk and pupil, Leonard Baier, and his friend Link. He arrived Oct. 7, 1518, and was kindly received by Dr. Conrad Peutinger and two counselors of the Elector, who advised him to behave with prudence, and to observe the customary rules of etiquette. Everybody was anxious to see the man who, like a second Herostratus, had kindled such a flame.

On Oct. 11, he received the letter of safe-conduct; and on the next day he appeared before the papal legate, Cardinal Cajetan (Thomas de Vio of Gaëta), who represented the Pope at the German Diet, and was to obtain its consent to the imposition of a heavy tax for the war against the Turks.

Cajetan was, like Prierias, a Dominican and zealous Thomist, a man of great learning and moral integrity, but fond of pomp and ostentation. He wrote a standard commentary on the *Summa* of Thomas Aquinas (which is frequently appended to the *Summa*); but in his later years, till his death (1534), — perhaps in consequence of his interview with

Luther, — he devoted himself chiefly to the study of the Scriptures, and urged it upon his friends. He labored with the aid of Hebrew and Greek scholars to correct the Vulgate by a more faithful version, and advocated Jerome's liberal views on questions of criticism and the canon, and a sober grammatical exegesis against allegorical fancies, without, however, surrendering the Catholic principle of tradition.

There was a great contrast between the Italian cardinal and the German monk, the shrewd diplomat and the frank scholar ; the expounder and defender of mediæval scholasticism, and the champion of modern biblical theology ; the man of church authority, and the advocate of personal freedom.

They had three interviews (Oct. 12, 13, 14). Cajetan treated Luther with condescending courtesy, and assured him of his friendship.[1] But he demanded retraction of his errors, and absolute submission to the Pope. Luther resolutely refused, and declared that he could do nothing against his conscience ; that one must obey God rather than man ; that he had the Scripture on his side ; that even Peter was once reproved by Paul for misconduct (Gal. 2: 11), and that surely his successor was not infallible. Still he asked the cardinal to intercede with Leo X., that he might not harshly condemn him. Cajetan threatened him with excommunication, having already the papal mandate in his hand, and dismissed him with the words: "Revoke, or do not come again into my presence." He urged Staupitz to do his best to convert Luther, and said he was unwilling to dis-

---

[1] Luther received at first a favorable impression, and wrote in a letter to Carlstadt, Oct. 14 (De Wette, I. 161): "The cardinal calls me constantly his dear son, and assures Staupitz that I had no better friend than himself. . . . I would be the most welcome person here if I but spoke this one word, *revoco.* But I will not turn a heretic by revoking the opinion which made me a Christian : I will rather die, be burnt, be exiled, be cursed." Afterwards he wrote in a different tone about Cajetan, e.g., in the letter to the Elector Frederick, Nov. 19 (I. 175 sqq.), and to Staupitz, Dec. 13 (De Wette, I. 194).

pute any further with that "deep-eyed German beast filled with strange speculations." [1]

Under these circumstances, Luther, with the aid of friends who provided him with an escort, made his escape from Augsburg, through a small gate in the city-wall, in the night of the 20th of October, on a hard-trotting hack, without pantaloons, boots, or spurs. He rode on the first day as far as the town of Monheim [2] without stopping, and fell utterly exhausted upon the straw in a stable.[3]

He reached Wittenberg, in good spirits, on the first anniversary of his Ninety-five Theses. He forthwith published a report of his conference with a justification of his conduct. He also wrote (Nov. 19) a long and very eloquent letter to the Elector, exposing the unfairness of Cajetan, who had misrepresented the proceedings, and demanded from the Elector the delivery of Luther to Rome or his expulsion from Saxony.

Before leaving Augsburg, he left an appeal from Cajetan to the Pope, and "from the Pope ill informed to the Pope to be better informed" (*a papa male informato ad papam melius informandum*). Soon afterwards, Nov. 28, he formally and

---

[1] "*Ego nolo amplius cum hac bestia loqui. Habet enim profundos oculos et mirabiles speculationes in capite suo.*" This characteristic dictum is not reported by Luther, but by Myconius, *Hist. Ref.* p. 73. Comp. Löscher, II. 477. The national antipathy between the Germans and the Italians often appears in the transactions with Rome, and continues to this day. Monsignor Eugenio Cecconi, Archbishop of Florence, in his tract *Martino Lutero*, Firenze, 1883, says : "*Lutero non amava gl' italiani, e gl' italiani non hanno mai avuto ne stima ne amore per quest' uomo. Il nostro popolo, col suo naturale criterio, lo ha giudicato da un pezzo.*" He declared the proposal to celebrate Luther's fourth centennial at Florence to be an act of insanity.

[2] In Bavaria; not Mannheim, as Kahnis (I. 228) has it.

[3] "*Dr. Staupitz*" (says Luther, in his Table-Talk) "*hatte mir ein Pferd verschafft und gab mir den Rath, einen alten Ausreuter zu nehmen, der die Wege wüsste, und half mir Langemantel (Rathsherr) des Nachts durch ein klein Pförtlein der Stadt. Da eilte ich ohne Hosen, Stiefel, Sporn, und Schwert, und kam bis gen Wittenberg. Den ersten Tag ritt ich acht* (German) *Meilen und wie ich des Abends in die Herberge kam, war ich so müde, stieg im Stalle ab, konnte nicht stehen, fiel stracks in die Streu.*"

solemnly appealed from the Pope to a general council, and
thus anticipated the papal sentence of excommunication.
He expected every day maledictions from Rome, and was
prepared for exile or any other fate.[1] He was already tormented with the thought that the Pope might be the Anti-
Christ spoken of by St. Paul in the Second Epistle to the
Thessalonians, and asked his friend Link (Dec. 11) to give
him his opinion on the subject.[2] Ultimately he lost faith
also in a general council, and appealed solely to the Scriptures and his conscience. The Elector urged him to moderation through Spalatin, but Luther declared: "The more those
Romish grandees rage, and meditate the use of force, the less
do I fear them, and shall feel all the more free to fight
against the serpents of Rome. I am prepared for all, and
await the judgment of God."

§ 36. *Luther and Miltitz. January, 1519.*

LÖSCHER, II. 552–569 ; III. 6–21, 820–847. LUTHER'S *Werke*, WALCH, XV.
308 sqq.; Weimar ed., II. 66 sqq. Letters in DE WETTE, I. 207 sqq., 233
sqq.

JOH. K. SEIDEMANN: *Karl von Miltitz. . . . Eine chronol. Untersuchung.*
Dresden, 1844 (pp. 37). The respective sections in MARHEINEKE,
KAHNIS (I. 235 sqq.), and KÖSTLIN (I. 238 sqq. and 281 sqq.).

Before the final decision, another attempt was made to
silence Luther by inducing him to revoke his heresies.
Diplomacy sometimes interrupts the natural development
of principles and the irresistible logic of events, but only for
a short season. It usually resorts to compromises which
satisfy neither party, and are cast aside. Principles must
work themselves out.

Pope Leo sent his nuncio and chamberlain, Karl von
Miltitz, a noble Saxon by birth, and a plausible, convivial

---

[1] Letter to Spalatin, Nov. 25 and Dec. 2. De Wette, I. 188 sqq.

[2] "*Mittam ad te nugas meas, ut videas, an recte divinem Antichristum
illum verum juxta Paulum in Romana curia regnare : pejorem Turcis esse
hodie, puto me demonstrare posse.*" De Wette, I. 193.

gentleman,[1] to the Elector Frederick with the rare present of a golden rose, and authorized him to negotiate with Luther. He provided him with a number of the highest recommendations to civil and ecclesiastical dignitaries.

Miltitz discovered on his journey a wide-spread and growing sympathy with Luther. He found three Germans on his side, especially in the North, to one against him. He heard bad reports about Tetzel, and summoned him; but Tetzel was afraid to travel, and died a few months afterwards (Aug. 7, 1519), partly, perhaps, in consequence of the severe censure from the papal delegate. Luther wrote to his opponent a letter of comfort, which is no more extant. Unmeasured as he could be in personal abuse, he harbored no malice or revenge in his heart.[2]

Miltitz held a conference with Luther in the house of Spalatin at Altenburg, Jan. 6, 1519. He was exceedingly polite and friendly; he deplored the offence and scandal of the Theses-controversy, and threw a great part of the blame on poor Tetzel; he used all his powers of persuasion, and entreated him with tears not to divide the unity of the holy Catholic Church.

They agreed that the matter should be settled by a German bishop instead of going to Rome, and that in the mean time both parties were to keep silence. Luther promised to ask the pardon of the Pope, and to warn the people against the sin of separating from the holy mother-church. After this agreement they partook of a social supper, and parted with a kiss. Miltitz must have felt very proud of his masterpiece of ecclesiastical diplomacy.

Luther complied with his promises in a way which seems

---

[1] He was charged with intemperance, and is reported to have fallen from the boat in crossing the Rhine or the Main near Mainz in a state of intoxication, a. 1529. See the reports in Seidemann, *l.c.* p. 33 sqq.

[2] He speaks generously of Tetzel in a letter to Spalatin, Feb. 12, 1519 (De Wette, I. 223): " *Doleo Tetzelium et salutem suam in eam necessitatem venisse . . . multo mallem, si posset, servari cum honore,*" etc.

irreconcilable with his honest convictions and subsequent conduct. But we must remember the deep conflicts of his mind, the awful responsibility of his undertaking, the critical character of the situation. Well might he pause for a while, and shrink back from the idea of a separation from the church of his fathers, so intimately connected with his religious life as well as with the whole history of Christianity for fifteen hundred years. He had to break a new path which became so easy for others. We must all the more admire his conscientiousness.

In his letter to the Pope, dated March 3, 1519, he expressed the deepest personal humility, and denied that he ever intended to injure the Roman Church, which was over every other power in heaven and on earth, *save only Jesus Christ the Lord over all.* Yet he repudiated the idea of retracting his conscientious convictions.

In his address to the people, he allowed the value of indulgences, but only as a recompense for the "satisfaction" given by the sinner, and urged the duty of adhering, notwithstanding her faults and sins, to the holy Roman Church, where St. Peter and St. Paul, and many Popes and thousands of martyrs, had shed their blood.

At the same time, Luther continued the careful study of history, and could find no trace of popery and its extraordinary claims in the first centuries before the Council of Nicæa. He discovered that the Papal Decretals, and the Donation of Constantine, were a forgery. He wrote to Spalatin, March 13, 1519, "I know not whether the Pope is antichrist himself, or his apostle; so wretchedly is Christ, that is the truth, corrupted and crucified by him in the Decretals." [1]

[1] De Wette, I. 239.

§ 37. *The Leipzig Disputation. June 27–July 15, 1519.*

I. LÖSCHER, III. 203–819. Luther's *Works*, WALCH, XV. 954 sqq.; Weim. ed.
II. 153–435 (see the literary notices of Knaake, p. 156). Luther's letters
to Spalatin and the Elector, in DE WETTE, I. 284–324.

II. JOH. K. SEIDEMANN: *Die Leipziger Disputation im Jahre 1519.*
Dresden and Leipzig, 1843 (pp. 161). With important documents (pp.
93 sqq.) The best book on the subject. Monographs on *Carlstadt* by
JÄGER (Stuttgart, 1856), on *Eck* by WIEDEMANN (Regensburg, 1865),
and the relevant sections in MARHEINEKE, KAHNIS (I. 251–285), KÖST-
LIN, KOLDE, and the general histories of the Reformation. The account
by RANKE (I. 277–285) is very good. On the Roman side, see JANSSEN,
II. 83–88 (incomplete).

The agreement between Miltitz and Luther was only a
short truce. The Reformation was too deeply rooted in the
wants of the age to be suppressed by the diplomacy of ecclesiastical politicians. Even if the movement had been arrested
in one place, it would have broken out in another; indeed,
it had already begun independently in Switzerland. Luther
was no more his own master, but the organ of a higher power.
"Man proposes, God disposes."

Before the controversy could be settled by a German
bishop, it was revived, not without a violation of promise on
both sides,[1] in the disputation held in the large hall of the
Castle of Pleissenburg at Leipzig, under the sanction of
Duke George of Saxony, between Eck, Carlstadt, and Luther,
on the doctrines of the papal primacy, free-will, good works,
purgatory, and indulgences. It was one of the great intellectual battles; it lasted nearly three weeks, and excited universal attention in that deeply religious and theological age.
The vital doctrines of salvation were at stake. The debate

---

[1] Eck was the chief originator of the disputation, and not Luther (as
Janssen endeavors to show). Seidemann, who gives a full and authentic
account of the preliminary correspondence, says (p. 21): " *Es ist entschieden,
dass Eck die Disputation antrug, und zwar zunächst nur mit Karlstadt.
Aber auch Luther's Absehen war auf eine Disputation gerichtet.*"

was in Latin, but Luther broke out occasionally in his more vigorous German.

The disputation began with the solemnities of a mass, a procession, an oration of Peter Mosellanus, *De ratione disputandi*, and the singing of *Veni, Creator Spiritus*. It ended with a eulogistic oration by the Leipzig professor John Lange, and the *Te Deum*.

The first act was the disputation between Eck and Carlstadt, on the freedom of the human will, which the former maintained, and the latter denied. The second and more important act began July 4, between Eck and Luther, chiefly on the subject of the papacy.

Dr. Eck (Johann Mair), professor of theology at Ingolstadt in Bavaria, was the champion of Romanism, a man of great learning, well-stored memory, dialectical skill, ready speech, and stentorian voice, but over-confident, conceited, and boisterous. He looked more like a butcher or soldier than a theologian. Many regarded him as a mere charlatan, and expressed their contempt for his audacity and vanity by the nicknames *Keck* (pert) and *Geck* (fop), which date from this dispute.[1]

Carlstadt (Andreas von Bodenstein), Luther's impetuous and ill-balanced friend and colleague, was an unfortunate debater.[2] He had a poor memory, depended on his notes, got embarrassed and confused, and furnished an easy victory to Eck. It was ominous, that, on entering Leipzig, his wagon broke down, and he fell into the mud.

Luther was inferior to Eck in historical learning and flowing Latinity, but surpassed him in knowledge of the Bible, independent judgment, originality, and depth of thought, and had the law of progress on his side. While Eck looked to the fathers, Luther went back to the grandfathers; he ascended from the stream of church history to the fountain

[1] As he complained twenty years later: see Seidemann, p. 80.
[2] Luther calls him an *infelicissimus disputator*.

of God's Word; yet from the normative beginning of the apostolic age he looked hopefully into the future. Though pale and emaciated, he was cheerful, wore a little silver ring, and carried a bunch of flowers in his hand. Peter Mosellanus, a famous Latinist, who presided over the disputation, thus describes his personal appearance at that time:[1] —

"Luther is of middle stature; his body thin, and so wasted by care and study that nearly all his bones may be counted.[2] He is in the prime of life. His voice is clear and melodious. His learning, and his knowledge of Scripture are so extraordinary that he has nearly every thing at his fingers' ends. Greek and Hebrew he understands sufficiently well to give his judgment on interpretations. For conversation, he has a rich store of subjects at his command; a vast forest (*silva ingens*) of thoughts and words is at his disposal. He is polite and clever. There is nothing stoical, nothing supercilious, about him; and he understands how to adapt himself to different persons and times. In society he is lively and agreeable. He is always fresh, cheerful, and at his ease, and has a pleasant countenance, however hard his enemies may threaten him, so that one cannot but believe that Heaven is with him in his great undertaking.[3] Most people, however, reproach him with want of moderation in polemics, and with being rather imprudent and more cutting than befits a theologian and a reformer."

The chief interest in the disputation turned on the subject of the authority of the Pope and the infallibility of the Church. Eck maintained that the Pope is the successor of

---

[1] In a letter to Julius Pflug, a young Saxon nobleman. Mosellanus describes also Carlstadt and Eck, and the whole disputation. See Löscher, III. 242-251 (especially p. 247); Walch, XV. 1422; Seidemann, 51 and 56. I find the description also in an appendix to Melanchthon's *Vita Lutheri*, Göttingen, 1741, pp. 32-44.

[2] "*Ut omnia pene ossa liceat dinumerare.*" But in later years Luther grew stout and fleshy.

[3] "*Ut haud facile credas, hominem tam ardua sine numine Divûm moliri.*"

Peter, and the vicar of Christ by divine right; Luther, that this claim is contrary to the Scriptures, to the ancient church, to the Council of Nicæa, — the most sacred of all councils, — and rests only on the frigid decrees of the Roman pontiffs.

But during the debate he changed his opinion on the authority of councils, and thereby injured his cause in the estimation of the audience. Being charged by Eck with holding the heresy of Hus, he at first repudiated him and all schismatic tendencies; but on mature reflection he declared that Hus held some scriptural truths, and was unjustly condemned and burnt by the Council of Constance; that a general council as well as a Pope may err, and had no right to impose any article of faith not founded in the Scriptures. When Duke George, a sturdy upholder of the Catholic creed, heard Luther express sympathy with the Bohemian heresy, he shook his head, and, putting both arms in his sides, exclaimed, so that it could be heard throughout the hall, " A plague upon it!"[1]

From this time dates Luther's connection with the Bohemian Brethren.

Luther concluded his argument with these words: "I am sorry that the learned doctor only dips into the Scripture as the water-spider into the water — nay, that he seems to flee from it as the Devil from the Cross. I prefer, with all deference to the Fathers, the authority of the Scripture, which I herewith recommend to the arbiters of our cause."

Both parties, as usual, claimed the victory. Eck was rewarded with honors and favors by Duke George, and followed up his fancied triumph by efforts to ruin Luther, and to gain a cardinal's hat; but he was also severely attacked and ridiculed, especially by Willibald Pirkheimer, the famous humanist and patrician of Nürnberg, in his stinging satire,

---

[1] "*Das walt' die Sucht!*"

" *The Polished Corner*." [1] The theological faculties of Cologne, Louvain, and afterwards (1521) also that of Paris, condemned the Reformer.

Luther himself was greatly dissatisfied, and regarded the disputation as a mere waste of time. He made, however, a deep impression upon younger men, and many students left Leipzig for Wittenberg.   After all, he was more benefited by the disputation and the controversies growing out of it, than his opponents.

The importance of this theological tournament lies in this : that it marks a progress in Luther's emancipation from the papal system. Here for the first time he denied the divine right and origin of the papacy, and the infallibility of a general council. Henceforward he had nothing left but the divine Scriptures, his private judgment, and his faith in God who guides the course of history by his own Spirit, through all obstructions by human errors, to a glorious end. The ship of the Reformation was cut from its moorings, and had to fight with the winds and waves of the open sea.

From this time Luther entered upon a revolutionary crusade against the Roman Church until the anarchical dissensions in his own party drove him back into a conservative and even re-actionary position.

Before we proceed with the development of the Reformation, we must make the acquaintance of Melanchthon, who had accompanied Luther to the Leipzig disputation as a spectator, suggesting to him and Carlstadt occasional arguments,[2] and hereafter stood by him as his faithful colleague and friend.

---

[1] " *Der algehobelte Eck*."   The book appeared first anonymously in Latin, *Eccius dedolatus*, at Erfurt, March, 1520. Hagen, in his *Der Geist der Reformation* (Erlangen, 1843), I. p. 60 sqq., gives a good summary of this witty book. Luther sent it to Spalatin, March 2, 1520 (De Wette, I. 426), but expressed his dissatisfaction with this " mode of raging against Eck," and preferred an open attack to a " bite from behind the fence."

[2] This excited the anger of Eck, who broke out, " *Tace tu, Philippe, ac tua studia cura, ne me perturba*."

§ 38. *Philip Melanchthon. Literature (Portrait).*

The best Melanchthon collection is in the Royal Library of Berlin, which I
have consulted for this list (July, 1886). The third centenary of Mel.'s
death in 1860, and the erection of his monument in Wittenberg, called
forth a large number of pamphlets and articles in periodicals.

1526

VIVENTIS·POTVIT·DVRERIVS·ORA·PHILIPPI
MENTEM·NON·POTVIT·PINGERE·DOCTA
MANVS

MELANCHTHON.   (From a portrait by Dürer.)

I. Works of Melanchthon.   The first ed. appeared at Basel, 1541, 5 vols. fol.;
   another by PEUCER (his son-in-law), Wittenberg, 1562–64, 4 vols. fol.;
   again 1601.   Selection of his German works by KÖTHE.   Leipzig, 1829–
   30, 6 vols.   *Best ed. of *Opera omnia* (in the "Corpus Reformatorum")
   by BRETSCHNEIDER and BINDSEIL.   Halle, 1834–60, 28 vols. 4°.   The

most important vols. for church history are vols. i.-xi. and xxi.-xxviii.
The last vol. (second part) contains *Annales Vitæ* (pp. 1–143), and
very ample *Indices* (145–378).

Add to these: *Epistolæ, Judicia, Consilia, Testimonia*, etc., ed. H. E.
BINDSEIL. Halle, 1874. 8°. A supplement to the "Corpus Reform."
Compare also BINDSEIL's *Bibliotheca Melanthoniana*. Halis, 1868 (pp.
28). CARL KRAUSE: *Melanthoniana, Regesten und Briefe über die
Beziehungen Philipp Mel. zu Anhalt und dessen Fürsten*. Zerbst, 1885.
pp. 185.

II. Biographies of Mel. An account of his last days by the Wittenberg professors: *Brevis narratio exponens quo fine vitam in terris suam clauserit
D. Phil. Mel. conscripta a professoribus academiæ Vitebergensis, qui
omnibus quæ exponuntur interfuerunt*. Viteb. 1560. 4°. The same in
German. A funeral oration by HEERBRAND: *Oratio in obitum Mel.
habita in Academia Tubingensi die decima quinta Maji*. Vitebergæ,
1560. *JOACHIM CAMERARIUS: *Vita Mel*. Lips. 1566; and other edd.,
one with notes by Strobel. Halle, 1777; one with preface by Neander
in the *Vitæ quatuor Reformatorum*. Berlin, 1841.

STROBEL: *Melanchthoniana*. Altdorf, 1771; *Die Ehre Mel. gerettet*, 1773;
and other works. A. H. NIEMEYER: *Phil. Mel. als Præceptor Germaniæ*. Halle, 1817. FR. AUG. COX : *Life of Mel., comprising an account of the Reform*. Lond. 1815, 2d ed. 1817. G. L. FR. DELBRÜCK:
Ph. Mel. der Glaubenslehrer. Bonn, 1826. HEYD: *Mel. und Tübingen,
1512–18*. Tüb. 1839. *FR. GALLE: *Characteristik Melanchth. als Theol.
und Entw. seines Lehrbegr*. Halle, 1840. *FR. MATTHES: *Ph. Mel. Sein
Leben u. Wirken aus den Quellen*. Altenb. 1841. 2d ed. 1846. LED-
DERHOSE: *Phil. Mel. nach seinem aüsseren u. inneren Leben dargestellt*.
Heidelberg, 1847 (English translation by Dr. KROTEL. Phila. 1855).
By the same: *Das Leben des Phil. Mel. für das Volk*. Barmen, 1858.
*MOR. MEURER: *Phil. Mel.'s Leben*. Leipzig u. Dresden, 1860. 2d ed.
1869. HEPPE: *Phil. Mel. der Lehrer Deutschlands*. Marburg, 1860.
*CARL SCHMIDT: *Philipp Melanchthons Leben und ausgewählte
Schriften*. Elberfeld, 1861 (in the "Reformatoren der Luth. Kirche").
*HERRLINGER: *Die Theologie Mel.'s in ihrer geschichtl. Entwicklung*.
Gotha, 1879.

III. Brief sketches, by NEANDER, in Piper's "Evang.-Kalender" for 1851.
By NITZSCH, in the "Deutsche Zeitschrift für christl. Wissenschaft,"
1855. Is. AUG. DORNER: *Zum dreihundertjährigen Gedächtniss des Todes
Melanchthons*, 1860. VOLBEDING: *Mel. wie er liebte und lebte* (Leipz.
1860). KAHNIS: *Rede zum Gedächtniss Mel.'s* (Leipz. 1860). WOHL-
FAHRT: *Phil. Mel.* (Leipzig, 1860). W. THILO: *Mel. im Dienste der heil.
Schrift* (Berlin, 1860). PAUL PRESSEL: *Phil. Mel. Ein evang. Lebensbild* (Stuttg. 1860). *Festreden zur Erinnerung an den 300 jährigen Todes-
tag Phil. Mel.'s und bei der Grundsteinlegung zu dessen Denkmal zu*

Wittenberg, herausgeg. von LOMMATZCH (Wittenb. 1860). HENKE: *Das Verhältniss Luthers und Mel. zu einander* (Marburg, 1860), and *Memoria B. Phil. Mel.* (Marburg, 1860). AD. PLANCK: *Mel. Præceptor Germ.* (Nördlingen, 1860). TOLLIN: *Ph. Mel. und Mich. Servet. Eine Quellenstudie* (Berlin, 1876). LANDERER: *Mel.*, in Herzog[1] and Herzog[2] ix. 471–525, revised by HERRLINGER. THIERSCH: *Mel.* (Augsburg, 1877, and New York, Am. Tract Soc. 1880). LUTHARDT: *Melanchthon's Arbeiten im Gebiete der Moral* (Leipz. 1884). WAGENMANN: *Ph. Mel.* (in the "Allgem. Deutsche Biographie"). PAULSEN in "Gesch. des gelehrten Unterrichts" (Leipz. 1885. pp. 34 sqq.). SCHAFF in *St. Augustin, Melanchthon, Neander* (New York and London, 1886. pp. 107–127).

IV. On Mel.'s *Loci*, see STROBEL: *Literärgesch. von Ph. Mel.'s locis theologicis.* Altdorf and Nürnberg, 1776. PLITT: *Melanchthons Loci in ihrer Urgestalt.* Erlangen, 1864.

§ 39. *Melanchthon's Training.*

On the twenty-fifth day of August, 1518, ten months after the publication of Luther's *Theses*, when he most needed a learned helper in his work, and two years before the papal excommunication, a modest but highly gifted youth arrived in Wittenberg, as professor of philosophy and Greek literature, who was predestinated to become the second leader of the Lutheran Reformation, and the "Teacher of Germany."[1]

Philip Melanchthon, or Melanthon,[2] was born of honest and pious parents, at Bretten in the Palatinate, Feb. 16, 1497, fourteen years after Luther, twelve years before Cal-

---

[1] "*Præceptor Germaniæ.*" Luther was the "*Reformator Germaniæ.*" This is the shortest expression of the difference of the two.

[2] He spelled his name *Melanchthon* (from μέλαν and χθών), but after 1531 *Melanthon*, for the sake of brevity and euphony. Bretschneider and Bindseil have adopted the latter form; but the older is more usual, and preserves the etymology. His original name was *Schwarzerd*, i.e., *Blackearth*, which his grand-uncle Reuchlin changed, according to the literary fashion of the age, into the corresponding Greek. See Förstemann, *Die Schwarzerde, oder Zusammenstellung der Nachrichten über Melanchthon's Geschlecht*, in the "Theol. Studien und Kritiken" for 1830, p. 119 sqq. D. Fr. Strauss conjectures that Mel.'s original name was not *Schwarzerd*, but *Schwarzert* or *Schwarzer*, i.e., *Black*, and has nothing to do with the earth, any more than kindred names derived from color, as Weissert, Grunert, Gelbert. (*Gesammelte Schriften*, ed. by Zeller, vol. ii. 337, and *Ulrich v. Hutten*, p. 18.) But Reuchlin must have known better.

vin. In his theology, as in age, he stood a mediator between the two. His father was a skillful manufacturer of arms for the Elector Philip and the Emperor Maximilian I.; his mother a niece of the celebrated Hebraist Reuchlin, who presented him with a Bible, and directed his studies at Pforzheim, Heidelberg, and Tübingen.

He was one of those rare scholars who mature early, and yet continue their productive labors in undiminished vigor to old age. He mastered all the branches of knowledge, especially classical philology, and graduated as Master of Arts in Tübingen, Jan. 25, 1514, when only seventeen years of age. He wrote and spoke Greek and Latin better than his native German, and composed poetry in those languages. He began his public career in the University of Tübingen, as lecturer on ancient literature, and editor of the comedies of Terence (1516), and translator of Aratus, and Plutarch (1518). He made preparations for a correct edition of Aristotle, who had been "mutilated, barbarously translated, and become darker than the sibylline oracles," though he never carried it out. In 1518 he published a Greek grammar, which passed through many editions.

Erasmus, the first scholar of his age, and best judge of literary merit, foresaw the future significance of this precocious youth, and paid him, in 1516, a glowing tribute of admiration for eminence in the classics, acumen in demonstration, purity and elegance of style, rare learning and comprehensive reading, tenderness and refinement.[1] Melanchthon wrote

---

[1] In his *Com. on Thessal.* (*Annotat. in N. Test.*, Basel, 1515, p. 555): "*At Deum immortalem, quam non spem de se præbet admodum etiam adolescens ac pene puer Philippus ille Melanchthon, utraque literatura pene ex æquo suspiciendus* [not *suscipiendus*]! *Quod inventionis acumen! Quæ sermonis puritas* [*et elegantia*]! *Quanta reconditarum rerum memoria! Quam varia lectio! Quam verecundiæ regiæque prorsus indolis festivitas!*" Erasmus dates the preface of these *Annotationes* from 1515, but they were not published till 1516, together with the first edition of his Greek Testament. In the second ed. of the *Annot.*, Bas. 1520, and in the ed. of 1522, as well as in vol. vii. of his *Opera*, Bas. 1540, the eulogy on Melanchthon is

a eulogy on Erasmus in Greek verse (September, 1516), and never forgot his eminent services to classical and biblical studies. A modern Catholic historian, notwithstanding his doctrinal objections, calls Melanchthon "the most brilliant phenomenon which proceeded from the Erasmian school, equal to his master Erasmus in many respects, superior to him in others. Riches of knowledge, the choicest classical culture, facility of expression, versatility of composition, rhetorical fullness and improvisation, united to untiring industry, — this rare combination of excellences fitted him above all others for the literary leadership of the mighty movement."[1]

Melanchthon embraced theology in his encyclopædic studies, without having the priesthood in view, but was rather repelled by the dry scholasticism which then prevailed in Tübingen. He quietly and naturally grew into his theological position, without violent changes and struggles like those of Luther. His experience was that of John rather than of Paul. He had received a pious training at home; he delighted in public worship, the lives of saints, and especially in the careful study of the Bible, which accompanied him even on his walks. His eyes were opened to the abuses in the Church, and the need of reform. His classical tastes and his intimacy with Reuchlin, the noble champion of Hebrew learning against monkish ignorance and obscurantism, predisposed him in favor of the evangelical movement which had broken out at Wittenberg a few months before he left Tübingen.

---

omitted. (I examined these various editions in the Royal Library of Berlin, July, 1886, to verify conflicting and inaccurate statements of historians.) In a letter to Melanchthon, April 22, 1519, Erasmus shows a little sensitiveness, but still professes great admiration for him, and hopes that he may more than fulfill that most favorable expectation which Germany had formed of his genius and piety. "Corp Ref.," I. 76 sq.; comp. Mel.'s letter to Erasmus, *ibid.* fol. 59 sq.

[1] Dr. Döllinger, *Die Reformation* (1846), vol. i. 349.

His fame spread so rapidly that he received calls from the universities of Ingolstadt, Leipzig, and Wittenberg. He concluded to go to Wittenberg as professor of Greek, at the modest salary of one hundred guilders. This salary was doubled in 1526, but Luther and the Elector had difficulty to induce him to accept.[1]

Reuchlin had strongly recommended him to the Elector Frederick. "I know no man among the Germans," he wrote, "who is superior to Master Philip Schwarzerd except Erasmus Roterodamus, who is a Hollander, and surpasses us all in Latin."[2] He applied to his nephew, in prophetic anticipation, the promise of God to Abraham, Gen. 12: 1–3.[3]

So far the aged scholar did great service to the cause of the Reformation. But when it threatened to end in a split of the Church, Reuchlin withdrew, like Erasmus and Staupitz. He was afraid of being called a heretic. He moved from Stuttgart to Ingolstadt in 1519, and lived for a while in the house of Dr. Eck. He even tried to draw Melanchthon from Wittenberg to Ingolstadt, but in vain; he recalled his promise to bequeath to him his valuable library, and gave it to his native city of Pforzheim. The pestilence drove him from Bavaria back to Würtemberg; he taught Greek and Hebrew grammar at Tübingen in 1521, and died at Stuttgart in the communion of the Roman Church, June 30, 1522.[4]

---

[1] Luth. ad Principem Electorem, Feb. 9, 1526: "*Es hat E. K. F. G. in der Ordnung der Universität befehlen lassen M. Philippsen 200 fl. jährlich zu geben. Nun beschwert sich der Mensch, solches zu nehmen; denn weil er nicht vermag so steif und täglich in der Schrift zu lesen, möcht er's nicht mit gutem Gewissen nehmen*," etc.

[2] In a German letter to Frederick, dated July 25, 1518. See "Corp. Reform.," I. 33.

[3] He wrote to him from Stuttgart, July 24, 1518 (*ibid.* I. 32): "*Egredere de terra tua . . . et magnificabo nomen tuum, erisque benedictus. Hæc Genesis xii. Ita mihi præsagit animus, ita spero futurum de te, mi Philippe, meum opus et meum solatium.*"

[4] Geiger, *Joh. Reuchlin, sein Leben und seine Werke*, Leipz., 1871; Horawitz, *Zur Biographie und Correspondenz J. Reuchlin's*, Wien, 1877; Strauss, *Ulrich v. Hutten*, Bk. I. chap. 7 (p. 132 sqq. of the 4th ed.); and Klüpfel, in Herzog[2] xii. 715–724.

§ 40. *Melanchthon's Early Labors.*

Although yet a youth of twenty-one years of age, Melanchthon at once gained the esteem and admiration of his colleagues and hearers in Wittenberg. He was small of stature, unprepossessing in his outward appearance, diffident and timid. But his high and noble forehead, his fine blue eyes, full of fire, the intellectual expression of his countenance, the courtesy and modesty of his behavior, revealed the beauty and strength of his inner man. His learning was undoubted, his moral and religious character above suspicion. His introductory address, which he delivered four days after his arrival (Aug. 29), on " The Improvement of the Studies of Youth," [1] dispelled all fears : it contained the programme of his academic teaching, and marks an epoch in the history of liberal education in Germany. He desired to lead the youth to the sources of knowledge, and by a careful study of the languages to furnish the key for the proper understanding of the Scriptures, that they might become living members of Christ, and enjoy the fruits of His heavenly wisdom. He studied and taught theology, not merely for the enrichment of the mind, but also and chiefly for the promotion of virtue and piety.[2]

He at first devoted himself to philological pursuits, and did more than any of his contemporaries to revive the study of Greek for the promotion of biblical learning and the cause of the Reformation. He called the ancient languages the swaddling-clothes of the Christ-child : Luther compared them to the sheath of the sword of the Spirit. Melanchthon was master of the ancient languages ; Luther, master of the

---

[1] *De Corrigendis Adolescentium Studiis,* in the "Corpus Reformatorum," XI. 15 sqq. See Schmidt, *l.c.* 29 sq.

[2] He wrote to his friend Camerarius, Jan. 22, 1525 ("Corp. Ref." I. 722): "*Ego mihi ita conscius sum, non aliam ob causam unquam* τεθεολογηκέναι *nisi ut vitam emendarem.*"

German.   The former, by his co-operation, secured accuracy
to the German Bible; the latter, idiomatic force and poetic
beauty.

In the year 1519 Melanchthon graduated as Bachelor of
Divinity; the degree of Doctor he modestly declined.   From
that time on, he was a member of the theological faculty, and
delivered also theological lectures, especially on exegesis.   He
taught two or three hours every day a variety of topics, including ethics, logic, Greek and Hebrew grammar; he explained
Homer, Plato, Plutarch, Titus, Matthew, Romans, the Psalms.
In the latter period of his life he devoted himself exclusively to sacred learning.   He was never ordained, and never
ascended the pulpit; but for the benefit of foreign students
who were ignorant of German, he delivered every Sunday in
his lecture-room a Latin sermon on the Gospels.   He became
at once, and continued to be, the most popular teacher at
Wittenberg.   He drew up the statutes of the University,
which are regarded as a model.   By his advice and example
the higher education in Germany was regulated.

His fame attracted students from all parts of Christendom,
including princes, counts, and barons.   His lecture-room was
crowded to overflowing, and he heard occasionally as many
as eleven languages at his frugal but hospitable table.   He
received calls to Tübingen, Nürnberg, and Heidelberg, and
was also invited to Denmark, France, and England; but he
preferred remaining in Wittenberg till his death.

At the urgent request of Luther, who wished to hold him
fast, and to promote his health and comfort, he married (having no vow of celibacy to prevent him) as early as August,
1520, Catharina Krapp, the worthy daughter of the burgomaster of Wittenberg, who faithfully shared with him the
joys and trials of domestic life.   He had from her four children, and was often seen rocking the cradle with one hand,
while holding a book in the other.   He used to repeat the
Apostles' Creed in his family three times a day.   He esteemed

his wife higher than himself. She died in 1557 while he was on a journey to the colloquy at Worms: when he heard the sad news at Heidelberg, he looked up to heaven, and exclaimed, "Farewell! I shall soon follow thee."

Next to the "Lutherhaus" with the "Luthermuseum," the most interesting dwelling in the quaint old town of Wittenberg on the banks of the Elbe is the house of Melanchthon in the Collegienstrasse. It is a three-story building, and belongs to the Prussian government, King Friedrich Wilhelm IV. having bought it from its former owner. Melanchthon's study is on the first story; there he died. Behind the house is a little garden which was connected with Luther's garden. Here, under the shade of the tree, the two Reformers may often have exchanged views on the stirring events of the times, and encouraged each other in the great conflict. The house bears in German the inscription on the outer wall: —

> "Here lived, taught, and died
> PHILIPP MELANCHTHON."

§ 41. *Luther and Melanchthon.*

P. SCHAFF: *Luther und Melanchthon*, in his "Der Deutsche Kirchenfreund," Mercersburg, Pa., vol. III. (1850), pp. 58–64. E. L. HENKE: *Das Verhältniss Luthers und Melanchthons zu einander. Festrede am 19 April*, 1860. Marburg (28 pages). Compare also DÖLLINGER: *Die Reformation*, vol. i. 349 sqq.

> "Wo sich das Strenge mit dem Zarten,
> Wo Starkes sich und Mildes paarten,
> Da giebt es einen guten Klang." (*Schiller.*)

In great creative epochs of the Church, God associates congenial leaders for mutual help and comfort. In the Reformation of the sixteenth century, we find Luther and Melanchthon in Germany, Zwingli and Œcolampadius, Farel and Viret, Calvin and Beza in Switzerland, Cranmer, Latimer, and Ridley in England, Knox and Melville in Scotland, working together with different gifts, but in the same spirit and for the same end. The Methodist revival of the eighteenth century was carried on by the co-operation of the two Wesleys and Whitefield; and the Anglo-Catholic movement of the nineteenth, by the association of Pusey, Newman, and Keble.

Immediately after his arrival at the Saxon University, on the Elbe, Melanchthon entered into an intimate relation with Luther, and became his most useful and influential co-laborer. He looked up to his elder colleague with the veneration of a son, and was carried away and controlled (sometimes against his better judgment) by the fiery genius of the Protestant Elijah; while Luther regarded him as his superior in learning, and was not ashamed to sit humbly at his feet. He attended his exegetical lectures, and published them, without the author's wish and knowledge, for the benefit of the Church. Melanchthon declared in April, 1520, that "he would rather die than be separated from Luther;" and in November of the same year, "Martin's welfare is dearer to me than my own life." Luther was captivated by Melanchthon's first lecture; he admired his scholarship, loved his character, and wrote most enthusiastically about him in confidential letters to Spalatin, Reuchlin, Lange, Scheurl, and others, lauding him as a prodigy of learning and piety.[1]

The friendship of these two great and good men is one of the most delightful chapters in the religious drama of the sixteenth century. It rested on mutual personal esteem and

---

[1] Lutherus ad Reuchlinum, Dec. 14, 1518: "*Philippus noster Melanchthon, homo admirabilis, imo pene nihil habens, quod non supra hominem sit, familiarissimus tamen et amicissimus mihi.*" To Billikan he wrote in 1523 (De Wette, II. 407): "*Den Philippus achte ich nicht anders als mich selbst, ausgenommen in Hinsicht auf seine Gelehrsamkeit und die Unbescholtenheit seines Lebens, wodurch er mich, dass ich nicht blos sage, übertrifft.*" In his humorous way he once invited him (Oct. 18, 1518) to supper under the address: "*Philippo Melanchthoni, Schwarzerd, Græco, Latino, Hebræo, Germano, nunquam Barbaro.*" The testimonies of Luther on Mel. are collected in the first and last vols. of the "Corp. Reform." (especially xxviii[b]. 9 and 10).

hearty German affection, but especially on the consciousness of a providential mission intrusted to their united labors. Although somewhat disturbed, at a later period, by slight doctrinal differences and occasional ill-humor,[1] it lasted to the end; and as they worked together for the same cause, so they now rest under the same roof in the castle church at Wittenberg, at whose doors Luther had nailed the war-cry of the Reformation.

Melanchthon descended from South Germany, Luther from North Germany; the one from the well-to-do middle classes of citizens and artisans, the other from the rough but sturdy peasantry. Melanchthon had a quiet, literary preparation for his work: Luther experienced much hardship and severe moral conflicts. The former passed to his Protestant conviction through the door of classical studies, the latter through the door of monastic asceticism; the one was fore-ordained to a professor's chair, the other to the leadership of an army of conquest.

Luther best understood and expressed the difference of temper and character; and it is one of his noble traits, that he did not allow it to interfere with the esteem and admiration for his younger friend and colleague. "I prefer the books of Master Philippus to my own," he wrote in 1529.[2] "I am rough, boisterous, stormy, and altogether warlike. I am born to fight against innumerable monsters and devils. I must remove stumps and stones, cut away thistles and thorns, and clear the wild forests; but Master Philippus comes along softly and gently, sowing and watering with joy, according to the gifts which God has abundantly bestowed upon him."

Luther was incomparably the stronger man of the two,

---

[1] Melanchthon hints also, in one of his confidential letters, at female influence, the γυναικοτυράννις, as an incidental element in the disturbance. "Corp. Ref.," III. 398.

[2] In his preface to Melanchthon's *Commentary on Colossians.*

and differed from Melanchthon as the wild mountain torrent
differs from the quiet stream of the meadow, or as the rushing tempest from the gentle breeze, or, to use a scriptural
illustration, as the fiery Paul from the contemplative John.
Luther was a man of war, Melanchthon a man of peace.
Luther's writings smell of powder; his words are battles; he
overwhelms his opponents with a roaring cannonade of argument, eloquence, passion, and abuse. Melanchthon excels
in moderation and amiability, and often exercised a happy
restraint upon the unmeasured violence of his colleague.
Once when Luther in his wrath burst out like a thunder-
storm, Melanchthon quieted him by the line, —

" Vince animos iramque tuam qui cœtera vincis."

Luther was a creative genius, and pioneer of new paths;
Melanchthon, a profound scholar of untiring industry. The
one was emphatically the man for the people, abounding in
strong and clear sense, popular eloquence, natural wit, genial
humor, intrepid courage, and straightforward honesty. The
other was a quiet, considerate, systematic thinker; a man
of order, method, and taste, and gained the literary circles
for the cause of the Reformation. He is the principal
founder of a Protestant theology, and the author of the Augsburg Confession, the chief symbol of the Lutheran Church.
He very properly represented the evangelical cause in all
the theological conferences with the Roman-Catholic party
at Augsburg, Speier, Worms, Frankfort, Ratisbon, where
Luther's presence would only have increased the heat of controversy, and widened the breach. Luther was unyielding
and uncompromising against Romanism and Zwinglianism:
Melanchthon was always ready for compromise and peace,
as far as his honest convictions would allow, and sincerely
labored to restore the broken unity of the Church. He was
even willing, as his qualified subscription to the Articles of
Smalcald shows, to admit a certain supremacy of the Pope

(*jure humano*), provided he would tolerate the free preaching of the gospel. But Popery and evangelical freedom will never agree

Luther was the boldest, the most heroic and commanding; Melanchthon, the most gentle, pious, and conscientious, of the Reformers. Melanchthon had a sensitive and irritable temperament, though under good control, and lacked courage; he felt, more keenly and painfully than any other, the tremendous responsibility of the great religious movement in which he was engaged. He would have made any personal sacrifice if he could have removed the confusion and divisions attendant upon it.[1] On several occasions he showed, no doubt, too much timidity and weakness; but his concessions to the enemy, and his disposition to compromise for the sake of peace and unity, proceeded always from pure and conscientious motives.

The two Wittenberg Reformers were brought together by the hand of Providence, to supply and complete each other, and by their united talents and energies to carry forward the German Reformation, which would have assumed a very different character if it had been exclusively left in the hands of either of them.

Without Luther the Reformation would never have taken hold of the common people: without Melanchthon it would never have succeeded among the scholars of Germany. Without Luther, Melanchthon would have become a second Erasmus, though with a profounder interest in religion; and the Reformation would have resulted in a liberal theological school, instead of giving birth to a Church. However much the humble and unostentatious labors and merits of Melanchthon are overshadowed by the more striking and brilliant deeds of the heroic Luther, they were, in their own way, quite as useful and indispensable. The "still

---

[1] "*Der Schmerz der Kirchenspaltung ist tief durch seine schuldlose Seele gegangen.*" Hase, *Kirchengesch.*, 11th ed. (1886), p. 372.

small voice" often made friends to Protestantism where the earthquake and thunder-storm produced only terror and convulsion.

Luther is greatest as a Reformer, Melanchthon as a Christian scholar. He represents in a rare degree the harmony of humanistic culture with biblical theology and piety. In this respect he surpassed all his contemporaries, even Erasmus and Reuchlin. He is, moreover, the connecting link between contending churches, and a forerunner of Christian union and catholicity which will ultimately heal the divisions and strifes of Christendom. To him applies the beatitude: "Blessed are the peacemakers; for they shall be called the children of God."

The friendship of Luther and Melanchthon drew into its charming circle also some other worthy and remarkable residents of Wittenberg, — Lucas Cranach the painter, who lent his art to the service of the Reformation; Justus Jonas, who came to Wittenberg in 1521 as professor and provost of the castle church, translated several writings of Luther and Melanchthon into German, and accompanied the former to Worms (1521), and on his last journey to Eisleben (1546); and Johann Bugenhagen, called Doctor Pomeranus, who moved from Pomerania to Wittenberg in 1521 as professor and preacher, and lent the Reformers most effective aid in translating the Bible, and organized the Reformation in several cities of North Germany and in Denmark.

§ 42. *Ulrich von Hutten and Luther.*

Böcking's edition of Ulrichi Hutteni *equitis Germani Opera.* Lips, 1859–1861. 5 vols. with three supplements, 1864–1870. David. Friedrich Strauss (the author of the *Leben Jesu*): *Gespräche von Ulrich von Hutten, übersetzt und erläutert,* Leipz. 1860, and his biography of *Ulrich von Hutten,* 4th ed., Bonn, 1878 (pp. 567). A masterly work by a congenial spirit. Compare K. Hagen, *Deutschlands liter. und rel. Verh. in Reformationszeitalter,* II. 47–60; Ranke, *D. Gesch.* I. 289–294; Janssen, II. 53 sqq. Werckshagen: *Luther u. Hutten,* 1888.

While Luther acquired in Melanchthon, the head of the Christian and theological wing of the humanists, a permanent and invaluable ally, he received also temporary aid and comfort from the pagan and political wing of the humanists, and its ablest leader, Ulrich von Hutten.

This literary knight and German patriot was descended from an ancient but impoverished noble family of Franconia. He was born April 21, 1488, and began life, like Erasmus, as an involuntary monk; but he escaped from Fulda in his sixteenth year, studied humanities in the universities of Erfurt, Cologne, and Frankfurt-on-the-Oder, law at Pavia and Bologna, traveled extensively, corresponded with the most prominent men of letters, was crowned as poet by the Emperor Maximilian at Augsburg (1517), and occupied an influential position at the court of Archbishop Albrecht of Mainz (1517–1520), who had charge of the sale of indulgences in Germany.

He took a lively part in Reuchlin's conflict with the obscurantism of the Dominicans of Cologne.[1] He is, next to his friend Crotus of Erfurt, the chief author of the *Epistolæ obscurorum Virorum*, that barbarous ridicule of barbarism, in which the ignorance, stupidity, bigotry, and vulgarity of the monks are exposed by factitious letters in their own wretched Latin with such success that they accepted them at first as genuine, and bought a number of copies for distribution.[2] He vigorously attacked the abuses and corruptions of the

---

[1] *Triumphus Capnionis* (κάπνιος = Reuchlin), a poem written in 1514, but not published till 1518 under the pseudo-name of Eleutherius Byzenus. *Works*, III. 413–447; Strauss, *U. v. H.*, 155 sq.

[2] First published 1515 [at Hagenau], and 1517 at Basel; best ed. by Böcking, in Hutten's *Opera*, Suppl. i. Lips. (1864), and commentary in Suppl. ii. (1869); an excellent critical analysis by Strauss, *l.c.* 165 sqq. He compares them with Don Quixote. The first book of the *Epist.* is chiefly from Crotus, the second chiefly from Hutten. The comic impression arises in great part from the barbarous Latinity, and is lost in a translation. There is, however, a good German translation by Dr. Wilhelm Binder : *Briefe von Dunkelmännern*. Stuttgart, 1876. The translator says he knew twenty-seven Latin editions, but no translation.

Church, in Latin and German pamphlets, in poetry and prose, with all the weapons of learning, common-sense, wit, and satire. He was, next to Luther, the boldest and most effective polemical writer of that period, and was called the German Demosthenes on account of his philippics against Rome. His Latin is better than Luther's, but his German far inferior. In wit and power of ridicule he resembles Lucian; at times he reminds one of Voltaire and Heine. He had a burning love of German liberty and independence. This was his chief motive for attacking Rome. He laid the axe at the root of the tree of tyranny. His motto was, "*Iacta est alea. Ich hab's gewagt.*"[1]

He republished in 1518 the tract of Laurentius Valla on the Donation of Constantine, with an embarrassing dedication to Pope Leo X., and exposed on German soil that gigantic fraud on which the temporal power of the papacy over all Christian Europe was made to rest. But his chief and most violent manifesto against Rome is a dialogue which he published under the name "*Vadiscus, or the Roman Trinity,*" in April, 1520, a few months before Luther's "Address to the German Nobility" (July) and his "Babylonian Captivity" (October). He here groups his experiences in Rome under several triads of what abounds in Rome, of what is lacking in Rome, of what is forbidden in Rome, of what one brings home from Rome, etc. He puts them into the mouth of a Roman consul, Vadiscus, and makes variations on them. Here are some specimens:[2] —

"Three things keep Rome in power: the authority of the Pope, the bones of saints, and the traffic in indulgences.

"Three things are in Rome without number: strumpets, priests, and scribes.

---

[1] "The die is cast. I have ventured it." An allusion to the exclamation of Cæsar when he crossed the Rubicon, and marched to Rome.

[2] Strauss, *U. v. H.*, p. 285 sqq., 289; and his translation, in *Hutten's Gespr.* p. 94 sqq., 114 sqq. I have omitted the interlocutories in the dialogue. Vadiscus is Hutten's friend Crotus of Erfurt (also Luther's friend); and Ernhold is his friend Arnold Glauberger, with whom he had been in Rome.

"Three things abound in Rome: antiquities, poison, and ruins.

"Three things are banished from Rome: simplicity, temperance, and piety (or, in another place: poverty, the ancient discipline, and the preaching of the truth).

"Three things the Romans trade in: Christ, ecclesiastical benefices, and women.

"Three things everybody desires in Rome: short masses, good gold, and a luxurious life.

"Three things are disliked in Rome: a general council, a reformation of the clergy, and the fact that the Germans begin to open their eyes.

"Three things displease the Romans most: the unity of the Christian princes, the education of the people, and the discovery of their frauds.

"Three things are most valued in Rome: handsome women, fine horses, and papal bulls.

"Three things are in general use in Rome: luxury of the flesh, splendor in dress, and pride of the heart.

"Three things Rome can never get enough of: money for the episcopal pallium, monthly, and annual incomes from vacant benefices.[1]

"Three things are most praised and yet most rare in Rome: devotion, faith, and innocence.

"Three things Rome brings to naught: a good conscience, devotion, and the oath.

"Three things are necessary in Rome to gain a lawsuit: money, letters of recommendation, and lies.

"Three things pilgrims usually bring back from Rome: a soiled conscience, a sick stomach, and an empty purse.

"Three things have kept Germany from getting wisdom: the stupidity of the princes, the decay of learning, and the superstition of the people.

"Three things are feared most in Rome: that the princes get united, that the people begin to open their eyes, and that Rome's frauds are coming to light.

"Three things only could set Rome right: the determination of the princes, the impatience of the people, and an army of Turks at her doors."

This epigrammatic and pithy form made the dialogue popular and effective. Even Luther imitated it when, in his " Babylonian Captivity," he speaks of three walls, and three rods of the Papists. Hutten calls the Roman court a sink of

---

[1] Allusion to the papal claims to fill the ecclesiastical vacancies which occurred during the long months (January, March, etc.), and to receive the *annates*, i.e , the first year's income from every spiritual living worth more than twenty-four ducats per annum. Luther, in his Address to the German Nobility, characterizes this papal avarice as downright robbery.

iniquity, and says that for centuries no genuine successor of Peter had sat on his chair in Rome, but successors and imitators of Simon Magus, Nero, Domitian, and Heliogabalus.

As a remedy for these evils, he advises, not indeed the abolition of the papacy, but the withdrawal of all financial support from Germany, a reduction of the clerical force, and the permission of clerical marriage; by these means, luxury and immorality would at least be checked.

It is characteristic of the church of that age, that Hutten was on terms of intimacy with the first prelate of Germany, even while he wrote his violent attacks on Rome, and received a salary, and afterwards a pension, from him. But he lauded Albrecht to the skies for his support of liberal learning. He knew little of, and cared less for, doctrinal differences. His policy was to fight the big Pope of Rome with the little Pope of Germany, and to make the German emperor, princes, and nobles, his allies in shaking off the degrading yoke of foreign tyranny. Possibly Albrecht may have indulged in the dream of becoming the primate of an independent Catholic Church of Germany.

Unfortunately, Hutten lacked moral purity, depth, and weight. He was frank, brave, and bold, but full of conceit, a restless adventurer, and wild stormer; able to destroy, but unable to build up. In his twentieth year he had contracted a disgusting disease which ruined him physically, and was used by his Roman opponents to ruin him morally. He suffered incredibly from it and from all sorts of quack remedies, for ten years, was attacked by it again after his cure, and yet maintained the vigor and freshness of his spirit.[1]

Hutten hailed the Wittenberg movement, though at first only as " a quarrel between two hot-headed monks who are

---

[1] He himself speaks very frankly of his *Morbus Gallicus*, or *Malum Franciæ* and its horrible effects, without asserting his innocence. Strauss discusses it fully with a belief in his guilt, yet pity for his sufferings and admiration for his endurance. " *Er hatte*," he says (*U. v. H.*, p. 241), " *den Jugendfehler, dessen wir ihn schuldig achten, in einem Grade zu büssen*,

shouting and screaming against each other," and hoped "that they would eat each other up." After the Leipzig disputation, he offered to Luther (first through Melanchthon) the aid of his pen and sword, and, in the name of his noble friend the knight Franz von Sickingen, a safe retreat at Ebernburg near Kreuznach, where Martin Bucer, Johann Œcolampadius, and other fugitives from convents, and sympathizers with reform, found a hospitable home. He sent him his books with notes, that he might republish them.

But Luther was cautious. He availed himself of the literary and political sympathy, but only as far as his theological and religious position allowed. He respected Reuchlin, Erasmus, Crotus, Mutian, Pirkheimer, Hutten, and the other humanists, for their learning and opposition to monkery and priestcraft; he fully shared the patriotic indignation against Romish tyranny: but he missed in them moral earnestness, religious depth, and that enthusiasm for the pure gospel which was his controlling passion. He aimed at reformation, they at illumination. He did not relish the frivolous satire of the *Epistolæ obscurorum virorum;* he called them silly, and the author a *Hans Wurst* (Jack Sausage); he would grow indignant, and weep rather than laugh, over the obscurantism and secret vices of the monks, though he had as keen a sense of the ridiculous as Crotus and Hutten. He deprecated, moreover, the resort to physical force in a spiritual warfare, and relied on the power of the Word of God, which had founded the Church, and which must reform the Church. His letters to Hutten are lost, but he wrote to Spalatin (Jan. 16, 1521): "You see what Hutten wants. I would not have the gospel defended by violence and murder. In this sense I wrote to him. By the Word the world was conquered; by

welcher selbst des unerbittlichsten Sittenrichters Strenge in Mitleid verwandeln muss. . . . Man weiss nicht was schrecklicher ist, die Beschreibung die uns Hutten von seinem Zustande, oder die er uns von den Quälereien macht, welche von unverständigen Aerzten als Curen über ihn verhängt wurden."

the Word the Church was preserved; by the Word she will be restored. Antichrist, as he began without violence, will be crushed without violence, by the Word."

Hutten was impatient. He urged matters to a crisis. Sickingen attacked the Archbishop and Elector of Trier (Treves) to force the Reformation into his territory; but he was defeated, and died of his wounds in the hands of his enemies, May 7, 1522. Within one month all his castles were captured and mostly burnt by the allied princes; two of his sons were banished, a third was made prisoner. Luther saw in this disaster a judgment of God, and was confirmed in his aversion to the use of force.[1]

Hutten fled, a poor and sick exile, from Germany to Basel, and hoped to find a hospitable reception by Erasmus, his former friend and admirer; but he was coldly refused by the cautious scholar, and took bitter revenge in an unsparing attack on his character. He then went to Zürich, and was kindly and generously treated by Zwingli, who provided him with books and money, and sent him first to the hot bath of Pfeffers, and then to a quiet retreat on the island of Ufnau in the Lake of Zürich, under medical care. But he soon died there, of the incurable disease of his youth, in August, 1523, in the prime of life (thirty-five years and four months of age), leaving nothing but his pen and sword, and the lesson: "Not by might, nor by power, but by my Spirit, saith the Lord of hosts" (Zech. 4: 6).

With Hutten and Sickingen the hope of a political reconstruction of Germany through means of the Reformation and physical force was destroyed. What the knights failed to accomplish, the peasants could still less secure by the general revolt two years later. But notwithstanding these checks, the Reformation was bound to succeed with spiritual weapons.

[1] E. Münch, *Fr. v. Sickingen*. Stuttgart, 1827 sqq. 3 vols. Strauss, *l.c.* p. 488. Ullmann, *Franz v. Sickingen*, Leipzig, 1872.

§ 43. *Luther's Crusade against Popery. 1520.*

After the disputation at Leipzig, Luther lost all hope of a reformation from Rome, which was preparing a bull of excommunication.

Here begins his storm and pressure period,[1] which culminated in the burning of the Pope's bull, and the protest at the Diet of Worms.

Under severe mental anguish he was driven to the conviction that the papacy, as it existed in his day, was an antichristian power, and the chief source and support of abuses in the Church. Prierias, Eck, Emser, and Alveld defended the most extravagant claims of the papacy with much learning, but without any discrimination between fact and fiction. Luther learned from the book of Laurentius Valla, as republished by Ulrich von Hutten, that the Donation of Constantine, by which this emperor conferred on Pope Sylvester and his successors the temporal sovereignty not only over the Lateran Palace, but also over Rome, Italy, and all the West, was a baseless forgery of the dark ages. He saw through the "devilish lies," as he called them, of the canon law and the pseudo-Isidorian Decretals. "It must have been a plague sent by God," he says (in his "Address to the German Nobility"), "that induced so many people to accept such lies, though they are so gross and clumsy that one would think a drunken boor could lie more skillfully." Genuine Catholic scholars of a later period have exposed with irrefragable arguments this falsification of history. His view of the Church expanded beyond the limits of the papacy, and took in the Oriental Christians, and even such men as Hus, who was burned by an œcumenical council for doctrines derived from St. Paul and St. Augustin. Instead of confining the Church, like the Romanists, to an external visible communion under the Pope, he regarded it now as a spiritual communion

---

[1] *Sturm- und Drangperiode* is an expressive German phrase.

of all believers under Christ the only Head. All the powers of indignation and hatred of Roman oppression and corruption gathered in his breast. " I can hardly doubt," he wrote to Spalatin, Feb. 23, 1520, "that the Pope is the Antichrist." In the same year, Oct. 11, he went so far as to write to Leo X. that the papal dignity was fit only for traitors like Judas Iscariot whom God had cast out.[1]

Luther was much confirmed in his new convictions by Melanchthon, who had independently by calm study arrived at the same conclusion. In the controversy with Eck, August, 1519, Melanchthon laid down the far-reaching principle that the Scriptures are the supreme rule of faith, and that we must not explain the Scriptures by the Fathers, but explain and judge the Fathers by the Scriptures. He discovered that even Ambrose, Jerome, and Augustin had often erred in their exegesis. A little later (September, 1519), he raised the same charge against the councils, and maintained that a Catholic Christian could not be required to believe any thing that was not warranted by the Scriptures. He expressed doubts about transubstantiation and the whole fabric of the mass. His estimate of the supreme value of the Scriptures, especially of Paul, rose higher and higher, and made him stronger and bolder in the conflict with mediæval tradition.

Thus fortified by the learning of Melanchthon, encouraged by the patriotic zeal of Hutten and Sickingen, goaded by the fury of his enemies, and impelled, as it were, by a preternatural impulse, Luther attacked the papal power as the very stronghold of Satan. Without personal ill-will against anybody, he had a burning indignation against the system, and

---

[1] In the midst of a Latin letter to Spalatin, from the beginning of June, 1520 (De Wette, I. 453), he gives vent to his wrath against popery in these German words: "*Ich meine, sie sind zu Rom alle toll, thöricht, wüthend, unsinnig, Narren, Stock, Stein, Hölle, und Teufel geworden.*" In the same letter he mentions his intention to publish a book "*ad Carolum et totius Germaniæ nobilitatem adversus Romanæ curiæ tyrannidem et nequitiam.*"

transcended all bounds of moderation.[1] He felt the inspiration of a prophet, and had the courage of a martyr ready to
die at any moment for his conviction.

He issued in rapid succession from July till October, 1520,
his three most effective reformatory works: the "Address to
the German Nobility," the "Babylonian Captivity of the
Church," and the "Freedom of a Christian Man."[2] The first
two are trumpets of war, and the hardest blows ever dealt
by human pen to the system of popery; while the third
is peaceful, and shines like a rainbow above the thunder-
clouds. A strange contrast! Luther was the most conservative of radicals, and the most radical of conservatives. He
had all the violence of a revolutionary orator, and at the
same time the pious spirit of a contemplative mystic.

The sixteenth century was the age of practical soteriology.
It had to settle the relation of man to God, to bring the believer into direct communion with Christ, and to secure to
him the personal benefits of the gospel salvation. What was
heretofore regarded as the exclusive privilege of the priest
was to become the common privilege of every Christian. To
this end, it was necessary to break down the walls which
separated the clergy from the laity, and obstructed the
approach to God. This was most effectually done by Luther's
anti-papal writings. On the relation of man to God rests the
relation of man to his fellow-men; this is the sociological
problem which forms one of the great tasks of the nineteenth
century.

[1] See the remarkable passage in his letter to Conrad Pellicanus, January
or February, 1521 (De Wette, I. 555): "*Recte mones modestiæ me: sentio et
ipse, sed compos mei non sum; rapior nescio quo spiritu, cum nemini me
male velle conscius sim: verum urgent etiam illi furiosissime, ut Satanam
non satis observem.*"

[2] L. Lemme: *Die drei grossen Reformationsschriften Luthers vom Jahre
1520.* Gotha, 1875, 2d ed., 1884. WACE and BUCHHEIM: *First Principles
of the Reformation,* London, 1883.

§ 44. *Address to the German Nobility.*

An den christlichen Adel deutscher Nation: von des christlichen Standes Besserung.   In Walch's ed., X. 296 sqq.; Erl. ed., XXI. 274–360; Weimar ed., VI. 404. Köstlin (in his shorter biography of Luther, p. 197 New-York ed.) gives a facsimile of the title-page of the second edition.   Dr. Karl Benrath of Bonn published a separate ed., with introduction and notes, as No. 4 of the "Schriften des Vereins für Reformationsgeschichte," Halle, 1886 (114 pages).

"The time for silence is gone, and the time for speaking has come." With these words (based on Eccles. 3 : 7) of the dedicatory preface to Amsdorf, Luther introduces his address "to his most Serene and Mighty Imperial Majesty, and to the Christian Nobility of the German Nation, respecting a Reformation of the Christian Estate." The preface is dated on the Eve of St. John the Baptist (June 23), 1520 ; the book was hastily completed July 20,[1] and before Aug. 18 no less than four thousand copies — an enormous number for those days — were published, and a new edition called for, besides reprints which soon appeared in Leipzig and Strassburg.

The book is a most stirring appeal to the German nobles, who, through Hutten and Sickingen, had recently offered their armed assistance to Luther. He calls upon them to take the much-needed Reformation of the Church into their own hands; not, indeed, by force of arms, but by legal means, in the fear of God, and in reliance upon his strength. The bishops and clergy refused to do their duty; hence the laity must come to the front of the battle for the purity and liberty of the Church.

Luther exposes without mercy the tyranny of the Pope, whose government, he says, "agrees with the government of the apostles as well as Lucifer with Christ, hell with heaven,

---

[1] On that date he informed Wencislaus Link: "*Editur noster libellus in Papam de reformanda ecclesia vernaculus, ad universam nobilitatem Germaniæ, qui summe offensurus est Romam. . . . Vale, et ora pro me.*" De Wette, I. 470.

night with day; and yet he calls himself Christ's Vicar, and the Successor of Peter."

The book is divided into three parts: —

1. In the first part, Luther pulls down what he calls the three walls of Jericho, which the papacy had erected in self-defense against any reformation; namely, the exclusion of the laity from all control, the exclusive claim to interpret the Scriptures, and the exclusive claim to call a Council.

Under the first head, he brings out clearly and strongly, in opposition to priestcraft, the fundamental Protestant principle of the general priesthood of all baptized Christians. He attacks the distinction of two estates, one spiritual, consisting of Pope, bishops, priests, and monks; and one temporal, consisting of princes, lords, artificers, and peasants. There is only one body, under Christ the Head. All Christians belong to the spiritual estate. Baptism, gospel and faith, — these alone make spiritual and Christian people.[1] We are consecrated priests by baptism; we are a royal priesthood, kings and priests before God (1 Pet. 2: 9; Rev. 5: 10). The only difference, then, between clergy and laity, is one of office and function, not of estate.

Luther represents here the ministerial office as the creature of the congregation; while at a later period, warned by democratic excesses, and the unfitness of most of the congregations of that age for a popular form of government, he laid greater stress upon the importance of the ministry as an institution of Christ. This idea of the general priesthood necessarily led to the emancipation of the laity from priestly control, and their participation in the affairs of the Church, although this has been but very imperfectly carried out in Protestant state churches. It destroyed the distinction between higher (clerical and monastic), and lower morality; it gave sanctity to the natural relations, duties, and

---

[1] " *Was aus der Taufe gekrochen ist, das mag sich rühmen, dass es schon Priester, Bischof, und Papst geweihet sei.*"

virtues; it elevated the family as equal in dignity to virginity; it promoted general intelligence, and sharpened the sense of individual responsibility to the Church. But to the same source may be traced also the undue interference of kings, princes, and magistrates in ecclesiastical matters, and that degrading dependence of many Protestant establishments upon the secular power. Kingcraft and priestcraft are two opposite extremes, equally opposed to the spirit of Christianity. Luther, and especially Melanchthon, bitterly complained, in their later years, of the abuse of the episcopal power assumed by the magistrate, and the avarice of princes in the misappropriation of ecclesiastical property.

The principle of the general priesthood of the laity found its political and civil counterpart in the American principle of the general kingship of men, as expressed in the Declaration of Independence, that "all men are born free and equal."

2. In the second part, Luther chastises the worldly pomp of the Pope and the cardinals, their insatiable greed, and exactions under false pretenses.

3. In the third part, he deals with practical suggestions. He urges sweeping reforms in twenty-seven articles, to be effected either by the civil magistrate, or by a general council of ministers and laymen.

He recommends the abolition of the *annates*, of the worldly pomp and idolatrous homage paid to the Pope (as kissing his feet), and of his whole temporal power, so that he should be hereafter merely a spiritual ruler, with no power over the emperor except to anoint and crown him, as a bishop crowns a king, as Samuel crowned Saul and David.

He strongly demands the abrogation of enforced clerical celibacy, which destroys instead of promoting chastity, and is the cause of untold misery. Clergymen should be allowed to marry, or not to marry, according to their gift and sense of duty.

Masses for the dead should be abolished, since they have become a solemn mockery, and devices for getting money, thus exciting the anger of God.

Processions, saints' days, and most of the public festivals, except Sunday, should be abrogated, since holy days have become most unholy by drinking, gambling, and idling.

Monasteries should be reduced in number, and converted into schools, with freedom to enter and to leave without binding vows.

Certain punishments of the canon law should cease, especially the interdict which silences God's word and service, — a greater sin than to kill twenty Popes at once.

Fasts should be voluntary and optional; for whilst at Rome they laugh at fasts, they let us abroad eat oil which they would not think fit for greasing their boots, and then sell us the liberty of eating butter and other things; whereas the apostle says that the gospel has given us liberty in all such matters (1 Cor. 10: 25 sq.).

He also would forbid all begging in Christendom; each town should support its own poor, and not allow strange beggars to come in, whether pilgrims or mendicant monks; it is not right that one should work that another may be idle, and live ill that another may live well, but "if any would not work, neither should he eat" (2 Thess. 3: 10).

He counsels a reduction of the clerical force, and the prohibition of pluralities. "As for the fraternities, together with indulgences, letters of indulgence, dispensations, masses, and all such things, let them all be drowned and abolished."

He recommends (Art. 24) to do justice to, and make peace with, the Bohemians; for Hus and Jerome of Prague were unjustly burnt, in violation of the safe-conduct promised by the Pope and the Emperor. Heretics should be overcome with books, not with fire; else "the hangmen would be the most learned doctors in the world, and there would be no need of study."

In Art. 25, Luther urges a sound reformation of the universities, which had become "schools of Greek fashion" and
"heathenish manners" (2 Macc. 4: 12, 13), and are "full
of dissolute living." He is unjustly severe upon Aristotle,
whom he calls a "dead, blind, accursed, proud, knavish heathen teacher." His logic, rhetoric, and poetic might be
retained; but his physics, metaphysics, ethics, and the book
"Of the Soul" (which teaches that the soul dies with the
body) ought to be banished, and the study of the languages,
mathematics, history, and especially of the Holy Scriptures,
cultivated instead. "Nothing is more devilishly mischievous," he says, "than an unreformed university." He would
also have the canon law banished, of which there is "nothing good but the name," and which is no better than
"waste paper."

He does not spare national vices. He justly rebukes the
extravagance in dress, the usury, and especially the intemperance in eating and drinking, for which, he says, "we Germans
have an ill reputation in foreign countries, as our special vice,
and which has become so common, and gained so much the
upper hand, that sermons avail nothing." (His frequent protest against the "*Saufteufel*" of the Germans, as he calls their
love of drink, is still unheeded. In temperance the Southern nations of Europe are far ahead of those of the North.)

In conclusion, he expresses the expectation that he will be
condemned upon earth. "My greatest care and fear is, lest
my cause be not condemned by men; by which I should
know for certain that it does not please God. Therefore let
them freely go to work, Pope, bishop, priest, monk, or doctor: they are the true people to persecute the truth, as they
have always done. May God grant us all a Christian understanding, and especially to the Christian nobility of the German nation true spiritual courage, to do what is best for our
unhappy Church. Amen."

The book was a firebrand thrown into the headquarters of

the papal church. It anticipated a reply to the papal bull,
and prepared the public mind for it. It went right to the
heart of the Germans, in their own language wielded with
a force as never before, and gave increased weight to the
hundred grievances of long standing against Rome. But
it alarmed some of his best friends. They condemned or
regretted his biting severity.[1] Staupitz tried at the eleventh
hour to prevent the publication, and soon afterwards (Aug.
23, 1520) resigned his position as general vicar of the Augustinians, and retired to Salzburg, feeling himself unequal
to the conflict. John Lange called the book a "blast for
assault, atrocious and ferocious." Some feared that it might
lead to a religious war. Melanchthon could not approve the
violence, but dared not to check the spirit of the new Elijah.
Luther defended himself by referring to the example of Paul
and the prophets: it was necessary to be severe in order to
get a hearing; he felt sure that he was not moved by desire
for glory or money or pleasure, and disclaimed the intention
of stirring up sedition and war; he only wished to clear the
way for a free general council; he was perhaps the forerunner of Master Philippus in fighting Ahab and the prophets
of Baal after the example of Elijah (1 Kings 18).[2]

NOTES.

The following extracts give a fair idea of Luther's polemic against the
Pope in this remarkable book: —

"The custom of kissing the Pope's feet must cease. It is an un-Chris-
tian, or rather an anti-Christian example, that a poor sinful man should suffer his feet to be kissed by one who is a hundred times better than he. If it
is done in honor of his power, why does he not do it to others in honor
of their holiness? Compare them together: Christ and the Pope. Christ
washed his disciples' feet, and dried them, and the disciples never washed
his. The Pope, pretending to be higher than Christ, inverts this, and considers it a great favor to let us kiss his feet: whereas if any one wished to

---

[1] "*Omnes ferme [fere] in me damnant mordacitatem,*" he says in letter
to Link, Aug. 19, 1520.

[2] See his letters to John Lange (Aug. 18, 1520) and to Wenceslaus Link
(Aug. 19) in De Wette, I. 477–479.

do so, he ought to do his utmost to prevent them, as St. Paul and Barnabas would not suffer themselves to be worshiped as gods by the men at Lystra, saying, 'We also are men of like passions with you' (Acts 14:14 seq.). But our flatterers have brought things to such a pitch, that they have set up an idol for us, until no one regards God with such fear, or honors him with such reverence, as they do the Pope. This they can suffer, but not that the Pope's glory should be diminished a single hair's-breadth. Now, if they were Christians, and preferred God's honor to their own, the Pope would never be willing to have God's honor despised, and his own exalted; nor would he allow any to honor him, until he found that God's honor was again exalted above his own.

"It is of a piece with this revolting pride, that the Pope is not satisfied with riding on horseback or in a carriage, but, though he be hale and strong, is carried by men like an idol in unheard-of pomp. I ask you, how does this Lucifer-like pride agree with the example of Christ, who went on foot, as did also all his apostles? Where has there been a king who lived in such worldly pomp as he does, who professes to be the head of all whose duty it is to despise and flee from all worldly pomp — I mean, of all Christians? Not that this need concern us for his own sake, but that we have good reason to fear God's wrath, if we flatter such pride, and do not show our discontent. It is enough that the Pope should be so mad and foolish, but it is too much that we should sanction and approve it."

After enumerating all the abuses to which the Pope and his canon law give sanction, and which he upholds with his usurped authority, Luther addresses him in this impassioned style: —

"Dost thou hear this, O Pope! not the most holy, but the most sinful? Would that God would hurl thy chair headlong from heaven, and cast it down into the abyss of hell! Who gave you the power to exalt yourself above God? to break and to loose what he has commanded? to teach Christians, more especially Germans, who are of noble nature, and are famed in all histories for uprightness and truth, to be false, unfaithful, perjured, treacherous, and wicked? God has commanded to keep faith and observe oaths even with enemies: you dare to cancel his command, laying it down in your heretical, antichristian decretals, that you have power to do so; and through your mouth and your pen Satan lies as he never lied before, teaching you to twist and pervert the Scriptures according to your own arbitrary will. O Lord Christ! look down upon this, let thy day of judgment come and destroy the Devil's lair at Rome. Behold him of whom St. Paul spoke (2 Thess. 2:3, 4), that he should exalt himself above thee, and sit in thy Church, showing himself as God — the man of sin and the child of damnation. . . . The Pope treads God's commandments under foot, and exalts his own: if this is not Antichrist, I do not know what it is."

Janssen (II. 100) calls Luther's "Address to the German Nobility" "*das eigentliche Kriegsmanifest der Lutherisch-Huttenschen Revolutionspartei,*"

and " *ein Signal zum gewaltsamen Angriff.*" But the book nowhere counsels war; and in the letter to Link he says expressly: "*nec hoc a me agitur,
ut seditionem moveam, sed ut concilio generali libertatem asseram*" (De
Wette, I. 479). Janssen quotes (p. 103) a very vehement passage from
Luther's contemporaneous postscript to a book of Prierias which he republished (*De juridica et irrefragabili veritate Romanæ Ecclesiæ Romanique
Pontificis*), expressing a wish that the Emperor, kings, and princes would
make a bloody end to Pope and cardinals and the whole rabble of the Romish
Sodom. But this extreme and isolated passage is set aside by his repeated
declarations against carnal warfare, and was provoked by the astounding
assertions of Prierias, the master of the papal palace, that the Pope was the
infallible judge of all controversies, the head of all spiritual, the father of all
secular princes, the head of the Church and of the whole universe (*caput
totius orbis universi*). Against such blasphemy Luther breaks out in these
words: "*Mihi vero videtur, si sic pergat furor Romanistarum, nullum
reliquum esse remedium, quam ut imperator, reges et principes vi et armis
accincti aggrediantur has pestes orbis terrarum, remque non jam verbis, sed
ferro decernant. . . . Si fures furca, si latrones gladio, si hæreticos igne
plectimus, cur non magis hos magistros perditionis, hos cardinales, hos papas
et totam istam romanæ Sodomæ colluviem, quæ ecclesiam Dei sine fine cor-
rumpit, omnibus armis impetimus, et manus nostras in sanguine eorum lava-
mus? tanquam a communi et omnium periculosissimo incendio nos nostrosque
liberaturi.*" Erl. ed., *Opera Latina*, II. 107. He means a *national* resistance
under the guidance of the Emperor and rightful rulers.

§ 45. *The Babylonian Captivity of the Church. October, 1520.*

De Captivitate Babylonica Ecclesiæ Prœludium D. Martini Lutheri. Wittenb. 1520. Erl. ed. *Opera Lat.*, vol. V. 13–118; German translation
(*Von der Babylonischen Gefängniss*, etc.) by an unknown author, 1520,
reprinted in WALCH, XIX. 5–153, and in O. v. GERLACH, IV. 65–199;
the Lat. original again in the Weimar ed., vol. V. An English translation by BUCHHEIM in *First Principles of the Reformation* (London,
1883), pp. 141–245.

In closing the "Address to the Nobility," Luther announces: "I have another song still to sing concerning
Rome. If they wish to hear it, I will sing it to them, and
sing with all my might. Do you understand, my friend
Rome, what I mean?"

This new song, or second war-trumpet, was the book on the
"Babylonian Captivity of the Church," published in the be-

ginning of October, 1520.[1] He calls it a "prelude," as if the
real battle were yet to come. He intended it for scholars and
the clergy, and therefore wrote in Latin. It is a polemical,
theological work of far-reaching consequences, cutting one of
the roots of Romanism, and looking towards a new type
of Christian life and worship. He attacks the sacramental
system of the Roman Church, by which she accompanies and
controls the life of the Christian from the cradle to the grave,
and brings every important act and event under the power
of the priest. This system he represents as a captivity, and
Rome as the modern Babylon. Yet he was very far from
undervaluing the importance and benefit of the sacrament;
and as far as the doctrine of baptism and the eucharist is
concerned, he agreed better with the Catholic than with the
Zwinglian view.

Luther begins by thanking his Romish opponents for
promoting his theological education. "Two years ago," he
says, "I wrote about indulgences when I was still involved
in superstitious respect for the tyranny of Rome; but now I
have learned, by the kind aid of Prierias and the friars, that
indulgences are nothing but wicked devices of the flatterers
of Rome. Afterwards Eck and Emser instructed me concerning the primacy of the Pope. While I denied the divine
right, I still admitted the human right; but after reading
the super-subtle subtilties of those coxcombs in defense of
their idol, I became convinced that the papacy is the kingdom
of Babylon and the power of Nimrod the mighty hunter.
Now a learned professor of Leipzig writes against me on the
sacrament in both kinds, and is about to do still greater wonders.[2] He says that it was neither commanded nor decreed,
whether by Christ or the apostles, that both kinds should
be administered to the laity."

---

[1] On Oct. 3, 1520, Luther wrote to Spalatin: "*Liber de captivitate Ecclesiæ sabbato exibit, et ad te mittetur.*" (De Wette, I. 491.)

[2] He means Alveld's *Tractatus de communione sub utraque specie quantum ad laicos*, 1520. He contemptuously omits his name.

1. Luther first discusses the sacrament of the *Holy Communion*, and opposes three errors as a threefold bondage; namely, the withdrawal of the cup from the laity, the doctrine of transubstantiation, and the sacrifice of the mass.

(*a*) As regards the *withdrawal of the cup*, he refutes the flimsy arguments of Alveld, and proves from the accounts of Matthew, Mark, Luke, and Paul, that the *whole* sacrament was intended for the laity as well as the clergy, according to the command, "Drink ye *all* of this." Each writer attaches the mark of universality to the cup, not to the bread, as if the Spirit foresaw the (Bohemian) schism. The blood of Christ was shed for all for the remission of sins. If the laymen have the thing, why should they be refused the sign which is much less than the thing itself? The Church has no more right to take away the cup from the laity than the bread. The Romanists are the heretics and schismatics in this case, and not the Bohemians and the Greeks who take their stand on the manifest teaching of the Word of God. "I conclude, then, that to deny reception in both kinds to the laity is an act of impiety and tyranny, and one not in the power of any angel, much less of any Pope or council whatsoever." . . . "The sacrament does not belong to the priests, but to all; nor are the priests lords, but servants, whose duty it is to give both kinds to those who seek them, as often as they seek them." . . . "Since the Bishop of Rome has ceased to be a bishop, and has become a tyrant, I fear absolutely none of his decrees; for I know that neither he, nor even a general council, has authority to establish new articles of faith."

(*b*) The doctrine of *transubstantiation* is a milder bondage, and might be held alongside with the other and more natural view of the real presence, which leaves the elements unchanged. It is well known that Luther was to the end of life a firm believer in the real presence, and oral manducation of the very body and blood of Christ by unworthy as well as worthy communicants (of course, with opposite effects). He denied a miraculous change of the substance of the elements, but maintained the co-existence of the body and blood in, with, and under bread and wine, both being real, the one invisible and the other visible.[1] In this book he claims toleration for both theories, with a personal preference for the latter. "Christians are at liberty, without peril to their salvation, to imagine, think, or believe in either of the two ways, since here there is no necessity of faith." . . . "I will not listen to those, or make the slightest account of them, who will cry out that this doctrine is Wiclifite, Hussite, heretical, and opposed to the decisions of the Church." The Scripture does not say that the elements are transubstantiated: Paul calls them real bread and real wine, just as the cup was real. Moreover, Christ speaks (figuratively), "This *cup* is the new covenant in my blood," meaning his blood contained in the cup. Transubstantiation is a scholastic or Aristotelian figment of the twelfth century.[2] "Why should Christ not be able to include his body within the substance of bread, as well as within the accidents? Fire and iron, two different substances, are so mingled in red-hot iron, that in every part of it are both fire and iron. Why may not the glorious body of Christ much more be in every part of the substance of the bread?" Common people do not understand the difference between substance and accidents, nor argue about it, but "believe with simple faith that the body and blood of Christ are truly contained in the elements." So also the incarnation does not require a transubstantiation of the human nature, that so the Godhead may be contained beneath the accidents of the human nature; "but each nature is entire,

---

[1] This view is usually called *consubstantiation;* but Lutherans object to the term in the sense of *impanation,* or local inclusion, mixture, and circumscription. They mean an illocal presence of a ubiquitous body.

[2] This is not strictly historical. Transubstantiation was clearly taught by Paschasius Radbertus in the ninth century, though not without contradiction from Ratramnus. See Schaff, *Ch. Hist.*, vol. IV. 544 sqq.

and we can say with truth, This man is God; this God is man."

(c) The *sacrifice of the mass:* that is, the offering to God of the very body and blood of Christ by the hands of the priest when he pronounces the words of institution ; in other words, an actual repetition of the atoning sacrifice of the cross, only in an unbloody manner. This institution is the very heart of Roman-Catholic (and Greek-Catholic) worship. Luther attacks it as the third bondage, and the most impious of all. He feels the difficulty, and perhaps impossibility, of a task which involves an entire revolution of public worship. "At this day," he says, "there is no belief in the Church more generally received, or more firmly held, than that the mass is a good work and a sacrifice. This abuse has brought in an infinite flood of other abuses, until faith in the sacrament has been utterly lost, and they have made this divine sacrament a mere subject of traffic, huckstering, and money-getting contracts; and the entire maintenance of priests and monks depends upon these things." He goes back to the simplicity of the primitive institution of the Lord's Supper, which is a thankful commemoration of the atoning death of Christ, with a blessing attached to it, namely, the forgiveness of sins, to be appropriated by faith. The substance of this sacrament is promise and faith. It is a gift of God to man, not a gift of man to God. It is, like baptism, to be received, and not to be given. The Romanists have changed it into a good work of man and an *opus operatum,* by which they imagine to please God; and have surrounded it with so many prayers, signs, vestments, gestures, and ceremonies, that the original meaning is obscured. "They make God no longer the bestower of good gifts on us, but the receiver of ours. Alas for such impiety!" He proves from the ancient Church that the offering of the eucharist, as the name indicates, was originally a thank-offering of the gifts of the communicants for the benefit of the poor. The true sacrifice which we are to offer to God is our thanks, our possessions, and our whole person. He also objects to the use of the Latin language in the mass, and demands the vernacular.

2. The sacrament of *Baptism*. Luther thanks God that this sacrament has been preserved uninjured, and kept from "the foul and impious monstrosities of avarice and superstition." He agrees essentially with the Roman doctrine, and considers baptism as a means of regeneration; while Zwingli and Calvin regarded it merely as a sign and seal of preceding regeneration and church-membership. He even makes more of it than the Romanists, and opposes the prevailing view of St. Jerome, that penitence is a second plank of refuge after shipwreck. Instead of relying on priestly absolution, it is better to go back to the remission of sins secured in baptism. "When we rise out of our sins, and exercise penitence, we are simply reverting to the efficacy of baptism and to faith in it, whence we had fallen; and we return to the promise then made to us, but which we had abandoned through our sin. For the truth of the promise once made always abides, and is ready to stretch out the hand and receive us when we return."

As to the *mode* of baptism, he gives here, as elsewhere, his preference to immersion, which then still prevailed in England and in some parts of the Continent, and which was not a point of dispute either between Romanists and Protestants, or between Protestants and Anabaptists; while on the question of *infant*-baptism the Anabaptists differed from both. "Baptism," he says, "is that dipping into water whence it takes its name. For, in Greek to baptize signifies to dip, and baptism is a dipping." "Baptism signifies two things, — death and resurrection; that is, full and complete justification. When the minister dips the child into the water, this signifies death; when he draws him out again, this signifies life. Thus Paul explains the matter (Rom. 6:4). . . . I could wish that the baptized should be totally immersed, according to the meaning of the word and the signification of the mystery; not that I think it necessary to do so, but that it would be well that so complete and perfect a thing as baptism should also be completely and perfectly expressed in the sign."

Luther's view of baptismal regeneration seems to be inconsistent with his chief doctrine of justification by faith alone. He says, " It is not baptism which justifies any man, or is of any advantage; but faith in that word of promise to which baptism is added: for this justifies and fulfills the meaning of baptism. For faith is the submerging of the old man, and the emerging of the new man." But how does this apply to baptized infants, who can not be said to have faith in any proper sense of the term, though they have undoubtedly the capacity of faith? Luther here brings in the vicarious faith of the parents or the Church. But he suggests also the idea that faith is produced in the children, through baptism, on the ground of their religious receptivity.

3. Lastly, Luther attacks the traditional *number* of the sacraments. He allows " only two sacraments in the Church of God, Baptism and Bread; since it is in these alone that we see both a sign divinely instituted, and a promise of remission of sins." In some sense he retains also the sacrament of Penance, as a way and means of return to baptism.

The rest of the seven Roman sacraments — confirmation, marriage, ordination, and extreme unction — he rejects because they can not be proved from Scripture, and are not commanded by Christ.

Matrimony has existed from the beginning of the world, and belongs to all mankind. Why, then, should it be called a sacrament? Paul calls it a " mystery," but not a sacrament, as translated in the Vulgate (Ep. 5: 32); or rather he speaks there of the union of Christ and the Church, which is reflected in matrimony as in a sort of allegory. But the Pope has restricted this universal human institution by rigorous impediments derived from spiritual affinity and legal relationship. He forbids it to the clergy, and claims the power to annull rightful marriages, even against the will of one of the parties. "Learn, then, in this one matter of matrimony, into what an unhappy and hopeless state of confusion, hindrance, entanglement, and peril all things that are done in the Church have been brought by the pestilent and impious traditions of men! There is no hope of a remedy, unless we do away with all the laws of men, call back the gospel of liberty, and judge and rule all things according to it alone."

Luther closes with these words: "I hear a report that fresh bulls and papal curses are being prepared against me, by which I am urged to recant, or else to be declared a heretic. If this is true, I wish this little book to be a part of my future recantation, that they may not complain that their tyranny has puffed itself up in vain. I shall also shortly publish, Christ being my helper, such a recantation as the See of Rome has never yet seen or heard, thus abundantly testifying my obedience in the name of our Lord Jesus Christ.[1] Amen.

> " ' *Hostis Herodes impie,*
> *Christum venire quid times?*
> *Non arripit mortalia*
> *Qui regna dat cœlestia.*' "

§ 46. *Christian Freedom. — Luther's Last Letter to the Pope. October, 1520.*

Von der Freiheit eines Christenmenschen, Wittenberg, 1520; often reprinted separately, and in the collected works of Luther. See WALCH, XIX. 1206 sqq.; Erl. ed., XXVII. 173–200 (from the first ed.); Gerlach's ed. V. 5–46. The Latin edition, *De Libertate Christiana*, was finished a little later, and has some additions; see Erl. ed. *Opera Lat.*, IV. 206–255. Luther's letter to the Pope in Latin and German is printed also in DE WETTE, I. 497–515. English version of the tract and the letter by BUCHHEIM, *l. c.* 95–137.

---

[1] Perhaps he means the burning of the Pope's bull, rather than, as O. v. Gerlach conjectures, the appendix to his later book against Ambrosius Catharinus, in which he tries to prove that the Pope is the Antichrist predicted by Dan. viii. 23–25.

Although Rome had already condemned Luther, the papal delegate Miltitz still entertained the hope of a peaceful settlement. He had extracted from Luther the promise to write to the Pope. He had a final interview with him and Melanchthon at Lichtenberg (now Lichtenburg, in the district of Torgau), in the convent of St. Antony, Oct. 11, 1520, a few days after Luther had seen the bull of excommunication. It was agreed that Luther should write a book, and a letter in Latin and German to Leo X., and assure him that he had never attacked his person, and that Dr. Eck was responsible for the whole trouble. The book was to be finished in twelve days, but dated back to Sept. 6 in order to avoid the appearance of being occasioned by the Pope's bull.

This is the origin of two of the most remarkable productions of Luther, — his little book on "Christian Freedom," and a dedicatory letter to Leo X.

The beautiful tract on "Christian Freedom" is a pearl among Luther's writings. It presents a striking contrast to his polemic treatises against Rome, which were intended to break down the tyranny of popery. And yet it is a positive complement to them, and quite as necessary for a full understanding of his position. While opposing the Pope's tyranny, Luther was far from advocating the opposite extreme of license. He was thoroughly imbued with the spirit of the Epistle to the Galatians, which protests against both extremes, and inspired the keynote to Luther's tract. He shows wherein true liberty consists. He means liberty according to the gospel; liberty *in* Christ, not *from* Christ; and offers this as a basis for reconciliation. He presents here a popular summary of Christian life. He keeps free from all polemics, and writes in the best spirit of that practical mysticism which connected him with Staupitz and Tauler.

The leading idea is: The Christian is the lord of all, and subject to none, by virtue of faith; he is the servant of all, and subject to every one, by virtue of love. Faith and love constitute the Christian: the one binds him to God, the other to his fellow-man. The idea is derived from St. Paul, who says, "Though I was free from all men, I brought myself under bondage to all, that I might gain the more" (1 Cor. 9:19); and "Owe no man any thing, save to love one another" (Rom. 13:8). It was carried out by Christ, who was Lord of all things, yet born of a woman, born under the law that he might redeem them who were under the law (Gal. 4:4); who was at once in the form of God, and in the form of a servant (Phil. 2:6, 7). The Christian life is an imitation of the life of Christ, — a favorite idea of the mediæval mystics.

Man is made free by faith, which alone justifies; but it manifests itself in love, and all good works. The person must first be good before good works can be done, and good works proceed from a good person; as Christ says, "A good tree cannot bring forth evil fruit, neither can a corrupt tree bring forth good fruit" (Matt. 7:18). The fruit does not bear the tree, nor does the tree grow on the fruit; but the tree bears the fruit, and the fruit grows on the tree. So it is in all handicrafts. A good or bad house does not make a good or bad builder, but the good or bad builder makes a good or bad house. Such is the case with the works of men. Such as the man himself is, whether in faith or in unbelief, such is his work; good if it is done in faith, bad if in unbelief. Faith, as it makes man a believer, so also it makes his works good; but works do not make a believing man, nor a justified man. We do not reject works; nay, we commend them, and teach them in the highest degree. It is not on their own account that we condemn them, but on account of the perverse notion of seeking justification by them. "From faith flow forth love and joy in the Lord; and from love, a cheerful, willing, free spirit, disposed to serve our neighbor voluntarily, without taking any account of gratitude or ingratitude, praise or blame, gain or loss. Its object is not to lay men under obligations; nor does it distinguish between friends and enemies, or look to gratitude or ingratitude; but most freely and willingly it spends itself and its goods, whether it loses them through ingratitude, or gains good-will. For thus did its Father, distributing all things to all men abundantly and freely, making his sun to rise upon the just and the unjust. Thus, too, the child does and endures nothing except from the free joy with which it delights through Christ in God, the giver of such great gifts." . . .

"Who, then, can comprehend the riches and glory of the Christian life? It can do all things, has all things, and is in want of nothing; is lord over sin, death, and hell, and, at the same time, is the obedient and useful servant of all. But alas! it is at this day unknown throughout the world; it is neither preached nor sought after, so that we are quite ignorant about our own name, why we are and are called Christians. We are certainly called so from Christ, who is not absent, but dwells among us, provided we believe in him; and are reciprocally and mutually one the Christ of the other, doing to our neighbor as Christ does to us. But now, in the doctrine of men, we are taught only to seek after merits, rewards, and things which are already ours; and we have made of Christ a task-master far more severe than Moses." . . .

"We conclude, then, that a Christian man does not live in and for himself, but in Christ and in his neighbor, or else is no Christian; in Christ by faith, in his neighbor by love. By faith he is carried upwards above himself to God, and by love he descends below himself to his neighbor, still always abiding in God and his love; as Christ says, 'Verily I say unto you, hereafter ye shall see the heaven opened, and the angels of God ascending and descending upon the Son of man'" (John 1:51).

In the Latin text Luther adds some excellent remarks against those who misunderstand and distort spiritual liberty, turn it into an occasion of carnal license, and show their freedom by their contempt of ceremonies, traditions, and human laws. St. Paul teaches us to walk in the middle path, condemning either extreme, and saying, " Let not him that eateth despise him that eateth not; and let not him that eateth not judge him that eateth " (Rom. 14: 3). We must resist the hardened and obstinate ceremonialists, as Paul resisted the Judaizers who would compel Titus to be circumcised; and we must spare the weak who are not yet able to apprehend the liberty of faith. We must fight against the wolves, but on behalf of the sheep, not against the sheep.

This *Irenicon* must meet with the approval of every true Christian, whether Catholic or Protestant. It breathes the spirit of a genuine disciple of St. Paul. It is full of heroic faith and childlike simplicity. It takes rank with the best books of Luther, and rises far above the angry controversies of his age, during which he composed it, in the full possession of the positive truth and peace of the religion of Christ.[1]

Luther sent the book to Pope Leo X., who was too worldly-minded a man to appreciate it; and accompanied the same with a most singular and undiplomatic, yet powerful polemic letter, which, if the Pope ever read it, must have filled him with mingled feelings of indignation and disgust. In his first letter to the Pope (1518), Luther had thrown himself at his feet as an obedient son of the vicar of Christ; in his

---

[1] Köstlin (*Mart. Luth.*, vol. I. 395 sq.): "*Die Schrift von der Freiheit eines Christenmenschen ist ein tief-religiöser Traktat. . . . Sie ist ein ruhiges, positives Zeugnis der Wahrheit, vor welcher die Waffen und Bande der Finsternis von selbst zu nichte werden müssen. Sie zeigt uns den tiefsten Grund des christlichen Bewusstseins und Lebens in einer edlen, seligen Ruhe und Sicherheit, welche die über ihm hingehenden Wogen und Stürme des Kampfes nicht zu erschüttern vermögen. Sie zeigt zugleich, wie fest Luther selbst auf diesem Grunde stand, indem er eben im Höhepunkt des Kampfgedränges sie zu verfassen fähig war.*" It is perhaps characteristic that Janssen, who gives one-sided extracts from the two other reformatory works of Luther, passes the tract on " Christian Liberty " in complete silence. Cardinal Hergenröther likewise ignores it.

second letter (1519), he still had addressed him as a humble
subject, yet refusing to recant his conscientious convictions:
in his third and last letter he addressed him as an equal,
speaking to him with great respect for his personal character
(even beyond his deserts), but denouncing in the severest
terms the Roman See, and comparing him to a lamb among
wolves, and to Daniel in the den of lions. The Popes, he
says, are vicars of Christ because Christ is absent from
Rome.[1] Miltitz and the Augustinian brethren, who urged
him to write an apologetic letter to Leo, must have been
sorely disappointed; for it destroyed all prospects of reconciliation, if they had not been destroyed already.

After some complimentary words about Leo, and protesting that he had never spoken disrespectfully of his person,
Luther goes on to say, —

"The Church of Rome, formerly the most holy of all churches, has
become the most lawless den of thieves, the most shameless of all brothels,
the very kingdom of sin, death, and hell; so that not even Antichrist, if he
were to come, could devise any addition to its wickedness.

"Meanwhile you, Leo, are sitting like a lamb in the midst of wolves, like
Daniel in the midst of lions, and, with Ezekiel, you dwell among scorpions.
What opposition can you alone make to these monstrous evils? Take to
yourself three or four of the most learned and best of the cardinals. What
are these among so many? You would all perish by poison, before you could
undertake to decide on a remedy. It is all over with the court of Rome: the
wrath of God has come upon her to the uttermost. She hates councils, she
dreads to be reformed, she cannot restrain the madness of her impiety; she fills
up the sentence passed on her mother, of whom it is said, 'We would have
healed Babylon, but she is not healed; let us forsake her.' It had been your
duty, and that of your cardinals, to apply a remedy to these evils; but this
gout laughs at the physician's hand, and the chariot does not obey the reins.
Under the influence of these feelings I have always grieved that you, most
excellent Leo, who were worthy of a better age, have been made pontiff in
this. For the Roman court is not worthy of you and those like you, but of
Satan himself, who in truth is more the ruler in that Babylon than you are.

"Oh, would that, having laid aside that glory which your most abandoned
enemies declare to be yours, you were living rather in the office of a private

---

[1] " *Ein Statthalter ist in Abwesenheit seines Herrn ein Statthalter.*"

priest, or on your paternal inheritance! In that glory none are worthy to glory, except the race of Iscariot, the children of perdition. For what happens in your court, Leo, except that, the more wicked and execrable any man is, the more prosperously he can use your name and authority for the ruin of the property and souls of men, for the multiplication of crimes, for the oppression of faith and truth, and of the whole Church of God? O Leo! in reality most unfortunate, and sitting on a most perilous throne: verily I tell you the truth, because I wish you well; for if Bernard felt compassion for his Anastasius at a time when the Roman See, though even then most corrupt, was as yet ruling with better hope than now, why should not we lament, to whom so much additional corruption and ruin has happened in three hundred years?

"Is it not true that there is nothing under the vast heavens more corrupt, more pestilential, more hateful, than the court of Rome? She incomparably

LEO X. From his Portrait by Raphael.

surpasses the impiety of the Turks, so that in very truth she, who was formerly the gate of heaven, is now a sort of open mouth of hell, and such a mouth as, under the urgent wrath of God, can not be blocked up; one course alone being left to us wretched men, — to call back and save some few, if we can, from that Roman gulf.

"Behold, Leo my father, with what purpose and on what principle it is that I have stormed against that seat of pestilence. I am so far from having felt any rage against your person, that I even hoped to gain favor with you and to aid in your welfare, by striking actively and vigorously at that your prison, nay, your hell. For, whatever the efforts of all intellects can contrive against the confusion of that impious court will be advantageous to you and to your welfare, and to many others with you. Those who do harm to her are doing your work; those who in every way abhor her are glorifying Christ; in short, those are Christians who are not Romans. . . .

"In fine, that I may not approach your Holiness empty-handed, I bring with me this little book,[1] published under your name, as a good omen of the establishment of peace and of good hope. By this you may perceive in what pursuits I should prefer and be able to occupy myself to more profit, if I were allowed, or had been hitherto allowed, by your impious flatterers. It is a small book, if you look to the paper; but, unless I mistake,

[1] *De Libertate Christiana.*

it is a summary of the Christian life put together in small compass, if you apprehend its meaning. I, in my poverty, have no other present to make you; nor do you need any thing else than to be enriched by a spiritual gift. I commend myself to your Holiness, whom may the Lord Jesus preserve for ever. Amen.

"WITTENBERG, 6th September, 1520."

§ 47. *The Bull of Excommunication.* June 15, 1520.

The Bull "*Exurge, Domine,*" in the *Bullarium Romanum*, ed. CAR. COCQUE-LINES, Tom. III., Pars III. (ab anno 1431 ad 1521), pp. 487–493, and in RAYNALDUS (continuator of Baronius): *Annal. Eccl.*, ad ann. 1520, no. 51 (Tom. XX. fol. 303–306). Raynaldus calls Luther "*apostatam nefandissimum,*" and takes the bull from Cochlæus, who, besides Eck and Ulemberg (a Protestant apostate), is the chief authority for his meager and distorted account of the German Reformation. A copy of the original edition of the bull is in the Astor Library, New York. See NOTES.

U. V. HUTTEN published the bull with biting glosses: *Bulla Decimi Leonis contra errores Lutheri et sequacium*, or *Die glossirte Bulle* (in Hutten's *Opera*, ed. Böcking, V. 301–333; in the Erl. ed. of Luther's *Op. Lat.*, IV. 261–304; also in German in WALCH, XV. 1691 sqq.; comp. STRAUSS: *U. v. Hutten*, p. 338 sqq.). The glosses in smaller type interrupt the text, or are put on the margin. LUTHER: *Von den neuen Eckischen Bullen und Lügen* (Sept. 1520); *Adv. execrabilem Antichristi bullam* (Nov. 1520); *Wider die Bullen des Endchrists* (Nov. 1520; the same book as the preceding Latin work, but sharper and stronger); *Warum des Papsts und seiner Jünger Bücher verbrannt sind* (Lat. and Germ., Dec. 1520); all in WALCH, XV. fol. 1674–1917; Erl. ed., XXIV. 14–164, and *Op. Lat.* V. 132–238; 251–271. LUTHER's letters to Spalatin and others on the bull of excommunication, in De Wette, I. 518–532.

RANKE: I. 294–301. MERLE D'AUBIGNÉ, Bk. VI. ch. III. sqq. HAGENBACH, III. 100–102. KAHNIS: I. 306–341. KÖSTLIN: I. 379–382. KOLDE: I. 280 sqq. JANSSEN: II. 108 sqq.

After the Leipzig disputation, Dr. Eck went to Rome, and strained every nerve to secure the condemnation of Luther and his followers.[1] Cardinals Campeggi and Cajetan, Prierias and Aleander, aided him. Cajetan was sick, but had him-

---

[1] As Luther said, to rouse "the abyss of hell" (*Abgrund der Hölle*) against him. Eck seems to have been acting also in the interest of the banking firm of Fugger in Augsburg, which carried on the financial transactions between Germany and Italy, including the transmission of indulgence-money. See Ranke, I. 297.

self carried on his couch into the sessions of the consistory.
With considerable difficulty the bull of excommunication
was drawn up in May, and after several amendments completed June 15, 1520.[1]

Nearly three years had elapsed since the publication of
Luther's Ninety-five Theses. In the mean time he had
attacked with increasing violence the very foundations of
the Roman Church, had denounced popery as an antichristian tyranny, and had dared to appeal from the Pope to a
general council, contrary to the decisions of Pius II. and
Julius II., who declared such an appeal to be heresy. Between the completion and the promulgation of the bull, he
went still further in his "Address to the German Nobility,"
and the book on the "Babylonian Captivity," and made a
reconciliation impossible except by an absolute surrender,
which was a moral impossibility for him. Rome could not
tolerate Lutheranism any longer without ceasing to be Rome.
She delayed final action only for political and prudential considerations, especially in view of the election of a new German Emperor, and the influential voice of the Elector Frederick, who was offered, but declined, the imperial crown.

The bull of excommunication is the papal counter-mani-
festo to Luther's Theses, and condemns in him the whole
cause of the Protestant Reformation. Therein lies its historical significance. It was the last bull addressed to Latin
Christendom as an undivided whole, and the first which was
disobeyed by a large part of it. Instead of causing Luther

---

[1] Ranke (I. 298) dates the bull from June 16; Walch (XV. 1691) from
June 24; but most historians (Gieseler, Kahnis, Köstlin, Lenz, Janssen, Hergenröther, etc.) from June 15. The last is correct, for the bull is dated
" MDXX. xvii. Kal. Julii." According to the Roman mode of reckoning
backwards, counting the day of departure, and adding two to the number of
days of the preceding month, the *Kalendæ Julii* fall on June 15. Ranke
probably overlooked the fact that June had only twenty-nine days in the
Julian Calendar. Janssen refers to an essay of Druffel on the date of the
bull in the "Sitzungsberichte der Bayer Academie," 1880, p. 572; but he
does not give the result.

and his friends to be burnt, it was burnt by Luther. It is an elaborate document, prepared with great care in the usual heavy, turgid, and tedious style of the curia. It breathes the genuine spirit of the papal hierarchy, and mingles the tones of priestly arrogance, concern for truth, abomination of heresy and schism, fatherly sorrow, and penal severity. The Pope speaks as if he were the personal embodiment of the truth, the infallible judge of all matters of faith, and the dispenser of eternal rewards and punishments.

He begins with the words of Ps. 74: 22: " Arise, O God, plead thine own cause: remember how the foolish man reproacheth thee daily. Forget not the voice of thine enemies: the tumult of those that rise up against thee increaseth continually." He calls St. Peter, St. Paul, and the whole body of the saints, to aid against " the boar out of the wood " and " the wild beast of the field " that had broken into the vineyard of the Lord, to waste and destroy it (Ps. 80: 13). He expresses deep sorrow at the revival of the Bohemian and other heresies in the noble German nation which had received the empire from the Pope, and shed so much precious blood against heresy. Then he condemns forty-one propositions selected from Luther's books, as heretical, or at least scandalous and offensive to pious ears, and sentences all his books to the flames. Among the errors named are those relating to the sacramental and hierarchical system, especially the authority of the Pope and the (Roman) Church. The denial of free will (*liberum arbitrium*) after the fall is also condemned, though clearly taught by St. Augustin. But Luther's fundamental doctrine of justification by faith is not expressly mentioned. The sentences are torn from the connection, and presented in the most objectionable form as mere negations of Catholic doctrines. The positive views of the Reformer are not stated, or distorted.

For the person of Luther, the Pope professes fatherly love and forbearance, and entreats him once more, by the mercies of God and the blood of Christ, to repent and recant within sixty days after the publication of the bull in the Branden- burg, Meissen, and Merseburg dioceses, and promises to re- ceive him graciously like the prodigal son. But failing to repent, he and his adherents will be cut off, as withered branches, from the vine of Christ, and be punished as obsti- nate heretics. This means that they shall be burned; for the bull expressly condemns the proposition of Luther which denounces the burning of heretics as "contrary to the will of the Holy Spirit." All princes, magistrates, and citizens are exhorted, on threat of excommunication and promise of re- ward, to seize Luther and his followers, and to hand him over to the apostolic chair. Places which harbor him or his fol- lowers are threatened with the interdict. Christians are forbidden to read, print, or publish any of his books, and are commanded to burn them.

We may infer from this document in what a state of intel- lectual slavery Christendom would be at the present time if the papal power had succeeded in crushing the Reformation. It is difficult to estimate the debt we owe to Martin Luther for freedom and progress.

The promulgation and execution of the bull were intrusted to two Italian prelates, Aleander and Caraccioli, and to Dr. Eck. The personal enemy of Luther, who had been especially active in procuring the bull, was now sent back in triumph with the dignity of a papal nuncio, and even with the ex- traordinary power of including by name several followers of Luther, among whom he singled out Carlstadt and Dolzig of Wittenberg, Adelmann of Augsburg, Egranus of Zwickau, and the humanists Pirkheimer and Spengler of Nürnberg. The selection of Eck, the most unpopular man in Germany, was a great mistake of the Pope, as Roman historians admit, and it helped the cause of the Reformation.[1]

---

[1] Pallavicini and Muratori censure Leo for commissioning Eck. Janssen says (II. 109): "*Es war ein trauriger Missgriff, dass mit der Verkündigung*

The bull was published and carried out without much difficulty in Mayence, Cologne, and Louvain; and Luther's books
were committed to the flames, with the sanction of the new
Emperor. But in Northern Germany, which was the proper
seat of the conflict, it met with determined resistance, and was
defeated. Eck printed and placarded the bull at Ingolstadt,
at Meissen (Sept. 21), at Merseburg (Sept. 25), and at Brandenburg (Sept. 29). But in Leipzig, where a year before he
had achieved his boasted victory over Luther in public debate,
he was insulted by the students (one hundred and fifty had
come over from Wittenberg), and took flight in a convent;
the bull was bespattered, and torn to pieces.[1] He fared still
worse in Erfurt, where he had been ridiculed and held up to
scorn as a second Hochstraten in the satire *Eccius dedolatus*
(printed at Erfurt in March, 1520) : the theological faculty
refused to publish the bull; and the students threw the
printed copies into the water, saying, "It is only a water-
bubble (*bulla*), let it float on the water."[2]

und *Vollstreckung der Bulle in mehreren deutschen Diöcesen Luther's Gegner Johann Eck beauftragt wurde.*" The same view was previously expressed by Kampschulte (*Die Universität Erfurt in ihrem Verh. zu dem
Humanismus und der Reformation*, Trier, 1858–60, Th. II., p. 36), although
he fully justified the papal bull as a necessity for the Roman Church,
and characterized its tone as comparatively mild in view of Luther's *radicale
Umsturzgedanken* and his violence of language. Audin and Archbishop
Spalding defend the Pope.

[1] Letter of Miltitz to Fabian von Feilitzsch, Oct. 2, 1520. In Walch, XV.
1872. Luther wrote to Spalatin, Oct. 3, 1520 (De Wette, I. 492), that he
had just heard of the bad reception and danger of Eck at Leipzig, and hoped
that he might escape with his life, but that his devices might come to naught.

[2] "*Bulla est, in aqua natet.*" So Luther reports in a letter to Greffen-
dorf, Oct. 20 (De Wette, I. 520), and in a letter to Spalatin, Nov. 4 (I. 522
sq.). Kampschulte (*l.c.* II. 37 sqq.) gives a full account of Eck's troubles at
Erfurt, from a rare printed placard, *Intimatio Erphurdiana pro Martino
Luthero* (preserved by Riederer, and quoted also by Gieseler, III. I. 81,
Germ. ed., or IV. 53, Anglo-Am. ed.), to the effect that the whole theological
faculty stirred up all the students, calling upon them to resist "with hand
and foot" the furious Pharisees and slanderers of Luther, who wished to cast
him out of the Church and into hell. Luther makes no mention of such a
strange action of the faculty, which is scarcely credible as it included strict
Catholics.

Eck sent the bull to the rector of the University of Wittenberg, Oct. 3, 1520, with the request to prohibit the teaching of any of the condemned propositions of Luther, and
threatening that, in case of disobedience, the Pope would
recall all the liberties and privileges of the university. The
professors and counselors of the Elector declined the promulgation for various reasons.

The Elector Frederick was on the way to Aachen to assist
at the coronation of Charles V., but was detained at Cologne
by the gout. There he received the bull from Aleander
after the mass, Nov. 4, and was urged with eloquent words
to execute it, and to punish Luther or to send him to Rome;
but he cautiously deferred an answer, and sought the advice
of Erasmus in the presence of Spalatin. The famous scholar
gave it as his judgment, that Luther's crime consisted in
having touched the triple crown of the Pope and the stom-
achs of the monks;[1] he also wrote to Spalatin, after the
interview, that the Pope's bull offended all upright men
by its ferocity and was unworthy of a meek vicar of Christ.[2]
The Elector was thus confirmed in his favorable view of
Luther. He sent Spalatin to Wittenberg, where some students had left in consequence of the bull; but Spalatin was
encouraged, and found that Melanchthon had about six hundred, Luther four hundred hearers, and that the church was
crowded whenever Luther preached. A few weeks afterward
the Pope's bull was burnt.

[1] " *Lutherus peccavit in duobus, nempe quod tetigit coronam Pontificis et
ventres monachorum.*" Spalatin, *Annal.* 28 sq.

[2] " *Bullæ sævitia probos omnes offendit, ut indigna mitissimo Christi
vicario.*" Erasmus soon afterwards called back his *Axiomata pro causa
Lutheri*, which he had sent to Spalatin. They were, however, published
(Erl. ed. of Luther's *Op. Lat.*, vol. V. 238–242). About the same time he
advised the Emperor to submit the case of Luther to impartial judges of
different nations, or to a general council. See Gieseler, IV. 53 sq., Am. ed.

LEO Epiſcopus Serſ
uus Seruoruz Dei/ Ad
perpetuam rei memoriam.
Exurge dñc & iudica cauſaʒ
tuam/ memor eſto imprope
riorum tuorum/ eoruʒ quæ
ab inſipientibus fiunt tota
die / inclina aurem tuam ad
preces noſtras/ quoniam ſur
rexerũt uulpes querentes de
moliri uineam/ cuius tu Torcular calcaſti ſolus/ & aſcē
ſurus ad patrem/ eius curam/ regimen / & adminiſtra/
tionem Petro tanquā capiti/ et tuo Vicario/ eiuſ͉ ſuc/
ceſſoribus inſtar triumphantis Eccleſie cōmiſiſti/ exter
minare nititur eam, Aper de ſilua/ & ſingularis fetus de
paſci eam. Exurge Petre/ & pro paſtorali cura prefata ti
bi(ut prefertur)diuinitus demandata/ intende in cauſaʒ
ſanctæ Romañ. Eccleſiæ/ Matris omnium eccleſiaruʒ/
ac fidei Magiſtre/ quam tu/ iubente Deo/ tuo ſanguine
conſecraſti/ contra quam ſicut tu premonere dignatus
es/ inſurgunt Magiſtri mendaces introducentes ſectas
perditionis ſibi celerem interitum ſuperducentes/ quoʒ
lingua ignis eſt/ itꝫ ̄ ectum malum/ plena ueneno mor
tifero/ qui Zelum amarum habentes/ & contentiones
in cordibus ſuis/ gloriantur/ & mendaces ſunt aduerſus
ueritatem. Exurge tu quoqꝫ queſumus Paule/ qui eam
tua doctrina/ ac pari martyrio illuminaſti/ atcꝫ illuſtra/
ſti. Iam eni ſurgit nouus Porphirius/ qui ſicut ille olim
ſanctos Apoſtolos iniuſte momordit, Ita hic ſanctos
Pontifices predeceſſores noſtros cōtra tuam doctriná

234

NOTES. — THE BULL OF EXCOMMUNICATION.

As I do not find the bull in any of the Protestant or Roman-Catholic church histories which I have consulted (except the *Annals* of Raynaldus), I give it here in full as transcribed from an original copy in possession of the Astor Library, New York (probably the only one on the American Continent), together with facsimiles of titlepage and first page. The pamphlet contains twenty pages, small quarto, and is printed continuously, like ancient MSS. I have divided it into sections, with headings, and noted the departures of Cocquelines and Raynaldus from the original.

BULLA CONTRA ERRORES MARTINI LUTHERI ET SEQUACIUM.

LEO Episcopus Servus Servorum Dei.[1]

Ad perpetuam rei memoriam.

[Proömium. The Pope invokes God, St. Peter and St. Paul, and all the saints, against the new enemies of the Church.]

Exurge, Domine, et judica causam tuam, memor esto improperiorum tuorum, eorum, quæ ab insipientibus fiunt totâ die; inclina aurem tuam ad preces nostras, quoniam surrexerunt vulpes quærentes demoliri vineam, cujus tu torcular calcasti solus, et ascensurus ad Patrem ejus curam, regimen et administrationem Petro tanquam capiti et tuo vicario, ejusque successoribus instar triumphantis Ecclesiæ commisisti: exterminare nititur eam aper de silva, et singularis ferus depasci [tur] eam. Exurge, Petre, et pro pastorali cura præfata tibi (ut præfertur) divinitus demandata, intende in causam sanctæ Romanæ Ecclesiæ, Matris omnium ecclesiarum, ac fidei magistræ, quam tu, jubente Deo, tuo sanguine consecrasti, contra quam, sicut tu præmonere dignatus es, insurgunt magistri mendaces introducentes sectas perditionis, sibi celerem interitum superducentes,[2] quorum lingua ignis est, inquietum malum, plena veneno mortifero, qui zelum amarum habentes et contentiones in cordibus suis, gloriantur, et mendaces sunt adversus veritatem. Exurge tu quoque, quæsumus, Paule, qui eam tuâ doctrinâ et pari martyrio illuminasti atque illustrasti. Jam enim surgit novus Porphyrius; quia sicut ille olim sanctos Apostolos injuste momordit, ita hic sanctos Pontifices prædecessores nostros contra tuam doctrinam eos non obsecrando, sed increpando, mordere, lacerare, ac ubi causæ suæ[3] diffidit, ad convicia accedere non veretur, more hæreticorum, quorum (ut inquit Hieronymus) ultimum præsidium est, ut cum conspiciant causas suas damnatum iri, incipiant virus serpentis linguâ diffundere; et cum se victos conspiciant, ad contumelias prosilire. Nam licet hæreses esse ad exercitationem fidelium tu dixeris oportere, eas tamen, ne incrementum accipiant, neve vulpeculæ coalescant, in ipso ortu, te intercedente et adjuvante, extingui necesse est.

---

[1] The heading is omitted by Raynaldus.   [2] Raynaldus: *superinducentes.*

[3] Cocquelines omits *suæ.*

Exurgat denique,[1] omnis sanctorum, ac reliqua universalis Ecclesia, cujus vera sacrarum literarum interpretatione posthabitâ, quidam, quorum mentem pater mendacii excæcavit, ex veteri hæreticorum instituto, apud semetîpsos sapientes, scripturas easdem aliter quam Spiritus sanctus flagitet, proprio dumtaxat sensu ambitionis, auræque popularis causâ, teste Apostolo, interpretantur, immo vero torquent et adulterant, ita ut juxta Hieronymum jam non sit evangelium Christi, sed hominis, aut quod pejus est, diaboli.   Exurgat, inquam, præfata Ecclesia sancta Dei, et una cum beatissimis Apostolis præfatis[2] apud Deum omnipotentem intercedat, ut purgatis ovium suarum erroribus, eliminatisque a fidelium finibus hæresibus universis Ecclesiæ suæ sanctæ pacem et unitatem conservare dignetur.

[The errors of the Greeks and Bohemians revived by Luther and his followers.]

Dudum siquidem[3] quod præ animi angustia et mœrore exprimere vix possumus, fide dignorum relatu ac famâ publicâ referente ad nostrum pervenit auditum, immo vero, proh dolor! oculis nostris vidimus ac legimus, multos et varios errores quosdam videlicet jam per Concilia ac Prædecessorum nostrorum constitutiones damnatos, hæresim etiam Græcorum et Bohemicam expresse continentes: alios vero respective, vel hæreticos, vel falsos, vel scandalosos, vel piarum aurium offensivos, vel simplicium mentium seductivos, a falsis fidei cultoribus, qui per superbam curiositatem mundi gloriam cupientes, contra Apostoli doctrinam plus sapere volunt, quam oporteat; quorum garrulitas (ut inquit Hieronymus) sine scripturarum auctoritate non haberet fidem, nisi viderentur perversam doctrinam etiam divinis testimoniis, male tamen interpretatis, roborare: a quorum oculis Dei timor recessit, humani generis hoste suggerente, noviter suscitatos, et nuper apud quosdam leviores in inclyta natione Germanica seminatos.

[The Germans, who received the empire from the Pope, were formerly most zealous against heresy, but now give birth to the most dangerous errors.]

Quod eo magis dolemus ibi[4] evenisse, quod eandem nationem et nos et Prædecessores nostri in visceribus semper gesserimus caritatis.   Nam post translatum ex Grecis a Romana Ecclesia in eosdem Germanos imperium, iidem Prædecessores nostri et nos ejusdem Ecclesiæ advocatos defensoresque ex eis semper accepimus; quos quidem Germanos, Catholicæ veritatis vere germanos, constat hæresum [hæresium] acerrimos oppugnatores[5] semper fuisse: cujus rei testes sunt laudabiles illæ constitutiones Germanorum Imperatorum pro libertate Ecclesiæ, proque expellendis exterminandisque ex omni Germania hæreticis, sub gravissimis pœnis, etiam amissionis terrarum et dominiorum, contra receptatores vel non expellentes olim editæ, et à nostris Prædecessoribus confirmatæ, quæ si hodie servarentur, et nos et ipsi utique hac molestiâ careremus.   Testis est in Concilio Constantiensi Hussitarum ac Wiccleffistarum, necnon Hieronymi Pragensis damnata ac punita perfidia.

---

[1] Raynaldus omits *denique*.   [2] Raynaldus omits *præfatis*.   [3] Omitted by Raynaldus.
[4] Omitted by Raynaldus.   [5] Raynaldus: *propugnatores*.

Testis est totiens contra Bohemos Germanorum sanguis effusus. Testis denique est prædictorum errorum, seu multorum ex eis per Coloniensem et Lovaniensem Universitates, utpote agri dominici piissimas religiosissimasque cultrices, non minus docta quam vera ac sancta confutatio, reprobatio, et damnatio. Multa quoque alia allegare possemus, quæ, ne historiam texere videamur, prætermittenda censuimus.

Pro pastoralis igitur officii, divinâ gratiâ nobis injuncti cura, quam gerimus, prædictorum errorum virus pestiferum ulterius tolerare seu dissimulare sine Christianæ religionis nota, atque orthodoxæ fidei injuria nullo modo possumus. Eorum autem errorum aliquos præsentibus duximus inferendos, quorum tenor sequitur, et est talis: —

[Forty-one heretical sentences selected from Luther's writings.]

I. Hæretica sententia est, sed usitata, Sacramenta novæ legis justificantem gratiam illis dare, qui non ponunt obicem.

II. In puero post baptismum negare remanens peccatum, est Paulum et Christum simul conculcare.

III. Fomes peccati, etiam si nullum adsit actuale peccatum, moratur exeuntem a corpore animam ab ingressu cœli.

IV. Imperfecta caritas morituri fert secum necessario magnum timorem, qui se solo satis est facere pœnam purgatorii, et impedit introitum regni.

V. Tres esse partes pœnitentiæ, contritionem, confessionem, et satisfactionem, non est fundatum in sacra scriptura, nec in antiquis sanctis Christianis doctoribus.

VI. Contritio, quæ paratus per discussionem, collectionem,[1] et detestationem peccatorum, qua quis recogitat annos suos in amaritudine animæ suæ, ponderando peccatorum gravitatem, multitudinem, fœditatem, amissionem æternæ beatitudinis, ac æternæ damnationis acquisitionem, hæc contritio facit hypocritam, immo magis peccatorem.

VII. Verissimum est proverbium, et omnium doctrina de contritionibus hucusque data præstantius, de cetero non facere, summa pœnitentia, optima pœnitentia, nova vita.

VIII. Nullo modo præsumas confiteri peccata venialia, sed nec omnia mortalia, quia impossibile est, ut omnia mortalia cognoscas: unde in primitiva Ecclesia solum manifesta mortalia confitebantur.

IX. Dum volumus omnia pure confiteri, nihil aliud facimus, quam quod misericordiæ Dei nihil volumus relinquere ignoscendum.

X. Peccata non sunt illi remissa, nisi remittente sacerdote credat sibi remitti; immo peccatum maneret nisi remissum crederet; non enim sufficit remissio peccati et gratiæ donatio, sed oportet etiam credere esse remissum.

XI. Nullo modo confidas absolvi propter tuam contritionem, sed propter verbum Christi: "Quodcumque solveris," etc. Sic, inquam, confide, si sacer-

---

[1] Cocquelines reads *collationem*, contrary to the original which plainly reads *collectionem*.

dotis obtinueris absolutionem, et crede fortiter te absolutum; et absolutus vere eris,[1] quidquid sit de contritione.

XII. Si per impossibile confessus non esset contritus, aut sacerdos non serio, sed joco absolveret, si tamen credat se absolutum, verissime est absolutus.

XIII. In sacramento pœnitentiæ ac remissione culpæ non plus facit Papa aut episcopus, quam infimus sacerdos; immo ubi non est sacerdos, æque tantum quilibet Christianus, etiam si mulier, aut puer esset.

XIV. Nullus debet sacerdoti respondere, se esse contritum, nec[2] sacerdos requirere.

XV. Magnus est error eorum, qui ad sacramenta Eucharistiæ accedunt huic innixi, quod sint confessi, quod non sint sibi conscii alicujus peccati mortalis; quod præmiserint orationes suas et præparatoria; omnes illi ad[3] judicium sibi manducant et bibunt; sed si credant et confidant se gratiam ibi consecuturos, hæc sola fides facit eos puros et dignos.

XVI. Consultum videtur, quod Ecclesia in communi concilio[4] statueret, laicos sub utraque specie communicandos; nec Bohemi communicantes sub utraque specie[5] sunt hæretici, sed schismatici.

XVII. Thesauri Ecclesiæ, unde Papa dat indulgentias, non sunt merita Christi et sanctorum.

XVIII. Indulgentiæ sunt piæ fraudes fidelium, et remissiones bonorum onerum, et sunt de numero eorum, quæ licent, et non de numero eorum, quæ expediunt.

XIX. Indulgentiæ his, qui veraciter eas consequuntur, non valent ad remissionem pœnæ pro peccatis actualibus debitæ ad divinam justitiam.

XX. Seducuntur credentes indulgentias esse salutares, et ad fructum spiritûs utiles.

XXI. Indulgentiæ necessariæ sunt solum publicis criminibus, et proprie conceduntur duris solummodo et impatientibus.

XXII. Sex generibus hominum indulgentiæ nec sunt necessariæ, nec utiles; videlicet mortuis seu morituris, infirmis, legitime impeditis, his qui non commiserunt crimina, his qui crimina commiserunt, sed non publica, his qui meliora operantur.

XXIII. Excommunicationes sunt tantum externæ pœnæ, nec privant hominem communibus spiritualibus Ecclesiæ orationibus.

XXIV. Docendi sunt Christiani plus diligere excommunicationem quam timere.

XXV. Romanus Pontifex, Petri successor, non est Christi vicarius super omnes mundi ecclesias ab ipso Christo in beato Petro institutus.

XXVI. Verbum Christi ad Petrum: "Quodcumque solveris super terram," etc., extenditur duntaxat ad ligata ab ipso Petro.

---

[1] Cocquelines: *et absolutum vere esse.* Raynaldus is right here, according to the original.
[2] Cocquelines: *sed.*   [3] Raynaldus omits *ad.*   [4] Rayn. omits *concilio.*
[5] Rayn. omits *specie.*

XXVII. Certum est in manu Ecclesiæ aut Papæ prorsus non esse statuere articulos fidei, immo nec leges morum, seu bonorum operum.

XXVIII. Si Papa cum magna parte Ecclesiæ sic vel sic sentiret, nec etiam erraret, adhuc non est peccatum aut hæresis contrarium sentire, præsertim in re non necessaria ad salutem, donec fuerit per Concilium universale alterum reprobatum, alterum approbatum.

XXIX. Via nobis facta est enarrandi auctoritatem Conciliorum, et libere contradicendi eorum gestis, et judicandi eorum decreta, et confidenter confitendi quidquid verum videtur, sive probatum fuerit, sive reprobatum a quocunque concilio.

XXX. Aliqui articuli Joannis Husz condemnati in concilio Constantiensi sunt Christianissimi, verissimi et evangelici, quos non universalis Ecclesia posset damnare.

XXXI. In omni opere bono justus peccat.

XXXII. Opus bonum optime factum veniale est peccatum.

XXXIII. Hæreticos comburi est contra voluntatem Spiritûs.[1]

XXXIV. Præliari adversus Turcas est repugnare Deo visitanti iniquitates nostras per illos.

XXXV. Nemo est certus se non semper peccare mortaliter propter occultissimum superbæ vitium.

XXXVI. Liberum arbitrium post peccatum est res de solo titulo, et dum facit quod in se est, peccat mortaliter.

XXXVII. Purgatorium non potest probari ex sacra scriptura, quæ sit in canone.

XXXVIII. Animæ in purgatorio non sunt securæ de earum salute, saltem omnes; nec probatum est ullis aut rationibus aut scripturis, ipsas esse extra statum merendi, aut[2] agendæ caritatis.

XXXIX. Animæ in purgatorio peccant sine intermissione, quamdiu quærunt requiem, et horrent pœnas.

XL. Animæ ex purgatorio liberatæ suffragiis viventium minus beantur, quam si per se satisfecissent.

XLI. Prælati ecclesiastici et principes seculares non malefacerent si omnes saccos mendicitatis[3] delerent.

[These propositions are condemned as heretical, scandalous, offensive, and contrary to Catholic truth.]

Qui quidem errores respective quam sint pestiferi, quam perniciosi, quam scandalosi, quam piarum et simplicium mentium seductivi, quam denique sint contra omnem charitatem, ac sanctæ Romanæ Ecclesiæ matris omnium fidelium et magistræ fidei reverentiam atque nervum ecclesiasticæ disciplinæ, obedientiam scilicet, quæ fons est et origo omnium virtutum, sine qua facile

---

[1] This is an indirect approval of the burning of heretics. Rome never has disowned this theory.

[2] Cocquelines reads *nec — nec* for *aut*. Raynaldus is right here.

[3] Raynaldus: *medicitatis* (a typographical error).

unusquisque infidelis esse convincitur, nemo sanæ mentis ignorat. Nos igitur in præmissis, utpote gravissimis, propensius (ut decet) procedere, necnon hujusmodi pesti morboque canceroso, ne in agro Dominico tanquam vepris nociva ulterius serpat, viam præcludere cupientes, habita super prædictis erroribus, et eorum singulis diligenti trutinatione, discussione, ac districto examine, maturaque deliberatione, omnibusque rite pensatis ac sæpius ventilatis cum venerabilibus fratribus nostris sanctæ Romanæ Ecclesiæ Cardinalibus, ac regularium ordinum Prioribus, seu ministris generalibus, plurisbusque aliis sacræ theologiæ, necnon utriusque juris professoribus sive magistris, et quidem peritissimis, reperimus eosdem errores respective (ut præfertur) aut articulos non esse catholicos, nec tanquam tales esse dogmatizandos, sed contra Ecclesiæ Catholicæ doctrinam sive traditionem, atque ab ea veram divinarum scripturarum receptam interpretationem, cujus auctoritati ita acquiescendum censuit Augustinus, ut dixerit, se Evangelio non fuisse crediturum, nisi Ecclesiæ Catholicæ intervenisset auctoritas. Nam ex eisdem erroribus, vel eorum aliquo, vel aliquibus, palam sequitur, eandem Ecclesiam, quæ Spiritu sancto regitur, errare, et semper errasse. Quod est utique contra illud, quod Christus discipulis suis in ascensione sua (ut in sancto Evangelio Matthæi legitur) promisit dicens: "Ego vobiscum sum usque ad consummationem seculi;" necnon contra sanctorum Patrum determinationes, Conciliorum quoque et summorum Pontificum expressas ordinationes seu canones, quibus non obtemperasse omnium hæresum et schismatum, teste Cypriano, fomes et causa semper fuit.

De eorundem itaque venerabilium fratrum nostrorum consilio et assensu, ac omnium et singulorum prædictorum maturâ deliberatione prædicta, auctoritate omnipotentis Dei, et beatorum Apostolorum Petri et Pauli, et nostra, præfatos omnes et singulos articulos seu errores, tanquam (ut præmittitur) respective hæreticos, aut scandalosos, aut falsos, aut piarum aurium offensivos, vel simplicium mentium seductivos, et veritati Catholicæ obviantes, damnamus, reprobamus, ac omnino rejicimus, ac pro damnatis, reprobatis, et rejectis ab omnibus utriusque sexûs Christi fidelibus haberi debere, harum serie decernimus et declaramus.[1]

[Prohibition of the defence and publication of these errors.]

Inhibentes in virtute sanctæ obedientiæ ac sub majoris excommunicationis latæ sententiæ, necnon quoad Ecclesiasticas et Regulares personas, Episcopalium omnium, etiam Patriarchalium, Metropolitanarum et aliarum Cathedralium Ecclesiarum, Monasteriorum quoque et Prioratuum etiam Conventualium et quarumcunque[2] dignitatum aut Beneficiorum Ecclesiasticorum, Sæcularium aut quorum vis Ordinum Regularium, privationis et inhabilitatis ad illa, et alia in posterum obtinenda. Quo vero ad Conventus,

---

[1] Raynaldus (fol. 305) omits all the specifications of punishments from here down to the next section beginning *Insuper.*

[2] The original reads *quorumcnq.* (an *o* for an *a*).

Capitula seu domos, aut pia loca sæcularium, vel regularium, etiam Mendicantium, necnon Universitatis etiam studiorum generalium, quorumcunque
privilegiorum indultorum a Sede Apostolica, vel ejus Legatis, aut alias quomodolibet habitorum, vel obtentorum, cujuscumque tenoris existant: necnon nominis et potestatis studium generale tenendi, legendi, ac interpretandi
quasvis scientias et facultates et inhabilitatis ad illa et alia in posterum obtinenda: Prædicationis quoque officii ac amissionis studii generalis et omnium privilegiorum ejusdem. Quo vero ad sæculares ejusdem excommunicationis, necnon amissionis cujuscumque emphyteosis, seu quorumcunque
feudorum, tam a Romana Ecclesia, quam alias quomodolibet obtentorum, ac
etiam inhabilitatis ad illa et alia in posterum obtinenda. Necnon quo ad
omnes et singulos superius nominatos, inhibitionis Ecclesiasticæ sepulturæ
inhabilitatisque ad omnes et singulos actus legitimos, infamiæ ac diffidatio-
nis et criminis læsæ majestatis, et hæreticorum et fautorum eorundem in
jure expressis pœnis, eo ipso et absque ulteriori declaratione per omnes et
singulos supradictos, si (quod absit) contrafecerint, incurrendis. A quibus
vigore cujuscumque facultatis et clausularum etiam in confessionalibus quibusvis personis, sub quibusvis verborum formis contentarum, nisi a Romano
Pontifice vel alio ab eo ad id in specie facultatem habente, præterquam in
mortis articulo constituti, absolvi nequeant. Omnibus et singulis utriusque
sexus Christifidelibus, tam Laicis quam Clericis, Sæcularibus et quorumvis
Ordinum Regularibus, et aliis quibuscumque personis cujuscumque status,
gradus, vel conditionis existant, et quarumque ecclesiastica vel mundana
præfulgeant dignitate, etiam S. R. E. Cardinalibus, Patriarchis, Primatibus,
Archiepiscopis, Episcopis, Patriarchalium, Metropolitanarum et aliarum
Cathedralium, Collegiatarum ac inferiorum ecclesiarum Prælatis, Clericis
aliisque personis Ecclesiasticis, Sæcularibus et quorumvis Ordinum etiam
Mendicantium regularibus, Abbatibus, Prioribus vel Ministris generalibus
vel particularibus, Fratribus, seu Religiosis, exemptis et non exemptis:
Studiorum quoque Universitatibus Sæcularibus et quorumvis Ordinum etiam
Mendicantium regularibus, necnon Regibus, Imperatori, Electoribus, Principibus, Ducibus, Marchionibus, Comitibus, Baronibus, Capitaneis, Conductoribus, Domicellis, omnibusque Officialibus, Judicibus, Notariis Ecclesiasticis et Sæcularibus, Communitatibus, Universitatibus, Potentatibus,
Civitatibus, Castris, Terris et locis, seu eorum vel earum civibus, habitatoribus et incolis, ac quibusvis aliis personis Ecclesiasticis, vel Regularibus (ut
præfertur) per universum orbem, ubicumque, præsertim in Alemania exis-
tentibus, vel pro tempore futuris, ne præfatos errores, aut eorum aliquos,
perversamque doctrinam hujusmodi asserere, affirmare, defendere, prædicare,
aut illi quomodolibet, publice vel occulte, quovis quæsito ingenio vel colore,
tacite vel expresse favere præsumant.

[The writings of Luther are forbidden, and ordered to be burnt.]

Insuper quia errores præfati, et plures alii continentur in libellis seu
scriptis Martini Luther, dictos libellos, et omnia dicti Martini scripta, seu

prædicationes in Latino, vel quocumque alio idiomate reperiantur, in quibus
dicti errores, seu eorum aliquis continentur, similiter damnamus, reprobamus, atque omnino rejicimus, et pro damnatis, reprobatis, ac rejectis (ut
præfertur) haberi volumus, mandantes in virtute sanctæ obedientiæ, et sub
pœnis prædictis eo ipso incurrendis, omnibus et singulis utriusque sexûs
Christifidelibus superius nominatis, ne hujusmodi scripta, libellos, prædicationes, seu schedulas, vel in eis contenta capitula, errores, aut articulos
supradictos continentia legere, asserere, prædicare, laudare, imprimere, publicare, sive defendere per se vel alium, seu alios directe vel indirecte, tacite
vel expresse, publice vel occulte, aut in domibus suis sive aliis publicis vel
privatis locis tenere quoquo modo præsumant; quinimmo illa statim post
harum publicationem ubicumque fuerint, per ordinarios et alios supradictos
diligenter quæsita, publice et solemniter in præsentia cleri et populi sub
omnibus et singulis supradictis pœnis comburant.

[Martin Luther was often warned with paternal charity to desist from these errors, and cited
to Rome with the promise of safe-conduct.]

Quod vero ad ipsum Martinum attinet, (bone Deus) quid prætermisimus,
quid non fecimus, quid paternæ charitatis omisimus, ut eum ab hujusmodi
erroribus revocaremus ? Postquam enim ipsum citavimus, mitius cum eo
procedere volentes, illum invitavimus, atque tam per diversos tractatus cum
legato nostro habitos, quam per literas nostras hortati fuimus, ut a prædictis
erroribus discederet, aut oblato etiam salvo conductu et pecuniâ ad iter neces-
sariâ, sine metu seu timore aliquo quem perfecta charitas foras mittere de-
buit, veniret, ac Salvatoris nostri Apostolique Pauli exemplo, non occulto,
sed palam et in facie loqueretur. Quod si fecisset, pro certo (ut arbitramur)
ad cor reversus errores suos cognovisset, nec in Romana curia, quam tanto-
pere vanis malevolorum rumoribus plusquam oportuit tribuendo vituperat,
tot reperisset errata; docuissemusque eum luce clarius, sanctos Romanos
Pontifices, quos præter omnem modestiam injuriose lacerat, in suis canoni-
bus, seu constitutionibus, quas mordere nititur, nunquam errasse; quia juxta
prophetam, nec in Galahad resina, nec medicus deest. Sed obaudivit semper, et prædicta citatione omnibus et singulis supradictis spretis venire con-
tempsit, ac usque in præsentem diem contumax, atque animo indurato cen-
suras ultra annum sustinuit: et quod deterius est, addens mala malis, de
citatione hujusmodi notitiam habens, in vocem temerariæ appellationis pro-
rupit ad futurum concilium contra constitutionem Pii Secundi ac Julii Secundi, prædecessorum nostrorum, qua cavetur, taliter appellantes hæreticorum
pœnâ plectendos (frustra etiam Consilii auxilium imploravit, qui illi se non
credere palam profitetur); ita ut contra ipsum tanquam de fide notorie sus-
pectum, immo vere hæreticum absque ulterori citatione vel mora ad con-
demnationem et damnationem ejus tanquam hæretici, ac ad omnium et
singularum suprascriptarum pœnarum et censurarum severitatem procedere
possemus.

[Luther is again exhorted to repent, and promised the reception of the prodigal son.]

Nihilominus de eorundem fratrum nostrorum consilio, omnipotentis Dei imitantes clementiam, qui non vult mortem peccatoris, sed magis ut convertatur et vivat, omnium injuriarum hactenus nobis et Apostolicæ sedi illatarum obliti, omni qua possumus pietate uti decrevimus, et quantum in nobis est, agere, ut propositâ mansuetudinis viâ ad cor revertatur, et a prædictis recedat erroribus, ut ipsum tanquam filium illum prodigum ad gremium Ecclesiæ revertentem benigne recipiamus.   Ipsum igitur Martinum et quoscumque ei adhærentes, ejusque receptatores et fautores per viscera misericordiæ Dei nostri, et per aspersionem sanguinis Domini nostri Jesu Christi. quo et per quem humani generis redemptio, et sanctæ matris Ecclesiæ ædificatio facta est, ex tote corde hortamur et obsecramus, ut ipsius Ecclesiæ pacem, unitatem et veritatem, pro qua ipse Salvator tam instanter oravit ad Patrem, turbare desistant, et a prædictis tam perniciosis erroribus prorsus abstineant, inventuri apud nos si effectualiter paruerint, et paruisse per legitima documenta nos certificaverint, paternæ charitatis affectum, et apertum mansuetudinis et clementiæ fontem.

[Luther is suspended from the functions of the ministry, and given sixty days, after the publication of the bull, to recant.]

Inhibentes nihilominus eidem Martino ex nunc, ut interim ab omni prædicatione seu prædicationis officio omnino desistat.   Alioquin in ipsum Martinum si forte justitiæ et virtutis amor a peccato non retrahat, indulgentiæque spes ad pœnitentiam non reducat, pœnarum terror coërceat disciplinæ: eundem Martinum ejusque adhærentes complices, fautores, et receptatores tenore præsentium requirimus, et monemus in virtute sanctæ obedientiæ, et sub prædictis omnibus et singulis pœnis eo ipso incurrendis districte præcipiendo mandamus, quatenus infra sexaginta dies, quorum viginti pro primo, viginti pro secundo, et reliquos viginti dies pro tertio et peremptorio termino assignamus ab affixione præsentium in locis infrascriptis immediate sequentes numerandos, ipse Martinus, complices, fautores, adhærentes, et receptatores prædicti a præfatis erroribus, eorumque prædicatione, ac publicatione, et assertione, defensione quoque et librorum seu scripturarum editione super eisdem, sive eorum aliquo omnino desistant, librosque ac scripturas omnes et singulas præfatos errores seu eorum aliquos quomodolibet continentes comburant, vel comburi faciant.   Ipse etiam Martinus errores et assertiones hujusmodi omnino revocet, ac de revocatione hujusmodi per publica documenta in forma juris valida in manibus duorum Prælatorum consignata ad nos infra alios similes sexaginta dies transmittenda, vel per ipsummet (si ad nos venire voluerit, quod magis placeret) cum præfato plenissimo salvo conductu, quem ex nunc concedimus deferenda, nos certiores efficiat, ut de ejus vera obedientia nullus dubitationis scrupulus valeat remanere.

[In case Luther and his followers refuse to recant within sixty days, they will be excommunicated, and dealt with according to law.]

Alias si (quod absit) Martinus præfatus, complices, fautores, adhærentes
et receptatores prædicti secus egerint, seu prœmissa omnia et singula infra
terminum prædictum cum effectu non adimpleverint, Apostoli imitantes
doctrinam, qui hæreticum hominem post primam et secundam correctionem
vitandum docuit, ex nunc prout ex tunc, et e converso eundem Martinum,
complices, adhærentes, fautores et receptatores præfatos et eorum quemlibet
tanquam aridos palmites in Christo non manentes, sed doctrinam contra-
riam, Catholicæ fidei inimicam, sive scandalosam seu damnatam, in non
modicam offensam divinæ majestatis, ac universalis Ecclesiæ, et fidei Catholicæ detrimentum et scandalum dogmatizantes, claves quoque Ecclesiæ vili-
pendentes, notorios et pertinaces hæreticos eâdem auctoritate fuisse et esse
declarantes, eosdem ut tales harum serie condemnamus, et eos pro talibus
haberi ab omnibus utriusque sexus Christi fidelibus supradictis volumus et
mandamus.   Eosque omnes et singulos omnibus supradictis et aliis contra
tales a jure inflictis pœnis præsentium tenore subjicimus, et eisdem irretitos
fuisse et esse decernimus et declaramus.

[All Catholics are admonished not to read, print, or publish any book of Luther and his
followers, but to burn them.]

Inhibemus præterea sub omnibus et singulis præmissis pœnis eo ipso
incurrendis, omnibus et singulis Christi fidelibus superius nominatis, ne
scripta, etiam præfatos errores non continentia, ab eodem Martino quomodolibet condita vel edita, aut condenda vel edenda, seu eorum aliqua tanquam ab homine orthodoxæ fidei inimico, atque ideo vehementer suspecta,
et ut ejus memoria omnino deleatur de Christifidelium consortio, legere,
asserere, prædicare, laudare, imprimere, publicare, sive defendere, per se vel
alium seu alios, directe vel indirecte, tacite vel expresse, publice vel occulte,
seu in domibus suis, sive aliis locis publicis vel privatis tenere quoquomodo
præsumant, quinimmo illa comburant, ut præfertur.[1]

[Christians are forbidden, after the excommunication, to hold any intercourse with Luther
and his followers, or to give them shelter, on pain of the interdict; and magistrates are
commanded to arrest and send them to Rome.]

Monemus insuper omnes et singulos Christifideles supradictos, sub eadem
excommunicationis latæ sententiæ pœna, ut hæreticos prædictos declaratos
et condemnatos, mandatis nostris non obtemperantes, post lapsum termini
supradicti evitent et quantum in eis est, evitari faciant, nec cum eisdem, vel
eorum aliquo commercium aut aliquam conversationem seu communionem
habeant, nec eis necessaria ministrent.

Ad majorem præterea dicti Martini suorumque complicum, fautorum et
adhærentium ac receptatorum prædictorum, sic post lapsum termini prædicti
declaratorum hæreticorum et condemnatorum confusionem universis et sin-

---

[1] The remainder of the bull is briefly summarized by Raynaldus.

gulis utriusque sexus Christifidelibus Patriarchis, Archiepiscopis, Episcopis,
Patriarchalium, Metropolitanarum, et aliarum cathedralium, collegiatarum
ac inferiorum ecclesiarum Prælatis, Capitulis, aliisque personis ecclesiasticis,
sæcularibus et quoramvis Ordinum etiam Mendicantium (præsertim ejus con-
gregationis cujus dictus Martinus est professus, et in qua degere vel morari
dicitur) regularibus exemptis et non exemptis, necnon universis et singulis
principibus, quacumque ecclesiastica vel mundana fulgentibus dignitate Regibus, Imperatoris [1] Electoribus, Ducibus, Marchionibus, Comitibus, Baronibus, Capitaneis, Conductoribus, Domicellis, Communitatibus, Universitatibus, Potentatibus, Civitatibus, Terris, Castris et locis, seu eorum
habitatoribus, civibus et incolis omnibusque aliis et singulis supradictis per
universum Orbem, præsertim in eadem Alemania constitutis mandamus, quatenus sub prædictis omnibus et singulis pœnis, ipsi vel eorum quilibet, præfatum Martinum, complices, adhærentes, receptantes et fautores personaliter
capiant et captos ad nostram instantiam retineant et ad nos mittant: repor-
taturi pro tam bono opere a nobis et Sede Apostolica remunerationem, præ-
miumque condignum vel saltem eos et eorum quemlibet, de Metropolitanis,
Cathedralibus, Collegiatis, et aliis ecclesiis, domibus, Monasteriis, Conventibus, Civitatibus, Dominiis, Universitatibus, Communitatibus, Castris, Terris,
ac locis respective, tam clerici et regulares quam laici omnes et singuli supradicti omnino expellant.

[The places which harbor Luther and his followers are threatened with the Interdict.]

Civitates vero, Dominia, Terras, Castra, Villas, comitatus, fortilicia,
Oppida et loca quæcumque ubilibet consistentia earum et eorum respective
Metropolitanas, Cathedrales, Collegiatas et alias ecclesias, Monasteria, Prior-
atus, Domus, Conventus et loca religiosa vel pia cujuscunque ordinis (ut
præfertur) ad quæ præfatum Martinum vel aliquem ex prædictis declinare
contigerit, quamdiu ibi permanserint et triduo post recessum, ecclesiastico
subjicimus interdicto.

[Provision for the promulgation and execution of the bull.]

Et ut præmissa omnibus innotescant, mandamus insuper universis Patriarchis, Archiepiscopis, Episcopis, Patriarchalium, Metropolitanarum et aliarum cathedralium ac collegiatarum ecclesiarum Prælatis, Capitulis aliisque
personis ecclesiasticis, sæcularibus et quorumvis Ordinum supradictorum regularibus, fratribus religiosis, monachis exemptis et non exemptis supradictis,
ubilibet, præsertim in Alemania constitutis quatenus ipsi vel eorum quilibet
sub similibus censuris et pœnis eo ipso incurrendis, Martinum omnesque et
singulos supradictos qui elapso termino hujusmodi mandatis seu monitis nostris non paruerint, in eorum ecclesiis, dominicis et aliis festivis diebus, dum
inibi major populi multitudo ad divina convenerit, declaratos hæreticos et
condemnatos publice nuncient faciantque et mandent ab aliis nunciari et ab

---

[1] Cocquelines: *Imperatori*. Then there should be a comma after *Imperatori*. The seven
Electors of the Emperor are meant.

omnibus evitari. Necnon omnibus Christifidelibus ut eos evitent, pari modo sub prædictis censuris et pœnis. Et præsentes literas vel earum transumptum sub forma infrascripta factum in eorum ecclesiis, monasteriis, domibus, conventibus et aliis locis legi, publicari atque affigi faciant. Excommunicamus quoque et anathematizamus omnes et singulos cujuscumque status, gradus, conditionis, præ-eminentiæ, dignitatis aut excellentiæ fuerint qui quo minus præsentes literæ vel earum transumpta, copiæ seu exemplaria in suis terris et dominiis legi, affigi et publicare possint, fecerint vel quoquomodo procuraverint per se vel alium seu alios, publice vel occulte, directe vel indirecte, tacite vel expresse.

Postremo quia difficile foret præsentes literas ad singula quæque loca deferri in quibus necessarium foret, volumus et apostolica authoritate decernimus, quod earum transumptis manu publici notarii confectis et subscriptis, vel in alma Urbe impressis et sigillo alicujus ecclesiastici Prælati munitis ubique stetur et plena fides adhibeatur, prout originalibus literis staretur, si forent exhibitæ vel ostensæ.

Et ne præfatus Martinus omnesque alii supradicti, quos præsentes literæ quomodolibet concernunt, ignorantiam earundem literarum et in eis contentorum omnium et singulorum prætendere valeant, literas ipsas in Basilicæ Principis Apostolorum et Cancellariæ Apostolicæ, necnon Cathedralium ecclesiarum Brandeburgen., Misnen. et Morspergen. [Merseburg] valvis affigi et publicari debere [1] volumus, decernentes, quod earundem literarum publicatio sic facta, supradictum Martinum omnesque alios et singulos prænominatos, quos literæ hujusmodi quomodolibet concernunt, perinde arctent, ac si literæ ipsæ die affixionis et publicationis hujusmodi eis personaliter lectæ et intimatæ forent, cum non sit verisimile, quod ea quæ tam patenter fiunt debeant apud eos incognita remanere.

Non obstantibus constitutionibus et ordinationibus apostolicis, seu si supradictis omnibus et singulis vel eorum alicui aut quibusvis aliis a Sede Apostolica prædicta, vel ab ea potestatem habentibus sub quavis forma, etiam confessionali et cum quibusvis etiam fortissimis clausulis, aut ex quavis causa, seu grandi consideratione, indultum vel concessum existat, quod interdici, suspendi, vel excommunicari non possint per literas Apostolicas, non facientes plenam et expressam ac de verbo ad verbum, non autem per clausulas generales id importantes, de indulto hujusmodi mentionem, ejusdem indulti tenores, causas [2] et formas perinde ac si de verbo ad verbum insererentur, ita ut omnino tollatur, præsentibus pro expressis habentes.

Nulli ergo omnino hominum liceat hanc paginam nostræ damnationis, reprobationis, rejectionis, decreti, declarationis, inhibitionis, voluntatis, mandati, hortationis, obsecrationis, requisitionis, monitionis, assignationis, concessionis, condemnationis, subjectionis, excommunicationis, et anathematizationis infringere, vel ei ausu temerario contraire. Si quis autem hoc

---

[1] Cocquelines omits *debere*.   [2] Cocquelines : *clausulas*. A plausible correction.

attentare præsumpserit, indignationem Omnipotentis Dei ac Beatorum Petri et Pauli Apostolorum ejus se noverit incursurum.

Dat. Romæ apud S. Petrum anno incarnationis Dominicæ Milesimo Quingentesimo Vigesimo. XVII. Kls. Julii. Pontificatûs Nostri Anno Octavo.

Visa. R. Milanesius.

Albergatus.

Impressum Romæ per Iacobum Mazochium
De Mandato S. D. N. Papæ.[1]

§ 48. *Luther burns the Pope's Bull, and forever breaks with Rome. Dec. 10, 1520.*

Literature in § 47.

Luther was prepared for the bull of excommunication. He could see in it nothing but blasphemous presumption and pious hypocrisy. At first he pretended to treat it as a forgery of Eck.[2] Then he wrote a Latin and German tract, "Against the Bull of Antichrist,"[3] called it a "cursed, impudent, devilish bull," took up the several charges of heresy, and turned the tables against the Pope, who was the heretic according to the standard of the sacred Scriptures. Hutten ridiculed the bull from the literary and patriotic standpoint with sarcastic notes and queries. Luther attacked its contents with red-hot anger and indignation bordering on frenzy. He thought the last day, the day of Antichrist, had come. He went so far as to say that nobody could be saved who adhered to the bull.[4]

In deference to his friends, he renewed the useless appeal from the Pope to a free general council (Nov. 17, 1520),

---

[1] Subscriptions are omitted by Cocquelines and Raynaldus.

[2] "*Ich höre auch sagen, Dr. Eck habe eine Bulle mit sich von Rom wider mich gebracht, die ihm so ähnlich sei, dass sie wohl möchte auch Dr. Eck heissen, so voll Lügen und Irrthum sie sein soll; und er gebe vor, den Leuten das Maul zu schmieren, sie sollen glauben, es sei des Papsts Werk, so es sein Lügenspiel ist. Ich lasse es geschehen, muss des Spiels in Gottes Namen warten; wer weiss, was göttlicher Rath beschlossen hat.*" *Von den neuen Eckischen Bullen und Lügen.*

[3] *Widder die Bullen des Endchrists*, Weimar ed. vol. VI. 613–629.

[4] He wrote to Spalatin, Nov. 4 (in De Wette, I. 522): "*Impossibile est salvos fieri, qui huic Bullæ aut faverunt, aut non repugnaverunt.*" He told his students, Dec. 11: "*Nisi toto corde dissentistis a regno papali, non potestis assequi vestrarum animarum salutem.*"

which he had made two years before (Nov. 28, 1518) ; and in his appeal he denounced the Pope as a hardened heretic, an antichristian suppresser of the Scriptures, a blasphemer and despiser of the holy Church and of a rightful council.[1]

At the same time he resolved upon a symbolic act which cut off the possibility of a retreat. The Pope had ordered his books, good and bad, without any distinction, to be burned ; and they were actually burned in several places, at Cologne even in the presence of the Emperor. They were to be burned also at Leipzig. Luther wanted to show that he too could burn books, which was an old custom (Acts 19:19) and easy business. He returned fire for fire, curse for curse. He made no distinction between truth and error in the papal books, since the Pope had ordered his innocent books to be destroyed as well. He gave public notice of his intention.

On the tenth day of December, 1520, at nine o'clock in the morning, in the presence of a large number of professors and students, he solemnly committed the bull of excommunication, together with the papal decretals, the canon law, and several writings of Eck and Emser, to the flames, with these words (borrowed from Joshua's judgment of Achan the thief, Josh. 7:25) : "As thou [the Pope] hast vexed the Holy One of the Lord, may the eternal fire vex thee !"[2]

The spot where this happened is still shown outside the Elster Gate at Wittenberg, under a sturdy oak surrounded by an iron railing.[3]

---

[1] Walch, XV. 1909 sqq. Erl. ed., XXIV. 28–35; and *Op. Lat.*, V. 119–131. The appeal was published in Latin and German.

[2] The "Holy One" refers to Christ, as in Mark 1:24; Acts 2:27; not to Luther, as ignorance and malignity have misinterpreted the word. Luther spoke in Latin: "*Quia tu conturbasti Sanctum Domini, ideoque te conturbet ignis æternus.*" The Vulgate translates Josh. 7:25: "*Quia turbasti nos, exturbet te Dominus in die hac.*" In the Revised E. V., the whole passage reads: "Why hast thou troubled us ? The Lord shall trouble thee this day. And all Israel stoned him with stones, and burnt them [in Hebrew אֹתָם] with fire after they had stoned them with stones."

[3] A tablet contains the inscription: "*Dr. Martin Luther verbrannte an dieser Stätte am 10 Dec. 1520 die päpstliche Bannbulle.*"

Several hundred students tarried at the fire, which had been kindled by a master of the university, some chanting the *Te Deum*, others singing funeral dirges on the papal laws; then they made a mock procession through the town, collected piles of scholastic and Romish books, and returning to the place of execution, threw them into the flames.

Luther, with Melanchthon, Carlstadt, and the other doctors and masters, returned home immediately after the act. He at first had trembled at the step, and prayed for light; but after the deed was done, he felt more cheerful than ever. He regarded his excommunication as an emancipation from all restraints of popery and monasticism. On the same day he calmly informed Spalatin of the event as a piece of news.[1] On the next day he warned the students in the lecture-room against the Romish Antichrist, and told them that it was high time to burn the papal chair with all its teachers and abominations.[2] He publicly announced his act in a Latin and German treatise, " Why the Books of the Pope and his Disciples were burned by Dr. Martin Luther." He justified it by his duties as a baptized Christian, as a sworn doctor of divinity, as a daily preacher, to root out all unchristian doctrines. He cites from the papal law-books thirty articles and errors in glorification of the papacy, which deserve to be burned; and calls the whole canon-law "the abomination of desolation" (Matt. 24: 15) and antichristian (2 Thess. 2: 4), since the sum of its teaching was, that "the Pope is God on

---

[1] "*Anno MDXX, decima Decembris, hora nona, exusti sunt Wittembergœ ad orientalem portam, juxta S. Crucem, omnes libri Papœ: Decretum, Decretales, Sext. Clement. Extravagant., et Bulla novissima Leonis X.: item summa Angelica* [a work on casuistry by Angelus Carletus de Clavasio, or Chiavasso, d. 1495], *Chrysoprasus* [*De prœdestinatione centuriœ sex, 1514*] *Eccii, et alia ejusdem autoris, Emseri, et quœdam alia, quœ adjecta per alios sunt: ut videant incendiarii Papistœ, non esse magnarum virium libros exurere, quos confutare non possunt. Hœc erunt nova.*" De Wette, I. 532. Further details about the burning and the conduct of the students we learn from the report of an unnamed pupil of Luther: *Excustionis antichristianarum decretalium Acta*, in the Erl. ed. of *Op. Lat.*, V. 250–256.

[2] Ranke, i. 307; Köstlin, i. 407; Kolde, i. 290.

earth, above all things, heavenly and earthly, spiritual and temporal; all things belong to the Pope, and no one dare ask, What doest thou?" Simultaneously with this tract, he published an exhaustive defense of all his own articles which had been condemned by the Pope, and planted himself upon the rock of God's revelation in the Scriptures.

Leo X., after the expiration of the one hundred and twenty days of grace allowed to Luther by the terms of the bull, proceeded to the last step, and on the third day of January, 1521, pronounced the ban against the Reformer and his followers, and an interdict on the places where they should be harbored. But Luther had deprived the new bull of its effect.

The burning of the Pope's bull was the boldest and most eventful act of Luther. Viewed in itself, it might indeed have been only an act of fanaticism and folly, and proved a *brutum fulmen*. But it was preceded and followed by heroic acts of faith in pulling down an old church, and building up a new one. It defied the greatest power on earth, before which emperors, kings, and princes, and all the nations of Europe bowed in reverence and awe. It was the fiery signal of absolute and final separation from Rome, and destroyed the effect of future papal bulls upon one-half of Western Christendom. It emancipated Luther and the entire Protestant world from that authority, which, from a wholesome school of discipline for young nations, had become a fearful and intolerable tyranny over the intellect and conscience of men.

Luther developed his theology before the eyes of the public; while Calvin, at a later period, appeared fully matured, like Minerva from the head of Jupiter. "I am one of those," he says, "among whom St. Augustin classed himself, who have gradually advanced by writing and teaching; not of those who at a single bound spring to perfection out of nothing."

He called the Pope the most holy and the most hellish father of Christendom. He began in 1517 as a devout papist and monk, with full faith in the Roman Church and its divinely appointed head, protesting merely against certain abuses; in 1519, at the Leipzig disputation, he denied the divine right, and shortly afterwards also the human right, of the papacy; a year later he became fully convinced that the papacy was that antichristian power predicted in the Scriptures, and must be renounced at the risk of a man's salvation.

There is no doubt that in all these stages he was equally sincere, earnest, and conscientious.

Luther adhered to the position taken in the act of Dec. 10, 1520, with unchanging firmness. He never regretted it for a moment. He had burned the ship behind him; he could not, and he would not, return. To the end of his life he regarded and treated the Pope of Rome in his official capacity as the very Antichrist, and expected that he soon would be destroyed by spiritual force at the second coming of Christ. At Schmalkalden in 1537 he prayed that God might fill all Protestants with hatred of the Pope. One of his last and most violent books is directed "Against the Papacy at Rome, founded by the Devil," Wittenberg, 1545.[1] He calls Paul III. the "Most hellish Father," and addresses him as "Your Hellishness," instead of "Your Holiness." He promises at the close to do still better in another book, and prays that in

---

[1] *Wider das Papstthum zu Rom, vom Teufel gestiftet* (in the Erl. ed., XXVI. 108–228). A rude wood-cut on the title-page represents the Pope with long donkey-ears going into the jaws of hell, while demons are punching and jeering at him. Luther calls the Pope (p. 228) "*Papstesel mit langen Eselsohren und verdammtem Lügenmaul.*" The book was provoked by two most presumptuous letters of Pope Paul III. to the Emperor Charles V., rebuking him for giving rest to the Protestants at the Diet of Speier, 1544, till the meeting of a general council, and reminding him of the terrible end of those who dare to violate the priestly prerogatives. King Ferdinand, the Emperor's brother, read the book through, and remarked, "*Wenn die bösen Worte heraus wären, so hätte der Luther nicht übel geschrieben.*" But not a few sincere friends of Luther thought at the time that he did more harm than good to his own cause by this book.

case of his death, God may raise another one "a thousand-fold more severe; for the devilish papacy is the last evil on earth, and the worst which all the devils with all their power could contrive. God help us. Amen." Thus he wrote, not under the inspiration of liquor or madness, as Roman historians have suggested, but in sober earnest. His dying words, as reported by Ratzeburger, his physician, were a prediction of the approaching death of the papacy: —

> *"Pestis eram vivus, moriens tua mors ero Papa."*

From the standpoint of his age, Luther regarded the Pope and the Turk as "the two arch-enemies of Christ and his Church," and embodied this view in a hymn which begins, —

> " *Erhalt uns, Herr, bei deinem Wort*
> *Und steur' des Papst's und Türken Mord.*" [1]

This line, like the famous eightieth question of the Heidelberg Catechism which denounces the popish mass as an "accursed idolatry," gave much trouble in mixed communities, and in some it was forbidden by Roman-Catholic magistrates. Modern German hymn-books wisely substitute "all enemies," or "enemies of Christ," for the Pope and the Turk.

In order to form a just estimate of Luther's views on the papacy, it must not be forgotten that they were uttered in the furnace-heat of controversy, and with all the violence of his violent temper. They have no more weight than his equally sweeping condemnation of Aristotle and Thomas Aquinas.

§ 49. *The Reformation and the Papacy.*

Here is the place to interrupt the progress of events, and to reflect on the right or wrong of the attitude of Luther and the Reformation to the papacy.

---

[1] It appeared in Klug's *Gesangbuch*, Wittenberg, 1543, under the title: " *Ein Kinderlied zu singen, wider die zween Ertzfeinde Christi und seiner heiligen Kirchen, den Papst und Türken.*"

The Reformers held the opinion that the papacy was an antichristian institution, and some of the Protestant confessions of faith have given symbolical sanction to this theory.   They did not mean, of course, that every individual Pope was an Antichrist (Luther spoke respectfully of Leo X.), nor that the papacy as such was antichristian : Melanchthon, at least, conceived of the possibility of a Christian papacy, or a general superintendence of the Church for the preservation of order and unity.[1]

They had in view simply the institution as it was at their time, when it stood in open and deadly opposition to what they regarded as the truth of the gospel of Christ, and the free preaching of the same.   Their theory does not necessarily exclude a liberal and just appreciation of the papacy before and after the Reformation.

And in this respect a great change has taken place among Protestant scholars, with the progress of exegesis and the knowledge of church history.

1. The prophetic Scripture texts to which the Reformers and early Protestant divines used to appeal for their theory of the papacy, must be understood in accordance with the surroundings and conditions of the writers and their readers who were to be benefited.   This does not exclude, of course, an application to events and tendencies of the distant future, since history is a growing and expanding fulfillment of prophecy ; but the application must be germane to the original design and natural meaning of the text.   Few commentators would now find the Pope of Rome in "the little horn" of Daniel (7 : 8, 20, 21), who had in view rather Antiochus Epiphanes ; or in the Apocalyptic beast from the abyss (Rev. 13 : 1), and "the mother of harlots" (17 : 5), which evidently apply to the persecuting heathen Rome of Nero and his successors.

---

[1] See his appendix to the Smalcald Articles, 1537: *De autoritate et primatu Papæ.*

St. John is the only biblical writer who uses the term "Antichrist;"[1] but he means by it, in the first instance, the Gnostic heresy of his own day, which denied the incarnation; for he represents this denial as the characteristic sign of Antichrist, and represents him as being already in the world; yea, he speaks of "many" antichrists who had gone out of the Christian churches in Asia Minor. The Pope has never denied the incarnation, and can never do it without ceasing to be Pope.

It is quite legitimate to use the terms "antichrist" and "antichristian" in a wider sense, of all such men and tendencies as are opposed to Christ and his teaching; but we have no right to confine them to the Pope and the Roman Church. "Many shall come in my name, saying, I am Christ, and shall deceive many" (Matt. 24:4, 11, 23, 24).

St. Paul's prediction of the great apostasy, and the "man of sin, the son of perdition, who opposes and exalts himself against all that is called God or that is worshiped; so that he sits in the temple of God, setting himself forth as God,"[2] sounds much more than any other passage like a description of the papacy with its amazing claim to universal and infallible authority over the Church of God. But the application becomes more than doubtful when we remember that the apostle characterizes this antichristian apostasy as "the mystery of lawlessness," already at work in his day, though restrained from open manifestation by some conservative power.[3] The papacy did not yet exist at the time; and its besetting sin is not lawless freedom, but the very opposite.

[1] 1 John 2:18, 22; 4:3; 2 John 7.

[2] 2 Thess. 2:3-7. This is the passage quoted by the Westminster Confession against the Pope, chap. xxv. 6.

[3] τὸ γὰρ μυστήριον ἤδη ἐνεργεῖται τῆς ἀνομίας· μόνον ὁ κατέχων ἄρτι ἕως ἐκ μέσου γένηται. The Roman government was at first (before the Neronian persecution of 64) a protector of Christianity, and more particularly of Paul, who could effectually appeal to his Roman citizenship at Philippi, before the centurion at Jerusalem, and before Festus at Cæsarea.

If we would seek for Scripture authority against the sins and errors of popery, we must take our stand on our Lord's opposition to the traditions of the elders, which virtually set aside the word of God; on Paul's Epistles to the Galatians and Romans, where he defends Christian freedom against legalistic bondage, and teaches the great doctrines of sin and grace, forgotten by Rome, and revived by the Reformation; and on St. Peter's protest against hierarchical presumption and pride.

There was in the early Church a general expectation that an Antichrist in the emphatic sense, an incarnation of the antichristian principle, a pseudo-Christ of hell, a "world-deceiver" (as he is called in the newly discovered "Teaching of the Apostles"[1]), should appear, and lead astray many Christians immediately before the second coming of Christ. The Reformers saw this Antichrist in the Pope, and looked for his speedy destruction; but an experience of more than three hundred and fifty years proves that in this expectation they were mistaken, and that the *final* Antichrist is still in the future.

2. As regards church history, it was as yet an unexplored field at the time of the Reformation; but the Reformation itself roused the spirit of inquiry and independent, impartial research. The documentary sources of the middle ages have only recently been made accessible on a large scale by such collections as the *Monumenta Germaniæ*. "The keys of Peter," says Dr. Pertz, the Protestant editor of the *Monumenta*, "are still the keys of the middle ages." The greatest Protestant historians, ecclesiastical and secular, — I need only

---

[1] Ch. 16:4; κοσμοπλάνος, a very significant term, which unites the several marks of the Antichrist of John (2 John 7: ὁ πλάνος καὶ ἀντίχριστος), of the Apocalypse (12:9: ὁ πλανῶν τὴν οἰκουμένην), and of Paul, since the *Didaché* connects the appearance of the world-deceiver with the increase of lawlessness (ἀνομία, as in 2 Thess. 2:7). Comp. my monograph on the *Didaché*, pp. 77 and 214 sq.

mention Neander and Ranke, — agree in a more liberal view of the papacy.[1]

After the downfall of the old Roman Empire, the papacy was, with all its abuses and vices, a necessary and wholesome training-school of the barbarian nations of Western and Northern Europe, and educated them from a state of savage heathenism to that degree of Christian civilization which they reached at the time of the Reformation. It was a check upon the despotism of rude force; it maintained the outward unity of the Church; it brought the nations into communication; it protected the sanctity of marriage against the lust of princes; it moderated slavery; it softened the manners; it inspired great enterprises; it promoted the extension of Christianity; it encouraged the cause of learning and the cultivation of the arts of peace.

And even now the mission of the papacy is not yet finished. It seems to be as needful for certain nations, and a lower stage of civilization, as ever. It still stands, not a forsaken ruin, but an imposing pyramid completed to the very top. The Roman Church rose like a wounded giant from the struggle with the Reformation, abolished in the Council of Trent some of the worst abuses, reconquered a considerable portion of her lost territory in Europe, added to her dominion one-half of the American Continent, and completed her doctrinal and governmental system in the decrees of the

---

[1] Comp. especially Ranke's classical work, *Die römischen Päpste in den letzten vier Jahrhunderten*, 8th edition, Leipzig, 1885, 3 vols. The first edition appeared 1834–36. Ranke has found a worthy successor in an English scholar, Dr. M. Creighton (professor of Church history in Cambridge), the author of an equally impartial *History of the Papacy during the Period of the Reformation*, beginning with the Great Schism, 1378. London and Boston, 1882 sqq. (so far 4 vols.). But the same period of the papacy is now being written with ample learning and ability from the modern Roman point of view, by Dr. Ludwig Pastor (professor of Church history at Innsbruck) in his *Geschichte der Päpste seit dem Ausgang des Mittelalters*, of which the first volume appeared at Freiburg-i.-B. 1886, and extends from 1305 to the election of Pius II. The author promises six volumes. He had the advantage of using the papal archives by the effectual favor of Pope Leo XIII.

Vatican Council.   The Pope has lost his temporal power by
the momentous events of 1870; but he seems to be all the
stronger in spiritual influence since 1878, when Leo XIII. was
called to occupy the chair of Leo X.   An aged Italian priest
shut up in the Vatican controls the consciences of two hundred millions of human beings, — that is, nearly one-half of
nominal Christendom, — and rules them with the claim of infallibility in all matters of faith and duty.   It is a significant
fact, that the greatest statesman of the nineteenth century,
and founder of a Protestant empire, who at the beginning of
the *Kulturkampf* declared that he would never go to Canossa
(1872), found it expedient, after a conflict of ten years,
to yield to an essential modification of the anti-papal May-
laws of 1873, without, however, changing his religious conviction, or sacrificing the sovereignty of the State; he even
conferred an extraordinary distinction upon the Pope by
selecting him as arbiter in an international dispute between
Germany and Spain (1885).[1]   But it is perhaps still more
remarkable, that Leo XIII. in return sent to Prince Bismarck,
the political Luther of Germany, the Christ Order, which was
never given to a Protestant before, and that he supported
him in the political campaign of 1887.

3. How can we justify the Reformation, in view of the
past history and present vitality of the Papacy?

Here the history of the Jewish Church, which is a type of
the Christian, furnishes us with a most instructive illustration
and conclusive answer.   The Levitical hierarchy, which culminated in the high priest, was of divine appointment, and a
necessary institution for the preservation of the theocracy.
And yet what God intended to be a blessing became a
curse by the guilt of man: Caiaphas, the lineal descendant
of Aaron, condemned the Messiah as a false prophet and

---

[1] Alexander VI., by a stroke of his pen, divided America between Spain
and Portugal: Leo XIII., in 1886, gave the insignificant Caroline Islands in
the Pacific to Spain, but the free commerce to Germany.

blasphemer, and the synagogue cast out His apostles with curses.

What happened in the old dispensation was repeated on a larger scale in the history of Christianity. An antichristian element accompanied the papacy from the very beginning, and culminated in the corruptions at the time of the Reformation. The greater its assumed and conceded power, the greater were the danger and temptation of abuse. One of the best of Popes, Gregory the Great, protested against the title of " universal bishop," as an antichristian presumption. The Greek Church, long before the Reformation, charged the Bishop of Rome with antichristian usurpation; and she adheres to her protest to this day. Not a few Popes, such as Sergius III., John XII., Benedict IX., John XXIII., and Alexander VI., were guilty of the darkest crimes of depraved human nature: and yet they called themselves successors of Peter, and vicars of Christ. Who will defend the papal crusades against the Albigenses and Waldenses, the horrors of the Inquisition, the papal jubilee over the massacre of St. Bartholomew, and all those bloody persecutions of innocent people for no other crime but that of opposing the tyranny of Rome, and dissenting from her traditions? Liberal and humane Catholics would revolt at an attempt to revive the dungeon and the fagot against heresy and schism; but the Church of Rome in her official capacity has never repudiated the principle of persecution by which its practice was justified: on the contrary, Pope Gregory XVI. declared liberty of conscience and worship an insanity (*deliramentum*), and Pius IX. in his " Syllabus " of 1864 denounced it among the pernicious and pestilential errors of modern times. And what shall we say of the papal schism in the fifteenth century, when two or three rival Popes laid all Christendom under the curse of excommunication? What of the utter secularization of the papacy just before the Reformation, its absorption in political intrigues and wars and schemes of

aggrandizement, its avarice, its shameless traffic in indulgences, and all those abuses of power which called forth the
one hundred and one *gravamina* of the German nation?
Who will stand up for the bull of excommunication against
Luther, with its threats of burning him and his books, and
refusing the consolations of religion to every house or community which should dare to harbor him or any of his followers?   If that bull be Christian, then we must close our
eyes against the plain teaching of Christ in the Gospels.

Even if the Bishop of Rome should be the legitimate successor of Peter, as he claims, it would not shield him against
the verdict of history.   For the carnal Simon revived and re-
asserted himself from time to time in the spiritual Peter.
The same disciple whom Christ honored as the "Rock," on
whose confession he promised to build his Church, was soon
afterwards called "Satan" when he presumed to divert his
Master from the path of suffering; the same Peter was
rebuked when he drew the sword against Malchus; the same
Peter, notwithstanding his boast of fidelity, denied his Lord
and Saviour; and the same Peter incurred the severe remon-
strance of Paul at Antioch when he practically denied the
rights of the Gentile converts, and virtually excluded them
from the Church.   According to the Roman legend, the
prince of the apostles relapsed into his consistent inconsistency, even a day before his martyrdom, by bribing the jailer,
and fleeing for his life till the Lord appeared to him with the
cross at the spot of the memorial chapel *Domine quo vadis.*
Will the Pope ever imitate Peter in his bitter repentance for
denying Christ?

If the Apostolic Church typically foreshadows the whole
history of Christianity, we may well see in the temporary
collision between Peter and Paul the type of the antagonism
between Romanism and Protestantism.   The Reformation
was a revolt against legal bondage, and an assertion of evangelical freedom.   It renewed the protest of Paul against

Peter, and it succeeded. It secured freedom in religion, and as a legitimate consequence, also intellectual, political, and civil freedom. It made the Word of God with its instruction and comfort accessible to all. This is its triumphant vindication. Compare for proof Protestant Germany under William I., with Roman-Catholic Germany under Maximilian I.; England under Queen Victoria, with England under Henry VII.; Calvinistic Scotland and Lutheran Scandinavia in the nineteenth century, with Roman Scotland and Scandinavia in the fifteenth. Look at the origin and growth of free Holland and free North America. Contrast England with Spain of the present day; Prussia with Austria; Holland with Portugal; the United States and Canada with the older Mexico and Peru or Brazil. Consider the teeming Protestant literature in every department of learning, science and art; and the countless Protestant churches, schools, colleges, universities, charitable institutions and missionary stations scattered all over the globe. Surely, the Reformation can stand the test: "By their fruits ye shall know them."

NOTES.

Opinions of representative Protestant historians who can not be charged with partisan bias or Romanizing tendency: —

"Whatever judgment," says LEOPOLD VON RANKE, who was a good Lutheran (*Die römischen Päpste*, I. 29), "we may form of the Popes of former times, they had always great interests in view: the care of an oppressed religion, the conflict with heathenism, the propagation of Christianity among the Northern nations, the founding of an independent hierarchical power. It belongs to the dignity of human existence to will and to execute something great. These tendencies the Popes kept in higher motion."

In the last volume of his great work, published after his death (*Weltgeschichte*, Siebenter Theil, Leipzig, 1886, pp. 311–313), RANKE gives his estimate of the typical Pope Gregory VII., of which this is a condensed translation: —

"The hierarchical system of Gregory rests on the attempt to make the clerical power the basis of the entire human existence. This explains the two principles which characterize the system, — the command of [clerical] celibacy, and the prohibition of investiture by the hands of a layman. By the first, the lower clergy were to be made a corporation free from all personal relations to human society; by the second, the higher clergy were to be secured against all influence of the secular power. The great hierarch had well considered his standpoint: he thereby met a want of the times, which regarded the clergy, so to say, as higher beings. All his words had dignity, consistency and power. He had a native talent for worldly affairs. Peter Damiani probably had this in view when he called him, once, the holy Satan. . . . Gregory's deliverances contain no profound doctrines; nearly all were known before. But they are summed up by him in a system, the sincerity of which no one could call in question. His dying words: 'I die in exile, because I loved justice,' express his inmost conviction. But we must not forget that it was only the hierarchical justice which he defended to his last breath." — In the thirteenth chapter, entitled "Canossa," Ranke presents his views on the conflict between Gregory VII. and Henry IV., or between the hierarchical and the secular power.

ADOLF HARNACK, a prominent historian of the present generation, in his commemorative address on *Martin Luther* (Giessen, 1883, p. 7), calls "the idea of the papacy the greatest and most humane idea (*die grösste und humanste Idee*) which the middle age produced."

It was in a review of Ranke's *History of the Popes*, that Lord MACAULAY, a Protestant of Scotch ancestry, penned his brilliant eulogy on the Roman Church as the oldest and most venerable power in Christendom, which is likely to outlast all other governments and churches. "She was great and respected," he concludes, "before the Saxon set his foot on Britain, before the Frank had passed the Rhine, when Grecian eloquence still flourished at Antioch, when idols were still worshiped in the Temple of Mecca. And she may still exist in undiminished vigor, when some traveler from New Zealand shall, in the midst of a vast solitude, take his stand on a broken arch of London Bridge to sketch the ruins of St. Paul's." [1]

But we must not overlook a later testimony, in which the eloquent historian supplemented and qualified this eulogy: —

"From the time," says MACAULAY in the first chapter of his *History of England*, "when the barbarians overran the Western Empire, to the time of the revival of letters, the influence of the Church of Rome had been generally favorable to science, to civilization, and to good government. But, during the last three centuries, to stunt the growth of the human mind has been her chief object. Throughout Christendom, whatever advance has been made in knowledge, in freedom, in wealth, and in the arts of life, has been made in spite of her, and has everywhere been in inverse proportion to her power. The loveliest and most fertile provinces of Europe have, under her rule, been sunk in poverty, in political servitude, and in intellectual tor-

---

[1] First published in the Edinburgh Review, October, 1840. The passage is often quoted by Roman Catholics, e.g., by Archbishop Spalding, in his *History of the Prot. Ref.*, p. 217 sqq.; but they find it convenient to ignore the other passage from his *History of England*.

por; while Protestant countries once proverbial for sterility and barbarism, have been turned, by skill and industry, into gardens, and can boast of a long list of heroes and statesmen, philosophers and poets. Whoever, knowing what Italy and Scotland naturally are, and what, four hundred years ago, they actually were, shall now compare the country round Rome with the country round Edinburgh, will be able to form some judgment as to the tendency of papal domination. The descent of Spain, once the first among monarchies, to the lowest depths of degradation; the elevation of Holland, in spite of many natural disadvantages, to a position such as no commonwealth so small has ever reached, — teach the same lesson. Whoever passes, in Germany, from a Roman-Catholic to a Protestant principality, in Switzerland from a Roman-Catholic to a Protestant canton, in Ireland from a Roman-Catholic to a Protestant county, finds that he has passed from a lower to a higher grade of civilization. On the other side of the Atlantic, the same law prevails. The Protestants of the United States have left far behind them the Roman Catholics of Mexico, Peru, and Brazil. The Roman Catholics of Lower Canada remain inert, while the whole continent round them is in a ferment with Protestant activity and enterprise. The French have doubtless shown an energy and an intelligence which, even when misdirected, have justly entitled them to be called a great people. But this apparent exception, when examined, will be found to confirm the rule; for in no country that is called Roman-Catholic has the Roman-Catholic Church, during several generations, possessed so little authority as in France.

"It is difficult to say whether England owes more to the Roman-Catholic religion or to the Reformation. For the amalgamation of races and for the abolition of villenage, she is chiefly indebted to the influence which the priesthood in the middle ages exercised over the laity. For political and intellectual freedom, and for all the blessings which political and intellectual freedom have brought in their train, she is chiefly indebted to the great rebellion of the laity against the priesthood."

§ 50. *Charles V.*

LITERATURE.

Most of the works on Charles V. are histories of his times, in which he forms the central figure. Much new material has been brought to light from the archives of Brussels and Simancas. He is extravagantly lauded by Spanish, and indiscriminately censured by French historians. The Scotch Robertson, the American Prescott, and the German Ranke are impartial.

I. Joh. Sleidan (d. 1556): *De Statu Religionis et Reipublicæ Carlo V. Cæsare Commentarii*, Argentor. 1555 fol. (best ed. by Am Ende, Frf.-a.-M., 1785). Ludw. v. Seckendorf: *Com. hist. et apol. de Lutheranismo sive de Reformatione Religionis*, Leipzig, 1694. Goes to the year

1546. — The English *Calendars of State-Papers,* — *Spanish,* published by
the Master of the Rolls. — DE THOU: *Historia sui Temporis* (from the
death of Francis I.). — The Histories of Spain by MARIANA (Madrid,
1817–22, 20 vols. 8vo); ZURITA (Çaragoça, 1669–1710, 6 vols. fol.); FER-

PROGENIES · DIVVM · QVINTVS · SIC · CAROLVS · ILLE
IMPERII · CAESAR · LVMINA · ET · ORA · TVLIT
AET · SVAE · XXXI
ANN · M · D · XXXI

CHARLES V.　From an engraving by B. Beham, in 1531.

RERAS (French trans., Amsterdam, 1751, 10 vols. 4to); SALAZAR DE
MENDOZA (Madrid, 1770–71, 3 vols. fol.); MODESTO LAFUENTE (vols.
XI. and XII., 1853), etc.

II. Biographies.　Charles dictated to his secretary, William van Male, while
leisurely sailing on the Rhine, from Cologne to Mayence, in June, 1550,

and afterwards at Augsburg, under the refreshing shade of the Fugger
gardens, a fragmentary autobiography, in Spanish or French, which was
known to exist, but disáppeared, until Baron KERVYN DE LETTENHOVE,
member of the Royal Academy of Belgium, discovered in the National
Library at Paris, in 1861, a Portuguese translation of it, and published
a French translation from the same, with an introduction, under the
title: *Commentaires de Charles-Quint*, Brussels, 1862. An English translation by LEONARD FRANCIS SIMPSON : *The Autobiography of the Emperor Charles V.*, London, 1862 (161 and xlviii. pp.]. It is a summary
of the Emperor's journeys and expeditions (" *Summario das Viages e
Jornadas* "), from 1516 to 1548. It dwells upon the secular events; but
incidentally reveals, also, his feelings against the Protestants, whom he
charges with heresy, obstinacy, and insolence, and against Pope Paul
III., whom he hated for his arrogance, dissimulation, and breach of
promise. Comp. on this work, the introduction of Lettenhove (translated by Simpson), and the acute criticism of Ranke, vol. vi. 75 sqq.

ALFONSO ULLOA: *Vita di Carlo V.*, Venet., 1560. SANDOVAL: *Historia
de la Vida y Hechos del Emperadòr Carlos Quinto*, Valladolid, 1606
(Pampelona, 1618; Antwerp, 1681, 2 vols.). SEPULVEDA (whom the
Emperor selected as his biographer): *De Rebus Gestis Caroli V. Imperatoris*, Madrid, 1780 (and older editions). G. LETI: *Vita del Imperatore
Carlo V.*, 1700, 4 vols. A. DE MUSICA (in Menckenius, *Scriptores Rerum
Germanicarum*, vol. I., Leipzig, 1728). WILLIAM ROBERTSON (d.
1793): *The History of the Reign of the Emperor Charles V.*, London,
1769, 3 vols.; 6th ed., 1787, 4 vols.; new ed. of his *Works*, London,
1840, 8 vols. (vols. III., IV., V.); best ed., Phila. (Lippincott) 1857,
3 vols., with a valuable supplement by W. H. PRESCOTT on the Emperor's life after his abdication, from the archives of Simancas (III., 327–
510). HERMANN BAUMGARTEN: *Geschichte Karls V.*, Stuttgart, 1885
sqq. (to embrace 4 vols.; chiefly based on the English Calendars and the
manuscript diaries of the Venetian historian Marino Sanuto).

III. Documents and Treatises on special parts of his history. G. CAMPOSI:
Carlo V. in Modena (in *Archivio Storico Italiano*, Florence, 1842–53,
25 vols., App.). D. G. VAN MALE: *Lettres sur la vie intérieure de
l'Empéreur Charles-Quint*, Brussels, 1843. K. LANZ: *Correspondenz des
Kaisers Karl V. aus dem kaiserlichen Archiv und der Bibliothèque de
Burgogne in Brussel*, Leipzig, 1844–46, 3 vols.; *Staatspapiere zur Ge-
schichte des Kaisers Karl V.*, Stuttgart, 1845; and *Actenstücke und
Briefe zur Geschichte Karls V.*, Wien, 1853–57. G. HEINE: *Briefe an
Kaiser Karl V., geschrieben von seinem Beichtvater* (Garcia de Loaysa) *in
den Jahren 1530-32*, Berlin, 1848 (from the Simancas archives). Sir W.
MAXWELL STIRLING: *The Cloister-Life of Charles V.*, London, 1852.
F. A. A. MIGNET: *Charles-Quint ; son abdication, son séjour et sa mort
au monastère de Yuste*, Paris, 1854; and *Rivalité de François I. et de*

Charles-Quint, 1875, 2 vols. AMÉDÉE PICHOT: *Charles-Quint, Chronique de sa vie intérieure et de sa vie politique, de son abdication et de sa retraite dans le cloître de Yuste*, Paris, 1854. GACHART (keeper of the Belgic archives): *Retraite et mort de Charles-Quint au monastère de Yuste* (the original documents of Simancas), Brussels. 1854–55, 2 vols.; *Correspondance de Charles-Quint et de Adrien VI.*, Brussels, 1859. HENNE: *Histoire du règne de Charles V. en Belgique*, Brussels, 1858 sqq., 10 vols. TH. JUSTE: *Les Pays-bas sous Charles V.*, 1861. GIUSEPPE DE LEVA: *Storia documentata di Carlo V. in correlazione all' Italia*, Venice, 1863. RÖSLER: *Die Kaiserwahl Karls V.*, Wien, 1868. W. MAURENBRECHER: *Karl V. und die deutschen Protestanten, 1545–1555*, Düsseldorf, 1865; *Studien und Skizzen zur Geschichte der Reformationszeit*, Leipzig, 1874, pp. 99–133. A. v. DRUFFEL : *Kaiser Karl V. und die röm. Curie 1544–1546*. 3 Abth. München, 1877 sqq.

IV. Comp. also RANKE: *Deutsche Geschichte*, I. 240 sqq., 311 sqq.; and on Charles's later history in vols. II., III., IV., V., VI. JANSSEN: *Geschichte des deutschen Volkes*, II. 131 sqq., and vol. III. WEBER: *Allgemeine Weltgeschichte*, vol. X. (1880), 1 sqq. PRESCOTT's *Philip II.*, Bk. 1, chaps. 1 and 9 (vol. I. 1–26; 296–359). MOTLEY's *Rise of the Dutch Republic*, vol. I., Introduction.

Before passing to the Diet of Worms, we must make the acquaintance of Charles V. He is, next to Martin Luther, the most conspicuous and powerful personality of his age. The history of his reign is the history of Europe for more than a third of a century (from 1520–1556).

In the midst of the early conflicts of the Reformation, the Emperor Maximilian I. died at Wels, Jan. 12, 1519. He had worn the German crown twenty-six years, and is called "the last knight." With him the middle ages were buried, and the modern era dawned on Europe.

It was a critical period for the Empire: the religion of Mohammed threatened Christianity, Protestantism endangered Catholicism. From the East the Turks pushed their conquests to the walls of Vienna, as seven hundred years before, the Arabs, crossing the Pyrenees, had assailed Christian Europe from the West; in the interior the Reformation spread with irresistible force, and shook the foundations of the Roman Church. Where was the genius who could save both Christianity and the Reformation, the unity of the Empire and the unity of the Church? A most difficult, yea, an impossible task.

The imperial crown descended naturally on Maximilian's grandson, the young king of Spain, who became the most powerful monarch since the days of Charles the Great. He was the heir of four royal lines which had become united by a series of matrimonial alliances.

Never was a prince born to a richer inheritance, or entered upon public life with graver responsibilities, than Charles V. Spanish, Burgundian, and German blood mingled in his veins, and the good and bad qualities of his ramified ancestry entered into his constitution. He was born with his eventful century (Feb. 24, 1500), at Ghent in Flanders, and educated under the tuition of the Lord of Chièvres, and Hadrian of Utrecht, a theological professor of strict Dominican orthodoxy and severe piety, who by his influence became the successor of Leo X. in the papal chair. His father, Philip I., was the only son of Maximilian and Mary of Burgundy (daughter of Charles the Bold), and cuts a small figure among the sovereigns of Spain as "Philip the Handsome" (Filipe el Hermoso), — a frivolous, indolent, and useless prince. His mother was Joanna, called "Crazy Jane" (Juana la Loca), second daughter of Ferdinand and Isabella, and famous for her tragic fate, her insanity, long imprisonment, and morbid devotion to the corpse of her faithless husband, for whom, during his life, she had alternately shown passionate love and furious jealousy. She became, after the death of her mother (Nov. 26, 1504), the nominal queen of Spain, and dragged out a dreary existence of seventy-six years (she died April 11, 1555).[1]

[1] Her sad story is told by the contemporary historians Gomez, Peter Martyr, Zurita, and Sandoval (from whom the scattered account of Prescott is derived in his *Ferdinand and Isabella*, III. 94, 170 sqq., 212 sqq., 260 sqq.), and more fully revealed in the Simancas and Brussels documents. It has been ably discussed by several modern writers with reference to the unproved

Charles inherited the shrewdness of Ferdinand, the piety of Isabella, and the melancholy temper of his mother which plunged her into insanity, and induced him to exchange the imperial throne for a monastic cell. The same temper reappeared in the gloomy bigotry of his son Philip II., who lived the life of a despot and a monk in his cloister-palace of the Escorial. The persecuting Queen Mary of England, a granddaughter of Isabella, and wife of Philip of Spain, had likewise a melancholy and desponding disposition.

From his ancestry Charles fell heir to an empire within whose boundaries the sun never set. At the death of his father (Sept. 25, 1506), he became, by right of succession, the sovereign of Burgundy and the Netherlands; at the death of Ferdinand (Jan. 23, 1516), he inherited the crown of Spain with her Italian dependencies (Naples, Sicily, Sardinia), and her newly acquired American possessions (to which were afterwards added the conquests of Mexico and Peru); at the death of Maximilian, he succeeded to the hereditary provinces of the house of Habsburg, and soon afterwards to the empire of Germany. In 1530 he was also crowned king of Lombardy, and emperor of the Romans, by the Pope.

The imperial crown of Germany was hotly contested between him and Francis I. All the arts of diplomacy and enormous sums of money were spent on electioneering by

hypothesis of Bergenroth that she was never insane, but suspected and tortured (?) for heresy, and cruelly treated by Charles. But her troubles began long before the Reformation, and her melancholy disposition was derived from her grandmother. She received the extreme unction from priestly hands, and her last word was: "Jesus, thou Crucified One, deliver me." See Gustav Bergenroth (a German scholar then residing in London), *Letters, Despatches, and State Papers relating to the negotiations between England and Spain preserved in the archives of Simancas and elsewhere.* Suppl. to vol. I. and II., London, 1868; Gachard, *Jeanne la Folle,* Bruxelles, 1869; and *Jeanne la Folle et Charles V.*, in the Bulletin of the Brussels Academy, 1870 and 1872; Rösler, *Johanna die Wahnsinnige, Königin von Castilien,* Wien, 1870; Maurenbrecher, *Johanna die Wahnsinnige,* in his "Studien und Skizzen zur Gesch. der Reformationszeit," Leipzig, 1874, pp. 75-98.

both parties. The details reveal a rotten state of the political morals of the times. Pope Leo at first favored the claims of King Francis, who was the natural rival of the Austrian and Burgundian power, but a stranger to the language and manners of Germany. The seven electors assembled at Frankfurt offered the dignity to the wisest of their number, Frederick of Saxony; but he modestly and wisely declined the golden burden lined with thorns. He would have protected the cause of the Reformation, but was too weak and too old for the government of an empire threatened by danger from without and within.[1] He nominated Charles; and this self-denying act of a Protestant prince decided the election, June 28, 1520. When the ambassadors of Spain offered him a large reward for his generosity, he promptly refused for himself, and declared that he would dismiss any of his servants for taking a bribe.

Charles was crowned with unusual splendor, Oct. 23, at Aachen (Aix-la-Chapelle), where the founder of the German Empire lies buried. In his oath he pledged himself to protect the Catholic faith, the Roman Church, and its head the Pope.

The new emperor was then only twenty years of age, and showed no signs of greatness. "*Nondum*" ("Not yet") was the motto which he had adopted for his maiden shield in a tournament at Valladolid two years before. He afterwards exchanged it for "*Plus Ultra.*" He was a good rider, and skilled in military exercises; he could break a lance with any knight, and vanquish a bull in the ring, like an expert espada; but he was in feeble health, with a pale, beardless, and melancholy face, and without interest in public affairs. He had no sympathy with the German nation, and was ignorant of their language. But as soon as he took the reins of power into his own hands, he began to develop a rare genius

---

[1] Martin (*Histoire de France*, VII. 496) says: "*L'électeur Frédéric n'a vait ni la hardiesse ni le génie d'un tel rôle.*"

for political and military government. His beard grew, and he acquired some knowledge of most of the dialects of his subjects. He usually spoke and wrote French and Spanish.

Charles V. as Emperor.

Without being truly great, he was an extraordinary man, and ranks, perhaps, next to Charlemagne and Otho I. among the German emperors.

He combined the selfish conservatism of the house of Habsburg, the religious ardor of the Spaniard, and the warlike spirit of the Dukes of Burgundy. He was the shrewdest prince in Europe, and an indefatigable worker. He usually slept only four hours a day. He was slow in forming his resolutions, but inflexible in carrying them into practice, and unscrupulous in choosing the means. He thought much, and spoke little; he listened to advice, and followed his own judgment. He had the sagacity to select and to keep the ablest men for his cabinet, the army and navy, and the diplomatic service. He was a good soldier, and could endure every hardship and privation except fasting. He was the first of the three great captains of his age, the Duke of Alva being the second, and Constable Montmorency the third.

His insatiable ambition involved him in several wars with France, in which he was generally successful against his bold but less prudent rival, Francis I. It was a struggle for supremacy in Italy, and in the councils of Europe. He twice marched upon Paris.[1]

He engaged in about forty expeditions, by land and sea, in times when there were neither railroads nor steamboats. He seemed to be ubiquitous in his vast dominions. His greatest service to Christendom was his defeat of the army

---

[1] Martin, from his French standpoint, calls the controversy between Francis I. and Charles V. "*la lutte de la nationalité française contre la monstrueuse puissance, issue des combinaisons artificielles de l'hérédité féodale, qui tend à l'asservissement des nationalités européennes.*" (*Hist. de France*, VIII., 2.)

of Solyman the Magnificent, whom he forced to retreat to Constantinople (1532), and his rescue of twenty thousand Christian slaves and prisoners from the grasp of the African corsairs (1535), who, under the lead of the renowned Barbarossa, spread terror on the shores of the Mediterranean. These deeds raised him to the height of power in Europe.

But he neglected the internal affairs of Germany, and left them mostly to his brother Ferdinand. He characterized the Germans as "dreamy, drunken, and incapable of intrigue." He felt more at home in the rich Netherlands, which furnished him the greatest part of his revenues. But Spain was the base of his monarchy, and the chief object of his care. Under his reign, America began to play a part in the history of Europe as a mine of gold and silver.

He aimed at an absolute monarchy, with a uniformity in religion, but that was an impossibility; France checked his political, Germany his ecclesiastical ambition.

His Personal Character.

In his private character he was superior to Francis I., Henry VIII., and most contemporary princes, but by no means free from vice. He was lacking in those personal attractions which endear a sovereign to his subjects.[1] Under a cold and phlegmatic exterior he harbored fiery passions. He was calculating, revengeful, implacable, and never forgave an injury. He treated Francis I., and the German Protestant princes in the Schmalkaldian war, with heartless severity. He was avaricious, parsimonious, and gluttonous. He indulged in all sorts of indigestible delicacies, — anchovies, frogs' legs, eel-pasties, — and drank large quantities of iced beer and Rhine wine; he would not listen to the frequent remonstrances of his physicians and confessors, and would rather endure the discomforts of dyspepsia and gout than

---

[1] Motley (I. 118) calls him "a man without a sentiment and without a tear." But he did shed tears at the death of his favorite sister Eleanore (Prescott, I. 324).

restrain his appetite, which feasted on twenty dishes at a
single meal. In his autobiography he speaks of a fourteenth
attack of gout, which "lasted till the spring of 1548."[1]

He had taste for music and painting. He had also some
literary talent, and wrote or dictated an autobiography in
the simple, objective style of Cæsar, ending with the defeat
of the Protestant league (1548); but it is dry and cold,
destitute of great ideas and noble sentiments.

He married his cousin, Donna Isabella of Portugal, at
Seville, 1526, and lived in happy union with her till her
sudden death in 1539; but during his frequent absences
from Spain, where she always remained, as well as before
his marriage, and after her death, he indulged in ephemeral
unlawful attachments.[2] He had at least two illegitimate
children, the famous Margaret, Duchess of Parma, and Don
Juan of Austria, the hero of Lepanto (1547–1578), who lies
buried by his side in the Escorial.

Charles has often been painted by the master hand of Titian, whom he greatly admired. He was of middle size,
broad-shouldered, deep-chested, with a commanding forehead,
an aquiline nose, a pale, grave, and melancholy countenance.
His blue and piercing eye, his blonde, almost reddish hair,
and fair skin, betokened his German origin, and his project-
ing lower jaw, with its thick, heavy lip, was characteristic
of the princes of Habsburg; but otherwise he looked like a
Spaniard, as he was at heart.

Incessant labors and cares, gluttony, and consequent gout,
undermined his constitution, and at the age of fifty he was
prematurely old, and had to be carried on a litter like a help-

---

[1] English translation, p. 157.
[2] Motley (I. 123) says, on the authority of the Venetian ambassador,
Badovaro: "He was addicted to vulgar and miscellaneous incontinence."
On the same authority he reports of Philip II.: "He was grossly licentious.
It was his chief amusement to issue forth at night, disguised, that he might
indulge in vulgar and miscellaneous incontinence in the common haunts of
vice." (I. 145.)

less cripple. Notwithstanding his many victories and successes, he was in his later years an unhappy and disappointed man, but sought and found his last comfort in the religion of his fathers.

§ 51. *The Ecclesiastical Policy of Charles V.*

The ecclesiastical policy of Charles was Roman Catholic without being ultramontane. He kept his coronation oath. All his antecedents were in favor of the traditional faith. He was surrounded by ecclesiastics and monks. He was thoroughly imbued with the Spanish type of piety, of which his grandmother is the noblest and purest representative. Isabella the Catholic, the greatest of Spanish sovereigns, "the queen of earthly queens,"[1] conquered the Moors, patronized the discoverer of America, expelled the Jews, and established the Inquisition, — all for the glory of the Virgin Mary and the Catholic religion.[2] A genuine Spaniard believes, with Gonzalo of Oviedo, that "powder against the infidels is incense to the Lord." With him, as with his Moorish antipode, the measure of conviction is the measure of intolerance, and persecution the evidence of zeal. The burning of heretics became in the land of the Inquisition a sacred festival, an "act of faith;"[3] and such horrid spectacles were

---

[1] So Shakespeare calls her, and praises her "sweet gentleness," "saint-like meekness," "wife-like government, obeying in commanding."

[2] The inscription on the tomb of Ferdinand and Isabella in the Capilla Real of the cathedral at Granada is characteristic: "*Mahometice secte prostratores et heretice pervicacie extinctores Ferdinandus Aragonum et Helisabetha Castelle vir et uxor unanimes Catholici appellati Marmores clauduntur hoc tumulo.*" The sepulcher is wrought in delicate alabaster ; on it are extended the life-size marble figures of the Catholic sovereigns; their faces are portraits; Ferdinand wears the garter, Isabella the cross of Santiago; the four doctors of the Church ornament the corners, the twelve apostles the sides. Under the same monument rest the ashes of their unfortunate daughter Joanna and her worthless husband. I have seen no monument which surpasses this in chaste and noble simplicity (unless it be that of King Frederick William III. and Queen Louisa at Charlottenburg), and none which is more suggestive of historical meditation and reflection.

[3] *Actus fidei ; auto-de-fé* in Spanish ; *auto-da-fé* in Portuguese.

in the reign of Philip II. as popular as the bull-fights which still flourish in Spain, and administer to the savage taste for blood.

Charles heard the mass daily, listened to a sermon on Sunday and holy days, confessed and communed four times a year, and was sometimes seen in his tent at midnight on his knees before the crucifix. He never had any other conception of Christianity than the Roman-Catholic, and took no time to investigate theological questions.

He fully approved of the Pope's bull against Luther, and ordered it to be executed in the Netherlands. In his retreat at Yuste, he expressed regret that he had kept his promise of safe-conduct; in other words, that he had not burned the heretic at Worms, as Sigismund had burned Hus at Constance. He never showed the least sympathy with the liberal tendencies of the age, and regarded Protestantism as a rebellion against Church and State. He would have crushed it out if he had had the power; but it was too strong for him, and he needed the Protestant support for his wars against France, and against the Turks. He began in the Netherlands that fearful persecution which was carried on by his more bigoted son, Philip II., but it provoked the uprising of the people, and ended in the establishment of the Dutch Republic.[1] He subdued the Lutheran league in the Schmal-

---

[1] Motley (*Dutch Republic*, I. 80) says: " Thousands and tens of thousands of virtuous, well-disposed men and women, who had as little sympathy with anabaptistical as with Roman depravity, were butchered in cold blood, under the sanguinary rule of Charles, in the Netherlands. In 1533, Queen Dowager Mary of Hungary, sister of the Emperor, Regent of the provinces, the 'Christian widow' admired by Erasmus, wrote to her brother, that 'in her opinion, all heretics, whether repentant or not, should be prosecuted with such severity as that error might be at once extinguished, care being only taken that the provinces were not entirely depopulated.' With this humane limitation, the 'Christian widow' cheerfully set herself to superintend as foul and wholesale a system of murder as was ever organized. In 1535, an imperial edict was issued at Brussels, condemning all heretics to death; repentant males to be executed with the sword, repentant females to be buried alive, the obstinate, of both sexes, to be burned. This and similar edicts were the law of the land for twenty years, and rigidly enforced."

kaldian war; pale as death, but trusting in God, he rushed into the hottest of the fight at Mühlberg, and greeted the decisive victory of 1547 with the words: "I came, I saw, and God conquered."[1] But the height of his power was the beginning of his decline. The same Saxon Elector, Moritz, who had aided him against the Protestant princes, turned against him in 1552, and secured in the treaty of Passau, for the first time, some degree of legal toleration to the Lutherans in Germany.

But while Charles was a strict Roman Catholic from the beginning to the end of his life, he was, nevertheless, by no means a blind and slavish papist. Like his predecessors on the German throne, he maintained the dignity and the sovereignty of the state against the claims of hierarchical supremacy. He hated the French, or neutral, politics of the papal court. His troops even captured Rome, and imprisoned Clement VII., who had formed a league with Francis I. against him (1527). He quarreled with Pope Paul III., who in turn severely protested against his tolerant or hesitating policy towards the Protestants in Germany. He says, in his Autobiography,[2] that "the Pope's emissaries, and some ecclesiastics, were incessantly endeavoring to induce him to take up arms against the Protestants (*tomar as armas contra os protestantes*)," but that he "hesitated on account of the greatness and difficulty of such an enterprise."

Moreover, Charles had a certain zeal for a limited reformation of church discipline on the basis of the Catholic doctrine and the papal hierarchy. He repeatedly urged a general council, against the dilatory policy of the Popes, and exhorted Protestants and Catholics alike to submit to its

---

[1] "*Vine, y vi, y Dios vencio.*" But it was hardly a battle. Ranke (vol. IV. 377): "*Es war keine Schlacht, sondern ein Ansprengen auf der einen, ein Auseinanderstieben auf der anderen Seite; in einem Augenblicke war alles vollendet.*" He says of the Emperor (p. 376): "*Wie ein einbalsamirter Leichnam, wie ein Gespenst rückte er gegen sie [die Protestanten] an.*"

[2] Ch. VI., in Simpson's translation, p. 91 sq.

decisions as final. Speaking of the Diet of Augsburg, held in 1530, he says that he "asked his Holiness to convoke and assemble a general council, as most important and necessary to remedy what was taking place in Germany, and the errors which were being propagated throughout Christendom."[1] This was likewise consistent with Spanish tradition. Isabella the Catholic, and Cardinal Ximenes, had endeavored to reform the clergy and monks in Spain.[2]

This Roman-Catholic reformation was effected by the Council of Trent, but turned out to be a papal counter-reformation, and a weapon against Protestantism in the hands of the Spanish order of the Jesuits.

The Emperor and the Reformer.

Charles and Luther saw each other once, and only once, at the Diet of Worms. The Emperor was disgusted with the monk who dared to set his private judgment and conscience against the time-honored creed of Christendom, and declared that he would never make him a heretic. But Luther wrote him a respectful letter of thanks for his safe-conduct.[3]

Twenty years later, after his victory over John Frederick of Saxony at Mühlberg on the Elbe (April 24, 1547), Charles stood on the grave of Luther in the castle church of Wittenberg, and was advised by the bloodthirsty Duke of Alva to

---

[1] *Autobiography*, p. 19. On p. 73 sqq. he complains of Clement VII. and Paul III., on account of their violation of promise to convoke such a council. He does not conceal his hatred of Paul III.

[2] Comp. Maurenbrecher, *Die Kirchenreformation in Spanien*, in his "Studien und Skizzen," pp. 1–40, and his *Geschichte der katholischen Reformation* (Nördlingen, 1880), vol. I., pp. 37–55. Maurenbrecher shows that there were two reformation-currents in the sixteenth century, one proceeding from Spain, and led by Charles V., which aimed at a restoration of the mediæval Church in its purity and glory; the other proceeding from Germany, and embodied in Luther, which aimed at an emancipation of the human mind from the authority of Rome, and at a reconstruction of the Church on the inner religiosity of the individual.

[3] April 28, 1521; in De Wette, I. 589–594.

dig up and burn the bones of the arch-heretic, and to scatter the ashes to the winds of heaven; but he declined with the noble words: "I make war on the living, not on the dead." This was his nearest approach to religious toleration. But the interesting incident is not sufficiently authenticated.[1]

For twenty-six years the Emperor and the Reformer stood at the head of Germany, the one as a political, the other as a religious, leader; working in opposite directions, — the one for the preservation of the old, the other for the creation of the new, order of things. The one had the army and treasure of a vast empire at his command; the other had nothing but his faith and pen, and yet made a far deeper and more lasting impression on his and on future ages. Luther died peacefully in his birthplace, trusting in the merits of Christ, and commending his soul to the God who redeemed him. Ten years later Charles ended his life as a monk in Spain, holding a burning candle in the right hand, and pressing with the left the crucifix to his lips, while the Archbishop of Toledo intoned the Psalm *De Profundis.* The last word of the dying Emperor was "Jesus."

§ 52. *The Abdication of Charles, and his Cloister Life.*

The abdication of Charles, and his subsequent cloister life, have a considerable interest for ecclesiastical as well as general history, and may by anticipation be briefly noted in this place.

In the year 305, the last of the imperial persecutors of Christianity, who was born a slave and reached his power by military achievements, voluntarily resigned the throne of the Cæsars, and retired for the remaining eight years of his

---

[1] In his Autobiography (ch. X., 151 sqq.) Charles speaks of the siege and capitulation of Wittenberg, but says nothing of a visit to Luther's grave, nor does he even mention his name. I looked in vain for an allusion to the fact in Sleidan, and Lindner (in his extensive Appendix to Seckendorf, from 1546 to 1555). Ranke ignores it, though he is very full on this chapter in Charles's history (vol. IV. 378 sqq.).

life to his native Salona in Dalmatia to raise cabbages. In the year 1555 (Oct. 25), Charles V., who was born an heir of three kingdoms, wearied of the race of politics, diplomacy, and war, defeated by the treason of Moritz, and tormented by gout, abdicated his crown to live and die like an humble monk.

The abdication of Charles took place in the royal palace at Brussels, in the same hall in which, forty years before, he had been declared of age, and had assumed the reign of Brabant. He was dressed in mourning for his unfortunate mother, and wore only one ornament, — the superb collar of the Golden Fleece. He looked grave, solemn, pale, broken : he entered leaning on a staff with one hand, and on the arm of William of Orange with the other; behind him came Philip II., his son and heir, small, meager, timid, but magnificently dressed, — a momentous association with the two youthful princes who were to be afterwards arrayed in deadly conflict for the emancipation of the Netherlands from the yoke of Spanish tyranny and bigotry.[1]

The Emperor rose from the throne, and with his right hand resting on the shoulder of the Prince of Orange, — who was one day to become the most formidable enemy of his house, — and holding a paper in the other hand, he addressed his farewell in French before the members of the royal family, the nobility of the Netherlands, the Knights of the Golden Fleece, the royal counselors, and the great officers of the household. He assured them that he had done his duty to the best of his ability, mindful of his dear native land, and especially of the interests of Christianity against

---

[1] "*Ein Moment voll Schicksal und Zukunft!*" says Ranke (V. 295). "*Da war der mächtige Kaiser, der bisher die grossen Angelegenheiten der Welt verwaltet hatte; von denen, die ihm zunächst standen, beinahe der Generation, die ihn umgab, nahm er Abschied. Neben ihm erschienen die Männer, denen die Zukunft gehörte, Philipp II. und der Prinz von Oranien, in denen sich die beiden entgegengesetzten Directionen repräsentirten, die fortan um Weltherrschaft kämpfen sollten.*"

infidels and heretics. He had shrunk from no toil; but a cruel malady now deprived him of strength to endure the cares of government, and this was his only motive for carrying out a long-cherished wish of resigning the scepter. He exhorted them above all things to maintain the purity of the faith. He had committed many errors, but only from ignorance, and begged pardon if he had wronged any one.

He then resigned the crown of the Netherlands to his son Philip with the exhortation, "Fear God: live justly; respect the laws; above all, cherish the interests of religion."

Exhausted, and pale as a corpse, he fell back upon his seat amid the tears and sobs of the assembly.[1]

On the 16th of January, 1556, he executed the deeds by which he ceded the sovereignty of Castile and Aragon, with their dependencies, to Philip. His last act was to resign the crown of Germany into the hands of his brother Ferdinand; but, as affairs move slowly in that country, the resignation was not finally acted on till Feb. 28, 1558, at the Diet at Frankfurt.[2]

His Retirement to Yuste.

On the 17th of September Charles sailed from the harbor of Flushing for Spain with a fleet of fifty-six sails, his two sisters (Mary, formerly queen of Hungary, and regent of the Low Countries, and Eleanor, the widow of King Francis of France), and a hundred and fifty select persons of the imperial household.

After a boisterous voyage, and a tedious land-journey, he arrived, Feb. 3, 1557, at the Convent of St. Gerome in Yuste, which he had previously selected for his retreat.

The resolution to exchange the splendors of the world for monastic seclusion was not uncommon among the rulers and

[1] Sandoval, II. 597 sqq.; Gachart, *Analectes belgiques*, 87; Prescott, *Philip the Second*, I. 10 sqq.; Ranke, V. 293 sqq. Prescott calls this abdication one of the most remarkable scenes in history.

[2] The negotiations with Ferdinand and the German Diet are detailed by Ranke, V. 297 sqq.

nobles of Spain; and the rich convents of Montserrat and
Poblet (now in ruins) had special accommodations for royal
and princely guests. Charles had formed it during the lifetime of the Empress Isabella, and agreed with her that they
would spend the rest of their days in neighboring convents,
and be buried under the same altar. In 1542 he announced
his intention to Francisco de Borgia; but the current of
events involved him in a new and vain attempt to restore
once more the Holy Roman Empire in the fullness of its
power. Now his work was done, and he longed for rest.
His resolution was strengthened by the desire to atone for
sins of unchastity committed after the death of his wife.[1]

Yuste is situated in the mountainous province of Estrema-
dura, about eight leagues from Plasencia and fifty leagues
from Valladolid (then the capital of Spain), in a well-
watered valley and a salubrious climate, and was in every
way well fitted for the wishes of the Emperor.[2]

Here he spent about eighteen months till his death, — a remarkable instance of the old adage, *Sic transit gloria mundi.*

His Cloister Life.

There is something grand and romantic, as well as sad and
solemn, in the voluntary retirement of a monarch who had
swayed a scepter of unlimited power over two hemispheres,
and taken a leading part in the greatest events of an event-

[1] He regretted that, from regard to his son, he had not married again.
Ranke, V. 297.

[2] It is often miscalled *Saint* Yuste, or *St. Justus*, even by Robertson in
Book XII., Eng. ed. III. 294; Amer. ed. III. 226, etc.; and more recently
by Dr. Stoughton, *Spanish Reformers*, Lond., 1883, p. 168. Yuste is not
named after a saint, but after a little stream. The convent was founded in
1404, and its proper name is *El monasterio de San Geronimo de Yuste.* It
lies on the route from Madrid to Lisbon, but is somewhat difficult of access.
It was sacked and almost destroyed by the French soldiers under Soult,
1809. The bedroom of Charles, and an overgrown walnut-tree under whose
shade he used to sit and muse, are still shown. Yuste is now in possession
of the Duke of Montpensier. See descriptions in the works of Stirling,
Mignet, and Prescott, above quoted, and by Ford in Murray's *Handbook
of Spain,* I. 294 (sixth edition).

ful century. There is also an idyllic charm in the combination of the innocent amusements of country life with the exercises of piety.

The cloister life of Charles even more than his public life reveals his personal and religious character. It was represented by former historians as the life of a devout and philosophic recluse, dead to the world and absorbed in preparation for the awful day of judgment;[1] but the authentic documents of Simancas, made known since 1844, correct and supplement this view.

He lived not in the convent with the monks, but in a special house with eight rooms built for him three years before. It opened into gardens alive with aromatic plants, flowers, orange, citron, and fig trees, and protected by high walls against intruders. From the window of his bedroom he could look into the chapel, and listen to the music and prayers of the friars, when unable to attend. He retained over fifty servants, mostly Flemings, including a major-domo (who was a Spaniard), an almoner, a keeper of the wardrobe, a keeper of the jewels, chamberlains, secretaries, physician, confessor, two watchmakers, besides cocks, confectioners, bakers, brewers, game-keepers, and numerous valets.[2] Some of them lived in a neighboring village, and

---

[1] By Sandoval, Strada, and by his most elaborate historian, Dr. Robertson, who says: "There he buried, in solitude and silence, his grandeur, his ambition, together with those projects which, during almost half a century, had alarmed and agitated Europe, filling every kingdom in it, by turns, with the terror of his arms, and the dread of being subdued by his power." Sepulveda, who visited Charles in his retreat, seems to be the only early historian who was aware of his deep interest in public affairs, so fully confirmed by the documents.

[2] "*Aus den Legaten seines Testamentes lernt man die Mitglieder derselben kennen, — eine ganze Anzahl Kammerdiener, besondere Diener für die Fruchtkammer, Obstkammer, Lichtbeschliesserei, Aufbewahrung der Kleider, der Juwelen, meist Niederländer, jedoch unter einem spanischen Haushofmeister, Louis Quixada. Der Leibarzt und eine Apotheke fehlten nicht.*" Ranke, V. 305. The codicil of Charles, executed a few days before his death, specifies the names and vocations of these servants. Sandoval and Gachart give the list, the latter more correctly, especially in the orthography of Flemish names.

would have preferred the gay society of Brussels to the dull monotony of solitude.   He was provided with canopies, Turkish carpets, velvet-lined arm-chairs, six cushions and a footstool for his gouty limbs, twenty-five suits of tapestry, sixteen robes of silk and velvet lined with ermine or eider-down, twelve hangings of the finest black cloth, four large clocks of elaborate workmanship, and a number of pocket-watches. The silver furniture for his table and kitchen amouted to fourteen thousand ounces in weight.   The walls of his room were adorned with choice pictures, nine from the pencil of Titian (including four portraits of himself and one of the Empress). He had also a small library, mostly of devotional books.[1]

He took exercise in his gardens, carried on a litter.   He constructed, with the aid of a skilled artisan, a little handmill for grinding wheat, puppet soldiers, clocks and watches, and endeavored in vain to make any two of them run exactly alike.   The fresh mountain air and exercise invigorated his health, and he never felt better than in 1557.

He continued to take a lively interest in public affairs, and the events of the times.   He greeted with joy the victory of St. Quentin ; with partial dissatisfaction, the conclusion of peace with the Pope (whom he would have treated more severely) ; with regret, the loss of Calais ; with alarm, the advance of the Turkish fleet to Spain, and the progress of the Lutheran heresy.   He received regular dispatches and messengers, was constantly consulted by his son, and freely gave advice in the new complications with France, and especially also in financial matters.   He received visits from his two sisters, — the dowager queens of Hungary and France, who had accompanied him to Spain, — and from the nobles of the surrounding country; he kept up a constant correspondence with his daughter Joanna, regent of Castile, and with his sister, the regent of Portugal.

---

[1] These and other articles of furniture and outfit are mentioned in the inventory.   See Sterling, Pichot, and Prescott, I. 302 sqq.

He maintained the stately Castilian etiquette of dining alone, though usually in the presence of his physician, secretary, and confessor, who entertained him on natural history or other topics of interest. Only once he condescended to partake of a scanty meal with the friars. He could not control, even in these last years, his appetite for spiced capons, pickled sausages, and eel-pies, although his stomach refused to do duty, and caused him much suffering.

But he tried to atone for this besetting sin by self-flagellation, which he applied to his body so severely during Lent that the scourge was found stained with his blood. Philip cherished this precious memorial of his father's piety, and bequeathed it as an heirloom to his son.[1]

From the beginning of his retreat, and especially in the second year, Charles fulfilled his religious duties with scrupulous conscientiousness, as far as his health would permit. He attended mass in the chapel, said his prayers, and listened to sermons and the reading of selections from the Fathers (Jerome, Augustin, Bernard), the Psalms, and the Epistles of Paul. He favored strict discipline among the friars, and gave orders that any woman who dared to approach within two bow-shots of the gate should receive a hundred stripes. He enjoyed the visits of Francisco Borgia, Duke of Gandia, who had exchanged a brilliant position for membership in the Society of the Jesuits, and confirmed him in his conviction that he had acted wisely in relinquishing the world. He wished to be prayed for only by his baptismal name, being no longer emperor or king. Every Thursday was for him a feast of *Corpus Christi*.

He repeatedly celebrated the exequies of his parents, his wife, and a departed sister.

Yea, according to credible contemporary testimony, he celebrated, in the presentiment of approaching death, his own funeral, around a huge catafalque erected in the dark

---

[1] Prescott, *l.c.*, I. 311.

chapel. Bearing a lighted taper, he mingled with his house-hold and the monks in chanting the prayers for the departed, on the lonely passage to the invisible world, and concluded the doleful ceremony by handing the taper to the priest, in token of surrendering his spirit to Him who gave it. According to later accounts, the Emperor was laid alive in his coffin, and carried in solemn procession to the altar.[1]

This relish for funeral celebrations reveals a morbid trait in his piety. It reminds one of the insane devotion of his mother to the dead body of her husband, which she carried with her wherever she went.

His Intolerance.

We need not wonder that his bigotry increased toward the end of life. He was not philosopher enough to learn a lesson of toleration (as Dr. Robertson imagines) from his inability to harmonize two timepieces. On the contrary, he regretted his limited forbearance towards Luther and the German Protestants, who had defeated his plans five years before. They were now more hateful to him than ever.

To his amazement, the same heretical opinions broke out in Valladolid and Sevilla, at the very court and around the throne of Spain. Augustin Cazalla,[2] who had accompanied

---

[1] The story is told with its later embellishments by Robertson and many others. The papers of Simancas, and the private letters of the Emperor's major-domo (Quixada) and physician, are silent on the subject; and hence Tomas Gonzalez, Mignet (1854 and 1857), and Maurenbrecher ("Studien und Skizzen," 1874, p. 132, note) reject the whole as a monkish fiction. But the main fact rests on the testimony of a Hieronymite monk of Yuste, who was present at the ceremony, and recorded the deep impression it made; and it is confirmed by Sandoval, who derived his report directly from Yuste. A fuller account is given by Siguença, prior of the Escorial, in his general history of the Order of St. Jerome (1605); and by Strada, who wrote a generation later, and leaves the Emperor in a swoon upon the floor. Stirling, Pichot, Juste, Gachard (1855), Prescott (*Phil. II.*, Vol. I., 327 sqq.), and Ranke (Vol. V., 309 sq.), accept the fact as told in its more simple form by the oldest witness. It is quite consistent with the character of Charles; for, as Prescott remarks (p. 332), "there was a taint of insanity in the royal blood of Castile."

[2] Commonly called Dr. Cazalla. See on him Dr. Stoughton, *The Spanish Reformers*, p. 204 sq.

him as chaplain in the Smalkaldian war, and had preached before him at Yuste, professed Lutheran sentiments. Charles felt that Spain was in danger, and repeatedly urged the most vigorous measures for the extermination of heresy with fire and sword. "Tell the Grand Inquisitor, from me," he wrote to his daughter Joanna, the regent, on the 3d of May, 1558, "to be at his post, and to lay the ax at the root of the evil before it spreads farther. I rely on your zeal for bringing the guilty to punishment with all the severity which their crimes demand." In the last codicil to his will, he conjures his son Philip to cherish the Holy Inquisition as the best instrument for the suppression of heresy in his dominions. "So," he concludes, "shall you have my blessing, and the Lord shall prosper all your undertakings."[1]

Philip II., who inherited the vices but none of the virtues of his father, faithfully carried out this dying request, and by a terrible system of persecution crushed out every trace of evangelical Protestantism in Spain, and turned that beautiful country into a graveyard adorned by somber cathedrals, and disfigured by bull-rings.

His Death.

The Emperor's health failed rapidly in consequence of a new attack of gout, and the excessive heat of the summer, which cost the life of several of his Flemish companions. He died Sept. 21, 1558, a consistent Catholic as he had lived. A few of his spiritual and secular friends surrounded his death-bed. He confessed with deep contrition his sins; prayed repeatedly for the unity of the Church; received, kneeling in his bed, the holy communion and the extreme unction; and placed his hope on the crucified Redeemer. The Archbishop of Toledo, Bartolomé de Carranza, read the one hundred and thirtieth Psalm, and, holding up a crucifix, said: "Behold Him who answers for all. There is no more sin; all is forgiven;" while another of his preachers

---

[1] Gachard, II. 461. Ranke, V. 308. Prescott, I. 325 sq.

commended him to the intercession of saints, namely, St. Matthew, on whose day he was born, and St. Matthias, on whose day he was in a few moments to leave this world.

"Thus," says Mignet, "the two doctrines which divided the world in the age of Charles V. were once more brought before him on the bed of death."

It is an interesting fact, that the same archbishop who had taken a prominent part in the persecution of English Protestants under Queen Mary, and who administered the last and truly evangelical comfort to the dying Emperor, became a victim of persecution, and that those very words of comfort were used by the Emperor's confessor as one of the grounds of the charge of heresy before the tribunal of the Spanish Inquisition. Bartolomé de Carranza was seven years imprisoned in Spain, then sent to Rome, lodged in the Castle of St. Angelo, after long delay found guilty of sixteen Lutheranizing propositions in his writings, suspended from the exercise of his episcopal functions, and sentenced to be shut up for five years in a convent of his order. He died sixteen days after the judgment, in the Convent Sopra Minerva, May 2, 1576, "declaring his innocence with tears in his eyes, and yet with strange inconsistency admitting the justice of his sentence." [1]

In less than two months after the decease of the Emperor, Queen Mary, his cousin, and wife of his son, died, Nov. 17, 1558, and was borne to her rest in Westminster Abbey. With her the Roman hierarchy collapsed, and the reformed religion, after five years of bloody persecution, was permanently restored on the throne and in the Church of England. In view of this coincidence, we may well exclaim with Ranke, "How far do the thoughts of Divine Providence exceed the thoughts and purposes of men!" [2]

---

[1] His long trial is told by Prescott, *Philip the Second*, I. 337, 437 sqq.; and by Stoughton, *The Spanish Reformers*, pp. 185 sqq.

[2] *Deutsche Gesch.*, vol. V. 311.

His Tomb.

From Yuste the remains of the once mighty Emperor were removed in 1574 to their last resting-place under the altar of the cathedral of the Escorial. That gloomy structure, in a dreary mountain region some thirty miles north of Madrid, was built by his order as a royal burial-place (between 1563 and 1584), and combines a palace, a monastery, a cathedral, and a tomb (called Pantheon). Philip II., "el Escorialense," spent there fourteen years, half king, half monk, boasting that he ruled the Old and New World from the foot of a mountain with two inches of paper. He died, after long and intense suffering, Sept. 13, 1598, in a dark little room facing the altar of the church.

Father and son are represented in gilt-bronze statues, opposite each other, in kneeling posture, looking to the high altar; Charles V., with his wife Isabella, his daughter Maria, and his sisters Eleonora and Maria; Philip II., with three of his wives, and his weak-minded and unfortunate son, Don Carlos.

The Escorial, like Spain itself, is only a shadow of the past, inhabited by the ghost of its founder, who entombed in it his own gloomy character.[1]

---

[1] The convent was robbed of its richest treasures by the French invaders in 1808, and by the Carlists in 1837. Some of the finest pictures were removed to the museum of Madrid. There still remains a considerable library; the books are richly bound, but their gilt backs are turned inside. The Rev. Fritz Fliedner, an active and hopeful Protestant evangelist in Madrid, with whom I visited the Escorial in May, 1886, bought there the ruins of a house and garden, which was built and temporarily occupied by Philip II. (while the palace-monastery was in process of construction), and fitted it up for an orphan-home, in which day by day the Scriptures are read, and evangelical hymns are sung, in the Spanish tongue.

§ 53. *The Diet of Worms.* 1521.

I. Sources. *Acta et res gestæ D. M. Luth. in Comitiis Principum Wormatiæ.* Anno 1521. 4°. *Acta Lutheri in Comitiis Wormatiæ ed. Pollicarius,* Viteb. 1546. These and other contemporary documents are reprinted in the Jena ed. of Luther's *Opera* (1557), vol. II.; in WALCH's German ed., vols. XV., 2018–2325, and XXII., 2026 sqq.; and the Erlangen-Frankf. ed. of the *Opera Lat.,* vol. VI. (1872); *Vermischte deutsche Schriften,* vol. XII. (or *Sämmtl. Werke,* vol. LXIV., pub. 1855), pp. 363–383. FÖRSTEMANN: *Neues Urkundenbuch,* 1842, vol. I. LUTHER's Letters to Spalatin, Cuspinianus, Lucas Cranach, Charles V., etc., see in DE WETTE, I. 586 sqq. SPALATIN: *Ann.* Spalatin is also, according to Köstlin, the author of the contemporary pamphlet: *Etliche wunderliche fleissige Handlung in D. M. Luther's Sachen durch geistliche und weltliche Fürsten des Reich's;* but Brieger (in his "Zeitschrift für Kirchengesch.," Gotha, 1886, p. 482 sqq.) ascribes it to Rudolph von Watzdorf.

On the Roman-Cath. side, COCHLÄUS (who was present at Worms): PALLAVICINI (who used the letters of Aleander); and especially the letters and dispatches of ALEANDER, now published as follows: JOHANN FRIEDRICH: *Der Reichstag zu Worms im Jahr 1521. Nach den Briefen des päpstlichen Nuntius Hieronymus Aleander.* In the "Abhandlungen der Bayer. Akad.," vol. XI. München, 1870. PIETRO BALAN (R. Cath.): *Monumenta Reform. Lutheranæ ex tabulariis S. Sedis secretis.* 1521–1525. Ratisb. Fasc. I., 1883. Contains Aleander's reports from the papal archives, and is one of the first fruits of the liberal policy of Leo XIII. in opening the literary treasures of the Vatican. THEOD. BRIEGER (Prof. of Ch. Hist. in Leipzig): *Aleander und Luther, 1521. Die vervollständigten Aleander-Depeschen nebst Untersuchungen über den Wormser Reichstag.* 1 Abth. Gotha, 1884 (315 pages). Gives the Aleander dispatches in Italian and Latin from a MS. in the library of Trent, and supplements and partly corrects, in the chronology, the edition of Balan.

II. Special Treatises. BOYE: *Luther zu Worms.* Halle, 1817, 1824. ZIMMER: *Luther zu Worms.* Heidelb. 1521. TUZSCHMANN: *Luther in Worms.* Darmstadt, 1860. SOLDAN: *Der Reichstag zu Worms.* Worms, 1863. STEITZ: *Die Melanchthon- und Luther-Herbergen zu Frankfurt-a.-M.* Frankf., 1861. Contains the reports of the Frankfurt delegate Fürstenberg, and other documents. HENNES (R. Cath.): *M. Luther's Aufenthalt in Worms.* Mainz, 1868. WALTZ: *Der Wormser Reichstag und seine Beziehungen zur reformator. Bewegung,* in the "Forschungen zur deutschen Gesch." Göttingen, 1868, VIII. pp. 21–44. DAN. SCHENKEL: *Luther in Worms.* Elberfeld, 1870. JUL. KÖSTLIN: *Luther's Rede in Worms am 18. April, 1521.* Halle, 1874 (the best on

Luther's famous declaration). MAURENBRECHER: *Der Wormser Reichs-tag von 1521*, in his "Studien und Skizzen zur Gesch. der Reform. Zeit," Leipzig, 1874 (pp. 241–275); also in his *Gesch. der kathol. Reformation*, Nördlingen, 1880, vol. I., pp. 181–201. KARL JANSEN (not to be confounded with the Rom.-Cath. Janssen): *Aleander am Reichstage zu Worms, 1521.* Kiel, 1883 (72 pages). Corrects Friedrich's text of Aleander's letters. TH. KOLDE: *Luther und der Reichstag zu Worms.* 2d ed. Halle, 1883. BRIEGER: *Neue Mittheilungen über L. in Worms.* Program to the Luther jubilee, Marburg, 1883 (a critique of Balan's *Monumenta*). KALKOFF: Germ. transl. of the Aleander Dispatches, Halle, 1886. ELTER: *Luther u. der Wormser Reichstag.* Bonn, 1886.

III. RANKE, I. 311–343. GIESELER, IV. 56–58 (Am. ed.). MERLE D'AUB., Bk. VII. chs. I.–XI. HAGENBACH, III. 103–109. G. P. FISHER, pp. 108–111. KÖSTLIN, chs. XVII. and XVIII. (I. 411–466). KOLDE, I. 325 sqq. JANSSEN (R. Cath.), II. 131–166. G. WEBER: *Das Zeitalter der Reformation* (vol. X. of his *Weltgeschichte*), Leipzig, 1886, pp. 162–178. BAUMGARTEN: *Gesch. Karls V.* Leipzig, 1885, vol. I. 379–460.

On the 28th of January, 1521, Charles V. opened his first Diet at Worms. This was a free imperial city on the left bank of the Rhine, in the present grand-duchy of Hesse.[1] It is famous in German song as the scene of the *Niebelungenlied*, which opens with King Günther of Worms and his sister Chriemhild, the world's wonder for grace and beauty. It is equally famous in ecclesiastical history for "the Concordat of Worms," which brought to an end the long contest between the Emperor and the Pope about investiture (Sept. 23, 1122). But its greatest fame the city acquired by Luther's heroic stand on the word of God and the rights of conscience, which made the Diet of 1521 one of the most important in the history of German Diets. After that event two conferences of Protestant and Roman-Catholic leaders were held in Worms, to heal the breach of the Reformation, — one in 1541, and one in 1557; but both failed of their object. In

[1] Worms is 26 miles S. S. E. of Mainz (Mayence or Mentz, the ancient Moguntiacum, the capital of Rhenish Hesse since 1815), and has now over 20,000 inhabitants, about one-half of them Protestants, but in the beginning of the seventeenth century it had 70,000. It was almost destroyed under Louis XIV. (1683). The favorite German wine, *Liebfrauenmilch*, is cultivated in its neighborhood. H. Boos, *Urkundenbuch der Stadt Worms*, Berlin, 1886.

1868 (June 25) a splendid monument to Luther and his fellow-laborers by Rietschel was erected at Worms, and dedicated with great national enthusiasm.[1]

The religious question threw all the political and financial questions into the background, and absorbed the attention of the public mind.

At the very beginning of the Diet a new papal brief called upon the Emperor to give, by an imperial edict, legal force to the bull of January 3, by which Luther was finally excommunicated, and his books condemned to the flames. The Pope urged him to prove his zeal for the unity of the Church. God had girded him with supreme earthly power, that he might use it against heretics who were much worse than infidels.[2] On Maundy Thursday, March 28, the Pope, in proclaiming the terrible bull *In Cœna Domini*, which is annually read at Rome, expressly condemned, among other heretics, Martin Luther by name with all his adherents. This was the third or fourth excommunication, but produced little effect.[3]

The Pope was ably represented by two Italian legates, who were afterwards created cardinals, — Marino Caracciolo (1459–1538) for the political affairs, and Jerome Aleander (1480–1542) for the ecclesiastical interests. Aleander was at that time librarian of the Vatican, and enjoyed great reputation as a Greek scholar. He had lectured at Paris before two thousand hearers of all classes. He stood in friendly

---

[1] See description of the celebration by Dr. Friedrich Eich, *Gedenkblätter*, Worms, 1868; and his book on the controversy about the locality of the Diet, *In welchem Locale stand Luther zu Worms vor Kaiser und Reich?* Leipzig, 1863. He decides for the *Bishofshof* (against the *Rathhaus*).

[2] "*Multo deteriores hœreticos.*" The new papal bull of condemnation, together with a brief to the Emperor, arrived in Worms the 10th of February. Aleander addressed the Diet three days after, on Ash Wednesday. Ranke, I. 329. Köstlin, I., 422 sq.

[3] Luther published this bull afterwards with biting, abusive, and contemptuous comments, under the title, *Die Bulla vom Abendfressen des allerheiligsten Herrn, des Papsts.* In Walch XV. 2127 sqq. Merle d'Aubigné gives characteristic extracts, Bk. VII. ch. 5.

relations to Erasmus; but when the latter showed sympathy
with the Reformation, he denounced him as the chief founder
of the Lutheran heresy.   He was an intense papist, and
skilled in all the arts of diplomacy.   His religious wants
were not very pressing.   During the Diet of Worms he
scarcely found time, in the holy week, "to occupy himself a
little with Christ and his conscience."   His sole object was
to maintain the power of the Pope, and to annihilate the new
heresy.   In his letters he calls Luther a fool, a dog, a basilisk, a ribald.   He urged everywhere the wholesale burning
of his books.[1]   He employed argument, persuasion, promises,
threats, spies, and bribes.   He complained that he could not
get money enough from Rome for greedy officials.   He
labored day and night with the Emperor, his confessor, and
the members of the privy council.   He played on their fears
of a popular revolution, and reminded them of the example
of the Bohemians, the worst and most troublesome of heretics.   He did not shrink from the terrible threat, "If ye Germans who pay least into the Pope's treasury shake off his
yoke, we shall take care that ye mutually kill yourselves,
and wade in your own blood."   He addressed the Diet,
Feb. 13, in a speech of three hours, and contended that
Luther's final condemnation left no room for a further hearing of the heretic, but imposed upon the Emperor and the
Estates the simple duty to execute the requirements of the
papal bull.

The Emperor hesitated between his religious impulses —
which were decidedly Roman Catholic, though with a leaning towards disciplinary reform through a council — and
political considerations which demanded caution and forbearance.   He had already taken lessons in the art of dissimu-

---

[1] Janssen, who praises him very highly, remarks (II. 144): "*Um der
Häresie Einhalt zu thun, hielt Aleander die Verbrennung der lutherischen
Bücher für ein überaus geeignetes Mittel.*" But I can not see why he says
(p. 142) that Aleander prided himself on being "a German."   Aleander was
born in Italy, hated the Germans, and died in Rome.

lation, which was deemed essential to a ruler in those days. He had to respect the wishes of the Estates, and could not act without their consent. Public sentiment was divided, and there was a possibility of utilizing the dissatisfaction with Rome for his interest. He was displeased with Leo for favoring the election of Francis, and trying to abridge the powers of the Spanish Inquisition; and yet he felt anxious to secure his support in the impending struggle with France, and the Pope met him half-way by recalling his steps against the Inquisition. He owed a debt of gratitude to the Elector Frederick, and had written to him, Nov. 28, 1520, to bring Luther to Worms, that he might have a hearing before learned men; but the Elector declined the offer, fearing the result. On the 17th of December, the Emperor advised him to keep Luther at Wittenberg, as he had been condemned at Rome.

At first he inclined to severe measures, and laid the draft of an edict before the Diet whereby the bull of excommunication should be legally enforced throughout all Germany. But this was resisted by the Estates, and other influences were brought to bear upon him. Then he tried indirectly, and in a private way, a compromise through his confessor, John Glapio, a Franciscan friar, who professed some sympathy with reform, and respect for Luther's talent and zeal. He held several interviews with Dr. Brück (Pontanus), the Chancellor of the Elector Frederick. He assured him of great friendship, and proposed that he should induce Luther to disown or to retract the book on the "Babylonian Captivity," which was detestable; in this case, his other writings, which contained so much that is good, would bear fruit to the Church, and Luther might co-operate with the Emperor in the work of a true (that is, Spanish) reformation of ecclesiastical abuses. We have no right to doubt his sincerity any more than that of the like-minded Hadrian VI., the teacher of Charles. But the Elector would not listen to such a proposal, and refused a private audience to Glapio. His conference with Hutten and Sickingen on the Ebern-burg was equally unsuccessful.[1]

The Estates were in partial sympathy with the Reforma-tion, not from doctrinal and religious, but from political and patriotic motives; they repeated the old one hundred and one *gravamina* against the tyranny and extortions of the Roman See[2] (similar to the charges in Luther's Address to the Ger-man Nobility), and resisted a condemnation of Luther with-out giving him a hearing. Even his greatest enemy, Duke George of Saxony, declared that the Church suffered most from the immorality of the clergy, and that a general refor-mation was most necessary, which could be best secured by a general council.

During the Diet, Ulrich von Hutten exerted all his power of invective against the Pope and for Luther. He was har-bored at Ebernburg, a few leagues from Worms, with his friend, the valorous Francis of Sickingen. He poured contempt and ridicule on the speech of Aleander, and even attempted to catch him and Caracciolo by force.[3] But he and Sickingen favored, at the same time, the cause of the young Emperor, from whom they expected great things, and wished to bring about an anti-papal revolution with his aid. Hutten called upon him to dismiss his clerical counsellors, to stand on his own dignity, to give Luther a hearing, and to build up a free Germany. Freedom was now in the air, and all men

[1] See Brück's conversations with Glapio in Förstemann, I., pp. 53, 54. Erasmus and Hutten regarded him as a crafty hypocrite, who wished to ruin Luther. Strauss agrees, *Ulrich von Hutten*, p. 405. But Maurenbrecher, (*Studien*, etc., pp. 258 sqq., and *Gesch. der kath. Ref.*, I. 187 sqq.) thinks that Glapio presented the program of the imperial policy of reform. Janssen, II., 153 sq., seems to be of the same opinion.

[2] See the list in Walch, XV., 2058 sqq.

[3] Luther, in a letter to Spalatin (Nov. 23, 1520, in De Wette I. 523), in a moment of indignation expressed a wish that Hutten might have *intercepted* (*utinam* — INTERCEPISSET) the legates, but not *murdered*, as Romanists (Janssen, twice, II. 104, 143) misinterpret it. See Köstlin, I. 411, and note on p. 797.

of intelligence longed for a new and better order of things.[1]

Aleander was scarcely safe on the street after his speech of February 13. He reported to his master, that for nine-tenths of the Germans the name of Luther was a war-cry, and that the last tenth screamed "Death to the court of Rome!" Cochlæus, who was in Worms as the theological adviser of the Archbishop of Treves, feared a popular uprising against the clergy.

Luther was the hero of the day, and called a new Moses, a second Paul. His tracts and picture, surrounded by a halo of glory, were freely circulated in Worms.[2]

At last Charles thought it most prudent to disregard the demand of the Pope. In an official letter of March 6, he cited Luther to appear before the Diet within twenty-one days under the sure protection of the Empire. The Elector Frederick, Duke George of Saxony, and the Landgrave of Hesse, added letters of safe-conduct through their respective territories.[3]

Aleander now endeavored to make the appearance of Luther as harmless as possible, and succeeded in preventing any discussion with him. The heretic was simply to recant, or, in case of refusal, to suffer the penalties of excommunication.

[1] See Aleander's dispatches in Brieger, *l.c.* I. pp. 119 sqq.; Strauss, *Ulrich von Hutten*, 4th ed., pp. 395 sqq.; and Ullmann, *Franz von Sickingen* (Leipzig, 1872).

[2] Aleander reports (April 13) that Luther was painted with the Holy Spirit over his head (*el spirito santo sopra il capo, come lo depingono*). Brieger, I. 139.

[3] The letters of safe-conduct are printed in Walch, XV., 2122–2127, and Förstemann, *Neues Urkundenbuch*, I., 61 sq. In the imperial letter signed by Albert, Elector and Archbishop of Mayence and Chancellor of the Empire, Luther is addressed as "honorable, well-beloved, pious" (*Ehrsamer, Geliebter, Andächtiger;* in the Latin copy, *Honorabilis, Dilecte, Devote*), much to the chagrin of the Romanists.

§ 54.   *Luther's Journey to Worms.*

"*Mönchlein, Mönchlein, du gehest einen schweren Gang.*"

Luther, from the first intimation of a summons by the Emperor, regarded it as a call from God, and declared his determination to go to Worms, though he should be carried there sick, and at the risk of his life. His motive was not to gratify an unholy ambition, but to bear witness to the truth. He well knew the tragic fate which overtook Hus at Constance notwithstanding the safe-conduct, but his faith inspired him with fearless courage. "You may expect every thing from me," he wrote to Spalatin, "except fear or recantation. I shall not flee, still less recant. May the Lord Jesus strengthen me." [1]

He shared for a while the hope of Hutten and Sickingen, that the young Emperor would give him at least fair play, and renew the old conflict of Germany with Rome; but he was doomed to disappointment.

While the negotiations in Worms were going on, he used incessantly his voice and his pen, and alternated between devotional and controversial exercises. He often preached twice a day, wrote commentaries on Genesis, the Psalms, and the Magnificat (the last he finished in March), and published the first part of his *Postil* (Sermons on the Gospels and Epistles), a defense of his propositions condemned by Rome, and fierce polemical books against Hieronymus Emser, Ambrose Catharinus, and other papal opponents.

Emser, a learned Romanist, and secretary of Duke George of Saxony, had first attacked Luther after the Leipzig disputation, at which he was present. A bitter controversy followed, in which both forgot dignity and charity. Luther

---

[1] Letter of Dec. 21, 1520 (De Wette, I., 534, 536): "*Ego vero, si vocatus fuero, quantum per me stabit, vel ægrotus advehar, si sanus venire non possem. Neque enim dubitari fas est, a Domino me vocari, si Cæsar vocat. . . . Omnia de me præsumas præter fugam et palinodiam : fugere ipse nolo, recantare multo minus. Ita me comfortet Dominus Jesus.*"

called Emser "the Goat of Leipzig" (in reference to the escutcheon of his family), and Emser called Luther in turn "the Capricorn of Wittenberg." Luther's *Antwort auf das überchristliche, übergeistliche, und überkünstliche Buch Bock Emser's*, appeared in March, 1521, and defends his doctrine of the general priesthood of believers.[1] Emser afterwards severely criticised Luther's translation of the Bible, and published his own version of the New Testament shortly before his death (1527).

Catharinus,[2] an eminent Dominican at Rome, had attacked Luther toward the end of December, 1520. Luther in his Latin reply tried to prove from Dan. 8:25 sqq.; 2 Thess. 2:3 sqq.; 2 Tim. 4:3 sqq.; 2 Pet. 2:1 sqq.; and the Epistle of Jude, that popery was the Antichrist predicted in the Scriptures, and would soon be annihilated by the Lord himself at his second coming, which he thought to be near at hand.

It is astonishing that in the midst of the war of theological passions, he could prepare such devotional books as his commentaries and sermons, which are full of faith and practical comfort. He lived and moved in the heart of the Scriptures; and this was the secret of his strength and success.

On the second of April, Luther left Wittenberg, accompanied by Amsdorf, his friend and colleague, Peter Swaven, a Danish student, and Johann Pezensteiner, an Augustinian brother. Thus the faculty, the students, and his monastic order were represented. They rode in an open farmer's wagon, provided by the magistrate of the city. The imperial herald in his coat-of-arms preceded on horseback. Melanchthon wished to accompany his friend, but he was needed at home. "If I do not return," said Luther in taking leave

---

[1] On the Emser controversy see Erl. Frkf. ed., vol. XXVII.

[2] His proper name was Lancelot Politi. See Lämmer, *Vortridentinische Theologie*, p. 21, and Burkhardt, *Luther's Briefwechsel*, p. 38. Luther calls him "*insulsus et stolidus Thomista*," in a letter to Spalatin, March 7, 1521 (De Wette, I. 570).

of him, "and my enemies murder me, I conjure thee, dear
brother, to persevere in teaching the truth. Do my work
during my absence: you can do it better than I. If you
remain, I can well be spared. In thee the Lord has a more
learned champion."

At Weimar, Justus Jonas joined the company. He was
at that time professor and canon at Erfurt. In June of the
same year he moved to Wittenberg as professor of church
law and provost, and became one of the most intimate friends
and co-workers of Luther. He accompanied him on his last
journey to Eisleben, and left us a description of his closing days. He translated several of his and Melanchthon's
works.

The journey to Worms resembled a march of triumph, but
clouded with warnings of friends and threats of foes. In
Leipzig, Luther was honorably received by the magistrate,
notwithstanding his enemies in the University. In Thuringia, the people rushed to see the man who had dared to
defy the Pope and all the world.

At Erfurt, where he had studied law and passed three
years in a monastic cell, he was enthusiastically saluted, and
treated as "the hero of the gospel." Before he reached the
city, a large procession of professors and students of his *alma
mater*, headed by his friends Crotus the rector, and Eoban
the Latin poet, met him. Everybody rushed to see the procession. The streets, the walls, and roofs were covered with
people, who almost worshiped Luther as a wonder-working
saint. The magistrate gave him a banquet, and overwhelmed
him with demonstrations of honor. He lodged in the Augustinian convent with his friend Lange. On Sunday, April
7, he preached on his favorite doctrine, salvation by faith in
Jesus Christ, and against the intolerable yoke of popery.
Eoban, who heard him, reports that he melted the hearts
as the vernal sun melts the snow, and that neither Demosthenes nor Cicero nor Paul so stirred their audiences as

Luther's sermon stirred the people on the shores of the Gera.[1]

During the sermon a crash in the balconies of the crowded church scared the hearers, who rushed to the door; but Luther allayed the panic by raising his hand, and assuring them that it was only a wicked sport of the Devil.[2]

In Gotha and Eisenach he preached likewise to crowded houses. At Eisenach he fell sick, and was bled; but a cordial and good sleep restored him sufficiently to proceed on the next day. He ascribed the sickness to the Devil, the recovery to God. In the inns, he used to take up his lute, and to refresh himself with music.

He arrived at Frankfurt, completely exhausted, on Sunday, April 14. On Monday he visited the high school of William Nesse, blessed the children and exhorted them "to be diligent in reading the Scriptures and investigating the truth." He also became acquainted with a noble patrician family, von Holzhausen, who took an active part in the subsequent introduction of the Reformation in that city.[3]

As he proceeded, the danger increased, and with it his courage. Before he left Wittenberg, the Emperor had issued

[1] A full description of the reception at Erfurt, with extracts from the speech of Crotus and the poems of Eoban, is given by Professor Kampschulte (a liberal Catholic historian), in his valuable monograph, *Die Universität Erfurt*, vol. II. 95–100. "It seems," he says, "that the nation at this moment wished to make every effort to assure Luther of his vocation. The glorifications which he received from the 2d to the 16th of April no doubt contributed much to fill him with that self-confidence which he manifested in the decisive hour. Nowhere was he received more splendidly than at Erfurt."

[2] " *Seid still*," he said, " *liebes Volk, es ist der Teufel, der richtet so eine Spiegelfechterei an; seid still, es hat keine Noth.*" Some of his indiscreet admirers called this victory over the imaginary Devil the first miracle of Luther. The second miracle, they thought, he performed at Gotha, where the Devil played a similar trick in the church, and met with the same defeat.

[3] His brief sojourn at Frankfurt, and his contact with the Holzhausen family, is made the subject of an interesting historical novel: *Haman von Holzhausen. Eine Frankfurter Patriziergeschichte nach Familienpapieren erzählt von M. K.* [*Maria Krummacher*]. Bielefeld and Leipzig, 1885. See especially chap. XX., pp. 253, sqq.

an edict ordering all his books to be seized, and forbidding their sale.[1] The herald informed him of it already at Weimar, and asked him, "Herr Doctor, will ye proceed?" He replied, "Yes." The edict was placarded in all the cities. Spalatin, who knew the critical situation, warned him by special messenger, in the name of the Elector his patron, not to come to Worms, lest he might suffer the fate of Hus.[2] Luther comforted his timid friends with the words: Though Hus was burned, the truth was not burned, and Christ still lives. He wrote to Spalatin from Frankfurt, that he had been unwell ever since he left Eisenach, and had heard of the Emperor's edict, but that he would go to Worms in spite of all the gates of hell and the evil spirits in the air.[3] The day after, he sent him from Oppenheim (between Mainz and Worms) the famous words : —

"I shall go to Worms, though there were as many devils there as tiles on the roofs."[4]

A few days before his death at Eisleben, he thus described

---

[1] The edict is dated March 10. See Burkhardt, *Luther's Briefwechsel* (1866), p. 38, who refers to Spalatin's MS. Seidemann dates the letter from March 2. Ranke, in the sixth ed. (1881), I. 333, says that it was published March 27, on the doors of the churches at Worms. Luther speaks of it in his Eisleben report, and says that the edict was a device of the Archbishop of Mainz to keep him away from Worms, and tempt him to despise the order of the Emperor. *Works*, Erl. Frankf. ed., LXIV. 367.

[2] Notwithstanding this danger, Janssen thinks (II. 158) that it required no "special courage" for Luther to go to Worms.

[3] April 14 (De Wette, I. 587): "*Christus vivit, et intrabimus Wormatiam invitis omnibus portis inferni et potentatibus œris*" (Eph. 2:2).

[4] Spalatin reports the saying thus: "*Dass er mir Spalatino aus Oppenheim gen Worms schrieb: 'Er wollte gen Worms wenn gleich so viel Teufel darinnen wären als immer Ziegel da wären'*" (Walch, XV. 2174). A year afterwards, in a letter to the Elector Frederick, March 5, 1522 (De Wette, II. 139), Luther gives the phrase with this modification: "*Er* [the Devil] *sah mein Herz wohl, da ich zu Worms einkam, dass, wenn ich hätte gewusst, dass so viel Teufel auf mich gehalten hätten, als Ziegel auf den Dächern sind, wäre ich dennoch mitten unter sie gesprungen mit Freuden.*" In the verbal report he gave to his friends at Eisleben in 1546 (Erl. Frankf. ed., vol. LXIV. p. 368): "*Ich entbot ihm* [Spalatin] *wieder: 'Wenn so viel Teufel zu Worms wären als Ziegel auf den Dächern, noch* [doch] *wollt ich hinein.'*"

his feelings at that critical period: "I was fearless, I was
afraid of nothing; God can make one so desperately bold.
I know not whether I could be so cheerful now."[1] Mathesius
says, with reference to this courage: "If the cause is good,
the heart expands, giving courage and energy to evangelists
and soldiers."

Sickingen invited Luther, through Martin Bucer, in person,
to his castle Ebernburg, where he would be perfectly safe
under the protection of friends. Glapio favored the plan,
and wished to have a personal conference with Luther about
a possible compromise and co-operation in a moderate scheme
of reform. But Luther would not be diverted from his aim,
and sent word, that, if the Emperor's confessor wished, he
could see him in Worms.

Luther arrived in Worms on Tuesday morning, April 16,
1521, at ten o'clock, shortly before early dinner, in an open
carriage with his Wittenberg companions, preceded by the
imperial herald, and followed by a number of gentlemen on
horseback. He was dressed in his monastic gown.[2] The
watchman on the tower of the cathedral announced the
arrival of the procession by blowing the horn, and thousands
of people gathered to see the heretic.[3]

As he stepped from the carriage, he said, "God will be
with me."

The papal legate reports this fact to Rome, and adds that
Luther looked around with the eyes of a demon.[4] Cardinal

---

[1] Ibid: "*Denn ich war unerschrocken, fürchtete mich nichts; Gott kann
einen wohl so toll machen. Ich weiss nicht, ob ich jetzt auch so freudig
wäre.*"

[2] See Luther's picture of that year, by Cranach, in the small biography
of Köstlin, p. 237 (Scribner's ed.). It is very different from those to which
we are accustomed.

[3] "*Nun fuhr ich,*" says Luther (LXIV. 368), "*auf einem offenen Wäg-
lein in meiner Kappen zu Worms ein. Da kamen alle Leute auf die Gassen
und wollten den Mönch D. Martinum sehen.*"

[4] Aleander to Vice-Chancellor Medici, from Worms, April 16: "*Esso Luther in descensu currus versis huc et illuc demoniacis oculis disse: 'Deus
erit pro me.'*" Brieger, I. 143.

Cajetan was similarly struck at Augsburg with the mysterious fire of the "profound eyes," and the "wonderful speculations," of the German monk.

Luther was lodged in the house of the Knights of St. John with two counselors of the Elector. He received visitors till late at night.[1]

The city was in a fever-heat of excitement and expectation.

§ 55. Luther's Testimony before the Diet. April 17 and 18, 1521.

See Lit. in § 53.

On the day after his arrival, in the afternoon at four o'clock, Luther was led by the imperial marshal, Ulrich von Pappenheim, and the herald, Caspar Sturm, through circuitous side-streets, avoiding the impassable crowds, to the hall of the Diet in the bishop's palace where the Emperor and his brother Ferdinand resided. He was admitted at about six o'clock. There he stood, a poor monk of rustic manners, yet a genuine hero and confessor, with the fire of genius and enthusiasm flashing from his eyes and the expression of intense earnestness and thoughtfulness on his face, before a brilliant assembly such as he had never seen : the young Emperor, six Electors (including his own sovereign), the Pope's legates, archbishops, bishops, dukes, margraves, princes, counts, deputies of the imperial cities, ambassadors of foreign courts, and a numerous array of dignitaries of every rank ; in one word, a fair representation of the highest powers in Church and State.[2] Several thousand spectators were collected in and around the building and in the streets, anxiously waiting for the issue.

---

[1] "Tutto il mondo," writes Aleander in the same letter, "went to see Luther after dinner."

[2] Walch, XV. 2225–2231, gives a list of over two hundred members of the Diet that were present.

Dr. Johann von Eck,[1] as the official of the Archbishop of Treves, put to him, in the name of the Emperor, simply two questions in Latin and German, — first, whether he acknowledged the books laid before him on a bench (about twenty-five in number) to be his own; and, next, whether he would retract them. Dr. Schurf, Luther's colleague and advocate, who stood beside him, demanded that the titles of those books be read.[2] This was done. Among them were some such inoffensive and purely devotional books as an exposition of the Lord's Prayer and of the Psalms.

Luther was apparently overawed by the august assembly, nervously excited, unprepared for a summary condemnation without an examination, and spoke in a low, almost inaudible tone. Many thought that he was about to collapse. He acknowledged in both languages the authorship of the books; but as to the more momentous question of recantation he humbly requested further time for consideration, since it involved the salvation of the soul, and the truth of the word of God, which was higher than any thing else in heaven or on earth.

We must respect him all the more for this reasonable request, which proceeded not from want of courage, but from a profound sense of responsibility.

The Emperor, after a brief consultation, granted him "out of his clemency" a respite of one day.

Aleander reported on the same day to Rome, that the heretical "fool" entered laughing, and left despondent; that

---

[1] Not to be confounded with the more famous Dr. Eck of Ingolstadt. Aleander, who lodged with him on the same floor, calls him "*homo literatissimo*" and "*orthodoxo*," who had already done good service in the execution of the papal demands at Treves. Brieger, I. 146. In a dispatch of April 29, he solicits a present for him from the Roman See. ("*Al official de Treveri un qualche presente sarebbe util,*" etc., p. 174). Froude, in his *Luther* (pp. 32, 33, 35), confounds the Eck of Treves with the Eck of Ingolstadt, Aleander with Cajetan, and makes several other blunders, which spoil his lively description of the scene at Worms.

[2] "*Legantur tituli librorum,*" he cried aloud.

even among his sympathizers some regarded him now as a fool, others as one possessed by the Devil; while many looked upon him as a saint full of the Holy Spirit; but in any case, he had lost much of his reputation.[1]

The shrewd Italian judged too hastily. On the same evening Luther recollected himself, and wrote to a friend: "I shall not retract one iota, so Christ help me."[2]

On Thursday, the 18th of April, Luther appeared a second and last time before the Diet.

It was the greatest day in his life. He never appeared more heroic and sublime. He never represented a principle of more vital and general importance to Christendom.

On his way to the Diet, an old warrior, Georg von Frundsberg, is reported to have clapped him on the shoulder, with these words of cheer: "My poor monk, my poor monk, thou art going to make such a stand as neither I nor any of my companions in arms have ever done in our hottest battles. If thou art sure of the justice of thy cause, then forward in God's name, and be of good courage: God will not forsake thee."[3]

He was again kept waiting two hours outside the hall, among a dense crowd, but appeared more cheerful and confident than the day before. He had fortified himself by prayer and meditation, and was ready to risk life itself to his honest

---

[1] Letter to Vice-Chancellor Medici, Worms, April 17, 1521 (in Brieger, *l. c.* p. 147): "*El pazzo era entrato ridendo et coram Cesare girava il capo continuamente quà et là, alto e basso; poi nel partir non parea così allegro. Quì molti di quelli et [= etiam] che lo favoreggiavano, poi che l'hanno visto, l'hanno existimado chi pazzo, chi demoniaco, molti altri santo et pieno di spiritu santo; tutta volta ha perso in ogni modo molta reputatione della opinione prima.*"

[2] April 17, to John Cuspinianus, an imperial counsellor. See De Wette, I. 587 sq.

[3] "*Mönchlein, Mönchlein, du gehst jetzt einen Gang, dergleichen ich und mancher Oberster auch in unserer allerernstesten Schlachtordnung nicht gethan haben,*" etc. The saying is reported by Mathesius (who puts it on the second day of trial, not on the first, as Köstlin and others), by Spangenberg, and Seckendorf (Leipzig ed. of 1694, vol. I. 156, in Latin and German).

conviction of divine truth. The torches were lighted when he was admitted.

Dr. Eck, speaking again in Latin and German, reproached him for asking delay, and put the second question in this modified form: "Wilt thou defend *all* the books which thou dost acknowledge to be thine, or recant some part?"

Luther answered in a well-considered, premeditated speech, with modesty and firmness, and a voice that could be heard all over the hall.[1]

After apologizing for his ignorance of courtly manners, having been brought up in monastic simplicity, he divided his books into three classes:[2] (1) Books which simply set forth evangelical truths, professed alike by friend and foe: these he could not retract. (2) Books against the corruptions and abuses of the papacy which vexed and martyred the conscience, and devoured the property of the German nation: these he could not retract without cloaking wickedness and tyranny. (3) Books against his popish opponents: in these he confessed to have been more violent than was proper, but even these he could not retract without giving aid and comfort to his enemies, who would triumph and make things worse. In defense of his books he could only say in the words of Christ: "If I have spoken evil, bear witness of the evil; but if well, why smitest thou me?" If his opponents could convict him of error by prophetic and evangelical Scriptures, he would revoke his books, and be the first to commit them to the flames. He concluded with a warning to the young Emperor not to begin his reign by

---

[1] "*Respondit Doctor Martinus et ipse latine et germanice, quanquam suppliciter, non clamose, ac modeste, non tamen sine Christiana animositate et constantia.*" *Acta*, etc. (*Op. Lat.*, VI. 9). He began with the customary titles: "*Allerdurchlauchtigster, grossmächtigster Kaiser, Durchlauchtige Churfürsten, gnädigste und gnädige Herren!*" These fulsome titles are used to this day in Germany, as if a king or emperor were mightier than the Almighty!

[2] In his report at Eisleben, he calls the three classes briefly *Lehrbücher, Zankbücher*, and *Disputationes*.

condemning the word of God, and pointed to the judgments over Pharaoh, the king of Babylon, and the ungodly kings of Israel.

He was requested to repeat his speech in Latin.[1] This he did with equal firmness and with eyes upraised to heaven.

The princes held a short consultation. Eck, in the name of the Emperor, sharply reproved him for evading the question; it was useless, he said, to dispute with him about views which were not new, but had been already taught by Hus, Wiclif, and other heretics, and had been condemned for sufficient reasons by the Council of Constance before the Pope, the Emperor, and the assembled fathers. He demanded a round and direct answer "without horns."

This brought on the crisis.

Luther replied, he would give an answer "with neither horns nor teeth."[2] From the inmost depths of his conscience educated by the study of the word of God, he made in both languages that memorable declaration which marks an epoch in the history of religious liberty: —

"Unless I am refuted and convicted by testimonies of the Scriptures or by clear arguments (since I believe neither the Pope nor the councils alone; it being evident that they have often erred and contradicted themselves), I am conquered by the Holy Scriptures quoted by me, and my conscience is bound in the word of God: I can not and will not

---

[1] So Luther says himself (in his Eisleben report of the Worms events, in the Erl. Frkf. ed., vol. LXIV. 370): "*Dieweil ich redete, begehrten sie von mir, ich sollt es noch einmal wiederholen mit lateinischen Worten . . . Ich wiederholte alle meine Worte lateinisch. Das gefiel Herzog Friedrich, dem Churfürsten überaus wohl.*" Spalatin confirms this in *Epitome Actorum Lutheri*, etc.: "*Dixit primo germanice, deinde latine.*" Other reports put the Latin speech first; so the *Acta Luth.* (in the Erl. Frkf. ed. of *Op. Lat.*, VI. 9: *respondit D. Martinus et ipse latine et germanice*). Köstlin follows the latter report (I. 445, 451), and overlooked the testimony of Luther, who must have known best.

[2] In the German text, "*ein unstüssige und unbeissige Antwort*" (vol. LXIV. 382); i.e., an answer neither offensive nor biting — with reference, no doubt, to his concluding warning.

recant any thing, since it is unsafe and dangerous to do any thing against the conscience." [1]

So far the reports are clear and harmonious. What followed immediately after this testimony is somewhat uncertain and of less importance.

Dr. Eck exchanged a few more words with Luther, protesting against his assertion that councils may err and have erred. " You can not prove it," he said. Luther repeated his assertion, and pledged himself to prove it. Thus pressed and threatened, amidst the excitement and confusion of the audience, he uttered in German, at least in substance, that concluding sentence which has impressed itself most on the memory of men: —

" Here I stand. [I can not do otherwise.] God help me! Amen." [2]

The sentence, if not strictly historical, is true to the situa-

---

[1] We give also the German and Latin texts. " *Weil denn Eure Kaiserliche Majestät und Eure Gnaden eine schlichte Antwort begehren, so will ich eine Antwort ohne Hörner und Zähne geben diesermassen: 'Es sei denn, dass ich durch Zeugnisse der Schrift oder durch helle Gründe überwunden werde — denn ich glaube weder dem Papst, noch den Konzilien allein, dieweil am Tag liegt, dass sie öfters geirrt und sich selbst widersprochen haben, — so bin ich überwunden durch die von mir angeführten heiligen Schriften, und mein Gewissen ist gefangen in Gottes Wort; widerrufen kann ich nichts und will ich nichts, dieweil wider das Gewissen zu handeln unsicher und gefährlich ist.'* " See Köstlin, I. 452. The oldest reports vary a little in the language. Some have *scheinbarliche und merkliche Ursachen* for *helle Gründe,* and at the close: " *dieweil wider das Gewissen zu handeln beschwerlich und unheilsam, auch gefährlich ist.*" *Werke* (Erl. Frkf. ed.), vol. LXIV. 382.

The Latin text as given in the *Acta Lutheri Wormatiæ habita* is as follows: " *Hic Lutherus: Quando ergo serenissima Majestas vestra Dominationesque vestræ simplex responsum petunt, dabo illud, neque cornutum, neque dentatum, in hunc modum: 'Nisi convictus fuero testimoniis Scripturarum, aut ratione evidente (nam neque Papæ, neque Conciliis solis credo, cum constet eos errasse sæpius, et sibi ipsis contradixisse), victus sum Scripturis a me adductis captaque est conscientia in verbis Dei; revocare neque possum neque volo quidquam, cum contra conscientiam agere neque tutum sit, neque integrum.'* " *Opera Lat.* (Frankf. ed.), vol. VI. 13 sq.

[2] " *Hier steh' ich. [Ich kann nicht anders.] Gott helfe mir! Amen.*" The bracketed words cannot be traced to a primitive source. See the critical note at the close of this section.

tion, and expresses Luther's mental condition at the time, — the strength of his conviction, and prayer for God's help, which was abundantly answered. It furnishes a parallel to Galileo's equally famous, but less authenticated, "It does move, for all that" (*E pur si muove*).

The Emperor would hear no more, and abruptly broke up the session of the Diet at eight o'clock, amid general commotion.

On reaching his lodgings, Luther threw up his arms, and joyfully exclaimed, "I am through, I am through!" To Spalatin, in the presence of others, he said, "If I had a thousand heads, I would rather have them all cut off one by one than make one recantation."

The impression he made on the audience was different according to conviction and nationality. What some admired as the enthusiasm of faith and the strength of conviction, appeared to others as fanaticism and heretical obstinacy.

The Emperor, a stranger to German thought and speech,[1] declared after the first hearing: "This man will never make a heretic of me." He doubted the authorship of the famous books ascribed to him.[2] At the second hearing he was horrified at the disparagement of general councils, as if a German monk could be wiser than the whole Catholic Church. The Spaniards and Italians were no doubt of the same opinion; they may have been repelled also by his lowly appearance and want of refined manners. Some of the Spaniards pursued him with hisses as he left the room. The papal legates reported that he raised his hands after the manner of

---

[1] The little German he knew was only the *Platt-Deutsch* of the Low Countries. He always communicated with his German subjects in Latin or French, or by the mouth of his brother Ferdinand.

[2] Aleander (*l.c.* p. 170): "*Cesar palam dixit et sepissime postea repetiit, che mai crederà che l' habbii composto detti libri.*" The mixing of Latin and Italian is characteristic of the Aleander dispatches. He was inclined to ascribe the authorship of the greater part of Luther's books to Melanchthon, of whom he says that he has "*un belissimo, ma malignissimo ingegno*" (p. 172).

the German soldiers rejoicing over a clever stroke, and represented him as a vulgar fellow fond of good wine.[1] They
praised the Emperor as a truly Christian and Catholic prince
who assured them the next day of his determination to treat
Luther as a heretic. The Venetian ambassador, otherwise
impartial, judged that Luther disappointed expectations, and
showed neither much learning, nor much prudence, nor was
he blameless in life.[2]

But the German delegates received a different impression.
When Luther left the Bishop's palace greatly exhausted,
the old Duke Erik of Brunswick sent him a silver tankard
of Eimbeck beer, after having first drunk of it himself
to remove suspicion. Luther said, " As Duke Erik has
remembered me to-day, may the Lord Jesus remember him
in his last agony." The Duke thought of it on his death-
bed, and found comfort in the words of the gospel: " Whosoever shall give unto one of these little ones a cup of cold
water only, in the name of a disciple, he shall in no wise lose
his reward." The Elector Frederick expressed to Spalatin
the same evening his delight with Luther's conduct: "How
excellently did Father Martin speak both in Latin and German before the Emperor and the Estates! He was bold
enough, if not too much so."[3] The cautious Elector would
have been still better pleased if Luther had been more mod-

---

[1] Aleander and Caracciolo to the Vice-Chancellor Medici, April 19, 1521
(Brieger, I. 153): "*Martino uscito fuora della sala Cesarea alzò la mano in
alto more militum Germanorum, quando exultano di un bel colpo di giostra.*"
In a letter of April 27 (*l.c.* p. 166), they call Luther "*il venerabile ribaldo,*"
who before his departure drank in the presence of many persons "*molte
tazze di malvasia, della qual ne è forte amoroso.*" The charge of intemperance is repeated in a dispatch of April 29 (p. 170): "*la ebrietà, alla quale
detto Luther è deditissimo.*" That Luther used to drink beer and wine according to the universal custom of his age, is an undoubted fact; but that he
was intemperate in eating or drinking, is a slander of his enemies. Melanchthon, who knew him best, bears testimony to his temperance. See below,
the section on his private life.

[2] Contarenus ad Matthæum Dandalum, quoted by Ranke, I. 336.

[3] Walch, XV. 2246.

erate, and not attacked the Councils.   Persons of distinction called on him in his lodgings till late at night, and cheered him.   Among these was the young Landgrave Philip of Hesse, who afterwards embraced the cause of the Reformation with zeal and energy, but did it much harm by his bigamy.   After a frivolous jest, which Luther smilingly rebuked, he wished him God's blessing.[1]

The strongest sympathizers with Luther were outside of the Diet, among the common people, the patriotic nobles, the scholars of the school of Erasmus, and the rising generation of liberal men.   As he returned from the Diet to his lodgings, a voice in the crowd was heard to exclaim: "Blessed be the womb that bare this son."   Tonstal, the English ambassador, wrote from Worms, that "the Germans everywhere are so addicted to Luther, that, rather than he should be oppressed by the Pope's authority, a hundred thousand of the people will sacrifice their lives."[2]   In the imperial chambers a paper was found with the words: "Woe to the nation whose king is a child" (Eccl. x. 16).[3]   An uprising of four hundred German knights with eight thousand soldiers was threatened in a placard on the city hall; but the storm passed away.   Hutten and Sickingen were in the Emperor's service.

---

[1] The interview as related by Luther (Walch, XV. 2247; Erlangen-Frankfurt edition, LXIV. 373) is characteristic of this prince, and foreshadows his future conduct.   "*Der Landgraf von Hessen kam zu Worms erstlich zu mir.   Er war aber noch nicht auf meiner Seiten, und kam in Hof geritten, ging zu mir in mein Gemach, wollte mich sehen.   Er war aber noch sehr jung, sprach: Lieber Herr Doctor, wie geht's?   Da antwortete ich: Gnädiger Herr, ich hoff, es soll gut werden.   Da sagte er: Ich höre, Herr Doctor, ihr lehret, wenn ein Mann alt wird und seiner Frauen nicht mehr Ehepflicht leisten kann, dass dann die Frau mag einen anderen Mann nehmen, und lachte, denn die Hofräthe hatten's ihm eingeblasen.   Ich aber lachte auch und sagte: Ach nein, gnädiger Herr, Euer Fürstlich Gnad sollt nicht also reden.   Aber er ging balde wieder von mir hinweg, gab mir die Hand und sagte: Habt ihr Recht, Herr Doctor, so helfe euch Gott.*"

[2] In Fiddes' *Life of Wolsey*, quoted by Ranke, I. 337, note.

[3] Ranke (1. 337) says "*in den kaiserlichen Gemächern.*"   Other reports say that these words were placarded in public places at Worms.

"Hutten only barks, but does not bite," was a saying in
Worms.

The papal party triumphed in the Diet. Nothing else
could be expected if the historic continuity of the Latin
Church and of the Holy German Roman Empire was to be
preserved. Had Luther submitted his case to a general
council, to which in the earlier stages of the conflict he had
himself repeatedly appealed, the result might have been different, and a moderate reform of the mediæval Church under
the headship of the Pope of Rome might have been accomplished; but no more. By denying the infallibility of a
council, he openly declared himself a heretic, and placed
himself in opposition to the universal opinion, which regarded
œcumenical councils, beginning with the first of Nicæa in
325, as the ultimate tribunal for the decision of theological
controversies. The infallibility of the Pope was as yet an
open question, and remained so till 1870, but the infallibility
of a general council was at that time regarded as settled.
A protest against it could only be justified by a providential
mission and actual success.

It was the will of Providence to prepare the way, through
the instrumentality of Luther, for independent church-organi-
zations, and the development of new types of Christianity on
the basis of the word of God and the freedom of thought.

NOTE ON LUTHER'S SENTENCE: "HERE I STAND," ETC.

These words of Luther have been reported again and again, not only in
popular books, but in learned histories, without a doubt of their genuineness.
They are engraven on his monument at Worms.

But this very fact called forth a critical investigation of the Saxon Archi-
varius, Dr. C. A. H. Burkhardt (author of the learned work: *Luther's
Briefwechsel*), *Ueber die Glaubwürdigkeit der Antwort Luthers: "Hie steh'
ich, ich kann nicht anders, Gott helff mir. Amen,"* in the "Theol. Studien
und Kritiken" for 1869, III. pp. 517–531. He rejects all but the last three
words (not the *whole*, as Janssen incorrectly reports, in his History, II. 165,
note). His view was accepted by Daniel Schenkel (1870), and W. Maurenbrecher (*Gesch. d. kath. Reform.*, 1880, I. 398). The latter calls the words
even "improper and unworthy," because theatrical, which we cannot admit.

On the other hand, Professor Köstlin, the biographer of Luther, has come to the rescue of the whole sentence in his Easter-program: *Luther's Rede in Worms*, Halle, 1874; comp. his notes in the "Studien und Kritiken" for 1882, p. 551 sq., and his *Martin Luther*, I. 453, and the note, p. 800 sq. (second ed. 1883). His conclusion was accepted by Ranke in the sixth ed. of his Hist. of Germany (I. 336), and by Mönckeberg (pastor of St. Nicolai in Hamburg), who supports it by new proofs, in an essay, *Die Glaubwürdigkeit des Lutherwortes in Worms*, in the "Studien und Kritiken" for 1876, No. II. pp. 295–306.

The facts are these. In Luther's own Latin notes which he prepared, probably at Worms, for Spalatin, there is no such sentence except the words, "God help me." The prayer which he offered loudly in his chamber on the evening before his second appearance before the Diet, and which some one has reported, concludes with the words, "*Gott helfe mir, Amen!*" (Walch, X. 1721; Erl.-Frkf. ed., LXIV. 289 sq.). Spalatin in his (defective) notes on the acts of the Diet, preserved at Weimar (*Gesammtarchiv, Reichtagsacten*, 1521), and in his *Annals* (ed. by Cyprian, p. 41), vouches likewise only for the words, "*Gott helfe mir, Amen!*" With this agrees the original edition of the *Acta Lutheri Wormatiæ habita* which were published immediately after the Diet (reprinted in the Frankf. ed. of the *Opera Lat.*, vol. VI. p. 14, see second foot-note).

But other contemporary reports give the whole sentence, though in different order of the words. See the comparative table of Burkhardt, *l.c.* pp. 525–529. A German report (reprinted in the Erl.-Frkf. ed., vol. LXIV. p. 383) gives as the last words of Luther (in reply to Eck): "*Gott kumm mir zu Hilf! Amen. Da bin ich.*" The words "*Da bin ich*" (Here I am) are found also in another source. Mathesius reports the full sentence as coming from the lips of Luther in 1540. In a German contemporary print and on a fly-leaf in the University library of Heidelberg (according to Köstlin), the sentence appears in this order: "*Ich kann nicht anders ; hier steh' ich ; Gott helfe mir.*" In the first edition of Luther's Latin works, published 1546, the words appear in the present order: "*Hier steh' ich,*" etc. In this form they have passed into general currency.

Köstlin concludes that the only question is about the order of words, and whether they were spoken at the close of his main declaration, or a little afterwards at the close of the Diet. I have adopted the latter view, which agrees with the contemporary German report above quoted. Kolde, in his monograph on Luther at Worms (p. 60), agrees substantially with Köstlin, and says: "*Wir wissen nicht mehr, in welchem Zusammenhang diese Worte gesprochen worden sind, auch können sie vielleicht etwas anders gelautet haben ; bei der herrschenden Unruhe hat der eine Berichterstatter den Ausspruch so, der andere ihn so verstanden ; sicherlich drückten sie zu gleicher Zeit seine felsenfeste Überzeugung von der Wahrheit seines in sich gewissen Glaubens aus, wie das Bewusstsein, dass hier nur Gott helfen könne.*"

§ 56. *Reflections on Luther's Testimony at Worms.*

Luther's testimony before the Diet is an event of world-historical importance and far-reaching effect. It opened an intellectual conflict which is still going on in the civilized world. He stood there as the fearless champion of the supremacy of the word of God over the traditions of men, and of the liberty of conscience over the tyranny of authority.

For this liberty, all Protestant Christians, who enjoy the fruit of his courage, owe him a debt of gratitude. His recantation could not, any more than his martyrdom, have stopped the Reformation; but it would have retarded its progress, and indefinitely prolonged the oppressive rule of popery.

When tradition becomes a wall against freedom, when authority degenerates into tyranny, the very blessing is turned into a curse, and history is threatened with stagnation and death.[1] At such rare junctures, Providence raises those pioneers of progress, who have the intellectual and moral courage to break through the restraints at the risk of their lives, and to open new paths for the onward march of history. This consideration furnishes the key for the proper appreciation of Luther's determined stand at this historical crisis.

Conscience is the voice of God in man. It is his most sacred possession. No power can be allowed to stand be-

---

[1] The Devil sometimes tells the truth. So Mephistopheles, in Goethe's *Faust*, when he excuses the aversion of the student to the study of jurisprudence, and says with a wicked purpose: —

> " *Es erben sich Gesetz' und Rechte*
> *Wie eine ew'ge Krankheit fort;*
> *Sie schleppen von Geschlecht sich zum Geschlechte*
> *Und schleichen sacht von Ort zu Ort.*
> *Vernunft wird Unsinn, Wohlthat Plage;*
> *Weh dir, dass du ein Enkel bist!*
> *Vom Rechte, das mit uns geboren ist,*
> *Von dem ist, leider! nie die Frage.*"

tween the gift and the giver. Even an erring conscience must be respected, and cannot be forced. The liberty of conscience was theoretically and practically asserted by the Christians of the ante-Nicene age, against Jewish and heathen persecution; but it was suppressed by the union of Church and State after Constantine the Great, and severe laws were enacted under his successors against every departure from the established creed of the orthodox imperial Church. These laws passed from the Roman to the German Empire, and were in full force all over Europe at the time when Luther raised his protest. Dissenters had no rights which Catholics were bound to respect; even a sacred promise given to a heretic might be broken without sin, and was broken by the Emperor Sigismund in the case of Hus.[1]

This tyranny was brought to an end by the indomitable courage of Luther.

Liberty of conscience may, of course, be abused, like any other liberty, and may degenerate into heresy and licentiousness. The individual conscience and private judgment often do err, and they are more likely to err than a synod or council, which represents the combined wisdom of many. Luther himself was far from denying this fact, and stood open to correction and conviction by testimonies of Scripture and clear arguments. He heartily accepted all the doctrinal decisions of the first four œcumenical councils, and had the deepest

---

[1] Dr. (Bishop) Hefele discusses this case at length from the Roman Catholic standpoint, in his *Conciliengeschichte,* vol. VII. (1869), pp. 218 sqq. He defends Sigismund and the Council of Constance on the ground that a *salvus conductus* protects only against illegal violence, but not against the legal course of justice and deserved punishment, and that its validity for the return of Hus to Bohemia depended on his recantation. But no such condition was expressed in the letter of safe-conduct (as given by Hefele, p. 221), which grants Hus freedom to come, stay, and *return* (*transire, morari et redire libere*). Sigismund had expressly promised him "*ut salvus ad Bohemiam redirem*" (p. 226). Such a promise would have been quite unnecessary in case of his recantation.

respect for the Apostles' Creed on which his own Catechism is based.   But he protested against the Council of Constance for condemning the opinions of Hus, which he thought
were in accordance with the Scriptures.   The Roman Church
itself must admit the fallibility of councils if the Vatican
decree of papal infallibility is to stand; for more than one
œcumenical council has denounced Pope Honorius as a
heretic, and even Popes have confirmed the condemnation of
their predecessor.   Two conflicting infallibilities neutralize
each other.[1]

Luther did not appeal to his conscience alone, but first and
last to the Scripture as he understood it after the most earnest study.   His conscience, as he said, was bound in the
word of God, who cannot err.   There, and there alone, he
recognized infallibility.   By recanting, he would have committed a grievous sin.

One man with the truth on his side is stronger than a
majority in error, and will conquer in the end.   Christ was
right against the whole Jewish hierarchy, against Herod and
Pilate, who conspired in condemning him to the cross.   St.
Paul was right against Judaism and heathenism combined,
"*unus versus mundum;*"   St. Athanasius, "the father of orthodoxy," was right against dominant Arianism;   Galileo
Galilei was right against the Inquisition and the common
opinion of his age on the motion of the earth; Döllinger
was right against the Vatican Council when, "as a Christian, as a theologian, as an historian, and as a citizen," he
protested against the new dogma of the infallibility of the
Pope.[2]

[1]   See my *Church Hist.*, vol. **IV.** 500 sqq.; and *Creeds of Christendom*,
vol. I. 169 sqq.

[2]   Döllinger's declaration of March 28, 1871, for which he was excommunicated, April 17, 1871, notwithstanding his eminent services to the
Roman Catholic Church as her most learned historian, bears some resemblance to Luther's declaration at Worms.   See Schaff, *Creeds of Christendom*, I. 195 sqq.

That Luther was right in refusing to recant, and that he uttered the will of Providence in bearing testimony to the supremacy of the word of God and the freedom of conscience, has been made manifest by the verdict of history.

§ 57. *Private Conferences with Luther. The Emperor's Conduct.*

On the morning after Luther's testimony, the Emperor sent a message — a sort of personal confession of faith — written by his own hand in French, to the Estates, informing them, that in consistency with his duty as the successor of the most Christian emperors of Germany and the Catholic kings of Spain, who had always been true to the Roman Church, he would now treat Luther, after sending him home with his safe-conduct, as an obstinate and convicted heretic, and defend with all his might the faith of his forefathers and of the councils, especially that of Constance.[1]

Some of the deputies grew pale at this decision; the Romanists rejoiced. But in view of the state of public sentiment the Diet deemed it expedient to attempt private negotiations for a peaceful settlement, in the hope that Luther might be induced to withdraw or at least to moderate his dissent from the general councils. The Emperor yielded in spite of Aleander's protest.

The negotiations were conducted chiefly by Richard von Greiffenklau, Elector and Archbishop of Treves, and at his residence. He was a benevolent and moderate churchman, to whom the Elector Frederick and Baron Miltitz had once desired to submit the controversy. The Elector of Brandenburg, Duke George of Saxony, Dr. Vehus (chancellor of the Margrave of Baden), Dr. Eck of Treves, Dean Cochlæus of

---

[1] Walch, XV. 2235-2237.

Frankfort,[1] and the deputies of Strasburg and Augsburg, likewise took part in the conferences.

These men were just as honest as Luther, but they occupied the standpoint of the mediæval Church, and could not appreciate his departure from the beaten track. The archbishop was very kind and gracious to Luther, as the latter himself admitted. He simply required that in Christian humility he should withdraw his objections to the Council of Constance, leave the matter for the present with the Emperor and the Diet, and promise to accept the final verdict of a future council unfettered by a previous decision of the Pope. Such a council might re-assert its superiority over the Pope, as the reformatory councils of the fifteenth century had done.

But Luther had reason to fear the result of such submission, and remained as hard as a rock. He insisted on the supremacy of the word of God over all councils, and the right of judging for himself according to his conscience.[2] He declared at last, that unless convinced by the Scriptures or "clear and evident reasons," he could not yield, no matter what might happen to him; and that he was willing to abide

---

[1] John Cochlæus (his original name was Dobeneck; b. 1479, at Wendelstein in Franconia, d. at Bresau, 1552) was at first as a humanist an admirer of Luther, but turned against him shortly before the Diet of Worms, and became one of his bitterest literary opponents. He went to Worms unasked, and wished to provoke him to a public disputation. He was employed by the Archbishop of Treves as theological counsel, and by Aleander as a spy. Aleander paid him ten guilders "*per sue spese*" (see his dispatch of April 29 in Brieger, I. 175). Cochlæus wrote about 190 books, mostly polemical against the Reformers, and mostly forgotten. Luther treated him with great contempt, and usually calls him "Doctor Rotzlöffel," also "Kochlöffel." See *Works*, Erl. ed., XXXI. 270 sq., 276 sq., 302 sq.; LXII. 74, 78. Otto, *Johann Cochläus, der Humanist*, Breslau, 1874; Felician Gess, *Johannes Cochlæus, der Gegner Luthers*, Oppeln, 1886, IV. 62 pages.

[2] "*Gnädiger Herr*," he said to the Archbishop of Trier, "*ich kann alles leiden, aber die heilige Schrift kann ich nicht übergeben.*" And again: "*Lieber will ich Kopf und Leben verlieren, als das klare Wort Gottes verlassen.*"

by the test of Gamaliel, "If this work be of men, it will be overthrown; but if it is of God, ye will not be able to overthrow it" (Acts 5 : 38, 39).[1]

He asked the Archbishop, on April 25, to obtain for him the Emperor's permission to go home. In returning to his lodgings, he made a pastoral visit to a German knight, and told him in leaving: "To-morrow I go away."

Three hours after the last conference, the Emperor sent him a safe-conduct for twenty-one days, but prohibited him from writing or preaching on the way. Luther returned thanks, and declared that his only aim was to bring about a reformation of the Church through the Scriptures, and that he was ready to suffer all for the Emperor and the empire, provided only he was permitted to confess and teach the word of God. This was his last word to the imperial commissioners. With a shake of hands they took leave of each other, never to meet again in this world.

It is to the credit of Charles, that in spite of contrary counsel, even that of his former teacher and confessor, Cardinal Hadrian, who wished him to deliver Luther to the Pope for just punishment, he respected the eternal principle of truth and honor more than the infamous maxim that no faith should be kept with heretics. He refused to follow the example of his predecessor, Sigismund, who violated the promise of safe-conduct given to Hus, and ordered his execution at the stake after his condemnation by the Council of Con-

---

[1] See the reports on these useless conferences, in Walch, XV. 2237–2347, 2292–2319; Cochlæus, *Com. de Actis Lutheri*, and his *Colloquium cum Luthero Wormatiæ habitum;* the report of Hieronymus Vehus, published by Seidemann, in the "Zeitschrift für histor. Theol.," 1851, p. 80 sqq.; and the report of Aleander in Brieger, I. 157–166. Ranke says (I. 332), one might almost be tempted to wish that Luther had withdrawn his opposition to the councils, and contented himself for the present with the attack upon the abuses of the papacy, in which he had the nation with him; but he significantly adds, that the power of his spirit would have been broken if it had bound itself to any but purely religious considerations. "*Der ewig freie Geist bewegt sich in seinen eigenen Bahnen.*"

stance.[1] The protection of Luther is the only service which Charles rendered to the Reformation, and the best thing, in a moral point of view, he ever did.[2] Unfortunately, he diminished his merit by his subsequent regret at Yuste.[3] He had no other chance to crush the heretic. When he came to Wittenberg in 1547, Luther was in his grave, and the Reformation too deeply rooted to be overthrown by a short-lived victory over a few Protestant princes.

It is interesting to learn Aleander's speculations about Luther's intentions immediately after his departure. He reported to Rome, April 29, 1521, that the heretic would seek refuge with the Hussites in Bohemia, and do four "beastly things" (*cose bestiali*) : 1, write lying *Acta Wormaciensia*, to incite the people to insurrection ; 2, abolish the confessional ; 3, deny the real presence in the sacrament; 4, deny the divinity of Christ.[4]

---

[1] It is asserted by Gieseler and Ranke (I. 341) that the Council gave official sanction to this maxim by declaring with regard to Hus: "*Nec aliqua sibi* [*ei*] *fides aut promissio de jure naturali, divino vel humano fuerit in præjudicium catholicæ fidei observanda.*" Von der Hardt, *Conc. Const.* IV. 521; Mansi, *Concil.* XXVII. 791. Hefele (*Conciliengeschichte,* VII. 227 sq.) charges Gieseler with sinning against the Council and against truth itself, and maintains that this decree, which is only found in the Codex Dorrianus at Vienna, was merely proposed by a member, and not passed by the Council. But the undoubted decree of the 19th Sess., Sept. 23, 1415, declares that a safe-conduct, though it should be observed by him who gave it as far as he was able, affords no protection against the punishment of a heretic if he refuses to recant; and the fact remains that Hus was not permitted to return, and was burned in consequence of his condemnation by the Council and during its session, July 6, 1415. Aeneas Sylvius (afterwards Pope Pius II.) bears to him and Jerome of Prague the testimony: "*Nemo philosophorum tam forti animo mortem pertulisse traditur quam isti incendium.*" The traditional prophecy of Hus: "Now ye burn a goose (*anser*; Hus in Bohemian means goose); but out of my ashes shall rise a swan (*cygnus*, Luther), which you shall not be able to burn," is not authentic, and originated in Luther's time as a *vaticinium post eventum.*

[2] Ranke says (vol. V. 308): "*Es ist die universalhistorisch grösste Handlung Karls V., dass er damals das gegebene Wort höher stellte als die kirchliche Satzung.*"   [3] See above, p. 283.

[4] Brieger, I. 169 sqq. Aleander says in support of the fourth item, that the Lutheran "wretch," Martin Butzer (he calls him Putzer), had already fallen into the diabolical Arian heresy, as he had been told by the Emperor's confessor, Glapio, who had a conference with Butzer and Sickingen.

Luther did none of these things except the second, and this only in part. To prevent his entering Bohemia, Rome made provision to have him seized on the way.

§ 58. *The Ban of the Empire. May 8 (26), 1521.*

After Luther's departure (April 26), his enemies had full possession of the ground. Frederick of Saxony wrote, May 4: "Martin's cause is in a bad state: he will be persecuted; not only Annas and Caiaphas, but also Pilate and Herod, are against him." Aleander reported to Rome, May 5, that Luther had by his bad habits, his obstinacy, and his "beastly" speeches against councils, alienated the people, but that still many adhered to him from love of disobedience to the Pope, and desire to seize the church property.

The Emperor commissioned Aleander to draw up a Latin edict against Luther.[1] It was completed and dated May 8 (but not signed till May 26). On the same day the Emperor concluded an alliance with the Pope against France. They pledged themselves "to have the same friends and the same enemies," and to aid each other in attack and defense.

The edict was kept back till the Elector Frederick and the Elector of the Palatinate with a large number of other members of the Diet had gone home. It was not regularly submitted to, nor discussed and voted on, by the Diet, nor signed by the Chancellor, but secured by a sort of surprise.[2] On Trinity Sunday, May 26, Aleander went with the Latin and German copy to church, and induced the Emperor to sign both after high mass, "with his pious hand." The

---

[1] Aleander reports, May 5: "*Poi me fù commesso per Cesar et el Consilio* (the imperial council), *che io stesso facesse el decreto, con quelle più justificationi si potesse, acciochè il popolo se contentasse.*"

[2] "*Das Edict,*" says Ranke (i. 342), "*ward den Ständen nicht in ihrer Versammlung vorgelegt; keiner neuen Deliberation ward es unterworfen; unerwartet, in der kaiserlichen Behausung bekamen sie Kunde davon, nachdem man nichts versäumt, um sie günstig zu stimmen; die Billigung desselben, die nicht einmal formell genannt werden kann, ward ihnen durch eine Art von Ueberraschung abgewonnen.*"

Emperor said in French, "Now you will be satisfied." —
"Yes," replied the legate in the same language, "but much
more satisfied will be the Holy See and all Christendom, and
will thank God for such a good, holy, and religious Emperor."[1]

The edict is not so long, but as turgid, bombastic, intolerant, fierce, and cruel, as the Pope's bull of excommunication.[2]
It gave legal force to the bull within the German Empire.
It denounces Luther as a devil in the dress of a monk, who
had gathered a mass of old and new heresies into one pool,
and pronounces upon him the ban and re-ban.[3] It commands
the burning, and forbids the printing, publication, and sale,
of his books, the sheltering and feeding of his person, and
that of his followers, and directs the magistrates to seize him
wherever he may be found, and to hand him over to the Emperor, to be dealt with according to the penal laws against
heretics.   At the same time the whole press of the empire
was put under strict surveillance.[4]

This was the last occasion on which the mediæval union of
the secular empire with the papacy was expressed in official
form so as to make the German emperor the executor of the
decrees of the bishop of Rome.   The *gravamina* of the nation
were unheeded.   Hutten wrote: "I am ashamed of my fatherland."[5]

[1] Dispatch of May 26. Brieger, I. 224. The edict appeared in print on
the following Thursday, May 30, and on Friday the Emperor left Worms.

[2] Aleander himself calls it more terrible than any previous edict (*così hor-
ribile quanto mai altro editto*), June 27, 1521. Brieger, I. 241. Ranke says
(I. 343): "*Es war so scharf, so entschieden wie möglich.*"

[3] *Die Acht und Aberacht.* The *Acht* is the civil counterpart of the ecclesiastical excommunication and excludes the victim from all protection of
the law.   The *Aberacht* or *Oberacht* follows if the *Acht* remains without
effect.   It is in the German definition *die völlige Fried- und Rechtslos- oder
Vogelfrei-Erklärung.* The imperial *Acht* is called the *Reichsacht.*

[4] See the edict in full in Walch, XV. 2264–2280. It was published officially in Latin and German, and translated into the languages of the Dutch
and French dominions of Charles. Aleander himself, as he says, prepared
the French translation.

[5] Letter to Pirkheimer, May 1, 1521: "*Me pudere incipit patriæ.*"
Opera II. 59.

Thus Luther was outlawed by Church and State, condemned by the Pope, the Emperor, the universities, cast out of human society, and left exposed to a violent death.

But he had Providence and the future on his side. The verdict of the Diet was not the verdict of the nation.

The departure of the Emperor through the Netherlands to Spain, where he subdued a dangerous insurrection, his subsequent wars with Francis in Italy, the victorious advance of the Turks in Hungary, the protection of Luther by the Elector Frederick, and the rapid spread of Protestant doctrines, these circumstances, combined to reduce the imperial edict, as well as the papal bull, to a dead letter in the greater part of Germany. The empire was not a centralized monarchy, but a loose confederation of seven great electorates, a larger number of smaller principalities, and free cities, each with an ecclesiastical establishment of its own. The love of individual independence among the rival states and cities was stronger than the love of national union ; and hence it was difficult to enforce the decisions of the Diet against a dissenting minority or even a single recalcitrant member. An attempt to execute the edict in electoral Saxony or the free cities by military force would have kindled the flame of civil war which no wise and moderate ruler would be willing to risk without imperative necessity. Charles was an earnest Roman Catholic, but also a shrewd statesman who had to consult political interests. Even the Elector Albrecht of Mainz prevented, as far as he could, the execution of the bull and ban in the dioceses of Mainz, Magdeburg, and Halberstadt. He did not sign the edict as chancellor of the empire.[1] Capito, his chaplain and private counselor, described him in a letter to Zwingli, Aug. 4, 1521, as a promoter of " the gospel," who would not permit that Lu-

---

[1] Janssen, II. 208 sq.: "*Albrecht musste sich beugen vor Luther, der Primus vor dem excommunicirten Mönch, welcher ihm mit Enthüllungen drohte.*"

ther be attacked on the pulpit. And this was the prelate who had been intrusted by the Pope with the sale of indulgences. Such a change had been wrought in public sentiment in the short course of four years.

The settlement of the religious question was ultimately left to the several states, and depended very much upon the religious preferences and personal character of the civil magistrate. Saxony, Hesse, Brandenburg, the greater part of Northern Germany, also the Palatinate, Würtemberg, Nürnberg, Frankfurt, Strassburg, and Ulm, embraced Protestantism in whole or in part; while Southern and Western Germany, especially Bavaria and Austria, remained predominantly Roman Catholic. But it required a long and bloody struggle before Protestantism acquired equal legal rights with Romanism, and the Pope protests to this day against the Treaty of Westphalia which finally secured those rights.

§ 59. *State of Public Opinion. Popular Literature.*

K. Hagen: *Der Geist der Reformation und seine Gegensätze.* Erlangen, 1843. Bd. I. 158 sqq. Janssen, II. 181–197, gives extracts from revolutionary pamphlets to disparage the cause of the Reformation.

Among the most potent causes which defeated the ban of the empire, and helped the triumph of Protestantism, was the teeming ephemeral literature which appeared between 1521 and 1524, and did the work of the periodical newspaper press of our days, in seasons of public excitement. In spite of the prohibition of unauthorized printing by the edict of Worms, Germany was inundated by a flood of books, pamphlets, and leaflets in favor of true and false freedom. They created a public opinion which prevented the execution of the law.

Luther had started this popular literary warfare by his ninety-five Theses. He was by far the most original, fertile, and effective controversialist and pamphleteer of his age. He commanded the resources of genius, learning, courage, eloquence, wit, humor, irony, and ridicule, and had, notwithstanding his many physical infirmities, an astounding power of work. He could express the deepest thought in the clearest and strongest language, and had an abundant supply of juicy and forcible epithets.[1] His very opponents had to imitate his German speech if they wished to reach the masses, and to hit the nail on the head. He had a genial heart, but also a most violent temper, and used it as a weapon for popular effect. He felt himself called to the rough work of "removing stumps and stones, cutting away thistles and thorns, and clearing the wild forests." He found aid and comfort in the severe language of the prophets. He had, as he says, the threefold spirit of Elijah, — the storm, the earthquake, and the fire, which subverts mountains and tears the rocks in pieces. He thoroughly understood the wants and tastes of his countrymen who preferred force to elegance, and the club to the dagger. Foreigners, who knew him only from his Latin writings, could not account for his influence.

Roman historians, in denouncing his polemics, are apt to forget the fearful severity of the papal bull, the edict of Worms, and the condemnatory decisions of the universities.[2]

His pen was powerfully aided by the pencil of his friend Lucas Cranach, the court-painter of Frederick the Wise.

Melanchthon had no popular talent, but he employed his scholarly pen in a Latin apology for Luther "against the furious decree of the Parisian theologasters."[3] The Sor-

---

[1] *Kraftwörter*, as the Germans call them.

[2] Janssen says (II. 181 and 193): "*Den Ton für die ganze damalige polemische Literatur gab Luther an, wie durch seine früheren Schriften, so auch durch die neuen, welche er von der Wartburg aus in die Welt schickte.*" Then he quotes a number of the coarsest outbursts of Luther's wrath, and his disparaging remarks on some books of the New Testament (the Eusebian Antilegomena), all of which, however, are disowned by the Lutheran Church, and more than counterbalanced by his profound reverence for, and submission to, the undoubted writings (the Homologumena). See § 6, pp. 16 sqq.

[3] "*Adversus furiosum Parisiensium theologastrorum Decretum pro Luthero Apologia,*" 1521. In the "Corpus Reformat.," vol. I. 398–416. A copy of the original edition is in the Royal Library at Berlin. An extract, in Carl Schmidt's *Philipp Melanchthon*, pp. 55 sqq.

bonne, hitherto the most famous theological faculty, which in
the days of the reformatory councils had stood up for the
cause of reform, followed the example of the universities of
Louvain and Cologne, and denounced Luther during the sessions of the Diet of Worms, April 15, 1521, as an arch-heretic
who had renewed and intensified the blasphemous errors of
the Manichæans, Hussites, Beghards, Cathari, Waldenses,
Ebionites, Arians, etc., and who should be destroyed by fire
rather than refuted by arguments.[1] Eck translated the
decision at once into German. Melanchthon dared to charge
the faculty of Paris with apostasy from Christ to Aristotle,
and from biblical theology to scholastic sophistry. Luther
translated the Apology into German at the Wartburg, and,
finding it too mild, he added to it some strokes of his
"peasant's axe."[2]

Ulrich von Hutten was almost equal to Luther in literary
power, eloquence, wit, and sarcasm, as well as in courage,
and aided him with all his might from the Ebernburg during
his trial at Worms; but he weakened his cause by want of
principle. He had previously republished and ridiculed the
Pope's bull of excommunication. He now attacked the edict
of Worms, and wrote invectives against its authors, the
papal legates, and its supporters, the bishops.[3] He told the
former how foolish it was to proceed with such impudence
and violence against Luther, in opposition to the spirit of
the age, that the time of revenge would soon come; that the

[1] *Determinatio Theologorum Parisiensium super Doctrina Lutheriana.*
"Corp. Reform." I. 366–388.

[2] "*Mein lieber Philipp,*" he says, "*hat ihnen* [*den groben Pariser Eseln*]
*wohl meisterlich geantwortet, hat sie aber doch zu sanft angerührt und mit
dem leichten Hobel überlaufen ; ich sehe wohl, ich muss mit der Bauernaxt
über die groben Blöcke kommen.*" At the same time there appeared an
anoymous satire against the Paris theologians, in the style of the *Epistolæ
Obscurorum Virorum.* See Schmidt, *l.c.* p. 58.

[3] *In Hieron. Aleandrum et Marinum Caracciolum Oratores Leonis X.
apud Vormaciam Invectivæ singulæ. — In Cardinales, episcopos et Sacer-
dotes, Lutherum Vormaciæ oppugnantes, Invectiva. — Ad Carolum Imp. pro
Luthero exhortatoria.* See Strauss, *Ulrich v. Hutten*, pp. 397 sqq.

Germans were by no means so blind and indifferent as they imagined; that the young Emperor would soon come to a better knowledge. He indignantly reminded Aleander of his shameful private utterance (which was also reported to Luther by Spalatin), that, if the Germans should shake off the papal yoke, Rome would take care to sow so much seed of discord among them that they would eat each other up. He reproached the archbishops and higher clergy for using force instead of persuasion, the secular magistrate instead of the word of Christ against Luther. He told them that they were no real priests; that they had bought their dignities; that they violated common morality; that they were carnal, worldly, avaricious; that they were unable or ashamed to preach the gospel which condemned their conduct, and that if God raised a preacher like Luther, they sought to oppress him. But the measure is full. "Away with you," he exclaims, "ye unclean hogs, away from the pure fountains! Away with you, wicked traffickers, from the sanctuary! Touch no longer the altars with your profane hands! What right have ye to waste the pious benefactions of our fathers in luxury, fornication, and vain pomp, while many honest and pious people are starving? The measure is full. See ye not that the air of freedom is stirring, that men, disgusted with the present state of things, demand improvement? Luther and I may perish at your hands, but what of that? There are many more Luthers and Huttens who will take revenge, and raise a new and more violent reformation."

He added, however, to the second edition, a sort of apologetic letter to Albrecht, the head of the German archbishops, his former friend and patron, assuring him of his continued friendship, and expressing regret that he should have been alienated from the protection of the cause of progress and liberty.

In a different spirit Hans Sachs, the pious poet-shoemaker

of Nürnberg,[1] wrote many ephemeral compositions in prose and poetry for the cause of Luther and the gospel.   He met Luther at Augsburg in 1518, collected till 1522 forty books in his favor, and published in 1523 a poem of seven hundred verses under the title: "*Die Wittenbergisch Nachtigall, Die man jetzt hört überall*," and with the concluding words: "*Christus amator, Papa peccator*."   It was soon followed by four polemical dialogues in prose.

Among the most popular pamphleteers on the Protestant side were a farmer named "Karsthans," who labored in the Rhine country between Strassburg and Basel, and his imitator, "Neukarsthans."   Many pamphlets were anonymous or pseudonymous.

It is a significant fact, that the Reformation was defended by so many laymen.   All the great German classics who arose in more recent times (Klopstock, Lessing, Herder, Goethe, Schiller, Uhland, Rückert), as well as philosophers (Leibnitz, Kant, Fichte, Schelling, Hegel, Herbart, Lotze), are Protestants, at least nominally, and could not have grown on papal soil.

The newness and freshness of this fugitive popular literature called out by the Reformation, and especially by the edict of Worms, made it all the more effective.   The people were hungry for intellectual and spiritual food, and the appetite grew with the supply.

The polemical productions of that period are usually brief, pointed, and aimed at the common-sense of the masses.   They abound in strong arguments, rude wit, and coarse abuse.   They plead the cause of freedom against oppression, of the laity against priestcraft and monkery.   A favorite form of

---

[1] Characteristic for his poetry is the well-known rhyme (which is, however, not found in his works): —

> "*Hans Sachs war ein Schuh-*
> *Macher und Poet dazu.*"

A new edition of his poems appeared at Stuttgart, 1870 sqq.   He figures prominently in Kaulbach's picture of the Reformation.

composition was the dialogue in which a peasant or a laboring-man defeats an ecclesiastic.

The Devil figures prominently in league with the Pope, sometimes as his servant, sometimes as his master. Very often the Pope is contrasted with Christ as his antipode. The Pope, says one of the controversialists, proclaimed the terrible bull of condemnation of Luther and all heretics on the day commemorative of the institution of the holy communion; and turned the divine mercy into human wrath, brotherly love into persecuting hatred, the very blessing into a curse.

St. Peter also appears often in these productions: he stands at the gate of heaven, examining priests, monks, and popes, whether they are fit to enter, and decides in most cases against them. Here is a specimen: A fat and drunken monk knocks at the gate, and is angry that he is not at once admitted; Peter tells him first to get sober, and laughs at his foolish dress. Then he catechises him; the monk enumerates all his fasts, self-mortifications, and pious exercises; Peter orders that his belly be cut open, and, behold! chickens, wild game, fish, omelets, wine, and other contents come forth and bear witness against the hypocrite, who is forthwith sent to the place of punishment.

The writer of a pamphlet entitled " Doctor Martin Luther's Passion," draws an irreverent parallel between Luther's treatment by the Diet, with Christ's crucifixion: Luther's entry into Worms is compared to Christ's entry into Jerusalem, the Diet to the Sanhedrin, Archbishop Albrecht to Caiaphas, the papal legates to the Pharisees, the Elector of Saxony to Peter, Eck and Cochlæus to the false witnesses, the Archbishop of Treves to Pilate, the German nation to Pilate's wife; at last Luther's books and likeness are thrown into the fire, but his likeness will not burn, and the spectators exclaim, " Verily, he is a Christian."

The same warfare was going on in German Switzerland.

Nicolas Manuel, a poet and painter (died 1530), in a carnival play which was enacted at Berne, 1522, introduces first the whole hierarchy, confessing one after another their sins, and expressing regret that they now are to be stopped by the rising opposition of the people; then the various classes of laymen attack the priests, expose their vices, and refute their sophistries; and at last Peter and Paul decide in favor of the laity, and charge the clergy with flatly contradicting the teaching of Christ and the Apostles.[1]

These pamphlets and fugitive papers were illustrated by rude woodcuts and caricatures of obnoxious persons, which added much to their popular effect. Popes, cardinals, and bishops are represented in their clerical costume, but with faces of wolves or foxes, and surrounded by geese praying a *Paternoster* or *Ave Maria*. The "*Passion of Christ and Antichrist*" has twenty-six woodcuts, from the elder Lucas Cranach or his school, which exhibit the contrast between Christ and his pretended vicar in parallel pictures: in one Christ declines the crown of this world, in the other the Pope refuses to open the gate to the Emperor (at Canossa); in one Christ wears the crown of thorns, in the other the Pope the triple crown of gold and jewels; in one Christ washes the feet of his disciples, in the other the Pope suffers emperors and kings to kiss his toe; in one Christ preaches the glad tidings to the poor, in the other the Pope feasts with his cardinals at a rich banquet; in one Christ expels the profane traffickers, in the other the Pope sits in the temple of God; in one Christ rides meekly on an ass into Jerusalem, in the other the Pope and his cardinals ride on fiery steeds into hell.[2]

The controversial literature of the Roman-Catholic Church was far behind the Protestant in ability and fertility. The most popular and effective writer on the Roman side was the Franciscan monk and crowned poet, Thomas Murner. He

---

[1] See Grüneisen's *Nicolaus Manuels Leben und Werke* (1837), pp. 339-392.

[2] *Passional Christi und Antichristi, mit Luther's Nachrede*, 1521, in the Frankf. ed., LXIII., 240-248. Luther accompanied the pictures with texts.

was an Alsatian, and lived in Strassburg, afterwards at Luzern, and died at Heidelberg (1537). He had formerly, in his *Narrenbeschwörung* (1512) and other writings, unmercifully chastised the vices of all classes, including clergy and monks, and had sided with Reuchlin in his controversy with the Dominicans, but in 1520 he turned against Luther, and assailed his cause in a poetical satire: " *Vom grossen lutherischen Narren wie ihn Doctor Murner beschworen hat, 1522.*" [1]

---

[1] Newly edited by H. Kurz, Zürich, 1848. Janssen makes much use of this poem (II. 123–128, 190, 415, 416). Murner thus describes the Protestant attack on the sacraments: —

> " *Die Mess, die sol nim gelten*
> *Im Leben noch im Tod.*
> *Die Sacrament sie schelten,*
> *Die seien uns nit Not.*
> *Fünf hont sie gar vernichtet,*
> *Die andern lon sie ston,*
> *Dermassen zugerichtet,*
> *Dass sie auch bald zergon.*"

Of Luther's doctrine of the general priesthood of the laity he says: —

> " *Wir sein all Pfaffen worden,*
> *Beid Weiber und die Man,*
> *Wiewol wir hant kein Orden*
> *Kein Weihe gnomen an.*"

CHAPTER IV.

THE GERMAN REFORMATION FROM THE DIET OF WORMS
TO THE PEASANTS' WAR, A.D. 1521–1525.

§ 60. *A New Phase in the History of the Reformation.*

AT Worms, Luther stood on the height of his protest
against Rome. The negative part of his work was completed: the tyranny of popery over Western Christendom
was broken, the conscience was set free, and the way opened
for a reconstruction of the Church on the basis of the New
Testament. What he wrote afterwards against Rome was
merely a repetition and re-affirmation.

On his return to Wittenberg, he had a more difficult task
before him: to effect a positive reformation of faith and discipline, worship and ceremonies. A revolution is merely
destructive and emancipative: a reformation is constructive
and affirmative; it removes abuses and corruptions, but saves
the foundation, and builds on it a new structure.

In this home-work Luther was as conservative and churchly
as he had been radical and unchurchly in his war against the
foreign foe. The connecting link between the two periods
was his faith in Christ and the ever-living word of God,
with which he began and ended his public labors.

He now raised his protest against the abuse of liberty in
his own camp. A sifting process was necessary. Division
and confusion broke out among his friends and followers.
Many of them exceeded all bounds of wisdom and moderation; while others, frightened by the excesses, returned to
the fold of the mother Church. The German nation itself
was split on the question of the old or new religion, and

remains, ecclesiastically, divided to this day; but the political unification and reconstruction of the German Empire with a Protestant head, instead of the former Roman-Catholic emperor, may be regarded as a remote result of the Reformation, without which it could never have taken place. And it is a remarkable providence, that this great event of 1870 was preceded by the Vatican Council and the decree of papal infallibility, and followed by the overthrow of the temporal power of the Pope and the political unification of Italy with Rome as the capital.

Before Luther entered upon the new phase in his career, he had a short rest on what he called his "Patmos" (Rev. 1: 9), and his "wilderness." It is the most romantic, as his stand at Worms is the most heroic, chapter in his eventful life.

§ 61. *Luther at the Wartburg. 1521–1522.*

I. LUTHER's Letters, from April 28, 1521, to March 7, 1522, in DE WETTE, vol. I. 588–605; II. 1–141. Very full and very characteristic. WALCH, XV. 2324–2402.

II. C. KÖHLER: *Luther auf der Wartburg.* Eisenach, 1798. A. WITZSCHELL: *Luthers Aufenthalt auf der Wartburg.* Wien, 1876. J. G. MORRIS: *Luther at Wartburg and Coburg.* Philadelphia, 1882.

III. MARHEINEKE, Chap. X. (I. 276 sqq.). MERLE D'AUBIGNÉ, Bk. IX., chs. I. and II. HAGENBACH, III. 105 sqq. FISHER, p. 112. KÖSTLIN, I. 468–525.

Luther left Worms after a stay of ten days, April 26, 1521, at ten o'clock in the morning, quietly, in the same company with which he had made his entrance under the greatest popular commotion and expectation. His friend Schurf went along. The imperial herald joined him at Oppenheim so as not to attract notice.

In a letter to his friend Cranach, dated Frankfurt, April 28, he thus summarizes the proceedings of the Diet : "Have you written these books? Yes. Will you recant? No. Then get thee hence! O we blind Germans, how childish we are to allow ourselves to be so miserably fooled by the Roman-

ists!"[1] In the same letter he takes leave of his Wittenberg
friends, and intimates that he would be hidden for a while,
though he did not know where. He says that he would
rather have suffered death from the tyrants, especially "the
furious Duke George," but he could not despise the counsel
of good people. "A little while, and ye behold me no
more; and again a little while, and ye shall see me (John
16: 16). I hope it will be so with me. But God's will, the
best of all, be done in heaven and on earth."

At Friedberg he dismissed the herald, and gave him a
Latin letter to the Emperor, and a German letter of the same
import to the Estates. He thanked the former for the safe-
conduct, and defended his course at Worms. He could not
trust in the decision of one man or many men when God's
word and eternal interests were at stake, but was still willing
to recant if refuted from the Scriptures.[2]

At Hersfeld he was hospitably entertained in the Benedictine convent by the Abbot Crato, and urged to preach. He
did so in spite of the Emperor's prohibition, obeying God
rather than men. "I never consented," he says, "to tie up
God's word. This is a condition beyond my power."[3] He
preached also at Eisenach, but under protest of the priest
in charge of the parish. Several of his companions parted
from him there, and proceeded in the direction of Gotha
and Wittenberg.

From Eisenach he started with Amsdorf and Petzensteiner
for Möhra to see his relations. He spent a night with his
uncle Heinz, and preached on the next Sunday morning.
He resumed his journey towards Altenstein and Walters-
hausen, accompanied by some of his relatives. On the 4th
of May, a company of armed horsemen suddenly appeared
from the woods, stopped his carriage, amidst cursing and
swearing, pulled him out, put him on horseback, hurried

---

[1] De Wette, I. 588.   [2] De Wette, I. 589, 600.
[3] See his letter to Spalatin, May 14, in De Wette, II. 6.

away with him in full speed, and brought him about midnight to the Wartburg, where he was to be detained as a
noble prisoner of state in charge of Captain von Berlepsch,
the governor of the castle.

The scheme had been wisely arranged in Worms by the
Elector Frederick, whom Aleander calls "the fox of Saxony."
He wavered between attachment to the old faith and inclina-
tion to the new. He could not be sure of Luther's safety
beyond the term of three weeks when the Emperor's safe-
conduct expired; he did not wish to disobey the Emperor,
nor, on the other hand, to sacrifice the reformer, his own
subject, and the pride of his university. He therefore deemed
it best to withdraw him for a season from the public eye.
Melanchthon characterizes him truly when he says of Frederick: " He was not one of those who would stifle changes in
their very birth. He was subject to the will of God. He
read the writings which were put forth, and would not
permit any power to crush what he believed to be true."

The secret was strictly kept. For several months even
John, the Elector's brother, did not know Luther's abode,
and thought that he was in one of Sickingen's castles. Conflicting rumors went abroad, and found credence among the
crowds who gathered in public places to hear the latest news.
Some said, He is dead; others, He is imprisoned, and cruelly
treated. Albrecht Dürer, the famous painter, who was at
that time at Antwerp, and esteemed Luther as "a man
enlightened by the Holy Spirit and a confessor of the true
Christian faith," entered in his diary on Pentecost, 1521, the
prayer that God may raise up another man in his place, and
fill him with the Holy Spirit to heal the wounds of the
Church.

The Wartburg is a stately castle on a hill above Eisenach,
in the finest part of the Thuringian forest. It combines
reminiscences of mediæval poetry and piety with those of
the Reformation. It was the residence of the Landgraves

of Thuringia from 1073 to 1440. There the most famous Minnesängers, Walther von der Vogelweide, and Wolfram von Eschenbach, graced the court of Hermann I. (1190–1217); there St. Elizabeth (1207–1231), wife of Landgrave Ludwig, developed her extraordinary virtues of humility and charity, and began those ascetic self-mortifications which her heartless and barbarous confessor, Conrad of Marburg, imposed upon her. But the most interesting relics of the past are the *Lutherstube* and the adjoining *Reformationszimmer*. The plain furniture of the small room which the Reformer occupied, is still preserved: a table, a chair, a bedstead, a small bookcase, a drinking-tankard, and the knightly armor of Junker Georg, his assumed name. The famous ink-spot is seen no more, and the story is not authentic.[1] In the Wartburg the German students celebrated, in October, 1817, the third jubilee of the Reformation; in the Wartburg Dr. Merle d'Aubigné of Geneva received the inspiration for his eloquent history of the Reformation, which had a wider circulation, at least in the English translation, than any other book on church history; in the Wartburg the Eisenach Conference of the various Lutheran church-governments of Germany inaugurates its periodical sessions for the consultative discussion of matters of common interest, as the revision of the Luther-Bible. The castle was handsomely restored and decorated in mediæval style, in 1847.

Luther's sojourn in this romantic solitude extended through nearly eleven months, and alternated between recreation and work, health and sickness, high courage and deep despondency. Considering that he there translated the New Testament, it was the most useful year of his life. He gives a full

[1] On my last visit, July 31, 1886, I saw only scratches and disfigurements on the wall where the ink-spot was formerly pointed out. "No old reporter," says Köstlin, I. 472 sq., "knows any thing about the spot of the inkstand on the wall; the story arose probably from a spot of a different sort." Semler saw such an ink-spot at Coburg. The legend, however, embodies a true idea.

description of it in letters to his Wittenberg friends, especially to Spalatin and Melanchthon, which were transmitted by secret messengers, and dated from "Patmos," or "the wilderness," from "the region of the air," or "the region of the birds."

He was known and treated during this episode as Knight George. He exchanged the monastic gown for the dress of a gentleman, let his hair and beard grow, wore a coat of mail, a sword, and a golden chain, and had to imitate courtly manners. He was served by two pages, who brought the meals to his room twice a day. His food was much better than he had been accustomed to as a monk, and brought on dyspepsia and insomnia. He enjoyed the singing of the birds, "sweetly lauding God day and night with all their strength." He made excursions with an attendant. Sometimes he took a book along, but was reminded that a knight and a scholar were different beings. He engaged in conversation on the way, with priests and monks, about ecclesiastical affairs, and the uncertain whereabouts of Luther, till he was requested to go on. He took part in the chase, but indulged in theological thoughts among the huntsmen and animals. "We caught a few hares and partridges," he said, "a worthy occupation for idle people." The nets and dogs reminded him of the arts of the Devil entangling and pursuing poor human souls. He sheltered a hunted hare, but the dogs tore it to pieces; this suggested to him the rage of the Devil and the Pope to destroy those whom he wished to preserve. It would be better, he thought, to hunt bears and wolves.

He had many a personal encounter with the Devil, whose existence was as certain to him as his own. More than once he threw the inkstand at him — not literally, but spiritually. His severest blow at the archfiend was the translation of the New Testament. His own doubts, carnal temptations, evil thoughts, as well as the dangers threatening him and his work from his enemies, projected themselves into apparitions of the prince of darkness. He heard his noises at night, in a chest, in a bag of nuts, and on the staircase "as if a hundred barrels were rolled from top to bottom." Once he saw him in the shape of a big black dog lying in his bed; he threw the creature out of the window; but it did not bark, and disappeared.[1] Sometimes he resorted to jokes. The Devil, he said, will bear any thing better than to be despised and laughed at.[2]

Luther was brought up in all the mediæval superstitions concerning demons, ghosts, witches, and sorcerers. His imagination clothed ideas in concrete, massive forms. The Devil was to him the personal embodiment of all evil and mischief in the world. Hence he figures very largely in his theology and religious experience.[3] He is the direct antipode of God, and the archfiend of Christ and of men. As God is pure love, so the Devil is pure selfishness, hatred, and envy. He is endowed with high intellectual gifts, as bad men often surpass good men in prudence and understanding. He was originally an archangel, but moved by pride and envy against the Son of God, whose incarnation and saving work he fore-saw, he rose in rebellion against it. He commands an organized army of fallen angels and bad men in constant conflict with God and the good angels. He is the god of

---

[1] In Goethe's *Faust*, Mephistopheles appears in the disguise of a poodle, the *canis infernus*, and is conjured by the sign of a cross:

> "*Bist du, Geselle,*
> *Ein Flüchtling der Hölle?*
> *So sieh diess Zeichen,*
> *Dem sie sich beugen*
> *Die schwarzen Schaaren.*"

[2] "*Verachtung kann der stolze hoffährtige Geist nicht leiden.*" *Tischreden.* (LX. 75. Erl.-Frkf. ed.)

[3] In the alphabetical index of the Erlangen-Frankfurt edition of Luther's German Works, the title *Teufel* fills no less than ten closely printed pages (vol. LXVII. 243-253). His Table-Talk on the Devil occupies about 150 pages in vols. LIX. and LX. It is instructive and interesting to read it through. Michelet devotes a whole chapter to this subject (pp. 219-234). For a systematic view, see Köstlin, *Luther's Theologie*, vol. II. 313 sq.; 351 sqq.

this world, and knows how to rule it. He has power over nature, and can make thunder and lightning, hail and earth-quake, fleas and bed-bugs. He is the ape of God. He can imitate Christ, and is most dangerous in the garb of an angel of light. He is most busy where the Word of God is preached. He is proud and haughty, although he can appear most hum-ble. He is a liar and a murderer from the beginning. He understands a thousand arts. He hates men because they are creatures of God. He is everywhere around them, and tries to hurt and seduce them. He kindles strife and enmity. He is the author of all heresies and persecutions. He invented popery, as a counterpart of the true kingdom of God. He inflicts trials, sickness, and death upon individuals. He tempts them to break the Ten Commandments, to doubt God's word, and to blaspheme. He leads into infidelity and despair. He hates matrimony, mirth, and music. He can not bear singing, least of all "spiritual songs."[1] He holds the human will captive, and rides it as his donkey. He can quote Scripture, but only as much of it as suits his purpose. A Christian should know that the Devil is nearer him than his coat or shirt, yea, than his own skin. Luther reports that he often disputed with the Devil in the night, about the state of his soul, so earnestly that he himself perspired profusely, and trembled. Once the Devil told him that he was a great sinner. "I knew that long ago," replied Luther, "tell me something new. Christ has taken my sins upon himself, and forgiven them long ago. Now grind your teeth." At other times he returned the charge and tauntingly asked him, "Holy Satan, pray for me," or, "Physician, cure thyself." The Devil assumes visible forms, and appears as a dog or a

---

[1] "*Der Teufel ist ein trauriger Geist,*" he says in his *Table-Talk* (LX. 60), "*und macht traurige Leute ; darum kann er Fröhlichkeit nicht leiden. Daher kommt's auch, dass er von der Musica aufs Weiteste fleuget ; er bleibt nicht, wenn man singt, sonderlich geistliche Lieder. Also linderte David mit seiner Harfen dem Saul seine Anfechtung, da ihn der Teufel plagte.*"

hog or a goat, or as a flame or star, or as a man with horns. He is noisy and boisterous.[1] He is at the bottom of all witchcraft and ghost-trickery. He steals little children and substitutes others in their place, who are mere lumps of flesh and torment the parents, but die young.[2] Luther was disposed to trace many mediæval miracles of the Roman Catholic Church to the agency of Satan. He believed in *dæmones incubos et succubos.*

But, after all, the Devil has no real power over believers. He hates prayer, and flees from the cross and from the Word of God as from a flaming fire. If you cannot expel him by texts of Holy Scripture, the best way is to jeer and flout him. A pious nun once scared him away by simply saying: " *Christiana sum.*" Christ has slain him, and will cast him out at last into the fire of hell. Hence Luther sings in his battle hymn, —

> " And let the Prince of ill
> Look grim as e'er he will,
> He harms us not a whit:
> For why? His doom is writ,
> One little word shall slay him."

Luther was at times deeply dejected in spirit. He wrote to Melanchthon, July 13, under the influence of dyspepsia which paints every thing in the darkest colors: " You elevate me too high, and fall into the serious error of giving me too much credit, as if I were absorbed in God's cause. This high opinion of yours confounds and racks me, when I see myself insensible, hardened, sunk in idleness, alas! seldom in prayer, and not venting one groan over God's Church. My unsubdued flesh burns me with devouring fire. In short, I who ought to be eaten up with the spirit, am devoured by

---

[1] *Ein Polter-und Rumpel-Geist.*

[2] " *Solche Wechselbälge* [or *Wechselkinder,* changelings] *und Kielkröpfe supponit Satan in locum verorum filiorum, und plaget die Leute damit. Denn diese Gewalt hat der Satan, dass er die Kinder auswechselt und einem für sein Kind einen Teufel in die Wiegen legt.*" Erl. ed., LX. 41.

the flesh, by luxury, indolence, idleness, somnolence.   Is it that God has turned away from me, because you no longer pray for me?   You must take my place; you, richer in God's gifts, and more acceptable in his sight.   Here, a week has passed away since I put pen to paper, since I have prayed or studied, either vexed by fleshly cares, or by other temptations.   If things do not improve, I will go to Erfurt without concealment; there you will see me, or I you, for I must consult physicians or surgeons.   Perhaps the Lord troubles me so much in order to draw me from this wilderness before the public." [1]

Notwithstanding his complaints of illness and depression, and assaults from the evil spirit, he took the liveliest interest in the events of the day, and was anxious to descend to the arena of conflict.   He kept writing letters, books, and pamphlets, and sent them into the world.   His literary activity during those few months is truly astounding, and contrasts strangely with his repeated lament that he had to sit idle at Patmos, and would rather be burned in the service of God than stagnate there.

He had few books in the Wartburg.   He studied the Greek and Hebrew Scriptures very diligently; [2] he depended for news on the letters of his friends at Wittenberg; and for his writings, on the resources of his genius.

He continued his great Latin commentary on the Psalms, dwelling most carefully on Psalm 22 with reference to the crucifixion, and wrote special expositions of Psalms 68 and 37.   He completed his book on the Magnificat of the Holy Virgin, in which he still expresses his full belief in her sinlessness, even her immaculate conception.   He attacked auricular confession, which was now used as a potent power against the reading of Protestant books, and dedicated the

---

[1] De Wette, II. 21 sq.

[2] " *Bibliam Græcam et Hebraicam lego.* "   To Spalatin, May 14 (De Wette, II. 6).

tract to Sickingen (June 1). He resumed his sermons on
the Gospels and Epistles of the church year (*Kirchenpostille*),
which were afterwards finished by friends, and became one
of the most popular books of devotion in Germany. He
declared it once the best book he ever wrote, one which
even the Papists liked.[1] He replied in Latin to Latomus,
a Louvain theologian. He attacked in Latin and German
the doctrine of the mass, which is the very heart of Roman
Catholic worship, and monastic vows, the foundation of the
monastic system. He dedicated the book against vows to
his father who had objected to his becoming a monk.

He also dealt an effectual blow at Cardinal Albrecht of
Mainz, who had exposed in Halle a collection of nearly nine
thousand wondrous relics (including the manna in the wilderness, the burning bush of Moses, and jars from the wedding at Cana) to the view of pilgrims, with the promise of a
"surpassing" indulgence for attendance and a charitable
contribution to the Collegiate Church. Luther disregarded
the fact that his own pious Elector had arranged a similar
exhibition in Wittenberg only a few years before, and prepared a fierce protest against the "Idol of Indulgences"
(October, 1521). Spalatin and the Elector protested against
the publication, but he wrote to Spalatin: "I will not put
up with it. I will rather lose you and the prince himself,
and every living being. If I have stood up against the Pope,
why should I yield to his creature?" At the same time he
addressed a sharp letter to the archbishop (Dec. 1), and
reminded him that by this time he ought to know that indulgences were mere knavery and trickery; that Luther was still
alive; that bishops, before punishing priests for marrying,
better first expel their own mistresses. He threatened him
with the issue of the book against the Idol of Halle. The
archbishop submitted, and made a humble apology in a letter

---

[1] See Preface to the St. Louis ed. of Walch, XI. (1882), p. 1 sqq., and
Köstlin, I. 486-489.

of Dec. 21, which shows what a power Luther had acquired over him.[1]

§ 62.   *Luther's Translation of the Bible.*

I. Dr. Martin Luther's *Bibelübersetzung nach der letzten Original-Ausgabe, kritisch bearbeitet von* H. E. Bindseil *und* H. A. Niemeyer. Halle, 1845–55, in 7 vols. 8°. The N. T. in vols. 6 and 7. A critical reprint of the last edition of Luther (1545). Niemeyer died after the publication of the first volume. Comp. the *Probebibel* (the revised Luther-Version), Halle, 1883. Luther's *Sendbrief vom Dolmetschen und Fürbitte der Heiligen* (with a letter to Wenceslaus Link, Sept. 12, 1530), in Walch, XXI. 310 sqq., and the Erl. Frkf. ed., vol. LXV. 102–123. (Not in De Wette's collection, because of its polemical character.) A defense of his version against the attacks of the Romanists. Mathesius, in his thirteenth sermon on the Life of Luther.

II. On the merits and history of Luther's version. The best works are by Palm (1772), Panzer (*Vollständ. Gesch. der deutschen Bibelübers. Luthers,* Nürnb. 1783, 2d ed. 1791), Weidemann (1834), H. Schott (1835), Bindseil (1847), Hopf (1847), Mönckeberg (1855 and 1861), Karl Frommann (1862), Dorner (1868), W. Grimm (1874 and 1884), Düsterdieck (1882), Kleinert (1883), Th. Schott (1883), and the introduction to the *Probebibel* (1883). See Lit. in § 17, p. 103.

III. On the pre-Lutheran German Bible, and Luther's relation to it. Ed. Reuss: *Die deutsche Historienbibel vor der Erfindung des Bücherdrucks.* Jena, 1855. Jos. Kehrein (Rom. Cath.): *Zur Geschichte der deutschen Bibelübersetzung vor Luther.* Stuttgart, 1851. O. F. Fritzsche in Herzog, 2d ed., Bd. III. (1876), pp. 543 sqq. Dr. W. Krafft: *Die deutsche Bibel vor Luther, sein Verhältniss zu derselben und seine Verdienste um die deutsche Bibelübersetzung.* Bonn, 1883 (25 pages. 4°.) Also the recent discussions (1885–1887) of Keller, Haupt, Jostes, Rachel, Kawerau, Kolde, K. Müller, on the alleged Waldensian origin of the pre-Lutheran German version.

---

[1] Both letters in Walch, XIX. 656 sqq.; Luther's letter in De Wette, II. 112–115. Comp. Köstlin, I. 485 sq. The usual opinion that Albrecht revived the *traffic* in indulgences at Halle seems at least doubtful, and is denied by Albrecht Wolters in his Easter Program, *Hat Cardinal Albrecht von Mainz im J. 1521 den Tetzel'schen Ablasshandel erneuert?* Bonn, 1877 (pp. 24). He concludes: "*Somit war der 'Abgott,' welchen Luther bekämpfte, nicht die Erneuerung des Tetzel'schen Ablasshandels, sondern die Wiederaufrichtung der in Sachsen theils erloschenen, theils erlöschenden alten Ablasslehre, welche der Cardinal durch Ausstellung seiner mit Ablass begnadigten Reliquien zur Hebung des neuen Stifts und in der Stiftskirche zu Halle im Jahr 1521 versucht hat.*"

The richest fruit of Luther's leisure in the Wartburg, and the most important and useful work of his whole life, is the translation of the New Testament, by which he brought the teaching and example of Christ and the Apostles to the mind and heart of the Germans in life-like reproduction. It was a republication of the gospel. He made the Bible the people's book in church, school, and house. If he had done nothing else, he would be one of the greatest benefactors of the German-speaking race.[1]

His version was followed by Protestant versions in other languages, especially the French, Dutch, and English. The Bible ceased to be a foreign book in a foreign tongue, and became naturalized, and hence far more clear and dear to the common people. Hereafter the Reformation depended no longer on the works of the Reformers, but on the book of God, which everybody could read for himself as his daily guide in spiritual life. This inestimable blessing of an open Bible for all, without the permission or intervention of pope and priest, marks an immense advance in church history, and can never be lost.

[1] The testimony of the great philosopher Hegel is worth quoting. He says in his *Philosophie der Geschichte*, p. 503: "*Luther hat die Autorität der Kirche verworfen und an ihre Stelle die Bibel und das Zeugniss des menschlichen Geistes gesetzt. Dass nun die Bibel selbst die Grundlage der christlichen Kirche geworden ist, ist von der grössten Wichtigkeit; jeder soll sich nun selbst daraus belehren, jeder sein Gewissen daraus bestimmen können. Diess ist die ungeheure Veränderung im Principe: die ganze Tradition und das Gebäude der Kirche wird problematisch und das Princip der Autorität der Kirche umgestossen. Die Uebersetzung, welche Luther von der Bibel gemacht hat, is von unschätzbarem Werthe für das deutsche Volk gewesen. Dieses hat dadurch ein Volksbuch erhalten, wie keine Nation der katholischen Welt ein solches hat; sie haben wohl eine Unzahl von Gebetbüchlein, aber kein Grundbuch zur Belehrung des Volks. Trotz dem hat man in neueren Zeiten Streit desshalb erhoben, ob es zweckmässig sei, dem Volke die Bibel in die Hand zu geben; die wenigen Nachtheile, die dieses hat, werden doch bei weitem von den ungeheuren Vortheilen überwogen; die äusserlichen Geschichten, die dem Herzen und Verstande anstössig sein können, weiss der religiöse Sinn sehr wohl zu unterscheiden, und sich an das Substantielle haltend überwindet er sie.*" Froude (*Luther*, p. 42) calls Luther's translation of the Bible "the greatest of all the gifts he was able to offer to Germany."

Earlier Versions.

Luther was not the first, but by far the greatest translator of the German Bible, and is as inseparably connected with it as Jerome is with the Latin Vulgate. He threw the older translation into the shade and out of use, and has not been surpassed or even equaled by a successor. There are more accurate versions for scholars (as those of De Wette and Weizsäcker), but none that can rival Luther's for popular authority and use.

The civilization of the barbarians in the dark ages began with the introduction of Christianity, and the translation of such portions of the Scriptures as were needed in public worship.

The Gothic Bishop Wulfila or Wölflein (i.e., Little Wolf) in the fourth century translated nearly the whole Bible from the Greek into the Gothic dialect. It is the earliest monument of Teutonic literature, and the basis of comparative Teutonic philology.[1]

During the fourteenth century some unknown scholars prepared a new translation of the whole Bible into the Middle High German dialect. It slavishly follows the Latin Vulgate. It may be compared to Wiclif's English Version (1380), which was likewise made from the Vulgate, the original languages being then almost unknown in Europe. A copy of the New Testament of this version has been recently published, from a manuscript in the Premonstratensian convent of Tepl in Bohemia.[2] Another copy is preserved in the

---

[1] Hence repeatedly published from the remaining fragmentary MSS. in Upsala (Codex Argenteus, so called from its silver binding), Wolfenbüttel and Milan, by H. C. von Gabelenz and J. Loebe (1836), Massmann (1857), Bernhardt (1875), Stamm (1878), Uppström (1854–1868, the most accurate edition), R. Müller and H. Hoeppe (1881), W. W. Skeat (1882). Comp. also Jos. Bosworth, *The Gothic and Anglo-Saxon Gospels in Parallel Columns with the Versions of Wycliffe and Tyndale*, London, 2d ed., 1874 (with a fac-simile of the Codex Argenteus).

[2] By P. Philipp Klimesch (librarian of the convent), *Der Codex Teplen-*

college library at Freiberg in Saxony.[1] Both are from the fourteenth century, and agree almost word for word with the first printed German Bible, but contain, besides the New Testament, the apocryphal letter of St. Paul to the Laodiceans, which is a worthless compilation of a few sentences from the genuine writings of the apostle.[2]

After the invention of the printing-press, and before the Reformation, this mediæval German Bible was more frequently printed than any other except the Latin Vulgate.[3] No less than seventeen or eighteen editions appeared between 1462 and 1522, at Strassburg, Augsburg, Nürnberg, Cöln, Lübeck, and Halberstadt (fourteen in the High, three or four in the Low German dialect). Most of them are in large folio, in two volumes, and illustrated by wood-cuts. The editions present one and the same version (or rather two versions, — one High German, the other Low German) with dialectical alterations and accommodations to the textual

sis, enthaltend " Die Schrift des newen Gezeuges." Aelteste deutsche Handschrift, welche den im 15 Jahrh. gedruckten deutschen Bibeln zu Grunde gelegen. Augsburg and München, 1881–1884, in 3 parts. The Codex contains also homilies of St. Augustin and St. Chrysostom, and seven articles of faith. The last especially have induced Keller and Haupt to assign the translation to Waldensian origin. But these Addenda are not uncatholic, and at most would only prove Waldensian or Bohemian proprietorship of this particular copy, but not authorship of the translation. See NOTES below, p. 353.

[1] See Dr. M. Rachel's Gymnasial program: Ueber die Freiberger Bibelhandschrift, nebst Beiträgen zur Gesch. der vorlutherischen Bibelübersetzung, Freiberg, 1886 (31 pages).

[2] This apocryphal Epistle was also included in the Albigensian (Romance) version of the 13th century, in a Bohemian version, and in the early English Bibles, in two independent translations of the 14th or 15th century, but not in Wiclif's Bible. See Forshall and Maddan, Wycliffite Versions of the Bible (1850), IV. 438 sq.; Anger, Ueber den Laodicenerbrief (Leipzig, 1843); and Lightfoot, Com. on Ep. to the Colossians (London, 1875), p. 363 sq. On the other hand, the same pseudo-Pauline Epistle appears in many MSS. and early editions of the Vulgate, and in the German versions of Eck and Dietenberger. It can therefore not be used as an argument for or against the Waldensian hypothesis of Keller.

[3] Ninety-seven editions of the Vulgate were printed between 1450 and 1500, — 28 in Italy (nearly all in Venice), 16 in Germany, 10 in Basel, 9 in France. See Fritzsche in Herzog[lii], vol. VIII. 450.

variations of the MSS. of the Vulgate, which was in a very unsettled condition before the Clementine recension (1592). The revisers are as unknown as the translators.

The spread of this version, imperfect as it was, proves the hunger and thirst of the German people for the pure word of God, and prepared the way for the Reformation. It alarmed the hierarchy. Archbishop Berthold of Mainz, otherwise a learned and enlightened prelate, issued, Jan. 4, 1486, a prohibition of all unauthorized printing of sacred and learned books, especially the German Bible, within his diocese, giving as a reason that the German language was incapable of correctly rendering the profound sense of Greek and Latin works, and that laymen and women could not understand the Bible. Even Geiler of Kaisersberg, who sharply criticised the follies of the world and abuses of the Church, thought it "an evil thing to print the Bible in German."

Besides the whole Bible, there were numerous German editions of the Gospels and Epistles (*Plenaria*), and the Psalter, all made from the Vulgate.[1]

Luther could not be ignorant of this mediæval version. He made judicious use of it, as he did also of old German and Latin hymns. Without such aid he could hardly have finished his New Testament in the short space of three months.[2] But this fact does not diminish his merit in the least; for his version was made from the original Hebrew and Greek, and was so far superior in every respect that the older version entirely disappeared. It is to all intents a new work.

---

[1] In the royal library of Munich there are 21 MSS. of German versions of the Gospels and Epistles. The Gospels for the year were printed about 25 times before 1518; the Psalter about 13 times before 1513. See besides the works of Panzer, Kehrein, Keller, Haupt, above quoted, Alzog, *Die deutschen Plenarien im 15. und zu Anfang des 16. Jahrh.*, Freiburg-i-B., 1874.

[2] Luther's use of the older German version was formerly ignored or denied, but has been proved by Professor Krafft of Bonn (1883). He adds, however, very justly (*l.c.* p. 19): "*Es gereicht Luther zum grössten Verdienst, dass er auf den griechischen Grundtext zurückgegangen, den deutschen Wortschatz zunächst im N. T. wesentlich berichtigt, dann aber auch mit seiner Genialität bedeutend vermehrt hat.*" See Notes below, p. 352.

Luther's Qualifications.

Luther had a rare combination of gifts for a Bible translator: familiarity with the original languages, perfect mastery over the vernacular, faith in the revealed word of God, enthusiasm for the gospel, unction of the Holy Spirit. A good translation must be both true and free, faithful and idiomatic, so as to read like an original work. This is the case with Luther's version. Besides, he had already acquired such fame and authority that his version at once commanded universal attention.

His knowledge of Greek and Hebrew was only moderate, but sufficient to enable him to form an independent judgment.[1] What he lacked in scholarship was supplied by his intuitive genius and the help of Melanchthon. In the German tongue he had no rival. He created, as it were, or gave shape and form to the modern High German. He combined the official language of the government with that of the common people. He listened, as he says, to the speech of the mother at home, the children in the street, the men and women in the market, the butcher and various tradesmen in their shops, and "looked them on the mouth," in pursuit of the most intelligible terms. His genius for poetry and music enabled him to reproduce the rhythm and melody, the parallelism and symmetry, of Hebrew poetry and prose. His crowning qualification was his intuitive insight and spiritual sympathy with the contents of the Bible.

A good translation, he says, requires "a truly devout, faithful, diligent, Christian, learned, experienced, and practiced heart."

---

[1] "*Ich kann,*" he says in his *Tischreden,* "*weder griechisch noch ebræisch, ich will aber dennoch einem Ebræer und Griechen ziemlich begegnen. Aber die Sprachen machen für sich selbst keinen Theologen, sondern sind nur eine Hülfe. Denn soll einer von einem Dinge reden, so muss er die Sache* [*Sprache ?*] *zuvor wissen und verstehen.*" Erl.-Frkf. ed., vol. LXII. 313.

Progress of his Version.

Luther was gradually prepared for this work. He found for the first time a complete copy of the Latin Bible in the University Library at Erfurt, to his great delight, and made it his chief study. He derived from it his theology and spiritual nourishment; he lectured and preached on it as professor at Wittenberg day after day. He acquired the knowledge of the original languages for the purpose of its better understanding. He liked to call himself a " Doctor of the Sacred Scriptures."

He made his first attempt as translator with the seven Penitential Psalms, which he published in March, 1517, six months before the outbreak of the Reformation. Then followed several other sections of the Old and New Testaments, — the Ten Commandments, the Lord's Prayer, the Prayer of King Manasseh, the Magnificat of the Virgin Mary, etc., — with popular comments. He was urged by his friends, especially by Melanchthon, as well as by his own sense of duty, to translate the whole Bible.

He began with the New Testament in November or December, 1521, and completed it in the following March, before he left the Wartburg. He thoroughly revised it on his return to Wittenberg, with the effectual help of Melanchthon, who was a much better Greek scholar. Sturz at Erfurt was consulted about coins and measures; Spalatin furnished from the Electoral treasury names for the precious stones of the New Jerusalem (Rev. ch. 21). The translation was then hurried through three presses, and appeared already Sept. 21, 1522, but without his name.[1]

---

[1] Under the title: *Das Newe Testament Deutzsch. Wittemberg.* With wood-cuts by Lucas Cranach, one at the beginning of each book and twenty-one in the Apocalypse. The chapter division of the Latin Bible, dating from Hugo a St. Caro, was retained with some paragraph divisions; the versicular division was as yet unknown (Robert Stephanus first introduced it in his Latin edition, 1548, and in his Greek Testament of 1551). The order of

In December a second edition was required, which contained many corrections and improvements.[1]

He at once proceeded to the more difficult task of translating the Old Testament, and published it in parts as they were ready. Tke Pentateuch appeared in 1523; the Psalter, 1524.

In the progress of the work he founded a *Collegium Biblicum*, or Bible club, consisting of his colleagues Melanchthon, Bugenhagen (Pommer), Cruciger, Justus Jonas, and Aurogallus. They met once a week in his house, several hours before supper. Deacon Georg Rörer (Rorarius), the first clergyman ordained by Luther, and his proof-reader, was also present; occasionally foreign scholars were admitted; and Jewish rabbis were freely consulted. Each member of the company contributed to the work from his special knowledge and preparation. Melanchthon brought with him the Greek Bible, Cruciger the Hebrew and Chaldee, Bugenhagen the Vulgate, others the old commentators; Luther had always with him the Latin and the German versions besides the Hebrew. Sometimes they scarcely mastered three lines of the Book of Job in four days, and hunted two, three, and four weeks for a single word. No record exists of the discussions of this remarkable company, but Mathesius says that "wonderfully beautiful and instructive speeches were made."

At last the whole Bible, including the Apocrypha as "books not equal to the Holy Scriptures, yet useful and

---

the Epistles is changed, and the change remained in all subsequent editions. Some parallel passages and glosses are added on the margin. It contained many typographical errors, a very curious one in Gal. 5:6: "*Die Liebe, die durch den Glauben thätig ist,*" instead of "*Der Glaube, der durch die Liebe thätig ist.*"

A copy of this rare edition, without the full-page Apocalyptic pictures, but with the error just noticed, is in the Union Seminary Library, New York. It has the famous preface with the fling at the "*rechte stroern Epistel*" of St. James, which was afterwards omitted or modified.

[1] The woodcuts were also changed. The triple papal crown of the Babylonian woman in Rev. ch. 17 gave place to a simple crown.

good to read," was completed in 1534, and printed with numerous woodcuts.

In the mean time the New Testament had appeared in sixteen or seventeen editions, and in over fifty reprints.[1]

Luther complained of the many errors in these irresponsible editions.

He never ceased to amend his translation. Besides correcting errors, he improved the uncouth and confused orthography, fixed the inflections, purged the vocabulary of obscure and ignoble words, and made the whole more symmetrical and melodious.

He prepared five original editions, or recensions, of his whole Bible, the last in 1545, a year before his death.[2] This is the proper basis of all critical editions.[3]

The edition of 1546 was prepared by his friend Rörer, and contains a large number of alterations, which he traced to Luther himself. Some of them are real improvements, e.g., " *Die Liebe höret nimmer auf*," for " *Die Liebe wird nicht müde* (1 Cor. 13:8). The charge that he made the changes in the interest of Philippism (Melanchthonianism), seems to be unfounded.

---

[1] Fritzsche (*l.c.*, p. 549): " *Vom N. T. sind von 1522–1533 ziemlich sicher 16 original Ausgaben nachgewiesen. . . . Die Nachdrucke belaufen sich auf ungefähr 54, wobei Augsburg mit 14, Strassburg mit 13, und Basel mit 12 vertreten ist.*"

[2] Under the title: *Biblia, das ist die gantze Heilige Schrift, Deutsch. Auffs neu zugericht. D. Mart. Luther. Wittemberg. Durch Hans Lufft, M.D.XLV.* fol. with numerous woodcuts. A copy in the Canstein *Bibelanstalt* at Halle. The Union Theol. Seminary in New York has a copy of the edition of 1535 which bears this title: *Biblia das ist die | gantze Heilige | Schrifft Deutsch. | Mart. Luth. | Wittemberg. | Begnadet mit Kür- | furstlicher zu Sachsen | freiheit. | Gedruckt durch Hans Lufft. | M.D.-XXXV.* The margin is ornamented. Then follows the *imprimatur* of the Elector John Frederick of Saxony, a preface of Luther to the O. T., and a rude picture of God, the globe and paradise with Adam and Eve among trees and animals.

[3] Republished with the greatest care by Bindseil & Niemeyer. See Lit., p. 340.

Editions and Revisions.

The printed Bible text of Luther had the same fate as the written text of the old Itala and Jerome's Vulgate. It passed through innumerable improvements and mis-improvements. The orthography and inflections were modernized, obsolete words removed, the versicular division introduced (first in a Heidelberg reprint, 1568), the spurious clause of the three witnesses inserted in 1 John 5 : 7 (first by a Frankfurt publisher, 1574), the third and fourth books of Ezra and the third book of the Maccabees added to the Apocrypha, and various other changes effected, necessary and unnecessary, good and bad. Elector August of Saxony tried to control the text in the interest of strict Lutheran orthodoxy, and ordered the preparation of a standard edition (1581). But it was disregarded outside of Saxony.

Gradually no less than eleven or twelve recensions came into use, some based on the edition of 1545, others on that of 1546. The most careful recension was that of the Canstein Bible Institute, founded by a pious nobleman, Carl Hildebrand von Canstein (1667–1719) in connection with Francke's Orphan House at Halle. It acquired the largest circulation and became the *textus receptus* of the German Bible.

With the immense progress of biblical learning in the present century, the desire for a timely revision of Luther's version was more and more felt. Revised versions with many improvements were prepared by Joh. Friedrich von Meyer, a Frankfurt patrician (1772–1849), and Dr. Rudolf Stier (1800–1862), but did not obtain public authority.

At last a conservative official revision of the Luther Bible was inaugurated by the combined German church governments in 1863, with a view and fair prospect of superseding all former editions in public use.[1]

---

[1] See Note at the end of the next section.

The Success.

The German Bible of Luther was saluted with the greatest enthusiasm, and became the most powerful help to the Reformation. Duke George of Saxony, Duke William of Bavaria, and Archduke Ferdinand of Austria strictly prohibited the sale in their dominions, but could not stay the current. Hans Lufft at Wittenberg printed and sold in forty years (between 1534 and 1574) about a hundred thousand copies, — an enormous number for that age, — and these were read by millions. The number of copies from reprints is beyond estimate.

Cochlæus, the champion of Romanism, paid the translation the greatest compliment when he complained that " Luther's New Testament was so much multiplied and spread by printers that even tailors and shoemakers, yea, even women and ignorant persons who had accepted this new Lutheran gospel, and could read a little German, studied it with the greatest avidity as the fountain of all truth. Some committed it to memory, and carried it about in their bosom. In a few months such people deemed themselves so learned that they were not ashamed to dispute about faith and the gospel not only with Catholic laymen, but even with priests and monks and doctors of divinity."[1]

The Romanists were forced in self-defense to issue rival translations. Such were made by Emser (1527), Dietenberger (1534), and Eck (1537), and accompanied with annotations. They are more correct in a number of passages, but slavishly conformed to the Vulgate, stiff and heavy, and they frequently copy the very language of Luther, so that he could say with truth, " The Papists steal my German of which they knew little before, and they do not thank me for

---

[1] De Actis et Scriptis M. Lutheri ad ann. 1522. Gieseler (IV. 65 sq.) quotes the whole passage in Latin.

it, but rather use it against me." These versions have long since gone out of use even in the Roman Church, while Luther's still lives.[1]

NOTE.

THE PRE-LUTHERAN GERMAN BIBLE.

According to the latest investigations, fourteen printed editions of the whole Bible in the Middle High German dialect, and three in the Low German, have been identified. Panzer already knew fourteen; see his *Gesch. der nürnbergischen Ausgaben der Bibel*, Nürnberg, 1778, p. 74.

The first four, in large folio, appeared without date and place of publication, but were probably printed: 1, at Strassburg, by Heinrich Eggestein, about or before 1466 (the falsely so-called *Mainzer Bibel* of 1462); 2, at Strassburg, by Johann Mentelin, 1466 (?); 3, at Augsburg, by Jodocus Pflanzmann, or Tyner, 1470 (?); 4, at Nürnberg, by Sensenschmidt and Frissner, in 2 vols., 408 and 104 leaves, 1470–73 (?). The others are located, and from the seventh on also dated, viz.: 5, Augsburg, by Günther Zainer, 2 vols., probably between 1473–1475. 6, Augsburg, by the same, dated 1477 (Stevens says, 1475 ?). 7, The third Augsburg edition, by Günther Zainer, or Anton Sorg, 1477, 2 vols., 321 and 332 leaves, fol., printed in double columns; the first German Bible with a date. 8, The fourth Augsburg edition, by A. Sorg, 1480, folio. 9, Nürnberg, by Anton Koburger (also spelled Koberger), 1483. 10, Strassburg, by Johann Gruninger, 1485. 11 and 12, The fifth and sixth Augsburg editions, in small fol., by Hans Schönsperger, 1487 and 1490. 13, The seventh Augsburg edition, by Hans Otmar, 1507, small folio. 14, The eighth Augsburg edition, by Silvan Otmar, 1518, small folio.

The Low Dutch Bibles were printed: 1, at Cologne, in large folio, double columns, probably 1480. The unknown editor speaks of previous editions and his own improvements. Stevens (Nos. 653 and 654) mentions two copies of the O. T. in Dutch, printed at Delf, 1477, 2 vols. fol. 2, At Lübeck, 1491 (not 1494), 2 vols. fol. with large woodcuts. 3, At Halberstadt, 1522.

Comp. Kehrein (*l.c.*), Krafft (*l.c.*, pp. 4, 5), and Henry Stevens, *The Bibles in the Caxton Exhibition*, London, 1878. Stevens gives the full titles with descriptions, pp. 45 sqq., nos. 620 sqq.

Several of these Bibles, including the Koburger and those of Cologne and Halberstadt, are in the possession of the Union Theol. Seminary, New York. I examined them. They are ornamented by woodcuts, beginning with a picture of God creating the world, and forming Eve from the rib of Adam in Paradise. Several of them have Jerome's preface (*De omnibus divinæ historiæ libris, Ep. ad Paulinum*), the oldest with the remark: "*Da hebet an die epistel des heiligen priesters sant Jeronimi zu Paulinum von allen gott-lichen büchern der hystory. Das erst capitel.*"

---

[1] The last edition of Dr. Eck's Bible appeared in 1558, at Ingolstadt, Bavaria.

Dr. Krafft illustrates the dependence of Luther on the earlier version by several examples (pp. 13–18). The following is from the Sermon on the Mount, Matt. 5:21–27:—

THE NINTH BIBLE, 1483.	LUTHER'S NEW TESTAMENT, 1522.
Habt ir gehört, das gesaget ist den alten. du solt nit tödten, wellicher aber tödtet. der wird schuldig des gerichts. Aber ich sag euch, daz ein yeglicher der do zürnet seinem bruder. der wirt schuldig des gerichts. Der aber spricht zu seinem bruder. racha. der wirt schuldig des rats. Und der do spricht. tor. der wirt schuldig des hellischen fewrs. Darum ob du opfferst dein gab zu dem altar. und do wirst gedenckend. daz dein bruder ettwas hat wider dich, lasz do dein gab vor dem altar und gee zum ersten und versüne dich mit deim bruder und denn kum und opffer dein gab. Bis gehellig deim widerwertigen schyer. die weyl du mit im bist him weg. das dich villeycht der widersacher nit antwurt dem richter. und der richter dich antwurt dem diener und werdest gelegt in den kercker. Fürwar ich sag dir. du geest nit aus von dannen. und das du vergeltest den letzten quadranten.	*Ihr habt gehortt, das zu den alten gesagt ist, du sollt nit todten, wer aber todtet, der soll des gerichts schuldig seyn. Ich aber sage euch, wer mit seynem bruder zurnit, der ist des gerichts schuldig, wer aber zu seynem bruder sagt, Racha, der ist des rads schuldig, wer aber sagt, du narr, der ist des hellischen fewers schuldig.* *Darumb weñ du deyn gabe auff den altar opfferst, un wirst alda eyngedenken, das deyn bruder ettwas widder dich hab, so las alda fur dem altar deyn gabe, unnd gehe zuvor hyn, unnd versune dich mitt deynem bruder, unnd als denn kom unnd opffer deyn gabe.* *Sey willfertig deynem widersacher, bald, dieweyl du noch mit yhm auff dem wege bist, auff das dich der widdersacher nit der mal eyns ubirantwortte dem richter, uñ d. richter ubirantworte dich dem diener, uñ werdist yñ den kercker geworffen, warlich ich sage dyr, du wirst nit von dannen erauzs komen, bis du auch den letzten heller bezalest.*

To this I add two specimens in which the superiority of Luther's version is more apparent.

GEN. 1:1–3.

THE KOBURGER BIBLE OF NÜRNBERG, 1483.	LUTHER'S BIBLE, ED. 1535.
In dem anfang hat got beschaffen hymel und erden. aber dye erde was eytel und leere. und die vinsternus warn auff dem antlitz des abgrunds. vnd der geist gots swebet oder ward getragen auff den wassern. Uñ got der sprach. Es werde dz' liecht. Un das liecht ist worden.	*Im anfang schuff Gott himel und erden. Und die erde war wüst und leer, und es war finster auff der tieffe, und der Geist Gottes schwebet auff dem wasser.* *Und Gott sprach. Es werde liecht. Und es ward liecht.*

1 Cor. 13:1, 2.

THE STRASSBURG BIBLE OF 1485.	LUTHER'S NEW TESTAMENT, 1522.
Ob ich rede inn der zungen der engel vnd der menschen; aber habe ich der lieb nit, ich bin gemacht alls ein glockenspeyss lautend oder alls ein schell klingend. Vnd ob ich hab die weissagung und erkenn all heimlichkeit vnd alle kunst, und ob ich hab allen glauben, also das ich übertrag die berg, habe ich aber der lieb nit, ich bin nichts.	*Wenn ich mit menschen und mit engelzungen redet und hette die* [1] *liebe nit,* [2] *so wäre ich ein tönend ertz oder ein klingende schell.* [3] *Und wenn ich weissagen kündt, vnnd wüste alle geheymnuss vnd alle erkantnüss, vnd hette allen glauben, also das ich berg versetzete, und hett der liebe nicht, so were ich nichts.*

[1] Ed. of 1535: *der.*   [2] Ed. of 1535: *nicht.*   [3] Later eds.: *eine . . . schelle.*

The precise origin of the mediæval German Bible is still unknown. Dr. Ludwig Keller of Münster first suggested in his *Die Reformation und die älteren Reformparteien*, Leipzig, 1885, pp. 257–260, the hypothesis that it was made by Waldenses (who had also a Romanic version); and he tried to prove it in his *Die Waldenser und die deutschen Bibelübersetzungen*, Leipzig, 1886 (189 pages). Dr. Hermann Haupt, of Würzburg, took the same ground in his *Die deutsche Bibelübersetzung der mittelalterlichen Waldenser in dem Codex Teplensis und der ersten gedruckten Bibel nachgewiesen*, Würzburg, 1885 (64 pages); and again, in self-defense against Jostes, in *Der waldensische Ursprung des Codex Teplensis und der vor-lutherischen deutschen Bibeldrucke*, Würzburg, 1886. On the other hand, Dr. Franz Jostes, a Roman Catholic scholar, denied the Waldensian and defended the Catholic origin of that translation, in two pamphlets: *Die Waldenser und die vorlutherische Bibelübersetzung*, Münster, 1885 (44 pages), and *Die Tepler Bibelübersetzung. Eine zweite Kritik*, Münster, 1886 (43 pages). The same author promises a complete history of German Catholic Bible versions. The question has been discussed in periodicals and reviews, e.g., by Kawerau in Luthardt's "Theol. Literaturblatt," Leipzig, 1885 and 1886 (Nos. 32–34), by Schaff in the New York "Independent" for Oct. 8, 1885, and in the "Presbyterian Review" for April, 1887, pp. 355 sqq.; by Kolde, in the "Göttinger Gelehrte Anzeigen," 1887, No. I.; by Müller in the "Studien und Kritiken," 1887, No. III.; and Bornemann, in the "Jahrb. f. Prot. Theol.," 1888, 67–101.

The arguments for the Waldensian origin are derived from certain additions to the Codex Teplensis, and alleged departures from the text of the Vulgate. But the additions are not anti-Catholic, and are not found in the cognate Freiberger MS.; and the textual variations can not be traced to sectarian bias. The text of the Vulgate was in greater confusion in the middle ages than the text of the Itala at the time of Jerome, nor was there any authorized text of it before the Clementine recension of 1592. The only plausible argument which Dr. Keller brings out in his second publication (pp. 80 sqq.) is the fact that Emser, in his *Annotations to the New Test.* (1523), charges Luther with having translated the N. T. from a " *Wickleffisch oder hussisch exemplar.*" But this refers to copies of the Latin Vulgate; and in the examples quoted by Keller, Luther does not agree with the Codex Teplensis.

The hostility of several Popes and Councils to the circulation of vernacular translations of the Bible implies the existence of such translations, and could not prevent their publication, as the numerous German editions prove. Dutch, French, and Italian versions also appeared among the earliest prints. See Stevens, Nos. 687 and 688 (p. 59 sq.). The Italian edition exhibited in 1877 at London is entitled: *La Biblia en lingua Volgare (per Nicolo di Mallermi).* Venetia: per Joan. Rosso Vercellese, 1487, fol. A Spanish Bible by Bonif. Ferrer was printed at Valencia, 1478 (see Reuss, *Gesch. der heil. Schr. N. T.*, II. 207, 5th ed.).

The Bible is the common property and most sacred treasure of all Christian churches. The art of printing was invented in Catholic times, and its history goes hand in hand with the history of the Bible. Henry Stevens says (*The Bibles in the Caxton Exhibition*, p. 25): "The secular history of the Holy Scriptures is the sacred history of Printing. The Bible was the first book printed, and the Bible is the last book printed. Between 1450 and 1877, an interval of four centuries and a quarter, the Bible shows the progress and comparative development of the art of printing in a manner that no other single book can; and Biblical bibliography proves that during the first forty years, at least, the Bible exceeded in amount of printing all other books put together; nor were its quality, style, and variety a whit behind its quantity."

§ 63. *A Critical Estimate of Luther's Version.*

Luther's version of the Bible is a wonderful monument of genius, learning, and piety, and may be regarded in a secondary sense as inspired. It was, from beginning to end, a labor of love and enthusiasm. While publishers and printers made fortunes, Luther never received or asked a copper for this greatest work of his life.[1]

We must judge it from the times. A German translation from the original languages was a work of colossal magnitude if we consider the absence of good grammars, dictionaries,

---

[1] He could say with perfect truth: " *Ich habe meine Ehre nicht gemeint, auch keinen Heller dafür genommen, sondern habe es zu Ehren gethan den lieben Christen und zu Ehren einem, der droben sitzt.*"

and concordances, the crude state of Greek and Hebrew scholarship, and of the German language, in the sixteenth century. Luther wrote to Amsdorf, Jan. 13, 1522, that he had undertaken a task beyond his power, that he now understood why no one had attempted it before in his own name, and that he would not venture on the Old Testament without the aid of his friends.[1] He felt especially how difficult it was to make Job and the Hebrew prophets speak in barbarous German.[2] He jocosely remarked that Job would have become more impatient at the blunders of his translators than at the long speeches of his " miserable comforters."

As regards the text, it was in an unsettled condition. The science of textual criticism was not yet born, and the materials for it were not yet collected from the manuscripts, ancient versions, and patristic quotations. Luther had to use the first printed editions. He had no access to manuscripts, the most important of which were not even discovered or made available before the middle of the nineteenth century. Biblical geography and archæology were in their infancy, and many names and phrases could not be understood at the time.

In view of these difficulties we need not be surprised at the large number of mistakes, inaccuracies, and inconsistencies in Luther's version. They are most numerous in Job and the Prophets, who present, even to the advanced Hebrew scholars of our day, many unsolved problems of text and rendering. The English Version of 1611 had the great advan-

---

[1] " *Interim Biblia transferam, quanquam onus susceperim supra vires. Video nunc, quid sit interpretari, et cur hactenus a nullo sit attentatum, qui proficeretur nomen suum.* [This implies his knowledge of older German translations which are anonymous.] *Vetus Testamentum non potero attingere, nisi vobis præsentibus et cooperantibus.*"

[2] "*Ach Gott ! wie ein gross und verdriesslich Werk ist es, die hebräischen Schreiber zu zwingen deutsch zu reden ; wie sträuben sie sich und wollen ihre hebräische Art gar nicht verlassen und dem groben Deutschen nachfolgen, gleich als wenn eine Nachtigall . . . sollte ihre liebliche Melodei verlassen und dem Kukuk nachsingen.*" Walch, XVI. 508. Comp. his letter to Spalatin about the difficulties in Job, Feb. 23, 1524, in De Wette, II. 486.

tage of the labors of three generations of translators and revisers, and is therefore more accurate, and yet equally idiomatic.

The Original Text.

The basis for Luther's version of the Old Testament was the Massoretic text as published by Gerson Ben Mosheh at Brescia in 1494.[1] He used also the Septuagint, the Vulgate of Jerome [2] (although he disliked him exceedingly on account of his monkery), the Latin translations of the Dominican Sanctes Pagnini of Lucca (1527), and of the Franciscan Sebastian Münster (1534), the " *Glossa ordinaria* " (a favorite exegetical vade-mecum of Walafried Strabo from the ninth century), and Nicolaus Lyra (d. 1340), the chief of mediæval commentators, who, besides the Fathers, consulted also the Jewish rabbis.[3]

The basis for the New Testament was the second edition of Erasmus, published at Basel in Switzerland in 1519.[4] His

---

[1] Luther's copy of the Hebrew Bible is preserved in the Royal Library at Berlin. The *editio princeps* of the whole Hebrew Bible appeared 1488 (Soncino: Abraham ben Chayin de' Tintori). A copy in possession of Dr. Ginsburg in England. See Stevens, *l.c.* p. 60. Portions had been printed before.

[2] A copy of the Lyons ed. of 1519, and one of the Basel ed. of 1509, now in possession of the Brandenburg Provincial Museum at Berlin. Grimm, *Gesch. d. luther. Bibelübers.*, p. 8, note.

[3] Lyra acquired by his *Postillæ perpetuæ in V. et N. Test.* (first published in Rome, 1472, in 5 vols. fol., again at Venice, 1540) the title *Doctor planus et utilis.* His influence on Luther is expressed in the well-known lines: —

> " *Si Lyra non lyrasset,*
> *Lutherus non saltasset.*"

[4] Greek and Latin, 2 vols. folio. The first part contains Preface, Dedication to Pope Leo X., and the *Ratio seu Compendium veræ Theologiæ per Erasmum Roterodamum* (120 pages); the second part, the Greek Text, with a Latin version in parallel columns, with brief introductions to the several books (565 pages). At the end is a Latin letter of Frobenius, the publisher, dated " Nonis Febr. Anno M.D.XIX." A copy in the Union Theol. Seminary, New York. — Some say that Luther made use of Gerbel's reprint of Erasmus, 1521. But Dr. Reuss of Strassburg, who has the largest collection and best knowledge of Greek Testaments, denies this. *Gesch. der h. Schriften des N. T.*, 5th ed., II. 211, note.

first edition of the Greek Testament had appeared in 1516, just one year before the Reformation. He derived the text from a few mediæval MSS.[1] The second edition, though much more correct than the first ("*multo diligentius recognitum, emendatum,*" etc.), is disfigured by a large number of typographical errors.[2] He laid the foundation of the *Textus Receptus*, which was brought into its mature shape by R. Stephen, in his "royal edition" of 1550 (the basis of the English *Textus Receptus*), and by the Elzevirs in their editions of 1624 and 1633 (the basis of the Continental *Textus Receptus*), and which maintained the supremacy till Lachmann inaugurated the adoption of an older textual basis (1831).

Luther did not slavishly follow the Greek of Erasmus, and in many places conformed to the Latin Vulgate, which is based on an older text. He also omitted, even in his last edition, the famous interpolation of the heavenly witnesses in 1 John 5 : 7, which Erasmus inserted in his third edition (1522) against his better judgment.[3]

The German Rendering.

The German language was divided into as many dialects as tribes and states, and none served as a bond of literary union. Saxons and Bavarians, Hanoverians and Swabians, could scarcely understand each other. Each author wrote in the dialect of his district, Zwingli in his Schwyzerdütsch.

---

[1] See Schaff, *Companion to the Greek Testament,* etc., New York, 3d ed., 1888, pp. 229 sqq., and the facsimile of the Erasmian ed. on p. 532 sq. Tyndale's English version was likewise made from Erasmus.

[2] O. von Gebhardt, in his *Novum Test. Græce et Germanice,* Preface, p. xvi., says of the second ed. of Erasmus: "*Die Zahl der Druckfehler ist so gross, dass ein vollständiges Verzeichniss derselben Seiten füllen würde.*" Comp. Scrivener, *Introd. to the Criticism of the N. T.,* 3d ed. (1883), p. 432 sq.

[3] It first appeared in the Frankfort edition of Luther's Bible, 1574. The revised Luther-Bible of 1883 strangely retains the passage, but in small type and in brackets, with the note that it was wanting in Luther's editions. The *Probebibel* departs only in a few places from the Erasmian text as followed by Luther: viz., Acts 12 : 25; Heb. 10 : 34; 1 John 2 : 23; Rev. 11 : 2. In this respect the German revision is far behind the Anglo-American revision of 1881, which corrects the *Textus Receptus* in about five thousand places.

"I have so far read no book or letter," says Luther in the preface to his version of the Pentateuch (1523), "in which the German language is properly handled. Nobody seems to care sufficiently for it ; and every preacher thinks he has a right to change it at pleasure, and to invent new terms." Scholars preferred to write in Latin, and when they attempted to use the mother tongue, as Reuchlin and Melanchthon did occasionally, they fell far below in ease and beauty of expression.

Luther brought harmony out of this confusion, and made the modern High German the common book language. He chose as the basis the Saxon dialect, which was used at the Saxon court and in diplomatic intercourse between the emperor and the estates, but was bureaucratic, stiff, heavy, involved, dragging, and unwieldy.[1] He popularized and adapted it to theology and religion. He enriched it with the vocabulary of the German mystics, chroniclers, and poets. He gave it wings, and made it intelligible to the common people of all parts of Germany.

He adapted the words to the capacity of the Germans, often at the expense of accuracy. He cared more for the substance than the form. He turned the Hebrew shekel into a *Silberling*,[2] the Greek drachma and Roman denarius into a German

---

[1] He says in his *Tischreden* (Erl. ed., vol. lxii. 313): "*Ich habe keine gewisse, sonderliche eigene Sprache im Deutschen* [i.e., no special dialect], *sondern brauche der gemeinen deutschen Sprache, dass mich Oberländer und Niederländer verstehen mögen. Ich rede nach der sächsischen Canzelei, welcher nachfolgen alle Fürsten und Könige in Deutschland. Alle Reichstädte, Fürstenhöfe schreiben nach der sächsischen und unseres Fürsten Canzelei, darumb ists auch die gemeinste deutsche Sprache. Kaiser Maximilian und Kurfürst Friedrich, Herzog zu Sachsen, etc., haben im römischen Reich die deutschen Sprachen* [dialects] *also in eine gewisse Sprache gezogen.*" Formerly the Latin was the diplomatic language in Germany. Louis the Bavarian introduced the German in 1330. The founder of the diplomatic German of Saxony was Elector Ernst, the father of Elector Friedrich. See Wilibald Grimm, *Gesch. der luth. Bibelübersetzung* (Jena, 1884), p. 24 sqq.

[2] The same word *silverling* occurs once in the English version, Isa. 7:23, and is retained in the R. V. of 1885. The German *Probebibel* retains it in this and other passages, as Gen. 20:16; Judg. 9:4, etc.

Groschen, the quadrans into a *Heller*, the Hebrew measures into *Scheffel*, *Malter*, *Tonne*, *Centner*, and the Roman centurion into a *Hauptmann*. He substituted even *undeutsch* (!) for barbarian in 1 Cor. 14:11. Still greater liberties he allowed himself in the Apocrypha, to make them more easy and pleasant reading.[1] He used popular alliterative phrases as *Geld und Gut*, *Land und Leute*, *Rath und That*, *Stecken und Stab*, *Dornen und Disteln*, *matt und müde*, *gäng und gäbe*. He avoided foreign terms which rushed in like a flood with the revival of learning, especially in proper names (as Melanchthon for Schwarzerd, Aurifaber for Goldschmid, Œcolampadius for Hausschein, Camerarius for Kammermeister). He enriched the vocabulary with such beautiful words as *holdselig*, *Gottseligkeit*.

Erasmus Alber, a contemporary of Luther, called him the German Cicero, who not only reformed religion, but also the German language.

Luther's version is an idiomatic reproduction of the Bible in the very spirit of the Bible. It brings out the whole wealth, force, and beauty of the German language. It is the first German classic, as King James's version is the first English classic. It anticipated the golden age of German literature as represented by Klopstock, Lessing, Herder, Goethe, Schiller, — all of them Protestants, and more or less indebted to the Luther-Bible for their style. The best authority in Teutonic philology pronounces his language to be the foundation of the new High German dialect on account of its purity and influence, and the Protestant dialect on account of its freedom which conquered even Roman Catholic authors.[2]

---

[1] See Grimm, *Luther's Uebersetzung der Apocryphen*, in the "Studien und Kritiken" for 1883, pp. 376–400. He judges that Luther's version of Ecclesiasticus (Jesus Sirach) is by no means a faithful translation, but a model of a free and happy reproduction from a combination of the Greek and Latin texts.

[2] "*Luther's Sprache*," says Jakob Grimm, in the Preface to his German Grammar, "*muss ihrer edeln, fast wunderbaren Reinheit, auch ihres ge-*

The Protestant Spirit of Luther's Version.

Dr. Emser, one of the most learned opponents of the Reformation, singled out in Luther's New Testament several hundred linguistic blunders and heretical falsifications.[1] Many of them were silently corrected in later editions. He published, by order of Duke George of Saxony, a new translation (1527) for the purpose of correcting the errors of "Luther and other heretics."[2]

waltigen Einflusses halber für Kern und Grundlage der neuhochdeutschen Sprachniedersetzung gehalten werden, wovon bis auf den heutigen Tag nur sehr unbedeutend, meistens zum Schaden der Kraft und des Ausdrucks, abgewichen worden ist. Man darf das Neuhochdeutsche in der That als den protestantischen Dialekt bezeichnen, dessen freiheitathmende Natur längst schon, ihnen unbewusst, Dichter und Schriftsteller des katholischen Glaubens überwältigte. Unsere Sprache ist nach dem unaufhaltsamen Laufe der Dinge in Lautverhältnissen und Formen gesunken; was aber ihren Geist und Leib genährt, verjüngt, was endlich Blüten neuer Poesie getrieben hat, verdanken wir keinem mehr als Luthern." Comp. Wetzel, *Die Sprache Luthers in seiner Bibel,* Stuttgart, 1859. Heinrich Rückert, *Geschichte der neu-hochdeutschen Schriftsprache,* II. 15–175. Opitz, *Ueber die Sprache Luthers,* Halle, 1869. Dietz, *Wörterbuch zu Luther's deutschen Schriften,* Leipzig, 1870 sqq. Lehmann, *Luthers Sprache in seiner Uebersetzung des N. T.,* Halle, 1873.

[1] *Annotationes des hochgel. und christl. doctors Hieronymi Emsers über Luthers neuw Testament,* 1523. I have before me an edition of Freiburg-i.-B., 1535 (140 pages). Emser charges Luther with a thousand grammatical and fourteen hundred heretical errors. He suspects (p. 14) that he had before him "*ein sonderlich Wickleffisch oder Hussisch Exemplar.*" He does not say whether he means a copy of the Latin Vulgate or the older German version. He finds (p. 17) four errors in Luther's version of the Lord's Prayer: 1, that he turned *Vater unser* into *Unser Vater,* against the German custom for a thousand years (but in his Shorter Catechism he retained the old form, and the Lutherans adhere to it to this day); 2, that he omitted *der du bist;* 3, that he changed the *panis supersubstantialis (überselbständig Brot!)* into *panis quotidianus (täglich Brot);* 4, that he added the doxology, which is not in the Vulgate. In our days, one of the chief objections against the English Revision is the *omission* of the doxology.

[2] *Das gantz New Testament: So durch den Hochgelerten L. Hieronymum Emser seligen verteutscht, unter des Durchlauchten Hochgebornen Fürsten und Herren Georgen Hertzogen zu Sachsen, etc., ausgegangen ist.* Leipzig, 1528. The first edition appeared before Emser's death, which occurred Nov. 8, 1527. I find in the Union Seminary four octavo copies of his N. T., dated Coln, 1528 (355 pp.), Leipzig, 1529 (416 pp.), Freiburg-i.-B. 1535 (406 pp.).

The charge that Luther adapted the translation to his theological opinions has become traditional in the Roman Church, and is repeated again and again by her controversialists and historians.[1]

The same objection has been raised against the Authorized English Version.[2]

In both cases, the charge has some foundation, but no more than the counter-charge which may be brought against Roman Catholic Versions.

The most important example of dogmatic influence in Luther's version is the famous interpolation of the word

Cöln, 1568 (879 pp.), and a copy of a fol. ed., Cologne, 1529 (227 pp.), all with illustrations and marginal notes against Luther. On the concluding page, it is stated that 607 errors of Luther's are noted and corrected. The Cologne ed. of 1529 indicates, on the titlepage, that Luther arbitrarily changed the text according to the *Hussite* copy ("*wie Martinus Luther dem rechten Text, dem huschischen Exemplar nach, seins gefallens ab und zugethan und verendert hab*"). Most editions contain a Preface of Duke George of Saxony, in which he charges Luther with rebellion against all ecclesiastical and secular authority, and identifies him with the beast of the Apocalypse, ch. 13 ("*dass sein Mund wol genannt werden mag der Mund der Bestie von welcher Johannes schreibet in seiner Offenbarung am dreizehnten*").

[1] Dr. Döllinger, in his *Reformation*, vol. III. 139 sqq., 156 sqq., goes into an elaborate proof. In his *Luther, eine Skizze* (Freiburg-i.-B., 1851), p. 26, he calls Luther's version "*ein Meisterstück in sprachlicher Hinsicht, aber seinem Lehrbegriffe gemäss eingerichtet, und daher in vielen Stellen absichtlich unrichtig und sinnentstellend.*" So also Cardinal Hergenröther (*Lehrbuch der allg. Kirchengesch.*, vol. III. 40, third ed. of 1886): "*Die ganze Uebersetzung war ganz nach Luthers System zugerichtet, auf Verbreitung seiner Rechtfertigungslehre berechnet, oft durch willkührliche Entstellungen und Einschaltungen seinen Lehren angepasst.*"

[2] By older and more recent Romanists, as Ward, *Errata of the Protestant Bible*, Dublin, 1810. Trench considers the main objections in his book on the *Authorized Version and Revision*, pp. 165 sqq. (in the Harper ed. of 1873). The chief passages objected to by Romanists are Heb. 13:4 (where the E. V. translates "Marriage *is* honorable in all" for "*Let* marriage *be* honorable among all"); 1 Cor. 11:27 ("and" for "or"); Gal. 5:6 ("faith *which worketh* by love;" which is correct according to the prevailing sense of ἐνεργεῖσθαι, and corresponds to the Vulgate *operatur*, against the Roman view of the passive sense, "*wrought* by love," in conformity with the doctrine of *fides formata*), and the rendering of εἴδωλον by *image*, instead of *idol*. The E. V. has also been charged with a Calvinistic bias from its connection with Beza's Greek text and Latin notes.

alone in Rom. 3 : 28 (*allein durch den Glauben*), by which he intended to emphasize his solifidian doctrine of justification, on the plea that the German idiom required the insertion for the sake of clearness.[1] But he thereby brought Paul into direct *verbal* conflict with James, who says (2 : 24), " by works a man is justified, and *not only* by faith " ("*nicht durch den Glauben allein*"). It is well known that Luther deemed it impossible to harmonize the two apostles in this article, and characterized the Epistle of James as an "epistle of straw," because it had no evangelical character ("*keine evangelische Art*").

He therefore insisted on this insertion in spite of all out-cry against it. His defense is very characteristic. " If your papist," he says,[2] "makes much useless fuss about the word *sola, allein,* tell him at once : Doctor Martin Luther will have it so, and says : Papist and donkey are one thing; *sic volo, sic jubeo, sit pro ratione voluntas.* For we do not want to be pupils and followers of the Papists, but their masters and judges." Then he goes on in the style of foolish boasting against the Papists, imitating the language of St. Paul in dealing with his Judaizing opponents (2 Cor. 11 : 22 sqq.): " Are they doctors? so am I. Are they learned? so am I. Are they preachers? so am I. Are they theologians? so am I. Are they disputators? so am I. Are they philos-ophers? so am I. Are they the writers of books? so am I. And I shall further boast: I can expound Psalms and Prophets; which they can not. I can translate; which they can not. . . . Therefore the word *allein* shall remain in my

---

[1] But he omitted *allein* in Gal. 2 : 16, where it might be just as well justi-fied, and where the pre-Lutheran Bible reads "*nur durch den Glauben.*" However correct in substance and as an inference, the insertion has no busi-ness in the text as a translation. See Meyer on Rom. 3 : 28, 5th ed., and Weiss, 6th ed. (1881), also my annotations to Lange on Romans (p. 136).

[2] In his *Sendbrief vom Dolmetschen,* in the Erl.-Frkf. ed., vol. LXV., p. 107 sqq. It was published in September, 1530, with special reference to Emser, whom he does not name, but calls "the scribbler from Dresden" ("*der dresdener Sudler*").

New Testament, and though all pope-donkeys (*Papstesel*) should get furious and foolish, they shall not turn it out." [1]

The Protestant and anti-Romish character of Luther's New Testament is undeniable in his prefaces, his discrimination between chief books and less important books, his change of the traditional order, and his unfavorable judgments on James, Hebrews, and Revelation.[2] It is still more apparent in his marginal notes, especially on the Pauline Epistles, where he emphasizes throughout the difference between the law and the gospel, and the doctrine of justification by faith alone; and on the Apocalypse, where he finds the papacy in the beast from the abyss (ch. 13), and in the Babylonian harlot (ch. 17).[3] The anti-papal explanation of the Apocalypse became for a long time almost traditional in Protestant commentaries.

On the other hand, the Roman Catholic translators used the same liberty of marginal annotations and pictorial illustrations in favor of the doctrines and usages of their own church. Emser's New Testament is full of anti-Lutheran glosses. In Rom. 3: 28, he protests on the margin against Luther's *allein*, and says, " Paul by the words ' without works of the law ' does not mean that man is saved by faith alone, without good works, but only without works of the law, that is, external circumcision and other Jewish ceremonies." He

---

[1] The Revisers of the *Probebibel* retained the interpolated *allein* in Rom. 3:28, the *nur* in 4:15, and the incorrect rendering in 3:25, 26, — a striking proof of Luther's overpowering influence even over conscientious critical scholars in Germany. Dr. Grimm, the lexicographer (*l.c.*, p. 48), unjustly censures Meyer and Stier for omitting the word *allein*. I have an old copy of Luther's Testament, without titlepage, before me, where the word *allein* is printed in larger type with a marginal finger pointing to it.

[2] The Prefaces are collected in the 7th volume of Bindseil's edition of the Luther Bible, and in the 63d volume of the Erlangen ed. of Luther's works. The most important is his preface to the Epistle to the Romans, and his most objectionable that to the Epistle of James.

[3] He adds in the marginal note on ch. 17: " *Hie zeiget er die römische Kirche in ihrer Gestalt und Wesen, die verdammt soll werden.*" His friend Cranach, in the accompanying picture in the first ed., and also in the ed. of 1535, represents the harlot as riding on a dragon with a triple crown on her head.

therefore confines the "law" here to the ritual law, and "works" to Jewish works; while, according to the best modern commentators, Paul means the *whole* law, moral as well as ceremonial, and *all* works commanded by the law. And yet even in the same chapter and throughout the whole Epistle to the Romans, Emser copies verbatim Luther's version for whole verses and sections; and where he departs from his language, it is generally for the worse.

The same may be said of the other two German Catholic Bibles of the age of the Reformation. They follow Luther's language very closely within the limits of the Vulgate, and yet abuse him in the notes. Dr. Dietenberger adds his comments in smaller type after the chapters, and agrees with Emser's interpretation of Rom. 3: 28.[1] Dr. Eck's German Bible has few notes, but a strongly anti-Protestant preface.[2]

To be just, we must recognize the sectarian imperfections of Bible versions, arising partly from defective knowledge, partly from ingrained prejudices. A translation is an interpretation. Absolute reproduction is impossible in any work.[3] A Jew will give a version of the Old Testament differing

---

[1] *Biblia beider Allt unnd Newen Testamenten, fleissig, treulich vñ Christlich nach alter inn Christlicher Kirchen gehabter Translation, mit Aussslegung etlicher dunckeler ort und besserung vieler verrückter wort und sprüch.* . . . *Durch D. Johan Dietenberger, new verdeutscht. Gott zu ewiger ehre unnd wolfarth seiner heil. Christlichen Kirchen* . . Meynz, 1534, fol. From a copy in the Union Seminary (Van Ess library). Well printed and illustrated.

[2] I have before me three copies of as many folio editions of Eck's Bible, 1537, 1550, and 1558, bearing the title: *Bibel Alt und New Testament, nach dem Text in der heiligen Kirchen gebraucht, durch Doctor Johañ Ecken, mit fleiss, auf hochteutsch verdolmetscht, etc.* They were printed at Ingolstadt, and agree in the number of pages (1035), and vary only in the date of publication. They contain in an appendix the Prayer of Manasseh, the Third Book of Maccabees, and the spurious Epistle of Paul to the Laodiceans.

[3] There is an Italian proverb that translators are traitors (*Traduttori traditori*). Jerome speaks of *versiones* which are *eversiones*. As Trench says, there are in every translation "unavoidable losses inherent in the nature of the task, in the relations of one language to the other, in the lack of accurate correlations between them, in the different schemes of their construction."

from that of a Christian, because they look upon it in a different light, — the one with his face turned backward, the
other with his face turned forward. A Jew cannot understand the Old Testament till he becomes a Christian, and
sees in it a prophecy and type of Christianity. No synagogue would use a Christian version, nor any church a Jewish
version. So also the New Testament is rendered differently
by scholars of the Greek, Latin, and Protestant churches.
And even where they agree in words, there is a difference in
the pervading spirit. They move, as it were, in a different
atmosphere. A Roman Catholic version must be closely conformed to the Latin Vulgate, which the Council of Trent
puts on an equal footing with the original text.[1] A Protestant version is bound only by the original text, and breathes
an air of freedom from traditional restraint. The Roman
Church will never use Luther's Version or King James's
Version, and could not do so without endangering her creed;
nor will German Protestants use Emser's and Eck's Versions, or English Protestants the Douay Version. The
Romanist must become evangelical before he can fully apprehend the free spirit of the gospel as revealed in the New
Testament.

There is, however, a gradual progress in translation, which
goes hand in hand with the progress of the understanding of
the Bible. Jerome's Vulgate is an advance upon the Itala,
both in accuracy and Latinity; the Protestant Versions of
the sixteenth century are an advance upon the Vulgate, in

---

[1] Hence the stiffness of literalism and the abundance of Latinisms in the
Rhemish Version of the N. T. (first published in 1582, second ed. 1600,
third ed. at Douay, 1621), such as "supersubstantial bread" for daily or
needful bread (Jerome introduced *supersubstantialis* for the difficult ἐπιούσιος
in the Lord's Prayer, Matt. 6:11, but retained *quotidianus* in Luke), trans-
migration of Babylon, impudicity, coinquinations, postulations, agnition,
cogitation, prepuce, pasche, exinanite, contristate, domesticals, exemplars of
the cœlestials, etc. Some of them have been silently removed in modern
editions. The notes of the older editions abound in fulminations against
heretics.

spirit and in idiomatic reproduction; the revisions of the nineteenth century are an advance upon the versions of the sixteenth, in philological and historical accuracy and consistency. A future generation will make a still nearer approach to the original text in its purity and integrity. If the Holy Spirit of God shall raise the Church to a higher plane of faith and love, and melt the antagonisms of human creeds into the one creed of Christ, then, and not before then, may we expect perfect versions of the oracles of God.

NOTES.

THE OFFICIAL REVISION OF THE LUTHER-BIBLE, AND THE ANGLO-AMERICAN REVISION OF THE AUTHORIZED ENGLISH BIBLE.

An official revision of Luther's version was inaugurated, after long previous agitation and discussion, by the "Eisenach German Evangelical Church Conference," in 1863, and published under the title: *Die Bibel oder die ganze Heilige Schrift des Alten und Neuen Testaments nach der deutschen Uebersetzung D. Martin Luthers.* Halle (Buchhandlung des Waisenhauses), 1883. It is called the *Probebibel.* The revised New Testament had been published several years before, and is printed by Dr. O. von Gebhardt together with the Greek text, in his *Novum Testamentum Græce et Germanice,* Leipzig, 1881.

The revision was prepared with extraordinary care, but in an ultra-conservative spirit, by a number of distinguished biblical scholars appointed by the ecclesiastical authorities of the German governments, eleven for the New Testament (Nitzsch, Twesten, Beyschlag, Riehm, Ahlfeld, Brückner, Meyer, Niemann, Fronmüller, Schröder, Köstlin), and over twenty for the Old Testament, including some who had also served in the New Testament company (Tholuck, Schlottmann, Riehm, Dillmann, Kleinert, Delitzsch, Bertheau, Düsterdieck, Kamphausen, Baur of Leipzig, Ahlfeld, Thenius, Kübel, Kapff, Schröder, Diestel, Grimm, Kühn, Hoffmann, Clausen, Grill). Dorner, Mönckeberg, and Karl Frommann took a very active part as counsellors and promoters, the last (an eminent Germanist and Luther-scholar, but with strong archaic tastes) in the linguistic portion.

The work was very severely criticised by opposite schools for changing too much or too little, and was recommitted by the Eisenach Conference of 1886 for final action. The history of this revision is told in the preface and introduction to the *Probebibel,* and in Grimm's *Geschichte der luth. Bibelübersetzung,* Jena, 1884, pp. 48–76.

The Anglo-American revision of the Authorized English Version of 1611 was set in motion by the Convocation of Canterbury, and carried out in fifteen years, between 1870 and 1885, by two committees, — one in England and one in the United States (each divided into two companies, — one for the Old Testament, one for the New, and each consisting of scholars of various Protestant denominations). Dr. Dorner, on his visit to America in 1873, desired to bring about a regular co-operation of the two revision movements, but it was found impracticable, and confined to private correspondence.

The two revisions are similar in spirit and aim; and as far as they run parallel, they agree in most of the improvements. Both aim to replace the old version in public and private use; but both depend for ultimate success on the verdict of the churches for which they were prepared. They passed through the same purgatory of hostile criticism both from conservative and progressive quarters. They mark a great progress of biblical scholarship, and the immense labor bestowed upon them can never be lost. The difference of the two arises from the difference of the two originals on which they are based, and its relation to the community.

The authorized German and English versions are equally idiomatic, classical, and popular; but the German is personal, and inseparable from the over-awing influence of Luther, which forbids radical changes. The English is impersonal, and embodies the labors of three generations of biblical scholars from Tyndale to the forty-seven revisers of King James, — a circumstance which is favorable to new improvements in the same line. In Germany, where theology is cultivated as a science for a class, the interest in revision is confined to scholars; and German scholars, however independent and bold in theory, are very conservative and timid in practical questions. In England and America, where theology moves in close contact with the life of the churches, revision challenges the attention of the laity which claims the fruits of theological progress.

Hence the Anglo-American revision is much more thorough and complete. It embodies the results of the latest critical and exegetical learning. It involves a reconstruction of the original text, which the German Revision leaves almost untouched, as if all the pains-taking labors of critics since the days of Bengel and Griesbach down to Lachmann and Tischendorf (not to speak of the equally important labors of English scholars from Mill and Bentley to Westcott and Hort) had been in vain.

As to translation, the English Revision removes not only misleading errors, but corrects the far more numerous inaccuracies and inconsistencies in the minor details of grammar and vocabulary; while the German Revision is confined to the correction of acknowledged mistranslations. The German Revision of the New Testament numbers only about two hundred changes, the Anglo-American thirty-six thousand. The revised German New Testament is widely circulated; but of the provisional *Probebibel*, which embraces both Testaments, only five thousand copies were printed and sold by the Canstein Bibelanstalt at Halle (as I learned there from Dr. Kramer, July, 1886). Of the revised English New Testament, a million copies were ordered from the Oxford University Press before publication, and three million copies were sold in less than a year (1881). The text was telegraphed from New York to Chicago in advance of the arrival of the book. Over thirty reprints appeared in the United States. The Revised Old Testament excited less interest, but tens of thousands of copies were sold on the day of publication (1885), and several American editions were issued. The Bible, after all, is the most popular book in the world, and constantly increasing in power and influence, especially with the English-speaking race. (For particulars on the English Revision, see Schaff's *Companion to the Greek Testament and the English Version*, New York, 3d ed., 1888, pp. 404 sqq., and the extensive Revision literature, pp. 371 sqq.)

§ 64. *Melanchthon's Theology.*

See Literature in § 38, pp. 182 sq. The 21st vol. of the "Corpus Reformatorum" (1106 fol. pages) is devoted to the various editions of Melanchthon's *Loci Theologici*, and gives bibliographical lists (fol. 59 sqq.; 561 sqq.), and also an earlier outline from an unpublished MS. Comp. CARL SCHMIDT, *Phil. Mel.*, pp. 64–75; and on Melanchthon's doctrinal changes, SCHAFF, *Creeds of Christendom*, vol. I. 261 sqq.

While Luther translated the New Testament on the Wartburg, Melanchthon prepared the first system of Protestant theology at Wittenberg. Both drew from the same fountain, and labored for the same end, but in different ways. Luther built up the Reformation among the people in the German tongue; Melanchthon gave it methodical shape for scholars by his Latin writings. The former worked in the quarries, and cut the rough blocks of granite; the latter constructed the blocks into a habitable building. Luther expressed a modest self-estimate, and a high estimate of his friend, when he said that his superiority was more "in the rhetorical way," while Melanchthon was "a better logician and reasoner."

Melanchthon finished his "Theological Common-Places" or Ground-Thoughts (*Loci Communes* or *Loci Theologici*), in April, 1521, and sent the proof-sheets to Luther on the Wartburg. They appeared for the first time before the close of that year.[1]

---

[1] Under the title: *Loci communes rerum theologicarum seu hypotyposes theologicæ*, Wittenberg, 1521. Bindseil puts the publication in December.

This book marks an epoch in the history of theology. It grew out of exegetical lectures on the Epistle to the Romans, the Magna Charta of the evangelical system. It is an exposition of the leading doctrines of sin and grace, repentance and salvation. It is clear, fresh, thoroughly biblical, and practical. Its main object is to show that man cannot be saved by works of the law or by his own merits, but only by the free grace of God in Christ as revealed in the gospel. It presents the living soul of divinity, in striking contrast to the dry bones of degenerate scholasticism with its endless theses, antitheses, definitions, divisions, and subdivisions.

The first edition was written in the interest of practical Christianity rather than scientific theology. It is meagre in the range of topics, and defective in execution. It is confined to anthropology and soteriology, and barely mentions the metaphysical doctrines of the Trinity and the incarnation, as transcendent mysteries to be adored rather than curiously discussed. It has a polemical bearing against the Romanists, in view of the recent condemnation of Luther by the Sorbonne. It also contains some crude and extreme opinions which the author afterwards abandoned. Altogether in its first shape it was an unripe production, though most remarkable if we consider the youth of the author, who was then only twenty-four years of age.

Melanchthon shared at first Luther's antipathy to scholastic theology; but he learned to distinguish between pure and legitimate scholasticism and a barren formalism, as also between the Aristotelian philosophy itself and the skeleton of it which was worshiped as an idol in the universities at that time. He knew especially the value of Aristotle's ethics, wrote a commentary on the same (1529), and made important

I have a copy of the Leipzig ed. of M.D.LIX., which numbers 858 pages without indices, and bears the title: *Loci Præcipui Theologici. Nunc denuo cura et diligentia summa recogniti, multisque in locis copiose illustrati, cum appendice disputationis de conjugio*, etc.

original contributions to the science of Christian ethics in his *Philosophiæ Moralis Epitome* (1535).[1]

Under his improving hand, the *Loci* assumed in subsequent editions the proportions of a full, mature, and well-proportioned system, stated in calm, clear, dignified language, freed from polemics against the Sorbonne and contemptuous flings at the schoolmen and Fathers. He embraced in twenty-four chapters all the usual topics from God and the creation to the resurrection of the body, with a concluding chapter on Christian liberty. He approached the scholastic method, and even ventured, in opposition to the Anti-Trinitarians, on a new speculative proof of the Holy Trinity from psychological analogies. He never forsakes the scriptural basis, but occasionally quotes also the Fathers to show their supposed or real agreement with evangelical doctrines.

Melanchthon's theology, like that of Luther, grew from step to step in the heat of controversy. Calvin's Institutes came finished from his brain, like Minerva out of the head of Jupiter.

The *Loci* prepared the way for the Augsburg Confession (1530), in which Melanchthon gave to the leading doctrines official shape and symbolical authority for the Lutheran Church. But he did not stop there, and passed through several changes, which we must anticipate in order to form a proper estimate of that work.

The editions of his theological manual are divided into three classes: 1, those from 1521 to 1535; 2, those from 1535 to 1544; 3, those from 1544 to 1559. The edition of 1535 (dedicated to King Henry VIII. of England, and translated into German by Justus Jonas) was a thorough revision. This and the editions which followed embody, besides additions in matter and improvements in style, important modi-

---

[1] See his ethical writings in vol. XVI. of his *Opera*, in the "Corp. Reform.," and a discussion of their merits in Wuttke's *Handbuch der christl. Sittenlehre*, 3d ed. (1874), I. 148 sqq.

fications of his views on predestination and free will, on the
real presence, and on justification by faith. He gave up
necessitarianism for synergism, the corporeal presence in the
eucharist for a spiritual real presence, and solifidianism for
the necessity of good works. In the first and third article
he made an approach to the Roman-Catholic system, in the
second to Calvinism.

The changes were the result of his continued study of the
Bible and the Fathers, and his personal conferences with
Roman and Reformed divines at Augsburg and in the colloquies of Frankfort, Hagenau, Worms, and Ratisbon. He
calls them elucidations of obscurities, moderations of extreme
views, and sober second thoughts.[1]

1. He denied at first, with Luther and Augustin, all freedom of the human will in spiritual things.[2] He even held
the Stoic doctrine of the necessary occurrence of all actions,
bad as well as good, including the adultery of David and the
treason of Judas as well as the conversion of Paul.[3]

But on closer examination, and partly under the influence
of Erasmus, he abandoned this stoic fatalism as a dangerous error, inconsistent with Christianity and morality. He
taught instead a co-operation of the divine and human will
in the work of conversion; thus anticipating Arminianism,
and approaching the older semi-Pelagianism, but giving the
initiative to divine grace. "God," he said in 1535, "is not the
cause of sin, and does not will sin; but the will of the Devil

---

[1] See his letters to his friend Camerarius, 2 Sept. 1535 ("Corp. Ref." II.
936), and Dec. 24, 1535 (ib. II. 1027): "Ego nunc in meis Locis multa miti-
gavi." . . . "In Locis meis videor habere δευτέρας φροντίδας." His letters
are interspersed with Greek words and classical reminiscences.

[2] Loc. Theol., 1521, A. 7: "Quandoquidem omnia quæ eveniunt, necessario
juxta divinam prædestinationem eveniunt, nulla est voluntatis nostrae libertas." He refers to Rom. 9 and 11 and Matt. 10:29.

[3] In his Com. in Ep. ad Roman., 1524, cap. 8: "Itaque sit hæc certa sententia, a Deo fieri omnia tam bona quam mala. . . . Constat Deum omnia
facere non permissive sed potenter, — ita ut sit ejus proprium opus Judæ
proditio, sicut Pauli vocatio." Luther published this commentary without
Melanchthon's knowledge, and humorously dedicated it to him.

and the will of man are the causes of sin." Human nature is radically, but not absolutely and hopelessly, corrupt; it can not without the aid of the Holy Spirit produce spiritual affections such as the fear and love of God, and true obedience; but it can accept or reject divine grace. God precedes, calls, moves, supports us; but we must follow, and not resist. Three causes concur in the conversion, — the word of God, the Holy Spirit, and the will of man. Melanchthon quotes from the Greek Fathers who lay great stress on human freedom, and he accepts Chrysostom's sentence: "God draws the willing."

He intimated this synergistic view in the eighteenth article of the altered Augsburg Confession, and in the German edition of the Apology of the Confession. But he continued to deny the meritoriousness of good works; and in the colloquy of Worms, 1557, he declined to condemn the doctrine of the slavery of the human will, because Luther had adhered to it to the end. He was willing to tolerate it as a theological opinion, although he himself had rejected it.

2. As to the Lord's Supper, he first accepted Luther's view under the impression that it was supported by the ancient Church. But in this he was shaken by Œcolampadius, who proved (1530) that the Fathers held different opinions, and that Augustin did not teach an oral manducation. After 1534 he virtually gave up for himself, though he would not condemn and exclude, the conception of a corporeal presence and oral manducation of the body and blood of Christ; and laid the main stress on the spiritual, yet real presence and communion with Christ.

He changed the tenth article of the Augsburg Confession in 1540, and made it acceptable to Reformed divines by omitting the anti-Zwinglian clause. But he never accepted the Zwinglian theory of a mere commemoration. His later eucharistic theory closely approached that of Calvin; while on the subject of predestination and free will he differed from

him. Calvin, who had written a preface to the French translation of the *Loci Theologici*, expressed, in private letters, his
surprise that so great a theologian could reject the Scripture
doctrine of eternal predestination; yet they maintained an
intimate friendship to the end, and proved that theological
differences need not prevent religious harmony and fraternal
fellowship.

3. Melanchthon never surrendered the doctrine of justification by faith; but he laid in his later years, in opposition to
antinomian excesses, greater stress on the necessity of good
works of faith, not indeed as a condition of salvation and in a
sense of acquiring merit, but as an indispensable proof of the
duty of obedience to the divine will.

These doctrinal changes gave rise to bitter controversies
after Luther's death, and were ultimately rejected in the
Formula of Concord (1577), but revived again at a later
period. Luther himself never adopted and never openly
opposed them.

The *Loci* of Melanchthon met from the start with extraordinary favor. Edition after edition appeared in Wittenberg
during the author's lifetime, the last from his own hand in the
year 1559. besides a number of contemporaneous reprints at
Basel, Hagenau, Strassburg, Frankfurt, Leipzig, Halle, and
many editions after his death.

Luther had an extravagant opinion of them, and even
declared them worthy of a place in the canon.[1] He thought
that his translation of the Bible, and Melanchthon's *Loci*, were
the best outfit of a theologian, and almost superseded all
other books.[2]

---

[1] "*Invictus libellus non solum immortalitate, sed quoque canone ecclesiastico dignus.*" In the beginning of *De Servo Arbitrio* (1525), against
Erasmus.

[2] He says in his *Tischreden* (Erl. ed., LIX. 278 sq.): "*Wer itzt ein Theologus will werden, der hat grosse Vortheil. Denn erstlich hat er die Bibel,
die ist nu so klar, dass er sie kann lesen ohne alle Hinderung. Darnach lese
er darzu die locos communes Philippi; die lese er fleissig und wohl, also*

The *Loci* became the text-book of Lutheran theology in the universities, and took the place of Peter Lombard's Sentences. Strigel and Chemnitz wrote commentaries on them. Leonhard Hutter likewise followed them, till he published a more orthodox compend (1610) which threw them into the shade and even out of use during the seventeenth century.

The theological manual of Melanchthon proved a great help to the Reformation. The Romanists felt its power. Emser called it a new Koran and a pest. In opposition to them, he and Eck wrote *Loci Catholici*.[1]

Melanchthon's *Loci* are the ablest theological work of the Lutheran Church in the sixteenth century. Calvin's *Institutes* (1536) equal them in freshness and fervor, and surpass them in completeness, logical order, philosophical grasp, and classical finish.

It is remarkable that the first and greatest dogmatic systems of the Reformation proceeded from these two lay-theologians who were never ordained by human hands, but received the unction from on high.[2] So the twelve apostles were not baptized by Christ with water, but with the Holy Spirit on the day of Pentecost.

---

dass er sie gar im Kopfe habe. Wenn er die zwei Stücke hat, so ist er ein Theologus, dem weder der Teufel noch kein Ketzer etwas abbrechen kann, und ihm stehet die ganze Theologia offen, dass er Alles, was er will, darnach lesen kann ad œdificationem. Und wenn er will, so mag er auch dazu lesen Philippi Melanchthonis Commentarium in Epistolam Pauli ad Romanos. Lieset er alsdenn darzu meinen commentarium in Epistolam ad Galatas und in Deuteronomium, so gebe ich ihm denn eloquentiam et copiam verborum. Ihr findet.kein Buch unter allen seinen Büchern, da die summa religionis oder die ganze Theologia so fein bei einander ist, als in den locis communibus. Leset alle Patres und Sententiarios, so ist es doch Alles nichts dagegen. Non est melior liber post scripturam sanctam, quam ipsius loci communes. Philippus ist enger gespannet denn ich; ille pugnat et docet; ich bin mehr ein Rhetoricus oder ein Wäscher [Deutscher ?] "

[1] Eck's *Loci Communes adversus Lutheranos*, Landshut, 1525, passed through many editions.

[2] Melanchthon was simply professor, first of Greek, then of theology. Calvin was destined by his father for the clerical profession, and he received the tonsure; but there is no record of his ordination for the priesthood.

§ 65. *Protestant Radicalism. Disturbances at Erfurt.*

I. Letters of LUTHER from May, 1521, to March, 1522, to Melanchthon,
Link, Lange, Spalatin, etc., in De Wette, vol. II.

II. F. W. KAMPSCHULTE: *Die Universität Erfurt in ihrem Verh. zu dem
Humanismus und der Reformation.* Trier, 1858. Second part, chs. III.
and IV. pp. 106 sqq.

III. Biographies of Andreas Bodenstein von Carlstadt, by FÜSSLIN (1776),
JÄGER (Stuttgart, 1856), ERBKAM (in Herzog[ii], VII. 523 sqq.).

IV. GIESELER, IV. 61-65 (Am. ed.). MARHEINEKE, chs. X. and XI.
(I. 303 sqq.). MERLE D'AUB., Bk. IX. chs. 6-8. KÖSTLIN, Bk. IV.
chs. 3 and 4 (I. 494 sqq.). RANKE, II. 7-26. JANSSEN, II. 204-227.

While Luther and Melanchthon laid a solid foundation for
an evangelical church and evangelical theology, their work
was endangered by the destructive zeal of friends who turned
the reformation into a revolution. The best thing may be
undone by being overdone. Freedom is a two-edged sword,
and liable to the worst abuse as well as to the best use.
Tares will grow up in every wheat-field, and they sometimes
choke the wheat. But the work of destruction was overruled for the consolidation of the Reformation. Old rotten
buildings had to be broken down before a new one could be
constructed.

The Reformation during its first five years was a battle of
words, not of deeds. It scattered the seeds of new institutions all over Germany, but the old forms and usages still
remained. The new wine had not yet burst the old skin
bottles. The Protestant soul dwelt in the Catholic body.
The apostles after the day of Pentecost continued to visit the
temple and the synagogue, and to observe circumcision,
the sabbath, and other customs of the fathers, hoping for the
conversion of all Israel, until they were cast out by the Jewish hierarchy. So the Protestants remained in external communion with the mother Church, attending Latin mass, bowing
before the transubstantiated elements on the altar, praying
the Ave Maria, worshiping saints, pictures, and crucifixes,

making pilgrimages to holy shrines, observing the festivals of the Roman calendar, and conforming to the seven sacraments which accompanied them at every step of life from the cradle to the grave. The bishops were still in charge of their dioceses, and unmarried priests and deacons performed all the ecclesiastical functions. The convents were still occupied by monks and nuns, who went through their daily devotions and ascetic exercises. The outside looked just as before, while the inside had undergone a radical change.

This was the case even in Saxony and at Wittenberg, the nursery of the new state of things. Luther himself did not at first contemplate any outward change. He labored and hoped for a reformation of faith and doctrine within the Catholic Church, under the lead of the bishops, without a division; but he was now cast out by the highest authorities, and came gradually to see that he must build a new structure on the new foundation which he had laid by his writings and by the translation of the New Testament.

The negative part of these changes, especially the abolition of the mass and of monasticism, was made by advanced radicals among his disciples, who had more zeal than discretion, and mistook liberty for license.

While Luther was confined on the Wartburg, his followers were like children out of school, like soldiers without a captain. Some of them thought that he had stopped half way, and that they must complete what he had begun. They took the work of destruction and reconstruction into their own inexperienced and unskillful hands. Order gave way to confusion, and the Reformation was threatened with disastrous failure.

The first disturbances broke out at Erfurt in June, 1521, shortly after Luther's triumphant passage through the town on his way to Worms. Two young priests were excommunicated for taking part in the enthusiastic demonstrations. This created the greatest indignation. Twelve hundred students, workmen, and ruffians attacked and demolished in a few days sixty houses of the priests, who escaped violence only by flight.[1]

The magistrate looked quietly on, as if in league with the insurrection. Similar scenes of violence were repeated during the summer. The monks under the lead of the Augustinians, forgetting their vows, left the convents. laid aside the monastic dress, and took up their abode among the people to work for a living, or to become a burden to others, or to preach the new faith.

Luther saw in these proceedings the work of Satan, who was bringing shame and reproach on the gospel.[2] He feared that many left the cloister for the same reason for which they had entered, namely, from love of the belly and carnal freedom.[3]

During these troubles Crotus, the enthusiastic admirer of Luther, resigned the rectorship of the university, left Erfurt, and afterwards returned to the mother Church. The Peasants' War of 1525 was another blow. Eobanus, the Latin poet who had greeted Luther on his entry, accepted a call to Nürnberg. The greatest celebrities left the city, or were disheartened, and died in poverty.

From this time dates the decay of the university, once the flourishing seat of humanism and patriotic aspirations. It never recovered its former prosperity.

---

[1] Kampschulte, *l.c.*, II. 117 sqq., gives a full account of this *Pfaffensturm* and its consequences.

[2] See his letters to Melanchthon and Spalatin, in De Wette, II. 7 sq., 31. To the latter he wrote: "*Erfordiæ Satanas suis studiis nobis insidiatus est, ut nostros mala fama inureret, sed nihil proficiet: non sunt nostri, qui hæc faciunt.*"

[3] Letter to Lange, March 28, 1522, in De Wette, II. 175.

§ 66. *The Revolution at Wittenberg. Carlstadt and the New Prophets.*

See Lit. in § 65.

In Wittenberg the same spirit of violence broke out under the lead of Luther's older colleague, Andreas Carlstadt, known to us from his ill success at the Leipzig disputation. He was a man of considerable originality, learning, eloquence, zeal, and courage, but eccentric, radical, injudicious, ill-balanced, restless, and ambitious for leadership.

He taught at first the theology of mediæval scholasticism, but became under Luther's influence a strict Augustinian, and utterly denied the liberty of the human will.

He wrote the first critical work on the canon of the Scriptures, and anticipated the biblical criticism of modern times. He weighed the historic evidence, discriminated between three orders of books as of first, second, and third dignity, putting the Hagiographa of the Old Testament and the seven Antilegomena of the New in the third order, and expressed doubts on the Mosaic authorship of the Pentateuch. He based his objections to the Antilegomena, not on dogmatic grounds, as Luther, but on the want of historical testimony; his opposition to the traditional canon was itself traditional; he put ante-Nicene against post-Nicene tradition. This book on the canon, however, was crude and premature, and passed out of sight.[1]

He invented some curious and untenable interpretations of Scripture, e.g., of the words of institution of the Lord's Supper. He referred the word "this," not to the bread, but to the body of Christ, so as to mean: "I am now ready to offer this (body) as a sacrifice in death." He did not, how-

---

[1] *Libellus de Canonicis Scripturis*, Wittenb. 1520; also in German: *Welche Bücher heilig und biblisch seind.* Comp. Weiss, *Einleitung in's N. T.* (1886), p. 109, and Reuss, *Histoire du Canon* (1863), 357 sqq. (*Hunter's translation*, p. 336 sq.)

ever, publish this view till 1524, and afterwards made common cause with Zwingli.

Carlstadt preached and wrote, during Luther's absence, against celibacy, monastic vows, and the mass. At Christmas, 1521, he omitted in the service the most objectionable parts of the canon of the mass, and the elevation of the host, and distributed both wine and bread to a large congregation. He announced at the same time that he would lay aside the priestly dress and other ceremonies. Two days afterwards he was engaged to the daughter of a poor nobleman in the presence of distinguished professors of the university, and on Jan. 20, 1522, he was married. He gave improper notoriety to this act by inviting the whole university and the magistrate, and by publishing a book in justification of it.

He was not, however, the first priest who openly burst the chains of celibacy. Bartholomäus Bernhardi of Feldkirchen, a Wittenberg licentiate and newly elected *Probst* at Kemberg, and two other priests of less reputable character, had preceded him in 1521. Justus Jonas followed the example, and took a wife Feb. 10, 1522, to get rid of temptations to impurity (1 Cor. 7 : 12). Luther approved of these marriages, but did not intend at that time to follow the example.

Carlstadt went further, and maintained that no priest without wife and children should receive an appointment (so he explained "*must*" in 1 Tim. 3 : 2) ; that it was sin to commune without the cup ; and that the monastic vow of celibacy was not binding, at least not before the sixtieth year of age, chastity being a free gift of God, and not at man's disposal. He introduced a new legalism instead of the old, in violation of the principle of evangelical liberty and charity.

He also denounced pictures and images as dumb idols, which were plainly forbidden in the second commandment, and should be burnt rather than tolerated in the house of God. He induced the town council to remove them from the parish church ; but the populace anticipated the orderly removal, tore them down, hewed them to pieces, and burnt them. He assailed the fasts, and enjoined the people to eat meat and eggs on fast-days. He repudiated all titles and dignities, since Christ alone was our Master (Matt. 23:8). He expressed contempt for theology and all human learning, because God had revealed the truth unto babes (Matt. 11: 25), and advised the students to take to agriculture, and earn their bread in the sweat of their face (Gen. 3:19). He cast away his priestly and academic robes, put on a plain citizen's dress, afterwards a peasant's coat, and had himself called brother Andrew. He ran close to the border of communism. He also opposed the baptism of infants. He lost himself in the clouds of a confused mysticism and spiritualism, and appealed, like the Zwickau Prophets, to immediate inspirations.

In the beginning of November, 1521, thirty of the forty monks left the Augustinian convent of Wittenberg in a rather disorderly manner. One wished to engage in cabinet-making, and to marry. The Augustinian monks held a congress at Wittenberg in January, 1522, and unanimously resolved, in accordance with Luther's advice, to give liberty of leaving or remaining in the convent, but required in either case a life of active usefulness by mental or physical labor.

The most noted of these ex-monks was Gabriel Zwilling or Didymus, who preached in the parish church during Luther's absence, and was esteemed by some as a second Luther. He fiercely attacked the mass, the adoration of the sacrament, and the whole system of monasticism as dangerous to salvation.

About Christmas, 1521, the revolutionary movement was reinforced by two fanatics from Zwickau, Nicolaus Storch, a weaver, and Marcus Thomä Stübner.[1] The latter had previously studied with Melanchthon, and was hospitably

---

[1] Marcus (Marx) Thomä and Stübner are not two distinct persons, but identical. See Köstlin's note, vol. I. 804 sq.

entertained by him. A few weeks afterwards Thomas Münzer, a millennarian enthusiast and eloquent demagogue, who figures prominently in the Peasants' War, appeared in Wittenberg for a short time. He had stirred up a religious excitement among the weavers of Zwickau in Saxony on the Bohemian frontier, perhaps in some connection with the Hussites or Bohemian Brethren, and organized the forces of a new dispensation by electing twelve apostles and seventy-two disciples. But the magistrate interfered, and the leaders had to leave.

These Zwickau Prophets, as they were called, agreed with Carlstadt in combining an inward mysticism with practical radicalism. They boasted of visions, dreams, and direct communications with God and the Angel Gabriel, disparaged the written word and regular ministry, rejected infant baptism, and predicted the overthrow of the existing order of things, and the near approach of a democratic millennium.

We may compare Carlstadt and the Zwickau Prophets with the Fifth Monarchy Men in the period of the English Commonwealth, who were likewise millennarian enthusiasts, and attempted, in opposition to Cromwell, to set up the " Kingdom of Jesus " or the fifth monarchy of Daniel.

Wittenberg was in a very critical condition. The magistrate was discordant and helpless. Amsdorf kept aloof. Melanchthon was embarrassed, and too modest and timid for leadership. He had no confidence in visions and dreams, but could not satisfactorily answer the objections to infant baptism, which the prophets declared useless because a foreign faith of parents or sponsors could not save the child. Luther got over this difficulty by assuming that the Holy Spirit wrought faith in the child.

The Elector was requested to interfere ; but he dared not, as a layman, decide theological and ecclesiastical questions. He preferred to let things take their natural course, and trusted in the overruling providence of God. He believed in

Gamaliel's counsel, which is good enough in the preparatory and experimental stages of a new movement. His strength lay in a wise, cautious, peaceful diplomacy. But at this time valor was the better part of discretion.

The only man who could check the wild spirit of revolution, and save the ship of the Reformation, was Luther.

§ 67. *Luther returns to Wittenberg.*

WALCH, XV. 2374–2403. DE WETTE, II. 137 sqq.

Luther was informed of all these disturbances. He saw the necessity of some changes, but regretted the violence with which they had been made before public opinion was prepared, and he feared a re-action which radicalism is always likely to produce. The Latin mass as a sacrifice, with the adoration of the host, the monastic institution, the worship of saints, images and relics, processions and pilgrimages, and a large number of superstitious ceremonies, were incompatible with Protestant doctrines. Worship had sooner or later to be conducted in the vernacular tongue; the sacrifice of the mass must give way to a commemorative communion; the cup must be restored to the laity, and the right of marriage to the clergy. He acquiesced in these changes. But about clerical vestments, crucifixes, and external ceremonies, he was indifferent; nor did he object to the use of pictures, provided they were not made objects of worship. In such matters he asserted the right of Christian freedom, against coercion for or against them. As to the pretended revelations of the new prophets, he despised them, and maintained that an inspired prophet must either be ordinarily called by church authority, or prove his divine commission by miracles.

He first went to Wittenberg in disguise, and spent three days there in December, 1521. He stayed under the roof of Amsdorf, and dared not show himself in the convent or on the street.

When the disturbances increased, he felt it his duty to re-appear openly on the arena of conflict.   He saw from the Wartburg his own house burning, and hastened to extinguish the flames.   The Elector feared for his safety, as the Edict of Worms was still in force, and the Diet of Nürnberg was approaching.   He ordered him to remain in his concealment. Luther was all his life an advocate of strict submission to the civil magistrates in their own proper sphere ; but on this occasion he set aside the considerations of prudence, and obeyed the higher law of God and his conscience.   His reply to the Elector (whom he never met personally) bears noble testimony to his sublime faith in God's all-ruling providence.   It is dated Ash Wednesday (March 5, 1522), from Borne, south of Leipzig.   He wrote in substance as follows : [1] —

"Grace and peace from God our Father and our Lord Jesus Christ, and my most humble service.

"Most illustrious, high-born Elector, most gracious Lord! I received the letter and warning of your Electoral Grace on Friday evening [Feb. 26], before my departure [March 1]. That your Electoral Grace is moved by the best intention, needs no assurance from me.   I also mean well, but this is of no account. . . .   If I were not certain that we have the pure gospel on our side, I would despair. . . .   Your Grace knows, if not, I make known to you, that I have the gospel, not from men, but from heaven through our Lord Jesus Christ. . . .   I write this to apprise you that I am on my way to Wittenberg under a far higher protection than that of the Elector ; and I have no intention of asking your Grace's support.   Nay, I believe that I can offer your Highness better protection than your Highness can offer me.   Did I think that I had to trust in the Elector, I should not come at all.

---

[1] In De Wette, II. 137-141.   De Wette calls the letter " *ein bewunderungs-würdiges Denkmal des hohen Glaubensmuthes, von welchem Luther erfüllt war.*"

The sword is powerless here. God alone must act without man's interference. He who has most faith will be the most powerful protector. As I feel your Grace's faith to be still weak, I can by no means recognize in you the man who is to protect and save me. Your Electoral Grace asks me, what you are to do under these circumstances? I answer, with all submission, Do nothing at all, but trust in God alone. . . . If your Grace had faith, you would behold the glory of God; but as you do not yet believe, you have not seen it. Let us love and glorify God forever. Amen."

Being asked by the Elector to give his reasons for a return, he assigned, in a letter of March 7, from Wittenberg,[1] three reasons : the urgent written request of the church at Wittenberg; the confusion in his flock; and his desire to prevent an imminent outbreak. "My second reason," he wrote, "is that during my absence Satan has entered my sheepfold, and committed ravages which I can not repair by writing, but only by my personal presence and living word. My conscience would not allow me to delay longer; I was bound to disregard, not only your Highness's disfavor, but the whole world's wrath. It is my flock, the flock intrusted to me by God; they are my children in Christ. I could not hesitate a moment. I am bound to suffer death for them, and will cheerfully with God's grace lay down my life for them, as Christ commands (John 10:12)."

Luther rode without fear through the territory of his violent enemy, Duke George of Saxony, who was then urging the Elector to severe measures against him and the Wittenbergers. He informed the Elector that he would pass through Leipzig, as he once went to Worms, though it should rain Duke Georges for nine days in succession, each fiercer than the original in Dresden.

He safely arrived in Wittenberg on Thursday evening, the

---

[1] De Wette, II. 141–144.

6th of March, full of faith and hope, and ready for a fight against his false friends.

On this journey he had on the 3d or 4th of March an interesting interview with two Swiss students, Kessler and Spengler, in the tavern of the Black Bear at Jena. We have an account of it from one of them, John Kessler of St. Gallen, who afterwards became a reformer of that city.[1] It contrasts very favorably with his subsequent dealings with the Swiss, especially with Zwingli, which were clouded by prejudice, and embittered by intolerance. The episode was purely private, and had no influence upon the course of events; but it reveals a characteristic trait in this mighty man, who even in critical moments of intense earnestness did not lose his playful humor. We find the same combination of apparently opposite qualities when at Coburg he was watching the affairs of the Diet at Augsburg, and wrote a childlike letter to his little Hans. Such harmless humor is like the light of the sun breaking through dark clouds.

The two Swiss, who had studied at Basel, were attracted by the fame of Luther and Melanchthon, and traveled on foot to Wittenberg to hear them. They arrived at Jena after a terrible thunderstorm, fatigued and soaked through, and humbly sat down on a bench near the door of the guest-chamber, when they saw a knight seated at a table, sword in hand, and the Hebrew Psalter before him. Luther recognized the Swiss by their dialect, kindly invited them to sit down at his side, and offered them a drink. He inquired whether Erasmus was still living in Basel, what he was doing, and what the people in Switzerland thought of Martin Luther. The students replied that some lauded him to the

---

[1] Published by Bernet, *Joh. Kessler genannt Athenarius*, St. Gallen, 1826, and more fully by E. Götzinger in Kessler's *Sabbata*, St. Gallen, 1866 and 1868, 2 parts. See a good account in Hagenbach's *Ref. Gesch.*, pp. 141 sqq. In the Schwarze Bär hotel at Jena, where I stopped a few days in July, 1886, the "Lutherstube" is still shown with the likeness of Luther an old Bible, and Kessler's report.

skies as a great reformer; others, especially the priests, denounced him as an intolerable heretic.   During the conversation two traders came in; one took from his pocket Luther's
sermons on the Gospels and Epistles, and remarked that the
writer must be either an angel from heaven or a devil from
hell.   At dinner Luther gave them a rare feast of reason and
flow of soul.   The astonished students suspected that the
mysterious knight was Ulrich von Hutten, when Luther,
turning to the host, smilingly remarked, "Behold, I have
become a nobleman over the night: these Swiss think that I
am Hutten; you take me for Luther.   The next thing will
be that I am Marcolfus."   He gave his young friends good
advice to study the biblical languages with Melanchthon,
paid their bill, offered them first a glass of beer, but substituted for it a glass of wine, since the Swiss were not used to
beer, and with a shake of the hand he begged them to remember him to Doctor Jerome Schurf, their countryman, at
Wittenberg.   When they wished to know the name of the
sender of the salutation, he replied, "Simply tell him that
he who is coming sends greeting, and he will understand it."

When the students a few days afterwards arrived at Wittenberg, and called on Dr. Schurf to deliver the message
from "him who is coming," they were agreeably surprised to
find Luther there with Melanchthon, Jonas, and Amsdorf.
Luther greeted them heartily, and introduced them to Melanchthon, of whom he had spoken at Jena.

The same student has left us a description of Luther's
appearance at that time.   He was no more the meager, emaciated monk as at the Leipzig disputation three years previously,[1] but, as Kessler says, "somewhat stout, yet upright,
bending backwards rather than stooping, with a face upturned
to heaven, with deep dark eyes and eyebrows, twinkling and
sparkling like stars, so that one could hardly look steadily at

---

[1] See the description of Mosellanus, p. 180.

them." [1] These deep, dark eyes, full of strange fire, had struck
Cardinal Cajetan at Augsburg, and Cardinal Aleander at
Worms, as the eyes of a demon. They made the same impression on John Dantiscus, afterwards bishop of Culm and
Ermeland, who on his return from Spain to Poland in 1523
saw Luther in Wittenberg; he reported that his "eyes were
sharp, and had a certain terrible coruscation of lightning
such as was seen now and then in demoniacs," and adds that
"his features were like his books," and "his speech violent
and full of scorn." But friends judged differently. Another
student, Albert Burrer, who saw him after his return from
the Wartburg, praises his mild, kindly countenance, his
pleasant sonorous voice, his charming address, the piety of
his words and acts, the power of his eloquence which moved
every hearer not made of stone, and created a desire to hear
him again and again.[2]

§ 68. *Luther restores Order in Wittenberg. — The End of Carlstadt.*

I. *Eight Sermons of* LUTHER preached from Sunday, March 7 (*Invocavit*) to
the next Sunday (*Reminiscere*), after his return to Wittenberg. The
oldest editions, slightly varying in length, appeared 1523. Altenb. ed.,
II. 99 sqq.; WALCH, XV. 2423 sqq.: XX. 1–101; Erl. ed., XXVIII. 202–
285 (both recensions). LUTHER'S *Letters* to Spalatin, the Elector, and
others from March, 1522, in DE WETTE, II. 144 sqq.

II. Of modern historians, MARHEINCKE, MERLE D'AUBIGNÉ, RANKE,
HAGENBACH, and KÖSTLIN (I. 537–549) may be compared.

On the Sunday after his arrival, Luther ascended his old
pulpit, and re-appeared before his congregation of citizens
and students. Wittenberg was a small place; but what he
said and did there, and what Calvin did afterwards in Geneva,
had the significance of a world-historical fact, more influential
at that time than an encyclical from Rome.

---

[1] "*Mit tiefen, schwarzen Augen und Braunen blinzend und zwitzerlnd
wie ein Stern, dass die nit wohl mögen angesehen werden.*"

[2] Köstlin, I. 536, with references, p. 805.

Protestantism had reached a very critical juncture. Luther or Carlstadt, reformation or revolution, the written Word or illusive inspirations, order or confusion: that was the question. Luther was in the highest and best mood, full of faith in his cause, and also full of charity for his opponents, strong in matter, sweet in manner, and completely successful. He never showed such moderation and forbearance before or after.

He preached eight sermons for eight days in succession, and carried the audience with him. They are models of effective popular eloquence, and among the best he ever preached. He handled the subject from the stand-point of a pastor, with fine tact and practical wisdom. He kept aloof from coarse personalities which disfigure so many of his polemical writings. Not one unkind word, not one unpleasant allusion, escaped his lips. In plain, clear, strong, scriptural language, he refuted the errors without naming the errorists. The positive statement of the truth in love is the best refutation of error.[1]

The ruling ideas of these eight discourses are: Christian freedom and Christian charity; freedom from the tyranny of radicalism which would force the conscience against forms, as the tyranny of popery forces the conscience in the opposite direction; charity towards the weak, who must be trained like children, and tenderly dealt with, lest they stumble and fall. Faith is worthless without charity. No man has a right to compel his brother in matters that are left free; and among these are marriage, living in convents, private confession, fasting and eating, images in churches. Abuses which contradict the word of God, as private masses, should be abolished, but in an orderly manner and by proper authority. The Word of God and moral suasion must be allowed to do the work. Paul preached against the idols in Athens,

---

[1] The ἀληθεύειν ἐν ἀγάπῃ, Eph. 4:15.

without touching one of them; and yet they fell in consequence of his preaching.

" *Summa summarum,*" said Luther, "I will preach, speak,
write, but I will force no one; for faith must be voluntary.
Take me as an example. I stood up against the Pope, indulgences, and all papists, but without violence or uproar. I
only urged, preached, and declared God's Word, nothing
else. And yet while I was asleep, or drinking Wittenberg
beer with my Philip Melanchthon and Amsdorf, the Word
inflicted greater injury on popery than prince or emperor
ever did. I did nothing, the Word did every thing. Had I
appealed to force, all Germany might have been deluged with
blood; yea, I might have kindled a conflict at Worms, so that
the Emperor would not have been safe. But what would
have been the result? Ruin and desolation of body and soul.
I therefore kept quiet, and gave the Word free course through
the world. Do you know what the Devil thinks when he
sees men use violence to propagate the gospel? He sits with
folded arms behind the fire of hell, and says with malignant
looks and frightful grin: 'Ah, how wise these madmen are
to play my game! Let them go on; I shall reap the benefit.
I delight in it.' But when he sees the Word running and
contending alone on the battle-field, then he shudders and
shakes for fear. The Word is almighty, and takes captive
the hearts." [1]

Eloquence rarely achieved a more complete and honorable
triumph. It was not the eloquence of passion and violence,
but the eloquence of wisdom and love. It is easier to rouse
the wild beast in man, than to tame it into submission. Melanchthon and the professors, the magistrate and peaceful citizens, were delighted. Dr. Schurf wrote to the Elector, after

---

[1] Erl. ed., XXVIII. 219 and 260 (second sermon). The allusion to the
drinking of " *Wittenbergisch Bier mit meinem Philippo und Amsdorf*"
(p. 260) is omitted in the shorter edition, which has instead: " *wenn ich bin
guter Dinge gewesen* " (p. 219).

the sixth discourse: "Oh, what joy has Dr. Martin's return spread among us! His words, through divine mercy, are bringing back every day misguided people into the way of the truth. It is as clear as the sun, that the Spirit of God is in him, and that he returned to Wittenberg by His special providence."

Most of the old forms were restored again, at least for a season, till the people were ripe for the changes. Luther himself returned to the convent, observed the fasts, and resumed the cowl, but laid it aside two years afterwards when the Elector sent him a new suit. The passage in the mass, however, which referred to the unbloody repetition of the sacrifice and the miraculous transformation of the elements, was not restored, and the communion in both kinds prevailed, and soon became the universal custom. The Elector himself, shortly before his death (May 5, 1525), communed with the cup.

Didymus openly acknowledged his error, and declared that Luther preached like an angel.[1] But the Zwickau Prophets left Wittenberg for ever, and abused the Reformer as a new pope and enemy of spiritual religion. Münzer stirred up the Peasants' War, and met a tragic fate.[2]

Carlstadt submitted silently, but sullenly. He was a disappointed and unhappy man, and harbored feelings of revenge against Luther. Ranke characterizes him as "one of those men, not rare among Germans, who with an inborn tendency to profundity unite the courage of rejecting all that is established, and defending all that others reject, without ever rising to a clear view and solid conviction." He resumed his lectures in the university for a time; but in 1523 he retired to a

---

[1] Luther speaks favorably of him, and recommended him to a pastoral charge at Altenburg. See his letters in De Wette, II. 170, 183, 184.

[2] He published at Nürnberg, 1524, a self-defense "*Wider das geistlose sanftlebende Fleisch zu Wittenberg*," and called Luther an "Arch-heathen," "Arch-scamp," "Wittenberg Pope," "Babylonian Woman," "Dragon," "Basilisk," etc.

farm in the neighborhood, to live as " neighbor Andrew " with lowly peasants, without, however, resigning the emoluments of his professorship.   He devoted himself more fully than ever to his mystical speculations and imaginary inspirations. He entered into secret correspondence with Münzer, though he never fully approved his political movements.   He published at Jena, where he established a printing-press, a number of devotional books under the name of "a new layman," instead of Doctor of Theology.   He induced the congregation of Orlamünde to elect him their pastor without authority from the academic Senate of Wittenberg which had the right of appointment, and introduced there his innovations in worship, storming the altars and images.   In 1524 he openly came out with his novel theory of the Lord's Supper in opposition to Luther, and thus kindled the unfortunate eucharistic controversy which so seriously interfered with the peace and harmony of the Reformers.   He also sympathized with the Anabaptists.[1]   Luther after long forbearance gave him up as incorrigible.[2]   With his consent, Carlstadt was exiled from Saxony (1524), but allowed to return on a sort of revocation, and on condition of keeping silence (1525). He evaded another expulsion by flight (1528).   He wandered about in Germany in great poverty, made common cause with the Zwinglians, gave up some of his extravagant notions, sobered down, and found a resting-place first as pastor in Zürich, and then as professor of theology in Basel (1534–1541), where during the raging of a pestilence he finished his erratic career.

[1] Nevertheless, in 1526 he invited Luther and his wife, Melanchthon and Jonas, as sponsors at the baptism of a new-born son in the village of Segren near Wittenberg. He lived after his return from exile in very humble circumstances, barely making a living from the sale of cakes and beer.

[2] His writings against Carlstadt, in Walch, X., XV., and XX., and in Erl. ed., LXIV. 384–408. His book *Wider die himmlischen Propheten* (1525) is chiefly directed against Carlstadt. In the Table Talk (Erl. ed., LXI. 91/ he calls Carlstadt and Münzer incarnate devils.

§ 69.   *The Diets of Nürnberg, A.D. 1522–1524.   Adrian VI.*

I. WALCH, XV. 2504 sqq.   RANKE, vol. II. pp. 27–46, 70–100, 244–262.
   J. JANSSEN, vol. II. 256 sqq., 315 sqq.   KÖSTLIN, I. 622 sqq.

II. On Adrian VI.   GACHARD: *Correspondance de Charles Quint et d'Adrian VI.* Brux., 1859.   MORING: *Vita Adriani VI.*, 1535.   BURMANN: *Hadrianus VI.,* sive *Analecta Historica de Hadr. VI.* Trajecti 1727 (includes Moring).   RANKE: *Die röm. Päpste in den letzten vier Jarhh.*, I., 59–64 (8th ed. 1885).   C. HÖFLER (Rom. Cath.): *Wahl und Thronbesteigung des letzten deutschen Papstes, Adrian VI.* Wien, 1872; and *Der deutsche Kaiser und der letzte deutsche Papst, Carl V. und Adrian VI.* Wien, 1876.   FR. NIPPOLD: *Die Reformbestrebungen Papst Hadrian VI., und die Ursachen ihres Scheiterns.* Leipzig, 1875.   H. BAUER : *Hadrian VI.* Heidelb., 1876.   MAURENBRECHER: *Gesch. der kathol. Reformation*, I. 202–225.   Nördlingen, 1880.   See also the Lit. on Charles V., § 50 (p. 262 sqq.).

We must now turn our attention to the political situation, and the attitude of the German Diet to the church question.

The growing sympathies of the German nation with the Reformation and the political troubles made the execution of the papal bull and the Edict of Worms against Luther more and more impossible.   The Emperor was absent in Spain, and fully occupied with the suppression of an insurrection, the conquest of Mexico by Cortez, and the war with France.   Germany was threatened by the approach of the Turks, who had conquered Belgrad and the greater part of Hungary.   The dangers of the nation were overruled for the progress of Protestantism.

An important change took place in the papacy.   Leo X. died Dec. 1, 1521; and Adrian VI. (1459–1523) was unexpectedly elected in his absence, perhaps by the indirect influence of the Emperor, his former pupil.   The cardinals hardly knew what they did, and hoped he might decline.

Adrian formed, by his moral earnestness and monastic piety, a striking contrast to the frivolity and worldliness of his predecessors.   He was a Dutchman, born at Utrecht, a learned professor of theology in Louvain, then administrator and inquisitor of Spain, and a man of unblemished character.[1] He had openly denied the papal infallibility; but otherwise he was an orthodox Dominican, and opposed to a doctrinal reformation. He had combined with the Louvain professors in the condemnation of Luther, and advised Charles to take rigorous measures against him at Worms. Barefooted and without any ostentation, he entered Rome. He read daily mass at early dawn, took a simple meal, slept on a couch, and lived like a monk. He introduced strict economy in the papal household, and vigorously attacked the grossest abuses. He tried to gain the influence of Erasmus and Zwingli. But he encountered opposition everywhere.

Under these circumstances the Diet met at Nürnberg, March 23, 1522, and again Nov. 17, under the presidency of Ferdinand, the brother of the Emperor. To avert the danger of the Turks, processions and public prayers were ordered, and a tax imposed; but no army was raised.

Adrian demanded the execution of the Edict of Worms, and compared Luther to Mohammed; but he broke the force of his request by confessing with surprising frankness the corruptions of the Roman court, which loudly called for a radical moral reform of the head and members. Never before had the Curia made such a confession.

"We know," wrote the Pope in the instruction to his legate, Francesco Chieregati, "that for some time many abominations, abuses in ecclesiastical affairs, and violations of rights have taken place in the holy see; and that all things have been perverted into bad. From the head the corrup-

---

[1] Ranke (*Päpste*, I. 60): "*Adrian war von durchaus unbescholtenem Ruf: rechtschaffen, fromm, thätig; sehr ernsthaft, man sah ihn nie anders als leise mit den Lippen lächeln; aber voll wohlwollender, reiner Absichten: ein wahrer Geistlicher. Welch ein Gegensatz, als er nun dort einzog, wo Leo so prächtig und verschwenderisch Hof gehalten! Es existirt ein Brief von ihm, in welchem er sagt: er möchte lieber in seiner Propstei zu Löwen Gott dienen als Papst sein.*" Pallavicino calls him "*ecclesiastico ottimo, pontifice mediocre.*"

tion has passed to the limbs, from the Pope to the prelates: we have all departed; there is none that doeth good, no, not one." He regarded Protestantism as a just punishment for the sins of the prelates. He promised to do all in his power to remedy the evil, and to begin with the Curia whence it arose.[1]

The Emperor was likewise in favor of a reform of discipline, though displeased with Adrian for not supporting him in his war with France and his church-spoliation schemes.

The attempt to reform the church morally without touching the dogma had been made by the great councils of the fifteenth century, and failed. Adrian found no sympathy in Rome, and reigned too short a time (Jan. 9, 1522 to Sept. 14, 1523) to accomplish his desire. It was rumored that he died of poison; but the proof is wanting. Rome rejoiced. His successor, Clement VII. (1523–1534), adopted at once the policy of his cousin, Leo X.

Complaint was made in the Diet against the Elector Frederick, that he tolerated Luther at Wittenberg, and allowed the double communion, the marriage of priests, and the forsaking of convents, but his controlling influence prevented any unfavorable action. The report of the suppression of the radical movements in Wittenberg made a good impression. Lutheran books were freely printed and sold in Nürnberg. Osiander preached openly against the Roman Antichrist.

The Diet, in the answer to the Pope (framed Feb. 8 and published as an edict March 6, 1523), refused to execute the Edict of Worms, and demanded the calling of a free general council in Germany within a year. In the mean time, Luther should keep silence; and the preachers should

---

[1] " Ut primum curia hæc, unde forte omne hoc malum processit, reformetur." See the instruction in Raynaldus, ad ann. 1522, Tom. XI. 363. Luther published it with sarcastic comments. Pallavicino charges Adrian with exaggeration and want of prudence, which he thought was "often more important for the public good than personal holiness." See Hergenröther, III. 43.

content themselves with preaching the holy gospel according
to the approved writings of the Christian church. At the
same time the hundred gravamina of the German nation
were repeated.

This edict was a compromise, and did not decide the
church question ; but it averted the immediate danger to
the Reformation, and so far marks a favorable change, as
compared with the Edict of Worms. It was the beginning
of the political emancipation of Germany from the control of
the papacy. Luther was rather pleased with it, except the
prohibition of preaching and writing, which he did not obey.

The influence of the edict, however, was weakened by
several events which occurred soon afterwards.

At a new Diet at Nürnberg in January, 1524, where the
shrewd Pope Clement VII. was represented by Cardinal
Campeggio, the resolution was passed to execute the Edict
of Worms, though with the elastic clause, "as far as
possible."

At the earnest solicitation of the papal nuncio, the Archduke Ferdinand of Austria, and the Dukes William and
Louis of Bavaria, together with twelve bishops of South
Germany, concluded at Ratisbon, July 6, 1524, a league for
the protection of the Roman faith against the Reformation,
with the exception of the abolition of some glaring abuses
which did not touch doctrines.[1] The Emperor lent it his
influence by issuing a stringent edict (July 27, 1524). This
was an ominous event. The Romish league called forth a
Protestant counter-league of Philip of Hesse and John of
Saxony, at Torgau in June, 1526, although against the advice
of the Wittenberg Reformers, who feared more evil than
good from a union of politics with religion and trusted to
the power of the Word of God without any carnal weapons.

Thus the German nation was divided into two hostile
camps. From this unhappy division arose the political weak-

---

[1] See details in Ranke, II., 108 sqq. and in Janssen, II., 336 sqq.

ness of the empire, and the terrible calamities of the Smal-kaldian and the Thirty Years' Wars. In 1525 the Peasants' War broke out, and gave new strength to the reaction, but only for a short time.

§ 70. *Luther and Henry VIII.*

HENRICUS VIII.: *Adsertio VII. Sacram. adv. Luth.* Lond. 1521. A German translation by Frick, 1522, in Walch, XIX., 158 sqq. LUTHERUS: *Contra Henricum Regem.* 1522. Also freely reproduced in German by Luther. His letter to Henry, Sept. 1, 1525. *Auf des Königs in England Lästerschrift M. Luther's Antwort.* 1527. Afterwards also in Latin. See the documents in WALCH, XIX. 153–521; Erl. ed., XXVIII. 343 sqq.; XXX. 1–14. Comp. also Luther's letters of Feb. 4 and March 11, 1527, in DE WETTE, III. 161 and 163.

With all his opposition to Ultra-Protestantism in church and state, Luther did not mean to yield an inch to the Romanists. This appears from two very personal contro-versies which took place during these disturbances, — the one with Henry VIII. concerning the sacraments; the other with Erasmus about predestination and free-will. In both he forgot the admirable lessons of moderation which he had enjoined from the pulpit in Wittenberg. He used again the club of Hercules.

Henry VIII. of England urged Charles V. to exterminate the Lutheran heresy by force, and wrote in 1521 (probably with the assistance of his chaplain, Edward Lee), a scholastic defence of the seven sacraments, against Luther's "Babylon-ish Captivity." He dedicated the book to Pope Leo X. He treated the Reformer with the utmost contempt, as a blas-phemer and servant of Satan. He used the old weapons of church authority against freedom. He adhered to the dogma of transubstantiation, even after his breach with Rome. Pope Clement VII. judged that this book was written with the aid of the Holy Spirit, and promised indulgence to all who read it. At the same time he gratified the ambition of the vain

king by confirming the title "Defender of the Faith," which
Leo had already conferred upon him.[1]

The Protestant successors of Henry have retained the title
to this day, though with a very different view of its meaning.
The British sovereigns are defenders of the Episcopal Church
in England, and of the Presbyterian Church in Scotland, and
in both characters enemies of the Church of Rome.

Luther read the King a lecture (in Latin and German) such
as was rarely read to any crowned head.   He called him
" King Henry, of God's *disgrace* (or *wrath*), King of England,"
and heaped upon him the most abusive epithets.[2]   He incidentally hit other princes, saying that "King Henry helps to
prove the proverb that there are no greater fools than kings
and princes."   Such a style of polemics can not be justified
by the coarseness of the age, or the nature of the provocation, and did more harm to Luther than to Henry.   His best
friends regretted it; yet long afterwards he even surpassed
the violence, if possible, in his savage and scurrilous attack
upon Duke Henry of Brunswick.[3]

When there was a prospect of gaining Henry VIII. for the
cause of the Reformation, Luther made the matter worse by
a strange inconsistency.   In a most humble letter of Sept. 1,
1525, he retracted (not his doctrine, but) all the personal

---

[1] Pallavicino and Hergenröther (III. 41) show that Leo conferred the
title in a bull of Oct. 11, 1521, and that Clement confirmed it in a bull of
March 5, 1523.

[2] Especially in the German edition of his reply, where Henry is styled not
only a *gekrönter Esel* (crowned donkey) and *elender Narr* (miserable fool),
but even a *verruchter Schurke, unverschämter Lügner, Gotteslästerer*, etc.
" I say it before all the world, that the King of England is a liar and no
gentleman (*ein Unbiedermann*)."   He makes fun of his title "Defender of
Faith."   The papists who deny Christ may need such a defender; but "the
true church disdains a human patron, and sings, ' *Dominus mihi adjutor* '
(Ps. 9:10), and ' *Nolite confidere in principibus*' (Ps. 118:8, 9)."   In conclusion he apologizes for his violence, because he had to deal with "*unver-
nünftigen wilden Ungeheuern*."   Card. Hergenröther (*Kirchengesch.* III. 41,
3d, 1886) says: " *Luther antwortete in der gemeinsten und boshaftesten Weise,
die Grobheit zur Classicität ausbildend*."

[3] *Wider Hanswurst*, 1541.

abuse, asked his pardon, and offered to honor his name publicly. Henry in his reply refused the offer with royal pride and scorn, and said that he now despised him as heartily for his cowardice as he had formerly hated him for his heresy. He also charged him with violating a nun consecrated to God, and leading other monks into a breach of their vows and into eternal perdition. Emser published a German translation of Luther's letter and the King's answer (which was transmitted through Duke George of Saxony), and accompanied it with new vituperations and slanders (1527). All the Romanists regarded this controversy, and the similar correspondence with Duke George, as a great blow to the Reformation.

Luther now resumed his former sarcastic tone; but it was a painful effort, and did not improve the case. He suspected that the answer was written by Erasmus, who had "more skill and sense in his finger than the King with all his wiseacres." He emphatically denied that he had offered to retract any of his doctrines. "I say, No, no, no, as long as I breathe, no matter how it offend king, emperor, prince, or devil. . . . In short, my doctrine is the main thing of which I boast, not only against princes and kings, but also against all devils. The other thing, my life and person, I know well enough to be sinful, and nothing to boast of; I am a poor sinner, and let all my enemies be saints or angels. I am both proud and humble as St. Paul (Phil. 2:3)."

In December of the same year in which he wrote his first book against King Henry, Luther began his important treatise "On the Secular Power, and how far obedience is due to it." He defends here the divine right and authority of the secular magistrate, and the duty of passive obedience, on the ground of Matt. 5:39 and Rom. 13:1, but only in *temporal* affairs. While he forbade the use of carnal force, he never shrank from telling even his own prince the truth in the plainest manner. He exercised the freedom of speech and of the press to the fullest extent, both in favor of the

Reformation and against political revolution. The Reformation elevated the state at the expense of the freedom of the church; while Romanism lowered the dignity of the state to the position of an obedient servant of the hierarchy.

One wrong does not justify another. Yet those Roman-Catholic historians who make capital of this humiliating conduct of the Reformer, against his cause, should remember that Cardinal Pole, whom they magnify as one of the greatest and purest men of that age, in his book on the Unity of the Church, abused King Henry as violently and more keenly, although he was his king and benefactor, and had not given him any personal provocation; while Luther wrote in self-defense only, and was with all his passionate temper a man of kind and generous feelings.

Melanchthon regretted the fierce attack on King Henry; and when the king began to favor the Reformation, he dedicated to him the revised edition of his theological *Loci* (1535). He was twice called to England, but declined.[1]

§ 71. *Erasmus.*

I. ERASMUS: *Opera omnia*, ed. by *Beatus Rhenanus*, Basil. 1540–41; 8 vols. fol.; best ed. by *Clericus* (Le Clerk), Lugd. Bat. 1703–06; 10 tom. in 11 vols. fol. There are several English translations of his *Enchiridion, Encomium, Adagia, Colloquia*, and smaller tracts. His most important theological works are his editions of the Greek Test. (1516, '19, '22, '27, '35, exclusive of more than thirty reprints), his Annotations and Paraphrases, his *Enchiridion Militis Christiani*, his editions of Laur. Valla, Jerome, Augustin, Ambrose, Origen, and other Fathers. His *Moriæ Encomium*, or *Panegyric of Folly* (composed 1509), was often edited. His letters are very important for the literary history of his age. His most popular book is his *Colloquies*, which contain the wittiest exposures of the follies and abuses of monkery, fasting, pilgrimages, etc. English transl. by *N. Bailey*, Lond. 1724; new ed. with notes by Rev. *E. Johnson*, 1878, 2 vols. After 1514 all his works were published by his friend John Froben in Basel.

[1] He wrote in March: "*Ego jam alteris literis in Angliam vocor*" (*Op.* II. 708).

Comp. ADALB. HORAWITZ: *Erasmus v. Rotterdam und Martinus Lipsius*, Wien, 1882; *Erasmiana*, several numbers, Wien, 1882–85 (reprinted from the *Sitzungsberichte* of the Imperial Academy of Vienna; contains extracts from the correspondence of Er., discovered in a Codex at Louvain, and in the Codex Rehdigeranus, 254 of the city library at

ERASMUS. From the Portrait by A. Dürer.

Breslau, founded by Rehdiger). HORAWITZ and HARTFELDER: *Briefwechsel des Beatus Rhenanus*, Leipzig, 1886.

II. Biographies of Erasmus by himself and by Beatus Rhenanus, in vol. I. of the ed. of Clericus; by PIERRE BAYLE, in his "Dictionnaire" (1696); KNIGHT, Cambr. 1726; JORTIN, Lond. 1748, 2 vols.; 1808, 3 vols. (chiefly a summary of the letters of Erasmus with critical comments); BURIGNY, Paris, 1757, 2 vols.; HENKE, Halle, 1782, 2 vols.; HESS, Zürich, 1789, 2 vols.; BUTLER, London, 1825; AD. MÜLLER, Hamburg, 1828 (*Leben*

des E. v. Rotterdam . . . Eine gekrönte Preisschrift; comp. the excellent review of ULLMANN in the "Studien und Kritiken," 1829, No. I.);
GLASIUS (prize essay in Dutch), The Hague, 1850; STICHART (*Er. v.
Rotterd., seine Stellung zur Kirche und zu den kirchl. Bewegungen
seiner Zeit*), Leipz. 1870; DURAND DE LAUR (*Erasme, précurseur et
initiateur de l'esprit moderne*), Par. 1873, 2 vols.; R. B. DRUMMOND
(*Erasmus, his Life and Character*), Lond. 1873, 2 vols.; G. FEUGÈRE
(*Er., étude sur sa vie et ses ouvrages*), Par. 1874; PENNINGTON, Lond.
1875; MILMAN (in *Savonarola, Erasmus, and other Essays*), Lond. 1870;
NISARD, *Rénaissance et réforme, Paris*, 1877. — Also WOKER: *De Erasmi
Rotterodami studiis irenicis.* Paderborn, 1872. W. VISCHER: *Eras-
miana. Programm zur Rectoratsfeier der Univers. Basel.* Basel, 1876.
"Erasmus" in Ersch and Gruber, vol. XXXVI. (by ERHARD); in the
"Allg. Deutsche Biogr." VI. 160-180 (by KÄMMEL); in Herzog,[1] IV.
114-121 (by HAGENBACH), and in Herzog,[2] IV. 278-290 (by R. STÄHE-
LIN); in the "Encycl. Brit.," 9th ed., VIII. 512-518. SCHLOTTMANN:
Erasmus redivivus, Hal. 1883. Comp. Lit. in § 72.

The quarrel between King Henry and Luther was the
occasion of a far more serious controversy and open breach
between Erasmus and the Reformation. This involved a
separation of humanism from Protestantism.

The Position of Erasmus.

Desiderius Erasmus of Rotterdam[1] (1466-1536) was the
king among scholars in the early part of the sixteenth century. He combined native genius, classical and biblical learning, lively imagination, keen wit, and refined taste. He was
the most cultivated man of his age, and the admired leader
of scholastic Europe from Germany to Italy and Spain, from

[1] His double name is a Latin and Greek translation of his father's Christian name *Gerard (Roger)*, or *Gerhard = Gernhaber* or *Liebhaber, i.e.,* Be-
loved, in mediæval Latin *Desiderius*, in Greek *Erasmus*, or rather *Erasmius*
from 'Ερἀσμιος, *Lovely.* He found out the mistake when he became familiar with Greek, and accordingly gave his godson, the son of his publisher
Froben, the name *John Erasmius (Erasmiolus).* In dedicating to him an
improved edition of his *Colloquies* (1524), he calls this book "ἐράσμιον, the
delight of the Muses who foster sacred things." He was equally unfortunate
in the additional epithet *Roterodamus,* instead of *Roterodamensis.* But he
was innocent of both mistakes.

England to Hungary. The visible unity of the Catholic Church, and the easy interchange of ideas through the medium of one learned language, explain in part his unique position. No man before or since acquired such undisputed sovereignty in the republic of letters. No such sovereignty is possible nowadays when distinguished scholars are far more numerous, and when the Church is divided into hostile camps.[1]

Erasmus shines in the front rank of the humanists and forerunners of the Reformation, on the dividing line between the middle ages and modern times. His great mission was to revive the spirit of classical and Christian antiquity, and to make it a reforming power within the church. He cleared the way for a work of construction which required stronger hands than his. He had no creative and no organizing power. The first period of his life till 1524 was progressive and reformatory; the second, till his death, 1536, was conservative and reactionary.

He did more than any of his contemporaries to prepare the church for the Reformation by the impulse he gave to classical, biblical, and patristic studies, and by his satirical exposures of ecclesiastical abuses and monastic ignorance and bigotry. But he stopped half way, and after a period of hesitation he openly declared war against Luther, thereby injuring both his own reputation and the progress of the movement among scholars. He was a reformer against reform, and in league with Rome. Thus he lost the respect and confidence of both parties. It would have been better for his fame if he had died in 1516, just after issuing the Greek Testament, a year before the Reformation. To do justice to him, we must look backward. Men of transition, like Staupitz, Reuchlin, and Erasmus, are no less necessary than bold leaders of a new

---

[1] Drummond (II. 337) calls Erasmus "the greatest luminary of his age, the greatest scholar of any age." But his learning embraced only the literature in the Greek and Latin languages.

departure. They belong to the class of which John the Baptist is the highest type. Protestants should never forget the immense debt of gratitude which they owe to the first editor of the Greek Testament who enabled Luther and Tyndale to make their translations of the word of life from the original, and to lead men to the very fountain of all that is most valuable and permanent in the Reformation. His edition was hastily prepared, before the art of textual criticism was born; but it anticipated the publication of the ponderous Complutensian Polyglot, and became the basis of the popularly received text. His exegetical opinions still receive and deserve the attention of commentators. To him we owe also the first scholarly editions of the Fathers, especially of Jerome, with whom he was most in sympathy. From these editions the Reformers drew their weapons of patristic controversy with the Romanists, who always appealed to the fathers of the Nicene age rather than to the grandfathers of the apostolic age.

Erasmus was allied to Reuchlin and Ulrich von Hutten, but greater and far more influential than both. All hated monasticism and obscurantism. Reuchlin revived Hebrew, Erasmus Greek learning, so necessary for the cultivation of biblical studies. Reuchlin gave his nephew Melanchthon to Wittenberg, but died a good Catholic. Hutten became a radical ultra-reformer, fell out with Erasmus, who disowned him when he was most in need of a friend, and perished in disgrace. Erasmus survived both, to protest against Protestantism.

And yet he cannot be charged with apostasy or even with inconsistency. He never was a Protestant, and never meant to be one. Division and separation did not enter into his program. From beginning to end he labored for a reformation within the church and within the papacy, not without it. But the new wine burst the old bottles. The reform which he set in motion went beyond him, and left him behind. In some of his opinions, however, he was ahead of his age, and anticipated a more modern stage of Protestantism. He was as much a forerunner of Rationalism as of the Reformation.

Sketch of His Life.

Erasmus was the illegitimate son of a Dutch priest, Gerard, and Margaret, the daughter of a physician, — their last but not their only child.[1] He was born in Rotterdam, Oct. 27, in the year 1466 or 1467.[2] He received his early education in the cathedral school of Utrecht and in a flourishing classical academy at Deventer, where he began to show his brilliant talents, especially a most tenacious memory. Books were his chief delight. Already in his twelfth year he knew Horace and Terence by heart.

After the death of his mother, he was robbed of his inheritance by his guardians, and put against his will into a convent at Herzogenbusch, which he exchanged afterwards for one at Steyn (Emaus), near Gouda, a few miles from Rotterdam.

He spent five unhappy years in monastic seclusion (1486–1491), and conceived an utter disgust for monkery. Ulrich von Hutten passed through the same experience, with the same negative result ; while for Luther monastic life was his free choice, and became the cradle of a new religious life. Erasmus found relief in the study of the classics, which he pursued without a guide, by a secret impulse of nature. We have from this period a number of his compositions in poetry

---

[1] His father was ordained a priest after the birth of Erasmus; for he says that he lived with Margaret "*spe conjugii*," and became a priest in Rome on learning from his parents, who were opposed to the marriage, the false report that his beloved Margaret was dead.

[2] He says in his autobiographical sketch: "*Natus Roterodami vigilia Simonis et Judæ circa annum 67, supra millesimum quadringentesimum.*" His friend and biographer, Beatus Rhenanus, did not know the year of his birth. His epitaph in Basel gives 1466; the inscription on his statue at Rotterdam gives 1467; the historians vary from 1464 to 1469. Bayle, Burigny, Müller, and Drummond (I. 3 sq.) discuss the chronology.

and prose, odes to Christ and the holy Virgin, invectives against despisers of eloquence, and an essay on the contempt of the world, in which he describes the corruptions of the world and the vices of the monks.

He was delivered from his prison life in 1491 by the bishop of Cambray, his parsimonious patron, and ordained to the priesthood in 1492. He continued in the clerical profession, and remained unmarried, but never had a parish.

He now gave himself up entirely to study in the University of Paris and at Orleans. His favorite authors were Cicero, Terence, Plutarch, and Lucian among the classics, Jerome among the fathers, and Laurentius Valla the commentator. He led hereafter an independent literary life without a regular charge, supporting himself by teaching, and then supported by rich friends.[1] In his days of poverty he solicited aid in letters of mingled humility and vanity; when he became famous, he received liberal gifts and pensions from prelates and princes, and left at his death seven thousand ducats. The title of royal counsellor of the King of Spain (Charles V.) brought him an annual income of four hundred guilders after 1516. The smaller pensions were paid irregularly, and sometimes failed in that impecunious age. Authors seldom received copy money or royalty from publishers and printers, but voluntary donations from patrons of learning and persons to whom they dedicated their works. Froben, however, his chief publisher, treated Erasmus very generously. He traveled extensively, like St. Jerome, and made the personal acquaintance of the chief celebrities in church and state.

He paid two important visits to England, first on the invitation of his grateful and generous pupil, Lord Montjoy, between 1498 and 1500, and again in 1510. There he became intimate with the like-minded Sir Thomas More, Dean Colet,

---

[1] He calls himself, in his autobiographical sketch, "*dignitatum ac divitiarum perpetuus contemptor.*"

Archbishop Warham, Cardinal Wolsey, Bishop Fisher, and was introduced to King Henry VII. and to Prince Henry, afterwards Henry VIII. Colet taught him that theology must return from scholasticism to the Scriptures, and from dry dogmas to practical wisdom.[1] For this purpose he devoted more attention to Greek at Oxford, but never attained to the same proficiency in it as in Latin. On his second visit he was appointed Lady Margaret's professor of divinity, and reader of Greek, in Cambridge. His room in Queen's College is still shown. The number of his hearers was small, and so was his income. "Still," he wrote to a friend in London, "I am doing my best to promote sound scholarship." He had much to say in praise of England, where he received so much kindness, but also in complaint of bad beer and bad wine, and of his robbery at Dover, where he was relieved of all his money in the custom-house, under a law that no one should take more than a small sum out of the realm.

Between his visits to England he spent three years in Italy (1506-1509), and bathed in the fountain of the renaissance. He took the degree of doctor of divinity at Turin, and remained some time in Venice, Padua, Bologna, and Rome. He edited the classics of Greece and Rome, with specimens of translations, and superintended the press of Manutius Aldus at Venice. He entered into the genius of antiquity, and felt at home there. He calls Venice the most magnificent city of the world. But the lovely scenery of Italy, and the majestic grandeur of the Alps, seem to have made no more impression upon his mind than upon that of Luther; at least, he does not speak of it.

After he returned from his last visit to England, he spent his time alternately at Brussels, Antwerp, and Louvain (1515-1521). He often visited Basel, and made this ancient

[1] J. H. Lupton: *A Life of John Colet, D.D., Dean of St. Paul's and Founder of St. Paul's School.* London, 1887.

city of republican Switzerland, on the boundaries between France and Germany, his permanent home in 1521. There he lived several years as editor and adviser of his friend and publisher, John Froben, who raised his press to the first rank in Europe. Basel was neutral till 1529, when the Reformation was introduced. It suited his position and taste. He liked the climate and the society. The bishop of Basel and the magistrate treated him with the greatest consideration. The university was then in its glory. He was not one of the public teachers, but enjoyed the intercourse of Wyttenbach, Capito, Glarean, Pellican, Amerbach. "I am here," he wrote to a friend, "as in the most agreeable museum of many and very eminent scholars. Everybody knows Latin and Greek, most of them also Hebrew. The one excels in history, the other in theology; one is well versed in mathematics, another in antiquities, a third in jurisprudence. You know how rarely we meet with such a combination. I at least never found it before. Besides these literary advantages, what candor, hospitality, and harmony prevail here everywhere! You would swear that all had but one heart and one soul."

The fame of Erasmus brought on an extensive correspondence. His letters and books had the widest circulation. The "Praise of Folly" passed through seven editions in a few months, and through at least twenty-seven editions during his lifetime. Of his "Colloquies," a bookseller in Paris printed twenty-four thousand copies. His journeys were triumphal processions. Deputations received him in the larger cities with addresses of welcome. He was treated like a prince. Scholars, bishops, cardinals, kings, and popes paid him homage, sent him presents, or gave him pensions. He was offered by the Cardinal of Sion, besides a handsome board, the liberal sum of five hundred ducats annually, if he would live with him in Rome. He was in high favor with Pope Julius II. and Leo X., who patronized liberal learning. The former released him from his monastic vows; the latter invited him to Rome, and would have given him any thing if he had consented to remain. Adrian VI. asked his counsel how to deal with the Lutheran heresy (1523). Clement VII., in reply to a letter, sent him a present of two hundred florins. Paul III. offered him a cardinal's hat to reward him for his attack on Luther (1536), but he declined it on account of old age.

The humanists were loudest in his praise, and almost worshiped him. Eoban Hesse, the prince of Latin poets of the time, called him a " divine being," and made a pilgrimage on foot from Erfurt to Holland to see him face to face. Justus Jonas did the same. Zwingli visited him in Basel, and before going to sleep used to read some pages of his writings. To receive a letter from him was a good fortune, and to have a personal interview with him was an event. A man even less vain than Erasmus could not have escaped the bad effect of such hero-worship. But it was partly neutralized by the detractions of his enemies, who were numerous and unsparing. Among these were Stunica and Caranza of Spain, Edward Lee of England, the Prince of Carpi, Cardinal Aleander, the leaders of scholastic divinity of Louvain and Paris, and the whole crowd of ignorant monks.

His later years were disturbed by the death of his dearest and kindest friend, John Froben (1527), to whose memory he paid a most noble tribute in one of his letters; and still more by the progress of the Reformation in his own neighborhood. The optimism of his youth and manhood gave way to a gloomy, discontented pessimism. The Lutheran tragedy, he said, gave him more pain than the stone which tortured him. "It is part of my unhappy fate, that my old age has fallen on these evil times when quarrels and riots prevail everywhere." " This new gospel," he writes in another letter, " is producing a new set of men so impudent, hypocritical, and abusive, such liars and sycophants, who agree neither with one another nor with anybody else, so universally offensive and seditious, such madmen and ranters, and in short so utterly distasteful to me that if I knew of any city in which I should be free from them, I would remove there at once." His last letters are full of such useless lamentations. He had the mortification to see Protestantism triumph in a tumultuous way in Basel, through the labors of Œcolampadius, his former friend and associate. It is pleasant, however, and creditable to him, that his last interview with the reformer was friendly and cordial. The authorities of the city left him undisturbed. But he reluctantly moved to the Roman Catholic city of Freiburg in Baden (1529), wishing that Basel might enjoy every blessing, and never receive a sadder guest than he.[1] He bought a house in Freiburg, lived there six years, and was treated with every demonstration of respect, but did not feel happy, and yielded to the solicitations of the Queen Regent of the Netherlands to return to his native land.

On his way he stopped in Basel in the house of Jerome Froben, August, 1535, and attended to the publication of Origen. It was his last work. He fell sick, and died in his seventieth year, July 12, 1536, of his old enemies, the stone and the gout, to which was added dysentery. He retained his consciousness and genial humor to the last. When his three friends, Amerbach, Froben, and Episcopius, visited him on his death-bed, he reminded them of Job's three comforters, and playfully asked them about the torn garments, and the ashes that should be sprinkled on their heads. He died without a priest or any ceremonial of the Church (in wretched monastic Latin: "*sine crux, sine lux, sine Deus*"), but invoking the mercy of Christ. His last words, repeated again and

---

[1] He dictated these lines to his friend Amerbach on departing:—

"*Jam Basilea vale! qua non urbs altera multis*
Annis exhibuit gratius hospitium.
Hinc precor omnia læta tibi, simul illud, Erasmo
Hospes uti ne unquam tristior adveniat."

again, were, "O Jesus, have mercy; Lord, deliver me; Lord, make an end; Lord, have mercy upon me!"[1]

In his will, dated Feb. 12, 1536, he left his valuables to Froben, Rhenanus, and other friends, and the rest to the aged and poor and for the education of young men of promise.[2] The funeral was attended by distinguished men of both parties. He lies buried in the Protestant cathedral of Basel, where his memory is cherished.

Erasmus was of small stature, but well formed. He had a delicate constitution, an irritable temperament, fair skin, blonde hair, wrinkled forehead, blue eyes, and pleasant voice. His face had an expression of thoughtfulness and quiet studiousness.[3] In his behavior he combined dignity and grace. "His manners and conversation," says Beatus Rhenanus, "were polished, affable, and even charming."

He talked and wrote in Latin, the universal language of scholars in mediæval Europe. He handled it as a living language, with ease, elegance, and effect, though not with classical correctness. His style was Ciceronian, but modified by the ecclesiastical vocabulary of Jerome. In his dialogue "*Ciceronianus*," or on the best mode of speaking (1528), he ridicules those pedantic semi-pagans, chiefly Italians, who worshiped and aped Cicero, and avoided Christian themes, or borrowed names and titles from heathen mythology. He had, however, the greatest respect for Cicero, and hoped that "he is now living peacefully in heaven." He learned neither German nor English nor Italian, and had only an imperfect knowledge of French, and even of his native Dutch.

---

[1] "*O Jesu, misericordia; Domine, libera me; Domine, fac finem; Domine, miserere mei;*" and in German or Dutch, *Lieber God (Gott)*! — Beatus Rhenanus, in *Vita Er.*

[2] Drummond, II. 338–340, gives the document in full.

[3] See the interesting description of his face by Lavater in his *Physiognomik*, quoted by Ad. Müller, p. 108, and Hagenbach, *K. Gesch.*, III. 50. There are several portraits of him, — by Matsys (1517), Dürer (1523), and, the best, by Holbein who painted him repeatedly at Basel.

He had a nervous sensibility. The least draught made him feverish. He could not bear the iron stoves of Germany, and required an open fireplace. He could drink no wine but Burgundy. He abhorred intemperance. He could not eat fish on fast days; the mere smell of it made him sick: his heart, he said, was Catholic, but his stomach Lutheran. He never used spectacles either by day or by candle-light, and many wondered that study had not blinded his eyes. He walked firm and erect without a cane. His favorite exercise was horseback-riding.[1] He usually traveled on horseback with an attendant, and carried his necessaries, including a shirt, a linen nightcap, and a prayer-book, in a knapsack tied to the saddle. He shrank from the mere mention of death, and frankly confessed that he was not born to be a martyr, but would in the hour of trial be tempted to follow St. Peter. He was fond of children, and charitable to the poor.

His Theological Opinions.

Erasmus was, like most of the German and English humanists, a sincere and enlightened believer in Christianity, and differed in this respect from the frivolous and infidel humanists of France and Italy. When charged by Prince Albertus Pius of Carpi, who was in high favor at the papal court, with turning sacred things into ridicule, he answered, " You will much more readily find scoffers at sacred things in Italy among men of your own rank, ay, and in your much-lauded Rome, than with us. *I* could not endure to sit down at table with such men." He devoted his brilliant genius and classi-

---

[1] In thanking Archbishop Warham of Canterbury for the present of a horse, he thus humorously describes the animal: " I have received the horse, which is no beauty, but a good creature notwithstanding; for he is free from all the mortal sins, except gluttony and laziness; and he is adorned with all the virtues of a good confessor, being pious, prudent, humble, modest, sober, chaste, and quiet, and neither bites nor kicks." To Polydore Virgil, who sent him money to *procure* a horse, he replied, " I wish you could give me any thing to *cure* the rider." (" *Dedisti quo* PARETUR *equus, utinam dare possis quo* REPARETUR *eques.* " — Op. III. 934.)

cal lore to the service of religion. He revered the Bible as
a divine revelation, and zealously promoted its study. He
anticipated Luther in the supreme estimate of the word of
God as the true source of theology and piety. Œcolampadius confessed that he learned from Erasmus " *nihil in sacris
scripturis præter Christum quærendum.*"

He had a sharp eye to the abuses of the Church, and endeavored to reform them in a peaceful way. He wished to lead
theology back from the unfruitful speculations and frivolous
subtleties of scholasticism to Scriptural simplicity, and to
promote an inward, spiritual piety. He keenly ridiculed the
foolish and frivolous discussions of the schoolmen about for-
malities and quiddities, and such questions as whether God
could have assumed the form of a woman, or an ass, or a cu-
cumber, or a flint-stone; whether the Virgin Mary was learned
in the languages; and whether we would eat and drink after
the resurrection. He exposed the vices and follies, the ignorance and superstition, of the monks and clergy. He did not
spare even the papacy. " I have no desire," he wrote in 1523,
" that the primacy of the Roman See should be abolished, but
I could wish that its discipline were such as to favor every
effort to promote the religion of the gospel; for several ages
past it has by its example openly taught things that are
plainly averse to the doctrines of Christ."

At the same time he lacked a deeper insight into the doctrines of sin and grace, and failed to find a positive remedy
for the evils he complained of. In using the dangerous
power of ridicule and satire which he shared with Lucian,
he sometimes came near the line of profanity. Moreover, he
had a decidedly skeptical vein, and in the present century
he would probably be a moderate Rationalist.

With his critical faculty he saw the difficulties and differences in the human surroundings and circumstances of the
Divine Scriptures. He omitted in his Greek Testament the
forgery of the three witnesses, 1 John 5 : 7, and only inserted

it under protest in the third edition (1522), because he had
rashly promised to do so if a single Greek MS. could be found
to contain it.[1] He doubted the genuineness of the pericope
of the adulteress (John 8:1–11), though he retained it in
the text. He disputed the orthodox punctuation of Rom.
9:5. He rejected the Pauline origin of Hebrews, and questioned the Johannean authorship of the Apocalypse. He
judged Mark to be an abridgment of Matthew. He admitted
lapses of memory and errors of judgment in the Apostles.
He denied any other punishment in hell except "the perpetual anguish of mind which accompanies habitual sin." As
to the Lord's Supper, he said, when asked his opinion by the
magistrate of Basel about the book of Œcolampadius and
his figurative interpretation,[2] that it was learned, eloquent,
well written, and pious, but contrary to the general belief of
the church from which it was dangerous to depart. There
is good reason to believe that he doubted transubstantiation.
He was also suspected of leaning to Arianism, because he
summed up the teaching of Scripture on the Trinity in this
sentence: "The Father is very frequently called God, the
Son sometimes, the Holy Spirit never;" and he adds: "Many
of the fathers who worshiped the Son with the greatest piety,
yet scrupled to use the word *homoousion*, which is nowhere
to be found in Holy Scripture."[3] He moderated the doctrine of hereditary sin, and defended human freedom in his
notes on Romans. He emphasized the moral, and depreciated
the doctrinal, element in Christianity. He deemed the Apos-

---

[1] . . . "*ne cui sit ansa calumniandi. Tametsi suspicor codicem illum
ad nostros esse correctum.*" — *Opera*, VI. 1080. The Codex Montfortianus,
now in Dublin, was probably written between 1519–1522, and the disputed
passage interpolated with the purpose of injuring the reputation of Erasmus.
See J. R. Harris, *The Origin of the Leicester Codex of the N. Test.*, London
and Cambridge, 1887, p. 46 sqq.

[2] *De genuina verborum Domini : Hoc est corpus meum, etc., juxta vetustissimos auctores expositione liber.* Basil., 1525.

[3] See the Preface to his edition of St. Hilary on the Trinity, published at
Basel, 1523.

tles' Creed sufficient, and was willing to allow within this limit freedom for theological opinions. " Reduce the number of dogmas," he advised Archbishop Albrecht of Mainz, " to a minimum ; you can do it without injury to Christianity ; on other points, leave every one free to believe what he pleases ; then religion will take hold on life, and you can correct the abuses of which the world justly complains."

He had a high opinion of the morality and piety of the nobler heathen, such as Socrates, Cicero, and Plutarch. " The Scriptures," he says in his Colloquies, " deserve, indeed, the highest authority ; but I find also in the writings of the ancient heathen and in the poets so much that is pure, holy and divine, that I must believe that their hearts were divinely moved. The spirit of Christ is perhaps more widely diffused than we imagine, and many will appear among the saints who are not in our catalogue."[1]   Then, after quoting from Cicero and Socrates, he says, " I can often hardly restrain myself from exclaiming, ' Holy Socrates, pray for us.' "

The same liberal sentiments we find among the early Greek fathers (Justin Martyr, Clement of Alexandria, Origen), and in Zwingli.

Bigoted Catholics hated and feared him, as much as the liberal admired and lauded him. " He laid the egg," they said, " which Luther hatched."[2]   They perverted his name into *Errasmus* because of his errors, *Arasmus* because he ploughed up old truths and traditions, *Erasinus* because he had made himself an ass by his writings. They even called him Behemoth and Antichrist. The Sorbonne condemned thirty-seven articles extracted from his writings in 1527.

---

[1] " *Fortasse latius se fundit spiritus Christi quam nos interpretamur, et multi sunt in consortio sanctorum qui non sunt apud nos in catalogo.*"— *Coll.,* in the conversation entitled *Convivium Religiosum.*

[2] He himself alludes to this saying: " *Ego peperi ovum, Lutherus exclusit* " (*Op.* III. 840), but adds, " *Ego posui ovum gallinaceum, Lutherus exclusit pullum longe dissimillimum.*"

His books were burned in Spain, and long after his death placed on the Index in Rome.

In his last word to his popish enemies who identified him with Luther to ruin both together, he writes : " For the future I despise them, and I wish I had always done so ; for it is no pleasure to drown the croaking of frogs.   Let them say, with their stout defiance of divine and human laws, ' We ought to obey God rather than men.'   That was well said by the Apostles, and even on *their* lips it is not without a certain propriety ; only it is not the same God in the two cases. The God of the Apostles was the Maker of heaven and earth : *their* God is their belly.   Fare ye well." [1]

His Works.

The literary labors of Erasmus may be divided into three classes : —

I.   Works edited.   Their number proves his marvellous industry and enterprise.

He published the ancient Latin classics, Cicero, Terence, Seneca, Livy, Pliny ; and the Greek classics with Latin translations, Euripides, Xenophon, Demosthenes, Plutarch, Lucian.

He edited the principal church fathers (some for the first time from MSS.) ; namely, Jerome (1516–1518 ; ed. ii., 1526 ; ed. iii., a year after his death), Cyprian (1520), Athanasius (in a Latin version, 1522), Hilarius (1523), Irenæus (Latin, 1526, ed. princeps, very defective), Ambrose (1527), Augustin (1529), Epiphanius (1529), Chrysostom on Matthew (1530), Basil (in Greek, 1532 ; he called him the "Christian Demosthenes "), Origen (in Latin, 1536).   He wrote the prefaces and dedications.

He published the Annotations of Laurentius Valla on the New Testament (1505 and 1526), a copy of which he had found by chance on the shelves of an old library.

---

[1] *Des. Erasmi Epistola ad quosdam impudentissimos Graculos* (jackdaws). *Op.* IX. Pars II. (or vol. X.), p. 1745; Drummond, II. 265 sq.

The most important of his edited works is the Greek New Testament, with a Latin translation.[1]

II. Original works on general literature.

His " Adages" (*Adagia*), begun at Oxford, dedicated to Lord Mountjoy, first published in Paris in 1500, and much enlarged in subsequent editions,[2] is an anthology of forty-one hundred and fifty-one Greek and Latin proverbs, similitudes, and sentences, — a sort of dictionary and commonplace-book, brimful of learning, illustrations, anecdotes, historical and biographical sketches, attacks on monks, priests, and kings, and about ten thousand quotations from Greek poets, literally translated into the Latin in the metre of the original.

" The Praise of Folly " (*Encomium Moriæ*)[3] was written on a journey from Italy to England, and finished in the house of his congenial friend, Sir Thomas More (whose name in Greek means " Fool "), as a *jeu d'esprit*, in the manner of his favorite Lucian. It introduces Folly personified as a goddess, in ironical praise of the merits, and indirect ridicule of the perversities, of different classes of society. It abounds in irony, wit, and humor, in keen observations of men and things, and contains his philosophy of life. The wise man is the most miserable of men, as is proved by the case of Socrates, who only succeeded in making himself ridiculous; while the fool is the happiest man, has no fear of death or hell, no tortures of conscience, tells always the truth, and is indispensable to the greatest of monarchs, who cannot even dine

[1] On this see the critical introductions to the New Testament; Scrivener's *Introd. to the Criticism of the N.T.*, 3d ed., pp. 429–434; Schaff's *Companion to the Greek Test.*, 3d ed., pp. 229–232; and Drummond, I. 308 sqq.

[2] The last edition before me, *Adagiorum Chiliades . . . ex officina Frobenia, 1536*, contains 1087 pages folio, with an alphabetical index of the Proverbs. See vol. II. of the Leiden ed. For extracts see Drummond, I. ch. X.

[3] Μωρίας 'Εγκώμιον, *id est Stultitiæ Laus*, first printed 1510 or 1511. *Op.* IV. 405–507. There is a neat edition of the *Encomium* and the *Colloquia* by Tauchnitz, Leipzig, 1829. Drummond (I. 184 sqq.) gives a good summary of the contents.

without him. In conclusion Erasmus, rather irreverently, quotes Scripture proofs in praise of folly. Pope Leo X. read and enjoyed the book from beginning to end. Holbein illustrated it with humorous pictures, which are still preserved in Basel.

In his equally popular "Colloquies" (*Colloquia Familiaria*), begun in 1519, and enlarged in numerous editions, Erasmus aims to make better scholars and better men, as he says in his dedication to John Erasmius Froben (the son of his friend and publisher).[1] He gives instruction for Latin conversation, describes the good and bad manners of the times, and ventilates his views on a variety of interesting topics, such as courtesy in saluting, rash vows, a soldier's life, scholastic studies, the profane feast, a lover and maiden, the virgin opposed to matrimony, the penitent virgin, the uneasy wife, the shipwreck, rich beggars, the alchemist, etc. The "Colloquies" are, next to the "Praise of Folly," his most characteristic work, and, like it, abound in delicate humor, keen irony, biting satire. He pays a glowing tribute to Cicero, and calls him "*sanctum illud pectus afflatum cœlesti numine;*" and in the same conversation occurs the famous passage already referred to, "*Sancte Socrates, ora pro nobis.*" He shows his sympathy with the cause of Reuchlin in the dialogue *Apotheosis Reuchlini Capnionis*, by describing a vision in which the persecuted Hebrew scholar (who died June 22, 1522) was welcomed in heaven by St. Jerome, and, without leave of the Pope, enrolled in the number of saints. But during Reuchlin's life he had kept neutral in the Domini-

---

[1] The work which appeared in 1518 under this title, with a preface of Rhenanus, was disclaimed by Erasmus, except some portions which he had dictated more than twenty years previously to a pupil in Paris by way of amusement. He compared it to an ass in a lion's skin. The *Colloquia* are printed in *Opera*, I. 624–908. I have an edition *cum notis selectis variorum accurante Corn. Schrevelio.* Lugd., Bat. Bailey's translation, London, 1724, republished 1878, reproduces in racy colloquial English the idiomatic and proverbial Latinisms of the original.

can quarrel about Reuchlin's orthodoxy. He is very severe on " the coarse, over-fed monks," and indulges too freely in insinuations which offend modern taste.[1] He attacks war, which he hated even more than monkery ; and in his description of a reckless, extravagant, debauched, sick, poor and wretched soldier, he took unchristian revenge of Ulrich von Hutten after his miserable death. In the dialogue, " Unequal Marriage," he paints him in the darkest colors as an abandoned *roué*. He gives an amusing description of a German inn, which makes one thankful for the progress of modern civilization. The bedrooms, he says, are rightly so called ; for they contain nothing but a bed ; and the cleanliness is on a par with the rest of the establishment and the adjoining stable. The "Ichthyophagia" is a dialogue between a butcher and a fishmonger, and exposes the Pharisaical tendency to strain out a gnat and to swallow a camel, and to lay heavy burdens on others. "Would they might eat nothing but garlic who imposed these fish-days upon us!" "Would they might starve to death who force the necessity of fasting upon free men!" The form of the dialogue furnished the author a door of escape from the charge of heresy, for he could not be held responsible for the sentiments of fictitious characters ; moreover, he said, his object was to teach Latin, not theology. Nevertheless, the Sorbonne condemned the "Colloquies," and the Inquisition placed them in the first class of prohibited books.

[1] In the dialogue *Virgo* μισόγαμος, the maiden Catharine, who had resolved to become a nun, is advised by her lover Eubulus that she may keep her chastity more safely at home ; for the monks were by no means all "eunuchs," but often do all they can to deserve their name "fathers." ("*Patres vocantur, ac frequenter efficiunt, ut hoc nomen vere competat in ipsos.*") She is also told that "all are not virgins who wear the veil, unless there be many in our days who share the pecular privilege of the Virgin Mary, of being a virgin after childbirth." The maiden admits the force of her lover's arguments, but refuses to be convinced. In the colloquy that follows, entitled *Virgo pœnitens*, she acknowledges the wisdom of the advice when it was too late. She had scarcely been twelve days in the nunnery before she entreated her mother, and then her father, to take her home if they wished to save her life.

The numerous letters of Erasmus and to Erasmus throw much light upon contemporaneous literary and ecclesiastical history, and make us best acquainted with his personality. He corresponded with kings and princes, popes and cardinals, as well as with scholars in all parts of Europe. He tells us that he wrote sometimes forty letters in a day.[1]

III. Theological works. The edition of the Greek Testament, with a new Latin version and brief annotations, and the independent paraphrases, are the most important contributions of Erasmus to exegesis, and have appeared in very many editions. The paraphrastic form of commenting, which briefly explains the difficulties, and links text and notes in continuous composition, so as to make the writer his own interpreter,[2] was a great benefit to the incipient scholarship of his day, and facilitated a more general spread of the New Testament, which he eloquently defended. He did not penetrate into the deeper meaning of the Scriptures, but he made the surface more intelligible by the moonlight of philology and refined culture. His Paraphrases cover the whole New Testament, except the Apocalypse, and fill the seventh volume of Le Clerk's edition of his works. A translation was published in two volumes folio, in black-letter, at London, 1551, and appointed, by public authority, to be placed in all the parish churches of England.

His "Method of True Theology" (*Ratio veræ Theologiæ*)[3]

---

[1] The *Epistolæ* in Froben's ed. of 1540, Tom. III. fol. (1213 pp.), with his preface, dated Freiburg, 1529; in Le Clerk's ed., Tom. III. Pars I. and II. There is also a fine edition of the collected epistles of Erasmus, Melanchthon, Thomas More, and Lud. Vives, London, 1642, 2 vols. fol. 2146 and 116 pages, with a good portrait of Erasmus (a copy in the Union Seminary). Recent additions have been made by Horawitz (*Erasmiana*, 1883 sqq.). Jortin and Drummond give many extracts from the epistles.

[2] Erasmus well defines it in the dedicatory preface *ad Card. Grimanum*, before the Pauline Epistles : "*hiantia committere, abrupta mollire, confusa digerere, evoluta evolvere, nodosa explicare, obscuris lucem addere, hebraismum romana civitate donare . . . et ita temperare* παράφρασιν *ne fiat* παραφρόνησις, *h. e. sic aliter dicere ut non dicas alia.*"

[3] *Opera*, vol. V. 57 sqq.

was prefixed to his first edition of the Greek Testament, and afterwards expanded and separately published, and dedicated to Cardinal-Archbishop Albrecht of Mainz (1519), in a preface full of complaints over the evil times of violent controversy, which, in his judgment, destroyed charity and the peaceful cultivation of learning and practical piety. He maintains that the first requisite for the study of the Scriptures is a knowledge of Greek, Latin, and Hebrew. Nor are poetry and good letters to be neglected. Christ clothes his teaching in poetic parables; and Paul quotes from the poets, but not from Aristotle.

The *Enchiridion Militis Christiani*,[1] first published at Louvain, 1501 (or 1503),[2] and translated into several languages, is a treatise on practical piety in its conflict with the Devil and unruly passions. The author borrows his weapons from the Scriptures, the fathers, and the Greek and Roman philosophers, and shows that the end of all human effort is Christ, and that the way to Christ is faith abounding in good works. In a later edition he added a defense, with a sharp attack on the scholastic theology contrasted with the plain, practical teaching of Christ and the apostles. The book was condemned by the Sorbonne as heretical.

In the tract on the Confessional (1524), he enumerates the advantages and the perils of that institution which may be perverted into a means of propagating vice by suggesting it to young and inexperienced penitents. He leaves, on the whole, the impression that the confessional does more harm than good.

In the book on the Tongue (1525), he eloquently describes,

---

[1] Usually translated " The Manual of a Christian Soldier ;" but ἐγχειρίδιον means also a dagger, and he himself explains it, " *Enchiridion, hoc est, pugiunculum.*" *Op.* V. 1–65. The first English translation (1533) is believed to be by William Tyndale, the translator of the New Testament. Another, with notes, which I have before me, is by Philip Wyatt Crowther, Esq., London, 1816, under the title " The Christian's Manual," etc.

[2] On the disputed date see Drummond, I. 122.

and illustrates with many anecdotes, its use and abuse. After its publication he wrote to his friends, "Erasmus will henceforth be mute, having parted with his tongue."

But a year after appeared his book on the Institution of Christian Matrimony (1526), dedicated to Queen Catherine of England. It contains the views of an unmarried man on the choice of a mate, the duties of parents, and the education of children. He justly blames Tertullian and Jerome (he might have included all the fathers) for their extravagant laudation of celibacy, and suggests doubts on the sacramental character of marriage.

One of his last works was a Catechism on the Apostles' Creed, the Decalogue, and the Lord's Prayer, which he dedicated to the father of the unfortunate Anne Boleyn. For the same nobleman he wrote a short devotional work on preparation for death.

§ 72. *Erasmus and the Reformation.*

I. ERASMUS: *De Libero Arbitrio diatribe* (1524), in *Opera ed. Lugd.* IX. Pars I. 1215 sqq., in WALCH, XVIII. *Hyperaspistæ diatribes libri duo contra Servum Arbitr. M. Lutheri*, in 2 parts (1526 and 1527), in *Opera* IX. Pars II. 1249 sqq., and in WALCH, XVIII.

LUTHER: *De Servo Arbitrio ad Erasmum Roterodamum*, Wittembergæ, 1525. On the last p. of the first ed. before me is the date "*Mense Decembri, Anno MDXXV.*" German in WALCH, XVIII. Erl. ed. *Opera Lat.* VII. 113 sqq. Letters of Luther to Erasmus and about Erasmus in WALCH, XVIII., and in DE WETTE, I. pp. 39, 52, 87, 247; II. 49; III. 427; IV. 497.

II. CHLEBUS: *Erasmus und Luther*, in "Zeitschr. f. hist. Theol.," 1845. DÖLLINGER in his *Die Reformation*, 1846, vol. i. pp. 1–20. KERKER: *Er. u. sein theol. Standpunkt*, in the "Theol. Quartalschrift," 1859. D. F. STRAUSS: *Ulrich von Hutten*, 4th ed. Bonn, 1878, pp. 448–484, 511–514, and *passim*. PLITT: *Erasmus in s. Stellung zur Reformation*, Leipz., in the "Zeitschrift f. hist. Theol.," 1866, No. III. RUD. STÄHELIN: *Eras. Stellung z. Reformation*, Basel, 1873 (35 pp.; comp. his art. in Herzog², quoted in § 71). FROUDE: *Times of Erasmus and Luther.* Three Lect., delivered at Newcastle, 1867 (in the first series of his "Short Studies on Great Subjects," New York ed., 1873, pp. 37–127), brilliant but inaccurate, and silent on the free-will controversy. DRUM-

MOND: *Erasmus, etc.*, 1873, vol. II. chs. xiii.-xv. E. WALTER: *Eras-mus und Melanchthon*, Bernburg, 1879. A. GILLY: *Erasme de Rotterd., sa situation en face de l'église et de la libre pensée*, Arras, 1879. Comp. also KATTENBUSCH: *Luther's Lehre vom unfreien Willen*, Göttingen, 1875, and KÖSTLIN: *Luther's Theologie*, vol. II. 32-55.

Erasmus was eighteen years older than Luther, and stood at the height of his fame when the reformer began his work. He differed from him as Jerome differed from Augustin, or Eusebius from Athanasius. Erasmus was essentially a scholar, Luther a reformer; the one was absorbed in literature, the other in religion. Erasmus aimed at illumination, Luther at reconstruction; the former reached the intellect of the educated, the latter touched the heart of the people. Erasmus labored for freedom of thought, Luther for freedom of conscience. Both had been monks, Erasmus against his will, Luther by free choice and from pious motives; and both hated and

ERASMUS. From a Portrait by Holbein.

opposed monkery, but the former for its ignorance and bigotry, the latter for its self-righteousness and obstruction of the true way to justification and peace. Erasmus followed maxims of worldly wisdom; Luther, sacred principles and convictions. The one was willing, as he confessed, to sacrifice "a part of the truth for the peace of the church," and his personal comfort; the other was ready to die for the gospel at any moment. Erasmus was a trimmer and time-server, Luther every inch a moral hero.

Luther wrote upon his tablet (1536), "*Res et verba Philip-pus; verba sine re Erasmus; res sine verbis Lutherus; nec res nec verba Carolostadius.*" But Luther himself was the master of

words and matter, and his words were deeds. Melanchthon
was an improved Erasmus on the side of evangelical truth.

It is easy to see how far two men so differently consti-
tuted could go together, and where and when they had to
part. So long as the Reformation moved within the church,
Erasmus sympathized with it. But when Luther, who had
at first as little notion of leaving the Catholic Church, burnt
the Pope's bull and the decretals, and with them the bridge
behind him, Erasmus shrank back, and feared that the
remedy was worse than the evil. His very breadth of culture
and irresolution became his weakness; while Luther's narrowness and determination were his strength. In times of
war, neutrality is impossible, and we must join one of the
two contending armies. Erasmus was for unity and peace,
and dreaded a split of the church as the greatest calamity;
and yet he never ceased to rebuke the abuses. It was his
misfortune, rather than his fault, that he could not side with
the Reformation. We must believe his assertion that his
conscience kept him from the cause of the Lutherans. At
the same time he was concerned for his personal comfort and
literary supremacy, and anxious to retain the friendship of
his hierarchical and royal patrons. He wished to be a spectator, but not an actor in "the Lutheran tragedy."

Erasmus hailed the young Melanchthon with enthusiastic
praise of his precocious genius and learning, and continued
to respect him even after his breach with Luther. He stood
in friendly correspondence with Zwingli, who revered him
as the prince of humanists. He employed Œcolampadius as
his assistant, and spoke highly, though evasively, of his book
on the eucharist. He was not displeased with Luther's
attacks on indulgences and monasticism, and wrote to
Zwingli that he had taught nearly every thing that Luther
teaches, but without his coarseness and paradoxes.[1] In a

---

[1] "*Videor mihi fere omnia docuisse quæ docet Lutherus, nisi quod non tam
atrociter, quodque abstinui a quibusdam ænigmatibus et paradoxis.*" In
Zwingli's *Opera*, ed. Schuler and Schulthess, vol. VII. 310.

letter of reply, dated Louvain, May 30, 1519, he courteously but cautiously and condescendingly accepted Luther's compliments and friendship, but advised him to moderate his tone, and to imitate Paul, who abolished the law by allegorical interpretation; at the same time he frankly admitted that he had not read his books, except portions of the commentary on the Psalms,[1] and that he considered it his duty to keep neutral, in order to do the more for the revival of letters. In conclusion he expressed the wish: "May the Lord Jesus grant you daily more of his spirit for his glory and the general good." [2]

So far, then, he objected not so much to the matter as to the manner of Luther, whose plebeian violence and roughness offended his cultured taste. But there was a deeper difference. He could not appreciate his cardinal doctrine of justification by faith *alone*, and took offence at the denial of free-will and human merit. He held the Catholic views on these subjects. He wished a reform of the discipline, but not of the faith, of the church, and cared little for dogmatic controversies.

His gradual alienation may be seen in the following extracts from his letters.

To Albrecht, Cardinal-Archbishop of Mainz, he wrote from Louvain, Nov. 1, 1519: —

"Permit me to say that I have never had any thing to do either with the affair of Reuchlin or with the cause of Luther. I have never taken any interest in the Cabbala or the Talmud. Those virulent contentions between

---

[1] After the bull of excommunication, it required special permission to read the books of the heretic. In a letter to Bombasius, Sept. 23, 1521, Erasmus says that he begged Jerome Aleander for permission, but was denied unless he were to obtain it in express words from the Pope. Drummond, II. 85 sq.

[2] Eras., *Epist.* 427. See the first letter of Luther (March 28, 1519), the reply of Erasmus (May 30), and a second letter of Luther (April, 1524), and the reply of Erasmus (May 5), in Latin in Er. *Epist.*, in German in Walch, vol. XVIII., 1944 sqq., and in the Appendix to Müller's *Erasmus*, pp. 385-395. The two letters of Luther to Erasmus are also given in Latin by De Wette, I. 247-249, and II. 498-501.

Reuchlin and the party of Hochstraten have been extremely distasteful to me. Luther is a perfect stranger to me, and I have never had time to read his books beyond merely glancing over a few pages. If he has written well, no praise is due to me ; if not, it would be unjust to hold me responsible. . . . Luther had written to me in a very Christian tone, as I thought; and I replied, advising him incidentally not to write any thing against the Roman Pontiff, nor to encourage a proud or intolerant spirit, but to preach the gospel out of a pure heart. . . . I am neither Luther's accuser, nor advocate, nor judge; his heart I would not presume to judge — for that is always a matter of extreme difficulty — still less would I condemn. And yet if I were to defend him, as a good man, which even his enemies admit him to be; as one put upon his trial, a duty which the laws permit even to sworn judges; as one persecuted — which would be only in accordance with the dictates of humanity — and trampled on by the bounden enemies of learning, who merely use him as a handle for the accomplishment of their designs, — where would be the blame, so long as I abstained from mixing myself up with his cause ? In short, I think it is my duty as a Christian to support Luther in this sense, that, if he is innocent, I should not wish him to be crushed by a set of malignant villains; if he is in error, I would rather see him put right than destroyed: for thus I should be acting in accordance with the example of Christ, who, as the prophet witnesseth, quencheth not the smoking flax, nor breaketh the bruised reed."

To Pope Leo X., from Louvain, Sept. 13, 1520 (three months after the excommunication of Luther, June 15) : —

"I have no acquaintance with Luther, nor have I ever read his books, except perhaps ten or twelve pages, and that only by snatches. From what I then saw, I judged him to be well qualified for expounding the Scriptures in the manner of the Fathers, — a work greatly needed in an age like this, which is so excessively given to mere subtleties, to the neglect of really important questions. Accordingly, I have favored his good, but not his bad, qualities, or rather I have favored Christ's glory in him. I was among the first to foresee the danger there was of this matter ending in violence, and no one ever hated violence more than I do. Indeed, I even went so far as to threaten John Froben the printer, to prevent him publishing his books. I wrote frequently and industriously to my friends, begging that they would admonish this man to observe Christian meekness in his writings, and do nothing to disturb the peace of the church. And when he himself wrote to me two years ago, I lovingly admonished him what I wished him to avoid : and I would he had followed my advice. This letter, I am informed, has been shown to your Holiness, I suppose in order to prejudice me, whereas it ought rather to conciliate your Holiness's favor towards me."

On Dec. 5, 1520, five days before the burning of the Pope's bull, Erasmus, being asked for his opinion about Luther by the Elector Frederick of Saxony, whom he happened to meet at Cologne, hesitated a while, and looked blank; but being pressed by the Elector, who stood square before him and stared him in the face, he gave the well-known answer, —

"Luther has committed two sins, — he has touched the Pope on the crown, and the monks on the belly." [1]

The Elector smiled, and remembered the expression shortly before his death. Returned to his lodgings, Erasmus wrote down some axioms rather favorable to Luther and disapproving of the "Pope's unmerciful bull," and sent them to Spalatin, but concealed the manuscript from fear that Aleander might see it; but it had been already published.

From a letter to a friend in Basel (Louis Berus), dated Louvain, May 14, 1521: —

"By the bitterness of the Lutherans, and the stupidity of some who show more zeal than wisdom in their endeavors to heal the present disorders, things have been brought to such a pass, that I, for one, can see no issue but in the turning upside down of the whole world. What evil spirit can have sown this poisonous seed in human affairs? When I was at Cologne, I made every effort that Luther might have the glory of obedience and the Pope of clemency, and some of the sovereigns approved of this advice. But, lo and behold! the burning of the Decretals, the 'Babylonish Captivity,' those propositions of Luther, so much stronger than they need be, have made the evil, it seems, incurable. . . . The only thing that remains to us, my dear Berus, is to pray that Christ, supreme in goodness and in power, may turn all to good; for he alone can do so."

In the same month, during the sessions of the Diet of Worms, he wrote to Nicholas Everard, from Mechlin, 1521: —

"If Luther had written more moderately, even though he had written freely, he would both have been more honored himself, and done more good to the world; but fate has decreed otherwise. I only wonder that the man is still alive. . . . They say that an edict is in readiness far more severe than

[1] See p. 232.

the Pope's bull;[1] but from fear, or some other reason, it has not yet been published. I am surprised that the Pope should employ such agents, some of them illiterate men, and all of them headstrong and haughty, for the transaction of such affairs. Nothing can exceed the pride or violent temper of Cardinal Cajetan, of Charles Miltitz, of Marinus, of Aleander. They all act upon the principle of the young king who said, 'My little finger is thicker than my father's loins.' As to Aleander, he is a complete maniac, — a bad, foolish man."

After the Diet of Worms, several events occurred which seemed to confirm his worst fears about the effects of the Reformation, and imbittered him against its leaders; namely, the disturbances of Carlstadt at Wittenberg (1521), Luther's invective against Henry VIII. (1522), and the fierce attack of his former friend and admirer Ulrich von Hutten (1523).[2]

Nevertheless, he advised Pope Adrian VI. to avoid all harsh measures, to deal gently with errors, to pardon past misdoings, to reform abuses, and to call a general council of moderate men. The counsel was disregarded.

Glareanus (Loriti) of Basel described Erasmus very well, when he wrote to Zwingli, Jan. 20, 1523, "Erasmus is an old man, and desires rest. Each party would like to claim him, but he does not want to belong to any party. Neither party is able to draw him. He knows whom to avoid, but not whom to attach himself to." Glareanus added, however, that Erasmus confessed Christ in his writings, and that he never heard any unchristian word from his lips.[3]

---

[1] The edict was passed May 26, 1521, but dated back May 8. (See p. 318.)

[2] Erasmus had disowned the poor fugitive Hutten, who turned on him like a wild beast in his *Expostulatio cum Erasmo*, published at Strasburg, July, 1523. Erasmus wrote to Pirkheimer, "*Emoriar si crediturus eram, in universis Germanis esse tantum inhumanitatis, impudentiæ, vanitatis, virulentiæ quantum habet unus libellus Hutteni.*" He answered by *Spongia Erasmi adversus Adspergines Ulrici Hutteni*, Basel, 1523. (*Opera*, vol. IX. Pars II. 1631–73). Luther judged: "I am not pleased with Hutten's attack, but still less with Erasmus's reply." The *Expostulatio* and the *Spongia* were also translated into German. See on this bitter personal controversy, Strauss, *Ulrich von Hutten*, pp. 448–484; and Drummond, II. 120 sqq.

[3] *Opera Zw.*, VII. 263.

§ 73.   *The Free-will Controversy.   1524–1527.*

See Literature in § 73.

After halting some time between approval and disapproval, Erasmus found it impossible to keep aloof from the irre-pressible conflict.   Provoked by Hutten, and urged by King Henry and English friends, he declared open war against Luther, and broke with the Reformation.   He did so with great reluctance ; for he felt that he could not satisfy either party, and that he was out of his element in a strictly theo-logical dispute.   He chose for his attack Luther's doctrine of total depravity.

Here lay the chief dogmatic difference between the two. Erasmus was an admirer of Socrates, Cicero, and Jerome ; while Luther was a humble pupil of St. Paul and Augustin. Erasmus lacked that profound religious experience through which Luther had passed in the convent, and sympathized with the anthropology of the Greek fathers and the semi-Pelagian school.

In September, 1524, Erasmus appeared on the field with his work on the " Freedom of the Will."   It is a defence of freedom as an indispensable condition of moral responsibility, without which there can be no meaning in precept, repent-ance, and reward.   He maintains essentially the old semi-Pelagian theory, but in the mildest form, and more negatively than positively ; for he wished to avoid the charge of heresy. He gives the maximum of glory to God, and a minimum to man.   " I approve," he says, " of those who ascribe some-thing to free-will, but rely most upon grace."   We must exert our will to the utmost, but the will is ineffective without the grace of God.   He urged against Luther Christ's call upon Jerusalem to repent (Matt. 23: 37), and the will of God that no one should perish, but that all should be saved (Ezek. 33: 11 ; 1 Tim. 2: 4 ; 2 Pet. 3: 9).   He treated him with respect, but charged him with attempting to drive out one extreme by another.

Luther appreciated the merits of Erasmus, and frankly acknowledged his literary superiority.[1] But he knew his weakness, and expressed, as early as 1516, the fear that he understood too little of the grace of God.[2] He found in his writings more refutation of error than demonstration of truth, more love of peace than love of the cross. He hated his way of insinuating doubts. On June 20, 1523, he wrote to Œcolampadius:[3] "May the Lord strengthen you in your proposed explanation of Isaiah [in the University of Basel], although Erasmus, as I understand, does not like it. . . . He has done what he was ordained to do: he has introduced the ancient languages, in the place of injurious scholastic studies. He will probably die like Moses in the land of Moab. He does not lead to better studies which teach piety. I would rather he would entirely abstain from explaining and paraphrasing the Scriptures, for he is not up to this work. . . . He has done enough to uncover the evil; but to reveal the good and to lead into the land of promise, is not his business, in my opinion." In a letter to Erasmus, dated April, 1524, a few months before the open breach, he proposed to him that they should let each other alone, and apologized for his subserviency to the papists, and his want of courage, in a manner which could not but wound the sensitive scholar.[4]

[1] He wrote him a very respectful letter, March 28, 1519, thanking him for his great services to the cause of letters, and congratulating him for being heartily abused by the enemies of truth and light. Even in his book against Erasmus (*De Servo Arbitrio*), he says at the beginning: "*Viribus eloquentiæ et ingenio me longissime superas.*" And towards the close: "*Fateor, tu magnus es et multis iisque nobilissimis dotibus a Deo ornatus . . . ingenio, eruditione, facundia usque ad miraculum. Ego vero nihil habeo et sum, nisi quod Christianum esse me glorier.*" *Op. Lat.* VII. 367 (Erl. Frcf. ed.).

[2] See his letters to Lange and Spalatin in De Wette, I. 39 sq., 52; 87 sq. To Lange he wrote: "*Ich fürchte, Erasmus breitet Christum und die Gnade Gottes nicht genug aus, von der er gar wenig weiss. Das Menschliche gilt mehr bei ihm als das Göttliche.*"

[3] De Wette, II. p. 352 sqq.

[4] In De Wette, II. 498 sq. Erasmus answered, May 5, 1524.

Luther on the Slavery of the Human Will.

He waited a whole year before he published his reply on the "Slavery of the Will" (December, 1525). It is one of his most vigorous and profound books, full of grand ideas and shocking exaggerations, that border on Manichæism and fatalism.[1] He thanked Erasmus for going to the root of the controversy instead of troubling him "about the papacy, purgatory, indulgences, and other fooleries." He inseparably connects divine foreknowledge and foreordination, and infers from God's almighty power that all things happen by necessity, and that there can be no freedom in the creature.[2] He represents the human will as a horse or a donkey which goes just as the rider directs it; and that rider is the Devil in the state of fallen nature, and God in the state of grace. The will has no choice of master; it is God and the Devil who are fighting for its possession. The Scripture exhortations to repentance and holy living must not be understood seriously, but ironically, as if God would say to man: Only try to repent and to do good, and you will soon find out that you cannot do it. He deals with man as a mother with the child: she invites the child to walk, in order that he may stretch out the arm for help. God speaks in this fashion solely to convict us of our helplessness, if we do not implore his assistance. Satan said, "Thou art free to act." Moses said, "Act," in order to convict us, before Satan, of our inability to act.

In the same book Luther makes a distinction between the Word of God and God himself, or between the revealed will of God, which offers salvation to all, and the concealed or

---

[1] Köstlin (I. 773) says that it is not surpassed by any work of Luther, "for energy and acuteness." But Döllinger and Janssen (II. 379) judge that Luther borrowed it from the Koran rather than from the New Testament.

[2] "*Ipsa ratione teste nullum potest esse liberum arbitrium in homine vel angelo aut ulla creatura.*"   *Op. Lat.* VII. 366.

hidden will, which means to save only some, and to leave the
rest to deserved perdition.   In this way he escapes the force
of such passages as Ezek. 18 : 23; 33 : 11; 1 Tim. 2 : 4,
urged by Erasmus, that God does not wish the death but
the salvation of the sinner (namely, according to his *revealed*
will only).[1]   But this distinction puts a contradiction in
God, which is impossible and intolerable.

If we except the peculiar way of statement and illustration, Luther's view is substantially that of St. Augustin,
whom Erasmus, with all due reverence for the great man,
represents as teaching, " God works in us good and evil, and
crowns his good works in us, and punishes his bad works
in us."   The positive part is unobjectionable : God is the
author and rewarder of all that is good; but the negative
part is the great stumbling-block.   How can God in justice
command us to walk when we are lame, and punish us for
not walking?   The theory presupposes, of course, the apostasy and condemnation of the whole human race, on the
ground of its unconscious or impersonal pre-existence and
participation in the sin and guilt of Adam.

All the Reformers were originally Augustinians, that is,
believers in the total depravity of man's nature, and the absolute sovereignty of God's grace.   They had, like St. Paul and
St. Augustin, passed through a terrible conflict with sin,
and learned to feel in their hearts, what ordinary Christians
profess with their lips, that they were justly condemned, and
saved only by the merits of Christ.   They were men of
intense experience and conviction of their own sinfulness
and of God's mercifulness ; and if they saw others perish in
unbelief, it was not because they were worse, but because of
the inscrutable will of God, who gives to some, and withholds

---

[1] " *Multa facit Deus quæ verbo suo non ostendit nobis, multa quoque vult,
quæ verbo suo non ostendit sese velle.   Sic non vult mortem peccatoris, verbo
scilicet, vult autem illam voluntate illa imperscrutabili.*"   Vol. VII. p. 222.
Erl. ed. *Op. Lat.*   The scholastic divines made a similar distinction between
the *voluntas signi* and the *voluntas beneplaciti.*

from others, the gift of saving faith. Those champions of freedom taught the slavery of the will in all things pertaining to spiritual righteousness. They drew their moral strength from grace alone. They feared God, and nothing else. Their very fear of God made them fearless of men. The same may be said of the French Huguenots and the English Puritans. Luther stated this theory in stronger terms than Augustin or even Calvin; and he never retracted it, — as is often asserted, — but even twelve years later he pronounced his book against Erasmus one of his very best.[1] Melanchthon, no doubt in part under the influence of this controversy, abandoned his early predestinarianism as a Stoic error (1535), and adopted the synergistic theory. Luther allowed this change without adopting it himself, and abstained from further discussion of these mysteries. The Formula of Concord re-asserted in the strongest terms Luther's doctrine of the slavery of the human will, but weakened his doctrine of predestination, and assumed a middle ground between Augustinianism and semi-Pelagianism or synergism.[2] In like manner the Roman Catholic Church, while retaining the greatest reverence for St. Augustin and indorsing his anthropology, never sanctioned his views on total depravity and unconditional predestination, but condemned them, indirectly, in the Jansenists.[3]

[1] In 1537 he wrote to Capito, "*Nullum agnosco meum justum librum nisi forte De Servo Arbitrio et Catechismum.*" De Wette, V. 70. In the Articles of Smalkald he again denied the freedom of the will as a scholastic error; and in his last work, the Commentary on Genesis (ch. 6 : 6, and ch. 26), he re-affirmed the distinction of the secret and revealed will of God, which we are unable to harmonize, but for this reason he deems it safest to adhere to the revealed will and to avoid speculations on the impenetrable mysteries of the hidden will. "*Melius et tutius est consistere ad præsepe Christi hominis; plurimum enim periculi in eo est, si in illos labyrinthos divinitatis te involvas.*" On Gen. 6: 6, in the Erl. ed. of *Exeg. Opera*, II. 170.

[2] *Form. Conc.*, Art. II. and XI. See Schaff, *Creeds of Christendom*, I. 313 sq.

[3] *Ibid.*, I. 102 sqq. Among the condemned propositions of Quesnel are these: "The grace of Christ is necessary for every good work ; without it nothing can be done." "The will of man, before conversion by prevenient grace, is capable of all evil and incapable of good."

Final Alienation.

The Erasmus-Luther controversy led to some further personalities in which both parties forgot what they owed to their cause and their own dignity. Erasmus wrote a bitter retort, entitled "Hyperaspistes," and drove Luther's predestinarian views to fatalistic and immoral consequences. He also addressed a letter of complaint to Elector John. The outrages of the Peasants' War confirmed him in his apprehensions. He was alienated from Melanchthon and Justus Jonas. He gave up correspondence with Zwingli, and rather rejoiced in his death.[1] He spoke of the Reformation as a tragedy, or rather a comedy which always ended in a marriage. He regarded it as a public calamity which brought ruin to arts and letters, and anarchy to the Church.[2]

He was summoned to the Diet of Augsburg, 1530, as a counsellor of the Emperor, but declined because he was sick and conscious of his inability to please either party. He wrote, however, to Cardinal Campeggio, to the bishop of Augsburg, and other friends, to protest against settling questions of doctrine by the sword. His remedy for the evils of the Church was mutual forbearance and the correction of abuses. But his voice was not heeded; the time for compromises and half measures had passed, and the controversy took its course. He devoted his later years chiefly to the

[1] When he heard of it in 1531, he wrote to a friend, "It is a good thing that two of their leaders have perished, — Zwingli on the battle-field, and Œcolampadius shortly after of fever and abscess." — *Op.* III. 1422.

[2] He gives a deplorable picture of the demoralizing effects of the Reformation in a letter to Geldenhauer in 1526, *Opera* X. 1578-1580, quoted in full in Latin and German by Döllinger, *Die Reformation*, I. 13-15. The Strasburg preachers, Capito, Bucer, and Hedio, tried to refute the charges in 1530. Erasmus again came out·with the charge, among others, that luxury was never greater, nor adulteries more frequent, than among the self-styled evangelicals, and appeals in confirmation to admissions of Luther, Melanchthon, and Œcolampadius. Some of his last letters, discovered and published by Horawitz (*Erasmiana*, 1885, No. IV. p. 44 sqq.), contain similar complaints.

editing of new editions of his Greek Testament, and the writings of the church fathers.

Luther abandoned Erasmus, and abused him as the vainest creature in the world, as an enraged viper, a refined Epicurean, a modern Lucian, a scoffer, a disguised atheist, and enemy of all religion.[1] We gladly return from this gross injustice to his earlier estimate, expressed in his letter to Erasmus as late as April, 1524: "The whole world must bear witness to your successful cultivation of that literature by which we arrive at a true understanding of the Scriptures; and this gift of God has been magnificently and wonderfully displayed in you, calling for our thanks."

§ 74. *Wilibald Pirkheimer.*

BILIBALDI PIRKHEIMERI *Opera politica, historica, philologica, et epistolica,* ed. by *M. Goldast,* Francf., 1610, fol. With a portrait by A. Dürer. His *Encomium Podagræ* was translated into English by W. Est, *The Praise of the Gout, or the Gout's Apology, a paradox both pleasant and profitable.* Lond., 1617.

LAMPE: *Zum Andenken W. P.'s.* Nürnberg, 1828. KARL HAGEN: *Deutschlands literarische und relig. Verhältnisse im Ref. Zeitalter. Mit besonderer Rücksicht auf Wilibald Pirkheimer.* Erlangen, vol. I., 1841, pp. 188 sqq., 261 sqq., 2d ed. 1868. DÖLLINGER: *Reformation,* vol. I., 161–174. D. F. STRAUSS: *Ulrich von Hutten,* 4th ed., Bonn, 1878, pp. 118 sq.; 227–235; 514–518. LOCHNER: *Lebensläufe berühmter und verdienter Nürnberger,* Nürnb., 1861. RUD. HAGEN: *W. P. in seinem Verhältniss zum Humanismus und zur Reformation,* Nürnberg, 1882. Lic. P. DREWS: *Wilibald Pirkheimer's Stellung zur Reformation,* Leipz., 1887 (138 pp.).

About this time, and after the Peasants' War, the most eminent humanists withdrew from the Reformation, and followed Erasmus into the sheepfold of the mother church, disgusted with the new religion, but without being fully

---

[1] In his letter to Link, March 7, 1529 (in De Wette, III. 426 sq.), he calls Erasmus "ἄθεον, *Lucianumque, Epicurum,*" and in a letter to his son John, 1533 (De Wette, IV. 497), he says: "*Erasmus, hostis omnium religionum et inimicus singularis Christi, Epicuri Lucianique perfectum exemplar et idea.*" Comp. his judgments in the *Tischreden,* LXI. 93–113 (Erl. ed.).

reconciled to the old, and dying at last of a broken heart. In this respect, the apprehension of Erasmus was well founded; the progress of the Reformation arrested and injured the progress of liberal learning, although not permanently. Theology triumphed over classical culture, and fierce dogmatic feuds took the place of satirical exposures of ignorant monks. But the literary loss was compensated by a religious gain. In the judgment of Luther, truth proved mightier than eloquence, faith stronger than learning, and the foolishness of God wiser than the wisdom of men.[1]

Among the pupils, friends and admirers of Erasmus, who were first attracted and then repelled by the Reformation, are Wilibald Pirkheimer, Crotus Rubeanus, Mutianus Rufus, Ulrich Zasius, Vitus Amerpach, Georg Wizel, Jacob Strauss, Johann Wildenauer (Egranus), Johann Haner, Heinrich Loriti Glareanus, and Theobald Billicanus.[2]

Wilibald Pirkheimer (1470–1530), the most distinguished and influential of them, was descended from an ancient, rich, and noble family of Nürnberg, and received a liberal military and diplomatic education. He spent seven years in Italy (1490–1497), and became a leader in the Renaissance. He occupied also a high social position as senator of Nürnberg and imperial counsellor. He was honored by important diplomatic missions, and fulfilled them with great ability. He was not an original genius, but the most learned and most eloquent layman in Germany. He mastered philology, jurisprudence, geography, astronomy, music, painting, botany,

---

[1] See his letter to Caspar Börner, professor of literature in Leipzig, May 28, 1522, in De Wette, II. 199–201. The letter was intended also for Erasmus, and printed under the title, "*Judicium D. M. Lutheri de Erasmo Roterodamo. Epistola ad amicum 1522.*" He says that he would not provoke Erasmus, but was not afraid of his attack.

[2] Döllinger gives, from the R. Catholic standpoint, a full account of these scholars in the first volume of his work on the *Reformation* (Regensburg, 1846). On Wizel we have an interesting university program of Neander: *Commentatio de Georgio Vicelio.* Berlin, 1840. Strauss notices several of them from the rationalistic standpoint, in his *Ulrich von Hutten.*

and all the discoveries and sciences of the time. He collected a rare library of books and manuscripts and a cabinet of coins, and gave free access to visitors. He translated writings of Xenophon, Plato, Plutarch, Euclid, Ptolemy, Lucian, Gregory Nazianzen, and Nilus, into Latin.[1] He was called "the Nürnberg Xenophon," for his account of the rather inglorious Swiss campaign (1499) in which he took part as an officer.[2] He carried on an extensive correspondence with the leading humanists, especially Reuchlin, Ulrich von Hutten, and Erasmus, and also with the Reformers, Melanchthon, Zwingli, Œcolampadius, and Luther. He was the Mæcenas of Germany, and a gentleman of striking and commanding presence, social culture, charming manners, and princely liberality.[3] He constantly entertained distinguished strangers at his hospitable board. Nürnberg was then the first German city in politics, industry, and commerce. He made it also a centre of literature and illumination. At Venice there was a proverb : "All German cities are blind, except Nürnberg, which has one eye."

Pirkheimer hailed the beginnings of the Reformation with patriotic and literary enthusiasm, invited Luther to his house

[1] On his literary labors, see Karl Hagen, *l.c.*, I. 280 sqq.

[2] He tells in his narrative the following anecdote of a brave and quick-witted Swiss maiden. When asked by the imperial soldiers, "What are the Swiss guards doing on their post?" she replied, "Waiting for you to attack them." — "How strong is their number?" — "Strong enough to throw you all back." — "But how strong?" — "You might have counted them in the recent fight, but fright and flight made you blind." — "What do they live of?" — "Of eating and drinking." The soldiers laughed, but one drew his sword to kill her. "Verily," she said, "you are a brave man to threaten an unarmed girl. Go and attack yonder guard, who can answer you with deeds instead of words." Comp. Münch, *W. P.'s Schweizerkrieg und Ehrenhandel*. Basel, 1826. Drews, *l.c.*, p. 10.

[3] Unfortunately his moral character was not free from blemish. He became a widower in 1504, and lived in illicit intercourse with his servant, who bore him a son when he was already past fifty. Christoph Scheurl wrote: "I wish Melanchthon knew Pirkheimer better: he would then be more sparing in his praise. With the most he is in bad repute." See K. Hagen, *l.c.*, I. 347, and Drews, *l.c.*, 14 sq.

when he returned utterly exhausted from Augsburg in 1518, distributed his books, and, with his friends Albrecht Dürer and Lazarus Spengler, prepared the way for the victory of the new ideas in his native city. He wrote an apology of Reuchlin in his controversy with the Dominicans, contributed probably to the "Letters of Obscure Men," and ridiculed Dr. Eck in a satirical, pseudonymous dialogue, after the Leipzig disputation.[1] Eck took cruel revenge when he published the Pope's bull of excommunication, by naming Pirkheimer among the followers of Luther, and warning him through the magistrate of Nürnberg. Luther burnt the Pope's bull; but Pirkheimer helped himself out of the difficulty by an evasive diplomatic disclaimer, and at last begged absolution.

This conduct is characteristic of the humanists. They would not break with the authorities of the church, and had not the courage of martyrs. They employed against existing abuses the light weapons of ridicule and satire rather than serious argument and moral indignation. They had little sympathy with the theology and piety of the Reformers, and therefore drew back when the Reformers, for conscience' sake, broke with the old church, and were cast out of her bosom as the Apostles were cast out of the synagogue.

In a letter to Erasmus, dated Sept. 1, 1524, Pirkheimer speaks still favorably of Luther, though regretting his excesses, and deprecates a breach between the two as the greatest calamity that could befall the cause of sound learning. But soon after the free-will controversy, and under the influence of Erasmus, he wrote a very violent book against his former friend Œcolampadius, in defence of consubstantiation (he did not go as far as transubstantiation).[2]

---

[1] *Eccius dedolatus (Der abgehobelte Eck). Auctore Ioanne Francisco Cottalambergio, Poëta Laureato.* 1520. See p. 182.

[2] *Bilibaldi Birckheimheri de vera Christi carne et vero ejus sanguine, ad Ioan. Œcolampadium responsio.* Norembergae, 1526. *Bilibaldi Pirckhey-*

The distractions among Protestants, the Anabaptist disturbances, the Peasants' War, the conduct of the contentious Osiander, sickness, and family afflictions increased his alienation from the Reformation, and clouded his last years. The stone and the gout, of which he suffered much, confined him at home. Dürer, his daily companion (who, however, differed from him on the eucharistic question, and strongly leaned to the Swiss view), died in 1528. Two of his sisters, and two of his daughters, took the veil in the nunnery of St. Clara at Nürnberg. His sister Charitas, who is famous for her Greek and Latin correspondence with Erasmus and other luminaries, was abbess. The nunnery suffered much from the disturbances of the Reformation and the Peasants' War. When it was to be secularized and abolished, he addressed to the Protestant magistrate an eloquent and touching plea in behalf of the nuns, and conclusively refuted the charges made against them. The convent was treated with some toleration, and survived till 1590.

His last letters, like those of Erasmus, breathe discontent with the times, lament over the decline of letters and good morals, and make the evangelical clergy responsible for the same evils which he formerly charged upon the Roman clergy and monks. "I hoped," he wrote to Zasius (1527), a distinguished professor of jurisprudence at Freiburg, who likewise stood halting between Rome and Wittenberg, — "I hoped for spiritual liberty; but, instead of it, we have carnal license, and things have gotten much worse than before." Zasius was of the same opinion,[1] and Protestants of Nürnberg admitted the fact of the extensive abuse of the gospel

meri de vera Christi carne, etc., *reponsio secunda.* 1527. I give the titles, with the inconsistencies of spelling, from original copies in the Union Theol. Seminary. Pirkheimer calls Œcolampadius (his Greek name for *Hausschein*, *House-lamp*) "Cœcolampadius" (*Blindschein*, *Blind-lamp*), and deals with him very roughly. Drews (pp. 89–110) gives a full account of this unprofitable controversy.

[1] Comp. Döllinger, *Die Reform.* i. 174–182.

liberty.[1] In a letter to his friend Leib, prior of Rebdorf,
written a year before his death, Pirkheimer disclaims all
fellowship with Luther, and expresses the opinion that the
Reformer had become either insane, or possessed by an evil
spirit.[2] But, on the other hand, he remained on good terms
with Melanchthon, and entertained him on his way to the
Diet of Augsburg in 1530.

His apparent inconsistency is due to a change of the
times rather than to a change of his conviction. Like
Erasmus, he remained a humanist, who hoped for a reformation from a revival of letters rather than theology and
religion, and therefore hailed the beginning, but lamented
the progress, of the Lutheran movement.[3]

Broken by disease, affliction, and disappointment, he died

---

[1] Hans Sachs (in his *Gespräch eines evang. Christen mit einem katholischen*, Nürnberg, 1524) warns the Nürnbergers against their excesses of
intemperance, unchastity, uncharitableness, by which they brought the
Lutheran doctrine into contempt. Döllinger, *l.c.*, I. 174 sqq., quotes testimonies to the same effect from Konrad Wickner and Lazarus Spengler, both
prominent Protestants in Nürnberg, and from contemporaries in other parts
of Germany.

[2] Döllinger, I. p. 533 sq., gives this letter in Latin and German, and infers
from it that Pirkheimer died a member of the Catholic Church.

[3] This is substantially also the judgment of Drews, his most recent
biographer, who says (*l. c.*, p. 123): "*Pirkheimer ist jeder Zeit Humanist
geblieben. . . . In der Theorie war er ein Anhänger der neuen, gewaltigen
Bewegung ; aber als dieselbe anfing praktisch zu werden, erschrak er vor
den Gährungen, die unvermeidlich waren. Der Humanist sah die schönen
Wissenschaften bedroht; der Patrizier erschrak vor der Übermacht des
Volkes ; der Staatsmann erzitterte, als er den Bruch mit den alten Ver-
hältnissen als eine Notwendigkeit fühlte. Nur ein religiös fest gegründeter
Glaube war im Stande, über diesen Kämpfen den Sieg und den Frieden zu
sehen. Daran aber fehlte es gerade Pirkheimer ; alles theologische Interesse
vermag dieses persönliche religiöse Leben nicht zu ersetzen. Wohl besass
er ein lebendiges Rechtsgefühl, einen ethischen Idealismus, aber es fehlte ihm
die Kraft, im eignen Leben denselben zu verwirklichen. Ihm war das Leben
ein heiteres Spiel, solange die Tage sonnenhell waren ; als sie sich umdüs-
terten, wollten sich die Wolken weder hinwegscherzen, noch hinwegschmä-
hen lassen. Ein religiös, sittlicher Charakter war Pirkheimer nicht,
' Vivitur ingenio, caetera mortis erunt,' diese Worte hat er unter sein von
Dürer gezeichnetes Bild (1524) gesetzt. Sie enthalten das Glaubensbekennt-
nis Pirkheimers, das Geheimnis seines Lebens.*"

in the year of the Augsburg Confession, Dec. 22, 1530, praying for the prosperity of the fatherland and the peace of the church. He left unfinished an edition of Ptolemy's Geography, which Erasmus published with a preface. Shortly before his death, Erasmus had given him an unfavorable account of the introduction of the Reformation in Basel and of his intention to leave the city.

Pirkheimer made no permanent impression, and his writings are antiquated; but, as one of the most prominent humanists and connecting links between the mediæval and the modern ages, he deserves a place in the history of the Reformation.

§ 75. *The Peasants' War. 1523-1525.*

I. LUTHER : *Ermahnung zum Frieden auf die zwölf Artikel der Bauernschaft in Schwaben* (1525); *Wider die mörderischen und raüberischen Rotten der Bauern* (1525); *Ein Sendbrief von dem harten Büchlein wider die Bauern* (1525). WALCH, vols. XVI. and XXI. Erl. ed., XXIV. 257-318. MELANCHTHON : *Historie Thomæ Münzers* (1525), in WALCH, XVI. 204 sqq. COCHLÆUS (Rom. Cath.), in his writings against Luther.

II. Histories of the Peasants' War, by SARTORIUS (*Geschichte des deutschen Bauernkriegs*, Berlin, 1795); WACHSMUTH (Leipzig, 1834); OECHSLE (Heilbronn, 1830 and 1844); BENSEN (Erlangen, 1840); ZIMMERMANN (Stuttgart, 1841, second edition 1856, 3 vols.); JÖRG (Freiburg, 1851); SCHREIBER (Freiburg, 1863-66, 3 vols.); STERN (Leipzig, 1868); BAUMANN (Tübingen, 1876-78); L. FRIES, ed. by Schäffler and Henner (Würzburg, 1876, 1877); HARTFELDER (Stuttgart, 1884).

III. Monographs on Thomas Münzer by STROBEL (*Leben, Schriften und Lehren Thomä Müntzers*, Nürnberg and Altdorf, 1795); GEBSER (1831); STREIF (1835); SEIDEMANN (Dresden, 1842); LEO (1856); ERBKAM (in Herzog[2], vol. X. 365 sqq.).

IV. RANKE : II. 124-150. JANSSEN: II. 393-582. HÄUSSER : ch. VII. WEBER : *Weltgesch.*, vol. X. 229-273 (second edition, 1886).

The ecclesiastical radicalism at Wittenberg was the prelude of a more dangerous political and social radicalism, which involved a large portion of Germany in confusion and blood. Both movements had their roots in crying abuses; both received a strong impetus from the Reformation, and pretended to carry out its principles to their legitimate consequences; but both were ultra- and pseudo-Protestant, fanatical, and revolutionary.

Carlstadt and Münzer are the connecting links between the two movements, chiefly the latter. Carlstadt never went so far as Münzer, and afterwards retraced his steps. Their expulsion from Saxony extended their influence over Middle and Southern Germany.[1]

Condition of the Peasants.

The German peasants were the beasts of burden for society, and in no better condition than slaves. Work, work, work, without reward, was their daily lot, even Sunday hardly excepted. They were ground down by taxation, legal and illegal. The rapid increase of wealth, luxury, and pleasure, after the discovery of America, made their condition only worse. The knights and nobles screwed them more cruelly than before, that they might increase their revenues and means of indulgence.

The peasants formed, in self-protection, secret leagues among themselves: as the "Käsebröder" (Cheese-Brothers), in the Netherlands; and the "Bundschuh,"[2] in South Germany. These leagues served the same purpose as the labor unions of mechanics in our days.

Long before the Reformation revolutionary outbreaks took place in various parts of Germany, — A.D. 1476, 1492, 1493, 1502, 1513, and especially in 1514, against the lawless tyranny of Duke Ulrich of Würtemberg. But these rebellions were put down by brute force, and ended in disastrous failure.[3]

---

[1] Ranke (II. 126): "*Dass Münzer und Karlstadt, und zwar nicht ohne Zuthun Luthers, endlich aus Sachsen entfernt wurden, trug zur Ausbreitung und Verstärkung dieser Bewegung ungemein bei. Sie wandten sich beide nach Oberdeutschland.*" Ranke attributes too much influence to Carlstadt's false doctrine of the Lord's Supper, which he published after his expulsion.

[2] So called from the tied shoe which the peasants wore as a symbol of subjection, in contrast to the buckled shoe of the upper classes.

[3] On the connection of the earlier peasants' insurrections with the movements preparatory to the Reformation, compare Ullmann's essay on Hans Böheim of Niklashausen, in his *Reformatoren vor der Reformation*, vol. I. 419-446.

In England a communistic insurrection of the peasants and villeins occurred in 1381, under the lead of Wat Tyler and John Balle, in connection with a misunderstanding of Wiclif's doctrines.

The Reformation, with its attacks upon the papal tyranny, its proclamation of the supremacy of the Bible, of Christian freedom, and the general priesthood of the laity, gave fresh impulse and new direction to the rebellious disposition. Traveling preachers and fugitive tracts stirred up discontent. The peasants mistook spiritual liberty for carnal license. They appealed to the Bible and to Dr. Luther in support of their grievances. They looked exclusively at the democratic element in the New Testament, and turned it against the oppressive rule of the Romish hierarchy and the feudal aristocracy. They identified their cause with the restoration of pure Christianity.

Thomas Münzer.

Thomas Münzer, one of the Zwickau Prophets, and an eloquent demagogue, was the apostle and travelling evangelist of the social revolution, and a forerunner of modern socialism, communism, and anarchism. He presents a remarkable compound of the discordant elements of radicalism and mysticism. He was born at Stolberg in the Harz Mountain (1590); studied theology at Leipzig; embraced some of the doctrines of the Reformation, and preached them in the chief church at Zwickau; but carried them to excess, and was deposed.

After the failure of the revolution in Wittenberg, in which he took part, he labored as pastor at Altstädt (1523), for the realization of his wild ideas, in direct opposition to Luther, whom he hated worse than the Pope. Luther wrote against the "Satan of Altstädt." Münzer was removed, but continued his agitation in Mühlhausen, a free city in Thuringia, in Nürnberg, Basel, and again in Mühlhausen (1525).

He was at enmity with the whole existing order of society, and imagined himself the divinely inspired prophet of a new dispensation, a sort of communistic millennium, in which there should be no priests, no princes, no nobles, and no private property, but complete democratic equality. He inflamed the people in fiery harangues from the pulpit, and in printed tracts to open rebellion against their spiritual and secular rulers. He signed himself "Münzer with the hammer," and "with the sword of Gideon." He advised the killing of all the ungodly. They had no right to live. Christ brought the sword, not peace upon earth. "Look not," he said, "on the sorrow of the ungodly; let not your sword grow cold from blood; strike hard upon the anvil of Nimrod [the princes]; cast his tower to the ground, because the day is yours."

The Program of the Peasants.

At the beginning of the uprising, the Swabian peasants issued a program of their demands, a sort of political and religious creed, consisting of twelve articles.[1]

Professing to claim nothing inconsistent with Christianity as a religion of justice, peace, and charity, the peasants claim: 1. The right to elect their own pastors (conceded by Zwingli, but not by Luther). 2. Freedom from the small tithe (the great tithe of grain they were willing to pay). 3. The abolition of bond-service, since all men were redeemed by the blood of Christ (but they promised to obey the elected rulers ordained by God, in every thing reasonable and Christian). 4. Freedom to hunt and fish. 5. A share in the forests for domestic fuel. 6. Restriction of compulsory service. 7. Payment for extra labor above what the contract requires.

---

[1] They are given in German by Walch, Strobel, Oechsle, Gieseler, Weber. The authorship is uncertain. It is ascribed to Christoph Schappeler, a native Swiss, and preacher at Memmingen; but also to Heuglin of Lindau, Hubmeier, and Münzer. See the note of Ranke, II. 135.

8. Reduction of rents. 9. Cessation of arbitrary punishments. 10. Restoration of the pastures and fields which have been taken from the communes. 11. Abolition of the right of heriot, by which widows and orphans are deprived of their inheritance. 12. All these demands shall be tested by Scripture; and if not found to agree with it, they are to be withdrawn.

These demands are moderate and reasonable, especially freedom from feudal oppression, and the primitive right to elect a pastor. Most of them have since been satisfied. Had they been granted in 1524, Germany might have been spared the calamity of bloodshed, and entered upon a career of prosperity. But the rulers and the peasants were alike blind to their best interests, and consulted their passion instead of reason. The peasants did not stick to their own program, split up in parties, and resorted to brutal violence against their masters. Another program appeared, which aimed at a democratic reconstruction of church and state in Germany. Had Charles V. not been taken up with foreign schemes, he might have utilized the commotion for the unification and consolidation of Germany in the interest of an imperial despotism and Romanism. But this would have been a still greater calamity than the division of Germany.

Progress of the Insurrection.

The insurrection broke out in summer, 1524, in Swabia. on the Upper Danube, and the Upper Rhine along the Swiss frontier, but not on the Swiss side, where the peasantry were free. In 1525 it extended gradually all over South-Western and Central Germany. The rebels destroyed the palaces of the bishops, the castles of the nobility, burned convents and libraries, and committed other outrages. Erasmus wrote to Polydore Virgil, from Basel, in the autumn of 1525: "Every day there are bloody conflicts between the nobles and the peasants, so near us that we can hear the firing, and almost the groans of the wounded." In another letter he says: " Every day priests are imprisoned, tortured, hanged, decapitated, or burnt."

At first the revolution was successful. Princes, nobles, and cities were forced to submit to the peasants. If the middle classes, which were the chief supporters of Protestant doctrines, had taken sides with the peasants, they would have become irresistible.

But the leader of the Reformation threw the whole weight of his name against the revolution.

Luther advises a wholesale Suppression of the Rebellion.

The fate of the peasantry depended upon Luther. Himself the son of a peasant, he had, at first, considerable sympathy with their cause, and advocated the removal of their grievances; but he was always opposed to the use of force, except by the civil magistrate, to whom the sword was given by God for the punishment of evil-doers. He thought that revolution was wrong in itself, and contrary to Divine order; that it was the worst enemy of reformation, and increased the evil complained of. He trusted in the almighty power of preaching, teaching, and moral suasion. In the battle of words he allowed himself every license; but there he stopped. With the heroic courage of a warrior in the spiritual army of God, he combined the humble obedience of a monk to the civil authority.

He replied to the Twelve Articles of the Swabian peasants with an exhortation to peace (May, 1525). He admitted that most of them were just. He rebuked the princes and nobles, especially the bishops, for their oppression of the poor people and their hostility to the gospel, and urged them to grant some of the petitions, lest a fire should be kindled all over Germany which no one could extinguish. But he also warned the peasants against revolution, and reminded them of the duty of obedience to the ruling powers (Rom. 13: 1), and of the passage, that "They that take the sword shall perish with the sword" (Matt. 26: 52). He advised both parties to submit the quarrel to a committee of arbitration. But it was too late; he preached to deaf ears.

When the dark cloud of war rose up all over Germany, and obscured the pure light of the Reformation, Luther dipped his pen in blood, and burst out in a most violent manifesto "against the rapacious and murderous peasants." He charged them with doing the Devil's work under pretence of the gospel.[1] He called upon the magistrates to "stab, kill, and strangle" them like mad dogs. He who dies in defence of the government dies a blessed death, and is a true martyr before God. A pious Christian should rather suffer a hundred deaths than yield a hair of the demands of the peasants.[2]

So fierce were Luther's words, that he had to defend himself in a public letter to the chancellor of Mansfeld (June or July, 1525). He did not, however, retract his position. "My little book," he said, "shall stand, though the whole world should stumble at it." He repeated the most offensive passages, even in stronger language, and declared that it was

---

[1] "*Kurzum, eitel Teufelswerk treiben sie, und insonderheit ists der Erzteufel, der zu Mühlhausen regiert* [Münzer], *und nichts denn Raub, Mord, Blutvergiessen anricht, wie denn Christus von ihm sagt, Joh. 8:44, dass er sei ein Mörder von Anbeginn.*" Erl. ed., XXIV. 288.

[2] "*Darum, lieben Herren, löset hie, rettet hie, erbarmet euch der armen Leute* [i.e., not the peasants, but the poor people deluded by them]; *steche, schlage, würge hie wer da kann. Bleibst du darüber todt: wohl dir, seliglicheren Tod kannst du nimmermehr überkommen. Denn du stirbst im Gehorsam göttlichs Worts und Befehls, Rom. 13: 1.*" . . . "*So bitte ich nun, fliehe von den Bauern wer da kann, als vom Teufel selbst.*" Ibid., xxiv. 294. In his explanatory tract, p. 307, this passage is repeated more strongly. "*Der halsstarrigen, verstockten, verblendeten Bauern erbarme sich nur niemand, sondern haue, steche, würge, schlage drein, als unter die tollen Hunde, wer da kann und wie er kann. Und das alles, auf dass man sich derjenigen erbarme, die durch solche Bauern verderbt, verjagt und verführt werden, dass man Fried und Sicherheit erhalte.*"

useless to reason with rebels, except by the fist and the sword.[1]

Cruel as this conduct appears to every friend of the poor peasants, it would be unjust to regard it as an accommodation, and to derive it from selfish considerations. It was his sincere conviction of duty to the magistrate in temporal matters, and to the cause of the Reformation which was threatened with destruction.

Defeat of the Rebellion.

The advice of the Reformer was only too well executed by the exasperated princes, both Protestant and Roman Catholic, who now made common cause against the common foe. The peasants, badly armed, poorly led, and divided among themselves, were utterly defeated by the troops of the Landgrave Philip of Hesse, Duke Henry of Brunswick, the Elector John, and the Dukes George and John of Saxony. In the decisive battle at Frankenhausen, May 25, 1525, five thousand slain lay on the field and in the streets; three hundred were beheaded before the court-house. Münzer fled, but was taken prisoner, tortured, and executed. The peasants in South Germany, in the Alsace and Lorraine, met with the same defeat by the imperial troops and the forces of the electors of the Palatinate and Treves, and by treachery. In the castle of Zabern, in the Alsace (May 17), eighteen thousand peasants fell. In the Tyrol and Salzburg, the rebellion lasted longest, and was put down in part by arbitration.

The number of victims of war far exceeded a hundred thousand.[2] The surviving rebels were beheaded or mutilated.

---

[1] *Ibid.*, 298, 303, 307. See preceding note.

[2] Bishop Georg of Speier estimated the number of the killed at a hundred and fifty thousand. This does not include those who were made prisoners, beheaded, and hanged, or dreadfully mutilated. A hangman in the district of Würzburg boasted that he had executed by the sword three hundred and fifty in one month. Margrave George of Brandenburg had to remind his brother Casimir, that, unless he spared some peasants, they would have nothing to live on. Janssen, II. 563.

Their widows and orphans were left destitute. Over a thousand castles and convents lay in ashes, hundreds of villages were burnt to the ground, the cattle killed, agricultural implements destroyed, and whole districts turned into a wilderness. "Never," said Luther, after the end of the war, "has the aspect of Germany been more deplorable than now." [1]

The Peasants' War was a complete failure, and the victory of the princes an inglorious revenge. The reaction made their condition worse than ever. Very few masters had sufficient humanity and self-denial to loosen the reins. Most of them followed the maxim of Rehoboam: "My father chastised you with whips, but I will chastise you with scorpions" (1 Kings 12:14). The real grievances remained, and the prospect of a remedy was put off to an indefinite future.

The cause of the Reformation suffered irreparable injury, and was made responsible by the Romanists, and even by Erasmus, for all the horrors of the rebellion. The split of the nation was widened; the defeated peasantry in Roman Catholic districts were forced back into the old church; quiet citizens lost their interest in politics and social reform; every attempt in that direction was frowned down with suspicion. Luther had once for all committed himself against every kind of revolution, and in favor of passive obedience to the civil rulers who gladly accepted it, and appealed again and again to Rom. 13:1, as the popes to Matt. 16:18, as if they contained the whole Scripture-teaching on obedience to authority. Melanchthon and Bucer fully agreed with Luther on this point; and the Lutheran Church has ever since been strictly conservative in politics, and indifferent to the progress of civil liberty. It is only in the nineteenth century that

---

[1] Letter of Aug. 16, 1525, to Brismann (in De Wette, III. 22): "*Rusticorum res quievit ubique, cæsis ad centum millia, tot orphanis factis, reliquis vero in vita sic spoliatis, ut Germaniæ facies miserior nunquam fuerit. Ita sæviunt victores, ut impleant suas iniquitates.*"

serfdom has been entirely abolished in Germany and Russia, and negro slavery in America.

The defeat of the Peasants' War marks the end of the destructive tendencies of the Reformation, and the beginning of the construction of a new church on the ruins of the old.

CHAPTER V.

THE INNER DEVELOPMENT OF THE REFORMATION FROM THE
PEASANTS' WAR TO THE DIET OF AUGSBURG, A.D. 1525–1530.

§ 76. *The Three Electors.*

G. SPALATIN: *Friedrich d. Weise, Lebensgeschichte,* ed. by Neudecker and
Preller, Jena, 1851. TUTZSCHMANN: *Fr. d. W.,* Grimma, 1848. RANKE,
vol. II. KOLDE: *Friedrich der Weise und die Anfänge der Reformation,*
Erlangen, 1881. KÖSTLIN in the *Studien u. Kritiken,* 1882, p. 700,
(*vers.* Kolde). Comp. §§ 26 and 61.

SHORTLY before the close of the Peasants' War, Frederick
III., surnamed the Wise, Elector of Saxony (1486–1525),
died peacefully as he had lived, in his sixty-third year, May 5,
1525. His last hours at the castle of Lochau form a striking
contrast with the stormy and bloody scenes around him. He
hoped that the common people would not prevail, but admitted
that they had reason to complain of harsh treatment. "Dear
children," he said to his servants, "if I have wronged any
one of you, I beg you to forgive me for God's sake; we
princes do many naughty things to the poor people." Shortly
before his death, he partook of the holy communion in both
kinds. This is the only distinct Protestant act in his life.
His body was removed to Wittenberg, and buried in the
castle church at which Luther had posted his Ninety-Five
Theses. Melanchthon delivered a Latin oration; Luther
wrote letters of condolence to his brother and nephew, who
succeeded him, and praised his wisdom, his kindness to his
subjects, his love of justice and hatred of falsehood. Aleander, the Pope's legate at Worms, called him the old fox
of Saxony, but in history he bears the name of the Wise.
He had charge of the German Empire after the death of

Frederick the Wise.

John the Constant.

John Frederick.

The Saxon Electors. FREDERICK the WISE, JOHN, and JOHN FREDERICK.
From a Picture by Cranach. At Nüremberg.

451

Maximilian; he modestly declined the imperial crown; he decided the election of King Charles of Spain, and was the only Elector who did not sell his vote.

Frederick was a devout Catholic, a believer in relics and indulgences, but at the same time a lover of fair dealing, an admirer of Luther, and much concerned for his university. He saved the German Reformation by saving the Reformer, without openly breaking with the Catholic Church. He never saw Luther, except at a distance in the Diet of Worms, and communicated with him chiefly through his chaplain and secretary, Spalatin. His cautious reserve was the best policy for the time.

Frederick was succeeded by his brother, John the Steadfast or Constant (1525–1532). He was less prudent and influential in politics, but a more determined adherent of the Reformation. He was too fat to mount his horse without the aid of a machine. He went to sleep at times under Luther's sermons, but stood by him at every cost. His motto was: "The word of God abideth for ever," which was placed on his ensigns and liveries.[1] He was the first to sign the immortal protest of Speier in 1529, and the Confession of Augsburg in 1530.

His son and successor, John Frederick the Magnanimous (1532–1554), survived Luther. He founded the University of Jena. He suffered the disastrous defeat at Mühlberg (April 24, 1547), and would rather lose his Electorate and half of his estates than deny the evangelical faith in which he was brought up. How different was the conduct of Elector Augustus the Strong of Saxony, who sold the Lutheran faith of his ancestors for the crown of Poland (1697), and disgraced both by his scandulous life.

Luther has left some characteristic remarks about his three sovereigns. Of Frederick, whom he only knew from a distance, he said, "He was a wise, intelligent, able, and good

[1] "V. D. M. I. Æ." = *Verbum Dei manet in æternum.*

man, who hated all display and hypocrisy. He was never married.[1] His life was pure and modest. His motto ' *Tantum quantum possim* ' was a sign of his good sense. . . . He was a fine manager and economist. He listened patiently in his council, shut his eyes, and took notes of each opinion. Then he formed his own conclusion. Such a prince is a blessing from God." Of John he said, "He had six pages to wait on him. They read the Bible to him for six hours every day. He often went to sleep, but when he awoke he had always some good text in his mouth. At sermon he used to take notes in a pocket-book. Church government and secular affairs were well administered. The Emperor had only good to say of him. He had a strong frame, and a hard death. He roared like a lion." John Frederick he judged to be "too indulgent, though he hates untruth and loose living. He fears God, and has his five wits about him. You never hear an impure or dishonorable word from his lips. He is a chaste husband, and loves his wife, — a rare virtue among kings and princes. One fault he has: he eats and drinks too much. Perhaps so big a body requires more than a small one. Otherwise he works like a donkey; and, drink what he will, he always reads the Bible or some good book before he goes to sleep." [2]

These three Electors of Saxony are the model princes of the Lutheran Reformation, which owes much to their protection. Philip of Hesse was more intelligent, brilliant, liberal, and daring than any of them, but his bigamy paralyzed his influence. He leaned more to the Reformed side, and stood on good terms with Zwingli. The most pious of the princes of Germany in the sixteenth century was Frederick III., surnamed the Pious, Elector of the Palatinate (1559–1576), who introduced the Heidelberg Catechism.

The Protestant sovereigns became supreme bishops in

---

[1] But he left two illegitimate sons.

[2] Extracts from the *Tischreden*, Erl. ed., vol. LXI., 379, 380, 385, 387, 389, 393, 394.

their respective dominions.   They did not preach, nor administer the sacraments, but assumed the episcopal jurisdiction in the government of the Church, and exercised also the right of reforming the Church (*jus reformationis*) in their dominions, whereby they established a particular confession as the state religion, and excluded others, or reduced them to the condition of mere toleration.   This right they claimed by virtue of a resolution of the Diet of Speier, in 1526, which was confirmed by the Peace of Augsburg, 1555, and ultimately by the Peace of Westphalia, 1648.   The Reformers regarded this secular summepiscopate as a temporary arrangement which was forced upon them by the hostility of the bishops who adhered to the Pope.   They justified it by the example of Josiah and other pious kings of Israel, who destroyed idolatry and restored the pure worship of Jehovah. They accepted the protection and support of the princes at the sacrifice of the freedom and independence of the church, which became an humble servant of the state.   Melanchthon regretted this condition; and in view of the rapacity of the princes, and the confusion of things, he wished the old bishops back again, and was willing even to submit to the authority of a pope if the pope would allow the freedom of the gospel.   In Scandinavia and England the episcopal hierarchy was retained, or a new one substituted for the old, and gave the church more power and influence in the government.

§ 77. *Luther's Marriage. 1525.*

I. LUTHER's Letters of May and June, 1525, touching on his marriage, in De Wette's collection, at the end of second and beginning of third vols. His views on matrimonial duties, in several sermons, *e. g., Predigt vom Ehestand*, 1525 (Erl. ed., xvi. 165 sqq.), and in his Com. on 1 Cor. vii., publ. Wittenberg, 1523, and in Latin, 1525 (Erl. ed., xix. 1–69). He wished to prevent this chapter from being used as a *Schanddeckel der falsch-berühmten Keuschheit.* His views about Katie, in Walch, XXIV. 150. His table-talk about marriage and woman, in Bindseil's *Colloquia*, II. 332–336. A letter of JUSTUS JONAS to Spalatin (June 14, 1525), and one of MELANCHTHON to Camerarius (June 16).

II. The biographies of Katharina von Bora by WALCH (1752), BESTE (1843), HOFMANN (1845), MEURER (1854). UHLHORN: *K. v. B.*, in Herzog[2], vol. II. 564–567. KÖSTLIN: *Leben Luthers*, I. 766–772; II. 488 sqq., 605 sqq.; his small biography, Am. ed. (Scribner's), pp. 325–335, and 535 sqq. BEYSCHLAG: *Luther's Hausstand in seiner reform. Bedeutung.* Barmen, 1888.

III. BURK: *Spiegel edler Pfarrfrauen.* Stuttgart, 3d ed. 1885. W. BAUR (Gen. Superintendent of the Prussian Rhine Province): *Das deutsche evangelische Pfarrhaus, seine Gründung, seine Entfaltung und sein Bestand.* Bremen, 1877, 3d ed. 1884.

Amidst the disturbances and terrors of the Peasants' War, in full view of his personal danger, and in expectation of the approaching end of the world, Luther surprised his friends and encouraged his foes by his sudden marriage with a poor fugitive nun. He wrote to his friend Link : " Suddenly, and while I was occupied with far other thoughts, the Lord has plunged me into marriage."

The manner was highly characteristic, neither saint-like nor sinner-like, but eminently Luther-like. By taking to himself a wife, he wished to please his father, to tease the Pope, and to vex the Devil. Beneath was a deeper and nobler motive, to rescue the oldest ordinance of God on earth from the tyranny of Rome, and to vindicate by his own example the right of ministers to the benefit of this ordinance. Under this view, his marriage is a public event of far-reaching consequence. It created the home life of the evangelical clergy.

He had long before been convinced that vows of perpetual celibacy are unscriptural and unnatural. He held that God has created man for marriage, and that those who oppose it must either be ashamed of their manhood, or pretend to be wiser than God. He did not object to the marriage of Carlstadt, Jonas, Bugenhagen, and other priests and monks. But he himself seemed resolved to remain single, and continued to live in the convent. He was now over forty years of age ; eight years had elapsed since he opened the controversy with Rome in the Ninety-Five Theses ; and, although a man of powerful passions, he had strictly kept his monastic and clerical vow. His enemies charged him with drinking beer, playing the lute, leading a worldly life, but never dared to dispute his chastity till after his marriage. As late as Nov. 30, 1524, he wrote to Spalatin : " I shall never take a wife, as I feel at present. Not that I am insensible to my flesh or sex (for I am neither wood nor stone) ; but my mind is averse to wedlock, because I daily expect the death of a heretic." [1] But on April 10, 1525, he wrote to the same friend: " Why do you not get married? I find so many reasons for urging others to marry, that I shall soon be brought to it myself, notwithstanding that enemies never cease to condemn the married state, and our little wiseacres (*sapientuli*) ridicule it every day." [2] He got tired of his monastic seclusion ; the convent was nearly emptied, and its resources cut off; his bed, as Melanchthon tells us, was not properly made for months, and was mildewed with perspiration ; he lived of the plainest food ; he worked himself nearly to death; he felt the need of a helpmate.

In April, 1523, nine nuns escaped from the convent of Nimptsch near Grimma, fled to Wittenberg, and appealed to Luther for protection and aid. Among them was Catharina von Bora,[3] a virgin of noble birth, but poor, fifteen years younger than Luther,[4] not remarkable for beauty or culture, but healthy, strong, frank, intelligent, and high-minded. In looking at the portraits of Dr. and Mrs. Luther in their honeymoon, we must remember that they were painted by Cranach, and not by Raphael or Titian.[5]

---

[1] De Wette, II. 570.   [2] *Ibid.*, II. 643.

[3] Also spelled Bore or Boren.

[4] She was born Jan. 29, 1499, and was in the convent from 1509.

[5] Erasmus, in a letter of 1525, ascribed to Catharina from hearsay extraordinary beauty: " *Lutherus duxit uxorem, puellam mire venustam, ex clara familia Bornæ, sed ut narrant indotatam, quæ ante annos complures vestalis esse desierat.*" Michelet (*Life of Luther*, ch. V.), probably misled by this letter, calls her " a young girl of remarkable beauty."

LUTHER. From a Portrait by Cranach in 1525. At Wittenberg.

CATHARINE VON BORA, LUTHER'S WIFE. From a Portrait by Cranach about 1525. At Berlin.

457

Catharina had been attached and almost engaged to a former student of Wittenberg from Nürnberg; but he changed his mind, to her great grief, and married a rich wife (1523). After this Luther arranged a match between her and Dr. Glatz of Orlamünde (who was afterwards deposed) ; but she refused him, and intimated to Amsdorf, that she would not object to marry him or the Reformer. Amsdorf remained single. Luther at first was afraid of her pride, but changed his mind. On May 4, 1525, he wrote to Dr. Rühel (councilor of Count Albrecht of Mansfeld, and of Cardinal Albrecht of Mainz), that he would "take his Katie to wife before he died, in spite of the Devil."[1] He left his friends ignorant of the secret, deeming it unwise to talk much about such delicate matters. "A man," he said, "must ask God for counsel, and pray, and then act accordingly."

On the evening of June 13, on Tuesday after Trinity Sunday, he invited Bugenhagen, Jonas, Lucas Cranach and wife, and a professor of jurisprudence, Apel (an ex-dean of the Cathedral of Bamberg, who had himself married a nun), to his house, and in their presence was joined in matrimony to Catharina von Bora in the name of the Holy Trinity. Bugenhagen performed the ceremony in the customary manner. On the following morning he entertained his friends at breakfast. Justus Jonas reported the marriage to Spalatin through a special messenger. He was affected by it to tears, and saw in it the wonderful hand of God.[2]

On June 27 Luther celebrated his wedding in a more public, yet modest style, by a nuptial feast, and invited his father

---

[1] De Wette, II. 655. On June 2, 1525, he advised Cardinal Archbishop and Elector Albrecht of Mainz, in an open letter, to marry, and to secularize the archbishopric. *Ibid.*, p. 673.

[2] "*Lutherus noster duxit Catharinam de Bora. Heri adfui rei et vidi sponsum in thalamo jacentem.* [An indecent German custom of the time; see Köstlin, I. 767.] *Non potui me continere, adstans huic spectaculo, quin illachrymarem, nescio quo affectu animum percellente . . . mirabilis Deus in consiliis et operibus suis.*"

and mother and his distant friends to "seal and ratify" the union, and to "pronounce the benediction."[1] He mentioned with special satisfaction that he had now fulfilled an old duty to his father, who wished him to marry. The university presented him with a rich silver goblet (now in possession of the University of Greifswald), bearing the inscription: "The honorable University of the electoral town of Wittenberg presents this wedding gift to Doctor Martin Luther and his wife Kethe von Bora." The magistrate provided the pair with a barrel of Eimbeck beer, a small quantity of good wine, and twenty guilders in silver. What is very remarkable, Archbishop Albrecht sent to Katie through Rühel a wedding gift of twenty guilders in gold; Luther declined it for himself, but let Katie have it.[2] Several wedding-rings of doubtful genuineness have been preserved, especially one which bears the image of the crucified Saviour, and the inscription, "D. Martino Luthero Catharina v. Boren, 13 Jun. 1525." It has been multiplied in 1817 by several copies. They lived together in the old Augustinian convent, which was now empty. He was not much interrupted in his studies, and at the end of the same year he published his violent book against Erasmus, who wondered that marriage had not softened his temper.

The event was a rich theme for slander and gossip. His enemies circulated a slander about a previous breach of the vow of chastity, and predicted that, according to a popular tradition, the ex-monk and ex-nun would give birth to Antichrist. Erasmus contradicts the slander, and remarked that if that tradition was true, there must have been many thousands of antichrists before this.[3] Melanchthon (who had been in-

---

[1] See his letters of invitation in De Wette, III. 1, 2, 9, 10, 11, 12, 13.

[2] *Ibid.*, III. 103, 104. *Tischreden*, IV. 308. Köstlin, I. 772.

[3] In his letter to Franciscus Sylvius (1526): "*De conjugio Lutheri certum est, de partu maturo sponsæ vanus erat rumor, nunc tamen gravida esse dicitur. Si vera est vulgi fabula Antichristum nasciturum ex monacho et monacha quemadmodum isti jactitant, quot Antichristorum millia jam olim*

vited to the feast of the 27th of June, but not to the ceremony of the 13th), in a Greek letter to his friend Camerarius
(June 16), expressed the fear that Luther, though he might
be ultimately benefited by his marriage, had committed a
lamentable act of levity and weakness, and injured his influence at a time when Germany most needed it.[1]

Luther himself felt at first strange and restless in his new
relation, but soon recovered.   He wrote to Spalatin, June 16,
"I have made myself so vile and contemptible forsooth that
all the angels, I hope, will laugh, and all the devils weep."[2]
A year after he wrote to Stiefel (Aug. 11, 1526): "Catharina, my dear *rib*, salutes you, and thanks you for your letter.
She is, thanks to God, gentle, obedient, compliant in all
things, beyond my hopes.   I would not exchange my poverty
for the wealth of Crœsus."[3]   He often preached on the trials
and duties of married life truthfully and effectively, from
practical experience, and with pious gratitude for that holy
state which God ordained in paradise, and which Christ honored by his first miracle.   He calls matrimony a gift of God,
wedlock the sweetest, chastest life, above all celibacy, or else
a veritable hell.

§ 78.   *Luther's Home Life.*

Luther and Katie were well suited to each other.   They
lived happily together for twenty-one years, and shared the
usual burdens and joys.   Their domestic life is very characteristic, full of good nature, innocent humor, cordial affec-

---

*habet mundus ?   At ego sperabam fore, ut Lutherum uxor redderet magis
cicurem.   Verum ille præter omnem expectationem emisit librum in me
summa quidem cura elaboratum, sed adeo virulentum, ut hactenus in
neminem scripserit hostilius.*"

[1] The letter was published in the original Greek by W. Meyer, in the
reports of the München Academy of Sciences, Nov. 4, 1876, pp. 601–604.
The text is changed in the *Corp. Reform.*, I. 753.   Mel. calls Luther a very
reckless man (ἀνὴρ ὡς μάλιστα εὐχερής), but hopes that he will become more
solemn (σεμνότερος).

[2] De Wette, III. 3.   [3] *Ibid.*, III. 125.

tion, rugged simplicity, and thoroughly German. It falls below the refinement of a modern Christian home, and some of his utterances on the relation between the two sexes are coarse; but we must remember the rudeness of the age, and his peasant origin. No stain rests upon his home life, in which he was as gentle as a lamb and as a child among children.

"Next to God's Word," he said from his personal experience, "there is no more precious treasure than holy matrimony. God's highest gift on earth is a pious, cheerful, God-fearing, home-keeping wife, with whom you may live peacefully, to whom you may intrust your goods and body and life."

He loved his wife dearly, and playfully called her in his letters "my heartily beloved, gracious housewife, bound hand and foot in loving service, Catharine, Lady Luther, Lady Doctor, Lady of Zulsdorf,[1] Lady of the Pigmarket,[2] and whatever else she may be." She was a good German *Hausfrau*, caring for the wants of her husband and children; she contributed to his personal comfort in sickness and health, and enabled him to exercise his hospitality. She had a strong will, and knew how to take her own part. He sometimes speaks of her as his "Lord Katie," and of himself as her "willing servant." "Katie," he said to her, "you have a pious husband who loves you; you are an empress." Once in 1535 he promised her fifty guilders if she would read the Bible through; whereupon, as he told a friend, it became "a very serious matter with her." She could not understand why God commanded Abraham to do such a cruel thing as to kill his own child; but Luther pointed her to God's sacrifice of his only Son, and to the resurrection from the dead. To Katie and to Melanchthon he wrote his last letters (five to her, three to Melanchthon) from Eisleben shortly before his death, informing her of his journey, his diet and condition, complaining of fifty Jews under the protection of the

[1] From his little farm.   [2] *Saumärkterin.* They lived near the pigmarket.

widowed Countess of Mansfeld, sending greetings to Master Philip (Melanchthon), and quieting her apprehensions about his health.

"Pray read, dear Katie, the Gospel of John and the little Catechism. . . . You worry yourself about your God, just as if He were not Almighty, and able to create ten Doctor Martin Luthers for the old one drowned perhaps in the Saale, or fallen dead by the fireplace, or on Wolf's fowling floor. Leave me in peace with your cares; I have a better protector than you and all the angels. He — my Protector — lies in the manger and hangs upon a Virgin's breast, but He sits also at the right hand of God, the Father Almighty. Rest, therefore, in peace. Amen." [1]

In his will (1542), seventeen years after his marriage, he calls her a "pious, faithful, and devoted wife, full of loving, tender care towards him." At times, however, he felt oppressed by domestic troubles, and said once he would not marry again, not even a queen. Those were passing moods. "Oh, how smoothly things move on, when man and wife sit lovingly at table! Though they have their little bickerings now and then, they must not mind that. Put up with it." "We must have patience with woman, though she be at times sharp and bitter. She presides over the household machinery, and the servants deserve occasionally a good scolding." He put the highest honor of woman on her motherhood. "All men," he said, "are conceived, born, and nursed by women. Thence come the little darlings, the highly prized heirs. This honor ought in fairness to cover up all feminine weakness."

Luther had six children, — three daughters, two of whom died young, and three sons, Hans (John), Martin, and Paul. None inherited his genius. Hans gave him much trouble. Paul rose to some eminence as physician of the Elector, and died at Dresden, 1593. The sons accompanied their father on his last journey to Eisleben.[2] His wife's aunt, Magdalen von Bora, who had been a nun and head-nurse in the same cloister, lived with his family, and was esteemed like a grand-

[1] Feb. 7, 1546, in De Wette, V. 787.
[2] Nobbe, *Stammbaum der Familie des Dr. M. Luther*, Grimma, 1846.

mother by him and his children. Two orphan nieces, and
a tutor for the boys, an amanuensis, and a number of students as boarders, belonged to the household in a portion of
the former convent on the banks of the Elbe. The chief
sitting-room of the family, his bedroom, and the lecture hall
are still shown in "the Lutherhaus."

He began the day, after his private devotions, which were
frequent and ardent, with reciting in his family the Ten
Commandments, the Apostles' Creed, the Lord's Prayer, and
a Psalm. He went to bed at nine, but rose early, and kept
wide awake during the day. Of his private devotions we
have an authentic account from his companion, Veit Dietrich,
who wrote to Melanchthon during the Diet of Augsburg,
1530, when Luther was at Coburg, feeling the whole weight
of that great crisis: —

"No day passes that he does not give three hours to prayer, and those the
fittest for study. Once I happened to hear him praying. Good God! how
great a spirit, how great a faith, was in his very words! With such reverence
did he ask, as if he felt that he was speaking with God; with such hope and
faith, as with a Father and a Friend. 'I know,' he said, 'that Thou art our
Father and our God. I am certain, therefore, that Thou art about to destroy
the persecutors of Thy children. If Thou doest not, then our danger is
Thine too. This business is wholly Thine, we come to it under compulsion: Thou, therefore, defend.' . . . In almost these words I, standing afar
off, heard him praying with a clear voice. And my mind burned within me
with a singular emotion when he spoke in so friendly a manner, so weightily,
so reverently, to God."

Luther celebrated the festivals, especially Christmas, with
childlike joy. One of the most familiar scenes of Christian
family life in Germany is Luther with his children around
the Christmas-tree, singing his own Christmas hymn: —

"Good news from heaven the angels bring,
    Glad tidings to the earth they ring." [1]

[1] The Nativity hymn, —

"*Vom Himmel hoch da komm ich her*,"

was written for his children in 1535. He abridged it in 1543: —

"*Vom Himmel kam der Engel Schaar*."

Nothing can be more charming or creditable to his heart than the truly childlike letter he wrote to his oldest boy Hans, then four years of age, from Coburg, during the sessions of the Augsburg Diet in the momentous year 1530.[1]

"Grace and peace in Christ, my dear little boy. I am pleased to see that thou learnest thy lessons well, and prayest diligently. Go on thus, my dear boy, and when I come home, I will bring you a fine fairing. I know of a pretty, delightful garden, where are merry children that have gold frocks, and gather nice apples and pears, cherries and plums under the trees, and sing and jump and are happy; they also ride on fine little horses with gold bridles and silver saddles. I asked the man who owns the garden, who the children were. He said, 'These are the children who love to pray and to learn, and are good.' Then I said, 'Dear man, I also have a son who is called Hans Luther. May he not come to this garden and eat such pretty apples and pears, and ride on such fine little horses, and play with these children?' The man said, 'If he likes to pray and to learn, and is pious, he may come to the garden, and Lippus[2] and Jost[3] may come also; and if they all come together, they shall have pipes and drums and lutes and fiddles, and they shall dance and shoot with little crossbows.'

"Then he showed me a smooth lawn in the garden laid out for dancing, and there hung the golden pipes and drums and crossbows. But it was still early, and the children had not dined; therefore I could not wait for the dance. So I said, 'Dear sir, I will go straight home and write all this to my little boy; but he has an aunt, Lene,[4] that he must bring with him.' And the man answered, 'So it shall be; go and write as you say.'

"Therefore, dear little boy Johnny, learn and pray with a good heart, and tell Lippus and Jost to do the same, and then you will all come to the garden together. And now I commend you to Almighty God. Give my love to aunt Lene, and give her a kiss for me. Anno 1530.

"Thy loving father,

"MARTINUS LUTHER."

He was deeply grieved by the early death of his favorite daughter Lena (Magdalen), a pious, gentle, and affectionate girl of fourteen, with large, imaginative eyes, and full of

---

[1] De Wette, IV. 41 sq. Comp. *Luther's Brief an sein Söhnlein Hänsigen.* With woodcuts and original drawings by Ludwig Richter, Leipz. 1883. Froude calls it "the prettiest letter ever addressed by a father to a child." *Luther,* p. 53.

[2] Philip, son of Melanchthon.   [3] Jodocus, son of Jonas.

[4] Great-aunt, Magdalen.

promise.[1] "I love her very much," he prayed; "but, dear
God, if it is thy holy will to take her hence, I would gladly
leave her with Thee." And to her he said, "Lena dear, my
little daughter, thou wouldst love to remain here with thy
father: art thou willing to go to that other Father?"—"Yes,
dear father," she replied, "just as God wills." And when
she was dying, he fell on his knees beside her bed, wept
bitterly, and prayed for her redemption. As she lay in her
coffin, he exclaimed, "Ah! my darling Lena, thou wilt rise
again, and shine like a star,—yea, as a sun. I am happy in
the spirit, but very sorrowful in the flesh." He wrote to his
friend Jonas: "You will have heard that my dearest child is
born again into the eternal kingdom of God. We ought to
be glad at her departure, for she is taken away from the world,
the flesh, and the devil; but so strong is natural love, that we
cannot bear it without anguish of heart, without the sense
of death in ourselves." On her tomb he inscribed these
lines:—

> "Here do I Lena, Luther's daughter, rest,
>   Sleep in my little bed with all the blessed.
>   In sin and trespass was I born;
>   Forever would I be forlorn,
>   But yet I live, and all is good—
>   Thou, Christ, didst save me with thy blood."

Luther was simple, regular, and temperate in his habits.
The reports to the contrary are slanders of enemies. The
famous and much-abused adage,—

> "Who does not love wife, wine, and song,
>   Remains a fool his whole life long," [2]—

is not found in his works, nor in any contemporary writing,
but seems to have originated in the last century, on the basis

---

[1] Erl. ed., vol. LXV. 237, in Latin and German. Lena died Sept. 20, 1542.
See her picture by Cranach in Köstlin's small biography, p. 545.
  [2] "*Wer nicht liebt Weib, Wein und Gesang,*
      Der bleibt ein Narr sein Leben lang."

of some mediæval saying.[1]   He used beer[2] and common wine
according to the general custom of his age and country; but
he abhorred intemperance, and justly complained of the
drink-devil (*Saufteufel*) of the Germans.[3]   Melanchthon, his
daily companion, often wondered (as he reports after Luther's
death) how a man with such a portly frame could live on
so meager a diet; for he observed that Luther sometimes
fasted for four days when in good health, and was often
contented for a whole day with a herring and a piece of
bread.   He preferred "pure, good, common, homely fare."
Occasionally he received a present of game from the Elector,
and enjoyed it with his friends.

He had a powerful constitution, but suffered much of the
stone, of headache, and attacks of giddiness, and fainting;
especially in the fatal year 1527, which brought him to the
brink of the grave.   He did not despise physicians, indifferent as they were in those days, and called them "God's
menders (*Flicker*) of our bodies;" but he preferred simple
remedies, and said, "My best medical prescription is written

---

[1] The lines appeared first in the present form in the *Wandsbecker Bote*
for 1775, No. 75, p. 300, and then in 1777 in the *Musenalmanach* of J. H.
Voss (the poet, and translator of Homer), who was supposed to be the author,
and to have foisted them upon Luther.   Herder gave them a place among
his *Volkslieder*, 1778, I. 12.   Seidemann, in Schnorr's "Archiv," vol. VIII.
(1879), p. 440, has shown that the sentiment is substantially pre-Lutheran,
and quotes from Luther's *Table Talk*, Ser. IV., a sentence somewhat an-
alogous, but involving a reproach to the Germans for drunkenness: "*Wie
wollt ihr jetzt anders einen Deutschen vorthun denn* EBRIETATE, *præsertim
talem qui non diligit* MUSICAM *et* MULIERES?*"   See Köstlin, II. 678 sq.
Another similar sentence has since been found by L. Schulze in the "*Reforma-
torium viæ clericorum*" of 1494: "*Absque Venere et mero rite lætabitur nemo.*"

[2] He liked the beer of Eimbeck and Naumburg.   In one of his last letters
(Feb. 7, 1546) to his wife from Eisleben, where he was treated like a prince by
the counts of Mansfeld, he gives her this piece of information: "We live here
very well, and the town-council gives me for each meal half a pint of 'Rhein-
fall' (Rhine wine), which is very good.   Sometimes I drink it with my friends.
The wine of the country here is also good, and Naumburger beer is very good,
though I fancy its pitch fills my chest with phlegm.   The Devil has spoilt all
the beer in the world with pitch, and the wine with brimstone.   But here
the wine is pure, such as the country gives."   De Wette, V. 788.

[3] He preached some strong sermons against intemperance, and commends
the Italians and Turks for sobriety.   See *Colloquia*, ed. Bindseil, I. 195 sqq.

in John 3: 'God so loved the world.'" He was too poor to keep horse and carriage, but he kept a bowling-alley for exercise. He liked to throw the first ball himself, and elicited a hearty laugh when he missed the mark; he then reminded the young friends that by aiming to knock down all the pins at once, they might miss them all, as they would find out in their future calling. He warned Melanchthon against excess of study, and reminded him that we must serve God by rest and recreation as well as by labor, for which reason He has given us the fourth commandment, and instituted the Sabbath.

Luther exercised a generous hospitality, and had always guests at his table. He was indiscriminately benevolent to beggars, until rogues sharpened his wits, and made him more careful.[1] There was an unbroken succession of visitors — theologians, students, princes, noblemen, and ladies, anxious to see the great man, to get his advice and comfort; and all were favorably impressed with his frank, manly, and pleasant bearing. At times he was wrapt in deep thought, and kept a monkish silence at table; but at other times he talked freely, seriously and merrily, always interestingly, about every thing under the sun. His guests called his speeches their "table-spice," and recorded them faithfully without discrimination, even his most trivial remarks. Once he offered a premium for the shortest blessing. Bugenhagen began in Low German: —

> *Dit und dat,*
> *Trocken und nat*
> *Gesegne Gott.*"

Luther improved upon it in Latin: —

> " *Dominus Jesus*
> *Sit potus et esus.*"

But Melanchthon carried the palm with

> " *Benedictus benedicat.*"

---

[1] He wrote to Justice Menius, Aug. 24, 1535 (De Wette, IV. 624), that he was often deceived, "*per fictas Nonnas et generosas meretrices.*"

To the records of Veit Dietrich, Lauterbach, and Mathesius, which were often edited, though in bad taste, we owe
the most remarkable "Table-Talk" ever published.[1] Many
of his sayings are exceedingly quaint, and sound strange,
coarse, and vulgar to refined ears. But they were never
intended for publication; and making due allowance for
human weakness, the rudeness of the age, and his own
rugged nature, we may agree with the judgment of one of his
most accurate biographers, that "in all his words and deeds
Luther was guided constantly by the loftiest principles, by
the highest considerations of morality and religious truth,
and that in the simple and straightforward manner which was
his nature, utterly free from affectation or artificial effort."[2]

After dinner he indulged with his friends and children in
music, sacred and secular songs, German and Latin hymns.
He loved poetry, music, painting, and all the fine arts. In
this respect he was ahead of those puritanical Reformers
who had no taste for the beautiful, and banished art from
the church. He placed music next to theology. He valued
it as a most effectual weapon against melancholy and the
temptations of the Devil. "The heart," he said, "is satisfied,
refreshed, and strengthened by music." He played the lute,
sang melodiously, and composed tunes to his hymns, especially the immortal "*Ein feste Burg,*" which gives classic
expression to his heroic faith in God and the triumph of
the gospel. He never lost his love for Virgil and Cicero,
which he acquired as a student at Erfurt. He was fond of
legends, fables, and proverbs. He would have delighted in

[1] See St. Louis ed. of Walch, vol. XXII., much improved by Hoppe, 1887.

[2] Köstlin, small biography, N.Y. ed. p. 554, Ger. ed. p. 592. But in his
large work, vol. II. 519, he makes this just qualification: "*Derbe, plumpe,
unserm Ohre anstössige Worte kommen in Luther's Reden wie in seinen
Schriften, ja einigemale sogar in seinen Predigten vor. Seine Art war in
der That keine feine; sie steht aber auch so noch bedeutend über dem Ton,
der damals durchschnittlich in weltlichen und geistlichen Kreisen, bei Bür-
gern, hohen Herren und Kirchenfürsten herrschte, und jene ungünstigen
Eindrücke müssen der edeln Kraft, dem Salz und Mark gegenüber, die seine
Gespräche und Schriften durchdringen, auch für uns weit zurücktreten.*"

the stories of old "Mother Goose," and in Grimm's "Haus-mährchen." He translated some of Esop's Fables, and wrote a preface to an edition which was published after his death.

He enjoyed the beauties of nature, loved trees and flowers, was fond of gardening, watched with wonder the household of the bees, listened with delight to the singing birds, renewed his youth with the return of spring, and adored everywhere the wisdom and goodness of nature's God. Looking at a rose, he said, "Could a man make a single rose, we should give him an empire; but these beautiful gifts of God come freely to us, and we think nothing of them. We admire what is worthless, if it be only rare. The most precious of things is nothing if it be common." "The smallest flowers show God's wisdom and might. Painters cannot rival their color, nor perfumers their sweetness; green and yellow, crimson, blue, and purple, all growing out of the earth. And yet we trample on lilies as if we were so many cows." He delighted in a refreshing rain. "God rains," he said, "many hundred thousand guilders, wheat, rye, barley, oats, wine, cabbage, grass, milk." Talking of children, he said, "They speak and act from the heart. They believe in God without disputing, and in another life beyond the present. They have small intellect, but they have faith, and are wiser than old fools like us. Abraham must have had a hard time when he was told to kill Isaac. No doubt he kept it from Sarah. If God had given me such an order, I should have disputed the point with Him. But God has given his only begotten Son unto death for us."

He shared in the traditional superstitions of his age. He believed in witchcraft, and had many a personal encounter with the Devil in sleepless nights.[1] He was reluctant to accept the new Copernican system of astronomy, because "Joshua bade the sun stand still, not the earth." He regarded the comets, which he calls "harlot stars," as tokens

[1] See above, p. 334 sq.

of God's wrath, or as works of the Devil. Melanchthon and Zwingli held similar opinions on these irregular visitors. It was an almost universal belief of mankind, till recent times, that comets, meteors, and eclipses were fire-balls of an angry God to scare and rouse a wicked world to repentance.[1] On the other hand, he doubted the calculations of astrology. "I have no patience with such stuff," he said to Melanchthon, who showed him the nativity of Cicero from the stars. "Esau and Jacob were born of the same father and mother, at the same time, and under the same planets, but their nature was wholly different. You would persuade me that astrology is a true science! I was a monk, and grieved my father; I caught the Pope by his hair, and he caught me by mine; I married a runaway nun, and begat children with her. Who saw that in the stars? Who foretold that? Astronomy is very good, astrology is humbug. The example of Esau and Jacob disproves it."

Luther gave himself little concern about his household, and left it in the hands of his wife, who was prudent and economical. He calls himself a negligent, forgetful, and ignorant housekeeper, but gives great credit to his " Herr Kathie." He was contented with little, and called economy the best capital. All the Reformers were poor, and singularly free from avarice; they moved in a lofty sphere, and despised the vanities of the world.

Luther's income was very small, even for the standard of his times, and presents a striking contrast to the royal splendor and luxury of bishops and cardinals. His highest annual salary as professor was three hundred guilders; it was first a hundred guilders; on his marriage the Elector John doubled it; the Elector John Frederick added a hundred; a guilder being equal in value to about sixteen marks or

[1] See a curious tract of Andrew D. White, *A History of the Doctrine of Comets*, in the " Papers of the American Historical Association," N.Y., 1887, vol. II. 16.

shillings (four dollars) of the present day. He received no honorarium from the students, nor any salary as preacher in the town church; but regular payments in wood and grain, and occasional presents of a fine suit, a cask of wine, or venison, or a silver cup from the Elector, with his greetings. Admiring friends gave him rings, chains, and other valuables, which he estimated in 1542 at a thousand guilders. In his last years (from 1541) he, as well as Bugenhagen, Melanchthon, and Jonas, received an annual honorary pension of fifty guilders from the king of Denmark, who thereby wished to show his gratitude for the Lutheran Reformation, and had previously (1539) sent him a special present of a hundred guilders through Bugenhagen. From his father, who left twelve hundred and fifty guilders, he inherited two hundred and fifty guilders. The publishers offered him (as he reported in 1539) a yearly grant of four hundred guilders for the free use of his manuscripts, but he refused " to make money out of the gifts of God." If he had been rewarded according to modern ideas, the royalty of his German Bible Version alone would have amounted to a handsome fortune before his death. He bought in 1540 from his brother-in-law a little farm, Zulsdorf, between Leipzig and Borna, for six hundred and ten guilders, as a home for his family. His wife culti vated a little garden with fruit-trees, even mulberry and fig trees, raised hops and brewed beer for domestic use, as was then the custom. She also had a small fish-pond. She enjoyed hard work. Luther assisted her in gardening and fishing. In 1541 he purchased a small house near the convent, for his wife.[1] He willed all his property, which amounted to about nine thousand guilders, to his wife during her lifetime, wishing that "she should not receive from her children, but the children from her; that they must honor and obey her, as God has commanded."

[1] On Luther's *Vermögensumstände*, see Seidemann, *Luther's Grundbesitz*, 1860. Köstlin, II. 498 sqq., and his references, p. 678.

His widow survived him seven years, and suffered from poverty and affliction. The Elector, the Counts of Mansfeld, and the King of Denmark added small sums to her income; but the unfortunate issue of the Smalkaldian war (1547) disturbed her peace, and drove her from Wittenberg. She returned after the war. Melanchthon and Bugenhagen did for her what they could. When the pestilence broke out at Wittenberg in 1552, and the university was moved to Torgau, she followed with her children; but on the journey she was thrown from the wagon into a ditch, and contracted a cold which soon passed into consumption. She died Dec. 20, 1552, at Torgau; her last prayer was for her children and the Lutheran Church.

A few words about Luther's personal appearance. In early life, as we have seen, he looked like an ascetic monk, pale, haggard, emaciated.[1] But in latter years he grew stout and portly. The change is characteristic of his transition from legalistic gloom to evangelical cheerfulness. He was of middle stature, had a large head and broad chest, a bold and open face without any dissimulation lurking behind, prominent lips, short curly hair, and uncommonly brilliant and penetrating eyes. His enemies saw in them the fire of a demon. His countenance makes the impression of frankness, firmness, courage, and trust in God. He looks like a hero of faith, who, with the Bible in his hand, defies the world, the flesh, and the Devil. His feet are firmly planted on the ground, as if they could not be moved. "Here I stand, I cannot otherwise." His voice was not strong, but clear and sonorous. He was neat in his dress, modest and dignified in his deportment. He exchanged the monastic gown in 1524 for a clerical robe, a gift of the Elector. He disliked the custom of the students to rise when he entered into the lecture-room. "I wish," he said, "Philip would give up this

---

[1] See the description of Mosellanus, p. 180, and Cranach's engraving from the year 1520, in Köstlin, p. 120 (Scribner's ed.).

old fashion. These marks of honor always compel me to offer a few more prayers to keep me humble ; and if I dared, I would go away without reading my lecture."

The same humility made him protest against the use of his name by his followers, who nevertheless persisted in it. " I pray you," he said, " leave my name alone, and do not call yourselves Lutherans, but Christians. Who is Luther? My doctrine is not mine. I have not been crucified for any one. St. Paul would not that any one should call themselves of Paul, nor of Peter, but of Christ. How, then, does it befit me, a miserable bag of dust and ashes, to give my name to the children of Christ? Cease, my dear friends, to cling to those party names and distinctions, — away with them all! and let us call ourselves only Christians, after Him from whom our doctrine comes. It is quite proper, that the Papists should bear the name of their party; because they are not content with the name and doctrine of Jesus Christ, they will be Papists besides. Well, let them own the Pope, as he is their master. For me, I neither am, nor wish to be, the master of any one. I and mine will contend for the sole and whole doctrine of Christ, who is our sole master."

§ 79. *Reflections on Clerical Family Life.*

The Reformers present to us the first noted examples of clerical family life in the Christian Church. This is a new and important chapter in the history of civilization.

They restored a natural right founded in the ordinance of God. The priests and high priests of the Jewish theocracy down to the father of John the Baptist, as well as the patriarchs, Moses, and some of the prophets, lived in wedlock. The prince of the apostles, whom Roman Catholics regard as the first pope, was a married man, and carried his wife with him on his missionary journeys.[1] Paul claimed the same

---

[1] In spite of this fact attested by St. Paul, 1 Cor. 9:5, in the year 57, Dr. Spalding (in his *Hist. of the Prot. Reformation*, I. 177, 8th ed. 1875) asserts that Peter's wife was " probably dead before he became an apostle."

right as "other apostles, and the brothers of the Lord, and Cephas," though he renounced it for personal reasons. From the pastoral Epistles we may infer that marriage was the rule among the bishops and deacons of the apostolic age. It is therefore plainly a usurpation to deprive the ministers of the gospel of this right of nature and nature's God.

But from the second century the opinion came to prevail, and still prevails in the papal communion, which is ruled by an unmarried priest, that marriage is inconsistent with the sacerdotal office, and should be forbidden after ordination. This view was based on the distinction between a lower and higher morality with corresponding merit and reward, — the one for the laity or the common people; the other for priests and monks, who form a spiritual nobility. All the church fathers, Greek and Latin, even those who were themselves married (as Tertullian, Gregory of Nyssa, Synesius), are unanimous in praising celibacy above marriage; and the greatest of them are loudest in this praise, especially St. Jerome. And yet the mothers of Gregory Nazianzen, Chrysostom, and Augustin, are the brightest examples of Christian women in the ancient Church. Nonna, Anthusa, and Monica were more useful in giving birth to these luminaries of the Church than any nuns.

This ascetic feature marks a decided difference between the Fathers and the Reformers, as it does between the Catholic and Evangelical churches. Anglicanism, with all its respect for the Fathers, differs as widely from them in this respect as any other Protestant communion.

The Oriental churches, including that of Russia, stopped half way in this ascetic restriction of a divine right. They approve and even enjoin marriage upon the lower clergy (before ordination), but forbid it to bishops, and regard the directions of Paul, 1 Tim. 3:2, 12 (compare 5:9), as a concession to the weakness of the flesh, and as a prohibition of *second* marriage. The Latin Church, understanding the advice of Paul, 1 Cor. 7 : 7, 32, 33, as "a counsel of perfection," indicating a better way, imposed, as early as the fourth century, total abstinence from marriage upon all orders of the clergy, and brands the marriage of a priest as sinful concubinage. Pope Siricius, A. D. 385, issued the first prohibition of sacerdotal marriage. His successors followed, but it was not till Gregory VII. that the prohibition was rigidly enforced. It was done in the interest of hierarchical power, and at an enormous sacrifice of clerical purity. The Roman Catholic system makes marriage one of the seven sacraments; but by elevating celibacy above it, and by declaring it to be beneath the dignity of a priest of God, it degrades marriage as if it involved an element of impurity. According to the Gnostic and Manichæan theory, condemned by Paul as a doctrine of demons, 1 Tim. 4 : 1–3, marriage is a contact with sinful matter, and forbidden altogether.

In view of this state of public opinion and the long tradition of Latin Christendom, we need not wonder that the marriage of the Reformers created the greatest sensation, and gave rise to the slander that sensual passion was one of the strongest motives of their rebellion against popery. Erasmus struck the keynote to this perversion of history, although he knew well enough that Luther and Œcolampadius were Protestants several years before they thought of marrying. Clerical marriage was a result, not a cause, of the Reformation, as clerical celibacy was neither the first nor the chief objection to the papal system.[1]

---

[1] Archbishop Spalding, in his *History of the Reformation* (I. 176), following the example of unscrupulous Romish controversialists, thus echoes the joke of Erasmus: "Matrimony was, in almost all cases, the *dénouement* of the drama which signalized the zeal for reformation." He refers for proof to Moore's *Travels of an Irish Gentleman in Search of a Religion*, ch. XLVI., "where the great Irish poet enters into the subject at length, giving his authorities as he proceeds, and playing off his caustic wit on the hymeneal propensities of the Reformers." In looking at that chapter (for the first time), I find that it abounds in misstatements and abuse of the Reformers, whom the Irish poet calls not only "fanatics" and "bigots," but "the

On a superficial view one might wish that the Reformers had remained true to their solemn promise, like the Jansenist bishops in the seventeenth century, and the clerical leaders of the Old Catholic secession in the nineteenth.[1] But it was their mission to introduce by example as well as by precept, a new type of Christian morality, to restore and re-create clerical family life, and to secure the purity, peace, and happiness of innumerable homes.

Far be it from us to depreciate the value of voluntary celibacy which is inspired by the love of God. The mysterious word of our Lord, Matt. 19:12, and the advice and example of Paul, 1 Cor. 7:7, 40, forbid it. We cheerfully admire the self-denial and devotion of martyrs, priests, missionaries, monks, nuns, and sisters of charity, who sacrificed all for Christ and their fellow-men. Protestantism, too, has produced not a few noble men and women who, without vows and without seeking or claiming extra merit, renounced the right of marriage from the purest motives.[2] But according

coarsest hypocrites" and "slaves of the most vulgar superstition" (p. 246, Philad. ed. 1833). The same poet gives us the startling piece of information (p. 248) that the Protestants were subdivided on the eucharistic question alone into countless factions such as "Panarii, Accidentarii, Corporarii, Arrabonarii, Tropistæ, Metamorphistæ, Iscariotistæ, Schwenkenfeldians, etc., etc., etc.," and that "an author of Bellarmine's time counted no less than two hundred different opinions on the words, ' This is my body'"! Moore was evidently better at home in the history of Lord Byron than in the history of the church.

[1] The Old Catholic Bishop Reinkens and Bishop Herzog, Drs. Döllinger, Friederich, Reusch, and Langen, remained single after their excommunication in 1870. But Père Loyson-Hyacinthe, who occupies a similar position of Tridentine or rather Gallican Romanism *versus* Vatican Romanism, followed the example of the Reformers, and married an American widow, whom he had converted to the Roman Church by his eloquent sermons in Notre Dame, before she converted him to herself. They were joined together by Dean Stanley in Westminster Abbey. It is reported that Pope Pius IX., on being informed of the fact, and asked to excommunicate the ex-monk, wittily replied, "It is not necessary, since he has taken the punishment into his own arms." A Pope's view of the blessed estate of matrimony!

[2] We may mention the saintly Archbishop Leighton, Dr. Samuel Hopkins, the missionary Zeisberger, Dr. William Augustus Mühlenberg (the founder of St. Luke's Hospital in New York and of St. Johnland, and the singer of

to God's ordinance dating from the state of innocency, and sanctioned by Christ at the wedding feast at Cana, marriage is the rule for all classes of men, ministers as well as laymen. For ministers are men, and do not cease to be men by becoming ministers.

The Reformation has changed the moral ideal, and elevated domestic and social life. The mediæval ideal of piety is the flight from the evil world: the modern ideal is the transformation of the world. The model saint of the Roman Church is the monk separated from the enjoyments and duties of society, and anticipating the angelic life in heaven where men neither marry nor are given in marriage: the model saint of the Evangelical Church is the free Christian and useful citizen, who shows his piety in the performance of social and domestic duties, and aims at the sanctification of the ordinances of nature. The former tries to conquer the world by running away from its temptations — though after all he cannot escape the flesh, the world, and the Devil in his own heart: the latter tries to conquer the world by converting it. The one abstains from the wedding feast: the other attends it, and changes the water into wine. The one flees from woman as a tempter: the other takes her to his heart, and reflects in the marriage relation the holy union of Christ with his Church. The one aims to secure chastity by abstinence: the other proves it within the family. The one renounces all earthly possessions: the other uses them for the good of his fellow-men. The one looks for happiness in heaven : the other is happy already on earth by making others happy. The daily duties and trials of domestic and social life are a better school of moral discipline than monkish celibacy and poverty. Female virtues and graces are necessary to supplement and round out the character of man. Exceptions there are, but they prove the rule.

" I would not live alway "), the model pastor Ludwig Harms of Hermannsburg, the historian Neander and his sister, and the nurses or deaconesses of Kaiserswerth and similar institutions.

It may be expected that in the fervor and hurry of the first attempts in the transition from slavery to freedom, some indiscretions were committed; but they are as nothing compared with the secret *chronique scandaleuse* of enforced celibacy. It was reserved for later times to cultivate a more refined style of family life; but the Reformers burst the chains of papal tyranny, and furnished the practical proof that it is possible to harmonize the highest and holiest calling with the duties of husband and father. Though falling short of modern Protestant ideas of the dignity and rights of woman, they made her the rightful companion of the Christian pastor; and among those companions may be found many of the purest, most refined, and most useful women on earth. The social standing of woman is a true test of Christian civilization.

Melanchthon was the first among the Reformers who entered the state of matrimony; but being a layman, he violated no priestly or monastic vow. He married, at the urgent request of his friends, Katharina Krapp, the daughter of the burgomaster of Wittenberg, in November, 1520, and lived with his plain, pious, faithful, and benevolent wife, till her death in 1557. He was seen at times rocking the cradle while reading a book.[1]

Calvin was likewise free from the obligation of vows, but the severest and most abstemious among the Reformers. He married Idelette de Buren, the widow of an Anabaptist minister of Holland, whom he had converted to the Pædobaptist faith; he lived with her for nearly nine years, had three children who died in infancy, and remained a widower after her death. The only kind of female beauty which impressed him was, as he said, gentleness, purity, modesty, patience, and devotion to the wants of her husband; and these qualities he esteemed in his wife.[2]

[1] C. Schmidt, *Philipp Melanchthon*, pp. 47 sqq., 617, 710 sqq.

[2] Stähelin, *Johannes Calvin*, vol. I. 272 sqq.

Zwingli unfortunately broke his vow at Einsiedeln, while still a priest, and in receipt of a pension from the Pope. He afterwards married a worthy patrician widow with three children, Anna Reinhard von Knonau, who bore him two sons and two daughters, and lived to lament his tragic death on the field of battle, finding, like him, her only comfort in the Lord Jesus and the word of God.[1]

Ludwig Cellarius (Keller), Œcolampadius (the Reformer of Basel), Wolfgang Capito (the Reformer of Strassburg), and his more distinguished friend Martin Bucer (a widower who was always ready for union) were successively married to Wilibrandis Rosenblatt, the daughter of a knight and colonel aid-de-camp of the Emperor Maximilian I. She accompanied Bucer to Cambridge in England, and after his death returned to Basel, the survivor of four husbands! She died Nov. 1, 1564.[2] She must have had a remarkable attraction for Reformers. Œcolampadius thought her almost too young for his age of forty-five, but found her a "good Christian" and "free from youthful frivolity." She bore him three children, — Eusebius, Alitheia, and Irene.[3] It was on the occasion of his marriage that Erasmus wrote to a friend (March 21, 1528) : " Œcolampadius has lately married. His bride is not a bad-looking girl" [she was a widow]. "I suppose he wants to mortify his flesh. Some speak of the Lutheran cause as a tragedy, but to me it appears rather as a comedy, for it always ends in a wedding."[4]

---

[1] R. Christoffel, *Huldreich Zwingli*, pp. 336–339, 413. The slanderous exaggerations of Janssen have been refuted by Ebrard, Usteri, and Schweizer.

[2] Hagenbach (*Œkolampad*, p. 108, note) gives this date, and refers to the *Reformations-Almanach*, 1821.

[3] Herzog, *Leben Joh. Œkolampadius*, vol. II. 70 sqq.; Hagenbach, *Joh. Œkolampad und Oswald Myconius*, p. 107. Hagenbach says that the names of his children were the pillars of his home: godliness, truth, and peace.

[4] In a letter to Adrianus Arivulus: " *Nuper Œcolampadius duxit uxorem, puellam non inelegantem. Vult opinor affligere carnem. Quidam appellant Lutheranam tragœdiam, mihi videtur esse comœdia. Semper enim in nuptias exeunt tumultus.*" He afterwards apologized to Œcolampadius, and disclaimed any intention to satirize him. See his letter to Œcolampadius in

Archbishop Cranmer appears in an unfavorable light.   His first wife, " Black Joan," died in childbed before his ordination.   Early in 1532, before he was raised to the primacy of Canterbury by Henry VIII. (August, 1532), he married a niece of the Lutheran preacher Osiander of Nürnberg, and concealed the fact, the disclosure of which would have prevented his elevation.   The papal bulls of confirmation were dated February and March, 1533, and his consecration took place March 30, 1533.   The next year he privately summoned his wife to England; but sent her away in 1539, when he found it necessary to execute the bloody articles of Henry VIII., which included the prohibition of clerical marriage. He lent a willing hand to the divorces and re-marriages of his royal master.   And yet with all his weakness of character, and time-serving policy, Cranmer must have been an eminently devout man if he translated and reproduced (as he certainly edited) the Anglican liturgy, which has stood the test of many generations to this day.[1]

John Knox, the Luther of Scotland, had the courage, as a widower of fifty-eight (March, 1563–64), to marry a Scotch lass of sixteen, Margaret Stuart, of royal name and blood, to the great indignation of Queen Mary, who " stormed wonderfully " at his audacity.   The papists got up the story that he gained her affection by sorcery, and aimed to secure for his heirs, with the aid of the Devil, the throne of Scotland.   His wife bore him three daughters, and two years after his death

---

Drummond's *Erasmus*, II. 319.   Archbishop Spalding (*l. c.* I. 176) thus repeats the joke : " The gospel light seems to have first beamed upon Œcolampadius from the eye of a beautiful young lady, whom, in violation of his solemn vows plighted to Heaven, he espoused, probably, as Erasmus wittily remarked, to mortify himself."   He says nothing of the apology of Erasmus to his friend and associate.

[1] Strype's *Memorials of Cranmer* (Bk. I., chs. 1, 4, 19; Bk. III., chs. 8 and 38); Hook's *Lives of the Archbishops of Canterbury* (vols. VI. and VII.); Hardwick's *History of the Reformation*, ed. W. Stubbs (1873), p. 179; and art. Cranmer in Leslie Stephen's " Dictionary of National Biogr.," vol. XIII.

(1572) contracted a second marriage with Andrew Ker, a widower.[1]

The most unfortunate matrimonial incident in the Reformation is the consent of Luther, Melanchthon, and Bucer to the disgraceful bigamy of Landgrave Philip of Hesse. It is a blot on their character, and admits of no justification. When the secret came out (1540), Melanchthon was so overwhelmed with the reproaches of conscience and a sense of shame that he fell dangerously ill at Weimar, till Luther, who was made of sterner stuff, and found comfort in his doctrine of justification by faith alone, prayed him out of the jaws of death.

In forming a just estimate of this subject, we must not only look backward to the long ages of clerical celibacy with all its dangers and evils, but also forward to the innumerable clerical homes which were made possible by the Reformation. They can bear the test of the closest examination.

Clerical celibacy and monastic vows deprived the church of the services of many men who might have become shining stars. On the other hand, it has been calculated by Justus Möser in 1750, that within two centuries after the Reformation from ten to fifteen millions of human beings in all lands owe their existence to the abolition of clerical celibacy.[2] More important than this numerical increase is the fact that an unusual proportion of eminent scholars and useful men in church and state were descended from clerical families.[3]

There is a poetic as well as religious charm in the home of

---

[1] Dr. M'Crie's *Life of John Knox*, Philad. ed., pp. 269 and 477 (Append. Note HHH); and Dav. Laing's Preface to the 6th vol. of his ed. of *Works of John Knox*, pp. LXV. sqq.

[2] Ranke states this fact.

[3] Among distinguished sons of clergymen may be named Linné, the botanist; Berzelius, the chemist; Pufendorf, the lawyer; Schelling, the philosopher; Buxtorff, the Orientalist; Euler, the mathematician; Agassiz, the scientist ; Edward and Ottfried Müller, the classical philologists; John von Müller, Spittler, Heeren, Mommsen, Bancroft, among historians; Henry Clay, Senator Evarts, and two Presidents of the United States, Arthur and Cleveland, among statesmen; Charles Wesley, Gellert, Wieland, Lessing, the brothers Schlegel, Jean Paul, Emanuel Geibel, Emerson (also the female

a Protestant country pastor who moves among his flock as a father, friend, and comforter, and enforces his teaching of domestic virtues and affections by his example, speaking louder than words. The beauty of this relation has often been the theme of secular poets. Everybody knows Oliver Goldsmith's "Vicar of Wakefield," which describes with charming simplicity and harmless humor the trials and patience, the domestic, social, and professional virtues of a country pastor, and begins with the characteristic sentence: "I was ever of opinion, that the honest man who married, and brought up a large family, did more service than he who continued single, and only talked of population; from this motive I had scarcely taken orders a year, before I chose my wife, as she did her wedding-gown, not for a fine glossy face, but for such qualities as would wear well." Herder read this English classic four times, and commended it to his bride as one of the best books in any language. Goethe, who himself tasted the charm of a pastoral home in the days of his purest and strongest love to Friederike of Sesenheim, praises the "Vicar of Wakefield," as "one of the best novels, with the additional advantage of being thoroughly moral, yea in a genuine sense Christian," and makes the general assertion: "A Protestant country pastor is perhaps the most beautiful topic for a modern idyl; he appears like Melchizedek, as priest and king in one person. He is usually associated by occupation and outward condition with the most innocent conceivable estate on earth, that of the farmer; he is father, master of his house, and thoroughly identified with his congregation. On this pure, beautiful earthly foundation, rests his higher vocation: to introduce men into life,

writers Meta Heusser, Elizabeth Prentiss, Mrs. Stowe), among poets; John Wesley, Monod, Krummacher, Spurgeon, H. W. Beecher, R. S. Storrs, among preachers; Jonathan Edwards, Schleiermacher, Hengstenberg, Nitzsch, Julius Müller, Dorner, Dean Stanley, among divines; Swedenborg, the seer; with a large number of prominent and useful clergymen, lawyers, and physicians, in all Protestant countries.

to care for their spiritual education, to bless, to instruct, to strengthen, to comfort them in all the epochs of life, and, if the comfort for the present is not sufficient, to cheer them with the assured hope of a more happy future." [1]   In his idyl "Hermann und Dorothea," he introduces a clergyman as an ornament and benefactor of the community.   It is to the credit of this greatest and most cultured of modern poets, that he, like Shakspeare and Schiller, never disparaged the clerical profession.

In his "Deserted Village," Goldsmith gives another picture of the village preacher as

> "A man who was to all the country dear,
> And passing rich on forty pounds a year. . . .
> At church, with meek and unaffected grace,
> His looks adorned the venerable place;
> Truth from his lips prevailed with double sway,
> And fools who came to scoff remained to pray."

From a higher spiritual plane William Wordsworth, the brother of an Anglican clergyman and uncle of two bishops, describes the character of a Protestant pastor in his "Ecclesiastical Sonnets."

> "A genial hearth, a hospitable board,
> And a refined rusticity, belong
> To the neat mansion, where, his flock among,
> The learned Pastor dwells, their watchful lord.
> Though meek and patient as a sheathèd sword ;
> Though pride's least lurking thought appear a wrong
> To human kind; though peace be on his tongue,
> Gentleness in his heart — can earth afford
> Such genuine state, pre-eminence so free,
> As when, arrayed in Christ's authority,
> He from the pulpit lifts his awful hand;
> Conjures, implores, and labors all he can
> For re-subjecting to divine command
> The stubborn spirit of rebellious man!"

[1] From the tenth book of his *Wahrheit und Dichtung*.   Herder directed his attention to the "Vicar," while they studied at Strassburg, and read it to him aloud in German translation.   In the same book Goethe describes in fascinating style his visits to the parsonage of Sesenheim.

A Romish priest or a Russian pope depends for his influence chiefly upon his official character, though he may be despised for his vices. A Protestant minister stands or falls with his personal merits; and the fact of his high and honorable position and influence in every Protestant country, as a Christian, a gentleman, a husband and father, is the best vindication of the wisdom of the Reformers in abolishing clerical celibacy.

§ 80. *Reformation of Public Worship.*

I. LUTHER: *Deutsches Taufbüchlein*, 1523; *Ordnung des Gottesdienstes in der Gemeinde*, 1523; *Vom Gräuel der Stillmesse*, 1524; *Deutsche Messe und Ordnung des Gottesdienstes*, 1526; *Das Taufbüchlein verdeutscht, aufs neue zugerichtet*, 1526. In *Walch*, X.; in Erl. ed., XXII. 151 sqq. Comp. the Augsburg Confession, Pars II. art. 3 (*De missa*); Apol. of the Augsb. Conf. art. XXIV. (*De missa*); the Lutheran liturgies or *Kirchenagenden* (also *Kirchenordnungen*) of the 16th century, collected in DANIEL: *Codex Liturgicus Ecclesiæ Lutheranæ*, Lips. 1848 (Tom. II. of his *Cod. Lit.*), and HÖFLING: *Liturgisches Urkundenbuch* (ed. by G. Thomasius and Theodos. Harnack), Leipz. 1854.

II. TH. KLIEFOTH: *Die ursprüngliche Gottesdienstordnung in den deutschen Kirchen luth. Reformation, ihre Destruction und Reformation*, Rostock, 1847. GRÜNEISEN: *Die evang. Gottesdienstordnung in den oberdeutschen Landen*, Stuttgart, 1856. GOTTSCHICK: *Luthers Anschauungen vom christl. Gottesdienst und seine thatsächliche Reform desselben*, Freiburg i. B., 1887.

The reformation of doctrine led to a reconstruction of worship on the basis of Scripture and the guidance of such passages as "God is spirit,"[1] and must be worshiped "in spirit and in truth" (John 4:24), and "Let all things be done decently and in order" (1 Cor. 14:40). Protestantism aims at a rational or spiritual service,[2] as distinct from a

---

[1] *i.e.*, all spirit, nothing but spirit, (without the article, as in the margin of the Revised Version), according to the Greek: πνεῦμα (emphatically put first) ὁ Θεός, in opposition to all materialistic conceptions and local limitations. Compare the parallel expressions: "God is love" (1 John 4: 8), "God is light" (1 John 1: 5), where neither the definite nor the indefinite article is admissible.

[2] λογικὴ λατρεία, Rom. 12:1; comp. the "spiritual sacrifices" (πνευματικαὶ θυσίαι), 1 Pet. 2:5.

mechanical service of mere forms. It acts upon the heart through the intellect, rather than the senses, and through instruction, rather than ceremonies. It brings the worshiper into direct communion with God in Christ, through the word of God and prayer, without the obstruction of human mediators.

The Reformers first cleansed the sanctuary of gross abuses and superstitions, and cast out the money-changers with a scourge of cords. They abhorred idolatry, which in a refined form had found its way into the church. They abolished the sale of indulgences, the worship of saints, images, and relics, processions and pilgrimages, the private masses, and masses for the dead in purgatory.[1] They rejected five of the seven sacraments (retaining only baptism and the eucharist), the doctrine of transubstantiation, the priestly sacrifice, the adoration of the host, the withdrawal of the cup from the laity, and the use of a dead language in public worship. They also reduced the excessive ceremonialism and ritualistic display which obscured the spiritual service.

But the impoverishment was compensated by a gain; the work of destruction was followed by a more important and difficult work of reconstruction. This was the revival of primitive worship as far as it can be ascertained from the New Testament, the more abundant reading of the Scriptures and preaching of the cardinal truths of the gospel, the restoration of the Lord's Supper in its original simplicity, the communion in both kinds, and the translation of the Latin service into the vernacular language whereby it was made intelligible and profitable to the people. There was, how-

---

[1] *Missæ de sanctis, missæ votivæ, missæ pro defunctis.* Melanchthon, in the Apology of the Augsburg Confession, art. XXIV., says: "The fact that we hold only public or common mass is no offense against the Catholic Church. For in the Greek churches even to-day private masses are not held; but there is only a public mass, and that on the Lord's Day and festivals." Masses for the dead, which date from Pope Gregory I., imply, of course, the doctrine of purgatory, and were among the crying abuses of the church.

ever, much crude experimenting and changing until a new order of worship could be fairly established.

Uniformity in worship is neither necessary nor desirable, according to Protestant principles. The New Testament does not prescribe any particular form, except the Lord's Prayer, the words of institution of the Lord's Supper, and the baptismal formula.

The Protestant orders of worship differ widely in the extent of departure from the Roman service, which is one and the same everywhere. The Lutheran Church is conserv- ative and liturgical. She retained from the traditional usage what was not inconsistent with evangelical doctrine; while the Reformed churches of the Zwinglian and Calvinistic type aimed at the greatest simplicity and spirituality of worship after what they supposed to be the apostolic pattern. Some went so far as to reject all hymns and forms of prayer which are not contained in the Bible, but gave all the more attention to the Psalter, to the sermon, and to extemporane- ous prayer. The Anglican Church, however, makes an ex- ception among the Reformed communions: she is even more conservative than the Lutheran, and produced a liturgy which embodies in the choicest English the most valuable prayers and forms of the Latin service, and has maintained its hold upon the reverence and affection of the Episcopal churches to this day. They subordinate preaching to wor- ship, and free prayer to forms of prayer.

Luther began to reform public worship in 1523, but with caution, and in opposition to the radicalism of Carlstadt, who during the former's absence on the Wartburg had tumultu- ously abolished the mass, and destroyed the altars and pic- tures. He retained the term "mass," which came to signify the whole public service, especially the eucharistic sacrifice. He tried to save the truly Christian elements in the old order, and to reproduce them in the vernacular language for the benefit of the people. His churchly instincts were strength-

ened by his love of poetry and music. He did not object even
to the use of the Latin tongue in the Sunday service, and
expressed an impracticable wish for a sort of pentecostal
Sunday mass in German, Latin, Greek, and Hebrew.[1] At the
same time he desired also a more private devotional service
of converted Christians, with the celebration of the holy
communion (corresponding to the *missa fidelium* of the ante-
Nicene Church, as distinct from the *missa catechumenorum*),
but deemed it impossible for that time from the want of the
proper persons; for "we Germans," he said, "are a wild,
rough, rabid people, with whom nothing can be done except
under the pressure of necessity."

So he confined himself to provide for the public Sunday
service. He retained the usual order, the Gospels and Epistles, the collects, the *Te Deum*, the *Gloria in excelsis*, the
Benedictus, the Creed, the responses, the kneeling posture in
communion, even the elevation of the host and chalice (which
he afterwards abandoned, but which is still customary in the
Lutheran churches of Scandinavia), though without the adoration. He omitted the canon of the mass which refers to the
priestly sacrifice, and which, since the sixth century, contains
the kernel of the Roman mass, as an unbloody repetition of the
crucifixion and miraculous transformation of the elements.[2]
He had previously rejected this "horrible canon," as he calls

---

[1] "*Wenn ichs vermöchte,*" he says in his tract on the German Mass, January, 1526, "*und die griechische und ebräische Sprache wäre uns so gemein als
die lateinische, und hätte so viel feiner Musica und Gesangs als die lateinische
hat, so sollte man einen Sonntag um den andern in allen vier Sprachen,
deutsch, lateinisch, griechisch und ebräisch, Messe halten, singen, und lesen.*"
Such a polyglot service was never even attempted except at the Propaganda
in Rome. Melanchthon (*Apol. Conf. Aug.*, art. XXIV.) defends the use of
Latin along with German hymns in public worship.

[2] The *canon missæ* (" *Te igitur,*" etc.), embraces five or six prayers bearing upon the consecration and the offering of Christ's body. It begins with
an intercession for the Pope and all orthodox Catholics. Janssen says (III.
64): "*In der Messe liess Luther den Canon, den Kern und das Wesen der
katholischen Messe, fort,*" and unfairly adds: "*Das Volk jedoch sollte dieses
nicht wissen.*" As if Luther were the man to deceive the people!

it, in his "Babylonian Captivity," and in a special tract from the Wartburg. He assailed it again and again as a cardinal error in the papal system. He held indeed the doctrine of the real presence, but without the scholastic notion of transubstantiation and priestly sacrifice.

He gave the most prominent place to the sermon, which was another departure from previous custom. He arranged three services on Sunday, each with a sermon: early in the morning, chiefly for servants; the mass at nine or ten; and in the afternoon a discourse from a text in the Old Testament. On Monday and Tuesday in the morning the Ten Commandments, the Creed, and the Lord's Prayer were to be taught; on Wednesday, the Gospel of Matthew; on Saturday, the Gospel of John; on Thursday, the Epistle lessons should be explained. The boys of the school were to recite daily some Psalms in Latin, and then read alternately one or more chapters of the New Testament in Latin and German.

Luther introduced the new order with the approval of the Elector in October, 1525, and published it early in 1526.[1] The chief service on Sunday embraces a German hymn or psalm; the *Kyrie Eleison*, and *Gloria in Excelsis* (*Allein Gott in der Höh sei Ehr*); a short collect, and the Epistle for the day; a hymn; the Gospel for the day sung by the minister; the Nicene Creed recited by the whole congregation; a sermon on the Gospel; the Lord's Prayer; exhortation; the holy communion, the words of institution sung by the minister (this being the consecration of the elements), with singing of the *Sanctus* (Isa. 6:1-4, rendered into German by Luther), the *Benedictus*, the *Agnus Dei* (John 1:29) or in German " *O Lamm Gottes unschuldig* " (by Decius), followed by the distribution, the collection, and benediction. Omitting the *canon missæ*, or the offering of the sacrifice of Christ's body, the new order was substantially the same as the old, only translated into German.

---

[1] *Deutsche Messe und Ordnung des Gottesdiensts*, with musical notes for the parts to be sung.

Melanchthon says in the Augsburg Confession of 1530 :[1] "Our churches are wrongfully accused of having abolished the mass. For the mass is retained still among us, and celebrated with great reverence ; yea, and almost all the ceremonies that are in use, saving that with the things sung in Latin we mingle certain things sung in German at various parts of the service, which are added for the people's instruction. For therefore alone we have need of ceremonies, that they may teach the unlearned."

Luther regarded ceremonies, the use of clerical robes, candles on the altar, the attitude of the minister in prayer, as matters of indifference which may be retained or abolished. In the revision of the baptismal service, 1526, he abolished the use of salt, spittle, and oil, but retained the exorcism in an abridged form. He also retained the public confession and absolution, and recommended private confession of sin to the minister.[2]

The Lutheran churches in Northern Germany and in Scandinavia adopted the order of Wittenberg with sundry modifications ; but the Lutheran churches in Southern Germany (Würtemberg, Baden, Palatinate, Alsace) followed the simpler type of the Swiss service.

The Lutheran order of worship underwent some radical changes in the eighteenth century under the influence of rationalism ; the spirit of worship cooled down ; the weekly communion was abolished ; the sermon degenerated into a barren moral discourse ; new liturgies and hymnbooks with all sorts of misimprovements were introduced. But in recent times, we may say since the third centennial celebration of

[1] Part II. art. III. Comp. his "Apology of the Conf.," art. XXIV., *De missa*.

[2] The Augsburg Confession, Part II. art. IV., says: "Confession is not abolished in our churches. For it is not usual to communicate the body of our Lord, except to those who have been previously examined and absolved. . . . Men are taught that they should highly regard absolution, inasmuch as it is God's voice, and pronounced by God's command."

the Reformation (1817), there has been a gradual revival of the liturgical spirit in different parts of Germany, with a restoration of many devotional treasures of past ages. There is, however, no uniform Lutheran liturgy, like the Common Prayer Book of the Church of England. Each Lutheran state church has its own liturgy and hymnbook.

§ 81. *Prominent Features of Evangelical Worship.*

Taking a wider view of the subject, we may emphasize the following characteristic features of evangelical worship, as compared with that of the Latin and Greek churches: —

1. The prominence given to the sermon, or the exposition and application of the word of God. It became the chief part of divine service, and as regards importance took the place of the mass. Preaching was the special function of the bishops, but sadly neglected by them, and is even now in Roman-Catholic countries usually confined to the season of Lent. The Roman worship is complete without a sermon. The mass, moreover, is performed in a dead language, and the people are passive spectators rather than hearers. The altar is the throne of the Catholic priest; the pulpit is the throne of the Protestant preacher and pastor. The Reformers in theory and practice laid the greatest stress on preaching and hearing the gospel as an act of worship.

Luther set the example, and was a most indefatigable and popular preacher.[1] He filled the pulpit of the town church alternately with Bugenhagen, the pastor, on Sundays and week-days, sometimes twice a day. Even in the last days of his life he delivered four sermons from the pulpit at Eisleben in spite of physical infirmity and pain.[2] His most popular sermons are those on the Gospels and Epistles of the year, collected in the *Kirchenpostille*, which he completed in 1525

---

[1] His sermons fill 16 vols. in the Erl. ed. of his *Works.*

[2] They were taken down in short-hand, and first published by his companion Aurifaber. In the Erl. ed., XVI. 209 sqq.

and 1527. Another popular collection is his *Hauspostille*, which contains his sermons at home, as taken down by Veit Dietrich and Rörer, and published in 1544 and 1559. He preached without notes, after meditation, under the inspiration of the moment.

He was a Boanerges, the like of whom Germany never heard before or since. He had all the elements of a popular orator. Melanchthon said, "One is an interpreter, one a logician, another an orator, but Luther is all in all." Bossuet gives him credit for "a lively and impetuous eloquence by which he delighted and captivated his hearers." Luther observed no strict method. He usually followed the text, and combined exposition with application. He made Christ and the gospel his theme. He lived and moved in the Bible, and understood how to make it a book of life for his time. He always spoke from intense conviction and with an air of authority. He had an extraordinary faculty of expressing the profoundest thoughts in the clearest and strongest language for the common people. He hit the nail on the head. He was bold and brave, and spared neither the Devil nor the Pope nor the Sacramentarians. His polemical excursions, however, are not always in good taste, nor in the right spirit.

He disregarded the scholars among his hearers, and aimed at the common people, the women and children and servants. "Cursed be the preachers," he said, "who in church aim at high or hard things." He was never dull or tedious. He usually stopped when the hearers were at the height of attention, and left them anxious to come again. He censured Bugenhagen for his long sermons, of which people so often and justly complain. He summed up his homiletical wisdom in three rules: —

"Start fresh; Speak out; Stop short."[1]

---

[1] "*Tritt frisch auf; Mach's Maul auf; Hör' bald auf.*" Literally: Get up freshly; Open your mouth widely; Be done quickly. Comp. E. Jonas, *Die Kanzelberedtsamkeit Luthers*, Berlin, 1852; Beste, *Die bedeutendsten Kanzel-*

The mass and the sermon are the chief means of edification, — the one in the Greek and Roman, the other in the Protestant churches. The mass memorializes symbolically, day by day, the sacrifice of Christ for the sins of the world; the sermon holds up the living Christ of the gospel as an inspiration to holy living and dying. Both may degenerate into perfunctory, mechanical services; but Christianity has outlived all dead masses and dry sermons, and makes its power felt even through the weakest instrumentalities.

As preaching is an intellectual and spiritual effort, it calls for a much higher education than the reading of the mass from a book. A comparison of the Protestant with the Roman or Greek clergy at once shows the difference.

2. In close connection with preaching is the stress laid on catechetical instruction. Of this we shall speak in a special section.

3. The Lord's Supper was restored to its primitive character as a commemoration of the atoning death of Christ, and a communion of believers with Him. In the Protestant system the holy communion is a sacrament, and requires the presence of the congregation; in the Roman system it is chiefly a sacrifice, and may be performed by the priest alone. The withdrawal of the cup is characteristic of the over-estimate of the clergy and under-estimate of the laity; and its restoration was not only in accordance with primitive usage, but required by the doctrine of the general priesthood of believers.

Luther retained the weekly communion as the conclusion of the regular service on the Lord's Day. In the Reformed churches it was made less frequent, but more solemn.

4. The divine service was popularized by substituting the

redner der älteren luth. *Kirche*, 1856 (pp. 30–36); G. Garnier, *Sur la predication de Luther*, Montauban, 1876; Thomas S. Hastings, *Luther as a Preacher*, in the "Luther Symposiac" by the Professors of the Union Theological Seminary, New York, 1883.

vernacular for the Latin language in prayer and song, — a change of incalculable consequence.

5. The number of church festivals was greatly reduced, and confined to those which commemorate the great facts of our salvation; namely, the incarnation (Christmas), the redemption (Palm Sunday, Good Friday, and Easter), and the outpouring of the Holy Spirit (Ascension and Pentecost), with the concluding festival of the Holy Trinity. They constitute the nucleus of the Christian year, and a sort of chronological creed for the people. The Lutheran Church retained also (at least in some sections) the feasts of the Virgin Mary, of the Apostles and Evangelists, and of All Saints; but they have gradually gone out of use.

Luther held that church festivals, and even the weekly sabbath, were abolished in principle, and observed only on account of the requirements of public worship and the weakness of the laity.[1] The righteous need no laws and ceremonies. To them all time is holy, every day a day of rest, and every day a day of good work. But "although," he says, "all days are free and alike, it is yet useful and good, yea, necessary, to keep holy one day, whether it be sabbath or Sunday or any other day; for God will govern the world orderly and peacefully; hence he gave six days for work, and the seventh for rest, that men should refresh themselves by rest, and hear the word of God."[2]

In this view all the Reformers substantially agree, including Calvin and Knox, except that the latter made practically less account of the annual festivals, and more of the weekly festival. The Anglo-American theory of the Lord's Day, which is based on the perpetual essential obligation of the Fourth Commandment, as a part of the moral law to be observed with Christian freedom in the light of Christ's res-

---

[1] "*Propter necessitatem Verbi Dei*" and "*propter infirmos.*"
[2] On Luther's views of Sunday, see his explanation of the third (fourth) commandment in his catechisms, and Köstlin, *Luthers Theologie*, II. 82 sqq.

urrection, is of Puritan origin at the close of the sixteenth century, and was first symbolically sanctioned by the Westminster standards in 1647, but has worked itself into the flesh and blood of all English-speaking Christendom to the great benefit of public worship and private devotion.[1]

§ 82. *Beginnings of Evangelical Hymnody.*

I. The "Wittenberg Enchiridion," 1524. The "Erfurt Enchiridion," 1524. Walter's "Gesangbuch," with preface by Luther, 1524. Klug's "Gesangbuch," by Luther, 1529, etc. Babst's "Gesangbuch," 1545, 5th ed. 1553. Spangenberg's "Cantiones ecclesiasticæ," 1545. See exact titles in Wackernagel's *Bibliographie*, etc.

II. C. v. WINTERFELD: *Luther's geistl. Lieder nebst Stimmweisen.* Leipz. 1840. PH. WACKERNAGEL: *Luther's geistl. Lieder u. Singweisen.* Stuttgart, 1848. Other editions of Luther's Hymns by STIP, 1854; SCHNEIDER, 1856; DREHER, 1857. B. PICK: *Luther as a Hymnist.* Philad. 1875. EMIL FROMMEL: *Luther's Lieder und Sprüche. Der singende Luther im Kranze seiner dichtenden und bildenden Zeitgenossen.* Berlin, 1883. (Jubilee ed. with illustrations from Dürer and Cranach.) L. W. BACON and N. H. ALLEN: *The Hymns of Luther set to their original melodies, with an English Version.* New York, 1883. E. ACHELIS: *Die Entstehungszeit v. Luther's geistl. Liedern.* Marburg, 1884. DANNEIL: *Luther's geistl. Lieder nach seinen drei Gesangbüchern von 1524, 1529, 1545.* Frankf.-a-M., 1885.

III. AUG. H. HOFFMANN VON FALLERSLEBEN: *Geschichte des deutschen Kirchenlieds bis auf Luther's Zeit.* Breslau, 1832; third ed., Hannover, 1861. F. A. CUNZ: *Gesch. des deutschen Kirchenlieds.* Leipz. 1855, 2 parts. JULIUS MÜTZELL: *Geistliche Lieder der evangelischen Kirche aus dem 16ten Jahrh. nach den ältesten Drucken.* Berlin, 1855, in 3 vols. (The same publ. afterwards *Geistl. Lieder der ev. K. aus dem 17ten und Anfang des 18ten Jahrh.* Braunschweig, 1858.) K. MÜLLENHOFF and W. SCHERER: *Denkmäler deutscher Poesie und Prosa aus dem 8ten bis 12ten Jahrh.* Berlin, 1864.

*EDUARD EMIL KOCH (d. 1871): *Geschichte des Kirchenlieds der christlichen, insbesondere der deutschen evangelischen Kirche.* Third ed. completed and enlarged by RICHARD LAUXMANN. Stuttgart, 1866–1876, in 8 vols. (The first ed. appeared in 1847; the second in 1852 and 1853, in 4 vols.) A very useful book for German hymnody.

[1] On the history of Sunday observance, see Hessey, *Sunday: its Origin, History,* etc. (Oxford, 1860); Gilfillan, *The Sabbath* (Edinb. 1861); and the author's essay on the *Christian Sabbath* in "Christ and Christianity" (New York and London, 1885, pp. 213–291).

*PHILIPP WACKERNAGEL (d. 1877): *Das deutsche Kirchenlied von Luther bis N. Hermann und A. Blaurer.* Stuttgart, 1842, in 2 vols. By the same: *Bibliographie zur Geschichte des deutschen Kirchenliedes im 16ten Jahrhundert.* Frankf.-a-M., 1855. *By the same: *Das deutsche Kirchenlied von der ältesten Zeit bis zu Anfang des XVII Jahrhunderts.* Leipzig, 1864–77, in 5 vols. (his chief work, completed by his two sons). A monumental work of immense industry and pains-taking accuracy, in a department where "pedantry is a virtue." Vol. I. contains Latin hymns, and from pp. 365–884 additions to the bibliography. The second and following vols. are devoted to German hymnody, including the mediæval (vol. II.).

*A. F. W. FISCHER: *Kirchenlieder-Lexicon. Hymnologisch-literarische Nachweisungen über 4,500 der wichtigsten und verbreitetsten Kirchenlieder aller Zeiten.* Gotha, 1878, '79, in 2 vols. K. SEVERIN MEISTER and WILHELM BÄUMKER (R. C.): *Das katholische deutsche Kirchenlied in seinen Singweisen von den frühesten Zeiten bis gegen Ende des 17ten Jahrh.* Freiburg-i.-B. 1862, 2d vol. by Bäumker, 1883. Devoted chiefly to the musical part.

On the hymnody of the Reformed churches of Switzerland and France in the sixteenth century, *Les Psaumes mis en rime française par Clément Marot et Theodore de Beze. Mis en musique à quatre parties par Claude Goudimel.* Genève, 1565. It contains 150 Psalms, Symeon's Song, a poem on the Decalogue, and 150 melodies, many of which were based on secular tunes, and found entrance into the Lutheran Church. A beautiful modern edition by O. DOUEN: *Clément Marot et le Psautier Huguenot.* Paris, 1878 and 1879, 2 vols. WEBER: *Geschichte des Kirchengesangs in der deutschen reformirten Schweiz seit der Reformation.* Zürich, 1876.

On the hymnody of the Bohemian and Moravian Brethren, see WACKERNAGEL'S large work, III. 229–350 (Nos. 255–417), and KOCH, *l.c.* II. 114–132.

Comp. the hymnological collections and discussions of RAMBACH, BUNSEN, KNAPP, DANIEL, J. P. LANGE, STIER, STIP, GEFFKEN, VILMAR, etc. Also SCHAFF'S sketch of "German Hymnology," and other relevant articles in the forthcoming "Dictionary of Hymnology," edited by J. JULIAN, to be published by J. Murray in London and Scribner in New York, 1889. This will be the best work in the English language on the origin and history of Christian hymns of all ages and nations.

The most valuable contribution which German Protestantism made to Christian worship is its rich treasury of hymns. Luther struck the key-note; the Lutheran Church followed with a luminous train of hymnists; the Reformed churches, first with metrical versions of the Psalms and appropriate tunes, afterwards with new Christian hymns.

The hymn in the strict sense of the term, as a popular religious lyric, or a lyric poem in praise of God or Christ to be sung by the congregation in public worship, was born in Germany and brought to maturity with the Reformation and with the idea of the general priesthood of believers. The Latin Church had prepared the way, and produced some of the grandest hymns which can never die, as the " Dies Iræ," the " Stabat mater," and the " Jesu dulcis memoria." But these and other Latin hymns and sequences of St. Hilary, St. Ambrose, Fortunatus, Notker, St. Bernard, St. Thomas Aquinas, Thomas a Celano, Jacobus de Benedictis, Adam of St. Victor, etc., were sung by priests and choristers, and were no more intelligible to the common people than the Latin Psalter and the Latin mass.[1] The reign of the Latin language in public worship, while it tended to preserve the unity of the church, and to facilitate literary intercourse, kept back the free development of a vernacular hymnody. Nevertheless, the native love of the Germans for poetry and song produced for private devotion a large number of sacred lyrics and versified translations of the Psalms and Latin hymns. As there were German Bibles before Luther's version, so there were also German hymns before his time ; but they were limited in use, and superseded by the superior products of the evangelical church. Philip Wackernagel (the most learned German hymnologist, and an enthusiastic admirer of Luther) gives in the second volume of his large collection no less than fourteen hundred and forty-eight German hymns and sequences, from Otfrid to Hans Sachs (inclusive) or from A. D. 868 to 1518. Nor was vernacular hymnody confined to Germany. St. Francis of Assisi composed the " Cantico del Sol," and Jacopone da Todi (the author of the " Stabat Mater ") those pas-

---

[1] On Greek and Latin hymnology and the literature, see Schaff, *Church History*, III. 575 sqq., and IV. 402 sqq. and 416 sqq.

sionate dithyrambic odes which "vibrate like tongues of fire," for private confraternities and domestic gatherings.[1]

German Hymnody before the Reformation.

In order to form a just estimate of German Protestant hymnody, we must briefly survey the mediæval German hymnody.

The first attempts of Teutonic church poetry are biblical epics, and the leader of the Teutonic Christ-singers is the Anglo-Saxon monk Cædmon of Whitby (formerly a swine-herd), about 680, who reproduced in alliterative verse, as by inspiration, the biblical history of creation and redemption, and brought it home to the imagination and heart of Old England.[2] This poem, which was probably brought to Germany by Bonifacius and other English missionaries, inspired in the ninth century a similar production of an unknown Saxon (Westphalian) monk, namely, a poetic gospel harmony or life of Christ under the title "Heliand" (i.e., *Heiland*, Healer, Saviour).[3] About the same time (*c.* 870), Otfrid of Weissenburg in the Alsace, a Benedictine monk, educated at Fulda and St. Gall, versified the gospel history in the Alemannian dialect, in fifteen hundred verses, divided into stanzas, each stanza consisting of four rhymed lines.[4]

These three didactic epics were the first vernacular Bibles for the laity among the Western barbarians.[5]

[1] Comp. Ozanam, *Les poetes Franciscains en Italie au* 13me *siècle.* Paris, 1852.

[2] Bouterweck, *Cædmon's des Angelsachsen biblische Dichtungen*, Elberfeld, 1849-54. Bosanquet, *The Fall of Man, or Paradise Lost of Cædmon, translated in verse from the Anglo-Saxon*, London, 1860.

[3] E. Sievers, *Der Heliand und die angelsächsische Genesis.* Halle, 1875.

[4] Flacius first edited Otfrid's *Evangelienbuch* (*Evangeliorum liber*), Bas. 1571. Recent editions by Graff, under the title *Krist*, Königsberg, 1831; and Kelle, *Otfrid's Evang.-buch*, Regensb. 1856 and 1859, 2 vols. Specimens in Wackernagel's *D. Kirchenlied* (the large work), vol. ii. 3-21. A translation into modern German by G. Rapp, Gotha, 1858.

[5] Comp. Hammerich, *Aelteste christliche Epik der Angelsachsen, Deutschen und Nordländer.* Translated from the Danish by Michelsen, 1874.

The lyric church poetry and music began with the "Kyrie Eleison" and "Christe Eleison," which passed from the Greek church into the Latin as a response of the people, especially on the high festivals, and was enlarged into brief poems called (from the refrain) *Kirleisen,* or *Leisen,* also *Leichen.* These enlarged cries for mercy are the first specimens of German hymns sung by the people. The oldest dates from the ninth century, called the "Leich vom heiligen Petrus," in three stanzas, the first of which reads thus in English : —

> "Our Lord delivered power to St. Peter,
> That he may preserve the man who hopes in Him.
> Lord, have mercy upon us!
> Christ, have mercy upon us!"[1]

One of the best and most popular of these *Leisen,* but of much later date, is the Easter hymn, —

> "*Christ is erstanden*
> *von der marter alle,*
> *des sul [sollen] wir alle fro sein,*
> *Christ sol unser trost sein.*
> *Kyrie leyson."*[2]

Penitential hymns in the vernacular were sung by the Flagellants (the *Geisslergesellschaften*), who in the middle of the fourteenth century, during a long famine and fearful pestilence (the "Black Death," 1348), passed in solemn processions with torches, crosses, and banners, through Germany

[1] Wackernagel, II. 22, published the whole hymn from a manuscript in Munich.

[2] Wackernagel, II. 43 sq., gives several forms. They were afterwards much enlarged. In a Munich manuscript of the fifteenth century, a Latin verse is coupled with the German: —

> "*Christus surrexit,*
> *mala nostra texit,*
> *et quos hic dilexit*
> *hos ad coelum vexit*
> *Kyrie leyson.*"

and other countries, calling upon the people to repent and to prepare for the judgment to come.[1]

Some of the best Latin hymns, as the "Te Deum," the "Gloria in excelsis," the "Pange lingua," the "Veni Creator Spiritus," the "Ave Maria," the "Stabat mater," the "Lauda, Sion, Salvatorem," St. Bernard's "Jesu dulcis memoria," and "Salve caput cruentatum," were repeatedly translated long before the Reformation. Sometimes the words of the original were curiously mixed with the vernacular, as in the Christmas hymn, —

> "*In dulci jubilo*
> *Nun singet und seit fro!*
> *Unsres Herzens Wonne*
> *Leit in præsepio*
> *Und leuchtet wie die Sonne*
> *In matris gremio*
> *Alpha es et O.*" [2]

A Benedictine monk, John of Salzburg, prepared a number of translations from the Latin at the request of his archbishop, Pilgrim, in 1366, and was rewarded by him with a parish.[3]

The "Minnesänger" of the thirteenth century — among whom Gottfried of Strassburg and Walther von der Vogelweide are the most eminent — glorified love, mingling the earthly and heavenly, the sexual and spiritual, after the model of Solomon's Song. The Virgin Mary was to them the type of pure, ideal womanhood. Walther cannot find epithets enough for her praise.

The mystic school of Tauler in the fourteenth century produced a few hymns full of glowing love to God. Tauler is the author of the Christmas poem, —

> "*Uns kommt ein Schiff geladen,*"

---

[1] See specimens in Koch, I. 194 sq., and in Wackernagel, II. 333 sqq.

[2] Several forms in Wackernagel, II. 483–486.

[3] Wackernagel (II. 409 sqq.) gives forty-three of his hymns from several manuscripts in the libraries at Munich and Vienna.

and of hymns of love to God, one of which begins, —

> *" Ich muss die Creaturen fliehen*
> *Und suchen Herzensinnigkeit,*
> *Soll ich den Geist zu Gotte ziehen,*
> *Auf dass er bleib in Reinigkeit."* [1]

The "Meistersänger" of the fifteenth century were, like the "Minnesänger," fruitful in hymns to the Virgin Mary. One of them begins, —

> *" Maria zart von edler Art*
> *Ein Ros ohn alle Dornen."*

From the middle ages have come down also some of the best tunes, secular and religious.[2]

The German hymnody of the middle ages, like the Latin, overflows with hagiolatry and Mariolatry. Mary is even clothed with divine attributes, and virtually put in the place of Christ, or of the Holy Spirit, as the fountain of all grace. The most pathetic of Latin hymns, the "Stabat mater dolorosa," which describes with overpowering effect the piercing agony of Mary at the cross, and the burning desire of being identified with her in sympathy, is disfigured by Mariolatry, and therefore unfit for evangelical worship without some omissions or changes. The great and good Bonaventura, who wrote the Passion hymn, "Recordare sanctæ crucis," applied the whole Psalter to the Virgin in his "Psalterium B. Mariæ," or Marian Psalter, where the name of Mary is substituted for that of the Lord. It was also translated into German, and repeatedly printed.[3]

---

[1] Wackernagel, II. 302 sqq.; Koch, I. 191.

[2] Meister and Bäumker, in the *Katholische deutsche Kirchenlied in seinen Singweisen*, give a collection of these Catholic tunes, partly from unpublished manuscript sources. They acknowledge, however, the great merit of the Protestant hymnologists who have done the pioneer work in mediæval church poetry and music, especially Winterfeld and Wackernagel.

[3] Wackernagel, in his *Bibliogr.*, p. 454 sqq., gives extracts from an edition printed at Nürnberg, 1521.

"Through all the centuries from Otfrid to Luther" (says Wackernagel),[1] "we meet with the idolatrous veneration of the Virgin Mary. There are hymns which teach that she pre-existed with God at the creation, that all things were created in her and for her, and that God rested in her on the seventh day." One of the favorite Mary-hymns begins, —

> *"Dich, Frau vom Himmel, ruf ich an,*
> *In diesen grossen Nöthen mein."* [2]

Hans Sachs afterwards characteristically changed it into

> *"Christum vom Himmel ruf ich an."*

The mediæval hymnody celebrates Mary as the queen of heaven, as the "eternal womanly," which draws man insensibly heavenward.[3] It resembles the Sixtine Madonna who carries the Christ-child in her arms.

German Hymnody of the Reformation.

The evangelical church substituted the worship of Christ, as our only Mediator and Advocate, for the worship of his virgin-mother. It reproduced and improved the old Latin and vernacular hymns and tunes, and produced a larger number of original ones. It introduced congregational singing in the place of the chanting of priests and choirs. The hymn became, next to the German Bible and the German sermon, the most powerful missionary of the evangelical doctrines of sin and redemption, and accompanied the Reformation in its triumphal march. Printed as tracts, the hymns were scattered wide and far, and sung in the house, the school, the church, and on the street. Many of them survive to this day, and kindle the flame of devotion.

---

[1] II. p. xiii.; compare Nos. 222, 226, 728, 870, 876.

[2] Wackernagel, II. 799 sqq., gives this hymn in several forms. It was sung on the feast of the Nativity of Mary, and at other times.

[3] I allude, of course, to the mystic conclusion of the second part of Goethe's *Faust :* —

> *"Das Ewig-Weibliche zieht uns hinan."*

To Luther belongs the extraordinary merit of having given to the German people in their own tongue, and in a form eclipsing and displacing all former versions, the Bible, the catechism, and the hymn-book, so that God might speak directly to them in His word, and that they might directly speak to Him in their songs. He was a musician also, and composed tunes to some of his hymns.[1] He is the Ambrose of German church poetry and church music. He wrote thirty-seven hymns.[2] Most of them (twenty-one) date from the year 1524; the first from 1523, soon after the completion of his translation of the New Testament; the last two from 1543, three years before his death. The most original and best known, — we may say the most Luther-like and most Reformer-like — is that heroic battle- and victory-hymn of the Reformation, which has so often been reproduced in other languages, and resounds in all German lands with mighty effect on great occasions : —

> " *Ein' feste Burg ist unser Gott.*"
> (A tower of strength is this our God.)[3]

This mighty poem is based upon the forty-sixth Psalm (*Deus noster refugium et virtus*) which furnished the key-note. It was born of deep tribulation and conquering faith, in the

---

[1] According to Koch (I. 470), Luther is *certainly* the author of the tunes to " *Ein feste Burg,*" and to " *Jesaja dem Propheten das geschah,*" and *probably* of six more; the tunes to the other Luther-hymns are of older or of uncertain origin.

[2] Wackernagel, III. 1–31, gives fifty-four Luther-poems, including the variations, and some which cannot be called hymns, as the praise of " *Frau Musica,*" and " *Wider Herzog Heinrich von Braunschweig.*"

[3] Carlyle's translation, —

> " A safe stronghold our God is still,"

is upon the whole the best because of its rugged vigor and martial ring. Heine called this hymn the Marseillaise of the Reformation; but it differs as widely from the Marseillaise as the German Reformation differs from the godless French Revolution.

disastrous year 1527 (not 1521, or 1529, or 1530), and appeared first in print in 1528.[1]

Luther availed himself with his conservative tact of all existing helps for the benefit of public worship and private devotion. Most of his hymns and tunes rest on older foundations partly Latin, partly German. Some of them were inspired by Hebrew Psalms. To these belong, besides "Ein feste Burg" (Ps. 46), the following: —

> "*Aus tiefer Noth schrei ich zu dir*" (1523).
> (Out of the depths I cry to Thee. Ps. 130.)

> "*Ach Gott, vom Himmel sieh darein*" (1523).
> (Help, Lord, look down from heaven above. Ps. 12.)

On the second chapter of Luke, which is emphatically the gospel of children, are based his truly childlike Christmas songs, —

> "*Vom Himmel hoch da komm ich her*" (1535),
> (From heaven high to earth I come,)

and

> "*Vom Himmel kam der Engel Schaar*" (1543).
> (From heaven came the angel hosts.)

[1] The hymn appears in Joseph Klug's *Gesangbuch* of 1529 (and in a hymn-book of Augsburg, 1529), and to that year it is assigned by Wackernagel (III. 20), Koch, and also by Köstlin in the first ed. of his large biography of M. Luther (1875, vol. II. 127), as a protest against the Diet of Speier held in that year. But since the discovery of an older print apparently from February, 1528, Köstlin has changed his view in favor of 1527, the year of the pestilence and Luther's severest spiritual and physical trials. He says (*l.c.* II. 182, second and third ed.): "*Aus jener schwersten Zeit, welche Luther bis Ende des Jahres 1527 durchzumachen hatte, ist wohl das gewaltigste seiner Lieder, das 'Ein feste Burg ist unser Gott,' hervorgegangen.*" Schneider (1856) first fixed upon Nov. 1, 1527, as the birthday of this hymn from internal reasons, and Knaake (1881) added new ones. The deepest griefs and highest faith often meet. Justinus Kerner sings: —

> "*Poesie ist tiefes Schmerzen,*
> *Und es kommt das schönste Lied*
> *Nur aus einem Menschenherzen,*
> *Das ein tiefes Leid durchglüht.*"

Others are free reproductions of Latin hymns, either directly from the original, or on the basis of an older German version: as, —

"*Herr Gott, dich loben wir*" (1543).
(*Te Deum laudamus.*)

"*Komm, Gott, Schöpfer, heiliger Geist*" (1524).
(*Veni, Creator Spiritus.*)

"*Nun komm, der Heiden Heiland*" (1524).
(*Veni, Redemptor gentium.*)

"*Gelobet séist du, Jesus Christ*" (1524).
(*Grates nunc omnes reddamus.*)

"*Mitten wir im Leben sind*" (1524).
(*Media vita in morte sumus.*)

"*Nun bitten wir den heiligen Geist*" (1524).
(Now we pray to the Holy Ghost.)

"*Christ lag in Todesbanden*" (1524).
(In the bonds of death He lay.)
("*Surrexit Christus hodie.*")[1]

Among his strictly original hymns are, —

"*Nun freut euch, lieben Christen g'mein*" (1523).
(Rejoice, rejoice, dear flock of Christ.)

[1] The third stanza of this resurrection hymn is very striking: —

"*Es war ein wunderlicher Krieg,*
Da Tod und Leben rungen:
Das Leben das behielt den Sieg,
Es hat den Tod verschlungen.
Die Schrift hat verkündet das,
Wie da ein Tod den andern frass,
Ein Spott aus dem Tod ist worden.
Hallelujah!"

(That was a wondrous war, I trow,
　　When Life and Death together fought;
But Life hath triumphed o'er his foe.
　　Death is mocked and set at naught.
'Tis even as the Scripture saith,
　　Christ through death hath conquered Death.)

Bunsen calls this "the first (?) voice of German church-song, which flashed with the power of lightning through all German lands, in praise of the eternal decree of redemption of the human race and of the gospel of freedom."

> "*Erhalt uns Herr bei deinem Wort,*
> *Und steur des Papsts und Türken Mord*" (1541).

This is directed against the Pope and the Turk, as the chief enemies of Christ and his church in Luther's days.[1]

The stirring song of the two evangelical proto-martyrs at Brussels in 1523, —

> "*Ein neues Lied wir heben an,*" —

is chronologically his first, and not a hymn in the proper sense of the term, but had an irresistible effect, especially the tenth stanza, —

> "*Die Asche will nicht lassen ab,*
> *Sie staübt in allen Landen,*
> *Hie hilft kein Bach, Loch, Grub noch **Grab**,*
> *Sie macht den Feind zu Schanden.*
> *Die er im Leben durch den Mord,*
> *Zu schweigen hat gedrungen*
> *Die muss er todt an allem Ort*
> *Mit aller Stimm und Zungen*
> *Gar frölich lassen singen.*"[2]

(Their ashes will not rest and lie,
But scattered far and near,
Stream, dungeon, bolt, and grave defy,
Their foeman's shame and fear.
Those whom alive the tyrant's wrongs
To silence could subdue,
He must, when dead, let sing the songs
And in all languages and tongues
Resound the wide world through.)

[1] The second line, which was very offensive to the Papists, is changed in most modern hymnbooks into, —

> "*Und steure aller Feinde Mord.*"

[2] See the whole in Wackernagel, III. 3, 4. Thomas Fuller says of the ashes of Wiclif, that the brook Swift, into which they were cast (1428), "conveyed them into the Avon, the Avon into Severn, Severn into the narrow seas, they into the main ocean; and thus the ashes of Wiclif are the emblems of his doctrine, which now is dispersed all the world over."

Luther's hymns are characterized, like those of St. Ambrose, by simplicity and strength, and a popular churchly tone. But, unlike those of St. Ambrose and the Middle Ages, they breathe the bold, confident, joyful spirit of justifying faith, which was the beating heart of his theology and piety.

Luther's hymns passed at once into common use in church and school, and sung the Reformation into the hearts of the people. Hans Sachs of Nürnberg saluted him as the nightingale of Wittenberg.[1] How highly his contemporaries thought of them, may be inferred from Cyriacus Spangenberg, likewise a hymnist, who said in his preface to the "Cithara Lutheri" (1569): "Of all master-singers since the days of the apostles, Luther is the best. In his hymns you find not an idle or useless word. The rhymes are easy and good, the words choice and proper, the meaning clear and intelligible, the melodies lovely and hearty, and, *in summa,* all is so rare and majestic, so full of pith and power, so cheering and comforting, that you will not find his equal, much less his master."

Before Luther's death (1546), there appeared no less than forty-seven Lutheran hymn- and tune-books. The first German evangelical hymn-book, the so-called "Wittenberg Enchiridion," was printed in the year 1524, and contained eight hymns, four of them by Luther, three by Speratus, one by an unknown author. The "Erfurt Enchiridion" of the same year numbered twenty-five hymns, of which eighteen were from Luther. The hymn-book of Walther, also of 1524, contained thirty-two German and five Latin hymns, with a preface of Luther. Klug's Gesangbuch by Luther, Wittenberg, 1529, had fifty (twenty-eight of Luther); Babst's of 1545 (printed at Leipzig), eighty-nine; and the fifth edition of 1553, a hundred and thirty-one hymns.[2]

---

[1] "*Die wittenbergisch Nachtigall,*
Die man jetzt höret überall."

[2] See Koch, I. 246 sqq., and Wackernagel's *Bibliographie,* p. 66 sqq.

This rapid increase of hymns and hymn-books continued after Luther's death. We can only mention the names of the principal hymnists who were inspired by his example.

Justus Jonas (1493–1555), Luther's friend and colleague, wrote, —

> " *Wo Gott, der Herr, nicht bei uns hält* " (Ps. 124).
> (If God were not upon our side.)

Paul Ebert (1511–1569), the faithful assistant of Melanchthon, and professor of Hebrew in Wittenberg, is the author of

> " *Wenn wir in höchsten Nöthen sein,* "
> (When in the hour of utmost need,)

and

> " *Herr Jesu Christ, wahr'r Mensch und Gott.* "
> (Lord Jesus Christ, true man and God.)

Burkhard Waldis of Hesse (1486–1551) versified the Psalter.

Erasmus Alber (d. in Mecklenburg, 1553) wrote twenty hymns which Herder and Gervinus thought almost equal to Luther's.

Lazarus Spengler of Nürnberg (1449–1534) wrote about 1522 a hymn on sin and redemption, which soon became very popular, although it is didactic rather than poetic : —

> " *Durch Adam's Fall ist ganz verderbt.* "

Hans Sachs (1494–1576), the shoemaker-poet of Nürnberg, was the most fruitful "Meistersänger" of that period, and wrote some spiritual hymns as well; but only one of them is still in use : —

> " *Warum betrübst du dich, mein Herz ?* "
> (Why doest thou vex thyself, my heart ?)

Veit Dietrich, pastor of St. Sebaldus in Nürnberg (d. 1549), wrote : —

> " *Bedenk, o Mensch, die grosse Gnad.* "
> (Remember, man, the wondrous grace.)

Markgraf Albrecht of Brandenburg (d. 1557), is the author of : —

> "*Was mein Gott will, gescheh allzeit.*"
> (Thy will, my God, be always done.)

Paul Speratus, his court-chaplain at Königsberg (d. 1551), contributed three hymns to the first German hymn-book (1524), of which —

> "*Es ist das Heil uns kommen her*"
> (To us salvation now has come)

is the best, though more didactic than lyric, and gives rhymed expression to the doctrine of justification by faith.

Schneesing's

> "*Allein zu dir, Herr Jesu Christ*"
> (To Thee alone, Lord Jesus Christ)

appeared first in 1545, and is used to this day.

Mathesius, the pupil and biographer of Luther, and pastor at Joachimsthal in Bohemia (1504–65), wrote a few hymns. Nicolaus Hermann, his cantor and friend (d. 1561), is the author of a hundred and seventy-six hymns, especially for children, and composed popular tunes. Nicolaus Decius, first a monk, then an evangelical pastor at Stettin (d. 1541), reproduced the *Gloria in Excelsis* in his well-known

> "*Allein Gott in der Höh sei Ehr*" (1526),

and the eucharistic *Agnus Dei* in his

> "*O Lamm Gottes unschuldig*" (1531).

He also composed the tunes.

The German hymnody of the Reformation period was enriched by hymns of the Bohemian Brethren. Two of them, Michael Weisse (d. 1542) and Johann Horn, prepared free translations. Weisse was a native German, but joined the Brethren, and was sent by them as a delegate to Luther in 1522, who at first favored them before they showed their preference for the Reformed doctrine of the sacraments. One of the best known of these Bohemian hymns is the Easter song (1531) : —

" Christus ist erstanden."
(Christ the Lord is risen.)

We cannot follow in detail the progress of German hymnody. It flows from the sixteenth century down to our days in an unbroken stream, and reflects German piety in the sabbath dress of poetry. It is by far the richest of all hymnodies.[1]

The number of German hymns cannot fall short of one hundred thousand. Dean Georg Ludwig von Hardenberg of Halberstadt, in the year 1786, prepared a hymnological catalogue of the first lines of 72,733 hymns (in five volumes preserved in the library of Halberstadt). This number was not complete at that time, and has considerably increased since. About ten thousand have become more or less popular, and passed into different hymn-books. Fischer[2] gives the first lines of about five thousand of the best, many of which were overlooked by Von Hardenberg.

We may safely say that nearly one thousand of these hymns are classical and immortal. This is a larger number than can be found in any other language.

To this treasury of German song, several hundred men and women, of all ranks and conditions, — theologians and pastors, princes and princesses, generals and statesmen, physicians and jurists, merchants and travelers, laborers and private persons, — have made contributions, laying them on the common altar of devotion. The majority of German hymnists are Lutherans, the rest German Reformed (as Neander and

[1] It is characteristic of the voluminous Ultramontane work of Janssen, that it has not a word to say about the hymnological enrichment of public worship and Christian piety by Luther and his followers.

[2] In his *Kirchenlieder-Lexicon*, 1878.

Tersteegen), or Moravians (Zinzendorf and Gregor), or belong to the United Evangelical Church. Many of these hymns, and just those possessed of the greatest vigor and unction, full of the most exulting faith and the richest comfort, had their origin amid the conflicts and storms of the Reformation, or the fearful devastations and nameless miseries of the Thirty Years' War; others belong to the revival period of the pietism of Spener, and the Moravian Brotherhood of Zinzendorf, and reflect the earnest struggle after holiness, the fire of the first love, and the sweet enjoyment of the soul's intercourse with her heavenly Bridegroom; not a few of them sprang up even in the cold and prosy age of "illumination" and rationalism, like flowers from dry ground, or Alpine roses on fields of snow; others, again, proclaim, in fresh and joyous tones, the dawn of reviving faith in the land where the Reformation had its birth. Thus these hymns constitute a book of devotion and poetic confession of faith for German Protestantism, a sacred band which encircles its various periods, an abiding memorial of its struggles and victories, its sorrows and joys, a mirror of its deepest experiences, and an eloquent witness for the all-conquering and invincible life-power of the evangelical Christian faith.

The treasures of German hymnody have enriched the churches of other tongues, and passed into Swedish, Norwegian, Danish, French, Dutch, and modern English and American hymn-books.

John Wesley was the first of English divines who appreciated its value; and while his brother Charles produced an immense number of original hymns, John freely reproduced several hymns of Paul Gerhardt, Tersteegen, and Zinzendorf. The English Moravian hymn-book as revised by Montgomery contains about a thousand abridged (but mostly indifferent) translations from the German. In more recent times several accomplished writers, male and female, have vied with each other in translations and transfusions of German hymns.

Among the chief English translators are Miss Frances Eliza-
beth Cox;[1] Arthur Tozer Russell;[2] Richard Massie;[3] Miss
Catherine Winkworth;[4] Mrs. Eric Findlater and her sister,
Miss Jane Borthwick, of the Free Church of Scotland, who
modestly conceal their names under the letters "H. L. L."
(Hymns from the Land of Luther);[5] James W. Alexander,[6]

[1] *Sacred Hymns from the German*, London, 1841, new ed. with German
text, 1865.

[2] *Psalms and Hymns, partly original, partly selected, for the use of the
Church of England*, Cambridge, 1851. Many of the pieces are from the
German. He contributed most of the translations to Ernest Bunsen's
Hymns for Public Worship and Private Devotion, London, 1848.

[3] *Luther's Spiritual Songs*, London, 1854; and *Lyra Domestica*, translations from *Spitta's Psaltery and Harp*, London, 1860; second series, 1864.

[4] *Lyra Germanica*, first and second series, Lond. and N. Y., 1855 and 1858,
in several editions. Also the beautiful *Chorale Book for England*, London,
1863, which contains many hymns from the *Lyra Germanica*, partly re-
modelled, with seventy-two others translated by the same lady, together with
the old tunes edited by Bennet and Goldschmidt. Several translations of
Miss C. W., especially from Paul Gerhardt, have passed into hymn-books.
Comp. Theo. Kübler, *Historical Notices to the Lyra Germanica* (dedicated
to Miss C. W.), London, 1865.

[5] *Hymns from the Land of Luther, translated from the German by H. L. L.*,
Edinburgh and New York, in 4 parts, 1854; fifth ed., Edinb. 1884 (15th thousand), enlarged by the *Alpine Lyrics* of Mrs. Meta Heusser. The translations of Miss Borthwick reproduce the spirit rather than the letter of the
original. Several of them have become more widely known through hymn-
books and private collections: as Franck's eucharistic hymn, "*Schmücke
dich, o liebe Seele*," "Soul, arise, dispel thy sadness;" Gerhardt's "*Ich bin
ein Gast auf Erden*," "A pilgrim and a stranger, I journey here below;"
Tersteegen's "*Gott rufet noch*," "God calling yet;" Schmolck's "*Mein
Jesu, wie Du willst, So lass mich allzeit wollen*," "My Jesus, as Thou wilt;"
Zinzendorf's "*Jesu, geh voran*," "Jesus, still lead on;" Spitta's "*Was
macht ihr, dass ihr weinet*," "What mean ye by this wailing," and his
"Angel of Patience" (*Es zieht ein stiller Engel*," "A gentle angel walketh
throughout this world of woe"); Lange's "*Was kein Auge hat gesehen*,"
"What no human eye hath seen;" Mrs. Heusser's "*Noch ein wenig Schweiss
und Thränen*," "A few more conflicts, toils and tears;" "*O Jesu Christ,
mein Leben*," "O Christ, my Life, my Saviour;" besides other religious
lyrics which are not intended for hymns. Miss Borthwick has since published *Lyra Christiana, a Treasury of Sacred Poetry, edited by H. L. L.*,
Edinb. 1888, which contains a few German poems, but is mostly selected
from English sources.

[6] Presbyterian minister in New York City, died 1859. He is the best
translator of Gerhardt's "*O Haupt voll Blut und Wunden*" ("O sacred
Head, now wounded"), and several other famous hymns, German and Latin.

Henry Mills,[1] John Kelly,[2] not to mention many others who have furnished admirable translations of one or more hymns for public or private hymnological collections.[3]

English and American hymnody began much later than the German, but comes next to it in fertility, is enriching itself constantly by transfusions of Greek, Latin, and German, as well as by original hymns, and may ultimately surpass all hymnodies.

§ 83. *Common Schools.*

LUTHER: *An die Rathsherren aller Städte deutschen Landes, dass sie christ-liche Schulen aufrichten und halten sollen.* Wittenberg, 1524. The book appeared in the same year in Latin (*De constituendis scholis*), with a preface of Melanchthon, the probable translator, at Hagenau. In WALCH, x. 533; in the Erlangen. ed., xxii. 168–199.

Church and school go together. The Jewish synagogue was a school. Every Christian church is a school of piety and virtue for old and young. The mediæval church was the civilizer and instructor of the barbarians, founded the convent and cathedral schools, and the great universities of Paris (1209), Bologna, Padua, Oxford, Cambridge, St. Andrews, Glasgow, Salamanca, Alcala, Toledo, Prague (1348), Vienna (1365), Heidelberg (1386), Cologne (1388), Erfurt (1393), Leipzig (1409), Basel (1460), Ingolstadt (1472), Tübingen (1477), Wittenberg (1502), etc. But education in the middle ages was aristocratic, and confined to the clergy and a very few laymen of the higher classes. The common people were ignorant and superstitious, and could neither

His translations were first published in Schaff's " Kirchenfreund" for 1849–'51 (with the originals), then in the " Mercersburg Review" for 1869, pp. 304 sqq., 414 sqq., and have since passed into many American hymn-books.

[1] *Horae Germanicæ*, Auburn and New York, 1845, 2d ed. 1856. Mills was professor of biblical criticism in the Presbyterian Theol. Seminary at Auburn, N.Y., and died 1867.

[2] *Paul Gerhardt's Spiritual Songs*, London, 1867.

[3] *e. g.*, for Schaff's *Christ in Song*, New York, 1868, and London, 1870. In my German Hymn-book (Philad. 1859, revised and enlarged ed., 1874), I have noted the English translations as far as I knew them.

read nor write. Even noblemen signed their name with a cross. Books were rare and dear. The invention of the printing-press prepared the way for popular education. The Reformation first utilized the press on a large scale, and gave a powerful impulse to common schools. The genius of Protestantism favors the general diffusion of knowledge. It elevates the laity, emancipates private judgment, and stimulates the sense of personal responsibility. Every man should be trained to a position of Christian freedom and self-government.

Luther discussed this subject first in his Address to the German Nobility (1520). In 1524 he wrote a special book in which he urged the civil magistrates of all the cities of Germany to improve their schools, or to establish new ones for boys and girls; this all the more since the zeal for monastic institutions had declined, and the convents were fast getting empty. He wisely recommended that a portion of the property of churches and convents be devoted to this purpose, instead of being wasted on secular objects, or on avaricious princes and noblemen. He makes great account of the study of languages, and skillfully refutes the objections. A few extracts will give the best idea of this very useful little book on a most important subject.

"Grace and peace from God our Father, and the Lord Jesus Christ. . . . Although I am now excommunicated for three years, and should keep silent if I feared men more than God, . . . I will speak as long as I live, until the righteousness of Christ shall break forth in its glory. . . . I beg you all, my dear lords and friends, for God's sake to take care of the poor youth, and thereby to help us all. So much money is spent year after year for arms, roads, dams, and innumerable similar objects, why should not as much be spent for the education of the poor youth? . . . The word of God is now heard in Germany more than ever before. But if we do not show our gratitude for it, we run the risk of sinking back into a worse darkness.

"Dear Germans, buy while the market is at the door. Gather while the sun shines and the weather is good. Use God's grace and word while it is at hand. For you must know that God's grace and word is a travelling shower, which does not return where once it has been. It was once with the Jews, but gone is gone (*hin ist hin*); now they have nothing. Paul brought it into Greece, but gone is gone; now they have the Turk. Rome and Italy have also had it, but gone is gone; they have now the Pope. And ye Germans must not think that you will have it forever; for ingratitude and contempt will not let it abide. Therefore, seize and hold fast, whoever can.

"It is a sin and shame that we should need to be admonished to educate our children, when nature itself, and even the example of the heathen, urge us to do so. . . . You say, the parents should look to that, it is none of the business of counselors and magistrates. But how, if the parents neglect it? Most of the parents are incapable; having themselves learnt nothing, they cannot teach their children. Others have not the time. And what shall become of the orphans? The glory of a town consists not in treasure, strong walls, and fine houses, but in fine, educated, well-trained citizens. The city of old Rome trained her sons in Latin and Greek and all the fine arts. . . .

"We admit, you say, there should and must be schools, but what is the use of teaching Latin, Greek, and Hebrew, and other liberal arts? Could we not teach, in German, the Bible and God's word, which are sufficient for salvation? Answer: Yes, I well know, alas! that we Germans must ever be and abide brutes and wild beasts, as the surrounding nations call us, and as we well deserve to be called. But I wonder why you never say, Of what use are silks, wines, spices, and other foreign articles, seeing we have wine, corn, wool, flax, wood, and stones, in German lands, not only an abundance for sustenance, but also a choice and selection for elegance and ornament? The arts and languages, which do us no harm, nay, which are a greater ornament, benefit, honor, and advantage, both for understanding Holy Writ, and for managing civil affairs, we are disposed to despise; and foreign wares, which are neither necessary nor useful to us, and which, moreover, peel us to the very bone, these we are not willing to forego. Are we not deserving to be called German fools and beasts ? . . .

"Much as we love the gospel, let us hold fast to the languages. God gave us the Scriptures in two languages, the Old Testament in Hebrew, the New Testament in Greek. Therefore we should honor them above all other languages. . . . And let us remember that we shall not be able to keep the gospel without the languages. The languages are the sheath in which this sword of the Spirit is hid. They are the casket in which this treasure is kept. They are the vessels in which this drink is contained; they are the storehouse in which this food is laid by; and, as the gospel itself shows, they are the baskets in which these loaves and fishes and fragments are preserved. Yea, if we should so err as to let the languages go (which God forbid!), we shall not only lose the gospel, but it will come to pass at length that we shall not be able to speak or write correctly either Latin or German. . . .

"Herewith I commend you all to the grace of God. May He soften and kindle your hearts so that they shall earnestly take the part of these poor, pitiable, forsaken youth, and, through Divine aid, counsel and help them to a happy and Christian ordering of the German land as to body and soul with all fullness and overflow, to the praise and honor of God the Father, through Jesus Christ, our Saviour. Amen."

The advice of Luther was not unheeded. Protestant nations are far ahead of the Roman Catholic in popular education. In Germany and Switzerland there is scarcely a Protestant boy or girl that cannot read and write; while in some papal countries, even to this day, the majority of the people are illiterate.[1]

§ 84. *Reconstruction of Church Government and Discipline.*

AEMIL LUDW. RICHTER: *Die evangel. Kirchenordnungen des 16 Jahrh.*, Weimar, 1846, 2 vols. By the same: *Gesch. der evang. Kirchenverfassung in Deutschland.* Leipz., 1851. By the same: *Lehrbuch des kath. und evang. Kirchenrechts,* Leipzig, 5th ed., 1858. J. W. F. HÖFLING: *Grundsätze der evang.-lutherischen Kirchenverfassung.* Erlangen, third ed., 1853. STAHL: *Die Kirchenverfassung nach Recht und Lehre der Protestanten.* Erlangen, 1862. MEJER: *Grundl. des luth. Kirchenregiments,* Rostock, 1864. E. FRIEDBERG: *Lehrbuch des kath. u. evang. Kirchenrechts,* Leipz., 1884.

The papal monarchy and visible unity of Western Christendom were destroyed with the burning of the Pope's bull and the canon law. The bishops refused to lead the new movement; disorder and confusion followed. A reconstruction of government and discipline became necessary. The idea of an invisible church of all believers was not available for this purpose. The invisible is not governable. The question was, how to deal with the visible church as it existed in Saxony and other Protestant countries, and to

---

[1] In Spain, once the richest and proudest monarchy of Europe, sixty per cent of the adult population could not read in 1877, according to the official census. Compare this with the educational statistics of Prussia, which in the sixteenth century was a poor, semi-barbarous principality. The contrast between North America and South America in point of popular education is still more striking.

bring order out of chaos.   The lawyers had to be consulted,
and they could not dispense with the legal wisdom and
experience of centuries.   Luther himself returned to the
study of the canon law, though to little purpose.[1] He hated
it for its connection with popery, and got into conflict with
the lawyers, even his colleague, Professor Schurf, who had
accompanied him to the Diet of Worms as a faithful friend
and counselor, but differed from him on matrimonial legislation.   He abused the lawyers, even from the pulpit, as
abettors of the Pope and the Devil.[2] He was not a disciplinarian and organizer like John Calvin, or John Knox, or
John Wesley, and left his church in a less satisfactory condition than the Reformed churches of Switzerland and Scotland.   He complained that he had not the proper persons
for what he wished to accomplish; but he did what he could
under the circumstances, and regretted that he could do no
more.

Four ways were open for the construction of an evangelical church polity : —

1. To retain the episcopal hierarchy, without the papacy,
or to create a new one in its place.   This was done in the
Lutheran churches of Scandinavia, and in the Church of
England, but in the closest connection with the state, and
in subordination to it.   In Scandinavia the succession was
broken; in England the succession continued under the lead
of Cranmer as Archbishop of Canterbury, was interrupted
under Queen Mary, and restored under Queen Elizabeth.

Had the German bishops favored the Reformation, they
would, no doubt, have retained their power in Germany, and
naturally taken the lead in the organization of the new

---

[1] Letter to Spalatin, March 30, 1529 (De Wette, III. 433): "*Jura papistica
legere incipimus et inspicere.*"

[2] Comp. A. Kohler, *Luther und die Juristen*, Gotha, 1873; Köstlin, *M.
Luth.*, II. 476 sqq., 580 sq. In his *Table Talk* (Erl. ed., LXII. 214 sqq.),
Luther has much to say against the lawyers, and thinks that few of them
will be saved. "*Ein frommer Jurist*," he says, "*ist ein seltsames Thier.*"

church. Melanchthon was in favor of episcopacy, and even a sort of papacy by human (not Divine) right, on condition of evangelical freedom; but the hostility of the hierarchy made its authority impossible in Germany.[1] He had, especially in his later years, a stronger conception of the institutional character and historical order of the church than Luther, who cared nothing for bishops. He taught, however, the original equality of bishops and presbyters (appealing to the Pastoral Epistles and to Jerome); and held that when the regular bishops reject the gospel, and refuse to ordain evangelical preachers, the power of ordination returns to the church and the pastors.

2. To substitute a lay episcopate for the clerical episcopate; in other words, to lodge the supreme ecclesiastical power in the hands of the civil magistrate, who appoints ministers, superintendents, and church counselors as executive officers.

This was done in the Lutheran churches of Germany. The superintendents performed episcopal duties, but without constituting a distinct and separate grade of the ministry, and without the theory of the episcopal or apostolical succession. The Lutheran Church holds the Presbyterian doctrine of the parity of ministers.[2] The organization of the Lutheran churches was, however, for a number of years regarded as provisional, and kept open for a possible reconciliation with the episcopate. Hence the princes were called *Nothbischöfe*.

3. To organize a presbyterian polity on the basis of the

---

[1] *Apol. Conf. Aug.*, Art. XIV. (Müller's ed. of the Lutheran symbols, p. 205): "*Nos summa voluntate cupere conservare politiam ecclesiasticam et gradus in ecclesia, factos etiam humana auctoritate.*" He subscribed the Smalcald Articles (1537), with a clause in favor of a limited papal supervision.

[2] See the Appendix to the Smalcald Articles, which have symbolical authority, on the Power and Primacy of the Pope (Müller's ed., p. 341): "*Quum jure divino non sint diversi gradus episcopi et pastoris manifestum est ordinationem a pastore in sua ecclesia factam jure divino ratam esse. Itaque cum episcopi ordinarii fiunt hostes ecclesiæ aut nolunt impartire ordinationem, ecclesiæ retinent jus suum.*"

parity of ministers, congregational lay-elders, and deacons, and a representative synodical government, with strict discipline, and a distinction between nominal and communicant membership. This was attempted in Hesse at the Synod of Homberg (1526) by Lambert (a pupil of Zwingli and Luther), developed by Calvin in Geneva, and carried out in the Reformed churches of France, Holland, Scotland, and the Presbyterian churches of North America. Luther rather discouraged this plan in a letter to Philip of Hesse; but in 1540 he expressed a wish, with Jonas, Bugenhagen, and Melanchthon, to introduce Christian discipline with the aid of elders (*seniores*) in each congregation. Several Lutheran Church constitutions exclude adulterers, drunkards, and blasphemers from the communion.

4. Congregational independency; i.e., the organization of self-governing congregations of true believers in free association with each other. This was once suggested by Luther, but soon abandoned without a trial. It appeared in isolated attempts under Queen Elizabeth, and was successfully developed in the seventeenth century by the Independents in England, and the Congregationalists in New England.

The last two ways are more thoroughly Protestant and consistent with the principle of the general priesthood of believers; but they presuppose a higher grade of self-governing capacity in the laity than the episcopal polity.

All these forms of government admit of a union with the state (as in Europe), or a separation from the state (as in America). Union of church and state was the traditional system since the days of Constantine and Charlemagne, and was adhered to by all the Reformers. They had no idea of a separation; they even brought the two powers into closer relationship by increasing the authority of the state over the church. Separation of the two was barely mentioned by Luther, as a private opinion, we may say almost as a prophetic dream, but was soon abandoned as an impossibility.

Luther, in harmony with his unique personal experience, made the doctrine of justification the cardinal truth of Christianity, and believed that the preaching of that doctrine would of itself produce all the necessary changes in worship and discipline. But the abuse of evangelical freedom taught him the necessity of discipline, and he raised his protest against antinomianism. His complaints of the degeneracy of the times increased with his age and his bodily infirmities. The world seemed to him to be getting worse and worse, and fast rushing to judgment. He was so disgusted with the immorality prevailing among the citizens and students at Wittenberg, that he threatened to leave the town altogether in 1544, but yielded to the earnest entreaties of the university and magistrate to remain.[1]

The German Reformation did not stimulate the duty of self-support, nor develop the faculty of self-government. It threw the church into the arms of the state, from whose bondage she has never been able as yet to emancipate herself. The princes, nobles, and city magistrates were willing and anxious to take the benefit, but reluctant to perform the duties, of their new priestly dignity; while the common people remained as passive as before, without a voice in the election of their pastor, or any share in the administration of

---

[1] See his letters to Jonas, Lauterbach, Link, Probst, and others, in De Wette, vol. V. To Lauterbach he wrote, Nov. 10, 1541 (V. 407), "*Ego pœne de Germania desperavi, postquam recepit inter parietes veros illos Turkas seu veros illos diabolos, avaritiam, usuram, tyrannidem, discordiam et totam illam Lernam perfidiæ, malitiæ, et nequitiæ, in nobilitate, in aulis, in curiis, in oppidis, in villis, super hæc autem contemtum verbi et ingratitudinem inauditam.*" To Jonas he wrote, March 7, 1543 (V. 548), that the German nobility and princes were worse than the Turks, and bent upon enslaving Germany, and exhausting the people. To the same he gives, June 18, 1543 (V. 570), an account of the immorality of Wittenberg, and the indifference of the magistrate, and concludes, "*Es ist ein verdriesslich Ding um die Welt.*" He thought that the end of the wicked world was near (Letter to Probst, Dec. 5, 1544, vol. V. 703).

their congregational affairs. The Lutheran prince took the place of the bishop or pope ; the Lutheran pastor (*Pfarr-herr*), the place of the Romish priest, but instead of obeying the bishop he had to obey his secular patron.[1]

§ 85. *Enlarged Conception of the Church. Augustin, Wiclif, Hus, Luther.*

KÖSTLIN: *Luthers Lehre von der Kirche.* Stuttgart, 1853. Comp. his *Lu-thers Theologie in ihrer geschichtl. Entwicklung,* II. 534 sqq.; and his *Martin Luther,* Bk. VI. ch. iii. (II. 23 sqq.). JOH. GOTTSCHICK: *Hus', Luther's und Zwingli's Lehre von der Kirche,* in Brieger's "Zeitschrift für Kirchengeschichte," Bd. VIII., Gotha, 1886, pp. 345 sqq. and 543 sqq. (Very elaborate, but he ought to have gone back to Wiclif and Augustin. Hus merely repeated Wiclif.)

Comp. also on the general subject MÜNCHMEYER: *Das Dogma von der sichtbaren und unsichtbaren Kirche,* 1854. RITSCHL: *Ueber die Begriffe sichtbare und unsichtbare Kirche,* in the "Studien und Kritiken" for 1859. JUL. MÜLLER: *Die unsichtbare Kirche,* in his "Dogmatische Abhandlungen," Bremen, 1870, pp. 278–403 (an able defense of the idea of the invisible church against Rothe, Münchmeyer, and others who oppose the term *invisible* as inapplicable to the church. See especially Rothe's *Anfänge der christl. Kirche,* 1837, vol. I. 99 sqq.). ALFRED KRAUSS: *Das protestantische Dogma von der unsichtbaren Kirche,* Gotha, 1876. SEEBERG: *Der Begriff der christlichen Kirche,* Part I., 1885. JAMES S. CANDLISH: *The Kingdom of God.* Edinburgh, 1884.

Separation from Rome led to a more spiritual and more liberal conception of the church, and to a distinction between the one universal church of the elect children of God of all ages and countries, under the sole headship of Christ, and the several visible church organizations of all nominal Christians. We must trace the gradual growth of this distinction.

In the New Testament the term ἐκκλησία (a popular assem-

---

[1] Friedberg, *Kirchenrecht,* p. 57, correctly says, "*Die Reformation hat schliesslich wohl Pfarrsprengel geschaffen, aber keine Gemeinden.*" This is true even now of the Lutheran churches in Northern Germany; but in Westphalia, on the Rhine, and in America, the congregational life is more or less developed, partly through contact with Reformed churches.

bly, congregation) is used in two senses (when applied to religion): 1, in the general sense of the whole body of Christian believers (by our Lord, Matt. 16:18); and 2, in the particular sense of a local congregation of Christians (also by our Lord, Matt. 18:17). We use the equivalent term "church" (from κυριακόν, belonging to the Lord) in two additional senses: of a denomination (e.g., the Greek, the Roman, the Anglican, the Lutheran Church), and of a church edifice. The word ἐκκλησία occurs only twice in the Gospels (in Matthew), but very often in the Acts and Epistles; while the terms "kingdom of God" and "kingdom of heaven" are used very often in the Gospels, but rarely in the other books. This indicates a difference. The kingdom of God precedes the institution of the church, and will outlast it. The kingdom has come, is constantly coming, and will come in glory. It includes the government of God, and all the religious and moral activities of man. The visible church is a training-school for the kingdom. In many instances the terms may be interchanged, while in others we could not substitute the church for the kingdom without impropriety: e.g., in the phrase "of such is the kingdom of heaven" (Matt. 5:3; Mark 10:14); or, "thy kingdom come" (Matt. 6:10); or, "the kingdom of God cometh not with observation, . . . the kingdom of God is within you" (Luke 17:20, 21); or, "to inherit the kingdom" (Matt. 25:34; 1 Cor. 6:10; 15:30; Gal. 5:21); or, "the kingdom of God is not meat and drink, but righteousness and peace and joy in the Holy Ghost." A distinction between nominal and real, or outward and inward, membership of the church, is indicated in the words of our Lord, "Many are called, but few are chosen" (Matt. 22:14), and by Paul when he speaks of a circumcision of the flesh and a circumcision of the heart (Rom. 2:28, 29). Here is the germ of the doctrine of the visible and invisible church.

The Apostles' and Nicene Creeds include the holy catholic

church and the communion of saints among the articles of faith,[1] and do not limit them by the Greek, Roman, or any other nationality or age. "Catholic" means universal, and is as wide as humanity. It indicates the capacity and aim of the church; but the actualization of this universalness is a process of time, and it will not be completed till the whole world is converted to Christ.[2]

The mediæval schoolmen distinguished three stages in the catholic church as to its locality, — the militant church on earth (*ecclesia militans*), the church of the departed or the sleeping church in purgatory (*ecclesia dormiens*), and the triumphant church in heaven (*ecclesia triumphans*). This classification was retained by Wiclif, Hus, and other fore-runners of Protestantism; but the Reformers rejected the intervening purgatorial church, together with prayers for the departed, and included all the pious dead in the church triumphant.

In the militant church on earth, Augustin made an important distinction between "the true body of Christ" (*corpus Christi verum*), and "the mixed body of Christ" (*corpus Christi mixtum* or *simulatum*). He substitutes this for the less suitable designation of a "twofold body of Christ" (*corpus Domini bipartitum*), as taught by Tichonius, the Donatist grammarian (who referred to Cant. 1: 5). These two bodies are in this world externally in one com-

---

[1] Yet not in the strict and deeper sense in which the Father, Son, and Holy Spirit are articles of (saving) faith; hence the preposition εἰς, *in*, is omitted before *ecclesiam*, and the following articles, at least in the Latin forms (the Greek Nicene Creed has εἰς).

[2] The term "catholic" (καθολικός, from κατά and ὅλος, whole, entire, complete) does not occur in the New Testament (for the inscriptions of the Epistles of James, Peter, John, and Jude, ἐπιστολαὶ καθολικαί, or simply καθολικαί, are no part of the apostolic text, but added by transcribers), and is first used as an epithet of the Church by Ignatius of Antioch, the enthusiast for episcopacy and martyrdom (*Ad Smyrn.*, c. 8), and in the Martyrium of Polycarp (in Eusebius, *II. E.*, IV. 14). It was applied also to faith, tradition, people, and became equivalent with Christian, in distinction from Jews, idolaters, heretics, and schismatics.

munion, as the good and bad fish are in one net, but they will ultimately be separated.[1] To the true or pure church belong all the elect, and these only, whether already in the Catholic Church, or outside of it, yet predestinated for it. "Many," he says, "who are openly outside, and are called heretics, are better than many good Catholics; for we see what they are to-day; what they shall be to-morrow, we know not; and with God, to whom the future is already present, they already are what they shall be hereafter."[2] On the other hand, hypocrites are in the church, but not of the church.

It should be added, however, that Augustin confined the true church on earth to the limits of the visible, orthodox, catholic body of his day, and excluded all heretics, — Manichæans, Pelagians, Arians, etc., — and schismatics, — Donatists, etc., — as long as they remain outside of fellowship with that body. In explaining the article "the holy church," in his version of the Creed (which omits the epithet "catholic," and the additional clause "the communion of saints"), he says that this surely means "the Catholic Church;" and adds, "Both heretics and schismatics style their congregations churches. But heretics in holding false opinions regarding God do injury to the faith itself; while schismatics, on the other hand, in wicked separations break off from brotherly charity, although they may believe just what we believe. Wherefore, neither do the heretics belong to the Church Catholic, which loves God; nor do the schismatics form a part of the same, inasmuch as it loves the neighbor, and consequently readily forgives the neighbor's sin."[3] It is well known that this great and good man even defended the principle of forcible coercion of schismatics, on a false interpretation of Luke 14: 23, "Constrain them to come in."

[1] *De Doctr. Christ.*, III. 32 (in Schaff's "Nicene and Post-Nicene Library;" Works of St. Augustin, vol. II. 509).

[2] *De Bapt. contra Donat.*, IV. 5. For a fuller exposition of his doctrine of the church, see his Donatist writings, and Reuter's *Augustin. Studien* (1887).

[3] *De Fide et Symbolo*, c. 10 (in Schaff's ed., III. 331).

In the ninth century the visible Catholic Church was divided into two rival Catholic churches, — the patriarchal church in the East, and the papal church in the West. The former denied the papal claim of universal jurisdiction and headship, as an anti-Christian usurpation; the latter identified the Church Catholic with the dominion of the papacy, and condemned the Greek Church as schismatical. Hereafter, in Western Christendom, the Holy Catholic Church came to mean the Holy Roman Church.

The tyranny and corruptions of the papacy called forth the vigorous protest of Wiclif, who revived the Augustinian distinction between the true church and the mixed church, but gave it an anti-Roman and anti-papal turn (which Augustin did not). He defined the true church to be the congregation of the predestinated, or elect, who will ultimately be saved.[1] Nobody can become a member of this church except by God's predestination, which is the eternal foundation of the church, and determines its membership. No one who is rejected from eternity (*præscitus*, foreknown, as distinct from *prædestinatus*, foreordained) can be a member of this church. He may be in it, but he is not of it. As there is much in the human body which is no part of it, so there may be hypocrites in the church who will finally be removed. There is but one universal church, out of which there is no salvation. The only Head of this church is Christ; for a church with two heads would be a monster. The apostles declared themselves to be servants of this Head.

[1] *Tractatus de Ecclesia*, c. I., "*congregatio omnium prædestinatorum . . . Illa est sponsa Christi . . . Jerusalem mater nostra, templum Domini, regnum cœlorum et civitas regni magni.*" Then he quotes the distinction made by Augustin, to whom he refers throughout the book more frequently than to all other fathers combined. This important tract was recently published for the first time from three MSS. in Vienna and Prague by the "Wyclif Society," and edited by Dr. Johann Loserth (professor of history in the University of Czernowitz), London (Trübner & Co.), 1886, 600 pp. But the same view of the church is taught in other books of Wiclif, and correctly stated by Dr. Lechler in his *Joh. von Wiclif*, Leipz., 1873, vol. I. 541 sqq.

The Pope is only the head of a part of the church militant, and this only if he lives in harmony with the commandments of Christ. This conception of the church excludes all hypocrites and bad members, though they be bishops or popes; and it includes all true Christians, whether Catholics, or schismatics, or heretics. It coincides with the Protestant idea of the invisible church. But Wiclif and Hus denied the certainty of salvation, as taught afterwards by Calvinists, and herein they agreed with the Catholics; they held that one may be sure of his present state of grace, but that his final salvation depends upon his perseverance, which cannot be known before the end.

Wiclif's view of the true church was literally adopted by the Bohemian Reformer Hus, who depended for his theology on the English Reformer much more than was formerly known.[1]

From Hus it passed to Luther, Zwingli, and Calvin, who agreed in denying the claims of the papacy to exclusive catholicity, and in widening the limits of the church so as to include all true believers in Christ. But they distinguished more clearly between the invisible and visible church, or rather between one true invisible church and several mixed visible churches.[2] The invisible church is within the visible church as the soul is in the body, and the

---

[1] The close affinity has recently been shown by Joh. Loserth, *Hus und Wiclif; zur Genesis der hussitischen Lehre* (Prag and Leipz., 1884), and is especially apparent from a comparison of Wiclif's and Hus's treatises *De Ecclesia*. Wiclif's book exerted little influence in England, but became known in Bohemia in 1407 or before, and the reproduction of it by Hus created a great sensation. The arrangement, the ideas, and arguments of the two books are the same, and often the very language. Comp. Loserth's Introduction to Wiclif's *De Ecclesia*.

[2] Luther first used the term "invisible." Zwingli first added the term "visible" in his *Expositio christianæ fidei* (1531): "*Credimus et unam sanctam esse catholicam, h. e. universalem ecclesiam. Eam autem esse aut visibilem aut invisibilem.*" Zwingli was the only one among the Reformers who included the elect *heathen* in the invisible church. The clearest symbolical statement of the Protestant doctrine of the invisible and visible church is given in the Westminster Confession, ch. xxv. (Schaff's *Creeds of Christendom*, III. 657).

kernel in the shell. It is not a Utopian dream or Platonic commonwealth, but most real and historical. The term "invisible" was chosen because the operations of the Holy Spirit are internal and invisible, and because nobody in this life can be surely known to belong to the number of the elect, while membership of the visible church is recognizable by baptism and profession.

Important questions were raised with this distinction for future settlement. Some eminent modern Protestant divines object to the term "invisible church," as involving a contradiction, inasmuch as the church is essentially a visible institution; but they admit the underlying truth of an invisible, spiritual communion of believers scattered throughout the world.[1] As Protestantism has since divided and subdivided into a number of denominations and separate organizations, the idea of the church needs to be further expanded. We must recognize a number of visible churches, Greek, Latin, Lutheran, Reformed, Anglican, and all the more recent Christian denominations which acknowledge Christ as their Head, and his teaching and example as their rule of faith and duty. The idea of denominations or confessions, as applied to churches, is of modern date; but is, after all, only an expansion of the idea of a particular church, or a contraction of the idea of the universal church, and therefore authorized by the double Scripture usage of *ecclesia*. The denominational conception lies between the catholic and the local conception. The one invisible church is found in all visible denominations and congregations as far as true Christianity extends. Another distinction should also be made between the church, and the kingdom of God, which is

---

[1] Rothe (*Anfänge der christl. Kirche*, I. p. 101) says that the idea of a moral and spiritual union and communion of all believers in Christ, or of the communion of saints, is in the highest sense real (*ist nach unsrer innigsten Ueberzeugung eine im höchsten Sinne reale*), but cannot be called a church. He resolves and dissolves the church ultimately into the kingdom of God, which he identifies with the ideal state.

a more spiritual and more comprehensive idea than even this invisible catholic church, although very closely allied to it, and usually identified with it. But we cannot anticipate modern discussions. The Reformers were concerned first of all to settle their relation to the Roman Church as they found it, and to reconcile the idea of a truly catholic church which they could not and would not sacrifice, with the corruptions of the papacy on the one hand, and with their separation from it on the other.

Luther received a copy of Hus's treatise *De Ecclesia* from Prague in 1519.[1] He was driven to a defense of the Bohemian martyr in the disputation at Leipzig, and ventured to assert that Hus was unjustly condemned by the Council of Constance for holding doctrines derived from Augustin and Paul. Among these was his definition of the universal church as the totality of the elect (*universitas prædestinatorum*).

Luther developed this idea in his own way, and modified it in application to the visible church. He started from the article of the Creed, "I believe in the holy catholic church," but identified this article with the "communion of saints," as a definition of the catholic church.[1] He explained the

---

[1] Under the date of Oct. 3, 1519, he informed Staupitz that he had received from Prague letters of two priests, "*una cum libello Joannis Hus.*" De Wette, I. 341. An edition of the *Tractatus de Ecclesia* was published at Mainz and Hagenau in 1520.

[2] This identification may be questioned. The holy catholic church corresponds rather to the church visible, the communion of saints to the church invisible. The communion of saints means that inward and spiritual fellowship of true believers on earth and in heaven which is based on their union with Christ. It is their fellowship with God the Father, the Son, and the Spirit (comp. 1 John 1:3; 1 Cor. 1:9; Phil. 2:1), and with each other, a fellowship not broken by death, but extending to the saints above. A most precious idea.

> "The saints in heaven and on earth
> But one communion make;
> All join in Christ, their living Head,
> And of his grace partake."

The article of the *communio sanctorum* (as well as the epithet *catholica*) is a later insertion, and not found in the creeds before the fifth century. See

communion (*Gemeinschaft*) to mean the community or congregation (*Gemeinde*) of saints. He also substituted, in his Catechism, the word "Christian" for "catholic," in order to include in it all believers in Christ. Hence the term "catholic" became, or remained, identical in Germany with "Roman Catholic" or "papal;"[1] while the English Protestant churches very properly retained the word "catholic" in its true original sense of "universal," which admits of no sectarian limitation. The Romanists have no claim to the exclusive use of that title; they are too sectarian and exclusive to be truly catholic.

Luther held that the holy church in its relation to God is an article of faith, not of sight, and therefore invisible.[2] But as existing among men the true church is visible, and can be recognized by the right preaching of the gospel or the purity of doctrine, and by the right administration of the sacraments (i.e., baptism and the Lord's Supper). These are the two essential marks of a pure church. The first he emphasized against the Romanists, the second against what he called Enthusiasts (*Schwarmgeister*) and Sacramentarians (in the sense of *anti*-sacramentarians).

His theory acquired symbolical authority through the Augsburg Confession, which defines the church to be "the congregation of saints in which the gospel is rightly taught, and the sacraments are rightly administered."[3] Worship

Schaff, *Creeds of Christendom*, I. 22 and II. 52. The oldest commentators understood it of the communion with the saints in heaven. According to the Catechism of the Council of Trent, it means "a community of spiritual blessings," especially the sacraments enjoyed in the Catholic Church. A more comprehensive and satisfactory exposition is given by Pearson on the *Creed*, Art. IX., and in the Westminster Confession, Ch. XXVI.

[1] The German proverb, "*Das ist um katholisch zu werden*" (This is to turn Catholic), describes a condition of things that drives one to desperation or madness.

[2] In his second Commentary on the Galatians (Erl. ed., III. 38): "*Recte igitur fatemur in symbolo, nos* CREDERE *ecclesiam sanctam. Est enim* IN-VISIBILIS, *habitans in Spiritu, in loco inaccessibili, ideo non potest* VIDERI *ejus sanctitas.*"

[3] Art. VII., "*Est autem ecclesia congregatio sanctorum* [Germ. ed., *Versammlung aller Gläubigen*], *in qua evangelium recte* [*rein*] *docetur, et*

and discipline, rites and ceremonies, are made secondary or indifferent, and reckoned with human traditions which may change from time to time. The church has no right to impose what is not commanded in the Word of God. In such things everybody is his own pope and church. The Lutheran Confession has always laid great — we may say too great — stress on the unity of doctrine, and little, too little, stress on discipline. And yet in no other evangelical denomination is there such a diversity of theological opinions, from the strict orthodoxy of the Formula Concordiæ to every form and degree of Rationalism.

How far, we must ask here, did Luther recognize the dominion of the papacy as a part of the true catholic church? He did not look upon the Pope in the historical and legal light as the legitimate head of the Roman Church; but he fought him to the end of his life as the antagonist of the gospel, as the veritable Antichrist, and the papacy as an apostasy. He could not have otherwise justified his separation, and the burning of the papal bull and law-books. He assumed a position to the Pope and his church similar to that of the apostles to Caiaphas and the synagogue. Nevertheless, whether consistently or not, he never doubted the validity of the ordinances of the Roman Church, having himself been baptized, confirmed, and ordained in it, and he never dreamed of being re-baptized or re-ordained. Those millions of Protestants who seceded in the sixteenth century were of the same opinion, with the sole exception of the Anabaptists who objected to infant-baptism, partly on the ground that it was an invention of the popish Antichrist, and therefore invalid.

recte [*laut des Evangelii*] *administrantur sacramenta.*" Comp. the *Apol. Conf.*, Art. VII. and VIII. The same definition is substantially given in the Anglican Art. XIX. It would exclude the Quakers, who reject the external sacraments, yet are undoubted believers in Christ. The Calvinistic Confessions (e.g., *Conf. Belgica*, Art. XXIX.) add characteristically to those two marks a third one, the exercise of discipline in punishing sin.

Nor did Luther or any of the Reformers and sensible Protestants doubt that there always were and are still many true
Christians in the Roman communion, notwithstanding all her
errors and corruptions, as there were true Israelites even in
the darkest periods of the Jewish theocracy. In his controversy with the Anabaptists (1528), Luther makes the striking admission: " We confess that under the papacy there is
much Christianity, yea, the whole Christianity, and has from
thence come to us. We confess that the papacy possesses
the genuine Scriptures, genuine baptism, the genuine sacrament of the altar, the genuine keys for the remission of sins,
the true ministry, the true catechism, the Ten Commandments, the articles of the Creed, the Lord's Prayer. . . . I
say that under the Pope is the true Christendom, yea, the
very *élite* of Christendom, and many pious and great saints."[1]

For proof he refers, strangely enough, to the very passage
of Paul, 2 Thess. 2 : 3, 4, from which he and other Reformers
derived their chief argument that the Pope of Rome is Antichrist, "the man of sin," "the son of perdition." For Paul
represents him as sitting "in the temple of God;" that is,
in the true church, and not in the synagogue of Satan. As
the Pope is Antichrist, he must be among Christians, and
rule and tyrannize over Christians.[2] Melanchthon, who

---

[1] "*Ich sage, dass unter dem Papst die rechte Christenheit ist, ja der rechte
Ausbund der Christenheit, und viel frommer, grosser Heiligen.*" (*Von der
Wiedertaufe*, Erl. ed. XXVI. 257 sq.) The Roman Catholic Möhler does
not fail to quote this passage in his *Symbolik*, p. 422 sq. He says of
Luther's conception of the church (p. 424), that it is not false, but only one-
sided (*nicht falsch, obgleich einseitig*). He virtually admits the Protestant
distinction between the visible and the invisible church, but holds that the
Catholics put the visible church first as the basis of the invisible, while
the Protestants reverse the order.

[2] *Ibid.* p. 258. Critical commentators have long since abandoned this
interpretation. Whatever be the wider applicability of this passage, Paul
certainly meant a "mystery of lawlessness" (not tyranny) already at work
in his time (ἤδη ἐνεργεῖται, ver. 7), long before popery existed, or before there
was even a bishop of Rome (unless it be Peter). Moreover, "lawlessness,"
which is the proper translation of ἀνομία, is not characteristic of popery, but
the very opposite. If Paul refers to Rome at all, it is rather as a " restrain-

otherwise had greater respect for the Pope and the Roman Church, repeatedly expressed the same view.[1] Luther came nearer the true position when he said that the Roman Church might be called a "holy church," by synecdoche or *ex parte*, with the same restriction with which Paul called the Galatian Christians "churches," notwithstanding their apostasy from the true gospel.[2]

He combined with the boldest independence a strong reverence for the historical faith. He derives from the unbroken tradition of the church an argument against the Zwinglians for the real presence in the eucharist; and says, in a letter to Albrecht, Margrave of Brandenburg and Duke of Prussia (April, 1532, after Zwingli's death) : "The testimony of the entire holy Christian church (even without any other proof) should be sufficient for us to abide by this article, and to listen to no sectaries against it. For it is dangerous and terrible (*gefährlich und erschrecklich*) to hear or believe any thing against the unanimous testimony, faith, and doctrine of the entire holy Christian church as held from the beginning for now over fifteen hundred years in all the world. . . . To deny such testimony is virtually to condemn not only the holy Christian church as a damned heretic, but

ing" force, τὸ κατέχον, vers. 6, 7 (comp. Rom. 13: 1). The term "Antichrist" occurs only in the Epistles of John, and he speaks of "*many* Antichrists" in his own day. In a wider sense all is antichristian that is contrary to the spirit and aim of Christ in any church or any age.

[1] In his *Judicium de jure reformandi*, 1525 ("Corp. Ref.," I. 767): "It is written that the Antichrist will have a great and powerful reign in the last times, as Paul says, Antichrist will be seated and rule in the temple of God, that is, in the church." And again in the "Apology of the Augsburg Confession" (1530), arts. VII. and VIII. (Müller's ed., p. 152): "*Paulus prædicat futurum, ut Antichristus sedeat in templo Dei, hoc est, in* ECCLESIA *dominetur et gerat officia.*"

[2] *Com. in Ep. ad Gal.* (Erl. ed., I. 40 sq.): "*Paulus vocat ecclesias Galatiæ per synecdochen. . . . Sic et nos hodie vocamus ecclesiam romanam sanctam et omnes episcopatus sanctos, etiamsi sint subversi et episcopi et ministri eorum impii. Deus enim regnat in medio inimicorum suorum; item, Antichristus sedet in templo Dei, et Satan adest in medio filiorum Dei. . . . Manet in romana urbe quamquam Sodoma et Gomorra pejore baptismus, sacramentum, vox et textus evangelii, sacra scriptura, ministeria, nomen Christi, nomen Dei.*"

even Christ himself, with all his apostles and prophets, who have founded this article, 'I believe a holy Christian church,' as solemnly affirmed by Christ when he promised, 'Behold, I am with you all the days, even to the end of the world' (Matt. 28 : 20), and by St. Paul when he says, 'The church of God is the pillar and ground of the truth' (1 Tim. 3 : 15)." [1]

A Roman controversialist could not lay more stress on tradition than Luther does in this passage. But tradition, at least from the sixth to the sixteenth century, strongly favors the belief in transubstantiation, and the sacrifice of the mass, both of which he rejected. And if the same test should be applied to his doctrine of solifidian justification, it would be difficult to support it by patristic or scholastic tradition, which makes no distinction between justification and sanctification, and lays as much stress on good works as on faith. He felt it himself, that on this vital point, not even Augustin was on his side. His doctrine can be vindicated only as a new interpretation of St. Paul in advance of the previous understanding.

Calvin, if we may here anticipate his views as expounded in the first chapters of the fourth book of his " Institutes of the Christian Religion," likewise clearly distinguishes between the visible and invisible church,[2] and in the visible church again between the true evangelical church and the false papal church, which he assails as unmercifully as Luther; yet he also admits that the Roman communion, notwithstanding the antichristian character of the papacy, yea, for the very reason that Antichrist sits " in the temple of God," remains a church with the Scriptures and valid Christian ordinances.[3] So the Jewish synagogue under

---

[1] De Wette, *Briefe*, IV. 354.

[2] Lib. IV., c. i., §§ 4 and 7. He speaks most eloquently of the *ecclesia visibilis*, as our mother in whose womb we are conceived to enter into spiritual life.

[3] Lib. IV., c. ii., § 12: " *Antichristum in templo Dei sessurum prædixerunt Daniel et Paulus* (Dan. 9: 27; 2 Thess. 2: 4): *illius scelerati et abominandi*

Caiaphas retained the law and the prophets, the rites and ceremonies, of the theocracy.

The Westminster Confession implies the same theory, and supports it by the same questionable exegesis of 2 Thess. 2: 3 sqq. and Rev. 13: 1–8.[1]

The claims of the Roman Church rest on a broader and more solid base than the papacy, which is merely the form of her government. The papal hierarchy was often as corrupt as the Jewish hierarchy, and some popes were as wicked as Caiaphas;[2] but this fact cannot destroy the claims nor invalidate the ordinances of the Roman Church, which from the days of the apostles down to the Reformation has been identified with the fortunes of Western Christendom, and which remains to this day the largest visible church in the world. To deny her church character is to stultify history, and to nullify the promise of Christ.   (Matt. 16: 18; 28: 20.)

regni ducem et antesignanum, apud nos facimus Romanum Pontificem. Quod sedes ejus in templo Dei collocatur, ita innuitur, tale fore ejus regnum quod nec Christi nec ecclesiæ nomen aboleat.   Hinc igitur patet nos minime negare, quin sub ejus quoque tyrannide ecclesiæ maneant: sed quas sacrilega impietate profanarit, quas immani dominatione afflixerit, quas malis et exitialibus doctrinis, ceu venenatis potionibus, corruperit, et propemodum enecarit, in quibus semisepultus lateat Christus, obrutum Evangelium, profligata pietas, cultus Dei fere abolitus: in quibus denique omnia sic sint conturbata, ut Babylonis potius quam civitatis Dei sanctæ facies illic appareat."   Comp. IV., 7, § 25; and Calvin's commentary on 2 Thess. 2:3.

[1] Ch. XXV. 6: "The Pope of Rome . . . is that Antichrist, that man of sin and perdition, that exalteth himself in the Church against Christ and all that is called God." And yet there are American divines who derive from this passage the very opposite conclusion; namely, that the Roman Church is no church at all, and that all her ordinances are invalid. An attempt to sanction this conclusion was made at the General Assembly of the Presbyterian Church at Cincinnati in 1885, but failed. The Westminster Confession never calls the Roman Church Antichrist, but only the Pope, who is no more the Roman Church than the Moderator of the General Assembly is the General Assembly, or the President of the United States is the American people, or the Czar of Russia is Russia. The government is only one factor in the life of a nation or a church.

[2] Dante locates them in the _Inferno;_ and Möhler says, "Hell has swallowed them up."

NOTES.

LUTHER'S VIEWS ON THE CHURCH FATHERS.

WALCH, XXII. 2050–2065. ERLANGEN ed. LXII. 97 sqq. (*Tischreden*). BINDSEIL: *Mart. Lutheri Colloquia* (1863), 3 vols.

In this connection it may be interesting to collect from his writings and Table Talk some of Luther's characteristic judgments of the church fathers whose works began to be more generally known and studied through the editions of Erasmus.

Luther had no idea of a golden age of virgin purity of the church. He knew that even among the apostles there was a Judas, and that errors and corruptions crept into the Galatian, Corinthian, and other congregations, as is manifest from the censures, warnings, and exhortations of the Epistles of the New Testament. Much less could he expect perfection in any post-apostolic age. His view of the absolute supremacy of the Word of God over all the words of men, even the best and holiest, led him to a critical and discriminating estimate of the fathers and schoolmen. Besides, he felt the difference between the patristic and the Protestant theology. The Continental Reformers generally thought much less of the fathers than the Anglican divines.

"The fathers," says Luther, "have written many things that are pious and useful (*multa pia et salutaria*), but they must be read with discrimination, and judged by the Scriptures." "The dear fathers lived better than they wrote; we write better than we live." (*Melius vixerunt quam scripserunt: nos Deo juvante melius scribimus quam vivimus.* Bindseil, *l. c.* III. 140; Erl. ed., LXII. 103.) He placed their writings far below the Scriptures; and the more he progressed in the study of both, the more he was impressed with the difference (Erl. ed., LXII. 107). To reform the church by the fathers is impossible; it can only be done by the Word of God (XXV. 231). They were poor interpreters, in part on account of their ignorance of Hebrew and Greek (XXII. 185). All the fathers have erred in the faith. Nevertheless, they are to be held in veneration for their testimony to the Christian faith (*propter testimonium fidei omnes sunt venerandi.* Erl. ed. LXII. 98).

Of all the fathers he learned most from Augustin. For him he had the profoundest respect, and him he quotes more frequently than all others combined. He regards him as one of the four pillars of the church (the claims of Ambrose, Jerome, and Gregory, he disputed), as the best commentator, and the patron of theologians. "*Latina nostra ecclesia nullum habuit præstantiorem doctorem quam Augustinum*" (Bindseil, I. 456). "He pleased and pleases me better than all other doctors; he was a great teacher, and worthy of all praise" (III. 147). The Pelagians stirred him up to his best books, in which he treats of free-will, faith, and original sin. He first distinguished it from actual transgression. He is the only one among the fathers who had a worthy view of matrimony. The papists pervert his famous word: "I would not believe the gospel if the Catholic Church did not move me thereto," which was said against the Manichæans in this sense: Ye are heretics, I do not believe you; I go with the church, the bride of Christ, which cannot err (Erl. ed., XXX. 394 sq.). Augustin did more than all the bishops and popes who cannot hold a candle to him (XXXI. 358 sq.), and more than all the councils (XXV. 341). If he lived now, he would side with us, but Jerome would condemn us (Bindseil, III. 149). Yet with all his sympathy, Luther could not find his "*sola fide.*" Augustin, he says, has sometimes erred, and is not to be trusted. "Although good and holy, he was yet lacking in the true faith, as well as the other fathers." "When the door was opened to me for the understanding of Paul, I was done with Augustin" (*da war es aus mit ihm.* Erl. ed., LXII. 119).

Next to Augustin he seems to have esteemed Hilary on account of his work on the Trinity. "*Hilarius,*" he says, "*inter omnes patres luctator fuit strenuissimus adversus hæreticos, cui neque Augustinus conferri potest*" (Bindseil, III. 138). Ambrose he calls "a pious, God-fearing, and brave man," and refers to his bold stand against the Emperor Theodosius. But his six books on Genesis are very thin, and his hymns have not much matter, though his (?) "*Rex Christe, factor omnium,*" is "*optimus hymnus.*" He praises Prudentius for his poetry. Tertullian, whom he once calls the oldest of the fathers (though he lived after 200), was "*durus et superstitiosus.*" Of Cyprian he speaks favorably. As to Jerome, he had to admit that he was the greatest Bible translator, and will not be surpassed in this line (Erl. ed. LXII. 462). But he positively hated him on account of his monkery, and says: "He ought not to be counted among the doctors of the church; for he was a heretic, although I believe that he was saved by faith in Christ. I know no one of the fathers, to whom I am so hostile as to him. He writes only about fasting, virginity, and such things" (LXII. 119 sq.). He was tormented by carnal temptations, and loved Eustochium so as to create scandal. He speaks impiously of marriage. His commentaries on Matthew, Galatians, and Titus are very thin. Luther had no more respect for Pope Gregory I. He is the author of the fables of purgatory and masses for souls; he knew little of Christ and his gospel, and was entirely too superstitious. The Devil deceived him, and made him believe in appearances of spirits from purgatory. "His sermons are not worth a copper" (Erl. ed., LI. 482; LII. 187; LX. 189, 405; XXVIII. 98 sqq.; Bindseil, III. 140, 228). But he praises beyond its merits his hymn *Rex Christe*, which he wrongly ascribes to Ambrose (Bindseil, III. 149; comp. Daniel, *Thesaurus Hymnol.*, vol. I. 180 sq.).

With the Greek fathers, Luther was less familiar. He barely mentions Ignatius, Irenæus, Origen, Eusebius, and Epiphanius. He praises Athanasius as the greatest teacher of the Oriental Church, although he was nothing extra (*obwohl er nichts sonderliches war*). He could not agree with

Melanchethon's favorable judgment of Basil the Great. He thought Gregory of Nazianzen, the eloquent defender of the divinity of Christ during the Arian ascendency, to be of no account (" *Nazianzenus est nihil.*" Bindseil, III. 152). He speaks well of Theodoret's Commentary to Paul's Epistles, but unreasonably depreciates Chrysostom, the golden preacher and commentator, and describes him as a great rhetorician, full of words and empty of matter ; he even absurdly compares him to Carlstadt! " He is garrulous, and therefore pleases Erasmus, who neglects faith, and treats only of morals. I consulted him on the beautiful passage on the highpriest in Hebrews; but he twaddled about the dignity of priests, and let me stick in the mud " (Bindseil, III. 136; Erl. ed. LXII. 102).

Of mediæval divines Luther esteemed Nicolaus Lyra as a most useful commentator. He praises St. Bernard, who in his sermons "excels all other doctors, even Augustin." He speaks highly of Peter the Lombard, "the Master of Sentences," and calls him a " *homo diligentissimus et excellentissimi ingenii,*" although he brought in many useless questions (Bindseil, III. 151; Erl. ed. LXII. 114). He calls Occam, whom he studied diligently, " *summus dialecticus*" (Bindseil, III. 138, 270). But upon the whole he hated the schoolmen and their master, "the damned heathen Aristotle," although he admits him to have been " *optimus dialecticus,*" and learned from him and his commentators the art of logical reasoning. Even Thomas Aquinas, "the Angelic Doctor," whom the Lutheran scholastics of the seventeenth century highly and justly esteemed, he denounced as a chatterer (*loquacissimus*), who makes the Bible bend to Aristotle (Bindseil, III. 270, 286), and whose books are a fountain of all heresies, and destructive of the gospel (" *der Brunn und Grundsuppe aller Ketzerei, Irrthums und Verleugnung des Evangeliums.*" Erl. ed. XXIV. 240). This is, of course, the language of prejudice and passion. — His views on Augustin are the most correct, because he knew him best, and liked him most.

Melanchthon and Œcolampadius from fuller knowledge and milder temper judged more favorably and consistently of the fathers generally, and their invaluable services to Christian literature.

§ 86. *Changes in the Views on the Ministry. Departure from the Episcopal Succession. Luther ordains a Deacon, and consecrates a Bishop.*

The Reformers unanimously rejected the sacerdotal character of the Christian ministry (except in a spiritual sense), and hence also the idea of a literal altar and sacrifice. No priest, no sacrifice. " Priest " is an abridgment of " presbyter,"[1] and "presbyter" is equivalent to "elder." It does not

---

[1] Milton, in his discontent with the Presbyterians and zeal for independency, said, " Presbyter is priest writ large."

mean *sacerdos* in the New Testament, nor among the earliest ecclesiastical writers before Tertullian and Cyprian.[1] Moreover, in Scripture usage "presbyter" and "bishop" are terms for one and the same office (as also in the Epistle of Clement of Rome, and the recently discovered "Teaching of the Twelve Apostles").[2] This fact (conceded by Jerome and Chrysostom and the best modern scholars) was made the basis for presbyterian ordination in those Lutheran and Reformed churches which abolished episcopacy.[3]

In the place of a graded hierarchy, the Reformers taught the parity of ministers; and in the place of a special priesthood, offering the very body and blood of Christ, a general priesthood of believers, offering the sacrifices of prayer and praise for the one sacrifice offered for all time to come. Luther derived the lay-priesthood from baptism as an anointing by the Holy Spirit and an incorporation into Christ. "A layman with the Scriptures," he said, "is more to be believed than pope and council without the Scriptures."[4]

Nevertheless, he maintained, in opposition to the democratic radicalism of Carlstadt and the fanatical spiritualism of the Zwickau prophets, the necessity of a ministry, as a matter of order and expediency; and so far he asserted its divine origin. Every public teacher must be called of God through the Church, or prove his extraordinary call by miracles. And so the Augsburg Confession declares that "no man shall publicly teach in the church, or administer the sacraments, without a regular call."[5]

But what constitutes a regular call? Luther at first took

---

[1] The exceptional designation of the Christian prophets as "highpriests" (ἀρχιερεῖς), in the *Didaché*, ch. XIII. 3, is probably figurative. See Schaff, *The Oldest Church Manual*, p. 206 sq.

[2] See Schaff, *l.c.* p. 74 sq., and 211.

[3] See the passage in the Appendix to Luther's Articles of Smalcald, quoted above on p. 517, note 2.

[4] Comp. § 44, p. 207, and Melanchthon in his *Apology of the Augsb. Conf.*, arts. XIII. and XXIV.

[5] Art. XIV.

the ground of congregational independency in his writings
to the Bohemian Brethren (1523), and advocated the right
of a Christian congregation to call, to elect, and to depose its
own minister.[1] He meant, of course, a congregation of true
believers, not a mixed multitude of nominal professors. In
cases of necessity, which knows no law, he would allow any
one who has the gift, to pray and sing, to teach and preach; and
refers to the congregation of Corinth, and to Stephen, Philip,
and Apollos, who preached without a commission from the
apostles. In a conflagration everybody runs to lend a help-
ing hand, to save the town. But, in ordinary cases, no one
should be a teacher unless called and elected by the congregation. Even Paul did not elect elders without the concurrence
of the people. The bishops of our days are no bishops, but
idols. They neglect preaching, their chief duty, leaving it
to chaplains and monks : they confirm and consecrate bells,
altars, and churches, which is a self-invented business, neither
Christian nor episcopal. They are baby-bishops.[2]

But congregations of pure Christians, capable of self-
government, could not be found in Germany at that time,
and are impossible in state churches where churchmanship
and citizenship coincide. Luther abandoned this democratic
idea after the Peasants' War, and called on the arm of the
government for protection against the excesses of the popular will.

In the first years of the Reformation the congregations
were supplied by Romish ex-priests and monks. But who
was to ordain the new preachers educated at Wittenberg?
The bishops of Saxony (Naumburg-Zeiz, Meissen, and Merseburg) remained loyal to their master in Rome ; and there

---

[1] In the address *De instituendis ministris*, to the magistrate and people of
Prag, and in his tract " *Dass eine christliche Versammlung oder Gemeinde
Recht und Macht habe, alle Lehrer zu urtheilen und Lehrer zu berufen, ein-
und abzusetzen.*" (Erl. ed., XXII. 140 sqq.; and Walch, X. 1795 sqq.)

[2] " *Es sind verkehrte, verblendete Larven, und rechte Kinderbischöfe.*"
The last word of his German tract to the Bohemians. Erl. ed., XXII. 151.

was no other ordaining power according to law. Luther might have derived the succession from two bishops of Prussia, — Georg von Polenz, bishop of Samland, and Erhard von Queis, bishop of Pomesania, — who accepted the Reformation, and afterwards surrendered their episcopal rights to Duke Albrecht as the *summus episcopus* (1525).[1] But he did not wish to go outside of Saxony, and hated the whole hierarchy of pope and bishop as a human invention and spiritual tyranny. He congratulated the bishop of Samland that he, as by a miracle of grace, had been delivered from the mouth of Satan; while all other bishops raged like madmen against the reviving gospel, although he hoped that there were some timid Nicodemuses among them.[2]

With these views, and the conviction of his own divine authority to reform the church, he felt no reluctance to take the episcopal prerogative into his hands. He acted to the end of his life as an irregular or extraordinary bishop and pope *in partibus Protestantium*, being consulted by princes, magistrates, theologians, and people of all sorts.

He set the first example of a presbyterian ordination by laying hands on his amanuensis, Georg Rörer (Rorarius), and making him deacon at Wittenberg, May 14, 1525. Rörer is favorably known by his assistance in the Bible Version and the first edition of Luther's works. He died as librarian of the University of Jena, 1557. Melanchthon

---

[1] The conversion and attempted reformation of Archbishop Herrmann of Cologne occurred much later, in 1543.

[2] In the preface to his commentary on Deuteronomy, which he dedicated to the bishop of Samland, 1525 (Erl. ed. of *Opera Latina*, XIII. 6): "*Non enim te laudamus, sed insigne illud miraculum gratiæ Dei extollimus, quam in te valere, regnare et triumphare videmus et audimus cum gaudio ut . . . te unicum et solum inter omnes episcopos orbis elegerit Dominus et liberaverit ex ore Satanæ quod dilatavit sicut infernum et devorat omnes. Nihil enim videmus in ceteris episcopis (quanquam esse inter eos sperem aliquot Nicodemos) nisi quod subversis cæsare et regibus ac principibus fremunt et insaniunt contra resurgens vel potius oriens evangelion, ut denuo impleant illud Psalmi secundi,*" etc. Comp. his letter to Spalatin, Feb. 1, 1524, and to Briesmann, July 4, 1524, in De Wette, II. 474 and 525 sqq.

justified the act on the ground that the bishops neglected
their duty.[1]

But Luther ventured even to consecrate a bishop, or a
superintendent; as John Wesley did two hundred and fifty
years afterwards in the interest of his followers in the United
States. When the bishopric of Naumburg became vacant,
the chapter, backed by the Roman-Catholic minority of the
nobility and people, regularly elected Julius von Pflug, one
of the ablest, purest, and mildest opponents of the Reformation. This choice displeased the Protestants. The Elector
John Frederick, by an illegal use of power, confiscated the
property of the diocese, and appointed a counter-bishop in
the person of Nicolaus von Amsdorf, Luther's most devoted
friend, who was unmarried and a nobleman, and at that time
superintendent at Magdeburg. The consecration took place
on June 20, 1542, in the dome of Naumburg, in the presence
of the Elector, the Protestant clergy, and a congregation of
about five thousand people. Luther preached the sermon,
and performed the consecration with the assistance of three
superintendents (Medler, Spalatin, and Stein) and an abbot,
by the laying-on of hands, and prayer.[2] This bold and defiant
act created great sensation and indignation, and required
a public defense, which he prepared at the request of the
Elector.[3] He used the strongest language against popery

---

[1] *Corp. Ref.*, I. 765.   Comp. Seckendorf, *Hist. Lutheranismi*, vol. II. 29.

[2] See an account of the consecration in Seckendorf, III. 391 sqq.; Köstlin,
II. 561 sqq.; Janssen, III. 483–492.   Janssen describes the sickening details
of the violence, intrigues, and robberies connected with the Protestantizing
and secularizing of the three Saxon bishoprics.

[3] *Exempel, einen rechten christlichen Bischof zu weihen, 1542.*   Erl. ed.,
XXVI. 77–108; Walch, XVII. 122.   He begins with the characteristic sentence: " *Wir armen Ketzer haben abermal eine grosse Sünde begangen wider
die höllische unchristliche Kirche des allerhöllischten Vaters, des Papstes,
dass wir einen Bischof im Stift Naumburg ordinirt und eingeweihet haben
ohne allen Chresem [Chrisma, Salböl], auch ohne Butter, Schmalz, Speck,
Teer, Schmeer, Weihrauch, Kohlen und was derselben grossen Heiligkeit
mehr ist: dazu wider ihren Willen; doch nicht ohne ihr Wissen.*"   Comp.
also his letter to Jacob Probst, March 26, 1546 (De Wette, V. 451), where he
calls this consecration " *audax facinus et plenissimum odio, invidia et indignatione.*"

and episcopacy to overawe the opposition, and to make it contemptible. He even boasts of having made a bishop without chrism, butter, and incense. "I cannot repent," he says, "of such a great and horrible sin, nor expect absolution for it." He assigns, among the reasons for setting aside the election of a Catholic bishop, that God had in the first three commandments, as by a thunderstroke of judgment, forever condemned to hell the chapter of Naumburg, together with the pope, cardinals, and all their *régime*, for breaking those commandments by their idolatry and false worship. Christians are forbidden, on pain of eternal damnation, to hear and tolerate them. They must flee a false prophet, preacher, or bishop, and regard a popish bishop as no bishop at all, but as a wolf, yea, as a devil.[1] "And what does the most hellish father in his hellish Church? Does he not depose all bishops, abbots, priests, whom he finds heretics or apostates from his idolatry? . . . Yea, he interferes even with secular and domestic government, deposes emperors, kings, princes, separates man and wife, dissolves marriage, abolishes obedience, duty, and oath, simply for disobedience to his audacious devilish decretals and accursed bulls." But, as the holy Virgin sings in her *Magnificat*, "the Lord hath scattered the proud in the imagination of their hearts, and hath put down princes from their thrones" (Luke 1: 51, 52); and as St. Peter writes, "*Deus superbis resistit*" (1 Pet. 5: 5). The proud and haughty, whether he be pope, emperor, king, prince, nobleman, citizen, or peasant, will be humbled, and come to a bitter end. The chapter of Naumburg elected a bishop who would have been bound by obedience to the pope to persecute the gospel, "to worship the devil," and to let the pope, the archbishop of Mainz, and their courtiers rule and ruin at pleasure. The papists have been playing

---

[1] " . . . *gezwungen durch Gottes Gebot, sich von ihm zu sondern, und ihn für keinen Bischof, sondern für einen Wolf, ja für einen Teufel zu halten.*" Erl. ed., p. 80.

this game for more than twenty years. It is high time to stop it. He who rules in heaven and also here in our hearts turns the wise into fools, and "taketh the wise in their craftiness" (1 Cor. 3:19).

This is the spirit and language of this apologetic tract. It was followed by a still fiercer attack upon popery as an "invention of the Devil" (1545).

Amsdorf was forced upon the chapter and the people by the Elector, but lost his bishopric in the Smalcaldian War (1547), took a leading and ultra-Lutheran part in the bitter theological controversies which followed, and died at Eisenach, 1565, in his eighty-second year. His ephemeral episcopate was, of course, a mere superintendency.

Several of Luther's friends and pupils were appointed superintendents; as Lauterbach at Pirna (d. 1569); Heidenreich, or Heiderich, at Torgau (d. 1572), who with Mathesius, Dietrich, Weller, and others, preserved his "table spice" (*condimenta mensæ*), as they called his familiar conversations.

The appointment of these superintendents was in the hands of the prince as *summus episcopus* over his territory. The congregations had not even the power of electing their own pastors.[1]

In the cities the magistrate assumed the episcopal power, and appointed the superintendents.

The further development of the episcopal, territorial, and collegial system in the Lutheran Church lies beyond our limits.

§ 87. *Relation of Church and State.*

In January, 1523, Luther published a remarkable book on the civil magistrate, dedicated to Prince John, in which he proved from Rom. 13:1 and 1 Pet. 2:13 the duty to obey

---

[1] "*Die Gemeinde,*" says Friedberg, *l.c.*, p. 61, "*tritt bei dieser Organisation ganz zurück. Sie ist der 'Pöbel,' der unter der Zucht des Wortes und der Polizei des Kirchenregimentes steht. . . . Eine Mitwirkung an der Handhabung der Kirchenzucht findet sich nur in den Kirchenordnungen, wo reformirte Einflüsse bemerkbar sind.*"

the civil magistrate, and from Acts 5:29 the duty to obey God more than man.[1] On the ground of Christ's word, Matt. 22:21, which contains the wisest answer to an embarrassing question, he drew a sharp distinction between the secular and spiritual power, and reproved the pope and bishops for meddling with secular affairs, and the princes and nobles for meddling with spiritual matters. It sounds almost like a prophetic anticipation of the American separation of church and state when he says:—

"God has ordained two governments among the children of Adam,—the reign of God under Christ, and the reign of the world under the civil magistrate, each with its own laws and rights. The laws of the reign of the world extend no further than body and goods and the external affairs on earth. But over the soul God can and will allow no one to rule but himself alone.[2] Therefore where the worldly government dares to give laws to the soul, it invades the reign of God, and only seduces and corrupts the soul. This we shall make so clear that our noblemen, princes, and bishops may see what fools they are if they will force people with their laws and commandments to believe this or that.[3] . . . In matters which relate to the soul's salvation nothing should be taught and accepted but God's word. . . . As no one can descend to hell or ascend to heaven for me, as little can any one believe or disbelieve for me; as he cannot open or shut heaven or hell for me, neither can he force me to faith or unbelief. . . . Faith is a voluntary thing which cannot be forced. Yea, it is a divine work in the spirit. Hence it is a common saying which is also found in Augustin: Faith cannot and should not be forced on anybody."[4]

[1] *Von weltlicher Obrigkeit, wie weit man ihr Gehorsam schuldig sei.* Erl. ed. XXII. 59–105.

[2] The Westminster Confession, ch. XX. 2, says: "God alone is Lord of the conscience."

[3] *L. c.* p. 82: "*Das weltlich Regiment hat Gesetze, die sich nicht weiter strecken, denn über Leib und Gut, und was äusserlich ist auf Erden. Denn über die Seele kann und will Gott niemand lassen regieren, denn sich selbst alleine. Darumb wo weltlich Gewalt sich vermisset, der Seelen Gesetze zu geben, da greift sie Gott in sein Regiment, und verführet und verderbet nur die Seelen. Das wollen wir so klar machen, dass mans greifen solle, auf dass unsere Junkern, die Fürsten und Bischöfe sehen, was sie für Narren sind, wenn sie die Leut mit ihren Gesetzen und Geboten zwingen wollen, sonst oder so zu glauben.*"

[4] "*Zum Glauben kann und soll man niemand zwingen.*" As to St. Augustin, he changed his views on this subject, as Luther did afterwards. The anti-Manichæan Augustin was tolerant (he himself had been a Manichæan

Here is the principle of religious liberty which was proclaimed in principle by Christ, acted upon by the apostles,
re-asserted by the ante-Nicene fathers against the tyranny of
persecuting Rome, but so often violated by Christian Rome
in her desire for a worldly empire, and also by Protestant
churches and princes in their dealings with Romanists and
Anabaptists. Luther does not spare the secular rulers,
though this book is dedicated to the brother of the Elector.

"From the beginning of the world wise princes have been rare birds, and
pious princes still rarer. Most of them are the greatest fools or the worst
boobies on earth.[1] Therefore we must fear the worst from them, and expect
little good, especially in divine things which affect the soul's welfare. They
are God's hangmen, and his wrath uses them to punish evil-doers, and to
keep external peace."

He refers to Isa. 3 : 4, "I will give children to be their
princes, and babes shall rule over them ;" and to Hos. 13 : 11,
"I have given thee a king in mine anger, and have taken
him away in my wrath." "The world is too bad," he adds,
"and not worthy to have many wise and pious princes."

To the objection that the secular magistrate should afford
an external protection, and hinder heretics from seducing the
people, he replies : —

"This is the business of bishops, and not of princes. For heresy can
never be kept off by force; another grip is needed for that; this is another
quarrel than that of the sword. God's word must contend here. If this
fails, the worldly power is of no avail, though it fill the world with blood.
Heresy is a spiritual thing that cannot be hewn down by iron, nor burned
by fire, nor drowned by water.[2] But God's word does it, as Paul says, 'Our
weapons are not carnal, but mighty in God' (2 Cor. 10 : 4, 5)."

for nine years), but the anti-Donatist Augustin was intolerant. The former
said, "Credere non potest homo nisi volens ;" the latter misinterpreted the
words: "Compelle intrare ut impleatur domus mea" (Luke 14 : 23), as a
justification of forcible coercion. Comp. above, § 11, p. 54 sq.

[1] "Die grössten Narren oder die ärgsten Buben auf Erden" (p. 89).

[2] "Ketzerei ist ein geistlich Ding, das kann man mit keinem Eisen hauen,
mit keinem Feuer verbrennen, mit keinem Wasser ertränken."

In his exposition of the First Epistle of St. Peter, from the same year (1523), he thus comments on the exhortation "to fear God and honor the king:"[1]—

"If the civil magistrate interferes with spiritual matters of conscience in which God alone must rule, we ought not to obey at all, but rather lose our head. Civil government is confined to external and temporal affairs. . . . If an emperor or prince asks me about my faith, I would give answer, not because of his command, but because of my duty to confess my faith before everybody. But if he should go further, and command me to believe this or that, I would say, 'Dear sir, mind your secular business; you have no right to interfere with God's reign, and therefore I shall not obey you at all.'"

Similar views on the separation of church and state were held by Anabaptists, Mennonites, the English martyr-bishop Hooper, and Robert Browne the Independent; but they had no practical effect till a much later period.[2]

Luther himself changed his opinion on this subject, and was in some measure driven to a change by the disturbances and heresies which sprang up around him, and threatened disorder and anarchy. The victory over the peasants greatly increased the power of the princes. The Lutheran Reformers handed the work of re-organization largely over to them, and thus unwittingly introduced a cæsaropapacy; that is, such a union of church and state as makes the head of the state also the supreme ruler in the church. It is just the opposite of the hierarchical principle of the Roman Church, which tries to rule the state. Melanchthon justified this transfer chiefly by the neglect of the pope and bishops to do their duty. He says, if Christ and the apostles had waited till Annas and Caiaphas permitted the gospel, they would have waited in vain.[3]

The co-operation of the princes and magistrates in the cities secured the establishment of the Protestant Church,

---

[1] In the Erl. ed., vol. LI. p. 419 sq.
[2] See § 12, p. 76, note.
[3] *Judicium de jure reformandi* (1525), in the "*Corp. Reform.*," I. 763 sqq.

but brought it under the bondage of lawyers and politicians who, with some honorable exceptions, knew less and ruled worse than the bishops. The Reformers often and bitterly complained in their later writings of the rapacity of princes and nobles who confiscated the property of churches and convents, and applied it to their own use instead of schools and benevolent purposes. Romish historians make the most of this fact to the disparagement of the Reformation. But the spoliations of Protestant princes are very trifling, as compared with the wholesale confiscation of church property by Roman-Catholic powers, as France, Spain, and Italy in the last and present centuries.

The union of church and state accounts for the persecution of papists, heretics, and Jews; and all the Reformers justified persecution to the extent of deposition and exile, some even to the extent of death, as in the case of Servetus.[1]

The modern progress of the principle of toleration and religious liberty goes hand in hand with the loosening of the bond of union between church and state.

§ 88. *Church Visitation in Saxony.*

MELANCHTHON: *Articuli de quibus egerunt per visitatores in regione Saxoniæ.* Wittenb., 1527. Reprinted in the *Corpus Reform.*, vol. XXVI. (1858), 9–28. The same in German with preface by LUTHER: *Unterricht der Visitatoren an die Pfarrherrn im Kurfürstenthum zu Sachsen.* Wittenb., 1528. In WALCH, X. 1902, and in *Corp. Reform.*, XXVI. 29–40. Also LUTHER's *Letters to Elector John*, from the years 1525 to 1527, in DE WETTE, vol. III. 38 sqq.

BURKHARDT: *Gesch. der sächsischen Kirchen- und Schulvisitationen von 1524–45.* Leipzig, 1879. KÖSTLIN: *M.L.*, II. 23–49.

In order to abolish ecclesiastical abuses, to introduce reforms in doctrine, worship, and discipline, and to establish Christian schools throughout the electorate of Saxony, Luther proposed a general visitation of all the churches. This was properly the work of bishops. But, as there were none in

---

[1] See § 12, p. 59 sqq.

Saxony who favored the Reformation, he repeatedly urged
the Elector John, soon after he succeeded his brother Frederick, to institute an episcopal visitation of the churches in
his territory, and to divide it into three or four districts, each
to be visited by two noblemen or magistrates.[1] He presented to him, in his strong way, the deplorable condition of
the church: the fear of God, and discipline are gone; the
common people have lost all respect for the preachers, pay
no more offerings, and let them starve; since the Pope's tyranny is abolished, everybody does as he pleases. We shall
soon have no churches, no schools, no pupils, unless the
magistrates restore order, and take care at least of the youth,
whatever may become of the old people.[2]

It was a dangerous step, and the entering wedge of a new
cæsaropapacy, — the rule of statecraft over priestcraft. But
it seemed to be the only available help under the circumstances, and certainly served a very useful purpose. Luther
had full confidence in the God-fearing Elector, that he would
not abuse the authority thus temporarily conferred on him.

The Elector, after considerable delay, resolved upon the
visitation in July, 1527, on the *quasi*-legal basis of the Diet
of Speier, which a year before had temporarily suspended,
but by no means abolished, the Edict of Worms. He directed
Melanchthon to prepare a "formula of doctrine and rites"
for the instruction of the visitors. Melanchthon elaborated
in Latin, and more fully in German, a summary of the evangelical doctrines of faith and duty, which may be regarded
as the first basis of the Augsburg Confession. He treats, in
seventeen articles, of faith, the cross (affliction), prayer, the

---

[1] See his letters of Oct. 31, 1525, Nov. 30, 1525, Nov. 22, 1526, Feb. 5,
1527, Oct. 12, 1527.

[2] " *Wollen die Alten ja nicht, mögen sie immer zum Teufel hinfahren.
Aber wo die Jugend versäumet und unerzogen bleibt, da ist die Schuld der
Obrigkeit* " (De Wette, III. 136). In the same letter he says that the people
live " *wie die Säue: da ist keine Furcht Gottes, noch Zucht mehr, weil des
Papstes Bann ist abgegangen, und thut jedermann was er nur will.* "

fruits of the Spirit, the magistrate, the fear of God, righteousness, judgment, the sacraments (Baptism, the Lord's
Supper, and Confession), the sign of the eucharist, penitence,
marriage, prohibited cases, human traditions, Christian liberty, free-will, and the law.   The order is not very logical,
and differs somewhat in the German edition.   The work
was finished in December, 1527.

Luther wrote a popular preface and notes to the German
edition, and explained the object.   He shows the importance
of church visitation, from the example of the apostles and
the primary aim of the episcopal office ; for a bishop, as the
term indicates, is an overseer of the churches, and an archbishop is an overseer of the bishops.   But the bishops have
become worldly lords, and neglect their spiritual duties.
Now, as the pure gospel has returned, or first begun, we
need a true episcopacy ; and, as nobody has a proper authority or divine command, we asked the Elector, as our divinely
appointed ruler (Rom. 13), to exercise his authority for the
protection and promotion of the gospel.   Although he is
not called to teach, he may restore peace and order, as the
Emperor Constantine did when he called the Council of
Nicæa for the settlement of the Arian controversy.[1]

Melanchthon wisely abstained from polemics, and advised
the preachers to attack sin and vice, but to let the pope and
the bishops alone.   Luther was not pleased with this moderation, and added the margin : " But they shall violently condemn popery with its devotees, since it is condemned by
God ; for popery is the reign of Antichrist, and, by instiga-
tion of the Devil, it terribly persecutes the Christian church
and God's Word." [2]

---

[1] " *Denn obwol S. K. F. Gnaden zu lehren und geistlich regieren nicht
befohlen ist, so sind sie doch schuldig, als weltliche Obrigkeit, darob zu halten,
dass nicht Zwietracht, Rotten und Aufruhr sich unter den Unterthanen
erheben, wie auch der Kaiser Constantinus die Bischöfe gen Nicæa fordert,*"
etc.   *Corp. Ref.*, XXVI. fol. 46.

[2] See the note in full, *l.c.*, fol. 85.

The Elector appointed Luther, Melanchthon, Jonas, Spalatin, and Myconius, besides some prominent laymen, among the visitors. They carried on their work in 1528 and 1529. They found the churches in a most deplorable condition, which was inherited from the times of the papacy, and aggravated by the abuse of the liberty of the Reformation. Pastors and people had broken loose from all restraint, churches and schools were in ruins, the ministers without income, ignorant, indifferent, and demoralized. Some kept taverns, were themselves drunkards, and led a scandalous life. The people, of course, were no better. "The peasants," wrote Luther to Spalatin, "learn nothing, know nothing, and abuse all their liberty. They have ceased to pray, to confess, to commune, as if they were bare of all religion. As they despised popery, so they now despise us. It is horrible to behold the administration of the popish bishops." [1]

The strong arm of the law was necessary. Order was measurably restored. The property of churches and convents was devoted to the endowment of parishes and schools, and stipends for theological students (1531). The appointment of ministers passed into the hands of the Elector. The visitations were repeated from time to time under the care of regular superintendents and consistories which formed the highest ecclesiastical councils, under the sovereign as the supreme bishop.

In this way, the territorial state-church government was established and order restored in Saxony, Hesse, Braunschweig-Lüneburg, Mecklenburg, East Friesland, Silesia, and other Protestant sovereignties of Germany.

---

[1] Letter of February, 1529, in De Wette, III. 424. Comp. also the prefaces to his Catechisms. It is characteristic of the Ultramontane history of Janssen, that, while he dwells largely on the lamentations of Luther over the wretched condition of the churches in Saxony, and derives them from his doctrine of justification by faith alone (vol. III. 67–69), he completely ignores Luther's Catechisms which were to cure these evils.

§ 89. *Luther's Catechisms.* *1529.*

I. Critical editions of Luther's Catechisms in his *Works*, Erl. ed., vol. XXI.
(contains the two catechisms and some other catechetical writings); by
MÖNCKEBERG (Hamburg, 1851, second ed. 1868); SCHNEIDER (Berlin,
1853, a reprint of the standard ed. of 1531 with a critical introduction);
THEODOS. HARNACK (Stuttgart, 1856; a reprint of two editions of 1529
and 1539, and a table of the chief textual variations till 1842); ZEZ-
SCHWITZ (Leipz. 1881); CALINICH (Leipz. 1882). See titles in SCHAFF:
Creeds of Christendom, I. 245. The Catechisms are also printed in the
editions of the Symbolical Books of the Lutheran Church, and the Little
(or Small) Catechism, with English translation, in SCHAFF'S *Creeds*,
etc., vol. III. 74–92. The text in the Book of Concord is unreliable,
and should be compared with the works mentioned.

II. Discussions on the history and merits of Luther's Catech., by KÖCHER,
AUGUSTI, VEESENMEYER, ZEZSCHWITZ, and others, quoted by SCHAFF,
l. c. 245. Add KÖSTLIN: *M. L.*, Bk. VI. ch. IV. (II. 50–65).

The Catechisms of Luther are the richest fruit of the Saxon
church visitations. Intended as a remedy for the evils of
ignorance and irreligion, they have become symbolical standards of doctrine and duty, and permanent institutions in the
Lutheran Church. The Little Catechism, which is his best,
bears the stamp of his religious genius, and is, next to his
translation of the Bible, his most useful and enduring work
by which he continues a living teacher in catechetical classes
and Sunday schools as far as the Lutheran confession extends.
He here adapts the mysteries of the kingdom of heaven to
the capacity of children, and becomes himself a child with
children, a learner with the teacher, as he said, "I am a doctor and a preacher, yet I am like a child who is taught the
Catechism, and I read and recite word by word in the morning the Ten Commandments, the Articles of the Creed, and
the Lord's Prayer, and cheerfully remain a child and pupil
of the Catechism." A great little book, with as many
thoughts as words, and every word sticking to the heart as
well as the memory. It is strong food for men, and milk for
babes. It appeals directly to the heart, and can be turned
into prayer. In the language of the great historian Leopold

von Ranke, "it is as childlike as it is profound, as compre-
hensible as it is unfathomable, simple and sublime. Happy
he whose soul was fed by it, who clings to it! He possesses
an imperishable comfort in every moment; under a thin shell,
a kernel of truth sufficient for the wisest of the wise." [1]

Catechetical instruction was (after the model of the Jewish
synagogue) a regular institution of the Christian church
from the beginning, as a preparation for membership. In the
case of adult converts, it preceded baptism; in the case of
baptized infants, it followed baptism, and culminated in the
confirmation and the first communion. The oldest theological school, where Clement and the great Origen taught, grew
out of the practical necessity of catechetical teaching. The
chief things taught were the Creed (the Nicene in the Greek,
the Apostles' in the Latin Church) or what to believe, the
Lord's Prayer (*Pater Noster*) or how to pray, and the Ten
Commandments or how to live. To these were added sometimes special chapters on the sacraments, the Athanasian
Creed, the *Te Deum*, the *Gloria in excelsis*, the *Ave Maria*,
Scripture verses, and lists of sins and virtues. Cyril's Catechetical Lectures were a standard work in the Greek Church.
Augustin wrote, at the request of a deacon, a famous book
on catechising (*De catechizandis rudibus*), and a brief exposition of the Creed and the Lord's Prayer (*Enchiridion*), which
were intended for teachers, and show what was deemed necessary in the fifth century for the instruction of Christians.
In the middle ages the monks Kero (720) and Notker (912),
both of St. Gall, Otfrid of Weissenburg (870), and others
prepared catechetical manuals or primers of the simplest
kind. Otfrid's Catechism contains (1) the Lord's Prayer
with an explanation; (2) the deadly sins; (3) the Apostles'
Creed; (4) the Athanasian Creed; (5) the Gloria. The

[1] To this and other testimonies, may be added that of Köstlin, II. 63:
"*Der Kleine Katechismus steht in erster Reihe unter den Schriften des
Reformators.*"

anti-papal sects of the Albigenses, Waldenses, and Bohemian Brethren, paid special attention to catechetical instruction.

The first Protestant catechisms were prepared by Lonicer (1523), Melanchthon (1524), Brentius (1527), Althamer, Lachmann (1528), and later by Urbanus Rhegius (Rieger).[1] Luther urged his friends and colleagues, Justus Jonas and Agricola, to write one for Saxony (1525);[2] but after the doleful experience of popular ignorance during the church visitation, he took the task in hand himself, and completed it in 1529. He had previously published popular expositions of the Ten Commandments, the Creed, and the Lord's Prayer (1520).[3]

He wrote two Catechisms, both in the German language. The "Great Catechism" is a continuous exposition, and not divided into questions and answers; moreover, it grew so much under his hands, that it became unsuitable for the instruction of the young, which he had in view from the beginning. Hence he prepared soon afterwards (in July, 1529) a short or little Catechism under the name *Enchiridion*. It is the ripe fruit of the larger work, and superseded it for practical use. The same relation exists between the Larger and Shorter Catechisms of the Westminster Assembly.

With his conservative instinct, Luther retained the three essential parts of a catechism, — the Decalogue, the Creed, and the Lord's Prayer. He called the first the doctrine of all doctrines; the second, the history of all histories; the third, the highest of all prayers. To these three chief divisions he added, after the Catholic tradition and the example of the Bohemian Catechism, an instruction on the sacraments of Baptism and the Lord's Supper, in two separate parts,

---

[1] Hartmann, *Aelteste Katechetische Denkmale*, Stuttgart, 1844.

[2] Jonas is probably the author of the *Laienbiblia*, 1525 (republished by Schneider in 1853), and this was probably the basis of " Cranmer's Catechism," 1548. See Schaff, *Creeds*, I. 655, note 2.

[3] Erl. ed., vol. XXII. 1-32. Comp. also his *Taufbüchlein verdeutscht*, 1523, and reproduced 1526 (?), *ibid.* XXII. 157 sqq. and 290 sqq.

making five in all. He retained in the address of the Lord's
Prayer the old German *Vater unser* (*Pater Noster*), and the
translation " Deliver us from *evil* " (*a malo*) ; but in his Bible
he changed the former into *Unser Vater* (Matt. 6 : 9), and in
his Large Catechism he refers the Greek to the *evil one*, i.e.,
the Devil (ὁ πονηρός), as our arch-enemy. Yet in practice these
two differences have become distinctive marks of the Lutheran and German Reformed use of the Lord's Prayer.[1]

The later editions of the Little Catechism (since 1564)
contain a sixth part on "Confession and Absolution," or,
" The Power of the Keys," which is inserted either as Part
V., between Baptism and the Lord's Supper, or added as
Part VI., or as an appendix. The precise authorship of the
enlarged form or forms (for they vary) of this part, with
the questions, " What is the power of the keys?" etc., is
uncertain ; but the substance of it — viz. the questions on
private or auricular confession of sin to the minister, and
absolution by the minister, as given in the " Book of Concord " — date from Luther himself, and appear first substantially in the third edition of 1531, as introductory to the
fifth part on the Lord's Supper. He made much account of
private confession and absolution ; while the Calvinists abolished the same as a mischievous popish invention, and retained only the public act. " True absolution," says Luther,
" or the power of the keys, instituted in the gospel by
Christ, affords comfort and support against sin and an evil
conscience. Confession or absolution shall by no means be
abolished in the church, but be retained, especially on account
of weak and timid consciences, and also on account of un-
tutored youth, in order that they may be examined and
instructed in the Christian doctrine. But the enumeration
of sins should be free to every one, to enumerate, or not to
enumerate such as he wishes." [2] The practice of private

---

[1] If German farmers in Pennsylvania are asked, " What is the difference
between the Lutherans and the Reformed ? " the reply is, " The one pray
Vater unser, the other *Unser Vater*."

[2] *Articuli Smalcald.* P. III., cap. 8.

confession is still retained in some sections, but has entirely disappeared in other sections, of the Lutheran Church.

The Church of England holds a similar view on this subject. The Book of Common Prayer contains, besides two forms of public confession and absolution, a form of private confession and absolution. But the last is omitted in the liturgy of the Episcopal Church of the United States.

Besides these doctrinal sections, the Little Catechism, as edited by Luther in 1531 (partly, also, in the first edition of 1529) has three appendices of a devotional or liturgical character: viz., (1) A series of short family prayers; (2) a table of duties (*Haustafel*) for the members of a Christian household, consisting of Scripture passages; (3) a marriage manual (*Traubüchlin*), and (4) a baptismal manual (*Taufbüchlin*).

The first two appendices were retained in the "Book of Concord;" but the third and fourth, which are liturgical and ceremonial, were omitted because of the great diversity in different churches as to exorcism in baptism and the rite of marriage.

The Little Catechism was translated from the German original into the Latin (by Sauermann) and many other languages, even into the Greek, Hebrew, and Syriac. It is asserted by Lutheran writers that no book, except the Bible, has had a wider circulation. Thirty-seven years after its appearance, Mathesius spoke of a circulation of over a hundred thousand copies. It was soon introduced into public schools, churches, and families. It became by common consent a symbolical book, and a sort of "layman's Bible" for the German people.

Judged from the standpoint of the Reformed churches, the catechism of Luther, with all its excellences, has some serious defects. It gives the text of the Ten Commandments in an abridged form, and follows the wrong division of the Latin Church, which omits the Second Commandment altogether, and cuts the Tenth Commandment into two to make up the number. It allows only three questions and answers to the exposition of the creed, — on creation, redemption, and sanctification. It gives undue importance to the sacraments by making them co-ordinate parts with the three great divisions; and elevates private confession and absolution almost to the dignity of a third sacrament. It contains no instruction on the Bible, as the inspired record of Divine revelation and the rule of faith and practice. These defects are usually supplied in catechetical instruction by a number of preliminary or additional questions and answers.

§ 90. *The Typical Catechisms of Protestantism.*

In this connection we may anticipate a brief comparison between the most influential manuals of popular religious instruction which owe their origin to the Reformation, and have become institutions, retaining their authority and usefulness to this day.

These are Luther's Little Catechism (1529), the Heidelberg Catechism (1563), the Anglican Catechism (1549, enlarged 1604, revised 1661), and the Westminster Shorter Catechism (1647). The first is the standard catechism of the Lutheran Church; the second, of the German and Dutch Reformed, and a few other Reformed churches (in Bohemia and Hungary); the third, of the Episcopal Church of England and her daughters in the British Colonies and the United States; the fourth, of the Presbyterian churches in Scotland, England, and America. They follow these various churches to all their missionary fields in heathen lands, and have been translated into many languages.

They are essentially agreed in the fundamental doctrines of catholic and evangelical religion. They teach the articles of the Apostles' Creed, the Ten Commandments, and the Lord's Prayer; that is, all that is necessary for a man to believe and to do in order to be saved. They thus exhibit the harmony of the chief branches of orthodox Protestant Christendom.

But they also differ, and reflect the peculiar genius and

charisma of these churches. The Lutheran Catechism is the
simplest, the most genial and childlike; the Heidelberg Catechism, the fullest and the richest for a more mature age;
the Anglican Catechism, the shortest and most churchly,
though rather meagre; the Westminster Catechism, the
clearest, precisest, and most logical. The first three are
addressed to the learner as a church-member, who answers
the questions from his present or prospective experience. The
Westminster Catechism is impersonal, and gives the answers
in the form of a theological definition embodying the question. The first two breathe the affectionate heartiness and
inwardness which are characteristic of German piety; the
other two reflect the sober and practical type of English and
Scotch piety. The Lutheran and Anglican Catechisms begin
with the Ten Commandments, and regard the law in its
preparatory mission as a schoolmaster leading to Christ.
The other catechisms begin with an exposition of the articles
of faith, and proceed from faith to the law as a rule of Christian life, which the Heidelberg Catechism represents as an act
of gratitude for the salvation obtained (following in its order
the Epistle to the Romans, from sin to redemption, and from
redemption to a holy life of gratitude). Luther adheres to
the Roman division of the Decalogue, and abridges it; the
others give the better division of the Jews and the Greek
Church, with the full text. The Lutheran and Anglican
Catechisms assign to the sacraments an independent place
alongside of the Commandments, the Creed, and the Lord's
Prayer; while the Heidelberg and Westminster Catechisms
incoporate them in the exposition of the articles of faith.
The former teach baptismal regeneration, and Luther also
the corporeal real presence, and private confession and absolution; the latter teach the Calvinistic theory of the sacra-
ments, and ignore private confession and absolution. The
Anglican Thirty-nine Articles, however, likewise teach the
Reformed view of the Lord's Supper. The Westminster

Catechism departs from the catholic tradition by throwing the Apostles' Creed into an appendix, and substituting for the historical order of revelation a new logical scheme; while all the other catechisms make the Creed the basis of their doctrinal expositions.[1]

The difference is manifest in the opening questions and answers, which we give here in parallel columns: —

LUTHER'S CATECHISM.	HEIDELBERG CATECHISM.	ANGLICAN CATECHISM.	WESTMINSTER CATECHISM.
The First Commandment.	*What is thy only comfort in life and in death?*	*What is your name?* N. or M.	*What is the chief end of man?* Man's chief end is to glorify God, and to enjoy Him forever.
Thou shalt have no other gods.	That I, with body and soul, both in life and in death, am not my own, but belong to my faithful Saviour Jesus Christ, who with his precious blood has fully satisfied for all my sins, and redeemed me from all the power of the devil; and so preserves me that without the will of my Father in heaven not a hair can fall from my head; yea, that all things must work together for my salvation. Wherefore, by his Holy Spirit, He also assures me of eternal life, and makes me heartily willing and ready henceforth to live unto Him.	*Who gave you this name?* My *Godfathers* and *Godmothers*[2] in my Baptism; wherein I was made a member of Christ, the child of God, and an inheritor of the kingdom of heaven.	*What rule hath God given to direct us how we may glorify and enjoy Him?* The Word of God, which is contained in the Scriptures of the Old and New Testaments, is the only rule to direct us how we may glorify and enjoy Him.
What does this mean? We should fear and love God, and trust in Him, above all things.		*What did your godfathers and godmothers [sponsors] then for you?* They did promise and vow three things in my name. First, that I should renounce the devil and all his works, the pomps and vanity of this wicked world, and all the sinful lusts of the flesh. Secondly, that I should believe all the Articles of the Christian Faith. And thirdly, that I should keep God's holy will and commandments, and walk in them all the days of my life.	*What do the Scriptures principally teach?* The Scriptures principally teach what man is to believe concerning God and what duty God requires of man.
The Second [Third] Commandment. Thou shalt not take the name of thy God in vain.			*What is God?* God is a Spirit, infinite, eternal, and unchangeable, in his being, wisdom, power, holiness, justice, goodness, and truth.
What does this mean? We should so fear and love God as not to curse, swear, conjure, lie, or deceive, by his name; but call upon it in every time of need, pray, praise, and give thanks.	*How many things are necessary for thee to know, that thou in this comfort mayest live and die happily?* Three things: First, the greatness of my sin and misery. Secondly, how I am redeemed from all my sins and misery. Thirdly, how I am to be thankful to God for such redemption.		
The Third [Fourth] Commandment. Thou shalt keep holy the Sabbath day.			
What does this mean? We should so fear and love God as not to despise preaching and His Word, but deem it holy, and willingly hear and learn it.			

[1] For a fuller comparison, see Schaff, *Creeds of Christendom*, I. 543 sqq.

[2] The American Episcopal Prayer-book reads instead: My *Sponsors*.

CHAPTER VI.

PROPAGATION AND PERSECUTION OF PROTESTANTISM IN GERMANY TILL 1530.

§ 91. *Causes and Means of Progress.*

THE Reformation spread over Germany with the spontaneous and irresistible impulse of a great historical movement that struck its roots deep in the wants and necessities of the church. The only propaganda of Luther was the word and the pen, but these he used to the utmost of his time and strength. " There was no need of an arrangement," says Ranke, " or of a concerted agreement, or of any special mission. As at the first favor of the vernal sun the seed sprouts from the ploughed field, so the new convictions, which were prepared by all what men had experienced and heard, made their appearance on the slightest occasion, wherever the German language was spoken."[1]

The chief causes of progress were the general discontent with papal tyranny and corruption; the desire for light, liberty, and peace of conscience; the thirst for the pure word of God. The chief agencies were the German Bible, which spoke with Divine authority to the reason and conscience, and overawed the human authority of the pope; the German hymns, which sang the comforting doctrines of grace into the hearts of the people; and the writings of Luther, who discussed every question of the day with commanding ability and abundant knowledge, assuring the faith of friends, and crushing the opposition of foes. The force

---

[1] *Deutsche Geschichte*, etc., vol. II. 46 (6th ed.).

and fertility of his genius as a polemic are amazing, and without a parallel among fathers, schoolmen, and modern divines. He ruled like an absolute monarch in the realm of German theology and religion ; and, with the gospel for his shield and weapon, he was always sure of victory.[1]

What Luther did for the people, Melanchthon accomplished, in his gentle and moderate way, for scholars. In their united labors they were more than a match for all the learning, skill, and material resources of the champions of Rome.

No such progress of new ideas and principles had taken place since the first introduction of Christianity. No power of pope or emperor, no council or diet, could arrest it. The very obstacles were turned into helps. Had the Emperor and his brother favored the cause of progress, all Germany might have become nominally Lutheran. But it was better that Protestantism should succeed, in spite of their opposition, by its intellectual and moral force. A Protestant Constantine or Charlemagne would have extended the territory, but endangered the purity, of the Reformation.

Secular and selfish motives and passions were mingled with the pure enthusiasm for the gospel. Violence, intrigues, and gross injustice were sometimes employed in the suppression of the old, and the introduction of the new, faith.[2] But human sin and imperfection enter into all great movements

---

[1] "*Selbstherrschender, gewaltiger ist wohl nie ein Schriftsteller aufgetreten, in keiner Nation der Welt. Auch dürfte kein anderer zu nennen sein, der die vollkommenste Verständlichkeit und Popularität, gesunden, treuherzigen Menschenverstand mit so viel echtem Geist, Schwung und Genius vereinigt hätte. Er gab der Literatur den Charakter den sie seitdem behalten, der Forschung, des Tiefsinns, der Polemik.*" Ranke, II. 56. "*Fesselnder, ergreifender und packender hat kein Deutscher geschrieben. Dabei beherrschte er seine Muttersprache mit solcher Gewalt, dass er sie zur Schriftsprache zu erheben vermochte.*" Fr. Kapp, *Geschichte des deutschen Buchhandels*, vol. I. p. 407.

[2] Janssen dwells, we may say, exclusively on the lower motives, and by omitting the higher spiritual motives and aims utterly misrepresents the Reformers and the Reformation.

of history. Wherever God builds a church, the Devil is
sure to build a chapel close by. The Devil is mighty; but
God is almighty, and overrules the wrath and outwits the
wit of his great enemy. Nothing but the power of truth
and conviction could break down the tyranny of the papacy,
which for so many centuries had controlled church and
state, house and home, from the cradle to the grave, and held
the keys to the kingdom of heaven. It is an insult to reason
and faith to deny the all-ruling and overruling supremacy of
God in the history of the world and the church.

§ 92. *The Printing-Press and the Reformation.*

The art of printing, which was one of the providential
preparations for the Reformation, became the mightiest lever
of Protestantism and modern culture.

The books before the Reformation were, for the most part,
ponderous and costly folios and quartos in Latin, for limited
circulation. The rarity of complete Bibles is shown by the
fact that copies in the libraries were secured by a chain
against theft. Now small and portable books and leaflets
were printed in the vernacular for the millions.

The statistics of the book trade in the sixteenth century
reveal an extraordinary increase since Luther. In the year
1513, there appeared only ninety prints in Germany; in
1514, one hundred and six; in 1515, one hundred and forty-
five; in 1516, one hundred and five; in 1517, eighty-one.
They are mostly little devotional tracts, flying newspapers,
official notices, medical prescriptions, stories, and satirical
exposures of clerical and monastic corruptions. In 1518 the
number rose to one hundred and forty-six; in 1519, to two
hundred and fifty-two; in 1520, to five hundred and seventy-
one; in 1521, to five hundred and twenty-three; in 1522, to
six hundred and seventy-seven; in 1523, to nine hundred
and forty-four. Thus the total number of prints in the five
years preceding the Reformation amounted only to five hun-

dred and twenty-seven; in the six years after the Reformation, it rose to three thousand one hundred and thirteen.[1]

These works are distributed over fifty different cities of Germany. Of all the works printed between 1518 and 1523 no less than six hundred appeared in Wittenberg; the others mostly in Nürnberg, Leipzig, Cologne, Strassburg, Hagenau, Augsburg, Basel, Halberstadt, and Magdeburg. Luther created the book-trade in Northern Germany, and made the little town of Wittenberg one of the principal book-marts, and a successful rival of neighboring Leipzig as long as this remained Catholic. In the year 1523 more than four-fifths of all the books published were on the side of the Reformation, while only about twenty books were decidedly Roman Catholic. Erasmus, hitherto the undisputed monarch in the realm of letters, complained that the people would read and buy no other books than Luther's. He prevailed upon Froben not to publish any more of them. "Here in Basel," he wrote to King Henry VIII., "nobody dares to print a word against Luther, but you may write as much as you please against the pope." Romish authors, as we learn from Cochläus and Wizel, could scarcely find a publisher, except at their own expense; and the Leipzig publishers complained that their books were unsalable.

The strongest impulse was given to the book trade by Luther's German New Testament. Of the first edition, Sept. 22, 1522, five thousand copies were printed and sold before December of the same year, at the high price of one guilder and a half per copy (about twenty-five marks of the present value). Hans Luft printed a hundred thousand

---

[1] For these figures and several facts in this paragraph I am indebted to the instructive work of Friedrich Kapp, *Geschichte des deutschen Buchhandels* (published by the "Börsenverein der deutschen Buchhändler," Leipzig, 1886), vol. I. 407 sq. The statistics of Ranke (II. 56) are taken from Panzer's *Annalen der älteren deutschen Literatur* (1788 and 1802) and are superseded by the more recent and fuller investigations of Weller, Kuczynski, and Kapp.

copies on his press in Wittenberg. Adam Petri in Basel published seven editions between 1522 and 1525; Thomas Wolf of the same city, five editions between 1523 and 1525. Duke George commanded that all copies should be delivered up at cost, but few were returned. The precious little volume, which contains the wisdom of the whole world, made its way with lightning speed into the palaces of princes, the castles of knights, the convents of monks, the studies of priests, the houses of citizens, the huts of peasants. Mechanics, peasants, and women carried the New Testament in their pockets, and dared to dispute with priests and doctors of theology about the gospel.[1]

As there was no copyright at that time, the works of the Reformers were multiplied by reprints in Nürnberg, Augsburg, Strassburg, Basel. Republication was considered a legitimate and honorable business. Luther complained, not of the business itself, but of the reckless and scandalous character of many reprints of his books, which were so full of blunders that he could hardly recognize them.[2] Sometimes the printers stole his manuscript, and published it elsewhere. He was not hindered by any censorship, except that he received occasionally a gentle warning from the Elector when he did not spare the princes. He took no honorarium for his books, and was satisfied with a number of free copies for friends. Authors were usually supported by a professorship, and considered it beneath their dignity, or as ungentlemanlike, to receive a royalty, but were indirectly rewarded by free copies or other presents of the publishers or rich patrons, in return for dedications, which were originally, as they are now, nothing more than public testimonies of regard or gratitude, though often used, especially during the seven-

---

[1] This was the complaint of Cochlæus, see p. 350. Luther called him *Kochlöffel* and *Rotzlöffel* (*cochlear*=spoon).

[2] He called such printers thieves and highway robbers, and their work " *Bubenstück, den gemeinen Mann zu betrügen* " (September, 1525).

teenth century, for selfish purposes.[1] Cash payments to
authors were, down to the eighteenth century, rare and very
low. Few could make a decent living from writing books;
and, we may add, few publishers acquired wealth from their
trade, which is very uncertain, and subject to great losses.
" *Habent sua fata libelli.*"

But, while the progressive Reformation gave wings to the
printing-press, the conservative re-action matured gradually
a system of restriction, which, under the name of censorship
and under the direction of book-censors, assumed the control
of the publishing business with authority to prevent or suppress the publication and sale of books, pamphlets, and newspapers hostile to the prevailing religious, moral, or political
sentiments.[2] The Peasants' War, which was kindled by
inflammatory books, and threatened a general overthrow
of social order, strengthened the re-actionary tendencies of
Protestant, as well as Roman Catholic, governments.

The burning of obnoxious books by public authority of
church or state is indeed as old as the book-trade. A work
of Protagoras, in which he doubted the existence of the
Greek gods, was burned at the stake in Athens about twenty
years after the death of Pericles. The Emperor Augustus
subjected slanderous publications (*libelli famosi*) to legal
prosecution and destruction by fire. Christian emperors employed their authority against heathen, heretical, and infidel
books. Constantine the Great, backed by the Council of
Nicæa, issued an edict against the writings of Porphyry
and Arius; Accadius, against the books of the Eunomians
(398); Theodosius, against the books of the Nestorians (435).
Justinian commanded the destruction of sundry obnoxious

---

[1] Kapp (I. 318) mentions that the electors of Saxony from 1571–1670
received no less than a hundred and ninety-two "most humble" (*aller-
untherthänigste*) dedications from various authors, and that the magistrate
of Zürich received thirty-eight from 1670–1685.

[2] On the history of the book censorship (*Büchercensur*) and press persecutions, compare the ninth and tenth chapters of Kapp, I. 522 sqq.

works, and forbade their re-issue on pain of losing the right arm (536). The œcumenical synod of 680 at Constantinople burned the books which it had condemned, including the letters of the Monothelitic Pope Honorius.

Papal Rome inherited this practice, and improved upon it. Leo I. caused a large number of Manichæan books to be burnt (446). The popes claimed the right and duty to superintend the religious and moral literature of Christendom. They transferred the right in the thirteenth century to the universities, but they found little to do until the art of printing facilitated the publication of books. The Council of Constance condemned the books of Wiclif and Hus, and ordered the bishops to burn all the copies they could seize (1415).

The invention of the printing-press (c. 1450) called forth sharper measures in the very city where the inventor, John Gutenberg, lived and died (1400–1467). It gave rise also to the preventive policy of book-censorship which still exists in some despotic countries of Europe. Berthold, Archbishop of Mainz, took the lead in the restriction of the press. He prohibited, Jan. 10, 1486, the sale of all unauthorized German translations of Greek and Latin works, on the plea of the inefficiency of the German language, but with a hostile aim at the German Bible. In the same year Pope Innocent VIII. issued a bull against the printers of bad books. The infamous Pope Alexander VI. prohibited in 1498, on pain of excommunication, the printing and reading of heretical books; and in a bull of June 1, 1501, which was aimed chiefly against Germany, he subjected all kinds of literary publications to episcopal supervision and censorship, and required the four archbishops of Cöln, Mainz, Trier, and Magdeburg, or their officials, carefully to examine all manuscripts before giving permission to print them. He also ordered that books already printed should be examined, and burnt if they contained any thing contrary to the Catholic

religion. This bull forms the basis of all subsequent prohibitions and restrictions of the press by papal, imperial, or
other authority.[1]

Leo X., who personally cared more for heathen art than
Christian literature, went further, and prohibited, in a bull
of March 3, 1515, the publication of any book in Rome
without the imprimatur of the *magister sacri palatii* (the
book-censor), and in other states and dioceses without the
imprimatur of the bishop or the inquisitor of heretical
depravity.[2] Offenders were to be punished by the confiscation and public burning of their books, a fine of one hundred ducats, and excommunication. Archbishop and Elector
Albrecht of Mainz was the first, and it seems the only,
German prince who gave force to this bull for his own large
diocese by a mandate of May 17, 1517, a few months before
the outbreak of the Reformation. The papal bull of excommunication, June 15, 1520, consistently ordered the burning
of "all the books of Luther."[3] But he laughed it to scorn,
and burned in revenge the pope's bull, with all his decretals,
Dec. 10, 1520.

Thus, with the freedom of conscience, was born the freedom of the press. But it had to pass through a severe ordeal,
even in Protestant countries, and was constantly checked by
Roman authorities as far as their power extended. The
German Empire, by the Edict of Worms, made itself an
ally of the pope against free thought and free press, and
continued so until it died of old age in 1806.[4] Fortunately,

---

[1] The bull is not given in the *Bullarium*, but by Raynaldus *ad a.* 1501,
No. 36, Zaccaria, and Reusch (I. 54), in part also by Kapp (*l.c.* p. 530).

[2] The bull "*Inter solicitudines*" was promulgated in the fifth Lateran
Council. Labbe, XIV. 257, and Reusch, I. 55 sq.

[3] The bull "*Exurge, Domine*," is printed in full, p. 235 sqq.

[4] Kapp, *l.c.*, p. 536 sqq., shows that the Edict of Worms, drawn up by the
papal legate Aleander, is the beginning of the German book-censorship, and
not, as usually supposed, the recess of the Nürnberg Diet of 1524. "*Wie
Rom*," he says (539), "*die Wiege der Büchercensur für die ganze Welt, so
ist Worms ihre Geburtsstätte für Deutschland.*" The restriction of the
press, however, was begun in Germany, as we have seen, already in 1486, by
Elector Berthold of Mainz.

the weakness of the empire and the want of centralization prevented the execution of the prohibition of Protestant books, except in strictly papal countries, as Bavaria and Austria. But unfortunately, the Protestants themselves, who used the utmost freedom of the press against the Papists, denied it to each other; the Lutherans to the Reformed, and both to the Anabaptists, Schwenkfeldians and Socinians.[1] Protestant princes liked to control the press to protect themselves against popery, or the charges of robbery of church property and other attacks. The Elector John Frederick was as narrow and intolerant as Duke George on the opposite side. But these petty restrictions are nothing compared with the radical and systematic crusade of the Papists against the freedom of the press. King Ferdinand of Austria ordered, July 24, 1528, all printers and sellers of sectarian books to be drowned, and their books to be burnt. The wholesale burning of Protestant books, including Protestant Bibles, was a favorite and very effective measure of the Jesuitical re-action which set in before the middle of the sixteenth century, and was promoted by the political arm, and the internecine wars of the Protestants. Pope Paul IV. published in 1557 and 1559 the first official *Index Librorum prohibitorum;* Pius IV. in 1564, an enlarged edition, generally known as *Index Tridentinus,* as it was made by order of the Council of Trent. It contains a list of all the books forbidden by Rome, good, bad, and indifferent. This list has been growing ever since in size (1590, 1596, 1607, 1664, 1758, 1819, etc.), but declining in authority, till it became, like the bull against the comet, an anachronism and a *brutum fulmen.*[2]

---

[1] "*Derselbe Luther,*" says Kapp, p. 552, "*welcher das Papstthum für noch lange nicht genug zerscholten, zerschrieben, zersungen, zerdichtet und zermalet hielt, rief schon 1525 die Censur für seinen nunmehrigen Standpunkt zur Hilfe.*" He refers to his attempt to secure a prohibition of Carlstadt's writings in Saxony.

[2] Fr. Heinrich Reusch (Old Catholic Prof. at Bonn): *Der Index der verbotenen Bücher,* Bonn, 1883-85, 2 vols. Of older works we mention, Fr. Zaccaria, *Storia polemica delle proibizioni de' libri,* Rom., 1777; and

§ 93. *Protestantism in Saxony.*

H. G. HASSE: *Meissnisch-Albertinisch-Sächsische Kirchengesch.* Leipz. 1847, 2 parts. FR. SEIFERT: *Die Reformation in Leipzig*, Leipz. 1881. G. LECHLER: *Die Vorgeschichte der Reform. Leipzigs*, 1885. See also the literary references in KÖSTLIN, II. 426 and 672.

Electoral Saxony was the first conquest of the Reformation. Wittenberg was the centre of the whole movement, with Luther as the general in chief, Melanchthon, Jonas, Bugenhagen, as his aids. The gradual growth of Lutheranism in this land of its birth is identical with the early history of the Reformation, and has been traced already.

In close connection with the Electorate is the Duchy of Saxony, and may here be considered, although it followed the movement much later. The Duchy included the important cities of Dresden (the residence of the present kingdom of Saxony) and Leipzig with its famous university. Duke George kept the Reformation back by force during his long reign from 1500 to 1539. He hated the papal extortions, and advocated a reform of discipline by a council, but had no sympathy whatever with Luther. He took a dislike to him at the disputation in Leipzig, forbade his Bible, issued a rival version of the New Testament by Emser, sent all the Lutherans out of the land, and kept a close watch on the book-sellers.[1] He executed the Edict of Worms to the extent of his power, and would have rejoiced in the burning of Luther, who in turn abused him most unmercifully by his pen as a slave of the pope and the devil, though he prayed for his conversion.[2]

Jos. Mendham, *The Literary Policy of the Church of Rome exhibited in an account of her damnatory Catalogues or Indexes, both prohibitory and expurgatory*, London, 1826, 3d ed. 1844.

[1] One of them, Johann Herrgott, was executed in Leipzig, 1527 (not 1524) for selling Lutheran books, or rather for complicity with the Peasants' War, and for agrarian socialistic doctrines. See A. Kirchhoff, *Johann Herrgott, Buchführer von Nürnberg, und sein tragisches Ende*, 1527, and Kapp, *l. c.*, I. 438 sq. and 594.

[2] After George's death Luther said: "I would rather that he lived and be converted; now he has gone into the eternal fire [!], if the gospel is true." Köstlin, II. 424.

George made provision for the perpetuation of Romanism in his dominion; but his sons died one after another. His brother and heir, Heinrich the Pious, was a Lutheran (as was his wife). Though old and weak, he introduced the Reformation by means of a church visitation after the Wittenberg model and with Wittenberg aid. The Elector of Saxony, Luther, Melanchthon, Jonas, and Cruciger were present at the inaugural festivities in Leipzig, May, 1539. Luther had the satisfaction of preaching at Pentecost before an immense audience in the city, where twenty years before he had disputed with Eck, and provoked the wrath of Duke George. Yet he was by no means quite pleased with the new state of things, and complained bitterly of the concealed malice of the semi-popish clergy, and the overbearing and avaricious conduct of the nobles and courtiers.

Nevertheless, the change was general and permanent. Leipzig became the chief Lutheran university, and the center of the Protestant book-trade, and remains so to this day. Joachim Camerarius (Kammermeister), an intimate friend and correspondent of Melanchthon, labored there as professor from 1541–1546 for the prosperity of the university, and for the promotion of classical learning and evangelical piety.

We briefly allude to the subsequent changes. Moritz, the son and heir of Heinrich, was a shrewd politician, a master in the art of dissimulation, and a double traitor, who from selfish motives in turn first ruined and then saved the cause of the Reformation. He professed the Lutheran faith, but betrayed his allies by aiding the Emperor in the Smalcaldian war for the price of the Electoral dignity of his cousin (1547); a few years later he betrayed the Emperor (1552), and thereby prepared the way for the treaty of Passau and the peace of Augsburg, which secured temporary rest to the Lutherans (1555).

His next successors, Augustus I. (his brother, 1553–1586), Christian I. (1586–1591), and Christian II. (1591–1611), were intolerant Lutherans, and suppressed Crypto-Calvinism and every other creed. Frederick Augustus I. (1694–1733) sold the faith of his ancestors for the crown of Poland. Since that time the rulers of Saxony have been Roman Catholics, while the people remained Lutheran, but gradually grew more liberal than their ancestors. Freedom of worship was granted to the Roman Church in 1807, to the German Reformed in 1818, and more recently (since 1866) to other communions.

§ 94. *The Reformation in Nürnberg.*

PRIEM: *Geschichte von Nürnberg*, 1874. F. ROTH: *Die Einführung der Reformation in Nürnberg, 1517–28*, Würzburg, 1885 (pp. 271).

The imperial cities (*Reichsstädte*) of the old German Empire, such as Nürnberg, Augsburg, Frankfurt, Strassburg, enjoyed a larger measure of liberty than other cities. They had the sovereignty over their territory, with a constitutional government, and seat and vote in the Diet (*Reichstag*). They were the centres of intelligence, wealth, and influence. For this reason the Reformation made from the beginning rapid progress in them, though not without commotion and opposition.

Nürnberg (Nuremberg), the most picturesque mediæval city of Germany, was at that time the metropolis of German commerce, politics, letters, and art, and of an unusual constellation of distinguished men, most of whom sympathized with Erasmus and Luther. Pirkheimer, the Mæcenas of Nürnberg (1475–1530), prepared the way, although he afterwards withdrew, like his friend Erasmus and other humanists.[1] Albrecht Dürer, the famous painter (1471–1528), admired the heroic stand of Luther at Worms, and lamented his supposed death when removed out of sight; but during the eucharistic controversy he inclined to the view of Zwingli. Hans Sachs (1494–1576), the "Mastersinger" and

---

[1] See § 74, p. 434 sqq.

shoemaker-poet, saluted the "Nightingale" of Wittenberg (1523). Wenzeslaus Link, an Augustinian monk and intimate friend and correspondent of Luther, was sent by Staupitz from Wittenberg to the Augustinian convent at Nürnberg in 1518, and promoted the cause by his popular evangelical sermons. The preachers of the two splendid churches of St. Sebaldus and St. Lorenz followed the movement. The mass was abolished in 1524. The most effective promoters of the Reformation besides Link were Spengler, a layman, and Osiander, the preacher of St. Lorenz.

Lazarus Spengler (1479–1534), secretary of the magistrate, an admirer of Staupitz, wrote an apology of Luther, 1519, and a popular hymn on justification by faith (" *Durch Adam's Fall ist ganz verderbt*"), helped to found an evangelical college, and left a confession of faith in his testamen,t which Luther published with a preface, 1535. Joachim Camerarius, on the recommendation of Melanchthon, was called to the new college in 1526, as professor of history and Greek literature, and remained there till 1535, when he was called to the University of Tübingen, and afterwards (1541) to Leipzig.

Andreas Osiander (1498–1552), an able and learned, but opinionated and quarrelsome theologian, preached in St. Lorenz against the Roman Antichrist after 1522, fought as violently against Zwinglianism, married in 1525, attended the colloquy at Marburg, 1529, and the convent at Smalcald, 1537. He published a mechanical Gospel Harmony (1537), at the request of Archbishop Cranmer, who had married his niece (1532). He left Nürnberg in 1549, and became professor of theology at the newly founded university of Königsberg. There he stirred up a bitter theological controversy with the Wittenberg divines by his mystical doctrine of an effective and progressive justification by the indwelling of Christ (1551).

At Nürnberg several Diets were held during the Reformation period, and a temporary peace was concluded between Protestants and Roman Catholics in 1532.

§ 95. The Reformation in Strassburg. Martin Bucer.

JOH. W. BAUM: *Capito und Butzer*, Elberfeld, 1860 (partly from MSS. See a complete chronological list of Bucer's works, pp. 577–611). W. KRAFFT: art. "Butzer" in Herzog's Encykl.[2], vol. III. 35–46 (abridged in Schaff-Herzog). TIM. W. RÖHRICH: *Gesch. der Reformation in Elsass und besonders in Strassburg*, Strassb. 1830–32, 3 vols. A. ERICHSON: *L'Église française de Strasbourg au seizième siècle d'après des monuments inédits.* Strasb. 1885. MAX LENZ: *Briefwechsel Landgraf Philipps mit Bucer*, Leipzig, 1880 and 1887, 2 vols. AD. BAUM: *Magistrat und Reformation in Strassburg.* Strassb. 1887 (212 pages).

Strassburg, the capital of the Alsace, celebrated for its Gothic cathedral, university, and libraries, had been long before the Reformation the scene of the mystic revival preacher Tauler and the Friends of God. It was a thoroughly German city before Louis XIV. incorporated it with France (1681), and was re-conquered by Germany in 1870.

The Reformation began there in 1523. Zell, Bucer, Capito (Köpfel), Hedio (Heil), and for a few years Calvin also (1538 to 1541), labored there with great success. The magistrate abolished the mass, 1528, and favored the Protestant cause under the lead of Jacob Sturm, an enlightened patriot, who represented the city in all important transactions at home, in the Diet, and in conferences with the Romanists, till his death (1553). He urged the establishment of a Christian college, where classical learning and evangelical piety should be cultivated. His namesake, Johann Sturm, an eminent pedagogue, was called from Paris to preside over this college (1537), which grew into an academy, and ultimately into a university. Both were moderate men, and agreed with Capito and Bucer.[1] The church of Strassburg was much disturbed by the Peasants' War, the Anabaptists, and still more by the unfortunate sacramental controversies.

---

[1] On Jacob Sturm see the monograph of H. Baumgarten, Strassburg, 1876. Of John Sturm (who died 1589, in his eighty-second year), there are several biographies, by C. Schmidt (in French, 1855), Rieth (1864), Kückelhahn (1872), and Zaar (1872).

The chief reformer of Strassburg was Martin Bucer (1491–1552).[1] He was a native of Alsace, a Dominican monk, and ordained to the priesthood. He received a deep impression from Luther at the disputation in Heidelberg, 1518; obtained papal dispensation from his monastic vows (1521); left the Roman Church; found refuge in the castle of Francis of Sickingen; married a nun, and accepted a call to Strassburg in 1523.

Here he labored as minister for twenty-five years, and had a hand in many important movements connected with the Reformation. He attended the colloquy at Marburg (1529); wrote, with Capito, the Confessio Tetrapolitana (1530); brought about an artificial and short-lived armistice between Luther and Zwingli by the Wittenberg Concordia (1536); connived, unfortunately, at the bigamy of Philip of Hesse; and took a leading part, with Melanchthon, in the unsuccessful reformation of Archbishop Herrmann of Cologne (1542). Serious political troubles, and his resistance to the semi-popish Interim, made his stay in Strassburg dangerous, and at last impossible. Melanchthon in Wittenberg, Myconius in Basel, and Calvin in Geneva, offered him an asylum; but he accepted, with his younger colleague Fagius, a call of Cranmer to England (1549). He aided him in his reforms; was highly esteemed by the archbishop and King Edward VI., and ended his labors as professor of theology in Cambridge. His bones were exhumed in the reign of Bloody Mary (1556), but his memory was honorably restored by Queen Elizabeth (1560).

Bucer figures largely in the history of his age as the third (next to Luther and Melanchthon) among the Reformers of Germany, as a learned theologian and diplomatist, and especially as a unionist and peacemaker between the Lutherans and Zwinglians. He forms also a connecting link between Germany and England, and exerted some influence in framing

[1] Butzer in German, Bucerus in Latin.

the Anglican standards of doctrine and worship. His motto was: "We believe in Christ, not in the church."[1]

He impressed his character upon the church of Strassburg, which occupied a middle ground between Wittenberg and Zürich, and gave shelter to Calvin and the Reformed refugees of France. Strict Lutheranism triumphed for a period, but his irenical catholicity revived in the practical pietism of Spener, who was likewise an Alsacian. In recent times the Strassburg professors, under the lead of Dr. Reuss, mediated between the Protestant theology of Germany and that of France, in both languages, and furnished the best edition of the works of John Calvin.

§ 96. *The Reformation in North Germany.*

In Magdeburg the doctrines of Luther were preached in 1522 by Melchior Mirisch, an Augustinian prior, who had studied at Wittenberg. The magistrate shook off the authority of Archbishop Albrecht, invited Luther to preach in 1524, and secured the services of his friend Nicolaus von Amsdorf, who became superintendent, and introduced the necessary changes. During the Interim troubles the city was a stronghold of the Lutheran party headed by Flacius, and laid under the imperial ban (1548). In the Thirty Years' War it was burnt by Tilly (1631), but rose anew from destruction.[2]

In Magdeburg appeared the first Protestant church history, 1559–1574, in thirteen folio volumes, edited by Flacius, under the title "The Magdeburg Centuries," — a work of colossal industry, but utilizing history for sectarian purposes against popery. It called forth the *Annales* of Baronius in the opposite interest.

Breslau and Silesia were reformed chiefly by John Hess,

---

[1] "*Wir sind Christgläubig, nicht kirchgläubig.*"
[2] *Seckendorf*, I. 246. Wolter, *Gesch. der Stadt Magdeburg* (1845); Hoffmann, *Chronik der Stadt Magdeb.* (1850, 3 vols.); Rathmann, *Gesch. Magdeb.* ; Preger, *Matth. Flacius Illyricus und seine Zeit* (Erlangen, 1859–1861).

who studied at Wittenberg, 1519, a friend of Luther and Melanchthon. He held a successful disputation in Breslau in defense of the Protestant doctrines, 1524.[1]

Kaspar Schwenkfeld von Ossig (1490–1561), a nobleman in the service of the Duke Frederick II. of Liegnitz, was one of the earliest promoters of the Reformation in Silesia, but fell out with Luther in the eucharistic controversy (1524). He had peculiar views on the sacraments, similar to those of the Quakers. He also taught that the flesh of Christ was deified. He founded a new sect, which was persecuted in Germany, but is perpetuated among the Schwenkfeldian congregations in Eastern Pennsylvania.[2]

Among the later leaders of the Protestant cause in Breslau must be mentioned Crato von Crafftheim (d. 1585), who studied at Wittenberg six years as an inmate of Luther's household, and became an eminent physician of the Emperor Maximilian II. His younger friend, Zacharias Ursinus (d. 1583), is one of the two authors of the Heidelberg Catechism. Crato belonged to the Melanchthonian school, in distinction from the rigid Lutheranism which triumphed in the Formula of Concord.[3]

Bremen accepted Protestantism in November, 1522, by calling Heinrich Moller, better known as Heinrich von Zütphen (1468–1524), to the parish of Ansgari, and afterwards two other Protestant preachers. Moller had studied at Wittenberg, 1515, and taken a degree in 1521 under Melanchthon.

[1] Of this disputation Luther reported to Spalatin, May 11, 1524 (De Wette, II. 511): "*Vratislaviæ disputatio Joannis Hess processit feliciter, frustra resistentibus tot legatis regum et technis episcopi.*"

[2] Professor Hartranft, D.D., of Hartford, Conn., a descendant of the Pennsylvania Schwenkfelders, has investigated the Schwenkfeld literature at Breslau, and issued a prospectus for its publication (1887).

[3] Köstlin, biography of Hess in the "Zeitschrift des schlesischen Geschichtsvereins," vol. VI. Gilett, *Crato von Crafftheim und seine Freunde,* Frankfurt-a.-M. 1860, 2 parts. A very learned work. To Ursinus we shall return in the history of the Reformation in the Palatinate. In the cities of the Hanseatic League the Reformation was introduced at an early period.

He was prior of an Augustinian convent at Dort, and preached there and in Antwerp the doctrines of the Reformation, but had to flee for his life. He followed an invitation to preach in Ditmar, but met with opposition, and was burnt to death by a fanatical and drunken mob excited by the monks. Luther published an account of his death, and dedicated it to the Christians in Bremen, with an exposition of the tenth Psalm. He rejoiced in the return of the spirit of martyrdom, which, he says, "is horrible to behold before the world, but precious in the sight of God."[1]

In 1527 all the churches of Bremen were in charge of Protestant pastors, and afterwards divided between the Lutheran and Reformed Confessions. The convents were turned into schools and hospitals.

Hamburg, which shares with Bremen the supremacy in the North German and maritime commerce, followed in 1523. Five years later Dr. Bugenhagen, called Pomeranus (1485–1558), was called from Wittenberg to superintend the changes. This Reformer, Luther's faithful friend and pastor, had a special gift of government, and was the principal organizer of the Lutheran churches in Northern Germany and Denmark. For this purpose he labored in the cities of Braunschweig (1528), Hamburg (1529), Lübeck (1530–1532), in his native Pomerania (1534), and in Denmark, where he spent nearly five years (1537–1542). His church constitutions were models.[2]

Lübeck, a rich commercial city, and capital of the Hanseatic

---

[1] *Vom Bruder Heinrich in Ditmar verbrannt*, Wittenberg, 1525, in the Erl. ed. XXVI. 313–337; in Walch, XXI. 94 sqq. Comp. Paul Crocius, *Das grosse Martyrbuch*, Bremen, 1682. Klaus Harms, *Heinrich von Zütphen*, in Piper's "Evang. Kalender," 1852.

[2] Printed in Richter, *Die evang. Kirchenordnungen*, vol. I. C. Bertheau, *Bugenhagen's Kirchenordnung für die Stadt Hamburg vom J. 1529*, 1885. L. Hänselmann, *B.'s Kirchenordnung f. d. Stadt Braunschweig*, 1885. Frantz, *Die evangelische Kirchenverfassung in den deutschen Städten des 16. Jahrh.*, Halle, 1876. Vogt, *Johannes Bugenhagen Pomeranus*, Elberfeld, 1867. The year 1885, the fourth centennial of Bugenhagen's birth, called out several popular sketches of his life by Knauth, Petrich, Zitzlaff, and Hering (1888). See also O. Vogt, *Bugenhagen's Briefwechsel*, Stettin, 1888.

League, expelled the first Lutheran preachers, but recalled them, and removed the priests in 1529. Bugenhagen completed the work.

In Braunschweig-Lüneburg, Duke Ernst the Confessor favored the new doctrines in 1527, and committed the prosecution of the work to Urbanus Rhegius, whom he met at the Diet of Augsburg, 1530.

Rhegius [1] (1489–1541) belongs to the second class of Reformers. He was the son of a priest on the Lake of Constance, educated at Lindau, Freiburg-i.-B. (in the house of Zasius), and Ingolstadt under Dr. Eck, and ordained priest at Constance (1519). He joined the humanistic school, entered into correspondence with Erasmus, Faber, and Zwingli, and became an imperial orator and poet-laureate, though his poetry is stiff and conventional. He acquired the doctorate of divinity at Basel. He was called to Augsburg by the magistrate, and labored as preacher in the Dome from 1523 to 1530. He passed from Romanism to Lutheranism, from Lutheranism to Zwinglianism, and back to a moderate Lutheranism. He sympathized most with Bucer, and labored afterwards for the Wittenberg Concordia. The imperial prohibition of Protestant preaching, June 16, 1530, terminated his career in Augsburg, though he remained till Aug. 26, and conferred much with Bucer and Melanchthon.

He now entered upon his more important and permanent labors as general superintendent of Lüneberg, and took the leading part in the Reformation of Celle, Hannover, Minden, Soest, Lemgo, and other places; but he gives a doleful description of the moral condition. He attended the colloquy at Hagenau, and died soon after his return, May 27, 1541.

He wrote two catechisms and several devotional books. In his earlier career he was vain, changeable, and factious. He lacked originality, but had the talent of utilizing and popularizing the new ideas of others. Luther gives him the

---

[1] So he spells his name (Rieger in German), not Regius (König).

testimony : " He hated not only the popish abominations, but also all sectaries ; he sincerely loved the pure word, and handled it with all diligence and faithfulness, as his writings abundantly show." [1]

The Dukes of Mecklenburg, Heinrich and Albrecht, applied to Luther in 1524 for " evangelists," and Luther sent them two Augustinian monks. Heinrich favored the Reformation, but very cautiously. The university of Rostock, founded 1419, became at a later period a school of strict Lutheran orthodoxy.

§ 97. *Protestantism in Augsburg and South Germany.*

Augsburg, first known twelve years before Christ as a Roman colony (Augusta Vindelicorum), and during the middle ages an imperial city (since 1276), the seat of a bishop, the chief emporium for the trade of Northern Europe with the Mediterranean and the East, and the home of princely merchants and bankers (the Fuggers and Welsers), figures prominently in the early history of the Reformation, and gave the name to the standard confession of the Lutheran Church in 1530, and to the treaty of peace in 1555.[2]   Luther was there in 1518 at a conference with Cardinal Cajetan, and lodged with the Carmelite friar Frosch, who remained faithful to him.   Peutinger, the bishop (Christoph von Stadium), and two canons (Adelmann) were friendly to reform, at least for a time.   Urbanus Rhegius preached there from 1523 to 1530, and exerted great influence.   He distributed, with Frosch, the communion with the cup at Christmas, 1524.   Both married in 1526.

But the Zwinglians, under the lead of Michael Keller,

---

[1] Rhegius, *Opera latine edita*, Norimb. 1561; *Deutsche Bücher und Schriften*, Nürnb. 1562, and again Frankf. 1577. Döllinger, *Die Reform.* II. 58 sqq. Uhlhorn, *Urbanus Rhegius*, Elberfeld, 1862, and his sketch in Herzog[2], XIII. 147-155.

[2] Friedrich Roth, *Augsburgs Reformationsgeschichte, 1517-1527.* München, 1881.

gradually gained the upper hand among influential men. Zwingli took advantage of the situation in his famous letter to Alber, Nov. 16, 1524, in which he first fully developed his theory. Even Rhegius, who had written before against Carstadt and Zwingli, became a Zwinglian, though only for a short period.

The Anabaptist leaders, Hubmaier, Denck, Hetzer, Hut, likewise appeared in Augsburg, and gathered a congregation of eleven hundred members. They held a general synod in 1527. They baptized by immersion. Rhegius stirred up the magistrate against them: the leaders were imprisoned, and some executed.[1]

The confusion and strife among the Protestants strengthened the Roman party. The people did not know what to believe, and the magistrate hesitated. The moral condition of the city, as described by Rhegius, Musculus, and other preachers, was deplorable, and worse than under the papal rule. During the Diet of Augsburg in 1530, the Emperor prohibited all Protestant preaching in public: the magistrate made no objection, and dismissed the preachers. But the Augsburg Confession left a permanent impression on the place.

The South-German cities of Constance, Memmingen, and Lindau were, like Augsburg, influenced by Zwingli as well as Luther, and united with Strassburg in the Tetrapolitan Confession, which Bucer and Capito prepared in great haste during the Diet of Augsburg as a document of union between the two wings of Protestantism. It failed to meet the approval of the Diet, and was, like Zwingli's Confession, not even allowed to be read; but Bucer adhered to it to the end.

The most important and permanent conquest which the

---

[1] See the description of the congregation of the "Apostolic Brethren," as the Anabaptists called themselves, in Ludwig Keller, *Ein Apostel der Wiedertäufer* (i.e., Hans Denck), Leipzig, 1882, ch. VI. 94–119.

Reformation made in South Germany was that of the duchy (now kingdom) of Württemberg under Duke Ulrich, through the labors of Brenz, Blaurer, and Schnepf, after 1534.   The University of Tübingen (founded 1477) became one of the most fruitful nurseries of Protestant theology, in all its phases, from the strictest orthodoxy to the most radical criticism.[1]

§ 98. *The Reformation in Hesse, and the Synod of Homberg. Philip of Hesse, and Lambert of Avignon.*

I. LAMBERTUS AVENIONENSIS: *Paradoxa quæ Fr. L. A. apud sanctam Hessorum Synodum Hombergi congregatam pro Ecclesiarum Reformatione e Dei Verbo disputanda et definienda proposuit,* Erphordiæ, 1527. (Reprinted in Sculteti *Annales,* p. 68; in Hardt, *Hist. lit. Ref.* V. 98; an extract in Henke's *N. Kirchengesch.,* I. 101 sqq.)   N. L. RICHTER: *Die Kirchenordnungen des 16ten Jahrh.,* Weimar, 1846, vol. I. 56–69 (the Homberg Constitution).   C. A. CREDNER: *Philipp des Grossmüthigen hessische Kirchenreformations-Ordnung.   Aus schriftlichen Quellen herausgegeben, übersetzt, und mit Rücksicht auf die Gegenwart bevorwortet,* Giessen, 1852 (123 pp.)

II. F. W. HASSENCAMP: *Hessische Kirchengesch. seit dem Zeitalter der Reformation,* Marburg, 1852 and 1855.   W. KOLBE: *Die Einführung der Reformation in Marburg,* Marburg, 1871.   H. L. J. HEPPE: *Kirchengesch. beider Hessen,* Marburg, 1876.   (He wrote several other works on the church history of Hesse and of the Reformation generally, in the interest of Melanchthonianism and of the Reformed Church.)   E. L. HENKE: *Neuere Kirchengesch.* (ed. by Gass, Halle, 1874), I. 98–109. MEJER: *Homberger Synode,* in Herzog[2], VI. 268 sqq.   KÖSTLIN: *M. L.,* II. 48 sqq.

III. Works on Philip of Hesse by ROMMEL (*Philipp der Grossmüthige, Landgraf von Hessen,* Giessen, 1830, 3 vols.), and WILLE (*Philipp der Grossmäthige und die Restitution Herzog Ulrichs von Würtemberg,* Tübingen, 1882).   MAX LENZ: *Zwingli und Landgraf Philip,* in Brieger's "Zeitschrift für Kirchengeschichte," 1879; and *Briefwechsel Landgraf Philipps mit Bucer,* Leipz. 1880, vol. 2d, 1887 (important for the political and ecclesiastical history of Germany between 1541 and 1547).   The history of Philip is interwoven in RANKE's *Geschichte* (vols. I. to VI.), and in JANSSEN's *Geschichte* (vol. III.).   Against Janssen is directed G. BOSSERT: *Württemberg und Janssen,* Halle, 1884, 2 parts.

---

[1] Römer, *Kirchliche Geschichte Württembergs,* Stuttg. 1848.   Keim, *Schwäbische Reformationsgeschichte.*   Tübingen, 1855.   Schneider, *Würtemb. Reformationsgesch.*   Stuttgart, 1887.

IV. Biographies of Lambert of Avignon by BAUM (Strassb. 1840), HASSEN-CAMP (Elberfeld, 1860), RUFFET (Paris, 1873), and a sketch by WAGEN-MANN in Herzog², VIII. 371 sqq. (1881). The writings of Lambert of Avignon, mostly Theses and Commentaries, are very scarce, and have never been collected. His letters (some of them begging letters to the Elector of Saxony and Spalatin) are published by HERMINJARD in *Correspondance des Réformateurs*, vol. I. 112, 114, 118, 123, 131, 138, 142, 144, 146, 328, 344, 347, 371; vol. II. 239. Luther refers to him in several letters to Spalatin (see below).

Hesse or Hessia, in Middle Germany, was Christianized by St. Boniface in the eighth century, and subject to the jurisdiction of the archbishop of Mainz. It numbered in the sixteenth century fifty convents, and more than a thousand monks and nuns.

Hesse became, next to Saxony, the chief theater of the Reformation in its early history ; and its chief patron among the princes, next to Elector John, was Philip, Landgrave of Hesse, surnamed the "Magnanimous" (1504–1567). He figures prominently in the political history of Germany from 1525, when he aided in the suppression of the Peasants' War, till 1547, when he was defeated by the Emperor in the Smalcaldian War, and kept a prisoner for five years (1547–1552). The last years of his life were quiet and conciliatory, but his moral force was broken by his misconduct and the failure of his political combinations.

His connection with the Reformation presents two different aspects, which make it difficult to decide whether it was more beneficial or more injurious. He made the acquaintance of Luther at the Diet of Worms (1521), and asked and received instruction from Melanchthon, whom he met at Heidelberg (1524). He declared in 1525, that he would rather lose body and life, land and people, than depart from the word of God, and urged the ministers to preach it in its purity.[1] He openly embraced the Reformation in 1526, and remained faithful to it in his conviction and policy, though

---

[1] Ranke, II. 121.

not in his moral conduct. He boldly and bravely defended it with a degree of theological knowledge which is rare among princes, and with a conciliatory liberality in regard to doctrinal controversies which was in advance of prevailing narrowness. He brought about the Marburg Colloquy with the noble aim of uniting the Protestant forces of Germany and Switzerland against the common foe (1529). By restoring Württemberg to Duke Ulrich in the brilliant victory at Laufen, he opened the way for the introduction of the Reformation into that country (1534). But, on the other hand, he repeatedly endangered the Protestant cause by his rashness, and injured it and himself most seriously by his licentiousness, which culminated in the open scandal of bigamy (1540). He resembles in many respects Henry VIII. of England.[1]

The Landgrave was the first prince who took advantage of the recess of the Diet of Speier, Aug. 27, 1526, and construed it into a legal permission for the introduction of the Reformation into his own territory. For this purpose he convened a synod in the little Hessian town of Homberg.[2] It consisted

---

[1] See pp. 308 and 481; Seckendorf's Excursus on the bigamy, III. 277–281; Ranke, IV. 186 sqq.; Köstlin, Bk. VIII., ch. I. (II. 533 sqq.); and Janssen, III. 57, 439 sqq. This nasty subject lies beyond our period, but may be disposed of here in a few remarks. Philip was a man of powerful sensuality, and married very young a daughter of Duke George of Saxony. As she was unattractive, and gave him little satisfaction, he indulged freely and long before his bigamy in his carnal passions to the injury of his health; and for this reason his conscience would not allow him to partake of the holy communion more than once in fifteen years (from 1525 to 1540), as he confessed himself in a letter to Luther, April 5, 1540 (Lenz, *Briefwechsel Philipp's mit Bucer*, I. 361, and Ranke, IV. 186, note). If Fräulein Margaretha von der Sale, who captivated his passions, had consented to become his mistress, he would not have fallen upon the extraordinary device of bigamy. The worst feature in this shameful affair is the weak connivance of the Reformers, which furnished the Romanists a keen weapon of attack. See Janssen. But Protestantism is no more responsible for the sins of Philip of Hesse, than Romanism is for the sins of Louis XIV.

[2] In Kurhessen (which in 1866 was annexed to Prussia). Homberg must not be confounded with the better-known watering-place Homburg near Frankfort on the Main.

of the clergy, the nobility, and the representatives of cities, and was held Oct. 20–22, 1526. He himself was present, and his chancellor Feige presided over the deliberations. The synod is remarkable for a premature scheme of democratic church government and discipline, which failed for the time, but contained fruitful germs for the future and for other countries. It was suggested by the disputations which had been held at Zürich for the introduction of the Zwinglican Reformation.

The leading spirit of this synod was Francis Lambert of Avignon (1487–1530), the first French monk converted to Protestantism and one of the secondary reformers. He had been formerly a distinguished and efficient traveling preacher of the Franciscan order in the South of France. But he could find no peace in severe ascetic exercises; and, when he became acquainted with some tracts of Luther in a French translation, he took advantage of a commission of his convent to deliver letters to a superior of his order in Germany, and left his native land never to return. He traveled on a mule through Geneva, Bern, Zürich, Basel, Eisenach, to Wittenberg, as a seeker after light on the great question of the day. He was half converted by Zwingli in a public disputation (July, 1522), and more fully by Luther in Wittenberg, where he arrived in January, 1523. Luther, who was often deceived by unworthy ex-priests and ex-monks, distrusted him at first, but became convinced of his integrity, and aided him.[1] At his request Lambert delivered exegetical lectures

[1] He mentions him under the assumed name of Johannes Serranus in letters to Spalatin, Dec. 20 and 26, 1522, and Jan. 12 and 23, 1523 (in De Wette, II. 263, 272, 299, 302). In the last letter, after he had made his personal acquaintance, he writes, "*Adest Johannes ille Serranus, vero nomine Franciscus Lambertus. . . . De integritate viri nulla est dubitatio : testes sunt apud nos, qui illum et in Francia et in Basilea audierunt. . . . Mihi per omnia placet vir, et satis spectatus mihi est . . . ut dignus sit quem in exilio paululum feramus et juvemus.*" Then he asks Spalatin to secure for him from the Elector a contribution of twenty or thirty guilders for his support. In a letter of Feb. 25, 1523 (De Wette, II. 308), he repeats this request as a beggar for a poor exile of Christ. A last request he made Aug. 14, 1523 (II. 387).

in the university, translated reformatory tracts into French
and Italian, and published a book in defense of his leaving
the convent (February, 1523), and a commentary on the rule
of the Minorites to which Luther wrote a preface (March,
1523). He advocated the transformation of convents into
schools. He married a Saxon maiden (July 15, 1523), anticipating herein the Reformer, and lived with her happily, but
in great poverty, which obliged him to beg for assistance.
He spent over a year in Wittenberg; but, finding no prospect
of a permanent situation on account of his ignorance of
the German language, he suddenly left for Metz, against the
advice of Luther and Melanchthon, on invitation of a few
secret friends of the Reformation (March 24, 1524). He
addressed a letter to the king of France to gain him for
the Reformation, and announced a public disputation; but the
clergy prevented it, and the magistrate advised him to leave
Metz. He then proceeded to Strassburg (April, 1524), was
kindly received by Bucer, and presented with the right of
citizenship by the magistrate. He published practical commentaries on the Canticles, the Minor Prophets, a book
against Erasmus, on free-will, and a sort of dogmatic compend.[1] He was highly recommended to the Landgrave, who
took him into his service soon after the Diet of Speier (1526),
and made him one of the reformers of Hesse.

Lambert prepared for the Synod of Homberg, at the
request of the Landgrave, a hundred and fifty-eight Theses
(*Paradoxa*), as a basis for the reformation of doctrine, worship, and discipline. He advocated them with fiery and passionate eloquence in a long Latin speech.[2] Adam Kraft
spoke in German more moderately.

---

[1] *Farrago omnium fere rerum theologicarum.* It was translated into
English, 1536. This book and his *De Fidelium vocatione in Regnum Christi*
contain the views which he defended in Homberg.

[2] Hase says (p. 387): "*Die Mönche und Prälaten verstummten vor der
glühenden Beredtsamkeit des landflüchtigen Minoriten.*" But he was
opposed by Ferber, the guardian of the Marburg Franciscans, who denounced

His leading ideas are these. Every thing which has been deformed must be reformed by the Word of God. This is the only rule of faith and practice. All true Christians are priests, and form the church. They have the power of self-government, and the right and duty to exercise discipline, according to Matt. 18:15–18, and to exclude persons who give offense by immorality or false doctrine. The bishops (i.e., pastors) are elected and supported by the congregation, and are aided by deacons who attend to the temporalities. The general government resides in a synod, which should meet annually, and consist of the pastors and lay representatives of all the parishes. The executive body between the meetings of synod is a commission of thirteen persons. Three visitors, to be appointed first by the prince, and afterwards by the synod, should visit the churches once a year, examine, ordain, and install candidates. Papists and heretics are not to be tolerated, and should be sent out of the land. A school for training of ministers is to be established in Marburg.

It is a matter of dispute, whether Lambert originated these views, or derived them from the Franciscan, or Waldensian, or Zwinglian, or Lutheran suggestions. The last is most probable. It is certain that Luther in his earlier writings (1523) expressed similar views on church government and the ministry. They are legitimately developed from his doctrine of the general priesthood of believers.[1]

On the basis of these principles a church constitution was prepared in three days by a synodical commission, no doubt chiefly by Lambert himself. It is a combination of Congre-

---

him as a "runaway monk," and denied the legal competency of the synod. Lambert in turn called him a champion of Antichrist and a blasphemer, and exclaimed, "*Expellatur ex provincia!*" which Ferber misunderstood, "*Occidatur bestia!*" He confessed afterwards that he lost his temper. Hassencamp, *Fr. Lambert*, p. 39 sq., and Hencke, *l. c.* I. 103 sq.

[1] See above, pp. 518 and 538. Ritschl and Mejer assert that Lambert borrowed his church ideal from his own order of the Minorites.

gationalism and Presbyterianism. Its leading features are congregational self-government, synodical supervision, and strict discipline. The directions for worship are based on Luther's "*Deutsche Messe*," 1526.[1]

The constitution, with the exception of a few minor features, remained a dead letter. The Landgrave was rather pleased with it, but Luther, whom he consulted, advised postponement; he did not object to its principles, but thought that the times and the people were not ripe for it, and that laws in advance of public opinion rarely succeed.[2] Luther learned a bitter lesson from the Peasants' War and from the visitation of the churches in Saxony. Lambert himself, in his letters, complained of the prevailing corruptions and the abuse of evangelical liberty.[3] A good reason both for the necessity and difficulty of discipline, which should have begun with the prince. But self-government must be

---

[1] The Latin original of the constitution is lost, but two copies are extant from which the printed editions of Schminke, Richter, and Credner are derived. Janssen (III. 54) calls it, not quite accurately, "*ein vollständig ausgebildetes, rein demokratisches Presbyterialsystem.*"

[2] Letter to the Landgrave, Monday after Epiphany, 1527 (in the Erl. ed., vol. LVI. 170 sq.). He was reluctant to give an answer, from fear that non-approval might be construed as proceeding from Wittenberg jealousy of any rivalry. He does not mention Lambert, but cautions against rash proceedings. "*Fürschreiben und Nachthun ist weit von einander*" (theory and practice are wide apart). Köstlin (II. 50) says: "*Gegen die Principien des Entwurfs an sich wandte Luther nichts ein. Der Grund, weshalb er ihn ablehnte, war das Bedürfniss allmählicher Entwicklung im Gegensatz zur plötzlichen gesetzlichen Durchführung umfassender Ideen, für welche die Gegenwart nicht vorbereitet sei.*"

[3] See his letter to Myconius in Hassencamp, *Lamb. v. A.*, p. 50 sq., and Döllinger, *Die Reform.* II. 18 sq. The latter quotes the Latin (from Strieder, *Hessische Gelehrtengesch.* VII. 386): "*Dolens et gemens vivo, quod paucissimos videam recte uti evangelii libertate, et quod caritas ferme nulla sit, sed plena sint omnia obtrectationibus mendaciis, maledicentia, invidia.*" In a letter to Bucer, Lambert says, "*Horreo mores populi hujus ita ut putem me frustra in eis laborare.*" Herminjard (II. 242) adds in a note an extract from the letter of a student of Zürich, Rudolph Walther, who wrote to Bullinger from Marburg, June 17, 1540 (the year of the bigamy of the Landgrave): "*Mores [huius regionis] omnium corruptissimi. Nullum in hac Germaniæ parte inter Papistas et Evangelicæ doctrinæ professores discrimen cernas, si morum et vitæ censuram instituas.*"

acquired by actual trial and experience. Nobody can learn to swim without going into the water.

The Landgrave put himself at the head of the church, and reformed it after the Saxon model. He abolished the mass and the canon law, confiscated the property of the convents, endowed hospitals and schools, arranged church visitations, and appointed six superintendents (1531).

The combination of Lutheran and Reformed elements in the Hessian reformation explains the confessional complication and confusion in the subsequent history, and the present status of the Protestant Church in Hesse, which is claimed by both denominations.[1]

The best service which the Landgrave did to the cause of learning and religion, was the founding of the University of Marburg, which was opened July 1, 1527, with a hundred and four students. It became the second nursery of the Protestant ministry, next to Wittenberg, and remains to this day an important institution. Francis Lambert, Adam Kraft, Erhard Schnepf, and Hermann Busch were its first theological professors.

Lambert now had, after a roaming life of great poverty, a settled situation with a decent support. He lectured on his favorite books, the Canticles, the Prophets, and the Apocalypse; but he had few hearers, was not popular with his German colleagues, and felt unhappy. He attended the eucharistic Colloquy at Marburg in October, 1529, as a spectator,

[1] Dr. Vilmar of Marburg (originally Reformed) tried to prove that the Hessians were Lutherans, but did not know it. His colleague, Dr. Heppe, with equal learning tried to prove the opposite. A German proverb speaks of the "blind Hessians," and this applies at least to those unfortunate twenty thousand soldiers who allowed themselves to be sold by their contemptible tyrant (Frederick II., a convert to the Church of Rome, d. 1785), like so many heads of cattle, for twenty-one million thalers, to the king of England to be used as powder against the American colonies. Hence the ugly meaning of the term "Hessians" in America, which does great injustice to their innocent countrymen and descendants.

became a convert to the view of Zwingli, and defended it in his last work.[1] This must have made his position more uncomfortable. He wished to find " some little town in Switzerland where he could teach the people what he had received from the Lord."[2] But before this wish could be fulfilled, he died with his wife and daughter, of the pestilence, April 18, 1530. He was an original, but eccentric and erratic genius, with an over-sanguine temperament, with more zeal and eloquence than wisdom and discretion. His chief importance lies in the advocacy of the principle of ecclesiastical self-government and discipline. His writings are thoughtful; and the style is clear, precise, vivacious, and direct, as may be expected from a Frenchman.[3]

Lambert seems to have had a remote influence on Scotland, where principles of church government somewhat similar to his own were carried into practice after the model of the Reformed Church of Geneva. For among his pupils was Patrick Hamilton, the proto-martyr of the Scotch Reformation, who was burned at St. Andrews, Feb. 29, 1528.[4] According to the usual view, William Tyndale also, the pioneer of the English Bible Version, studied at Marburg about the same time; for several of his tracts contain on the titlepage or in the colophon the imprint, " Hans Luft at Marborow (Marburg) in the land of Hesse."[5]

---

[1] *De Symbolo Fœderis,* etc., published at Strassburg after his death, 1530. He says in the preface: " *Volo ut mundus sciat me sententiam circa Cœnam Domini demutasse.*" Herminjard, II. 240.

[2] Letter to Bucer, March 14, 1530, *ib.* II. 242.

[3] Dr. Döllinger, II. 18, uses his complaints of the prevailing immorality as a testimony against the Reformation, but judges favorably of his writings.

[4] His name is entered on the University Album of the year 1527, together with two other Scotchmen, John Hamilton and Gilbert Winram. See Jul. Cæsar, *Catalogus Studiorum scholœ Marpurgensis,* Marb. 1875, p. 2. Comp. Lorimer, *Patrick Hamilton,* Edinb. 1857, and the careful sketch of Professor Mitchell of St. Andrews, in the Schaff-Herzog "Encycl." II. 935 sqq.

[5] The fact of Tyndale's sojourn in Marburg has been disputed without good reason by Mombert in the preface to his facsimile edition of *Tyndale's Pentateuch,* New York, 1884 (p. XXIX.). He conjectures that " Marbo-

§ 99. *The Reformation in Prussia. Duke Albrecht and Bishop Geory Von Polenz.*

I. LUTHER'S Letters to *Albrecht* from May 26, 1525, to May 2, 1545 (17, see list in Erl. ed. LVI. 248), to *Briesmann* and *Georg von Polenz*, in the collections of De Wette and Enders. J. VOIGT: *Briefwechsel der berühmtesten Gelehrten des Zeitalters der Reformation mit Herzog Albrecht von Preussen,* Königsb. 1841.

II. HARTKNOCH: *Preussische Kirchenhistorie,* Königsberg, 1686. AR-NOLDT: *Preussische Kirchengeschichte,* Königsberg, 1769. BOCK: *Leben Albrechts des Aelteren,* Königsb. 1750. RHESA: *De primis sacrorum reformatoribus in Prussia,* Königsberg, 1823-1830 (seven University Programs containing biographies of Briesmann, Speratus, Poliander, Georg v. Polenz, Amandus). GEBSER: *Der Dom zu Königsberg,* 1835. ERDMANN: *Preussen, Ordensstaat,* in Herzog[1], XII. 117-165 (1860; omitted in the second ed.). PASTOR (R. Cath.): *Neue Quellenberichte über den Reformator Albrecht von Brandenburg,* Mainz, 1876 (in the "Katholik," LVI. February and March). C. A. HASE: *Herzog Albrecht von Preussen und sein Hofprediger. Eine königsberger Tragödie aus dem Zeitalter der Reformation,* Leipzig, 1879. RINDFLEISCH: *Herzog Albrecht von Hohenzollern, der letzte Hochmeister, und die Reformation in Preussen,* Danzig, 1880. P. TSCHACKERT (professor in Königsberg): *Georg von Polentz, Bischof von Samland,* Leipzig, 1888 (in "Kirchengeschichtl. Studien" by Brieger, Tschackert, etc., pp. 145-194).

III. The general histories of Prussia by STENZEL, DROYSEN, VOIGT (large work, 1827-39, in 9 vols.; condensed ed. 1850, in 3 vols.), COSEL, HAHN, PIERSON (4th ed. 1881, 2 vols.), RANKE (*Zwölf Bücher preussischer Gesch.* 1874), FÖRSTER, etc. For the history of the Teutonic order, see WATTERICH: *Die Gründung des deutschen Ordensstaates in Preussen,* Leipzig, 1857; and JOH. VOIGT: *Geschichte des deutschen Ritterordens,* Berlin, 1859, 2 vols.

IV. RANKE: Vol. II. 326 sqq. JANSSEN: III. 70-77.

Of greater prospective importance than the conversion of Hesse and even of Saxony to Protestantism, was the evangelization of Prussia, which from a semi-barbarous Duchy on the shores of the Baltic rose to the magnitude of a highly

row" is a fictitious name for Wittenberg. Tyndale's name does not appear in the University Register, but he may not have entered it. Hans Luft was the well-known printer of Luther's Bible in Wittenberg in Saxony, but he may have had an agent in Marburg "in the land of Hesse."

civilized kingdom, stretching from the borders of Russia beyond the banks of the Rhine, and which is now, in connection with the new German Empire, the leading Protestant power on the Continent of Europe.[1]

Old Prussia[2] was a colony of the Teutonic Knights (*Deutschorden*), one of the three military religious orders which arose during the crusades for the defense of the Holy Land and the protection of pilgrims. They had the same military and monastic constitution as the Knights Templars, and the Knights of St. John (*Johannitæ*); but their members were all Germans. They greatly distinguished themselves in the later crusades, and their chivalrous blood still flows in the veins of the old Prussian nobility. They wore a white mantle with a black silver-lined cross, and as a special favor an imperial eagle on their arms, which descended from them to the royal house of Prussia. After the fall of Jerusalem they removed their headquarters to Venice, and afterwards to Marienburg and Königsberg (the capital, where the kings of Prussia are crowned). Emperor Frederick II. and Pope Innocent III. granted them all the lands they might conquer from the heathen on the eastern borders of Germany, and the grand-masters received the dignity of princes of the Roman Empire. They were invited by the Duke of Poland to defend the frontiers of his country against the heathen Prussians (1240). The conquest was completed in 1283. The Knights Christianized, or rather Romanized and Ger-

---

[1] "*Bei weitem die merkwürdigste und durchgreifendste Veränderung fand in Preussen statt.*" Ranke, II. 326. Janssen can see in the Reformation of Prussia only a change for the worse. The best refutation of his view is the subsequent history and present condition of Prussia. The history of the past must be read in the light of the present. "By their fruits ye shall know them."

[2] Prussia proper is a division of the kingdom of Prussia, and comprises East or Ducal Prussia and West or Royal Prussia, with a total area of 24,114 square miles, and a population of about three millions and a half. East Prussia was united with Brandenburg by the Elector John Sigismund, 1618. West Prussia was severed from Poland by Frederick the Great in the first division of that kingdom, 1772.

manized, the Prussians, after the military fashion of Charlemagne in his dealings with the Saxons, and of Otho I. in subduing the Wends. The native heathenism was conquered, but not converted, and continued under Christian forms. Prussia is said to have contained under the Knights two millions of people and more than fifty cities, which carried on an extensive trade by means of the Hanseatic League. The chief cities were Marienburg, Königsberg, Thorn, Danzig, and Culm. But the common people were treated as slaves.

After nearly two centuries of rule the Knights degenerated, and their power declined by internal dissensions and the hostility of Poland. In 1466 they were forced by Casimir IV. in the Peace of Thorn to cede West Prussia with the richest cities to Poland, and to accept East Prussia as a fief of that kingdom. This was virtually the destruction of the political power of the order. The incompatibility of the military and monastic life became more and more apparent. Pope Adrian VI. urged Albrecht to restore the order to its former monastic purity and dignity. But this was impossible. The order had outlived itself.[1]

Luther saw this, and inaugurated a different kind of reform. He seized a favorable opportunity, and exhorted the Knights, in a public address, March 28, 1523, to forsake the false monastic chastity so often broken, and to live in true matrimonial chastity according to the ordinance of God in paradise (Gen. 2:18), which was older and wiser than popes and councils. "Your order," he argued, "is truly a singular order: it is both secular and spiritual, and neither; it is bound to wield the sword against infidels, and yet to

---

[1] "*Der deutsche Orden*," says Ranke (II. 334), "*und seine Herrschaft in Preussen war ohne Zweifel das eigenthümlichste Product des hierarchisch-ritterlichen Geistes der letzen Jahrhunderte in der deutschen Nation; er hatte eine grossartige Welteinwirkung ausgeübt und ein unermessliches Verdienst um die Ausbreitung des deutschen Namens erworben; aber seine Zeit war vorüber.*"

live in celibacy, poverty, and obedience, like other monks.
These things do not agree together, as is shown by reason and
by daily experience. The order is therefore of no use either
to God or the world." [1]

In the summer of the same year he sent, at the wish of
Albrecht, the pioneer of Protestant preachers, to Prussia, in
the person of his friend Dr. Johannes Briesmann (1488–
1549), a theologian of learning, piety, and executive ability,
who arrived in Königsberg, Sept. 27, 1523, and labored there
as preacher in the Dome, and successor of Bishop Georg von
Polenz, till his death, with the exception of four years which
he spent as evangelist in Riga (1527–1531).[2] He afterwards
sent two other gifted evangelists, known for their evangelical
hymns, namely, Paul Speratus (d. 1551), and John Poliander
(Graumann, d. 1541), who made themselves very useful. A
third one, Amandus, created disturbance by his radicalism,
which resembled that of Carlstadt, and caused his removal
from Königsberg.

With the help of these theologians and evangelists, Duke
Albrecht and Bishop Georg von Polenz brought about a
radical change in Prussia, and prepared the way for its great
future destiny. The religious reformation preceded the
political change.

Albrecht, Margrave of Brandenburg-Ansbach, last grand-
master of the Teutonic Knights, and first Duke of Prussia,
was born at Ansbach, May 16, 1490; destined for the clerical profession; received into the order of the Knights, and
elected its grand-master in 1511. He made his entry into
Königsberg, Nov. 22, 1512. His effort to make Prussia independent, and to refuse obedience to the king of Poland,

---

[1] *An die Herren deutsches Ordens, dass sie falsche Keuschheit meiden
und zur rechten ehelichen Keuschheit greifen, Ermahnung.* Wittenberg,
den 28 März, 1523. In the Erl. ed. XXIX. 16–33. Walch, XIX. 2157 sqq.

[2] He published several sermons. Extracts in Seckendorf, I. 272. See the
article "Briesmann" by Dr. Erdmann in Herzog[2], II. 629–631, with literature.

involved him in a disastrous war till 1521, when an armistice for four years was concluded. He attended, as one of the princes of the empire, the Diet of Nürnberg, 1522 and 1523, and sought protection against Poland, but in vain. He diligently heard, during that time, the sermons of Andreas Osiander, and was converted to the doctrines of the Reformation. He called him his "spiritual father in Christ, through whom God first rescued him from the darkness of popery, and led him to the true divine knowledge." On a journey to Berlin he had a private conference with Luther and Melanchthon, and asked their advice (September, 1523). "Trust in God," said Luther with the consent of Melanchthon, "rather than the empire; shake off the senseless rules of your order, and make an end to that hermaphrodite monster which is neither religious nor secular; abolish the unchaste chastity of monkery; take to thyself a wife, and found a legitimate secular sovereignty." At the same time he recommended to him Paul Speratus as his assistant, who afterwards became bishop of Pomesania. The prince smiled, but said nothing.[1] He wavered between obedience to the pope and to his conscience, and his open and secret instructions to the bishop of Samland were contradictory. His brother, Margrave Georg of Brandenburg, had previously given him the same advice as Luther, and he ultimately followed it.

In the mean time the evangelical doctrines had already spread in Prussia, and facilitated the proposed political change by undermining the monastic constitution of the order.

Two bishops of Prussia, differing from their brethren in Germany, favored the movement, George von Polenz of Samland, and Erhard von Queiss of Pomesania. The former took the lead. Luther was agreeably surprised, and expressed his joy that one, at least, of the bishops dared to profess the

---

[1] Letter to John Briesmann, July 4, 1524, in De Wette, II. 526 sq.

free gospel of Christ.[1] He dedicated to him his commentary on Deuteronomy, with a congratulatory letter full of gratitude for the rapid flight of the gospel to Prussia in the far North (1525).[2] The bishop did not reply, and seems to have preserved a dignified or prudent reserve towards the person of Luther, while allowing free course to his doctrines.[3]

Erhard von Queiss renounced popery in a public sermon, 1524, and resigned his worldly possessions and authority to the Duke (1527), in order to attend better to the spiritual duties of an evangelical bishop.

Georg von Polenz was the chancellor and chief counselor of Albrecht (we may say his Bismarck on a small scale) in this work of transformation. He was about five years older than Luther, and survived him four years. He descended from an old noble family of Meissen in Saxony, studied law in Italy, and was for a while private secretary at the court of Pope Julius II. Then he served as a soldier under Maximilian I. He became acquainted with Margrave Albrecht at Padua, 1509, and joined the Teutonic Knights. In 1519 he was raised to the episcopal chair, and consecrated by the neighboring bishops of Ermland and Pomesania in the Dome of Königsberg. The receipt of the Roman curia for a tax of

[1] "At last," he wrote to Spalatin, Feb. 1, 1524, "even a bishop has given the glory to the name of Christ, and proclaims the gospel in Prussia, namely the bishop of Samland, encouraged and instructed by John Briesmann, whom I sent, so that Prussia also begins to give farewell to the kingdom of Satan." De Wette, II. 474.

[2] Erl. ed., Op. Lat. XIII. The dedicatory letter dated April, 1525, is printed also in De Wette, II. 647–651. In this letter occurs the notable passage (p. 649): "Vide mirabilia, ad Prussiam pleno cursu plenisque telis currit Evangelion." Comp. the passage quoted p. 539, note 2.

[3] Professor Tschackert, his best biographer, says (l.c., p. 187): "The correspondence of Bishop Georg von Polentz, as far as known, contains not a syllable nor even an allusion to a letter of his to Luther. Even the name of Luther occurs after the reformatory mandate of 1524 only once, in a postscript to a letter to Paul Speratus, Aug. 22, 1535." In this letter he requested his colleague, Bishop Speratus of Pomesania, to give some noble students from Lithuania letters of introduction to Luther and Melanchthon ("literis tuis Martino et Philippo commendes.") See the letter, l.c., p. 191.

fourteen hundred and eighty-eight ducats is still extant in the archives of that city. The first years of his office were disturbed by war with Poland, for which he had to furnish men and means. During the absence of the Duke in Germany he took his place.

In September, 1523, he became acquainted with Dr. Briesmann, and learned from him the biblical languages, the elements of theology, which he had never studied before, and the doctrines of Luther. In January, 1524, he already issued an order that baptism be celebrated in the vernacular tongue, and recommended the clergy to read diligently the Bible, and the writings of Luther, especially his book on Christian Liberty. This was the beginning of the Reformation in Prussia. We have from him three sermons, and three only, which he preached in favor of the change, at Christmas, 1523, and at Easter and Pentecost, 1524. He echoes in them the views of Briesmann. He declares, "I shall with the Divine will hold fast to the word of God and to the gospel, though I should lose body and life, goods and honor, and all I possess." He despised the authority of Pope Clement VII., who directed his legate, Campeggio, Dec. 1, 1524, to summon the bishop as a rebel and perjurer, to induce him to recant, or to depose him.

In May, 1525, he resigned the secular part of his episcopal authority into the hands of the Duke, because it was not seemly and Christian for a bishop to have so much worldly glory and power. A few days afterwards he married, June 8, 1525, five days before Luther's marriage. In the next year the Duke followed his example, and invited Luther to the wedding (June, 1526). This double marriage was a virtual dissolution of the order as a monastic institution. In 1546 Georg von Polenz resigned his episcopal supervision into the hands of Briesmann. He died in peace, April 28, 1550, seventy two years old, and was buried in the cathedral of Königsberg, — the first Protestant bishop and chancellor of the first Prussian Hohenzollern, standing with him on the bridge of two ages with his hand on the Bible and his eye firmly fixed upon the future.

Albrecht, acting on the advice of Luther, changed the property of the Knights into a hereditary duchy. The king of Poland consented. On April 10, 1525, Albrecht was solemnly invested at Crakow with the rule of Prussia as a fief of Poland. Soon afterwards he received the homage of the Diet at Königsberg. The evangelical preachers saluted him under the ringing of the bells. The Emperor put him under the ban, but it had no effect. Most of the Knights received large fiefs, and married; the rest emigrated to Germany. Albrecht formally introduced the Reformation, July 6, 1525, and issued a Lutheran constitution and liturgy. The fasts were abolished, the number of holy days reduced, the ceremonies changed, the convents turned into hospitals, and worship conducted in the vernacular. All Romish and sectarian preaching was prohibited. He assumed all the ecclesiastical appointments, and became the supreme bishop of Prussia, the two Roman-Catholic bishops Georg and Queiss having surrendered to him their dignity. Their successors were mere superintendents. He felt, however, that the episcopal office was foreign to a worldly sovereign, and accepted it as a matter of necessity to secure order.[1] He founded the University of Königsberg, the third Protestant university (after Wittenberg and Marburg). It was opened in 1544.[2] He called Dr. Osiander from Nürnberg to the chief theological chair (1549); but this polemical divine, by his dissertations on the law and the gospel, and on the doctrine of justification, soon turned Prussia into a scene of violent and disgraceful theological controversies.[3]

---

[1] "*Coacti sumus,*" he said, "*alienum officium, i.e., episcopale in nos sumere, ut omnia ordine, et decenter fierent.*" Preface to the *Articuli ceremoniarum*, published by a general synod at Königsberg, May 12, 1530.

[2] Arnoldt, *Historie der königsberger Universität*, 1746.

[3] See above, p. 570. Osiander's son-in-law, Funke, Albrecht's chaplain

Albrecht did not enjoy his reign. It was sadly disturbed in this transition state by troubles from within and without. He repeatedly said that he would rather watch sheep than be a ruler. He was involved in heavy debts. The seven children of his first wife, a daughter of the king of Denmark, died young, except a daughter, Anna Sophia, who married a duke of Mecklenburg (1555). His pious and faithful wife died, 1547. In 1550 he married a princess of Braunschweig; her first daughter was born blind; only one son, Albrecht Friedrich, survived him, and spent his life in melancholy. But Albrecht remained true to his evangelical faith, and died (March 20, 1568), with the words of Psa. 31:5, upon his lips, "Into Thine hand I commend my spirit: Thou hast redeemed me, O Lord, Thou God of truth." He left proofs of his piety in prayers, meditations, and the testament to his son, who succeeded him, and died without male issue, 1618

SUBSEQUENT HISTORY.

A few glimpses of the later history are here in place to explain the present confessional status of the Protestant church in the kingdom of Prussia.

The Duchy of Prussia in 1618 fell as an inheritance to John Sigismund, Elector of Brandenburg (1608–1619), son-in-law of the second Prussian Duke (Albert Frederick), and a descendant of Frederick of Hohenzollern, who had become margrave of Brandenburg by purchase in 1415. In this way the connection of Prussia and Brandenburg was completed.

But Prussia remained in feudal subjection to Poland till 1656, when Frederick William, "the great Elector," conquered the independence by the victory of Warsaw. He is the first, as Frederick II., his great-grandson, is the second, founder of the greatness of Prussia. After the terrible devastations of the Thirty Years' War he gathered the broken fragments of his provinces into a coherent whole during his long and successful reign (1640–1688). He was the most enlightened and most liberal among the German princes of his age. He protected the independence of Germany against French aggression. He was married to Louisa Henrietta, princess of Orange, of the Calvinistic faith, and authoress of the popular resurrection hymn, "*Jesus, meine Zuver-*

and confessor, continued the controversies, but was at last beheaded with two others, 1566, as "*Ruhestörer, Landesverräther und Beförderer der osiandrischen Ketzerei.*"

sicht." [1] He secured toleration to the Reformed churches in the Treaty of Westphalia. He gave refuge to over twenty thousand French Huguenots, who with their descendants became an important element in the Prussian nationality and the Reformed church. His son Frederick became the first king of Prussia, and was crowned at Königsberg, Jan. 18, 1701. He founded the University of Halle, 1693, which ultimately absorbed the University of Wittenberg by incorporation (1815), and assumed an important position in the history of German theology as the nursery, first of pietism, then of rationalism, and (since Tholuck's appointment, 1827) of the evangelical revival.

With John Sigismund began an important confessional change, which laid the foundation for the union policy of his successors. He introduced the Reformed or Calvinistic element, which had been crushed out in Saxony, into the Court and Dome Church of Berlin, and gave the Heidelberg Catechism a place besides the Augsburg Confession. His grandson, "the great Elector," strengthened the Reformed element by his marriage to a princess from Holland, who adorned her faith, and by inviting a colony of French Huguenots who left their country for the sake of conscience. It was therefore quite natural that the Reformed rulers of a Lutheran country should cherish the idea of a union of the two confessions, which was realized in the present century.[2]

We have seen that Old Prussia was Lutheranized under the direct influence of the Wittenberg divines with whom Albrecht was in constant correspondence. In Brandenburg also, the Lutheran type of Protestantism, after many reverses and controversies, was established under John George (1571–1598); the Formula of Concord was forcibly introduced, and all Calvinistic teaching was strictly forbidden. The Brandenburg "Corpus Doctrinæ" of 1572 emphasizes Luther's word that Zwingli was no Christian, and the Brandenburg chancellor Dietelmeyer is known by his unchristian prayer: "*Impleat nos Deus odio Calvinistarum!*"

---

[1] Several English translations; one by Miss Winkworth, "Jesus my Redeemer lives." The hymn has a long and interesting history. See A. F. W. Fischer, *Kirchenlieder-Lexicon*, I. 390–396.

[2] For fuller information, see Schaff, *Creeds of Christendom*, I. 554 sqq. To the literature there given should be added Ranke, *Zwölf Bücher Preuss. Geschichte*, Leipz. 1874, I. 185–192; Kawerau in Herzog[2], XIV. 227–232; and Wangemann, *Joh. Sigismund und Paul Gerhard*, Berlin, 1884. The literature on the Prussian Union refers to the history after 1817, and is very large. We mention Nitzsch, *Urkundenbuch der evangelischen Union*, Berlin, 1853; Jul. Müller, *Die evangel. Union, ihr Wesen und göttliches Recht*, Berlin, 1854; Brandes, *Geschichte der kirchlichen Politik des Hauses Brandenburg*, 1872, '73, 2 vols.; Mücke, *Preussen's landeskirchliche Unionsentwicklung*, 1879; Wangemann, *Die preussische Union in ihrem Verhältniss zur Una Sancta*, Berlin, 1884.

But the Elector John Sigismund, who by travels and personal intercourse with Calvinistic princes and divines conceived a high regard for their superior Christian piety and courtesy, embraced the Reformed faith in 1606, and openly professed it in February, 1614, by declaring his assent to the four œcumenical symbols (including the *Chalcedonense*) and the *altered* Augsburg Confession of 1540, without imposing his creed upon his subjects, only prohibiting the preachers to condemn the Calvinists from the pulpit. In May, 1514, he issued a personal confession of faith, called the "Confession of Sigismund," or the "Brandenburg Confession" (*Confessio Marchica*). It teaches a moderate, we may say, Melanchthonian and unionistic Calvinism, and differs from the Lutheran Formula of Concord in the following points: It rejects Eutychianism and the ubiquity of Christ's body, consubstantiation in the Lord's Supper, the use of the wafer instead of the broken bread, and exorcism in baptism; on the other hand, it teaches the Calvinistic view of the spiritual real presence for believers, and unconditional election, but without an unconditional decree of reprobation; it distinctly declares that God sincerely wishes the salvation of *all* men, and is not the author of sin and damnation.

The change of Sigismund was the result of conscientious conviction, and not dictated by political motives. The people and his own wife remained Lutheran. He made no use of his territorial summepiscopate and the *jus reformandi*. He disclaimed all intention to coerce the conscience, since faith is a free gift of God, and cannot be forced. No man should presume to exercise dominion over man's religion. He thus set, in advance of his age, a noble example of toleration, which became the traditional policy of the Prussian rulers. The pietistic movement of Spener and Francke, which was supported by the theological faculty at Halle, weakened the confessional dissensus, and strengthened the consensus. The Moravian brotherhood exhibited long before the Prussian Union, in a small community, the real union of evangelical believers of both confessions.

Frederick the Great was an unbeliever, and had as little sympathy with Pietism and Moravianism as with Lutheranism and Calvinism; but he was a decided upholder of religious toleration, which found expression in his famous declaration that in his kingdom everybody must be at liberty to get saved "after his own fashion." The toleration of indifferentism, which prevailed in the last century, broke down the reign of bigotry, and prepared the way for the higher and nobler principle of religious liberty.

The revival of religious life at the beginning of the nineteenth century was a revival of general Christianity without a confessional or denominational type, and united for a time pious Lutherans, Reformed, and even Roman Catholics. It was accompanied by a new phase of evangelical theology, which since Schleiermacher and Neander laid greater stress on the consensus than the dissensus of the Protestant confessions in opposition to rationalism and infidelity. The ground was thus prepared for a new attempt to establish a mode of peaceful living between the two confessions of the Reformation.

King Frederick William III. (1797-1840), a conscientious and God-fearing monarch, who had been disciplined by sad reverses and providential deliverances of Prussia, introduced what is called the "Evangelical Union" of the Lutheran and Reformed confessions at the tercentennial celebration of the Reformation (Sept. 27, 1817). The term "evangelical," which was claimed by both, assumed thus a new technical sense. The object of the Union (as officially explained in 1834 and 1852) was to unite the two churches under one government and worship, without abolishing the doctrinal distinctions.[1] It was conservative, not absorptive, and differed in this respect from all former union schemes between the Greek and Latin, the Protestant and Roman Catholic, the Lutheran and Reformed Churches, which aimed at doctrinal uniformity or at best at a doctrinal compromise. The Prussian Union introduced no new creed; the Augsburg Confession, Luther's Catechisms, and the Heidelberg Catechism continued to be used where they had been in use before; but it was assumed that the confessional differences were not vital and important enough to exclude Christian fellowship. The opposition proceeded chiefly from the "Old Lutherans," so called, who insist upon "pure doctrine," as the basis of union, to the exclusion of the Calvinistic "heresies," and who took just offense at the forcible introduction of the new liturgy of the king (the *Agende* of 1822); but the opposition was silenced by granting them the liberty of separate organization and self-government (1845). The Prussian Union suffers from the defects of Erastianism, but no more than any other state-church, or the introduction of the Reformation in the sixteenth century by the civil power. Experience has proved that moderate Lutherans and Reformed Christians can live together, commune at the same altar, and co-operate in the work of the common Master. This experience is a great gain. The union type of Protestantism has become an important historic fact and factor in the modern theology and church life of Prussia and those other parts of Germany which followed her example.

The two sons and successors of the founder of the Prussian Union, King Frederick William IV. (1840-1858), and Emperor William I. (1858-1888), have faithfully adhered to it in theory and practice.

Frederick William IV. was well versed in theology, and a pronounced evangelical believer. He wished to make the church more independent, and as a means to that end he established the *Oberkirchenrath* (1850, modified 1852), which in connection with the *Cultusministerium* should administer the affairs of the church in the name of the king; while a general synod was to exercise the legislative function. Under his reign the principle of

---

[1] The *Cabinetsordre* of Feb. 18, 1834, declares: "*Die Union bezweckt und bedeutet kein Aufgeben des bisherigen Glaubensbekenntnisses; auch ist die Autorität, welche die Bekenntnisschriften der beiden evangelischen Confessionen bisher gehabt, durch sie nicht aufgehoben worden.*"

religious liberty made great progress, and was embodied in the Prussian Constitution of 1850, which guarantees in Article XII. the freedom of conscience and of private and public worship to all religious associations.[1]

William I., aided by Bismarck and Moltke, raised Prussia, by superior statesmanship and diplomacy, and by brilliant victories in the wars with Austria (1866) and France (1870), to her present commanding position. He became by common consent of the German sovereigns and people the first hereditary emperor of United Germany under the lead of Prussia. He adorned this position in eighteen years of peace by his wisdom, integrity, justice, untiring industry, and simple piety, and gained the universal esteem and affection of the German nation, yea, we may say, of the civilized world, which mourned for him when on the 9th of March, 1888, in the ninety-first year of an eventful life, he entered into his rest. History has never seen a more illustrious trio than the Emperor William, "the Iron Chancellor," and "the Battle-thinker," who "feared God, and nothing else."

The new German Empire with a Protestant head is the last outcome of the Reformation of Prussia, and would not have been possible without it.

§ 100. *Protestant Martyrs.*

No great cause in church or state, in religion or science, has ever succeeded without sacrifice. Blood is the price of liberty. "The blood of martyrs is the seed of Christianity." Persecution develops the heroic qualities of human nature, and the passive virtues of patience and endurance under suffering. Protestantism has its martyrs as well as Catholicism. In Germany it achieved a permanent legal existence only after the Thirty Years' War. The Reformed churches in France, Holland, England, and Scotland, passed through the fiery ordeal of persecution. It has been estimated that the victims of the Spanish Inquisition outnumber those of heathen Rome, and that more Protestants were executed by the Spaniards in a single reign, and in a single province of Holland, than Christians in the Roman empire during the first three centuries.[2] Jews and heathens have persecuted Christians, Christians have persecuted Jews and heathens, Roman-

---

[1] See Schaff, *Church and State in the United States,* New York, 1888, p. 97 sq.

[2] See Schaff, *Church Hist.* II. 78.

ists have persecuted Protestants, Protestants have persecuted Romanists, and every state-church has more or less persecuted dissenters and sects. It is only within a recent period that the sacred rights of conscience have been properly appreciated, and that the line is clearly and sharply drawn between church and state, religious and civil offenses, heresy and crime, spiritual and temporal punishments.

The persecution of Protestants began at the Diet of Worms in 1521. Charles V. issued from that city the first of a series of cruel enactments, or "placards," for the extermination of the Lutheran heresy in his hereditary dominion of the Netherlands. In 1523 two Augustinian monks, Henry Voes and John Esch, were publicly burnt, as adherents of Luther, at the stake in Brussels. After the fires were kindled, they repeated the Apostles' Creed, sang the "Te Deum laudamus," and prayed in the flames, "Jesus, thou Son of David, have mercy upon us." The heroic death of these Protestant proto-martyrs inspired Luther's first poem, which begins, —

"*Ein neues Lied wir heben an.*" [1]

The prior of their convent, Lampert Thorn, was suffocated in prison. The martyrdom of Henry of Zütphen has already been noticed.[2] Adolph Klarenbach and Peter Flysteden suffered at the stake in Cologne with constancy and triumphant joy, Sept. 28, 1529.[3]

George Winkler, a preacher in Halle, was cited by the Archbishop of Cologne to Aschaffenburg for distributing the communion in both kinds, and released, but murdered by unknown hands on his return, May, 1527.[4]

Duke George of Saxony persecuted the Lutherans, not by

---

[1] See above, p. 505, and Ranke, II. 119.   [2] § 96, p. 574, sq.

[3] See their biography in Piper's *Evang. Kalender*, VII. 408, and article "Klarenbach" by C. Krafft, in Herzog[2], VIII. 20–33.

[4] Luther wrote a letter of comfort to the Christians at Halle on the death of their minister. Walch, X. 2260. See also his letter, April 28, 1528, in De Wette, III. 305.

death, but by imprisonment and exile. John Herrgott, a traveling book-peddler, was beheaded (1527) for revolutionary political opinions, rather than for selling Lutheran books.[1]

In Southern Germany the Edict of Worms was more rigidly executed. Many executions by fire and sword, accompanied by barbarous mutilations, took place in Austria and Bavaria. In Vienna a citizen, Caspar Tauber, was beheaded and burnt, because he denied purgatory and transubstantiation, Sept. 17, 1524.[2] In Salzburg a priest was secretly beheaded without a trial, by order of the archbishop, for Lutheran heresy.[3] George Wagner, a minister at Munich, was burnt Feb. 8, 1527. Leonard Käser (or Kaiser) shared the same fate, Aug. 18, 1527, by order of the bishop of Passau. Luther wrote him, while in prison, a letter of comfort.[4]

But the Anabaptists had their martyrs as well, and they died with the same heroic faith. Hätzer was burnt in Constance, Hübmaier in Vienna. In Passau thirty perished in prison. In Salzburg some were mutilated, others beheaded, others drowned, still others burnt alive.[5] Unfortunately, the Anabaptists were not much better treated by Protestant governments; even in Zürich several were drowned in the river under the eyes of Zwingli. The darkest blot on Protestantism is the burning of Servetus for heresy and blasphemy, at Geneva, with the approval of Calvin and all the surviving Reformers, including Melanchthon (1553). He had been previously condemned, and burnt in effigy, by a Roman-Catholic tribunal in France. Now such a tragedy would be impossible in any church. The same human passions exist, but the ideas and circumstances have changed.

---

[1] See § 93, p. 567, note. [2] Ranke, II. 117 sq. [3] *Ibid.* p. 117.
[4] Letter dated May 20, 1527, in De Wette, III. 179 sq. But Käser seems to have been an Anabaptist, which Luther did not know. See Cornelius, *Gesch. des Münsterschen Aufruhrs,* II. 56. [5] Ranke, III. 369.

CHAPTER VII.

THE SACRAMENTARIAN CONTROVERSIES.

§ 101. *Sacerdotalism and Sacramentalism.*

THE Catholic system of Christianity, both Greek and Roman, is sacramental and sacerdotal. The saving grace of Christ is conveyed to men through the channel of seven sacraments, or "mysteries," administered by ordained priests, who receive members into the church by baptism, accompany them through the various stages of life, and dismiss them by extreme unction into the other world. A literal priesthood requires a literal sacrifice, and this is the repetition of Christ's one sacrifice on the cross offered by the priest in the mass from day to day. The power of the mass extends not only to the living, but even to departed spirits in purgatory, abridging their sufferings, and hastening their release and transfer to heaven.

The Reformers rejected the sacerdotal system altogether, and substituted for it the general priesthood of believers, who have direct access to Christ as our only Mediator and Advocate, and are to offer the spiritual sacrifices of prayer, praise, and intercession. They rejected the sacrifice of the mass, and the theory of transubstantiation, and restored the cup to the laity. They also agreed in raising the Word of God, as the chief means of grace, above the sacraments, and in reducing the number of the sacraments. They retained Baptism and the Lord's Supper, as instituted by Christ for universal and perpetual observance.

But here begins the difference. It consists in the extent of departure from the sacramental system of the Roman

Church. The Lutheran Confession is, we may say, semi-sacra-
mental, or much more sacramental than the Reformed (if we
except the Anglican communion).[1] It retained the doctrine
of baptismal regeneration, with the rite of exorcism, and the
corporal presence in the eucharist. The Augsburg Confession makes the sacraments an essential criterion of the
church. Luther's Catechism assigns to them an independent
place alongside of the Commandments, the Creed, and the
Lord's Prayer. It adds to baptism and the Lord's Supper
confession and absolution as a third sacrament. At a later
period, confirmation was restored to the position of a quasi-
sacrament as a supplement of infant-baptism.

Zwingli and Calvin reduced the sacraments to signs and
seals of grace which is inwardly communicated by the Holy
Spirit. They asserted the sovereign causality of God, and the
independence of the Spirit who "bloweth where it willeth"
(John 3:8). God can communicate his gifts freely as he
chooses. We are, however, bound to his prescribed means.
The Swiss Reformers also emphasized the necessity of faith,
not only for a profitable use of the sacrament (which is conceded by the Lutherans), but for the reception of the sacrament itself. Unworthy communicants receive only the
visible sign, not the thing signified, and they receive the sign
to their own injury.

The Anabaptists went still farther, and rejected infant-
baptism because it lacks the element of faith on the part of
the baptized. They were the forerunners of the Quakers,
who dispensed with the external sacraments altogether,
retaining, however, the spiritual fact of regeneration and

_____

[1] Claus Harms, a typical Lutheran of the nineteenth century, published in
1817 Ninety-five Theses against Rationalism in the Lutheran Church, one of
which reads thus (I quote from memory): "The Catholic Church is a glorious church; for it is built upon the Sacrament. The Reformed Church is a
glorious church; for it is built upon the Word. But more glorious than
either is the Lutheran Church; for it is built upon both the Word and the
Sacrament."

communion with Christ, which the sacraments symbolize to the senses. The Quakers protested against forms when they were made substitutes for the spirit, and furnished the historic proof that the spirit in cases of necessity may live without forms, while forms without the spirit are dead.

It was the will of Providence that different theories on the means of grace should be developed. These theories are not isolated; they proceed from different philosophical and theological standpoints, and affect other doctrines. Luther was not quite wrong when he said to Zwingli at Marburg: "You have a different spirit." Luther took his stand on the doctrine of justification by faith; Zwingli and Calvin, on the doctrine of divine causality and sovereignty, or eternal election. Luther proceeded anthropologically and soteriologically from man to God, Zwingli and Calvin proceeded theologically from God to man.

The difference culminates in the doctrine of the eucharistic presence, which called forth the fiercest controversies, and still divides Western Christendom into hostile camps. The eucharistic theories reveal an underlying difference of views on the relation of God to man, of the supernatural to the natural, of invisible grace to the visible means. The Roman doctrine of transubstantiation is the outgrowth of a magical supernaturalism which absorbs and annihilates the natural and human, leaving only the empty form. The Lutheran doctrine implies an interpenetration of the divine and human. The commemorative theory of Zwingli saves the integrity and peculiar character of the divine and human, but keeps them separate and distinct. The eucharistic theory affects Christology, the relation of church and state, and in some measure the character of piety. Lutheranism inclines to the Eutychian, Zwinglianism to the Nestorian, Christology. The former fosters a mystical, the latter a practical, type of piety.

Calvin, who appeared on the stage of public action five years after Zwingli's, and ten years before Luther's, death, advocated with great ability a eucharistic theory which mediates between the Lutheran realism and the Zwinglian spiritualism, and which passed into the Reformed confessions Luther had to deal with Zwingli, and never came into contact with Calvin. If he had, the controversy might have taken a different shape; but he would have maintained his own view of the real presence, and refused the figurative interpretation of the words of institution.

With the doctrine of the eucharist are connected some minor ritualistic differences, as the use of the wafer, and the kneeling posture of the communicants, which the Lutherans retained from the Catholic Church; while the Reformed restored the primitive practice of the breaking of bread, and the standing or sitting posture. Some Lutheran churches retained also the elevation of the host; Luther himself declared it a matter of indifference, and abolished it at Wittenberg in 1542.[1]

§ 102. *The Anabaptist Controversy. Luther and Hübmaier.*

LUTHER: *Von der Wiedertaufe, an zwei Pfarrherrn.* Wittenberg, 1528. In WALCH, XXVII. 2643 sqq.; Erl. ed. XXVI. 254–294. JUSTUS MENIUS: *Der Wiedertäufer Lehre und Geheimniss,* with a Preface by LUTHER, 1530. In the Erl. ed. LXIII. 290 sqq. MELANCHTHON: *Contra Anabaptistas Judicium,* "Corp. Reform." I. 953 sqq.

On the Baptist side the writings of HÜBMAIER, or, as he wrote his name, HÜBMÖR, which are very rare, and ought to be collected and republished. CALVARY, in "Mittheilungen aus dem Antiquariate," vol. I. Berlin, 1870, gives a complete list of them. The most important are *Von dem christlichen Tauf der Gläubigen* (1525); *Eine Stimme eines ganzen christlichen Lebens* (1525); *Von Ketzern und ihren Verbrennern; Schlussreden (Axiomata); Ein Form des Nachtmals Christi; Von der Freiwilligkeit des Menschen* (to show that God gives to all men an

---

[1] "*Vom Anbeten des Sacraments des heil. Leichnams Christi*" (1523), addressed to the Bohemians (Erl. ed. XXVIII. 389, 404, 410); *Kurzes Bekenntniss vom heil. Sacrament* (1544), Erl. ed. XXXII. 420 sqq. In a letter to Buchholzer in Berlin, Dec. 4, 1539 (De Wette, V. 236), Luther reports that the elevation was given up at Wittenberg. But this must refer to the castle church, for in the parish church it continued till June 25, 1542, when Bugenhagen abolished it. See Köstlin, II. 588 and 683.

opportunity to become his children by free choice); *Zwölf Artikel des christlichen Glaubens*, etc.

On Hübmaier, see SCHREIBER in the "Taschenbuch für Gesch. und Alterthum Süddeutschlands," Freiburg, 1839 and 40. CUNITZ in Herzog's "Encykl.," 2d ed. VI. 344. RANKE, II. 118, 126; III. 366, 369. JANSSEN, II. 387, 486.

All the Reformers retained the custom of infant-baptism, and opposed rebaptism (*Wiedertaufe*) as a heresy. So far they agreed with the Catholics against the Anabaptists, or Catabaptists as they were called, although they rejected the name, because in their view the baptism of infants was no baptism at all.

The Anabaptists or Baptists (as distinct from Pedobaptists) sprang up in Germany, Holland, and Switzerland, and organized independent congregations. Their leaders were Hübmaier, Denck, Hätzer, and Grebel. They thought that the Reformers stopped half-way, and did not go to the root of the evil. They broke with the historical tradition, and constructed a new church of believers on the voluntary principle. Their fundamental doctrine was, that baptism is a voluntary act, and requires personal repentance, and faith in Christ. They rejected infant-baptism as an anti-scriptural invention. They could find no trace of it in the New Testament, the only authority in matters of faith. They were cruelly persecuted in Protestant as well as Roman Catholic countries. We must carefully distinguish the better class of Baptists and the Mennonites from the restless revolutionary radicals and fanatics, like Carlstadt, Münzer, and the leaders of the Münster tragedy.

The mode of baptism was not an article of controversy at that time; for the Reformers either preferred immersion (Luther), or held the mode to be a matter of indifference (Calvin).

Luther agreed substantially with the Roman Catholic doctrine of baptism. His *Taufbüchlein* of 1523 is a translation of the Latin baptismal service, including the formula of exorcism, the sign of the cross, and the dipping. The second edition (1526) is abridged, and omits the use of chrisma, salt, and spittle.[1] He defeated Carlstadt, Münzer, and the Zwickau Prophets, who rejected infant-baptism, and embarrassed even Melanchthon. Saxony was cleared of Anabaptists; but their progress in other parts of Germany induced him a few years later to write a special book against Hübmaier, who appealed to his authority, and ascribed to him similar views.

Balthasar Hübmaier, or Hübmör, was born near Augsburg, 1480; studied under Dr. Eck at Freiburg-i.-B. and Ingolstadt, and acquired the degree of doctor of divinity. He became a famous preacher in the cathedral at Regensburg, and occasioned the expulsion of the Jews in 1519, whose synagogue was converted into a chapel of St. Mary. In 1522 he embraced Protestant opinions, and became pastor at Waldshut on the Rhine, on the borders of Switzerland. He visited Erasmus at Basel, and Zwingli at Zürich, and aided the latter in the introduction of the Reformation. The Austrian government threatened violent measures, and demanded the surrender of his person. He left Waldshut, and took refuge in a convent of Schaffhausen, but afterwards returned. He openly expressed his dissent from Zwingli and Œcolampadius on the subject of infant-baptism. Zwingli was right, he said, in maintaining that baptism was a mere sign, but the significance of this sign was the pledge of faith and obedience unto death, and such a pledge a child could not make; there-

---

[1] See above § 45, p. 218, and the two editions of the *Taufbüchlein* in the Erl. ed. XXII. 157, 291. In both editions dipping is prescribed ("*Da nehme er das Kind und tauche es in die Taufe*"), and no mention is made of any other mode. The Reformed churches objected to the retention of exorcism as a species of superstition. The first English liturgy of Edward VI. (who was baptized by immersion) prescribes trine-immersion (dipping); the second liturgy of 1552 does the same, but gives (for the first time in England) permission to substitute pouring when the child is weak.

fore the baptism of a child had no meaning, and was invalid.
Faith must be present, and cannot be taken for granted as a
future certainty. Instead of baptism he introduced a solemn
presentation or consecration of children before the congregation. He made common cause with the Anabaptists of
Zürich, and with Thomas Münzer, who came into the neighborhood of Waldshut, and kindled the flame of the Peasants'
War. He is supposed by some to be the author of the
Twelve Articles of the Peasants. He was re-baptized about
Easter, 1525, and re-baptized many others. He abolished the
mass, and removed the altar, baptismal font, pictures and
crosses, from the church.

The triumph of the re-action against the rebellious peasants
forced him to flee to Zürich (December, 1525). He had a
public disputation with Zwingli, who had himself formerly
leaned to the view that it would be better to put off baptism
to riper years of responsibility, though he never condemned
infant-baptism. He retracted under pressure and protest,
and was dismissed with some aid. He went to Nikolsburg
in Moravia, published a number of books in German, having
brought a printing-press with him from Switzerland, and
gathered the Baptist " Brethren " into congregations. But
when Moravia, after the death of Louis of Hungary, fell into
the possession of King Ferdinand of Austria, Hübmaier was
arrested with his wife, sent to Vienna, charged with complicity in the Peasants' War, and burned to death, March 10,
1528. He died with serene courage and pious resignation.
His wife, who had strengthened him in his faith, was drowned
three days later in the Danube. Zwingli, after his quarrel
with Hübmaier, speaks unfavorably of his character; Vadian
of St. Gall, and Bullinger, give him credit for great eloquence and learning, but charge him with a restless spirit of
innovation. He was an advocate of the voluntary principle,
and a martyr of religious freedom. Heretics, he maintained,
are those only who wickedly oppose the Holy Scriptures, and

should be won by instruction and persuasion. To use force is to deny Christ, who came to save, not to destroy.

A few months before Hübmaier's death, Luther wrote, rather hastily, a tract against the Anabaptists (January or February, 1528), in the shape of a letter to two unnamed ministers in Catholic territory.[1] " I know well enough," he begins, " that Balthasar Hübmör quotes me among others by name, in his blasphemous book on Re-baptism, as if I were of his foolish mind. But I take comfort in the fact that neither friend nor foe will believe such a lie, since I have sufficiently in my sermons shown my faith in infant-baptism." He expressed his dissent from the harsh and cruel treatment of the Anabaptists, and maintained that they ought to be resisted only by the Word of God and arguments, not by fire and sword, unless they preach insurrection and resist the civil magistrate.[2] At the same time he ungenerously depreciated the constancy of their martyrs, and compared them to the Jewish martyrs at the destruction of Jerusalem, and the Donatist martyrs.[3] He thought it served the papists right, to be troubled with such sectaries of the Devil in punishment for not tolerating the gospel. He then proceeds to refute their objections to infant-baptism.

1. Infant-baptism is wrong because it comes from the pope, who is Antichrist. But then we ought to reject the Scriptures, and Christianity itself, which we have in common

---

[1] He calls it in a letter to Spalatin, Feb. 5, 1528 (De Wette, III. 279), "*epistolam tumultuarie scriptam.*" He alludes to it in several other letters of the same year (III. 250, 253, 263).

[2] The passage is quoted in § 11, p. 60.

[3] Letter to Link, May 12, 1528 (De Wette, III. 311): "*Constantiam Anabaptistarum morientium arbitror similem esse illi, qua Augustinus celebrat Donatistas et Josephus Judæos in vastata Jerusalem, et multa talia furorem esse Satanæ non est dubium, præsertim ubi sic moriuntur cum blasphemia sacramenti. Sancti martyres, ut noster Leonardus Kaiser* [a Lutheran of Bavaria who was beheaded Aug. 18, 1527] *cum timore et humilitate magnaque animi erga hostes lenitate moriuntur: illi vero quasi hostium tædio et indignatione pertinaciam suam augere, et sic mori videntur.*"

with Rome. Christ found many abuses among the Pharisees and Sadducees and the Jewish people, but did not reject the Old Testament, and told his disciples to observe their doctrines (Matt. 23 : 3). Here Luther pays a striking tribute to the Roman church, and supports it by the very fact that the pope is Antichrist, and reveals his tyranny in the temple of God, that is, within the Christian Church, and not outside of it.[1] By such an argument the Anabaptists weaken the cause of Christianity, and deceive themselves.

2. Infants know nothing of their baptism, and have to learn it afterwards from their parents or sponsors. But we know nothing of our natural birth and of many other things, except on the testimony of others.

3. Infants cannot believe. Luther denied this, and appealed to the word of Christ, who declared them fit for the kingdom of heaven (Matt. 19 : 14), and to the example of John the Baptist, who believed in the mother's womb (Luke 1 : 41). Reformed divines, while admitting the capacity or germ of faith in infants, base infant-baptism on the vicarious faith of parents, and the covenant blessing of Abraham which extends to his seed (Gen. 17 : 7). Luther mentions this also.

4. The absence of a command to baptize children. But they are included in the command to baptize all nations (Matt. 28 : 19). The burden of proof lies on the Anabaptists to show that infant-baptism is forbidden in the Bible, before they abolish such an old and venerable institution of the whole Christian Church.

5. Among the positive arguments, Luther mentions the analogy of circumcision, Christ's treatment of children, the cases of family baptisms, Acts 2 : 39; 16 : 15, 33; 1 Cor. 1 : 16.

Melanchthon quoted also the testimonies of Origen, Cyprian, Chrysostom, and Augustin, for the apostolic origin of infant-baptism.

---

[1] See above, p. 529 sq.

§ 103. *The Eucharistic Controversy.*

I. Sources (1) Lutheran. LUTHER: *Wider die himmlischen Propheten*, Jan. 1525 (against Carlstadt and the Enthusiasts). *Dass die Worte, "Das ist mein Leib," noch fest stehen (wider die Schwarmgeister)*, 1527. *Grosses Bekenntniss vom Abendmahl*, March, 1528 (against Zwingli and Œcolampadius). *Kurzes Bekenntniss vom heil. Sacrament*, 1544. All these tracts in the Erl. ed. vols. XXVI. 254; XXIX. 134, 348; XXX. 14, 151; XXXII. 396. WALCH, vol. XX. 1–2955, gives the eucharistic writings, for and against Luther, together with a history.

BUGENHAGEN: *Contra novum errorem de sacramento corporis et sanguinis Christi*. 1525. Also in German. In Walch, XX. 641 sqq. BRENTZ and SCHNEPF: *Syngramma Suevicum super verbis cœnæ Dominicæ "Hoc est corpus meum,"* etc., signed by fourteen Swabian preachers, Oct. 21, 1525. Against Œcolampadius, see Walch, XX. 34, 667 sqq.

(2) On the Zwinglian side. ZWINGLI: Letter to Rev. Mathæus Alber, Nov. 16, 1524; *Commentarius de vera et falsa religione*, 1525; *Amica exegesis, id est, Expositio eucharistiæ negotii ad M. Lutherum*, 1526; *Dass diese Worte Jesu Christi: "Das ist myn Lychnam," ewiglich den alten eynigen Sinn haben werden*, 1527; and several other eucharistic tracts. ŒCOLAMPADIUS: *De genuina verborum Domini: "Hoc est corpus meum," juxta vetustissimos auctores expositione*, Basel, 1525; *Antisyngramma ad ecclesiastas Suevos* (with two sermons on the sacrament), 1526. ŒCOLAMPADIUS and ZWINGLI: *Ueber Luther's Buch Bekenntniss genannt, zwo Antworten*, 1528. See ZWINGLI: *Opera*, ed. Schuler and Schulthess, vol. II. Part II. 1–223; III. 145; 459 sqq.; 589 sqq.; 604 sqq. Also Walch, vol. XX. Extracts in Usteri and Vögelin, *M. H. Zwingli's Sämmtl. Schriften im Auszuge*, vol. II. Part I., pp. 3–187.

II. The historical works on the eucharistic controversies of the Reformation period, by LAVATER (*Historia Sacramentaria*, Tig. 1563); SELNECKER and CHEMNITZ (*Hist. des sacram. Streits*, Leipz., 1583 and 1593); HOSPINIAN (*Hist. Sacramentaria*, Tig. 1603, 2 vols.); LÖSCHER (*Hist. Motuum*, in 3 Parts, Leipz., second ed., 1723); EBRARD (*Das Dogma vom heil. Abendmahl und seine Geschichte*, 2 vols., 1846); KAHNIS (1851); DIECKHOFF (1854); H. SCHMID (1873).

III. The respective sections in the General Church Histories, and the Histories of the Reformation, especially SECKENDORF, GIESELER, BAUR, HAGENBACH, MERLE, FISHER. PLANCK, in his *Geschichte des Protest. Lehrbegriffs* (Leipz. second revised ed., 1792, vol. II., Books V. and VI.), gives a very full and accurate account of the eucharistic controversy, although he calls it "*die unseligste aller Streitigkeiten*" (II. 205).

IV. Special discussions. DORNER: *Geschichte der protestant. Theologie* (München, 1867), pp. 296–329. JUL. MÜLLER: *Vergleichung der Lehren Luther's und Calvin's über das heil. Abendmahl*, in his "Dogmatische Abhandlungen" (Bremen, 1870, pp. 404–467). KÖSTLIN: *Luther's Theologie*, II. 100 sqq., 511 sqq.; *Mart. Luther*, I. 715–725; II. 65–110 (*Luther und Zwingli*); 127 sqq.; 363–369. AUGUST BAUR: *Zwingli's Theologie* (Halle, 1885; second vol. has not yet appeared).

American discussions of the eucharistic controversies. J. W. NEVIN (Reformed, d. 1886): *The Mystical Presence*, Philadelphia, 1846; *Doctrine of the Reformed Church on the Lord's Supper*, in "The Mercersburg Review," 1850, pp. 421–549. CH. HODGE (Presbyt., d. 1878): in "The Princeton Review" for April, 1848; *Systematic Theology*, New York, 1873, vol. III., 626–677. C. P. KRAUTH (Luth., d. 1883): *The Conservative Reformation* (Philadelphia, 1872), p. 585 sqq. H. J. VAN DYKE (Calvinist): *The Lord's Supper*, 2 arts. in "The Presbyterian Review," New York, 1887, pp. 193 and 472 sqq. J. W. RICHARD (Luth.), in the "Bibliotheca Sacra" (Oberlin, O.), Oct. 1887, p. 667 sqq., and Jan. 1888, p. 110 sqq.

See, also, the lit. quoted in Schaff, *Church Hist.*, I. 471 sq. and IV. 543 sq.

While the Reformers were agreed on the question of infant-baptism against the Anabaptists, they disagreed on the mode and extent of the real presence in the Lord's Supper.

The eucharistic controversies of the sixteenth century present a sad and disheartening spectacle of human passion and violence, and inflicted great injury to the progress of the Reformation by preventing united action, and giving aid and comfort to the enemy; but they were overruled for the clearer development and statement of truth, like the equally violent Trinitarian, Christological, and other controversies in the ancient church. It is a humiliating fact, that the feast of union and communion of believers with Christ and with each other, wherein they engage in the highest act of worship, and make the nearest approach to heaven, should have become the innocent occasion of bitter contests among brethren professing the same faith and the same devotion to Christ and his gospel. The person of Christ and the supper of Christ have stirred up the deepest passions of love and hatred. Fortunately, the practical benefit of the sacrament depends upon God's promise, and simple and childlike faith in Christ, and not upon any scholastic theory, any more than the benefit of the Sacred Scriptures depends upon a critical knowledge of Greek and Hebrew.

The eucharist was twice the subject of controversy in the Middle Ages, — first in the ninth, and then in the eleventh, century. The question in both cases turned on a grossly realistic and a spiritual conception of the sacramental presence and fruition of Christ's body and blood ; and the result was the triumph of the Roman dogma of transubstantiation, as advocated by Paschasius Radbertus against Ratramnus, and by Lanfranc against Berengar, and as finally sanctioned by the fourth Lateran Council in 1215, and the Council of Trent in 1551.[1]

The Greek and Latin churches are substantially agreed on the doctrine of the communion and the mass, but divide on the ritual question of the use of leavened or unleavened bread. The withdrawal of the cup from the laity caused the bloody Hussite wars.

The eucharistic controversies of the Protestants assumed a different form. Transubstantiation was discarded by both parties. The question was not, whether the elements as to their substance are miraculously transformed into the body and blood of Christ, but whether Christ was corporally or only spiritually (though no less really) present with the natural elements; and whether he was partaken of by all communicants through the mouth, or only by the worthy communicants through faith.

The controversy has two acts, each with several scenes : first, between Luther and Zwingli; secondly, between the Lutherans and Philippists and Calvinists. At last Luther's theory triumphed in the Lutheran, Calvin's theory in the

[1] Schaff, *Church History*, vol. IV. 543–572; *Creeds of Christendom*, II. 130–139.

Reformed churches. The Protestant denominations which have arisen since the Reformation on English and American soil,—Independents, Baptists, Methodists, etc.,—have adopted the Reformed view. Luther's theory is strictly confined to the church which bears his name. But, as the Melanchthonian and moderate Lutherans approach very nearly the Calvinistic view, so there are Calvinists, and especially Anglicans, who approach the Lutheran view more nearly than the Zwinglian. The fierce antagonism of the sixteenth and seventeenth centuries has given way on both sides to a more dispassionate and charitable temper. This is a real progress.

We shall first trace the external history of this controversy, and then present the different theories with the arguments.

§ 104. *Luther's Theory before the Controversy.*

Luther rejected, in his work on the "Babylonish Captivity of the Church" (1520), the doctrine of the mass, transubstantiation, and the withdrawal of the cup, as strongholds of the Papal tyranny. From this position he never receded. In the same work he clearly intimated his own view, which he had learned from Pierre d'Ailly, Cardinal of Cambray (Cameracensis),[1] in these words:—

"Formerly, when I was imbibing the scholastic theology, the Cardinal of Cambray gave me occasion for reflection, by arguing most acutely, in the Fourth Book of the Sentences, that it would be much more probable, and that fewer superfluous miracles would have to be introduced, if real bread and real wine, and not only their accidents, were understood to be upon the altar, unless the Church had determined the contrary. Afterwards, when I saw what the church was, which had thus determined, — namely, the Thomistic, that is, the Aristotelian Church, — I became bolder; and, whereas I

---

[1] Petrus de Alliaco (1350–1420) was one of the leaders of the disciplinary reform movement during the papal schism, and in the councils of Pisa and Constance, the teacher of Gerson and Nicolaus de Clemanges. He gives his views on consubstantiation and transubstantiation, which resemble those of Occam, in his *Quæstiones super libros Sententiarum* (Argent. 1490), Lib. IV. Qu. VI. See Steitz, in his learned art. on transubstantiation, in Herzog[2] XV. 831; and Tschackert, *Peter von Ailli*, Gotha, 1877.

had been before in great straits of doubt, I now at length established my conscience in the former opinion: namely, that *there were real bread and real wine, in which were the real flesh and real blood of Christ in no other manner and in no less degree than the other party assert them to be under the accidents.*[1] . . . Why should not Christ be able to include his body within the substance of bread, as well as within the accidents ? Fire and iron, two different substances, are so mingled in red-hot iron that every part of it is both fire and iron. Why may not the glorious body of Christ much more be in every part of the substance of the bread ? . . . I rejoice greatly, that, at least among the common people, there remains a simple faith in this sacrament. They neither understand nor argue whether there are accidents in it or substance, but believe, with simple faith, that the body and blood of Christ are truly contained in it, leaving to these men of leisure the task of arguing as to what it contains."

At that time of departure from Romanism he would have been very glad, as he confessed five years later, to become convinced that there was nothing in the Lord's Supper but bread and wine. Yea, his old Adam was still inclined to such a view; but he dared not doubt the literal meaning of the words of institution.[2] In his book on the "Adoration of the Sacrament" (1523), addressed to the Waldensian Brethren in Bohemia, he rejects their symbolical theory, as well as the Romish transubstantiation, and insists on the real and substantial presence of Christ's body and blood in the eucharistic elements; but treats them very kindly, notwithstanding their supposed error, and commends them for

---

[1] " *Esse verum panem verumque vinum, in quibus Christi vera caro verusque sanguis non aliter nec minus sit, quam illi sub accidentibus suis ponunt.*"

[2] " *Das bekenne ich,*" he wrote, Dec. 15, 1524, to the Christians in Strassburg (De Wette, II. 577), "*wo D. Carlstadt oder jemand anders vor fünf Jahren mich hätte mögen berichten, dass im Sacrament nichts denn Brot und Wein wäre, der hätte mir einen grossen Dienst gethan. Ich habe wohl so harte Anfechtungen da erlitten und mich gerungen und gewunden, dass ich gern heraus gewesen wäre, weil ich wohl sah, dass ich damit dem Papstthum hätte den grössten Puff können geben. Ich hab auch zween gehabt, die geschickter davon zu mir geschrieben haben denn D. Carlstadt, und nicht also die Worte gemartert nach eigenem Dünken. Aber ich bin gefangen, kann nicht heraus: der Text ist zu gewaltig da, und will sich mit Worten nicht lassen aus dem Sinn reissen.*" The two persons alluded to are probably, as Ullmann conjectures, Wessel or Rhodius and Honius, who sent a letter to Luther with Wessel's books.

their piety and discipline, in which they excelled the Germans.[1]

In his conviction of the real presence, he was greatly strengthened by the personal attacks and perverse exegesis of Carlstadt. Henceforth he advocated the point of agreement with the Catholics more strenuously than he had formerly opposed the points in which he differed from them. He changed the tone of moderation which he had shown in his address to the Bohemians, and treated his Protestant opponents with as great severity as the Papists. His peculiar view of the eucharist became the most, almost the only, serious doctrinal difference between the two wings of the Reformation, and has kept them apart ever since.

§ 105. *Luther and Carlstadt.*

The first outward impulse to the eucharistic controversy came from Holland in the summer of 1522, when Henry Rhodius brought from Utrecht a collection of the writings of John Wessel to Wittenberg, which he had received from a distinguished Dutch jurist, Cornelius Honius (Hœn). Wessel, one of the chief forerunners of the Reformation (d. 1489), proposed, in a tract " De Cœna," a figurative interpretation of the words of institution, which seems to have influenced the opinions of Erasmus, Carlstadt, and Zwingli on this subject.[2]

---

[1] In Walch, XIX. 1593 sqq.; Erl. ed., XXVIII. 389 sqq. He says in the beginning: "We Germans believe that Christ is verily with his flesh and blood in the sacrament, as he was born of Mary, and hung on the holy cross." He rejects the figurative interpretation because it might deprive other passages of their force.

[2] Ullmann, *Reformatoren vor der Reformation* (1842), vol. II. 560–583. Melanchthon derived the controversy from Erasmus. " *Tota illa* tragœdia περὶ δείπνου κυριακοῦ *ab ipso* [*Erasmo*] *nata videri potest.*" Letter to Camerarius, July 26, 1529 (" Corpus Ref.," I. 1083). He was informed by Zwingli in Marburg: " *se ex Erasmi scriptis primum hausisse opinionem suam de cœna Domini.*" Letter to Acquila, Oct. 12, 1529 (IV. 970). Erasmus spoke very highly of the book of Œcolampadius on the Lord's Supper, and would have accepted his view if it were not for the consensus of the church:

But Luther was so much pleased with the agreement on other points that he overlooked the difference, and lauded Wessel as a theologian truly taught of God, and endowed with a high mind and wonderful gifts; yea, so fully in harmony with him, that the Papists might charge Luther with having derived all his doctrines from Wessel, had he known his writings before.[1]

The controversy was opened in earnest by Carlstadt, Luther's older colleague and former friend, who gave him infinite trouble, and forced him into self-defense and into the development of the conservative and churchly elements in his theology.[2] He smarted under the defeat he had suffered in 1522, and first silently, then openly, opposed Luther, regarding him henceforth as his enemy, and as the author of all his misfortunes. In this way he mixed, from the start, the gall of personal bitterness into the eucharistic controversy. Luther would probably have been more moderate if it had been free from those complications.

In 1524 Carlstadt came out with a new and absurd interpretation of the words of institution (Matt. 26 : 26 and parallel passages); holding that the Greek word for "this" being neuter (τοῦτο), could not refer to the bread, which is masculine in Greek (ἄρτος), but must refer to the body of Christ (τὸ σῶμα), to which the Saviour pointed, so as to say, "Take, eat! This here [this body] is my body [which will soon be] broken for you; this [blood] is my blood [which will be] shed for you." This resolves the words into a

---

"*Mihi non displiceret Œcolampadii sententia, nisi obstaret consensus ecclesiæ.*" Letter to Pirkheimer, June 6, 1526.

[1] Preface to "*Farrago rerum, theolog., Wesselo autore,*" published at Wittenberg, 1521 or 1522. *Op.*, VII. 493 sqq. See Ullmann, *l.c.* p. 564 sq. This edition, however, excludes the tract *De cœna*, — a proof that Luther did not altogether like it.

[2] See §§ 66 and 68, pp. 378 sqq. and 387. Carlstadt is the real author of the eucharistic controversy, not Luther, as Hospinian and Hottinger assumed. But Luther and Zwingli were the chief actors in it. Carlstadt's view passed out of sight, when the Swiss view was brought out.

tautology and platitude. At the same time Carlstadt opposed infant-baptism, and traced his crude novelties to higher inspiration.[1] After his expulsion from Saxony he propagated them, together with slanderous assaults upon Luther as "a double Papist," in several publications which appeared in Basel and Strasburg.[2] He excited some interest among the Swiss Reformers, who sympathized with his misfortunes, and agreed with his opposition to the theory of a corporal presence and oral manducation, but dissented entirely from his exegesis, his mysticism, and radicalism. Capito and Bucer, the Reformers of Strassburg, leaned to the Swiss view, but regretted the controversy, and sent a deacon with Carlstadt's tracts to Luther for advice.

Luther exhorted the Strassburgers, in a vigorous letter (Dec. 14, 1524), to hold fast to the evangelical doctrines, and warned them against the dangerous vagaries of Carlstadt. At the same time he issued an elaborate refutation of Carlstadt, in a book "Against the Heavenly Prophets" (December, 1524, and January, 1525, in two parts). It is written with great ability and great violence. "A new storm is arising," he begins. "Dr. Andreas Carlstadt is fallen away from us, and has become our worst enemy." He thought the poor man had committed the unpardonable sin.[3] He describes, in vivid colors, the wild and misty mysticism and false legalism of these self-styled prophets, and defends the real presence. He despised the objections of reason, which was the mistress of the Devil. It is characteristic, that, from this

---

[1] This is the reason why Luther called Carlstadt and his sympathizers enthusiasts and fanatics. *Schwarmgeister* or *Schwärmer.*

[2] His eucharistic tracts in crude and unreadable German are printed in Walch, XX. 138-158, 378-409, 2852-2929. Comp., also, vol. XV. 2414-2502. Carlstadt's earlier eucharistic writings of 1521 strongly defend the corporal presence, and even the adoration of bread and wine, because they were the body and blood of Christ. Planck, *l.c.*, II. 210 sqq., gives a full exposition of his earlier and later views. See, also, M. Göbel on *Carlstadt's Abendmahlslehre* in the "Studien und Kritiken," 1842.

[3] Letter to Briesmann, Jan. 11, 1525, De Wette, II. 612.

time on, he lowered his estimate of the value of reason in theology, although he used it very freely and effectually in this very book.[1]

§ 106. *Luther and Zwingli.*

But now two more formidable opponents appeared on the field, who, by independent study, had arrived at a far more sensible interpretation of the words of institution than that of Carlstadt, and supported it with strong exegetical and rational arguments. Zwingli, the Luther of Switzerland, and Œcolampadius, its Melanchthon, gave the controversy a new and more serious turn.

Zwingli received the first suggestion of a figurative interpretation (*est = significat*) from Erasmus and Wessel through Honius ; as Luther derived his first idea of a corporal presence in the unchanged elements from Pierre d'Ailly.[2] He communicated his view, in a confidential Latin letter, Nov. 16, 1524, to the Lutheran preacher, Matthaeus Alber in Reutlingen, an opponent of Carlstadt, and based it on Christ's word, John 6 : 63, as excluding a carnal or material manducation of his body and blood.[3]

---

[1] Köstlin (*M. L.*, I. 726) : *Luther's Widerwille gegen die menschliche Vernunft im Gebiete des Religiösen und Göttlichen wurde, seit er hier* [in Carlstadt's writings] *sie auftreten sah, noch stärker und heftiger als früher. Früher stellte er hin und wieder noch unbefangen die Berufung auf Schriftbeweise und auf helle, evidente, vernünftige Gründe nebeneinander, indem er durch die einen oder anderen widerlegt zu werden begehrte : so ja auch noch beim Wormser Reichstag ; solchen Ausdrücken werden wir fortan nicht leicht mehr begegnen.''* On Luther's views of the relation of reason to faith, see above, § 9, p. 29 sqq.

[2] The assertion of some biographers of Zwingli, that he already at Glarus became acquainted with the writings of Ratramnus and Wiclif, is without proof. He first intimates his view in a letter to his teacher Wyttenbach, June 15, 1523, but as a secret. (*Opera*, VII., I. 297.) He published the letter of Honius, which explains the *est* to be equivalent to *significat*, at Zürich in March, 1525, but had received it in 1521 from two learned visitors, Rhodius and Sagarus. See Gieseler, III. 1, 192 sq., note 27 (Germ. ed.); and especially Ullmann, *l.c.*, II. 569 sq.

[3] *Opera*, III. 589. Walch gives a German translation, XVII. 1881. Planck (II. 261 sqq.) quotes all the important points of this letter.

A few months later (March, 1525) he openly expressed his view with the same arguments in the "Commentary on the True and False Religion."[1] This was three months after Luther had published his book against Carlstadt. He does not mention Luther in either of these two writings, but evidently aimed at him, and speaks of his view almost as contemptuously as Luther had spoken of Carlstadt's view.

In the same year Œcolampadius, one of the most learned and pious men of his age, appeared with a very able work in defense of the same theory, except that he put the figure in the predicate, and explained the words of institution (like Tertullian) : " *hoc est* FIGURA *corporis mei.*" He lays, however, no stress on this difference, as the sense is the same. He wrote with as much modesty and moderation as learning and acuteness. He first made use of testimonies of the church fathers, especially Augustin, who favors a spiritual fruition of Christ by faith. Erasmus judged the arguments of Œcolampadius to be strong enough to seduce the very elect.[2]

The Lutherans were not slow to reply to the Swiss.

Bugenhagen, a good pastor, but poor theologian, published a letter to Hess of Breslau against Zwingli.[3] He argues, that, if the substantive verb in the words of institution is

---

[1] *Opera*, III. 145. The section on the Lord's Supper appeared also in a German translation. Planck, II. 265 sqq.

[2] *Ep. ad Budam Episc. Lingonensem*, Oct. 2, 1525 (*Op.*, III. 1, 892): " *Exortum est novum dogma, in Eucharistia nihil esse præter panem et vinum. Id ut sit difficillimum refellere, fecit Io. Œcolampadius qui tot testimoniis, tot argumentis eam opinionem communiit, ut seduci posse videantur etiam electi.*" Planck (II. 274): " *Dass Œcolampad in dieser Schrift die ausgebreitetste Gelehrsamkeit und den blendendsten oder treffendsten Scharfsinn zeigte, dies haben selbst seine parteyischsten Gegner niemals geläugnet ; aber sie hätten wohl auch gestehen dürfen, dass er die anständigste Bescheidenheit, die würdigste Mässigung und gewiss auch die redlichste Wahrheitsliebe darin gezeigt habe.*" Dr. Baur also, in his *Kirchengesch.* IV. 90, speaks very highly of the book of Œcolampadius, and gives a summary of it. Baur and Gieseler, among modern church historians, clearly betray their Swiss sympathy in this controversy, as well as Planck, although all of them are Germans of Lutheran descent.

[3] In German translation, Walch, XX. 641.

figurative, it must always be figurative; e.g., "Peter is a man," would mean, "Peter signifies a man."[1] He also appeals to 1 Cor. 11 : 27, where Paul says that unworthy communicants are guilty of the body and blood of Christ, not of bread and wine. Zwingli had easy work to dispose of such an opponent.[2]

Several Swabian preachers, under the lead of Brentius of Hall, replied to Œcolampadius, who (himself a Swabian by birth) had dedicated his book to them with the request to examine and review it. Their *Syngramma Suevicum* is much more important than Bugenhagen's epistle. They put forth the peculiar view that the word of Christ puts into bread and wine the very body and blood of Christ; as the word of Moses imparted a healing power to the brazen serpent; as the word of Christ, "Peace be unto you," imparts peace; and the word, "Thy sins be forgiven," imparts pardon. But, by denying that the body of Christ is broken by the hands, and chewed with the teeth, they unwittingly approached the Swiss idea of a purely spiritual manducation. Œcolampadius clearly demonstrated this inconsistency in his *Anti-syngramma* (1526).[3] Pirkheimer of Nürnberg, and Billicum of Nördlingen, likewise wrote against Œcolampadius, but without adding any thing new.

---

[1] Luther had used the same weak argument before, in his Address to the Bohemians (1523), where he says (Erl. ed., XXVIII. 393 sq.): " *Wo man solchen Frevel an einem Ort zuliesse, dass man ohn Grund der Schrift möcht sagen, das Wörtlin ' Ist' heisst so viel als das Wörtlin ' Bedeut,' so könnt mans auch an keinem andern Ort wehren, und würde die ganze Schrift zunichte; sintemal keine Ursach wäre, warum solcher Frevel an einem Ort gülte, und nicht an allen Oertern. So möcht man denn sagen, dass Maria ist Jungfrau und Mutter Gottes, sei so viel gesagt, Maria bedeut eine Jungfrau und Gottes Mutter. Item, Christus ist Gott und Mensch, das ist, Christus bedeut Gott und Mensch. Item, Rom. 1 : 16, Das Evangelium ist Gottes Kraft, das ist, das Evangelium bedeut Gottes Kraft. Siehe, welch ein greulich Wesen wollt hieraus werden.*"

[2] In his *Responsio ad Bugenhagii Epistolam*, 1525. *Opera*, III. 604–614. In German, Walch, XX. 648.

[3] Walch, XX. 667; Planck, II. 281–311. Köstlin and Dorner say that the *Syngramma* is more Calvinistic than Lutheran.

The controversy reached its height in 1527 and 1528, when Zwingli and Luther came into direct conflict. Zwingli combated Luther's view vigorously, but respectfully, *fortiter in re, suaviter in modo*, in a Latin book, under the peaceful title, "Friendly Exegesis," and sent a copy to Luther with a letter, April 1, 1527.[1] Luther appeared nearly at the same time (early in 1527), but in a very different tone, with a German book against Zwingli and Œcolampadius, under the title, "*That the Words of Christ: 'This is my Body,' stand fast. Against the Fanatics (Schwarmgeister)*."[2] Here he derives the Swiss view directly from the inspiration of the Devil. "How true it is," he begins, "that the Devil is a master of a thousand arts![3] He proves this powerfully in the external rule of this world by bodily lusts, tricks, sins, murder, ruin, etc., but especially, and above all measure, in spiritual and external things which affect God's honor and our conscience. How he can turn and twist, and throw all sorts of obstacles in the way, to prevent men from being saved and abiding in the Christian truth!" Luther goes on to trace the working of the Devil from the first corruptions of the gospel by heretics, popes, and councils, down to Carlstadt and the Zwinglians, and mentions the Devil on every page. This is characteristic of his style of polemics against the Sacramentarians, as well as the Papists. He refers all evil in the world to the Prince

---

[1] Even Löscher admits that Zwingli treated Luther with great respect in this book. Comp. Planck, II. 470 sq.; Köstlin, II. 94 sqq.

[2] He informed Stiefel, Jan. 1, 1527 (De Wette, III. 148), that he was writing a book against the "*sacramentarii turbatores.*" On March 21, 1527 (III. 165), he informed the preacher Ursinus that he had finished it, and warned him to avoid the "*Zwingliana et Œcolampadia sententia*" as the very pest, since it was "*blasphema in Christi verbum et fidem.*" The work was translated into German by M. Judex. The closing passages blaming Bucer for accompanying a Latin version of Luther's *Kirchenpostille* and Bugenhagen's commentary on the Psalms with Zwinglian notes are omitted in the Wittenberg edition of Luther's Works, 1548. Amsdorf complained of this omission, which was traced by some to Melanchthon, by others to Rörer, the corrector of Luft's printing establishment. See Walch, XX. 53, and Erl. ed., XXX. 15.

[3] *Ein Tausendkünstler*, a myriad-minded trickster.

of evil. He believed in his presence and power as much as in the omnipresence of God and the ubiquity of Christ's body.

He dwells at length on the meaning of the words of institution: "This is my body." They must be taken literally, unless the contrary can be proved. Every departure from the literal sense is a device of Satan, by which, in his pride and malice, he would rob man of respect for God's Word, and of the benefit of the sacrament. He makes much account of the disagreement of his opponents, and returns to it again and again, as if it were conclusive against them. Carlstadt tortures the word "this" in the sacred text; Zwingli, the word "is;" Œcolampadius, the word "body;"[1] others torture and murder the whole text. All alike destroy the sacraments. He allows no figurative meaning even in such passages as 1 Cor. 10:4; John 15:1; Gen. 41:26; Exod. 12:11, 12. When Paul says, Christ is a rock, he means that he is truly a *spiritual* rock. When Christ says, "I am the vine," he means a true *spiritual* vine. But what else is this than a figurative interpretation in another form?

A great part of the book is devoted to the proof of the ubiquity of Christ's body. He explains "the right hand of God" to mean his "almighty power." Here he falls himself into a figurative interpretation. He ridicules the childish notion which he ascribes to his opponents, although they never dreamed of it, that Christ is literally seated, and immovably fastened, on a golden throne in heaven, with a golden crown on his head.[2] He does not go so far as to deny the realness

---

[1] He coins new names for the three parties, *Tutisten, Tropisten, Deutisten.* Erl. ed. XXX. 336.

[2] " *Wie man den Kindern pflegt fürzubilden einen Gaukelhimmel, darin ein gülden Stuhl stehe und Christus neben dem Vater sitze in einer Chorkappen und gülden Krone, gleichwie es die Mäler malen. Denn wo sie nicht solche kindische, fleischliche Gedanken hätten von der rechten Hand Gottes, würden sie freilich sich nicht so lassen anfechten den Leib Christi im Abendmahl, oder sich bläuen mit dem Spruch Augustini (welchem sie doch sonst nichts gläuben noch keinem andern), Christus muss an einem Ort leiblich sein, aber seine Wahrheit [Gottheit?] is allenthalben.*" Erl. ed. XXX. 56.

of Christ's ascension, which implies a removal of his corporal presence. There is, in this reasoning, a strange combination of literal and figurative interpretation. But he very forcibly argues from the personal union of the divine and human natures in Christ, for the possibility of a real presence ; only he errs in confounding real with corporal. He forgets that the spiritual is even more real than the corporal, and that the corporal is worth nothing without the spiritual.

Nitzsch and Köstlin are right when they say that both Zwingli and Luther "assume qualities of the glorified body of Christ, of which we can know nothing ; the one by asserting a spacial inclusion of that body in heaven, the other by asserting dogmatically its divine omnipresence on earth." [1] We may add, that the Reformers proceeded on an assumption of the locality of heaven, which is made impossible by the Copernican system. For aught we know, heaven may be very near, and round about as well as above us.

Zwingli answered Luther without delay, in an elaborate treatise, likewise in German (but in the Swiss dialect), and under a similar title (" *That the words, 'This is my body,' have still the old and only sense,*" etc.).[2] It is addressed to the Elector John of Saxony, and dated June 20, 1527. Zwingli follows Luther step by step, answers every argument, defends the figurative interpretation of the words of institution by many parallel passages (Gen. 41:26 ; Exod. 12:11 ; Gal. 4:24 ; Matt. 11:14 ; 1 Cor. 10:4, etc.), and discusses also the relation of the two natures in Christ.

He disowns the imputed literal understanding of God's almighty hand, and says, " We have known long since that God's power is everywhere, that he is the Being of beings, and that his omnipresence upholds all things. We know that where Christ is, there is God, and where God is, there is

---

[1] Köstlin, *M. Luther*, II. 96 and 642; and *Luthers Theologie*, II. 172 sqq.

[2] *Werke*, vol. II. Part II. 16–93. Afterwards translated into Latin by Gualter, *Opera Lat.* II. 374–416.

Christ. But we distinguish between the two natures, and between the person of Christ and the body of Christ." He charges Luther with confounding the two. The attributes of the infinite nature of God are not communicable to the finite nature of man, except by an exchange which is called in rhetoric *allœosis*. The ubiquity of Christ's body is a contradiction. Christ is everywhere, but his body cannot be everywhere without ceasing to be a body, in any proper sense of the term.

This book of Zwingli is much sharper than his former writings on the subject. He abstains indeed from abusive language, and says that God's Word must decide the controversy, and not opprobrious terms, as fanatic, devil, murderer, heretic, hypocrite, which Luther deals out so freely.[1] But he and his friends applied also very unjust terms against the Lutherans, such as Capernaites, flesh-eaters, blood-drinkers, and called their communion bread a baked God.[2] Moreover, Zwingli assumes an offensive and provoking tone of superiority, which cut to the quick of Luther's sensibilities. Take the opening sentence : " To Martin Luther, Huldrych Zwingli wishes grace and peace from God through Jesus Christ the living Son of God, who, for our salvation, suffered death, and then left this world in his body and ascended to heaven, where he sits until he shall return on the last day, according to his own word, so that you may know that he dwells in our hearts by faith (Eph. 3 : 17), and not by bodily

---

[1] "*Es wirt hie Gottes Wort Oberhand gwünnen, nit ' Schwärmer, Tüfel, Schalk, Ketzer, Mörder, Ufrührer, Glychsner [Gleissner] oder Hüchler, trotz, potz, plotz, blitz, donder [Donner], po, pu, pa, plump,' und derglychen Schelt-, Schmütz-, und Schänzelwort.*" *Werke*, II. Part II. 29.

[2] *Fleischfresser, Blutsäufer, Anthropophagos, Capernaiten, brödern Gott, gebratener Gott.* Luther indignantly protests against these opprobrious epithets in his *Short Confession*, "*als wären wir solche tolle, unsinnige, rasende Leute, die Christum im Sacrament localiter hielten, und stückweise zerfrässen, wie der Wolf ein Schaaf, und Blut söffen, wie eine Kuh das Wasser.*" But in the same breath he pays the opponents back with interest, and calls them "*Brotfresser, Weinsäufer, Seelenfresser, Seelenmörder, eingeteufelt, durchteufelt, überteufelt.*" Erl. ed. XXXII. 402-404.

eating through the mouth, as thou wouldest teach without
God's Word." Towards the end he says, with reference to
Luther's attack upon Bucer: "Christ teaches us to return
good for evil. Antichrist reverses the maxim, and you have
followed him by abusing the pious and learned Bucer for
translating and spreading your books. . . . Dear Luther, I
humbly beseech you not to be so furious in this matter as
heretofore. If you are Christ's, so are we. It behooves us
to contend only with the Word of God, and to observe
Christian self-control. We must not fight against God, nor
cloak our errors by his Word. God grant unto you the
knowledge of truth, and of thyself, that you may remain
Luther, and not become λούτριον.[1] The truth will prevail.
Amen."

Œcolampadius wrote likewise a book in self-defense.[2]

Luther now came out, in March, 1528, with his *Great "Confession on the Lord's Supper*," which he intended to be his last
word in this controversy.[3] It is his most elaborate treatise
on the eucharist, full of force and depth, but also full of
wrath. He begins again with the Devil, and rejoices that he
had provoked his fury by the defense of the holy sacrament.
He compares the writings of his opponents to venomous
adders. I shall waste, he says, no more paper on their mad
lies and nonsense, lest the Devil might be made still more
furious. May the merciful God convert them, and deliver
them from the bonds of Satan! I can do no more. A heretic
we must reject, after the first and second admonition (Tit.

---

[1] Water that has been used in washing.

[2] *Secunda, justa et aequa responsio ad Mart. Lutherum.* The book is
mentioned by Hospinian, but must be very rare, since neither Löscher nor
Walch nor Planck has seen it.

[3] It was afterwards called the " Great " Confession, to distinguish it from
the " Small " Confession which he published sixteen years later (1544).
Erl. ed. XXX. 151–373 ; Walch, XX. 1118 sqq. In a letter dated March 28,
1528 (De Wette, III. 296), he informs Link that he sent copies of his Confession through John Hofmann to Nürnberg, and speaks with his usual contempt
of the Sacramentarians. " Zwingel," he says, " *est tam rudis, ut asino queat
comparari.*"

3 : 10).   Nevertheless, he proceeds to an elaborate assault on the Devil and his fanatical crew.

The "Confession" is divided into three parts.   The first is a refutation of the arguments of Zwingli and Œcolampadius; the second, an explanation of the passages which treat of the Lord's Supper; the third, a statement of all the articles of his faith, against old and new heresies.

He devotes much space to a defense of the ubiquity of Christ's body, which he derives from the unity of the two natures.   He calls to aid the scholastic distinction between three modes of presence, — local, definitive, and repletive.[1] He calls Zwingli's allœosis "a mask of the Devil."   He concludes with these words: "This is my faith, the faith of all true Christians, as taught in the Holy Scriptures.   I beg all pious hearts to bear me witness, and to pray for me that I may stand firm in this faith to the end.   For — which God forbid! — should I in the temptation and agony of death speak differently, it must be counted for nothing but an inspiration of the Devil.[2]   Thus help me my Lord and Saviour Jesus Christ, blessed forever.   Amen."

The "Confession" called out two lengthy answers of Zwingli and Œcolampadius, at the request of the Strassburg divines; but they add nothing new.[3]

---

[1] "*Es sind dreierlei Weise an einem Ort zu sein, localiter oder circumscriptive, definitive, repletive.*"   He explains this at length (XXX. 207 sqq., Erl. ed.).   Local or circumscriptive presence is the presence of wine in the barrel, where the body fills the space; definite presence is incomprehensible, as the presence of an angel or devil in a house or a man, or the passing of Christ through the tomb or through the closed door; repletive presence is the supernatural omnipresence of God which fills all space, and is confined by no space. When Christ walked on earth, he was locally present; after the resurrection, he appeared to the disciples definitively and incomprehensibly; after his ascension to the right hand of God, he is everywhere by virtue of the inseparable union of his humanity with his divinity.

[2] Zwingli made the biting remark that Luther ends this book with the Devil, with whom he had begun his former book.

[3] Zwingli's answer in German is printed in *Werke*, II. Part II. 94–223; in Latin, *Opera*, II. 416–521.   The answer of Œcolampadius, in Walch, XX. 1725 sqq.

This bitter controversy fell in the most trying time of Luther, when he suffered greatly from physical infirmity and mental depression, and when a pestilence raged at Wittenberg (1527), which caused the temporary removal of the University to Jena. He remained on the post of danger, escaped the jaws of death, and measurably recovered his strength, but not his former cheerfulness, good humor, and buoyancy of spirit.

§ 107. The Marburg Conference, A.D. 1529. (With Facsimile of Signatures.)

I. Contemporary Reports. (1) Lutheran. LUTHER's references to the Conference at Marburg, in Erl. ed. XXXII. 398, 403, 408; XXXVI. 320 sqq. (his report from the pulpit); LIV. 286; 83, 107 sq., 153; LV. 88. Letters of Luther to his wife, Philip of Hesse, Gerbel, Agricola, Amsdorf, Link, and Probst, from October, 1529, and later, in De Wette, III. 508 sqq; IV. 26 sq. Reports of MELANCHTHON, JONAS, BRENZ, and OSIANDER, in "Corpus Reform.," I. 1098, 1102 (Mel. in German); 1095 (Jonas), XXVI. 115; Seckendorf, II. 136; Walch, XVII. 2352–2379; Scultetus, *Annal. evang.*, p. 215 sqq.; Riederer, *Nachrichten*, etc., II. 109 sqq.

(2) Reformed (Swiss and Strassburg) reports of COLLIN, ZWINGLI, ŒCO-LAMPADIUS, are collected in Zwingli's *Opera*, ed. Schuler and Schulthess, vol. IV. 173–204, and Hospinian's *Hist. Sacram.*, II. 74 sqq., 123 sqq. BULLINGER: *Reformationsgesch.*, II. 223 sqq. The reports of BUCER and HEDIO are used by Baum in his *Capito und Butzer* (Elberf. 1860), p. 453 sqq., and Erichson (see below). The MS. of Capito's Itinerary was burned in 1870 with the library of the Protestant Seminary at Strassburg, but had previously been copied by Professor Baum.

II. The Marburg Articles in WALCH, XVII. 2357 sqq.; Erl. ed. LXV. 88 sqq.; "Corp. Reform.," XXVI. 121–128; H. HEPPE: *Die 15 Marburger Artikel vom 3 Oct., 1529, nach dem wieder aufgefundenen Autographon der Reformatoren als Facsimile veröffentlicht*, Kassel, 1847, 2d ed. 1854 (from the archives at Kassel); another ed. from a MS. in Zürich by J. M. USTERI in the "Studien und Kritiken," 1883, No. II., p. 400–413 (with facsimile). A list of older editions in the "Corpus Reform.," XXVI. 113–118.

III. L. J. K. SCHMITT: *Das Religionsgespräch zu Marburg im J. 1529*, Marb. 1840. J. KRADOLFER: *Das Marb. Religionsgesprach im J. 1529*, Berlin, 1871. SCHIRRMACHER: *Briefe und Akten zur Geschichte des Religionsgesprächs zu Marburg 1529 und des Reichstags zu Augsburg 1530 nach der Handschrift des Aurifaber*, Gotha, 1876. M. LENZ: *Zwingli und*

Landgraf Philipp, three articles in Brieger's "Zeitschrift für K. Gesch.,"
1879 (pp. 28, 220, and 429). OSWALD SCHMIDT: in Herzog[2], IX. (1881),
270–275. A. ERICHSON: *Das Marburger Religionsgespräch i. J. 1529,
nach ungedruckten strassburger Urkunden,* Strassb. 1880. (Based upon
Hedio's unpublished *Itinerarium ab Argentina Marpurgum super negotio
Eucharistiæ.*) FRANK H. FOSTER: *The Historical Significance of the
Marburg Colloquy, and its Bearing upon the New Departure* [of An-
dover], in the "Bibliotheca Sacra," Oberlin, Ohio, April, 1887, p.
363–369.

IV. See also the respective sections in HOSPINIAN, LÖSCHER (*Historia
Motuum,* I. 143 sqq.), PLANCK (II. 515 sqq.), MARHEINEKE, HAGEN-
BACH, ROMMEL (*Phil. der Grossmüthige,* I. 247 sqq., II. 219 sqq.), HAS-
SENCAMP (*Hessische K. G.,* II.), MERLE D'AUBIGNÉ (Bk. VIII. ch.
VII.), EBRARD (*Das Dogma vom heil. Abendmahl,* II. 268 sqq.), and
in the biographies of Luther, e. g., KÖSTLIN: *M. Luth.* II. 127 sqq.
(small biography, E. V. p. 391 sqq.), and of Zwingli, e. g., by CHRIS-
TOFFEL and MÖRIKOFER. Comp. also RANKE, III. 116 sqq.; JANS-
SEN, III. 149–154.

The eucharistic controversy broke the political force of
Protestantism, and gave new strength to the Roman party,
which achieved a decided victory in the Diet of Speier, April,
1529.

In this critical situation, the Elector of Saxony and the
Landgrave of Hesse formed at Speier "a secret agreement"
with the cities of Nürnberg, Ulm, Strassburg and St. Gall,
for mutual protection (April 22, 1529). Strassburg and St.
Gall sided with Zürich on the eucharistic question.

The situation became more threatening during the summer. The Emperor made peace with the Pope, June 29, and
with France, July 19, pledging himself with his allies to
extirpate the new deadly heresy; and was on the way to
Augsburg, where the fate of Protestantism was to be decided. But while the nations of Europe aimed to emancipate
themselves from the authority of the church and the clergy,
the religious element was more powerful, — the hierarchical
in the Roman, the evangelical in the Protestant party, — and
overruled the political. This is the character of the sixteenth
century: it was still a churchly and theological age.

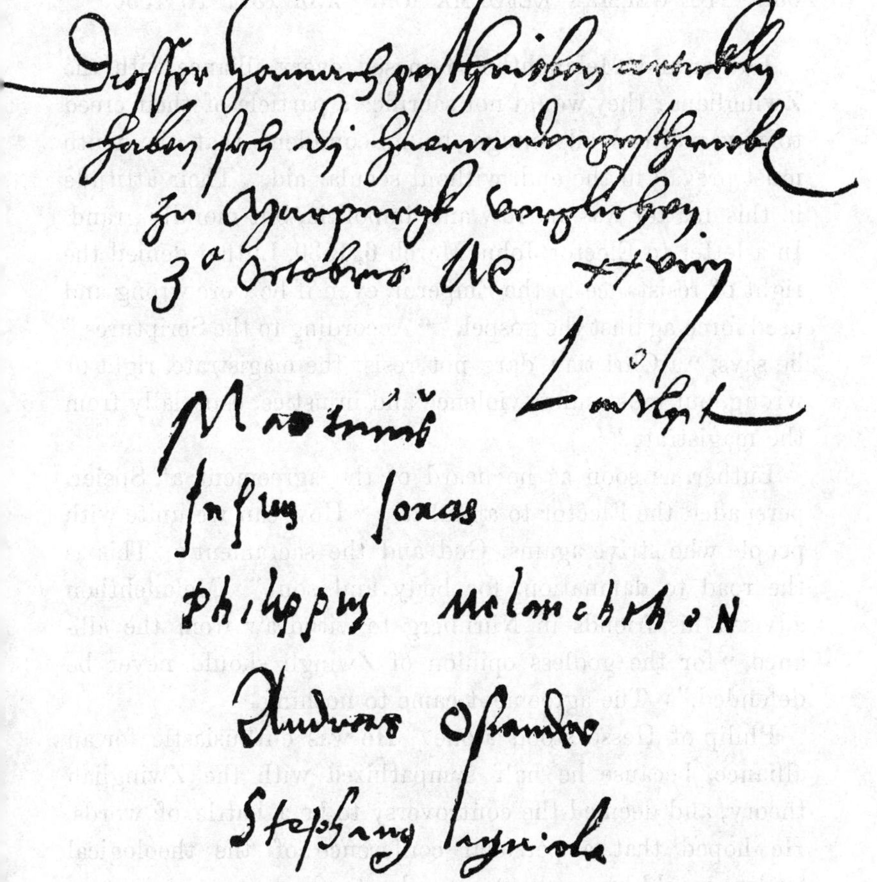

FIG. 39.

FACSIMILE OF THE SIGNATURES TO THE MARBURG ARTICLES.

(In the original copy at Zürich, the Swiss names are signed first.)

631

Luther and Melanchthon opposed every alliance with the
Zwinglians; they would not sacrifice a particle of their creed
to any political advantage, being confident that the truth
must prevail in the end, without secular aid. Their attitude
in this matter was narrow and impolitic, but morally grand.
In a letter to Elector John, March 6, 1530, Luther denied the
right of resistance to the Emperor, even if he were wrong and
used force against the gospel. "According to the Scriptures,"
he says, "a Christian dare not resist the magistrate, right or
wrong, but must suffer violence and injustice, especially from
the magistrate." [1]

Luther, as soon as he heard of the agreement at Speier,
persuaded the Elector to annul it. "How can we unite with
people who strive against God and the sacrament? This is
the road to damnation, for body and soul." Melanchthon
advised his friends in Nürnberg to withdraw from the alliance, "for the godless opinion of Zwingli should never be
defended." The agreement came to nothing.

Philip of Hesse stood alone. He was enthusiastic for an
alliance, because he half sympathized with the Zwinglian
theory, and deemed the controversy to be a battle of words.
He hoped that a personal conference of the theological
leaders would bring about an understanding.

After consulting Melanchthon personally in Speier, and
Zwingli by letter, the Landgrave issued formal invitations to
the Reformers, to meet at Marburg, and offered them a safe-
conduct through his territory.[2]

Zwingli received the invitation with joy, and hoped for the
best. The magistrate of Zürich was opposed to his leaving;
but he resolved to brave the danger of a long journey
through hostile territory, and left his home in the night of
Sept. 3, without waiting for the Landgrave's safe-conduct,

---

[1] De Wette, III. 560.
[2] The letters of invitation in *Monumenta Hassiaca,* tom. III., and Neudecker, *Urkunden,* p. 95.

and without even informing his wife of his destination, beyond Basel. Accompanied by a single friend, the Greek professor Collin, he reached Basel safely on horseback, and on the 6th of September he embarked with Œcolampadius and several merchants on the Rhine for Strassburg, where they arrived after thirteen hours. The Reformers lodged in the house of Matthew Zell, the preacher in the cathedral, and were hospitably entertained by his wife Catharine, who cooked their meals, waited at the table, and conversed with them on theology so intelligently that they ranked her above many doctors. She often alluded in later years, with joy and pride, to her humble services to these illustrious men. They remained in Strassburg eleven days, in important consultation with the ministers and magistrates. Zwingli preached in the minster on Sunday, the 12th of September, in the morning, on our knowledge of truth, and our duty to obey it; Œcolampadius preached in the afternoon, on the new creature in Christ, and on faith operative in love (Gal. 5:6). On the 19th of September, at six in the morning, they departed with the Strassburg delegates, Bucer, Hedio, and Jacob Sturm, the esteemed head of the city magistrate, under protection of five soldiers. They travelled on horseback over hills and dales, through forests and secret paths. At the Hessian frontier, they were received by forty cavaliers, and reached Marburg on the 27th of September, at four o'clock in the afternoon, and were cordially welcomed by the Landgrave in person.[1] The same journey can now be made in a few hours. On the next days they preached.

Zwingli and Philip of Hesse had political and theological sympathies. Zwingli, who was a statesman as well as a reformer, conceived about that time far-reaching political combinations in the interest of religion. He aimed at no less than a Protestant alliance between Zürich, Hesse, Strass-

---

[1] The 27th is given by Hedio in his Itinerary, as the day of their arrival, and is accepted by Baum, Erichson, and Köstlin. The usual date is the 29th.

burg, France, Venice, and Denmark, against the Roman empire and the house of Habsburg. He believed in muscular, aggressive Christianity, and in rapid movements to anticipate an attack of the enemy, or to be at least fully prepared for it. The fiery and enthusiastic young Landgrave freely entered into these plans, which opened a tempting field to his ambition, and discussed them with Zwingli, probably already at Marburg, and afterwards in confidential letters, till the catastrophe at Cappel made an end to the correspondence, and the projected alliance.[1]

The Wittenbergers, as already remarked, would have nothing to do with political alliances unless it were an alliance against foreign foes. They were monarchists and imperialists, and loyally attached to Charles V., "the noble blood," as Luther called him. They feared that an alliance with the Swiss would alienate him still more from the Reformation, and destroy the prospect of reconciliation. In the same year Luther wrote two vigorous works (one dedicated to Philip of Hesse) against the Turks, in which, as a Christian, a citizen, and a patriot, he exhorted the German princes to aid the Emperor in protecting the German fatherland against those invaders whom he regarded as the Gog and Magog of prophecy, and as the instruments of God's wrath for the punishment of corrupt Christendom.[2] He had a still stronger

---

[1] There are still extant ten letters from the Landgrave to Zwingli, and three from Zwingli to the Landgrave, to which should be added four letters from Duke Ulrich of Württemberg to Zwingli. They are published in Kuchenbecker's *Monumenta Hassiaca*, in Neudecker's *Urkunden aus der Reformationszeit*, and in Zwingli's *Opera*, vol. VIII., and are explained and discussed by Max Lenz in three articles quoted in the Literature. The correspondence began during the second Diet of Speier, April 22, 1529 (the date of the first epistle of Philip), and ended Sept. 30, 1531 (the date of Philip's last letter), eleven days before Zwingli's death. The letters of the Landgrave, before the Marburg Conference, treat of religion; those after that Conference, chiefly of politics, and are strictly confidential. The prince addresses the theologian as " Dear Master Ulrich," " Dear Zwingli," etc.

[2] *Vom Kriege wider die Türken*, April, 1529, and *Heerpredigt wider den Türken*, published at the end of 1529, and in a second edition, January, 1530. In the Erl. ed., XXXI. 31 sqq. and 80 sqq.

religious motive to discourage a colloquy. He had denounced the Swiss divines as dangerous heretics, and was unwilling to negotiate with them, except on terms of absolute surrender such as could not be expected from men of honor and conscientious conviction.

The Wittenbergers, therefore, received the invitation to a colloquy with distrust, and resisted it. Luther declared that such a conference was useless, since he would not yield an inch to his opponents. Melanchthon even suggested to the Elector that he should forbid their attendance. They thought that " honorable Papists " should be invited as judges on a question touching the real presence ! But the Elector was unwilling to displease the Landgrave, and commanded the Reformers to attend. When they arrived at the Hessian frontier, Luther declared that nothing could induce him to cross it without a safe-conduct from the Landgrave (which arrived in due time). They reached Marburg on the last of September, three days after the Swiss.

How different the three historic appearances of Luther in public ! In the Leipzig disputation with Eck, we see him struggling in the twilight for emancipation from the bondage of popery. At Worms he stood before the Emperor, with invincible courage, as the heroic witness of the liberty of conscience. Marburg he entered reluctantly, at the noon-day heat of his labors, in bad humor, firmly set in his churchly faith, imperious and obstinate, to face the Swiss Reformers, who were as honest and earnest as he, but more liberal and conciliatory. In Leipzig he protested as a Catholic against the infallibility of pope and council ; in Worms he protested against the papal tyranny over the Bible and private judgment ; in Marburg he protested as a conservative churchman against his fellow-Protestants, and in favor of the catholic faith in the mystery of the sacrament.[1] On all occasions he

---

[1] R. Rothe calls Luther an old Catholic, not a modern Protestant, though the greatest Reformer and a prophet. (*Kirchengesch.* II. 334.)

was equally honest, firm, and immovable, true to his words at
Worms, "Here I stand: I cannot do otherwise." The conduct of the two parties at that Conference is typical of the
two confessions in their subsequent dealings with each other.

The visitors stopped at an inn, but were at once invited
to lodge in the castle, and treated by the Landgrave with
princely hospitality.

The Reformed called upon the Lutherans, but met with a
cool reception. Luther spoke a kind word to Œcolampadius;
but when he first met his friend Bucer, who now sided with
Zwingli, he shook his hand, and said, smiling, and pointing
his finger at him, "You are a good-for-nothing knave."[1]

In that romantic old castle of Marburg which overlooks the
quaint city, and the beautiful and fertile valley of the Lahn,
the famous Conference was held on the first three days of
October. It was the first council among Protestants, and
the first attempt to unite them. It attracted general attention, and promised to become world-historical.[2] Euricius
Cordus, a professor of medicine at Marburg, addressed, in a
Latin poem, "the penetrating Luther, the gentle Œcolampadius, the magnanimous Zwingli, the eloquent Melanchthon,
the pious Schnepf, the brave Bucer, the true-hearted Hedio,"
and all other divines who were assembled in Marburg, with
an appeal to heal the schism. "The church," he says, "falls
weeping at your feet, and begs you, by the mercies of Christ,
to consider the question with pure zeal for the welfare of
believers, and to bring about a conclusion of which the world
may say that it proceeded from the Holy Spirit." Very
touching is the prayer with which Zwingli entered upon the
conference: "Fill us, O Lord and Father of us all, we
beseech Thee, with thy gentle Spirit, and dispel on both sides

---

[1] "*Du bist ein Schalk und ein Nebler.*" Melanchthon saluted Hedio in
Latin, "I am glad to see you. You are Hedio." Baum, p. 459. Erichson,
p. 16.

[2] "*Die Versammlung,*" says Ranke, III. 122, "*hatte etwas Erhabenes,
Weltbedeutendes.*"

all the clouds of misunderstanding and passion. Make an end to the strife of blind fury. Arise, O Christ, Thou Sun of righteousness, and shine upon us. Alas! while we contend, we only too often forget to strive after holiness which Thou requirest from us all. Guard us against abusing our powers, and enable us to employ them with all earnestness for the promotion of holiness."

§ 108. *The Marburg Conference continued. Discussion and Result.*

The work of the Conference began on Friday, the 1st of October, with divine service in the chapel of the castle. Zwingli preached on the providence of God, which he afterwards elaborated into an important treatise, "*De Providentia.*" It was intended for scholars rather than the people; and Luther found fault with the introduction of Hebrew, Greek, and Latin words into the pulpit. Luther, Bucer, and Osiander preached the morning sermons on the following days; Luther, on his favorite doctrine of justification by faith.

The Landgrave first arranged a private interview between the lions and the lambs; that is, between Luther and Œcolampadius, Zwingli and Melanchthon. The two pairs met after divine service, in separate chambers, and conferred for several hours. The Wittenberg Reformers catechised the Swiss about their views on the Trinity, original sin, and baptism, and were in a measure relieved of their suspicion that they entertained unsound views on these topics. Melanchthon had, a few months before the Conference, written a very respectful letter to Œcolampadius (April 8, 1529), in which he regrets that the "*horribilis dissensio de cœna Domini*" interfered with the enjoyment of their literary and Christian friendship, and states his own view of the eucharist very moderately and clearly to the effect that it was a communion with the present Christ rather than a commemoration of the absent Christ.[1] In the private conference with Zwingli, against whom he was strongly prejudiced, he is reported to have yielded the main point of dispute, as regards the literal interpretation of " This is my body," and the literal handing of Christ's body to his disciples, but added that he gave it to them "in a certain mysterious manner."[2] When Zwingli urged the ascension as an argument against the local presence, Melanchthon said, "Christ has ascended indeed, but in order to fill all things" (Eph. 4: 10). "Truly," replied Zwingli, "with his power and might, but not with his body." During the open debate on the following days, Melanchthon observed a significant silence, though twice asked by Luther to come to his aid when he felt exhausted.[3] He made only a few remarks. He was, however, at that time, of one mind with Luther, and entirely under his power. He was as strongly opposed to an alliance with the Swiss and Strassburgers, influenced in part by political motives, being anxious to secure, if possible, the favor of Charles and Ferdinand.[4]

Luther must have handled Œcolampadius more severely; for the latter, in coming from the conference room, whispered to Zwingli, "I am again in the hands of Dr. Eck" (as at the colloquy in Baden in 1526).

The general discussion took place on Saturday, the 2d of

---

[1] "Corpus Reform.," I. 1048 sqq. He says: "*Vos absentis Christi corpus tanquam in tragœdia repræsentari contenditis. Ego de Christo video exstare promissiones: ' Ego vobiscum usque ad consummationem seculi, et similes, ubi nihil est opus divellere ab humanitate divinitatem; proinde de sentio, hoc sacramentum veræ præsentiæ testimonium esse quod cum ita sit, sentio in illa cœna præsentis corporis κοινωνίαν esse.*" He does not enter into an interpretation of the words of institution.

[2] Erichson, p. 20, from Strassburg reports.

[3] "*Ich habe mich müde gewaschen,*" said Luther.

[4] Bucer, in a letter to Blaurer in Constance, Oct. 18, 1529, charged Melanchthon especially with the obstinate refusal of brotherhood, and made him, even more than Luther, responsible for the failure of the Conference, adding, as a reason, that he was unwilling to lose the favor of the Emperor Charles and his brother Ferdinand. Baum, *l.c.*, p. 463; Erichson, p. 45.

October, in a large hall (which cannot now be identified with certainty).[1] The Landgrave in plain dress appeared with his court as an eager listener, but not as an arbitrator, and was seated at a separate table. The official attendants on the Lutheran side were Luther (dressed as an Electoral courtier) and Melanchthon, behind them Jonas and Cruciger of Wittenberg, Myconius of Gotha, Osiander of Nürnberg, Stephen Agricola of Augsburg, Brentius of Hall in Swabia; on the Reformed side Zwingli and Œcolampadius, and behind them Bucer and Hedio of Strassburg: all men of eminent talent, learning, and piety, and in the prime of manhood and usefulness. Luther and Zwingli were forty-six, Œcolampadius forty-seven, Bucer thirty-eight, Hedio thirty-five, Melanchthon thirty-two, the Landgrave only twenty-five years of age. Luther and Melanchthon, Zwingli and Œcolampadius, as the chief disputants, sat at a separate table, facing each other.

Besides these representative theologians there were a number of invited guests, princes (including the exiled Duke Ulrich of Württemberg), noblemen, and scholars (among them Lambert of Avignon). Zwingli speaks of twenty-four, Brentius of fifty to sixty, hearers. Poor Carlstadt, who was then wandering about in Friesland, and forced to sell his Hebrew Bible for bread, had asked for an invitation, but was refused. Many others applied for admission, but were disappointed.[2] Zwingli advocated the greatest publicity and the employment of a recording secretary, but both requests were declined by Luther. Even the hearers were not allowed to make verbatim reports. Zwingli, who could not expect the Germans to understand his Swiss dialect, desired the

---

[1] "*In interiore hypocausto ad cubiculum Principis,*" says Jonas (Seckendorf, II. 140). It was not the *Rittersaal*, but the reception-room in the new east wing of the castle, adjoining the bedroom of the Landgrave. The castle has undergone many changes.

[2] Justus Jonas reports ("Corp. Ref.," I. 1097, and Seckendorf, II. 140): "*A Francofordia confluxerunt plerique, alii Rhenanis partibus, e Colonia, Argentina, Basilea, Helvetiis, etc., sed non sunt admissi in colloquium.*"

colloquy to be conducted in Latin, which would have placed him on an equality with Luther; but it was decided to use the German language in deference to the audience.

John Feige, the chancellor of the Landgrave, exhorted the theologians in an introductory address to seek only the glory of Christ and the restoration of peace and union to the church.

The debate was chiefly exegetical, but brought out no new argument. It was simply a recapitulation of the preceding controversy, with less heat and more gentlemanly courtesy. Luther took his stand on the words of institution in their literal sense: "This is my body;" the Swiss, on the word of Christ: "It is the Spirit that quickeneth; the flesh profiteth nothing; the words that I have spoken unto you are spirit and are life."

Luther first rose, and declared emphatically that he would not change his opinion on the real presence in the least, but stand fast on it to the end of life. He called upon the Swiss to prove the absence of Christ, but protested at the outset against arguments derived from reason and geometry. To give pictorial emphasis to his declaration, he wrote with a piece of chalk on the table in large characters the words of institution, with which he was determined to stand or fall: "*Hoc est corpus Meum.*"

Œcolampadius in reply said he would abstain from philosophical arguments, and appeal to the Scriptures. He quoted several passages which have an obviously figurative meaning, but especially John 6 : 63, which in his judgment furnishes the key for the interpretation of the words of institution, and excludes a literal understanding. He employed this syllogism: Christ cannot contradict himself; he said, "The flesh profiteth nothing," and thereby rejected the oral manducation of his body; therefore he cannot mean such a manducation in the Lord's Supper.

Luther denied the second proposition, and asserted that

Christ did not reject oral, but only material manducation, like that of the flesh of oxen or of swine. I mean a sublime spiritual fruition, yet with the mouth. To the objection that bodily eating was useless if we have the spiritual eating, he replied, If God should order me to eat crab-apples or dung, I would do it, being assured that it would be salutary. We must here close the eyes.

Here Zwingli interposed: God does not ask us to eat crab-apples, or to do any thing unreasonable. We cannot admit two kinds of corporal manducation; Christ uses the same word "to eat," which is either spiritual or corporal. You admit that the spiritual eating alone gives comfort to the soul. If this is the chief thing, let us not quarrel about the other. He then read from the Greek Testament which he had copied with his own hand, and used for twelve years, the passage John 6:52, "How can this man give us his flesh to eat?" and Christ's word, ver. 63.

Luther asked him to read the text in German or Latin, not in Greek. When Christ says, "The flesh profiteth nothing," he speaks not of his flesh, but of ours.

Zwingli: The soul is fed with the spirit, not with flesh.

Luther: We eat the body with the mouth, not with the soul. If God should place rotten apples before me, I would eat them.

Zwingli: Christ's body then would be a corporal, and not a spiritual, nourishment.

Luther: You are captious.

Zwingli: Not so; but you contradict yourself.

Zwingli quoted a number of figurative passages; but Luther always pointed his finger to the words of institution, as he had written them on the table. He denied that the discourse, John 6, had any thing to do with the Lord's Supper.

At this point a laughable, yet characteristic incident occurred. "Beg your pardon," said Zwingli, "that passage [John 6: 63] breaks your neck." Luther, understanding this literally, said, "Do not boast so much. You are in Hesse, not in Switzerland. In this country we do not break people's necks. Spare such proud, defiant words, till you get back to your Swiss."[1]

Zwingli: In Switzerland also there is strict justice, and we break no man's neck without trial. I use simply a figurative expression for a lost cause.

The Landgrave said to Luther, "You should not take offense at such common expressions." But the agitation was so great that the meeting adjourned to the banqueting hall.

The discussion was resumed in the afternoon, and turned on the christological question. I believe, said Luther, that Christ is in heaven, but also in the sacrament, as substantially as he was in the Virgin's womb. I care not whether it be against nature and reason, provided it be not against faith.

Œcolampadius: You deny the metaphor in the words of institution, but you must admit a synecdoche. For Christ does not say, This is bread and my body (as you hold), but simply, This is my body.

Luther: A metaphor admits the existence of a sign only; but a synecdoche admits the thing itself, as when I say, the sword is in the scabbard, or the beer in the bottle.

Zwingli reasoned: Christ ascended to heaven, therefore he cannot be on earth with his body. A body is circumscribed, and cannot be in several places at once.

Luther: I care little about mathematics.

The contest grew hotter, without advancing, and was broken up by a call to the repast.

The next day, Sunday, Oct. 3, it was renewed.

Zwingli maintained that a body could not be in different places at once. Luther quoted the Sophists (the Schoolmen) to the effect that there are different kinds of presence. The universe is a body, and yet not in a particular place.

---

[1] He added, "*Wo nicht, so will ich euch auch über die Schnauze fahren, dass es euch gereuen wird, dazu Ursach gegeben zu haben.*"

Zwingli: Ah, you speak of the Sophists, doctor! Are you really obliged to return to the onions and fleshpots of Egypt? He then cited from Augustin, who says, "Christ is everywhere present as God; but as to his body, he is in heaven."

Luther: You have Augustin and Fulgentius on your side, but we have all the other fathers. Augustin was young when he wrote the passage you quote, and he is obscure. We must believe the old teachers only so far as they agree with the Word of God.

Œcolampadius: We, too, build on the Word of God, not on the fathers; but we appeal to them to show that we teach no novelties.[1]

Luther, pointing again his finger to the words on the table: This is our text: you have not yet driven us from it. We care for no other proof.

Œcolampadius: If this is the case, we had better close the discussion.

The chancellor exhorted them to come to an understanding.

Luther: There is only one way to that. Let our adversaries believe as we do.

The Swiss: We cannot.

Luther: Well, then, I abandon you to God's judgment, and pray that he will enlighten you.

Œcolampadius: We will do the same. You need it as much as we.

At this point both parties mellowed down. Luther begged pardon for his harsh words, as he was a man of flesh and blood. Zwingli begged Luther, with tearful eyes, to forgive him his harsh words, and assured him that there were no men

---

[1] Luther hastily prepared a memorandum for the Landgrave, with quotations from Hilary, Ambrose, Chrysostom, Cyprian, and Irenæus, to counteract the quotations from Augustin. See Letters, ed. De Wette, III. 508-511.

in the world whose friendship he more desired than that of the Wittenbergers.[1]

Jacob Sturm and Bucer spoke in behalf of Strassburg, and vindicated their orthodoxy, which had been impeached. Luther's reply was cold, and displeased the audience. He declared to the Strassburgers, as well as the Swiss, "Your spirit is different from ours."[2]

The Conference was ended. A contagious disease, called the English sweat (*sudor Anglicus*), which attacked its victims with fever, sweat, thirst, intense pain, and exhaustion, had suddenly broken out in Marburg as in other parts of Germany, and caused frightful ravages that filled everybody with alarm. The visitors were anxious to return home. So were the fathers of the Council of Trent, when the Elector Moritz chased the Emperor through the Tyrol; and in like manner the fathers of the Vatican Council hurried across the Alps when France declared war against Germany, and left the Vatican decrees in the hands of Italian infallibilists.

But the Landgrave once more brought the guests together at his table on Sunday night, and urged upon every one the supreme importance of coming to some understanding.

On Monday morning he arranged another private conference between the Saxon and the Swiss Reformers. They met for the last time on earth. With tears in his eyes, Zwingli approached Luther, and held out the hand of brotherhood; but Luther declined it, saying again, "Yours is a different spirit from ours." Zwingli thought that differences in non-essentials, with unity in essentials, did not forbid

---

[1] As Luther reports the words, "*Es sind keine Leut auf Erden, mit denen ich lieber wollt' eins seyn als mit den Wittenbergern.*" In Zwingli's dialect, "*Es werend kine Lüt uff Erden, mit denen ich lieber wöllt' ins sin, denn mit den Wittenbergern.*"

[2] "*Ihr habt einen anderen Geist als wir.*"

Christian brotherhood. " Let us," he said, " confess our union in all things in which we agree ; and, as for the rest, let us remember that we are brethren. There will never be peace in the churches if we cannot bear differences on secondary points." Luther deemed the corporal presence a fundamental article, and construed Zwingli's liberality into indifference to truth. " I am astonished," he said, " that you wish to consider me as your brother. It shows clearly that you do not attach much importance to your doctrine." Melanchthon looked upon the request of the Swiss as a strange inconsistency.[1] Turning to the Swiss, the Wittenbergers said, " You do not belong to the communion of the Christian Church. We cannot acknowledge you as brethren." They were willing, however, to include them in that universal charity which we owe to our enemies.

The Swiss were ready to burst over such an insult, but controlled their temper.

On the same day Luther wrote the following characteristic letter to his wife : —

" Grace and peace in Christ. Dear Lord Keth, I do you to know that our friendly colloquy in Marburg is at an end, and that we are agreed in almost every point, except that the opposite party wants to have only bread in the Lord's Supper, and acknowledge the spiritual presence of Christ in the same. To-day the Landgrave wants us to come to an agreement, and, if not, to acknowledge each other as brethren and members of Christ. He labors very zealousy for this end. But we want no brothership and membership, only peace and good-will. I suppose to-morrow or day after to-morrow we shall break up, and proceed to Schleitz in the Voigtland whither his Electoral Grace has ordered us.

" Tell Herr Pommer [Bugenhagen] that the best argument of Zwingli was that *corpus non potest esse sine loco : ergo Christi corpus non est in pane.* Of Œcolampadius: This *sacramentum est signum corporis Christi.* I think God has blinded their eyes.

---

[1] He wrote to Agricola, Oct. 12, 1529 (" Corp. Ref.," I. 1108): "*Magnopere contenderunt, ut a nobis fratres appellarentur. Vide eorum stultitia! Cum damnent nos, cupiunt tamen a nobis fratres haberi ! Nos noluimus eis hac in re assentiri.*"

"I am very busy, and the messenger is in a hurry. Give to all a good night, and pray for us. We are all fresh and hale, and live like princes. Kiss for me little Lena and little Hans (*Lensgen und Hänsgen*).

"Your obedient servant,

"M. L."

"P. S. — John Brenz, Andrew Osiander, Doctor Stephen [Agricola] of Augsburg are also here.

"People are crazy with the fright of the sweating plague. Yesterday about fifty took sick, and two died." [1]

At last Luther yielded to the request of the Landgrave and the Swiss, retired to his closet, and drew up a common confession in the German language. It consists of fifteen articles expressing the evangelical doctrines on the Trinity, the person of Christ, his death and resurrection, original sin, justification by faith, the work of the Holy Spirit, and the sacraments.

The two parties agreed on fourteen articles, and even in the more important part of the fifteenth article which treats of the Lord's Supper as follows: —

"We all believe, with regard to the Supper of our blessed Lord Jesus Christ, that it ought to be celebrated in both kinds, according to the institution of Christ; that the mass is not a work by which a Christian obtains pardon for another man, whether dead or alive; that the sacrament of the altar is the sacrament of the very body and very blood of Jesus Christ; and that the spiritual manducation of this body and blood is specially necessary to every true Christian. In like manner, as to the use of the sacrament, we are agreed that, like the word, it was ordained of Almighty God, in order that weak consciences might be excited by the Holy Ghost to faith and charity.

"And although at present we are not agreed on the question whether the real body and blood of Christ are corporally present in the bread and wine, yet both parties shall cherish Christian charity for one another, so far as the conscience of each will permit; and both parties will earnestly implore Almighty God to strengthen us by his Spirit in the true understanding. Amen." [2]

---

[1] De Wette, III. 512 sq.

[2] I add the German original in the antiquated spelling, from the archives in Zürich (as published by Usteri in 1883): —

"*Vom Sacrament des leibs und bluts Christi.*

"*Zum fünffzehennden Gleuben unnd hallten wir alle | vonn dem Nacht-*

The Landgrave urged the insertion that each party should show Christian charity to the other. The Lutherans assented to this only on condition that the clause be added : "as far as the conscience of each will permit."

The articles were read, considered, and signed on the same day by Luther, Melanchthon, Osiander, Agricola, Brentius, on the part of the Lutherans; and by Zwingli, Œcolampadius, Bucer, and Hedio, on the part of the Reformed. They were printed on the next day, and widely circulated.[1]

On the fifth day of October, in the afternoon, the guests took leave of each other with a shake of hands. It was not the hand of brotherhood, but only of friendship, and not very cordial on the part of the Lutherans. The Landgrave left Marburg on the same day, early in the morning, with a painful feeling of disappointment.

Luther returned to Wittenberg by way of Schleitz, where he met the Elector John by appointment, and revised the Marburg Articles so as to adapt them to his creed, and so far to weaken the consensus.

Both parties claimed the victory. Zwingli complained in

---

male unnsers lieben herrn Jhesu Christi | das man bede gestallt nach Innset-
zung Christi prauchen soll | das ouch die Messe nicht ein werck ist | do mit
einer dem andren tod oder lebendig gnad erlangt. | Das auch das Sacrament
desz Altars | sey ein Sacrament desz waren leibs unnd pluts | Jhesu Christi
und die geistliche Niessung desselbigen leibs unnd pluts | einem Iden Chris-
ten fürnemlich vonn nöthen | deszgleichen der prauch desz Sacraments | wie
das wort | von Gott dem allmechtigen gegeben | unnd geordennt sey | damit
die schwachen Gewissen | zu gleuben | zubewegen | durch den heyligenn Geist.
Unnd wiewol aber wir unns | ob der war leyb unnd plut Christi | leiplich im
prot unnd wein sey | diser Zeit nit vergleicht haben | so soll doch ein theyl
gegen den anndern Christliche lieb | so fern Idesz gewissen ymmer leiden
kan | erzeigen | unnd bede theyl | Gott den Allmechtigen vleyssig bitten | das
er unns durch seinen Geist den rechten verstanndt bestetigen well. Amen."

[1] Three copies were signed at Marburg (according to Osiander's report, who took one to Nürnberg). They were long supposed to be lost, but two have been recovered and published by Heppe and Usteri from the archives at Cassel and Zürich (see Lit.). They agree almost verbatim, except in the order of signatures, the former giving the first place to the Lutheran, the latter to the Reformed names. The small differences are discussed by Usteri. *l.c.*

a letter to Vadian of the overbearing and contumacious spirit of Luther, and thought that the truth (i.e., his view of it) had prevailed, and that Luther was vanquished before all the world after proclaiming himself invincible. He rejoiced in the agreement which must destroy the hope of the papists that Luther would return to them.

Luther, on the other hand, thought that the Swiss had come over to him half way, that they had humbled themselves, and begged his friendship. "There is no brotherly unity among us," he said in the pulpit of Wittenberg after his return from Marburg, "but a good friendly concord ; they seek from us what they need, and we will help them."

Nearly all the contemporary reports describe the Conference as having been much more friendly and respectful than was expected from the preceding controversy. The speakers addressed each other as "Liebster Herr," "Euer Liebden," and abstained from terms of opprobrium. The Devil was happily ignored in the interviews ; no heresy was charged, no anathema hurled. Luther found that the Swiss were not such bad people as he had imagined, and said even in a letter to Bullinger (1538), that Zwingli impressed him at Marburg as "a very good man " (*optimus vir*). Brentius, as an eye-witness, reports that Luther and Zwingli appeared as if they were brothers. Jonas described the Reformed leaders during the Conference as follows : [1] "Zwingli has a certain rusticity and a little arrogance.[2] In Œcolampadius there is an admirable good-nature and clemency.[3] Hedio has no less humanity and liberality of spirit; but Bucer possesses the cunning of a fox,[4] that knows how to give himself the air of acumen and prudence. They are all learned men, no doubt, and more formidable opponents than the papists; but Zwingli

---

[1] In a Latin letter to Reiffenstein, dated Marburg, Oct. 4, 1529; in the "Corp. Reform.," I. 109, and Seckendorf, vol. II. 140.

[2] "*In Zwinglio agreste quiddam est et arrogantulum.*"

[3] "*Mira bonitas naturæ et clementia.*"

[4] "*Calliditas vulpina.*"

seems well versed in letters, in spite of Minerva and the Muses." He adds that the Landgrave was the most attentive hearer.

The laymen who attended the Conference seem to have been convinced by the Swiss arguments. The Landgrave declared that he would now believe the simple words of Christ, rather than the subtle interpretations of men. He desired Zwingli to remove to Marburg, and take charge of the ecclesiastical organization of Hesse. Shortly before his death he confessed that Zwingli had convinced him at Marburg. But more important is the conversion of Lambert of Avignon, who had heretofore been a Lutheran, but could not resist the force of the arguments on the other side. "I had firmly resolved," he wrote to a friend soon after the Conference, "not to listen to the words of men, or to allow myself to be influenced by the favor of men, but to be like a blank paper on which the finger of God should write his truth. He wrote those doctrines on my heart which Zwingli developed out of the word of God." Even the later change of Melanchthon, who declined the brotherhood with the Swiss as strongly as Luther, may perhaps be traced to impressions which he received at Marburg.

If the leaders of the two evangelical confessions could meet to-day on earth, they would gladly shake hands of brotherhood, as they have done long since in heaven.

The Conference did not effect the desired union, and the unfortunate strife broke out again. Nevertheless, it was by no means a total failure. It prepared the way for the Augsburg Confession, the chief symbol of the Lutheran Church. More than this, it served as an encouragement to peace movements of future generations.[1] It produced the first formulated consensus between the two confessions in four-

[1] Comp. the remarks of Ranke, III. 124 sqq. He sees the significance of the Conference in the fact that the two parties, in spite of the theological difference, professed the same evangelical faith.

teen important articles, and in the better part of the fifteenth, leaving only the corporal presence and oral manducation in dispute. It was well that such a margin was left. Without liberty in non-essentials, there can never be a union among intelligent Christians. Good and holy men will always differ on the mode of the real presence, and on many other points of doctrine, as well as government and worship. The time was not ripe for evangelical catholicity ; but the spirit of the document survived the controversies, and manifests itself wherever Christian hearts and minds rise above the narrow partition walls of sectarian bigotry. Uniformity, even if possible, would not be desirable. God's ways point to unity in diversity, and diversity in unity.

It was during the fiercest dogmatic controversies and the horrors of the Thirty Years' War, that a prophetic voice whispered to future generations the watchword of Christian peacemakers, which was unheeded in a century of intolerance, and forgotten in a century of indifference, but resounds with increased force in a century of revival and re-union :

"IN ESSENTIALS UNITY, IN NON-ESSENTIALS LIBERTY, IN ALL THINGS CHARITY."

NOTE

On the Origin of the Sentence: "*In necessariis unitas, in non-necessariis (or, dubiis) libertas, in utrisque (or, omnibus) caritas.*"

This famous motto of Christian Irenics, which I have slightly modified in the text, is often falsely attributed to St. Augustin (whose creed would not allow it, though his heart might have approved of it), but is of much later origin. It appears for the first time in Germany, A.D. 1627 and 1628, among peaceful divines of the Lutheran and German Reformed churches, and found a hearty welcome among moderate divines in England.

The authorship has recently been traced to RUPERTUS MELDENIUS, an otherwise unknown divine, and author of a remarkable tract in which the sentence first occurs. He gave classical expression to the irenic sentiments of such divines as Calixtus of Helmstädt, David Pareus of Heidelberg, Crocius of Marburg, John Valentin Andreæ of Württemberg, John Arnd of Zelle, Georg Frank of Francfort-on-the Oder, the brothers Bergius in

Brandenburg, and of the indefatigable traveling evangelist of Christian union, John Dury, and Richard Baxter. The tract of Meldenius bears the title, *Paraenesis votiva pro Pace Ecclesiæ ad Theologos Augustanæ Confessionis, Auctore Ruperto Meldenio Theologo*, 62 pp. in 4to, without date and place of publication. It probably appeared in 1627 at Francfort-on-the-Oder, which was at that time the seat of theological moderation. Mr. C. R. Gillett (librarian of the Union Theological Seminary) informs me that the original copy, which he saw in Berlin, came from the University of Francfort-on-the Oder after its transfer to Breslau.

Dr. Lücke republished the tract, in 1850, from a reprint in Pfeiffer's *Variorum Auctorum Miscellanea Theologiæ* (Leipzig, 1736, pp. 136–258), as an appendix to his monograph on the subject (pp. 87–145). He afterwards compared it with a copy of the original edition in the Electoral library at Cassel. Another original copy was discovered by Dr. Klose in the city library of Hamburg (1858), and a third one by Dr. Briggs and Mr. Gillett in the royal library of Berlin (1887).

The author of this tract is an orthodox Lutheran, who was far from the idea of ecclesiastical union, but anxious for the peace of the church and zealous for practical scriptural piety in place of the dry and barren scholasticism of his time. He belongs, as Lücke says ("Stud. und Kritiken," 1851, p. 906), to the circle of "those noble, genial, and hearty evangelical divines, like John Arnd, Valentin Andreæ, and others, who deeply felt the awful misery of the fatherland, and especially the inner distractions of the church in their age, but who knew also and pointed out the way of salvation and peace." He was evidently a highly cultivated scholar, at home in Hebrew, Greek, and Latin, and in controversial theology. He excels in taste and style the forbidding literature of his age. He condemns the pharisaical hypocrisy, the φιλοδοξία, φιλαργία, and φιλονεικία of the theologians, and exhorts them first of all to humility and love. By too much controversy about the truth, we are in danger of losing the truth itself. *Nimium altercando amittitur Veritas.* "Many," he says, "contend for the corporal presence of Christ who have not Christ in their hearts." He sees no other way to concord than by rallying around the living Christ as the source of spiritual life. He dwells on the nature of God as love, and the prime duty of Christians to love one another, and comments on the seraphic chapter of Paul on charity (1 Cor. 13). He discusses the difference between *necessaria* and *non-necessaria*. Necessary dogmas are, (1) articles of faith necessary to salvation; (2) articles derived from clear testimonies of the Bible; (3) articles decided by the whole church in a synod or symbol; (4) articles held by all orthodox divines as necessary. Not necessary, are dogmas (1) not contained in the Bible; (2) not belonging to the common inheritance of faith; (3) not unanimously taught by theologians; (4) left doubtful by grave divines; (5) not tending to piety, charity, and edification. He concludes with a defense of John Arnd (1555–1621), the famous author of "True Christianity," against the attacks of orthodox fanatics, and with a fervent and touching prayer to Christ to come to the rescue of his troubled church (Rev. 22 : 17).

The golden sentence occurs in the later half of the tract (p. 128 in Lücke's edition), incidentally and in hypothetical form, as follows: —

"*Verbo dicam : Si nos servaremus* IN NECESSARIIS UNITATEM, IN NON-NECESSARIIS LIBERTATEM, IN UTRISQUE CHARITATEM, *optimo certe loco essent res nostræ.*"

The same sentiment, but in a shorter sententious and hortative form, occurs in a book of GREGOR FRANK, entitled *Consideratio theologica de gradibus necessitatis dogmatum Christianorum quibus fidei, spei et charitatis officia reguntur*, Francf. ad Oderam, 1628. Frank (1585–1651) was first a Lutheran, then a Reformed theologian, and professor at Francfort. He distinguishes three kinds of dogmas: (1) dogmas necessary for salvation: the clearly revealed truths of the Bible; (2) dogmas which are derived by clear and necessary inference from the Scriptures and held by common consent of orthodox Christendom; (3) the specific and controverted dogmas of the several confessions. He concludes the discussion with this exhortation: —

"*Summa est: Servemus* IN NECESSARIIS UNITATEM, IN NON-NECESSARIIS LIBERTATEM, IN UTRISQUE CHARITATEM."

He adds, "*Vincat veritas, vivat charitas, maneat libertas per Jesum Christum qui est veritas ipsa, charitas ipsa, libertas ipsa.*"

Bertheau deems it uncertain whether Meldenius or Frank was the author. But the question is decided by the express testimony of Conrad Berg, who was a colleague of Frank in the same university between 1627 and 1628, and ascribes the sentence to Meldenius.

Fifty years later Richard Baxter, the Puritan pacificator in England, refers to the sentence, Nov. 15, 1679, in the preface to *The True and Only Way of Concord of All the Christian Churches*, London, 1680, in a slightly different form: "I once more repeat to you the pacificator's old despised words, '*Si in necessariis sit* [*esset*] *unitas, in non necessariis libertas, in utrisque charitas, optimo certo loco essent res nostræ.*'"

Lücke was the first to quote this passage, but overlooked a direct reference of Baxter to Meldenius in the same tract on p. 25. This Dr. Briggs discovered, and quotes as follows: —

"Were there no more said of all this subject, but that of Rupertus Meldenius, cited by Conradus Bergius, it might end all schism if well understood and used, viz." Then follows the sentence. Baxter also refers to Meldenius on the preceding page. This strengthens the conclusion that Meldenius was the "pacificator." For we are referred here to the testimony of a contemporary of Meldenius. Samuel Werenfels, a distinguished irenical divine of Basel, likewise mentions Meldenius and Conrad Bergius together as irenical divines, and *testes veritatis*, and quotes several passages from the *Parænesis votiva.*

Conrad Bergius (Berg), from whom Baxter derived his knowledge of the sentence, was professor in the university of Frankfurt-an-der-Oder, and then a preacher at Bremen. He and his brother John Berg (1587-1658), court chaplain of Brandenburg, were irenical divines of the German Reformed Church, and moderate Calvinists. John Berg attended the Leipzig Colloquy of March, 1631, where Lutheran and Reformed divines agreed on the basis of the revised Augsburg Confession of 1540 in every article of doctrine, except the corporal presence and oral manducation. The colloquy was in advance of the spirit of the age, and had no permanent effect. See Schaff, *Creeds of Christendom*, I. 558 sqq., and Niemeyer, *Collectio Confessionum in Ecclesiis Reformatis publicatarum*, p. LXXV. and 653-668.

Dr. Briggs has investigated the writings of Conrad Bergius and his associates in the royal library of Berlin. In his "*Praxis Catholica divini canonis contra quasvis hæreses et schismata,*" etc., which appeared at Bremen in 1639, Bergius concludes with the classical word of "Rupertus Meldenius Theologus," and a brief comment on it. This is quoted by Baxter in the form just given. In the autumn of 1627 Bergius preached two discourses at Frankfurt on the subject of Christian union, which accord with the sentence, and appeared in 1628 with the consent of the theological faculty. They were afterwards incorporated in his *Praxis Catholica*. He was thoroughly at home in the polemics and irenics of his age, and can be relied on as to the authorship of the sentence.

But who was Meldenius? This is still an unsolved question. Possibly he took his name from Melden, a little village on the borders of Bohemia and Silesia. His voice was drowned, and his name forgotten, for two centuries, but is now again heard with increased force. I subscribe to the concluding words of my esteemed colleague, Dr. Briggs: "Like a mountain stream that disappears at times under the rocks of its bed, and re-appears deeper down in the valley, so these long-buried principles of peace have reappeared after two centuries of oblivion, and these irenical theologians will be honored by those who live in a better age of the world, when Protestant irenics have well-nigh displaced the old Protestant polemics and scholastics."

The origin of the sentence was first discussed by a Dutch divine, Dr. Van der Hœven of Amsterdam, in 1847; then by Dr. Lücke of Göttingen, *Ueber das Alter, den Verfasser, die ursprüngliche Form und den wahren Sinn des kirchlichen Friedenspruchs 'In necessariis unitas,'* etc., Göttingen, 1850 (XXII. and 146 pages); with supplementary remarks in the "Studien und Kritiken" for 1851, p. 905-938. Lücke first proved the authorship of Meldenius. The next steps were taken by Dr. Klose, in the first edition of Herzog's "Theol. Encycl." sub Meldenius, vol. IX. (1858), p. 304 sq., and by Dr. Carl Bertheau, in the second edition of Herzog, IX. (1881), p. 528-530. Dr. Briggs has furnished additional information in two articles in the "Presbyterian Review," vol. VIII., New York, 1887, pp. 496-499, and 743-746.

§ 109.   *Luther's Last Attack on the Sacramentarians.   His Relation to Calvin.*

We anticipate the concluding act of the sad controversy of Luther with his Protestant opponents. It is all the more painful, since Zwingli and Œcolampadius were then sleeping in the grave; but it belongs to a full knowledge of the great Reformer.

The Marburg Conference did not really reconcile the parties, or advance the question in dispute; but the conflict subsided for a season, and was thrown into the background by other events. The persistent efforts of Bucer and Hedio to bring about a reconciliation between Wittenberg and Zürich soothed Luther, and excited in him the hope that the Swiss would give up their heresy, as he regarded it. But in this hope he was disappointed. The Swiss could not accept the " Wittenberg Concordia " of 1536, because it was essentially Lutheran in the assertion of the corporal presence and oral manducation.

A year and a half before his death, Luther broke out afresh. to the grief of Melanchthon and other friends, in a most violent attack on the Sacramentarians, the " *Short Confession on the Holy Sacrament* " (1544).[1] It was occasioned by Schwenkfeld,[2] and by the rumor that Luther had changed his

---

[1] Erl. ed. XXXII. 396-425; Walch, XX. 2195 sqq. Comp. Luther's letter to Hungarian ministers, April 21, 1544 (in De Wette, V. 644), where he announces his intention soon to add one more to his many confessions on the real presence. " *Cogor post tot confessiones meas adhuc unam facere, quam faciam propediem et novissimam.*" The Erlangen editor says that the book was not published till 1545; but the titlepage of Hans Luft's edition bears date " Am Ende : M.D. XLIIII." Melanchthon informed Bullinger of the appearance of the book in August, 1544; and Calvin heard of it in November, 1544.

[2] Schwenkfeld sent Luther some books with appeals to his authority (1543). Luther returned an answer by the messenger, in which he called Schwenkfeld " a nonsensical fool," and asked him to spare him his books, which were " spit out by the Devil." In the Short Confession, he calls him always Stenkefeld (Stinkfield), and *ein* " *verdampt Lügenmaul.*"

view, because he had abolished the elevation and adoration of the host.[1] Moreover he learned that Dévay, his former student, and inmate of his house, smuggled the sacramentarian doctrine under Luther's name into Hungary.[2] He was also displeased with the reformation program of Bucer and Melanchthon for the diocese of Cologne (1543), because it stated the doctrine of the eucharist without the specific Lutheran features, so that he feared it would give aid and comfort to the Sacramentarians.[3] These provocations and vexations, in connection with sickness and old age, combined to increase his irritability, and to sour his temper. They must be taken into account for an understanding of his last document on the eucharist. It is the severest of all, and forms a parallel to his last work against the papacy, of the same year, which surpasses in violence all he ever wrote against the Romish Antichrist.[4]

The "Short Confession" contains no argument, but the strongest possible re-affirmation of his faith in the real presence, and a declaration of his total and final separation from the Sacramentarians and their doctrine, with some concluding remarks on the elevation of the sacrament. Standing on the brink of the grave, and in view of the judgment-seat, he solemnly condemns all enemies of the sacraments wherever

---

[1] See above, p. 606, note.

[2] Dévay is the founder of the Reformed (Calvinistic) church in Hungary. See Revecz in Herzog[2], III. 572 sqq.

[3] "*Summa*," he wrote to Chancellor Brück, who sent him the program, and Amsdorf's censure, "*das Buch ist den Schwärmern nicht allein leidlich, sondern auch tröstlich, vielmehr für ihre Lehre als für unsere; . . . und ist alles zu lang und gross Gewäsche, dass ich das Klappermaul, den Butzer, hier wohl spüre.*" De Wette, V. 709; "Corp. Reform." V. 113, 461.

[4] Comp. above, p. 251. Melanchthon called the "Short Confession" "the most atrocious book of Luther" (*atrocissimum Lutheri scriptum, in quo bellum περὶ δείπνου κυριακοῦ instaurat*). Letter to Bullinger, Aug. 30, 1544, in "Corp. Ref." v. 475. He agreed with the judgment of Calvin, who wrote to him, June 28, 1545 : "I confess that we all owe the greatest thanks to Luther, and I should cheerfully concede to him the highest authority, if he only knew how to control himself. Good God! what jubilee we prepare for the Papists, and what sad example do we set to posterity!"

they are.[1] "Much rather," he says, "would I be torn to
pieces, and burnt a hundred times, than be of one mind and
will with Stenkefeld [Schwenkfeld], Zwingel, Carlstadt,
Œcolampad, and all the rest of the *Schwärmer*, or tolerate
their doctrine." He overwhelms them with terms of opprobrium, and coins new ones which cannot be translated into
decent English. He calls them heretics, hypocrites, liars,
blasphemers, soul-murderers, sinners unto death, bedeviled
all over.[2] He ceased to pray for them, and left them to their
fate. At one time he had expressed some regard for Œcolampadius,[3] and even for Zwingli, and sincere grief at his tragic
death.[4] But in this last book he repeatedly refers to his
death as a terrible judgment of God, and doubts whether he
was saved.[5] He was horrified at Zwingli's belief in the salvation of the pious heathen, which he learned from his last

[1] "*Denn ich*," he says after a few contemptuous words about Schwenkfeld, "*als der ich nu auf der Gruben gehe, will diess Zeugniss und diesen
Ruhm mit mir für meins lieben Herrn und Heilands Jesu Christi Richtstuhl
bringen, dass ich die Schwärmer und Sacramentsfeinde, Carlstadt, Zwingel,
Œcolampad, Stenkefeld und ihre Jünger zu Zürch* [Zürich], *und wo sie sind,
mit ganzem Ernst verdampt und gemieden habe, nach seinem Befehl Tit. 3 :
10, Einen Ketzer sollt du meiden.*"

[2] He ascribes to them indiscriminately "*ein eingeteufelt, durchteufelt,
überteufelt, lästerlich Herz und Lügenmaul*" (*l. c.*, p. 404).

[3] He wrote in 1527: "*Dem Œcolampad hat Gott viel Gaben geschenkt für*
[vor] *vielen andern, und mir ja herzlich für den Mann leid ist.*" Erl. ed.
XXX. 34.

[4] In an answer to Bullinger, Zwingli's successor, dated May 14, 1538 (De
Wette, V. 112): "*Libere enim dicam : Zwinglium, postquam Marpurgi mihi
visus et auditus est, virum optimum esse judicavi, sicut et Œcolampadium, ita
ut eorum casus me pœne exanimaverit . . . non quod invideam honori
Zwinglii, de cuius morte tantum dolorem concepi,*" etc.

[5] He had expressed the same doubt twelve years before, but in a milder
tone, in a letter to Duke Albrecht of Prussia, April, 1532 (De Wette, IV.
352 sq.): "*Sind sie*" [Zwingli and his followers who fell on the battle-field at
Cappel] "*selig worden, wie dasselb Gott nicht unmöglich ist, einen Menschen
in seinem letzten Ende, in einem Augenblick, zu bekehren, das gönnen und
wünschen wir ihnen von Grund unsers Herzens : aber Märtyrer zu machen,
da gehört mehr zu, denn schlecht selig werden.*" In the Short Confession
(p. 411) he seems to count Zwingli and Œcolampadius among "the Devil's
martyrs."

exposition of the Christian faith, addressed to the king of France. "If such godless heathen," he says, "as Socrates, Aristides, yea, even the horrible Numa who introduced all kinds of idolatry in Rome [1] (as St. Augustin writes), were saved, there is no need of God, Christ, gospel, Scriptures, baptism, sacrament, or Christian faith." He thinks that Zwingli either played the hypocrite when he professed so many Christian articles at Marburg, or fell away, and has become worse than a heathen, and ten times worse than he was as a papist.

This attitude Luther retained to the end. It is difficult to say whom he hated most, the papists or the Sacramentarians. On the subject of the real presence he was much farther removed from the latter. He remarks once that he would rather drink blood alone with the papists than wine alone with the Zwinglians. A few days before his death, he wrote to his friend, Pastor Probst in Bremen: "Blessed is the man that walketh not in the counsel of the *Sacramentarians*, nor standeth in the way of the *Zwinglians*, nor sitteth in the seat of the *Zurichers*." [2] Thus he turned the blessing of the first Psalm into a curse, in accordance with his growing habit of cursing the pope and the devil when praying to God. He repeatedly speaks of this habit, especially in reciting the Lord's Prayer, and justifies it as a part of his piety.[3]

---

[1] "*Solche gottlose Heiden, Socrates, Aristides, ja der gräuliche Numa, der zu Rom alle Abgötterei erst gestiftet.*"

[2] De Wette, V. 778. The German in Walch, XVII. 2633. It should be remembered that in this letter, dated Jan. 17, 1546, he describes himself as "*senex, decrepitus, piger, fessus, frigidus, monoculus,*" and "*infelicissimus omnium hominum*"

[3] In a book of March, 1531, against an anonymous layman of Dresden, who charged him with stirring up the Germans to open rebellion against the emperor, he defends this pious cursing as the necessary negative supplement to the positive petitions of the Lord's Prayer. "*Ich kann nicht beten,*" he says, "*ich muss dabei fluchen. Soll ich sagen: 'geheiligt werde dein Name,' muss ich dabei sagen: 'Verflucht, verdammt, geschändet müsse werden der Papisten Namen, und aller, die deinen Namen lästern.' Soll ich sagen: 'Dein Reich komme,' so muss ich dabei sagen: 'Verflucht, verdammt, verstört*"

It is befitting that with this last word against the Sacramentarians should coincide in time and spirit his last and most violent attack upon the divine gift of reason, which he had himself so often and so effectually used as his best weapon, next to the Word of God. On Jan. 17, 1546, he ascended the pulpit of Wittenberg for the last time, and denounced reason as "the damned whore of the Devil." The fanatics and Sacramentarians boast of it when they ask: "How can this man give us his flesh to eat?" Hear ye the Son of God who says : "This is my body," and crush the serpent beneath your feet.[1]

Six days later Luther left the city of his public labors for the city of his birth, and died in peace at Eisleben, Feb. 18. 1546, holding fast to his faith, and commending his soul to his God and Redeemer.

müsse werden das Papstthum sammt allen Reichen auf Erden, die deinem Reiche zuwider sind. Soll ich sagen: 'Dein Wille geschehe,' so muss ich dabei sagen: 'Verflucht, verdammt, geschändet und zu nichte müssen werden alle Gedanken und Anschläge der Papisten und aller die wider deinen Willen und Rath streben.' Wahrlich, so bete ich alle Tage mündlich, und mit dem Herzen ohne Unterlass, und mit mir alle, die an Christum gläuben, und fühle auch wohl, dass es erhört wird. Denn man muss Gottes Wunder sehen, wie er diesen schrecklichen Reichstag [the Diet of Augsburg, 1530], *und das unmässliche Dräuen und Wüthen der Papisten zu nichte macht, und auch ferner sie gründlich zu nichte machen wird. Dennoch behalte ich ein gut, freundlich, friedlich und christlich Herz gegen jedermann ; das wissen auch meine grössten Feinde."* (*Wider den Meuchler zu Dresden*, Walsh, XVI. 2085 ; Erl. ed. XXV. 108.) Seven years later (1538) he made a similar statement in a tract on the Pope's program of a Reformation : " *Man soll nicht fluchen (das ist wahr)* ; *aber beten muss man, dass Gottes Name geheiliget und geehrt werde, des Papsts Name geschändet und verflucht werde, sammt seinem Gott, dem Teufel, dass Gottes Reich komme, des Antichrists Reich zu Grunde gehe. Solchen paternosterlichen Fluch mag man wohl beten, und soll ihn jeder Christ beten, weil die letzten Erzbösewichte am Ende der Welt, Papst, Cardinal, und Bischof, so schändlich, böslich, muthwillig unsern lieben Herrn und Gott lästern und dazu spotten."* Erl. ed. XXV. 151. When once asked whether we may curse in praying, Luther replied: "Yes; for when I pray, 'Hallowed be thy name,' I curse Erasmus and all heretics who blaspheme God." *Tischreden*, vol. LIX. 22. In Marburg, at the dinner-table, he added after that petition, audibly, with a sharp voice, and closing his hands more tightly, " *Und dass unser Name für tausend Teufel verdammt werde."* Baum, *Capito u. Butzer*, p. 461.

[1] See above, § 9, p. 31 sq. Köstlin, *Luthers Theologie*, II. 226, 290.

In view of these last utterances we must, reluctantly, refuse
credit to the story that Luther before his death remarked to
Melanchthon: "Dear Philip, I confess that the matter of the
Lord's Supper has been overdone ; "[1] and that, on being asked
to correct the evil, and to restore peace to the church, he
replied: "I often thought of it; but then people might lose
confidence in my whole doctrine. I leave the matter in the
hands of the Lord. Do what you can after my death."[2]

But it is gratifying to know that Luther never said one
unkind word of Calvin, who was twenty-five years younger.
He never saw him, but read some of his books, and heard of
him through Melanchthon. In a letter to Bucer, dated Oct.
14, 1539, he sent his respectful salutations to John Sturm and
John Calvin, who lived at that time in Strassburg, and added
that he had read their books with singular delight. This
includes his masterly answer to the letter of Bishop Sadolet
(1539).[3] Melanchthon sent salutations from Luther and
Bugenhagen to Calvin, and informed him that he was "in
high favor with Luther,"[4] notwithstanding the difference of

---

[1] "*Der Sache vom Abendmahl ist viel zu viel gethan.*"

[2] Hardenberg, a Reformed minister at Bremen (d. 1574), reported such a
conversation as coming from the lips of his friend Melanchthon; but Melanchthon nowhere alludes to it. Stähelin (*John Calvin*, I. 228 sq.) accepts,
Köstlin (*M. L.*, II. 627) rejects the report, as resting on some misunderstanding. So also C. Bertheau in the article "Hardenberg" in Herzog[2], V. 596
sq. Comp. Diestelmann, *Die letzte Unterredung Luthers mit Melanchthon
über den Abendmahlsstreit*, Göttingen, 1874; Köstlin's review of Diestelmann, in the "Studien und Kritiken," 1876, p. 385 sqq.; and Walte in the
"Jahrb. für prot. Theol.," 1883. It is a pity that the story cannot be sufficiently authenticated, for it certainly expresses what *ought* to have been
Luther's last confession on the subject.

[3] De Wette, V. 211: "*Bene vale et salutabis Dr. Joannem Sturmium et
Johannem Calvinum reverenter, quorum libellos cum singulari voluptate legi.
Sadoleto optarem, ut crederet Deum esse creatorem hominum etiam extra
Italiam.*" From the last sentence it appears that he read Calvin's answer
to Bishop Sadolet. He is reported to have remarked to Cruciger: "This
answer has hand and foot, and I rejoice that God raises such men who will
give popery the last blow, and finish the war against Antichrist which I
began." Calvin alludes to these salutations in his *Secunda Defensio adv.
Westphalum* (*Opera*, ed. Reuss, IX. 92).

[4] "*Calvinus magnam gratiam iniit.*"

views on the real presence, and that Luther hoped for better
opinions, but was willing to bear something from such a good
man.[1]   Calvin had expressed his views on the Lord's Supper
in the first edition of his *Institutes*, which appeared in 1536,[2]
incidentally also in his answer to Sadolet, which Luther read
"with delight,"[3] and more fully in a special treatise, *De Cœna
Domini*, which was published in French at Strassburg, 1541,
and then in Latin, 1545.[4]   Luther must have known these
views.   He is reported to have seen a copy of Calvin's tract
on the eucharist in a bookstore at Wittenberg, and, after
reading it, made the remark: "The author is certainly a
learned and pious man: if Zwingli and Œcolampadius had
from the start declared themselves in this way, there would
probably not have arisen such a controversy."[5]

Calvin returned Luther's greetings through Melanchthon,
and sent him two pamphlets with a letter, dated Jan. 21,
1545, addressing him as "my much respected father," and
requesting him to solve the scruples of some converted
French refugees.   He expresses the wish that "he might
enjoy for a few hours the happiness of his society," though
this was impossible on earth.

Melanchthon, fearing a renewal of the eucharistic contro-

---

[1] This letter of Melanchthon is lost, but Calvin alludes to it in a letter
to Farel, 1539. *Opera*, X. 432. The words of Luther are: "*Spero ipsum
[Calvinum] olim de nobis melius sensurum, sed œquum est a bono ingenio nos
aliquid ferre.*"

[2] Ch. IV. p. 236 sqq. (*De Cœna Domini*), *Opera*, I. 118 sqq.

[3] *Opera Calc.*, ed. Reuss, vol. V. 385–416. On fol. 400 Calvin rejects the
"*localis corporis Christi præsentia*" in the eucharist, but asserts "*veram
carnis et sanguinis communicationem quæ fidelibus in cœna exhibetur.*"

[4] *Opera*, V. 429–460.

[5] Pezel, *Ausführliche Lehre vom Sacramentsstreit*, Bremen, 1600, p. 137
sqq. See Gieseler, vol. IV. 414 sq. (New York ed. of the E. transl.); Stähelin, *Joh. Calvin*, I. 227 (with Pezel's report in full); Müller, *Dogmat. Abhandlungen*, p. 406; Köstlin, *M. L.*, II. 615 and 687. It is remarkable in
this connection that Luther spoke in high terms of the Swabian *Syngramma*,
which was directed against the Swiss theory, but leaves no room for an oral
manducation, and comes nearest to the Calvinistic view. Comp. Köstlin,
Luthers Theologie, II. 147.

versy, had not the courage to deliver this letter — the only
one of Calvin to Luther — "because," he says, " Doctor
Martin is suspicious, and dislikes to answer such questions
as were proposed to him." [1]

Calvin regretted " the vehemence of Luther's natural temperament, which was so apt to boil over in every direction,"
and to " flash his lightning sometimes also upon the servants
of the Lord; " but he always put him above Zwingli, and
exhorted the Zurichers to moderation. When he heard of the
last attack of Luther, he wrote a noble letter to Bullinger,
Nov. 25, 1544, in which he says: [2] —

" I hear that Luther has at length broken forth in fierce invective, not so
much against you as against the whole of us. On the present occasion, I
dare scarce venture to ask you to keep silence, because it is neither just that
innocent persons should thus be harassed, nor that they should be denied the
opportunity of clearing themselves; neither, on the other hand, is it easy to
determine whether it would be prudent for them to do so. But of this I do
earnestly desire to put you in mind, in the first place, that you would consider how eminent a man Luther is, and his excellent endowments, with what
strength of mind and resolute constancy, with how great skill, with what
efficiency and power of doctrinal statement, he hath hitherto devoted his
whole energy to overthrow the reign of Antichrist, and at the same time
to diffuse far and near the doctrine of salvation. Often have I been wont to
declare, that even although he were to call me a devil, I should still not the
less esteem and acknowledge him as an illustrious servant of God. [3] . . . This,
therefore, I would beseech you to consider first of all, along with your colleagues, that you have to do with a most distinguished servant of Christ, to
whom we are all of us largely indebted. That, besides, you will do yourselves
no good by quarreling, except that you may afford some sport to the wicked,
so that they may triumph not so much over us as over the gospel. If they
see us rending each other asunder, they then give full credit to what we say,
but when with one consent and with one voice we preach Christ, they avail
themselves unwarrantably of our inherent weakness to cast reproach upon
our faith. I wish, therefore, that you would consider and reflect on these
things, rather than on what Luther has deserved by his violence; lest that

[1] *Opera*, ed. Reuss, XII. 6 sq., 61 sq. *Letters*, ed. Constable, I. 416 sq.
[2] *Letters*, I. 409 sq., *Opera*, XI. 774.
[3] " *Sæpe dicere solitus sum : etiam si me diabolum vocaret, me tamen hoc
illi honoris habiturum, ut insignem Dei servum agnoscam: qui tamen ut
pollet eximiis virtutibus, ita magnis vitiis laboret.*"

may happen to you which Paul threatens, that by biting and devouring one another, ye be consumed one of another. Even should he have provoked us, we ought rather to decline the contest than to increase the wound by the general shipwreck of the church."

This is the wisest Christian answer from Geneva to the thunderbolts of Wittenberg.

§ 110. *Reflections on the Ethics of the Eucharistic Controversy,*

Dogmatics and ethics, faith and conduct, should agree like the teaching and example of Christ from which they are to be drawn. But, in practice, they often conflict. History shows us many examples of ungodly champions of orthodoxy and godly champions of heterodoxy, of unholy churchmen and holy dissenters. The angel of Ephesus is commended for zeal against false apostles, and censured for leaving the first love; while the angel of Thyatira is praised for his good works, and reproved for tolerating error. Some are worse than their belief, and others are better than their misbelief or unbelief.

Luther and Zwingli are by no means opposed to each other as orthodox and heretic; they were essentially agreed in all fundamental articles of the evangelical faith, as the Marburg Conference proved. The difference between them is only a little more Catholic orthodoxy and intolerance in Luther, and a little more Christian charity and liberality in Zwingli. This difference is characteristic of the Reformers and of the denominations which they represent.

Luther had a sense of superiority, and claimed the credit of having begun the work of the Reformation. He supposed that the Swiss were indebted to him for what little knowledge they had of the gospel; while, in fact, they were as independent of him as the Swiss Republic was of the German Empire, and knew the gospel as well as he.[1]

---

[1] In his book, "*Dass die Worte Christi,*" etc. (1527, Erl. ed. XXX. 11), he calls the Sacramentarians "his tender children, his dear brethren, his golden friends" ("*meine zarte Kinder, meine Brüderlein, meine gülden*

But it would be great injustice to attribute his conduct to obstinacy and pride, or any selfish motive. It proceeded from his inmost conviction. He regarded the real presence as a fundamental article of faith, inseparably connected with the incarnation, the union of the two natures of Christ, and the mystical union of believers with his divine-human personality. He feared that the denial of this article would consistently lead to the rejection of all mysteries, and of Christianity itself. He deemed it, moreover, most dangerous and horrible to depart from what had been the consensus of the Christian Church for so many centuries. His piety was deeply rooted in the historic Catholic faith, and it cost him a great struggle to break loose from popery. In the progress of the eucharistic controversy, all his Catholic instincts and abhorrence of heresy were aroused and intensified. In his zeal he could not do justice to his opponents, or appreciate their position. His sentiments are shared by millions of pious and devout Lutherans to this day, whose conscience forbids them to commune with Christians of Reformed churches.[1] We may lament their narrowness, but must re-

---

Freundlein "), who would have known nothing of Christ and the gospel if Luther had not previously written ("*wo der Luther nicht zuvor hätte geschrieben*"). He compared Carlstadt to Absalom and to Judas the traitor. He treated the Swiss not much better, in a letter to his blind admirer Amsdorf, April 14, 1545 (De Wette, V. 728), where he says that they kept silence, while he alone was sustaining the fury of popery (*cum solus sudarem in sustinenda furia Papæ*), and that after the peril was over, they claimed the victory, and reaped the fruit of his labors (*tum erampebant triumphatores gloriosi. Sic, sic alius laborat, alius fruitur*). Dr. Döllinger (*Luther*, 1851, p. 29 sq.) derives the bitterness of Luther's polemics against the Swiss largely from "jealousy and wounded pride," and calls his refutation of their arguments "very weak," and even "dishonest" ("*seine Polemik war, wie immer und gegen jedermann, in hohem Grade unehrlich,*" p. 31). The charge of dishonesty we cannot admit.

[1] The philosopher Steffens, who was far from uncharitable bigotry, always went from Berlin to Breslau to commune with the orthodox Old Lutherans. Bishop Martensen, one of the profoundest Lutheran divines of the nineteenth century, thought that only in cases of necessity could a Lutheran commune with a Calvinist, who denies what Luther affirms, or evades the mystery of the real presence. *Briefwechsel zwischen Martensen und Dorner,*

spect their conviction, as we do the conviction of the far larger number of Roman Catholics, who devoutly believe in the miracle of transubstantiation and the sacrifice of the mass.

In addition to Luther's dogmatic standpoint we must take into account his ignorance of the true character of the Swiss, and their real doctrine. He had hardly heard of the Swiss Reformation when the controversy began. He did not even spell Zwingli's name correctly (he always calls him "Zwingel"), and could not easily understand his Swiss dialect.[1] He made a radical mistake by confounding him with Carlstadt and the fanatics. He charged him with reducing the Lord's Supper to a common meal, and bread and wine to empty signs; and, although he found out his mistake at Marburg, he returned to it again in his last book, adding the additional charge of hypocrisy or apostasy. He treated him as a heathen, yea, worse than a heathen, as he treated Erasmus.

Zwingli was clear-headed, self-possessed, jejune, and sober (even in his radical departures from Rome), and farther removed from fanaticism than Luther himself. He was a pupil of the classical and humanistic school of Erasmus; he had never been so deeply rooted in the mediæval faith, and it cost him much less trouble than Luther to break off from the old church; he was a man of reflection rather than of intuition, and had no mystic vein, but we may say a rationalistic bent. Nevertheless, he was as loyal to Christ, and believed in the Word of God and the supernatural as firmly,

Berlin, 1888, vol. I. 262 sq. He changed his view afterwards. I could name eminent living Lutheran divines who would hardly allow even this exception. In America the Lutheran theory had largely given way to the Zwinglian until it was revived by the German Missouri Synod, and found a learned advocate in Dr. Krauth, who went so far as to propose to the General Lutheran Council the so-called "Galesburg rule" (1875): "Lutheran pulpits for Lutheran ministers only, Lutheran altars for Lutheran communicants only."

[1] Zwingli's Latin is better than his *Züridütsch*, in which his answers to Luther's German attacks were written.

as Luther; and the Reformed churches to this day are as
pure, faithful, devoted, and active in Christian works as any,
and less affected by rationalism than the Lutheran, in part
for the very reason that they allow reason its legitimate
influence in dogmatic questions. If Zwingli believed in the
salvation of the pious heathen and unbaptized infants, it was
not because he doubted the absolute necessity of the saving
grace of Christ, which he very strongly asserted, but simply
because he extended this grace beyond the boundaries of the
visible church, and the ordinary means of grace ; and on this
point, as on others, he anticipated modern ideas. He was
inferior to Luther in genius, and depth of mind and heart,
but his superior in tolerance, liberality, and courtesy ; and in
these qualities also he was in advance of his age, and has the
sympathies of the best modern culture.

Making every allowance for Luther's profound religious
conviction, and for the misunderstanding of his opponent,
nothing can justify the spirit and style of Luther's polemics,
especially his last book against the sacramentarians. He
drew his inspiration for it from the imprecatory Psalms, not
from the Sermon on the Mount. He spoke the truth in
hatred and wrath, not in love.

This betrays an organic defect in his reformation ; namely,
the over-estimate of dogmatics over ethics, and a want of
discipline and self-government. In the same year in which
he wrote his fiercest book against the Sacramentarians, he
seriously contemplated leaving Wittenberg as a veritable
Sodom: so bad was the state of morals, according to his own
testimony, in the very centre of his influence.[1] It required
a second reformation, and such men as Arnd, Andreæ, Spener,
and Franke, to supplement the one-sided Lutheran orthodoxy

---

[1] In July, 1545 (De Wette, V. 732 sq.), he wrote to his wife from Leipzig
that he did not wish to return, and that she should sell house and home, and
move "from this Sodoma" to Zulsdorf. He would rather beg his bread than
torture his last days by the sight of the disorderly condition of Wittenberg.

by practical piety. Calvin, on the other hand, left at his death the church of Geneva in such a flourishing condition that John Knox pronounced it the best school of Christ since the days of the Apostles, and that sixty years later John Valentin Andreæ, one of the noblest and purest Lutheran divines of the seventeenth century, from personal observation held it up to the Lutheran Church as a model for imitation.

Luther's polemics had a bad effect on the Lutheran Church. He set in motion that theological fury which raged for several generations after his death, and persecuted some of the best men in it, from Melanchthon down to Spener. His blind followers, in their controversies among themselves and with the Reformed, imitated his faults, without his genius and originality; and in their zeal for what they regarded the pure doctrine, they forgot the common duties of courtesy and kindness which we owe even to an enemy.[1]

We may quote here a well-considered judgment of Dr. Dorner, one of the ablest and profoundest evangelical divines

---

[1] These champions of Lutheran orthodoxy were not simply *Lutherisch*, but *verluthert*, *durchluthert*, and *überluthert*. They fulfilled the prediction of the Reformer: "*Adorabunt stercora mea.*" Their mottoes were, —

> "*Gottes Wort und Luther's Lehr*
> *Vergehet nun und nimmermehr;*"

and

> "*Gottes Wort und Luther's Schrift*
> *Sind des Papst's und Calvini Gift.*"

They believed that Luther's example gave them license to exhaust the vocabulary of abuse, and to violate every rule of courtesy and good taste. They called the Reformed Christians "dogs," and Calvin's God "a roaring bull (*Brüllochse*), a blood-thirsty Moloch, and a hellish Behemoth." They charged them with teaching and worshiping the very Devil (*den leibhaftigen Teufel*), instead of the living God. One of them proved that "the damned Calvinistic heretics hold six hundred and sixty-six tenets [the apocalyptic number!] in common with the Turks." Another wrote a book to show that Zwinglians and Calvinists are no Christians at all, but baptized Jews and Mohammedans. *O sancta simplicitas!* On the intolerance of those champions of Lutheran orthodoxy, see the historical works of Arnold, Planck, Tholuck (*Der Geist der lutherischen Theologen Wittenbergs im 17ten Jahrh.*, 1852, p. 279 sqq.), and the fifth volume of Janssen.

of Germany, who says in a confidential letter to his lifelong friend, Bishop Martensen of Denmark, —

"I am more and more convinced that the deepest defect of Lutheran churchism heretofore has been a lack of the full appreciation of the ethical element of Christianity. This becomes manifest so often in the manner of the Lutheran champions. There is lacking the tenderness of conscience and thorough moral culture which deals conscientiously with the opponent. Justification by faith is made to cover, in advance, all sins, even the future ones ; and this is only another form of indulgence. The Lutheran doctrine leads, if we look at the principle, to an establishment of ethics on the deepest foundation. But many treat justification, not only as the beginning, but also as the goal. Hence we see not seldom the justified and the old man side by side, and the old man is not a bit changed. Lutherans who show in their literary and social conduct the stamp of the old Adam would deal more strictly with themselves, and fear to fall from grace by such conduct, if they had a keener conscience, and could see the necessary requirements of the principle of justification; for then they would shrink from such conduct as a sin against conscience. But the doctrine of justification is often misused for lulling the conscience to sleep, instead of quickening it." [1]

Zwingli's conduct towards Luther, judged from the ethical point of view, is much more gentlemanly and Christian, though by no means perfect. He, too, misunderstood and misrepresented Luther when he charged him with teaching a *local* presence and a *carnal* eating of Christ's body. He, too, knew how to be severe, and to use the rapier and the knife against the club and sledge-hammer of the Wittenberg Reformer. But he never forgot, even in the heat of controversy, the great services of Luther, and more than once paid him the tribute of sincere admiration.

[1] " *Die Rechtfertigungslehre wird vielfach zur Einschläferung statt zur Schärfung des Gewissens missbraucht.*" See Dorner's letter of May 14, 1871, in the *Briefwechsel* just quoted, vol. II. 114. Dorner and Martensen, both masters in Christian dogmatics and ethics, kept up a most instructive and interesting correspondence of friendship for more than forty years, on all theological and ecclesiastical questions of the day, even during the grave disturbances between Germany and Denmark on the Schleswig-Holstein controversy, which broke out at last in open war (1864). That correspondence is as remarkable in theology as the Schiller and Goethe correspondence is in poetry and art.

"For a thousand years," says Zwingli, "no mightier investigator of the Holy Scriptures has appeared than Luther. No one has equaled him in manly and immovable courage with which he attacked popery. But whose work is it? God's, or Luther's? Ask Luther himself, and he will say God's. He traces his doctrine to God and his eternal Word. As far as I have read his writings (although I have often purposely abstained from doing so), I find them well founded in the Scriptures: his only weak point is, that he yields too much to the Romanists in the matter of the sacraments, and the confession to the priest, and in tolerating the images in the churches. If he is sharp and racy in speech, it comes from a pious, honest heart, and a flaming love for the truth. . . . Others have come to know the true religion, but no one has ventured to attack the Goliath with his formidable armor; but Luther alone, as a true David, anointed by God, hurled the stones taken from the heavenly brook so skillfully that the giant fell prostrate on the ground. Therefore let us never cease to sing with joy: 'Saul has slain his thousands, and David his ten thousands' (1 Sam. 18 : 7). He was the Hercules who slew the Roman boar. . . . I have always been grateful to my teachers, how much more to that excellent man whom I can never expect to equal in honor and merit! With no men on earth would I rather be agreed than with the Wittenbergers. . . . Many have found the true religion before Luther became famous; I have learnt the gospel from the same fountain of the Scriptures, and began to preach it in 1516 (at Einsiedeln), when I diligently studied and copied with mine own hand the Greek epistles of Paul,[1] before I heard the name of Luther. He preaches Christ, so do I, thanks to God. And I will be called by no other name than that of my Captain Christ, whose soldiers we are."[2]

I may add here the impartial testimony of Dr. Köstlin, the best biographer of Luther, and himself a Lutheran: —

"Zwingli knew how to keep himself under control. Even where he is indignant, and intentionally sharp and pointed, he avoids the tone of passionate excitement, and uses the calm and urbane language of a gentleman of humanistic culture, and thereby proves his superiority over his opponent, without justifying the suspicion of Luther that he was uncertain in his own mind, and that the attitude he assumed was only a feint. His polemics forms thus the complete opposite to Luther's book, 'That the words of Christ,' etc. Yet it presents also another aspect. Zwingli characterizes, with select words of disregard, the writers and contents of the *Syngramma*, to which

[1] The neat manuscript is still preserved in the library of the Wasserkirche at Zürich, where I examined it in August, 1886.

[2] I have given the substance of several passages scattered through his polemical writings, and collected in the useful edition of *Zwingli's Sämmtliche Schriften* by Usteri and Vögelin, vol. II., Part II., p. 571 sqq.

Luther had given his assent, and clearly hints at Luther's wrath, spite, jealousy, audacity, and other faults poorly concealed under the cover of bravery, constancy, etc.; yea, here and there he calls his arguments 'childish' and 'fantastic,' etc. Hence his new writings were by no means so 'friendly' as the title indicates. What is more important, we miss in them a sense for the deeper, truly religious motives of Luther, as much as we miss in Luther an appreciation of like motives in Zwingli. . . . He sees in Luther obstinate blindness, while Luther discovered in him a devilish spirit." [1]

§ 111. *The Eucharistic Theories compared. Luther, Zwingli, Calvin.*

We now present, for the sake of clearness, though at the risk of some repetition, the three Protestant theories on the real presence, with the chief arguments.

Luther, Zwingli, and Calvin agree, negatively, in opposition to the dogma of transubstantiation, the sacrifice of the mass, and the withdrawal of the cup from the laity; positively, in these essential points: the divine institution and perpetuity of the Lord's Supper, the spiritual presence of Christ, the commemorative character of the ordinance as the celebration of Christ's atoning sacrifice, its importance as the highest act of worship and communion with Christ, and its special blessing to all who worthily partake of it.

They differ on three points, — the mode of Christ's presence (whether corporal, or spiritual); the organ of receiving his body and blood (whether by the mouth, or by faith); and the extent of this reception (whether by all, or only by believers). The last point has no practical religious value, though it follows from the first, and stands or falls with it. The difference is logical rather than religious. The Lord's Supper was never intended for unbelievers. Paul in speaking of "unworthily" receiving the sacrament (1 Cor. 11 : 27) does not mean theoretical unbelief, but moral unworthiness, irreverence of spirit and manner.

I. THE LUTHERAN THEORY teaches a real and substantial

---

[1] *Martin Luther*, II. 96 sq.

presence of the very body and blood of Christ, which was born of the Virgin Mary, and suffered on the cross, in, with, and under (*in*, *sub*, *cum*) the elements of bread and wine, and the oral manducation of both substances by all communicants, unworthy and unbelieving, as well as worthy and believing, though with opposite effects. The simultaneous co-existence or conjunction of the two substances is not a local inclusion of one substance in the other (impanation), nor a mixture or fusing-together of the two substances into one; nor is it permanent, but ceases with the sacramental action. It is described as a sacramental, supernatural, incomprehensible union.[1] The earthly elements remain unchanged and distinct in their substance and power, but they become the divinely appointed media for communicating the heavenly substance of the body and blood of Christ. They become so, not by priestly consecration, as in the doctrine of transubstantiation, but by the power and Word of God. The eating of the body is by the mouth, indeed, yet is not Capernaitic, and differs from the eating of ordinary food.[2] The

---

[1] The Lutheran divines of the seventeenth century describe the real presence as *sacramentalis, vera et realis, substantialis, mystica, supernaturalis, et incomprehensibilis*, and distinguish it from the *præsentia gloriosa, hypostatica, spiritualis, figurativa*, and from ἀπουσία (absence), ἐνουσία (inexistence), συνουσία (co-existence in the sense of coalescence), and μετουσία (transubstantiation).

[2] The *Formula Concordiæ* (Epitome, Art. VII., Negativa 21) indignantly rejects the notion of dental mastication as a malicious slander of the Sacramentarians. But Luther, in his instruction to Melanchthon, Dec. 17, 1534, gave it as his opinion, from which he would not yield, that "the body of Christ is distributed, eaten, and bitten with the teeth." "*Und ist Summa das unsere Meinung, dass wahrhaftig in und mit dem Brod der Leib Christi gessen wird, also dass alles, was das Brod wirket und leidet, der Leib Christi wirke und leide, dass er ausgetheilt, gessen, und mit den Zähnen zubissen [zerbissen] werde.*" De Wette, IV. 572. Comp. his letter to Jonas, Dec. 16, 1534, vol. IV. 569 sq. Dorner thinks that Luther speaks thus only *per synecdochen*; but this is excluded by the words, "What the bread does and suffers, that the body of Christ does and suffers." Melanchthon very properly declined to act on this instruction (see his letter to Camerarius, Jan. 10, 1535, in the "Corp. Reform." II. 822), and began about that time to change his view on the real presence. He was confirmed in his change by the renewal of the eucharistic controversy, and his contact with Calvin.

object and use of the Lord's Supper is chiefly the assurance of the forgiveness of sins, to the comfort of the believer.[1]

This is the scholastic statement of the doctrine, as given by the framers of the Formula Concordiæ, and the Lutheran scholastics of the seventeenth century.

The confessional deliverances of the Lutheran Church on the Lord's Supper are as follows: —

THE AUGSBURG CONFESSION OF 1530.

"ART. X. Of the Supper of the Lord they teach that the [true] body and blood of Christ [2] are truly present [under the form of bread and wine],[3] and are [there] [4] communicated to [and received by] [5] those that eat [6] in the Lord's Supper. And they disapprove of those that teach otherwise." [7]

[1] The Lutheran theory is generally designated by the convenient term *consubstantiation*, but Lutheran divines expressly reject it as a misrepresentation. The Zwinglians, with their conception of corporality, could not conceive of a corporal presence without a local presence; while Luther, with his distinction of three kinds of presence and his view of the ubiquity of Christ's body, could do so. The scholastic term *consubstantiatio* is not so well defined as *transubstantiatio*, and may be used in different senses: (1) a mixture of two substances (which nobody ever taught); (2) an inclusion of one substance in another (*impanatio*); (3) a sacramental co-existence of two substances in their integrity in the same place. In the first two senses the term is not applicable to the Lutheran theory. The *"in pane"* might favor impanation, but the *sub* and *cum* qualify it. Dr. Steitz, in a learned article on Transubstantiation, in Herzog,[1] XVI. 347, and in the second edition, XV. 829, attributes to the Lutheran Church the third view of consubstantiation, but to Luther himself the second; namely, *"die sacramentliche Durchdringung der Brotsubstanz von der Substanz des Leibes."* To this Luther's illustration of the fire in the iron might lead. But fire and iron remain distinct. At all events, he denied emphatically a *local* or *physical* inclusion. Lutheran divines in America are very sensitive when charged with consubstantiation.

[2] The Latin text reads simply: *corpus et sanguis Christi*; the German text: *wahrer Leib und Blut Christi.*

[3] *Vere adsint et distribuantur.* The German text adds: *unter der Gestalt des Brots und Weins.* The variations between the Latin and German texts of the original edition indicate a certain hesitation in Melanchthon's mind, if not the beginning of a change, which was completed in the altered confession.

[4] German: *da.*

[5] German addition: *und genommen wird.*

[6] *Vescentibus.* The German text has no equivalent for this verb.

[7] *Et improbant secus docentes.* In German: *Derhalben wird auch die Gegenlehre verworfen, wherefore also the opposite doctrine is rejected.* The

THE ALTERED AUGSBURG CONFESSION OF 1540.

Concerning the Supper of the Lord they teach that with bread and wine are truly exhibited[1] the body and blood of Christ to those that eat in the Lord's Supper.[2]

ARTICLES OF SMALKALD (BY LUTHER), 1537.

" Of this Sacrament of the Altar, we hold that the bread and wine in the Supper are the true body and blood of Christ, and are given to, and received by, not only the pious, but also to and by the impious Christians."

In the same articles Luther denounces transubstantiation as a "subtle sophistry (*subtilitas sophistica*)," and the Romish mass as "the greatest and most terrible abomination (*maxima et horrenda abominatio*)." Pars III., Art. VI., in Müller's ed., pp. 301, 320.

FORMULA OF CONCORD (1577).   EPITOME, ART. VII.   AFFIRMATIVE.

" I. We believe, teach, and confess that in the Lord's Supper the body and blood of Christ are truly and substantially present, and that they are truly distributed and taken together with the bread and wine.

" II. We believe, teach, and confess that the words of the Testament of Christ are not to be understood otherwise than as the words themselves literally sound, so that the bread does not signify the absent body of Christ, and the wine the absent blood of Christ, but that on account of the sacramental union the bread and wine are truly the body and blood of Christ.

" III. Moreover, as concerns the consecration, we believe, teach, and confess that no human work, nor any utterance of the minister of the Church, is the cause of the presence of the body and blood of Christ in the Supper, but that this is to be attributed to the omnipotent power of our Lord Jesus Christ alone.

" IV. Nevertheless, we believe, teach, and confess, by unanimous consent, that in the use of the Lord's Supper the words of the institution of Christ

sacramentarian (Zwinglian) doctrine is meant, but not the Calvinistic, which appeared six years afterward, 1536.   The term *improbant* for the papal *damnant*, and *anathema sit*, shows the progress in toleration.   The Zwinglian view is not condemned as a heresy, but simply disapproved as an error. The Formula of Concord made a step backwards in this respect, and uses *repudiamus* and *damnamus*.

[1] *Cum pane et vino vere exhibeantur*, instead of *vere adsint et distribuantur*.   The verb *exhibit* does not necessarily imply the actual *reception* by unbelievers, which the verb *distribute* does.   So Dorner also judges of the difference (*l.c.*, p. 324).

[2] The disapproval of those who teach otherwise is significantly omitted, no doubt in deference to Calvin's view, which had been published in the mean time, and to which Melanchthon himself leaned.

are by no means to be omitted, but are to be publicly recited, as it is written (1 Cor. 10: 16), 'The cup of blessing which we bless, is it not the communion of the blood of Christ?' etc. And this benediction takes place by the recitation of the words of Christ.

"V. Now the foundations on which we rest in this controversy with the Sacramentarians are the following, which, moreover, Dr. Luther has laid down in his Larger Confession concerning the Supper of the Lord:—

"The first foundation is an article of our Christian faith, to wit: Jesus Christ is true, essential, natural, perfect God and man in unity of person, inseparable and undivided.

"Secondly: That the right hand of God is everywhere; and that Christ, in respect of his humanity, is truly and in very deed seated thereat, and therefore as present governs, and has in his hand and under his feet, as the Scripture saith (Eph. 1: 22), all things which are in heaven and on earth. At this right hand of God no other man, nor even any angel, but the Son of Mary alone, is seated, whence also he is able to effect those things which we have said.

"Thirdly: That the Word of God is not false or deceiving.

"Fourthly: That God knows and has in his power various modes of being in any place, and is not confined to that single one which philosophers are wont to call local or circumscribed.

"VI. We believe, teach, and confess that the body and blood of Christ are taken with the bread and wine, not only spiritually through faith, but also by the mouth, nevertheless not Capernaitically, but after a spiritual and heavenly manner, by reason of the sacramental union. For to this the words of Christ clearly bear witness, in which he enjoins us to take, to eat, to drink; and that this was done by the Apostles the Scripture makes mention, saying (Mark 14: 23), 'And they all drank of it.' And Paul says, 'The bread which we break is the communion of the body of Christ;' that is, he that eats this bread eats the body of Christ.

"To the same, with great consent, do the chief of the most ancient doctors of the church — Chrysostom, Cyprian, Leo the First, Gregory, Ambrose, Augustin — bear witness.

"VII. We believe, teach, and confess that not only true believers in Christ, and such as worthily approach the Supper of the Lord, but also the unworthy and unbelieving receive the true body and blood of Christ; in such wise, nevertheless, that they derive thence neither consolation nor life, but rather so as that receiving turns to their judgment and condemnation, unless they be converted, and repent (1 Cor. 11: 27, 29).

"For although they repel from them Christ as a Saviour, nevertheless they are compelled, though extremely unwilling, to admit him as a stern Judge. And he no less present exercises his judgment over these impenitent guests than as present he works consolation and life in the hearts of true believers and worthy guests.

"VIII. We believe, teach, and confess that there is one kind only of unworthy guests: they are those only who do not believe. Of these it is written (John 3: 18), 'He that believeth not is condemned already.' And this judgment is enhanced and aggravated by an unworthy use of the holy Supper (1 Cor. 11: 29).

"IX. We believe, teach, and confess that no true believer, so long as he retains a living faith, receives the holy Supper of the Lord unto condemnation, however much weakness of faith he may labor under. For the Lord's Supper has been chiefly instituted for the sake of the weak in faith, who nevertheless are penitent, that from it they may derive true consolation and a strengthening of their weak faith (Matt. 9: 12; 11: 5, 28).

"We believe, teach, and confess that the whole worthiness of the guests at this heavenly Supper consists alone in the most holy obedience and most perfect merit of Christ. And this we apply to ourselves by true faith, and are rendered certain of the application of this merit, and are confirmed in our minds by the sacrament. But in no way does that worthiness depend upon our virtues, or upon our inward or outward preparations."

The three great arguments for the Lutheran theory are the words of institution taken in their literal sense, the ubiquity of Christ's body, and the prevailing faith of the church before the Reformation.

1. As to the literal interpretation, it cannot be carried out, and is surrendered, as inconsistent with the context and the surroundings, by nearly all modern exegetes.[1]

---

[1] I may mention among commentators (on Matt. 26: 26 and parallel passages), De Wette, Meyer, Weiss (in the seventh ed. of Meyer on Matt., p. 504 sq.), Bleek, Ewald, Van Oosterzee, Alford, Morison, etc.; and, among Lutheran and Lutheranizing theologians, Kahnis, Jul. Müller, Martensen, Dorner. The Bible, true to its Oriental origin and character, is full of parables, metaphors, and tropical expressions, from Genesis to Revelation. The substantive verb ἐστι (which was not spoken in the Aramaic original) is simply the logical copula, and may designate a figurative, as well as a real, identity of the subject and the predicate ; which of the two, depends on the connection and surroundings. I may say of a likeness of Luther, "This is Luther's," i.e., a figure or representation of Luther. It has a symbolical or allegorical sense in many passages, as Matt. 13: 38 sq.; Luke 12: 1; John 10. 6, 14: 6; Gal. 4: 24; Heb. 10: 20; Rev. 1: 20. But what is most conclusive, even in the words of institution, Luther himself had to admit a double metaphor; namely, a synecdoche *partis pro toto* ("This is my body" for "This is my body, *and bread;*" to avoid transubstantiation, which denies the substance of bread), and a synecdoche *continentis pro contento* ("This *cup* is the new covenant in my blood," instead of "This *wine,*" etc.). The whole

2. The ubiquity of Christ's body involves an important element of truth, but is a dogmatic hypothesis without sufficient Scripture warrant, and cannot well be reconciled with the fact of the ascension, or with the nature of a body, unless it be resolved into a mere potential or dynamic presence which makes it possible for Christ to make his divine-human power and influence felt wherever he pleases.[1]

The illustrations which Luther uses — as the sun shining everywhere, the voice resounding in a thousand ears and hearts, the eye seeing different objects at once — all lead to a dynamic presence, which Calvin fully admits.

3. The historic argument might prove too much (for transubstantiation and the sacrifice of the mass), unless we are satisfied with the substance of truth which underlies the imperfect human theories and formulas. The real presence of Christ with his people is indeed a most precious truth, which can never be surrendered. It is the very life of the church and the comfort and strength of believers from day to day. He promised the perpetual presence not only of his spirit or influence, but of his theanthropic person: "I am with you alway." It is impossible to make an abstract separation of

action is symbolical. At that time Christ, living and speaking to the disciples with his body yet unbroken, and his blood not yet shed, could not literally offer his body to them. They would have shuddered at such an idea, and at least expressed their surprise. Kahnis, an orthodox Lutheran, came to the conclusion (1861) that "the literal interpretation of the words of institution is an impossibility, and must be given up." (See the first ed. of his *Luth. Dogmatik*, I. 616 sq.) Dorner says (*Christl. Glaubenslehre*, II. 853), "That ἐστί may be understood figuratively is beyond a doubt, and should never have been denied. It is only necessary to refer to the parables." Martensen, an eminent Danish Lutheran (*Christl. Dogmatik*, p. 491), admits Zwingli's exegesis, and thinks that his "sober common-sense view has a greater importance than Lutheran divines are generally disposed to accord to it."

[1] The Lutheran divines were divided between the idea of an *absolute* ubiquity (which would prove too much for the Lutheran doctrine, and run into a sort of Panchristism or Christo-Pantheism), and a *relative* ubiquity or *multivolipræsentia* (which depends upon the will). The Formula of Concord inconsistently favors both views. See Dorner's History of Christology, II. 710 sqq. (Germ. ed.), and Schaff, *Creeds*, I. 322, 325 sq., and 348.

the divine and human in the God-man. He is the Head of the church, his body, and "filleth all in all." Nor can the church give up the other important truth that Christ is the bread of life, and nourishes, in a spiritual and heavenly manner, the soul of the believer which is vitally united to him as the branch is to the vine. This truth is symbolized in the miraculous feeding of the multitude, and set forth in the mysterious discourse of the sixth chapter of John.

As far as Luther contended for these truths, he was right against the Sacramentarians, though he erred in the form of conception and statement. His view is mystical but profound; Zwingli's view is clear but superficial. The former commends itself to devout feeling, the latter to the sober understanding and intellect.

II. THE ZWINGLIAN THEORY. — The Lord's Supper is a solemn commemoration of the atoning death of Christ, according to his own command: "Do this in remembrance of me," and the words of Paul: "As often as ye eat this bread, and drink the cup, ye proclaim the Lord's death till he come."[1] Zwingli emphasized this primitive character of the institution as a gift of God to man, in opposition to the Roman mass as a work or offering which man makes to God.[2] He compares the sacrament to a wedding-ring which seals the marriage union between Christ and the believer. He denied the corporal presence, because Christ ascended to heaven, and because a body cannot be present in more than one place at once, also because two substances cannot occupy the same space at the same time; but he admitted his spiritual presence, for Christ is eternal God, and his death

---

[1] Zwingli calls the sacrament *ein Wiedergedächtniss und Erneuern dessen was einst geschehen und in Ewigkeit kräftig ist.* His views on the Lord's Supper are conveniently put together by Usteri and Vögelin, in *Zwingli's Sämmtliche Schriften im Auszuge*, vol. II. 70–167.

[2] Dorner (*Gesch. der protest. Theol.*, p. 300): " *Das Charakteristische in allen Schriften Zwingli's vor 1524 ist sein Gegensatz gegen das heil. Abendmahl als Opfer und Messe.*" So also Ebrard.

is forever fruitful and efficacious.[1] He denied the corporal
eating as Capernaitic and useless, but he admitted a spiritual participation in the crucified body and blood by faith.
Christ is both "host and feast" in the holy communion.

His last word on the subject of the eucharist (in the Confession to King Francis I.) is this : —

> "We believe that Christ is truly present in the Lord's Supper; yea, that
> there is no communion without such presence. . . . We believe that the true
> body of Christ is eaten in the communion, not in a gross and carnal manner,
> but in a sacramental and spiritual manner by the religious, believing and
> pious heart." [2]

This passage comes so near the Calvinistic view that it
can hardly be distinguished from it. Calvin did injustice to
Zwingli, when once in a confidential letter he called his
earlier eucharistic doctrine "profane."[3] But Zwingli in his
polemic writings laid so much stress upon the absence of
Christ's body, that the positive truth of His spiritual presence
was not sufficiently emphasized. Undoubtedly the Lord's
Supper is a commemoration of the historic Christ of the
past, but it is also a vital communion with the ever-living
Christ who is both in heaven and in his church on earth.

Zwingli's theory did not pass into any of the leading
Reformed confessions; but it was adopted by the Arminians,

---

[1] He expressed at Marburg, and in his two confessions to Charles I. and to
Francis I., his full belief in the divinity of Christ in the sense of the Nicene
and Athanasian Creeds. Dorner says (*l. c.*, p. 302): "*Dass Zwingli Christum
gegenwärtig denkt, ist unleugbar ; er sei bei diesem Mahle Wirth und
Gastmahl (hospes et epulum).*"

[2] *Christum credimus vere esse in cœna, immo non esse Domini cœnam
nisi Christus adsit . . . Adserimus igitur non sic carnaliter et crasse man-
ducari corpus Christi in cœna, ut isti perhibent, sed verum Christi corpus
credimus in cœna sacramentaliter et spiritualiter edi, a religiosa, fideli et
sancta mente, quomodo et divus Chrysostomus sentit. Et hæc est brevis
summa nostræ, immo non nostræ, sed ipsius veritatis, sententia de hac con-
troversia.* Niemeyer, *Collectio Confess.*, pp. 71, 72.

[3] Letter to Viret, September, 1542: "*De scriptis Zwinglii sic sentire, ut
sentis, tibi permitto. Neque enim omnia legi. Et fortassis sub finem vitæ
retractavit ac correxit in melius quæ temere initio exciderant. Sed in scriptis prioribus memini, quam profana sit de Sacramentis sententia.*" *Opera*,
XI. 438.

Socinians, Unitarians, and Rationalists, and obtained for a time a wide currency in all Protestant churches, even the Lutheran. But the Rationalists deny what Zwingli strongly believed, the divinity of Christ, and thus deprive the Lord's Supper of its deeper significance and power.

III. THE CALVINISTIC THEORY. — Calvin was the greatest divine and best writer among the Reformers, and his " Institutes of the Christian Religion " have almost the same importance for Reformed theology as the "Summa" of Thomas Aquinas for that of the Roman Church. He organized the ideas of the Reformation into a clear, compact system, with the freshness and depth of genius, the convincing power of logic, and a complete mastery of the Latin and French languages.[1]

His theory of the Lord's Supper occupies a *via media* between Luther and Zwingli; he combines the realism of the one with the spiritualism of the other, and saves the substance for which Luther contended, but avoids the objectionable form. He rests on the exegesis of Zwingli. He accepts the symbolical meaning of the words of institution; he rejects the corporal presence, the oral manducation, the participation of the body and blood by unbelievers, and the ubiquity of Christ's body. But at the same time he strongly asserts a spiritual real presence, and a spiritual real participation of Christ's body and blood by faith. While Zwingli dwelt chiefly on the negative, he emphasizes the positive, element. While the mouth receives the visible signs of bread and wine, the soul receives by faith, and by faith alone, the things signified and sealed thereby; that is, the body and blood of

---

[1] Henri Martin (*Histoire de France*, Tom. VIII. 188 sq.) says of Calvin's *Institutes* that they gave a religious code to the Reform in France and in a great part of Europe," and that it is " *une vraie ' Somme' théologique, où se trouve impliqué l'ordre civil même, et qui n'est pas, comme celle de Thomas d'Aquin, le résumé d'un système établi, mais le programme et le code d'un système à établir. . . . Luther attire : Calvin impose et retient. . . . Volonté et logique, voilà Calvin*" (p. 185). He calls him " *le premier écrivain par la durée et l'influence de sa langue, de son style.*"

Christ with the benefit of his atoning death and the virtue of his immortal life.   He combines the crucified Christ with the glorified Christ, and brings the believer into contact with the whole Christ.   He lays great stress on the agency of the Holy Spirit in the ordinance, which was overlooked by Luther and Zwingli, but which appears in the ancient liturgies in the invocation of the Holy Spirit.   It is the Holy Spirit who unites in a supernatural manner what is separated in space, and conveys to the believing communicant the life-giving virtue of the flesh of Christ now glorified in heaven.[1]   When Calvin requires the communicant to ascend to heaven to feed on Christ there, he does, of course, not mean a locomotion, but that devotional *sursum corda* of the ancient liturgies, which is necessary in every act of worship, and is effected by the power of the Holy Spirit.

Calvin discussed the eucharistic question repeatedly and fully in his *Institutes* and in separate tracts.   I select a few extracts from his *Institutes* (Book IV., ch. XVII. 10 sqq.), which contain his first and last thoughts on the subject.

(10) "The sum is, that the flesh and blood of Christ feed our souls just as bread and wine maintain and support our corporal life.   For there would be no aptitude in the sign, did not our souls find their nourishment in Christ. This could not be, did not Christ truly form one with us, and refresh us by the eating of his flesh, and the drinking of his blood.   But though it seems an incredible thing that the flesh of Christ, while at such a distance from us in respect of place, should be food to us, let us remember how far the secret

---

[1] Some of the strongest passages on this point occur in his polemic tracts against Westphal.   In the Second Defense he says: " *Christum corpore absentem doceo nihilominus non tantum divina sua virtute, quæ ubique diffusa est, nobis adesse, sed etiam facere ut nobis vivifica sit sua caso* " (*Opera*, IX. 76). " *Spiritus sui virtute Christus locorum distantiam superat ad vitam nobis e sua carne inspirandam* " (p. 77).   And in his last admonition: " *Hæc nostræ doctrinæ summa est, carnem Christi panem esse vivificum, quia dum fide in eam coalescimus, vere animas nostras alit et pascit.   Hoc nonnisi spiritualiter fieri docemus, quia hujus sacræ unitatis vinculum arcana est et incomprehensibilis Spiritus Sancti virtus* " (p. 162).   For a good exposition of the Calvinistic theory which substantially agrees with ours, we may refer to Ebrard (*Abendmahl*, II. 550–570), Stähelin (*Calvin*, I. 222 sqq.), and Nevin (*Mystical Presence*).

virtue of the Holy Spirit surpasses all our conceptions, and how foolish it is to wish to measure its immensity by our feeble capacity. Therefore, what our mind does not comprehend, let faith conceive; viz., that the Spirit truly unites things separated by space. That sacred communion of flesh and blood by which Christ transfuses his life into us, just as if it penetrated our bones and marrow, he testifies and seals in the Supper, and that not by presenting a vain or empty sign, but by there exerting an efficacy of the Spirit by which he fulfils what he promises. And truly the thing there signified he exhibits and offers to all who sit down at that spiritual feast, although it is beneficially received by believers only who receive this great benefit with true faith and heartfelt gratitude." . . .

"(18) . . . Though Christ withdrew his flesh from us, and with his body ascended to heaven, he sits at the right hand of the Father; that is, he reigns in power and majesty, and the glory of the Father. This kingdom is not limited by any intervals of space, nor circumscribed by any dimensions. Christ can exert his energy wherever he pleases, in earth and heaven, can manifest his presence by the exercise of his power, can always be present with his people, breathing into them his own life, can live in them, sustain, confirm, and invigorate them, and preserve them safe, just as if he were with them in the body; in fine, can feed them with his own body, communion with which he transfuses into them. After this manner, the body and blood of Christ are exhibited to us in the sacrament.

"(19) The presence of Christ in the Supper we must hold to be such as neither affixes him to the element of bread, nor encloses him in bread, nor circumscribes him in any way (this would obviously detract from his celestial glory); and it must, moreover, be such as neither divests him of his just dimensions, nor dissevers him by differences of place, nor assigns to him a body of boundless dimensions, diffused through heaven and earth. All these things are clearly repugnant to his true human nature. Let us never allow ourselves to lose sight of the two restrictions. First, let there be nothing derogatory to the heavenly glory of Christ. This happens whenever he is brought under the corruptible elements of this world, or is affixed to any earthly creatures. Secondly, let no property be assigned to his body inconsistent with his human nature. This is done when it is either said to be infinite, or made to occupy a variety of places at the same time.

"But when these absurdities are discarded, I willingly admit any thing which helps to express the true and substantial communication of the body and blood of the Lord, as exhibited to believers under the sacred symbols of the Supper, understanding that they are received, not by the imagination or intellect merely, but are enjoyed in reality as the food of eternal life."

Calvin's theory was not disapproved by Luther, who knew it, was substantially approved by Melanchthon in 1540, and adopted by all the leading Reformed Confessions of faith. We select a few specimens from one of the earliest and from the latest Calvinistic standards: —

HEIDELBERG CATECHISM (1563).

Question 76. What is it to eat the crucified body, and drink the shed blood, of Christ?

Answer. It is not only to embrace with a believing heart all the sufferings and death of Christ, and thereby to obtain the forgiveness of sins and life eternal; but moreover also, to be so united more and more to his sacred body by the Holy Ghost, who dwells both in Christ and in us, that although He is in heaven, and we on the earth, we are nevertheless flesh of His flesh and bone of His bones, and live and are governed forever by one Spirit, as members of the same body are by one soul.

Q. 78. Do, then, the bread and wine become the real body and blood of Christ?

A. No: but as the water, in baptism, is not changed into the blood of Christ, nor becomes the washing away of sins itself, being only the divine token and assurance thereof; so also, in the Lord's Supper, the sacred bread does not become the body of Christ itself, though agreeably to the nature and usage of sacraments it is called the body of Christ.

Q. 79. Why, then, doth Christ call the bread His body, and the cup His blood, or the New Testament in His blood; and St. Paul, the communion of the body and blood of Christ?

A. Christ speaks thus not without great cause; namely, not only to teach us thereby, that, like as bread and wine sustain this temporal life, so also His crucified body and shed blood are the true meat and drink of our souls unto life eternal; but much more, by this visible sign and pledge to assure us that we are as really partakers of His true body and blood, through the working of the Holy Ghost, as we receive by the mouth of the body these holy tokens in remembrance of Him; and that all His sufferings and obedience are as certainly our own, as if we had ourselves suffered and done all in our own persons.

WESTMINSTER CONFESSION OF FAITH (1647).

Chapter XXIX., section VII.

Worthy receivers, outwardly partaking of the visible elements in this sacrament, do then also inwardly by faith, really and indeed, yet not carnally and corporally, but spiritually, receive and feed upon Christ crucified, and all benefits of his death: the body and blood of Christ being then not corporally or carnally in, with, or under the bread and wine; yet as really, but spiritually, present to the faith of believers in that ordinance, as the elements themselves are, to the outward senses.

WESTMINSTER LARGER CATECHISM (1647).

Question 170. How do they that worthily communicate in the Lord's Supper feed upon the body and blood of Christ therein?

Answer. As the body and blood of Christ are not corporally or carnally present in, with, or under the bread and wine in the Lord's Supper; and yet are spiritually present to the faith of the receiver, no less truly and really than the elements themselves are to their outward senses; so they that worthily communicate in the sacrament of the Lord's Supper, do therein feed upon the body and blood of Christ, not after a corporal or carnal, but in a spiritual manner; yet truly and really, while by faith they receive and apply unto themselves Christ crucified, and all the benefits of his death.

CHAPTER VIII.

THE POLITICAL SITUATION BETWEEN 1526 AND 1529.

§ 112. *The First Diet of Speier, and the Beginning of the Territorial System. 1526.*

I. The documents in WALCH, XVI. 243 sqq. *Neue Sammlung der Reichs-abschiede*, II. 273-75. BUCHHOLTZ: *Ferdinand I.*, Bd. III.

II. RANKE, II. 249 sqq. JANSSEN, III. 39 sqq. J. NEY (Prot. minister in Speier): *Analekten zur Gesch. des Reichstags zu Speier im J. 1526*, in Brieger's "Zeitschrift für Kirchengesch.," Gotha, 1885, p. 300 sqq., and 1887, p. 300 sqq. (New Documents from the archives of Karlsruh and Würzburg). WALTER FRIEDENSBURG: *Der Reichstag zu Speier*, 1526, *im Zusammenhang der polit. und kirchl. Entwicklung Deutschlands im Reformationszeitalter*, Berlin, 1887 (xiv. and 602 pages). Previous discussions by VEESEMEIER and KLUCKHOHN (in "Hist. Zeitschrift," 1886). Friedensburg used much new material preserved in the archives of Hamburg and other cities. CHARLES G. ALBERT: *The Diet of Speyer, the Rise and Necessity of Protestantism*, in the "Luth. Quart. Review" (Gettysburg, Penn.), for January, 1888.

WE must now consider the political situation which has in part been presupposed in previous sections.

As Protestantism advanced, the execution of the Edict of Worms became less and less practicable. This was made manifest at the imperial Diet of Speier, held in the summer of 1526 under Archduke Ferdinand, in the name of the Emperor.[1] The Protestant princes dared here for the first time to profess their faith, and were greatly strengthened by the delegates of the imperial cities in which the Reformation had

---

[1] Speier, or Speyer, is an old German city on the left bank of the Rhine, the seat of a bishop, with a cathedral and the graves of eight German kings, the capital of the Bavarian Palatinate. It became the birthplace of the name "Protestants" in 1529. See below, § 115, p. 692.

made great progress.   The threatening invasion of the Turks, and the quarrel of the Emperor with the Pope, favored the Protestant cause, and inclined the Roman Catholic majority to forbearance.

The Diet came with the consent of Ferdinand to the unanimous conclusion, Aug. 27, that a general or national council should be convened for the settlement of the church question, and that in the mean time, in matters concerning the Edict of Worms, "every State shall so live, rule, and believe as it may hope and trust to answer before God and his imperial Majesty." [1]

This important action was not meant to annul the Edict of Worms, and to be a permanent law of religious liberty, which gave to each member of the Diet the right to act as he pleased.[2]   It was no legal basis of territorial self-government, and no law at all.   It was, as indicated by the terms, only an armistice, or temporary suspension of the Edict of Worms till the meeting of a general council, and within the limits of obedience to the Catholic Emperor who had no idea of granting religious liberty, or even toleration, to Protestants.

But in its practical effect the resolution of 1526 went far

---

[1] "*Demnach haben wir uns jetzt einmüthiglich verglichen und vereiniget, mittlerzeit des Concilii, oder aber Nationalversammlung, nichtsdestoweniger mit unsern Unterthanen, ein jeglicher in Sachen so das Edict durch kaiserl. Majestät auf dem Reichstag zu Worms gehalten, ausgangen, belangen möchten, für sich also zu leben, zu regieren und zu halten, wie ein jeder solches gegen Gott und kaiserliche Majestät hoffet und vertraut zu verantworten.*"   See the *Reichsabschied* (recess) in Walch, XVI. 266, and in Giesefer, III. I. 223 (Germ. ed.; IV. 126 Am. ed.).   The acts are now published in full by Friedensburg.

[2] This was the view heretofore taken by most Protestant historians, *e.g.*, by Kurtz (II. 31, ed. 9th), who calls the recess "*die reichsgesetzliche Legitimation der Territorialverfassung,*" and by Fisher (*Hist. of the Christ. Ch.*, p. 304): "This act gave the Lutheran movement a legal existence."   The correct view is stated by Janssen (III. 51): "*Der Speierer Abschied bildet keineswegs eine positive Rechtsgrundlage, wohl aber den Ausgangspunkt für die Ausbildung neuer Landeskirchen.*"   Kluckhohn, Friedensburg, and his reviewer, Kawerau (in the "Theol. Literaturzeitung," Dec. 3, 1887), arrive at the same conclusion.

beyond its intention. It was a great help to the cause of Protestantism, especially as the council which the Diet contemplated, and which the Emperor himself repeatedly urged upon the Pope, was postponed for twenty years. In the mean time the Protestant princes, notably Philip of Hesse at the Synod of Homberg (Oct. 20, 1526), and the Elector of Saxony, interpreted the decree according to their wishes, and made the best use of the temporary privilege of independent action, regardless of its limitations or the views of the Emperor. Luther himself understood the Diet of Speier as having given him a temporary acquittal of heresy.[1]

At all events, from this time dates the exercise of territorial sovereignty, and the establishment of separate State churches in Germany. And as that country is divided into a number of sovereign States, there are there as many Protestant church organizations as Protestant States, according to the maxim that the ruler of the territory is the ruler of religion within its bounds (*cujus regio, ejus religio*).

Every Protestant sovereign hereafter claimed and exercised the so-called *jus reformandi religionem*, and decided the church question according to his own faith and that of the majority of his subjects. Saxony, Hesse, Prussia, Anhalt, Lüneburg, East-Friesland, Schleswig-Holstein, Silesia, and the cities of Nürnberg, Augsburg, Frankfurt, Ulm, Strassburg, Bremen, Hamburg, Lübeck, adopted the Reformation.

---

[1] He alludes to it in a polemical tract against Duke George of Saxony from the year 1529 as follows: "*Auch so bin ich auf dem Reichstage zu Speir durch ein öffentlichs kaiserlichs Reichsdecret wiederumb befreiet, oder zum wenigsten befristet* [freed at least for a season], *dass man mich nicht kann einen Ketzer schelten; weil daselbst beschlossen ist von Allen einträchtiglich, dass ein jeglicher solle und müge glauben, wie ers wisse gegen Gott und kaiserliche Majestät zu verantworten; und ich billig daraus als die Ungehorsamen dem Reich und Aufrührischen beklagen möcht alle die, so mich einen Ketzer schelten. Hat das Gebot zu Worms gegolten, da ich verdampt ward ohn Bewilligung der besten und höhesten Stände des Reichs: warumb sollt mir denn das Gebot zu Speir nicht auch gelten, welchs einträchtlich durch alle Stände des Reichs beschlossen und angenommen ist.*" Erl. ed., vol. VIII. p. 14.

The princes of the territories and the magistrates of the cities consulted the theologians and preachers; but the congregations had no voice, not even in the choice of their pastor, and submitted in passive obedience. The powerful house of Austria, with the Emperor, and the Dukes of Bavaria, adhered to the old faith, and hotly contested the principle of independent state action on the church question, as being contrary to all the traditions of the Empire and of the Roman Church, which is constitutionally exclusive and intolerant.

The Protestant princes and theologians were likewise intolerant, though in a less degree, and prohibited the mass and the Roman religion wherever they had the power. Each party was bent upon victory, and granted toleration only from necessity or prudence when the dissenting minority was strong enough to assert its rights. Toleration was the fruit of a bitter contest, and was at last forced upon both parties as a *modus vivendi*. Protestantism had to conquer the right to exist, by terrible sacrifices. The right was conceded by the Augsburg treaty of peace, 1555, and finally established by the Westphalian treaty, 1648, which first uses the term *toleration* in connection with religion, and remains valid to this day, in spite of the protest of the Pope. The same policy of toleration was adopted in England after the downfall of the Stuart dynasty in 1688, and included all orthodox Protestants, but excluded the Roman Catholics, who were not emancipated till 1829. In Germany, toleration was first confined to three confessions, — the Roman Catholic, the Lutheran, and the German Reformed, — but was gradually extended to other religious communions which are independent of state support and state control.

NOTES.

TOLERATION AND FREEDOM.

Toleration is far from religious liberty, but a step towards it. Toleration is a concession of the government on the ground of necessity or expediency, and may be withdrawn or extended. Even despotic Russia and Turkey are tolerant, the one towards Mohammedans, the other towards Christians, because they cannot help it. To kill or to exile all dissenters would be suicidal folly. But they allow no departure from the religion of the State, and no propagandism against its interests.

Religious liberty is an inviolable and inalienable right which belongs to all men, within the limits of public morals and safety. God alone is the Lord of conscience, and no power on earth has a right to interfere with it. The full enjoyment and public exercise of religious liberty require a peaceful separation of church and state, which makes each independent, self-governing, and self-supporting in its own sphere, and secures to the church the legal protection of the state, and to the state the moral support of the church. This is the American theory of religious freedom, as guaranteed by the Federal Constitution of 1787 : it prevents the state from persecuting the church, and the churches from persecuting each other, and confines them to their proper moral and spiritual vocation. The American principle of the *legal* equality of religious confessions was proposed by the Frankfort Parliament in 1849, triumphed in the new German empire, 1870, and is making steady progress all over the civilized world. (See the author's *Church and State in the United States*, N. Y., 1888.)

§ 113. *The Emperor and the Pope. The Sacking of Rome, 1527.*

Contemporary accounts of the sacking of Rome are collected by CARLO MILANESI: *Il Sacco di Roma del MDXXVII.*, Florence, 1867. ALFRED VON REUMONT: *Geschichte der Stadt Rom* (Berlin, 1870), vol. III. 194 sqq.; comp. the liter. he gives on p. 846 sq. RANKE: Bk. V. (vol. III. 1 sqq.). JANSSEN: vol. III. 124 sqq.

Charles V. neither signed nor opposed the edict of Speier. He had shortly before fallen out with Clement VII., because this Pope released King Francis I. from the hard conditions of peace imposed upon him after his defeat at Pavia, June 26, 1526, and placed himself at the head of a Franco-Italian league against the preponderance of Austria (" the Holy League " of Cognac, May 22, 1526). The league of the Emperor and the Pope had brought about the Edict of Worms ; the breach between the two virtually annulled it at the Diet of Speier. Had the Emperor now embraced the Protestant doctrines, he might have become the head of a German imperial state church. But all his instincts were against Protestantism.

His quarrel with the Pope was the occasion of a fearful calamity to the Eternal City. The Spanish and German troops of the Emperor, under the lead of Constable Charles de Bourbon, and the old warrior Frundsberg (both enemies of the Pope), marched to Rome with an army of twenty thousand men, and captured the city, May 6, 1527. Bourbon, the ablest general of Charles, but a traitor to his native France, was struck by a musket-ball in climbing a ladder, and fell dead in the moment of victory. The pope fled to the castle St. Angelo. The soldiers, especially the Spaniards, deprived of their captain, surpassed the barbarians of old in beastly and refined cruelty, rage and lust. For eight days they plundered the papal treasury, the churches, libraries, and palaces, to the extent of ten millions of gold; they did not spare even the tomb of St. Peter and the corpse of Julius II., and committed nameless outrages upon defenseless priests, monks, and nuns. German soldiers marched through the streets in episcopal and cardinal's robes, dressed a donkey like a priest, and by a grim joke proclaimed Luther as pope of Rome.

Never before had Rome suffered such indignities and loss. The sacking was a crime against civilization, humanity, and religion; but, at the same time, a fearful judgment of God upon the worldliness of the papacy, and a loud call to repentance.[1]

When the news reached Germany, many rejoiced "at the fall of Babylon." But Melanchthon, rising above bigotry, said in one of his finest addresses to the students of Wittenberg: "Why should we not lament the fall of Rome, which

---

[1] Reumont (*l. c.* III. 201) says: "*Wüster und andauernder ist keine Stadt geplündert, sind keine Einwohner misshandelt worden als Rom und die Römer. Spanier wie Teutsche haben bei diesem grausen Werke gewetteifert, jene mit erfinderischer Unmenschlichkeit, diese mit wilder Barbarei. Kirchen, Klöster, Palläste, Wohnhäuser, Hütten wurden mit gleicher Beutelust ausgeleert und verwüstet, Männer, Frauen, Kinder mit gleicher Grausamkeit misshandelt.*"

is the common mother-city of all nations? I indeed feel this
calamity no less than if it were my own native place. The
robber hordes were not restrained by considerations of the
dignity of the city, nor the remembrance of her services for
the laws, sciences, and arts of the world. This is what we
grieve over. Whatever be the sins of the Pope, Rome
should not be made to suffer." He acquitted the Emperor
of all blame, and held the army alone responsible.[1]

§ 114. *A War Panic, 1528.*

On the "*Packische Händel*," see WALCH (XVI. 444), GIESELER (III. 1, 229),
RANKE (III. 26), JANSSEN (III. 109), ROMMEL'S, and WILLE'S mono-
graphs on *Philip of Hesse;* and ST. EHSES: *Geschichte der Packschen
Händel*, Freiburg i. B. 1881.

The action of the Diet of 1526, and the quarrel between
the Emperor and the Pope, were highly favorable to the
progress of the Reformation. But the good effect was in
great part neutralized by a stupendous fraud which brought
Germany to the brink of a civil war.

Philip of Hesse, an ardent, passionate, impulsive, ambitious prince, and patron of Protestantism, was deceived by
an unprincipled and avaricious politician, Otto von Pack,
provisional chancellor of the Duchy of Saxony, into the
belief that Ferdinand of Austria, the Electors of Mainz and
Brandenburg, the Dukes of Saxony and Bavaria, and other
Roman Catholic rulers had concluded a league at Breslau,
May 15, 1527, for the extermination of Protestantism. He
procured at Dresden a sealed copy of the forged document,
for which he paid Pack four thousand guilders. He persuaded the Elector John of Saxony of its genuineness, and
concluded with him, in all haste, a counter-league, March 9,
1528. They secured aid from other princes, and made
expensive military preparations, to anticipate by a master-
stroke an attack of the enemy.

---

[1] "Corp. Ref.," XI. 130; C. Schmidt, *Phil. Melanchthon*, p. 135 sq.

Fortunately, the Reformers of Wittenberg were consulted, and prevented an open outbreak by their advice. Luther deemed the papists bad enough for any thing, but was from principle opposed to aggressive war;[1] Melanchthon saw through the forgery, and felt keenly mortified. When the fictitious document was published, the Roman Catholic princes indignantly denied it. Duke George denounced Pack as a traitor.[2] Archduke Ferdinand declared that he never dreamed of such a league.

The rash conduct of Philip put the Protestant princes in the position of aggressors and disturbers of the public peace, and the whole affair brought shame and disgrace upon their cause.

§ 115. *The Second Diet of Speier, and the Protest of 1529.*

WALCH, XVI. 315 sqq. J. J. MÜLLER: *Historie von der evang. Stände Protestation und Appellation wider den Reichsabschied zu Speier, 1529,* Jena, 1705. TITTMANN: *Die Protestation der evang. Stände mit hist. Erläuterungen,* Leipzig, 1829. A. JUNG: *Gesch. des Reichstags zu Speier, 1529,* Leipzig, 1830. J. NEY (Protest. pastor at Speier): *Geschichte des Reichstags zu Speier im Jahr 1529. Mit einem Anhange ungedruckter Akten und Briefe,* Hamburg, 1880. RANKE, III. 102–116. JANSSEN, III. 130–146.

Under these discouragements the second Diet of Speier was convened in March, 1529, for action against the Turks, and against the further progress of Protestantism. The Catholic dignitaries appeared in full force, and were flushed with hopes of victory. The Protestants felt that "Christ was again in the hands of Caiaphas and Pilate."[3]

The Diet neutralized the recess of the preceding Diet of 1526; it virtually condemned (without, however, annulling) the innovations made; and it forbade, on pain of the imperial

---

[1] See his letters on this subject in De Wette, III. 314 sqq.

[2] After a fugitive life, Pack was beheaded as a forger in the Netherlands, 1536, at the solicitation of Duke George.

[3] Words of Jacob Sturm, the ambassador of Strassburg, from the middle of March.

ban, any further reformation until the meeting of the council, which was now positively promised for the next year by
the Emperor and the Pope.   The Zwinglians and Anabaptists
were excluded even from toleration.   The latter were to be
punished by death.

The Lutheran members of the Diet, under the well-founded
impression that the prohibition of any future reformation
meant death to the whole movement, entered in the legal form
of an appeal for themselves, their subjects and for all who
now or shall hereafter believe in the Word of God, the famous
protest of April 25, 1529, against all those measures of the
Diet which were contrary to the Word of God, to their conscience, and to the decision of the Diet of 1526, and appealed
from the decision of the majority to the Emperor, to a
general or German council, and impartial Christian judges.[1]
The document was signed by the Elector John of Saxony,
Margrave George of Brandenburg, Dukes Ernest and Francis
of Braunschweig-Lüneburg, Landgrave Philip of Hesse,
Prince Wolfgang of Anhalt, and the representatives of fourteen imperial cities, including Strassburg and St. Gall of the
Zwinglian persuasion.   They were determined to defend
themselves against every act of violence of the majority.
Their motto was that of Elector John the Constant: "The
Word of God abideth forever."   They deserve the name of
confessors of the evangelical faith and the rights of conscience in the face of imminent danger.[2]

The protest of Speier was a renewal and expansion of
Luther's protest at Worms.   The protest of a single monk

[1] The great *Instrumentum appellationis* is given by Müller, Walch, Jung,
and in substance by Gieseler, *l.c.*   April 25 (a Sunday) is the date of the
legal completion of the protest (Ranke, III. 113).   The dates of the preparatory steps are April 19 and 22.

[2] Janssen denies the right of such protest, and dates from it the schism
of the German nation.   "*Von dem Tage zu Speier an,*" he says, III. 144,
"*beginnt die eigentliche Spaltung der deutschen Nation.*"   Fortunately, the
schism has been healed in 1870 by Providence, without the aid of the Pope
and against his wish and will.

had become the protest of princes and representatives of leading cities of the empire, who now for the first time appeared as an organized party. It was a protest of conscience bound in the Word of God against tyrannical authority.

The appeal was not entertained. The Emperor, who soon afterwards concluded peace with the Pope (June 29, 1529), and with the King of France (Aug. 5), refused even to grant the delegation of the Protestant States a respectful hearing at Piacenza (September), and kept them prisoners for a while.

From this protest and appeal the Lutherans were called *Protestants;* with good reason, if we look at their attitude to Rome, which remains the same to this day. It is the duty of the church at all times to protest against sin, error, corruption, tyranny, and every kind of iniquity. But the designation, which has since become a general term for evangelical Christians, is negative, and admits of an indiscriminate application to all who dissent from popery, no matter on what grounds and to what extent. It must be supplemented by the more important positive designation *Evangelical.* The gospel of Christ, as laid down in the New Testament, and proclaimed again in its primitive purity and power by the Reformation, is the basis of historical Protestantism, and gives it vitality and permanency. The protest of Speier was based objectively upon the Word of God, subjectively upon the right of private judgment and conscience, and historically upon the liberal decision of the Diet of 1526.[1]

---

[1] It is remarkable that one of the most conservative branches of Protestant Christendom, " the Protestant Episcopal Church in the United States of America," adopted the term as a part of its *official* title when, after the Revolutionary War, it assumed an independent organization. This could not be done in the state of churchly sentiment which has since come to prevail in that church. Vigorous efforts have been made within the last few years to get rid of the term *Protestant,* and to substitute for it *Catholic,* or *American,* or some other more or less presumptuous epithet, but without success so far. The secession from this body which was organized in 1873 took the name of " The Reformed Episcopal Church."

Unfortunately, the moral force of the protest of Speier was soon weakened by dissensions among the signers. Luther and Melanchthon, who at that time were quite agreed on the eucharistic question, seriously objected to all political and military alliances, and especially to an alliance with the Zwinglians, whom they abhorred as heretics.[1] They prevented vigorous measures of defense. Philip of Hesse, who was in full political, and in half theological, sympathy with the Swiss and Zwinglians, brought about in October of the same year the conference at Marburg in the hope of healing the Protestant schism : but the conference failed of its main object, and Protestantism had to carry on the conflict with Rome as a broken army.

§ 116. *The Reconciliation of the Emperor and the Pope. The Crowning of the Emperor. 1529.*

The Emperor expressed to the Pope his deep regret at the sacking of the holy city. His breach with him was purely political and temporary. The French troops again entered Lombardy. Henry VIII. of England sympathized with Francis and the Pope. The Spanish counselors of Charles represented to him that the imprisonment of the vicar of Christ was inconsistent with the traditional loyalty of Spain to the holy see.

On Nov. 26, 1527, the Emperor concluded an agreement with the Pope by which he was released from confinement, and reinstated in his temporal power (except over a few fortified places), on promise of paying the soldiers, and convening a council for the reformation of the church. For a while Clement distrusted the Emperor, and continued his Franco-Italian policy ; but at last they definitely made peace, June 29, 1529. The Pope acknowledged the sovereignty of the

---

[1] In a letter to Elector John, May 22, 1529 (De Wette, III. 455), Luther went so far as to call the Zwinglians "audacious enemies of God and his Word, who fight against God and the sacrament."

Emperor in Italy, which he had heretofore opposed; the Emperor guaranteed to him the temporal possessions, with a reservation of imperial rights.

They held a personal conference at Bologna in November of that year. They were well matched in political and diplomatic shrewdness, and settled their secular disputes as well as they could. Charles was crowned Roman emperor, Feb. 24, 1530, at Bologna, the only emperor crowned outside of St. Peter's at Rome, and the last German emperor crowned by the Pope. The dignitaries who graced the occasion were chiefly Spanish and Italian noblemen. Only one of the seven German electors was present, Philip of the Palatinate. The wooden awning which was constructed between the palace and the church of San Petronio broke down, but the Emperor escaped an accident. Clothed in a richly jewelled robe, he was anointed with oil, and received from the bishop of Rome the crown of Charlemagne as the temporal head of Western Christendom, and swore to protect the Pope and the Roman-Catholic Church with their possessions, dignities, and rights.[1]

This event was the sunset of the union of the German empire with the papal theocracy.

The German electors complained that they were not invited to the coronation, nor consulted about the treaties with the Italian States, and entered a formal protest.

Early in May, 1530, the Emperor crossed the Alps on his way to the Diet of Augsburg, which was to decide the fate of Lutheranism in Germany.

---

[1] How has the situation changed since! In the same once papal city where the Emperor was crowned by the Pope with all the splendor of the Catholic ceremonial, the eighth centennial of the University — the oldest in the world (" *Bononia docet* ") — was celebrated June 11–13, 1888, in the presence of the King and Queen, with unbounded enthusiasm for free and united Italy, which has shaken off the yoke of petty tyrants, and is determined to resist all attempts at a restoration of the temporal power of the papacy. The Italians are willing to take their religion from the Pope, but not their politics. Practically, church and state are almost as separate in Italy, since 1870, as in the United States.

CHAPTER IX.

THE DIET AND CONFESSION OF AUGSBURG. A.D. 1530.

§ 117. *The Diet of Augsburg.*

I. Sources. Collection in WALCH, XVI. 747-2142. LUTHER's Letters of
the year 1530, in De Wette, vol. IV. MELANCHTHON's Letters in the
"Corpus Reformatorum," ed. Bretschneider and Bindseil, vol. II., and
documents relating to the Augsb. Conf. in vol. XXVI. SPALATIN,
Annal., ed. by Cyprian, 131-289. The Roman Cath. representation:
*Pro Religione Christiana Res Gestæ in Comitiis Augustæ Vindelicorum
habitis, 1530*, reprinted in Cyprian's *Historie der Augsb. Conf.* BRÜCK
wrote a refutation published by Förstemann, "Archiv für Ref. Gesch.,"
1831. Collection of documents by FÖRSTEMANN: *Urkundenbuch zu der
Gesch. des Reichstages zu Augsburg in J. 1530.* Halle, 1833, '35, 2 vols.
By the same: *Neues Urkundenbuch*, Hamburg, 1842. SCHIRRMACHER :
*Briefe und Acten zur Gesch. des Religionsgesprächs zu Marburg, 1529,
und des Reichstages zu Augsburg, 1530, nach der Handschrift des Aurifaber*, Gotha, 1876.

II. Histories of the Augsburg Diet and Confession. See list in "Corp.
Ref." XXVI. 101-112. D. CHYTRÆUS (Kochhafe): *Historie der Augsb.
Conf.*, Rostock, 1576, Frcf. 1577, 1578, 1600. G. CŒLESTIN: *Hist. Comi-
tiorum a. 1530 Augustæ celebratorum*, Frcf. 1577, 4 vols. fol. E. SAL.
CYPRIAN: *Hist. der Augsb. Conf.*, Gotha, 1730. CHR. A. SALIG: *His-
torie der Augsb. Conf. und derselben Apologie*, Halle, 1730-35, in 3 parts.
WEBER: *Vollständige Gesch. der Augsb. Conf.*, Frcf. 1783-84, 2 vols.
PLANCK: *Gesch. des protest. Lehrbegriff's* (Leipz. 1792), vol. III. I.
1-178. FICKENSCHER: *Gesch. des Reichstages zu Augsb. 1530*, Nürnb.
1830. PFAFF: *Gesch. des Reichstags zu Augsburg, 1530*, Stuttg. 1830.
Add special works on the Augsb. Conf. mentioned in § 119.

III. The relevant sections in the general Church Histories of SCHROECKH,
MOSHEIM, GIESELER, etc. ; in the Histories of the Reformation by MAR-
HEINEKE, HAGENBACH, MERLE D'AUB., FISHER; in the general His-
tories of Germany by RANKE (Prot.), vol. III. 162-215, and JANSSEN
(Rom. Cath.), vol. III. 165-211. Also the numerous Lives of Luther
(e.g., KÖSTLIN, Book VI., chs. XI. and XII., vol. II. 198 sqq.), and
Melanchthon (e.g., C. SCHMIDT, 190-250).

IV. Special points. H. VIRK: *Melanchthon's Politische Stellung auf dem Reichstag zu Augsburg*, in Brieger's " Zeitschrift für Kirchengeschichte," 1887, pp. 67 and 293 sqq.

THE situation of Protestantism in 1530 was critical. The Diet of Speier had forbidden the further progress of the Reformation : the Edict of Worms was in full legal force ; the Emperor had made peace with the Pope, and received from him the imperial crown at Bologna; the Protestants were divided among themselves, and the Conference at Marburg had failed to unite them against the common foe. At the same time the whole empire was menaced by a foreign power. The Turks under Suleiman "the Magnificent," who called himself "Lord of all rulers, Dispenser of crowns to the monarchs of the earth, the Shadow of God over the world," had reached the summit of their military power, and approached the gates of Vienna in September, 1529. They swore by the beard of Mohammed not to rest till the prayers of the prophet of Mecca should be heard from the tower of St. Stephen. They were indeed forced to retire with a loss of eighty thousand men, but threatened a second attempt, and in the mean time laid waste a great part of Hungary.

Under these circumstances the Diet of Augsburg convened, April 8, 1530. Its object was to settle the religious question, and to prepare for war against the Turks. The invitation dated Jan. 21, 1530, from Bologna, carefully avoids all irritating allusions, sets forth in strong language the danger of foreign invasion, and expresses the hope that all would co-operate for the restoration of the unity of the holy empire of the German nation in the one true Christian religion and church.

But there was little prospect for such co-operation. The Roman majority meant war against the Protestants and the Turks as enemies of church and state ; the Protestant minority meant defense against the Papists and the Turks as the enemies of the gospel. In the eyes of the former, Luther was worse than Mohammed; in the eyes of the Lutherans, the Pope was at least as bad as Mohammed. Their motto was, —

> " *Erhalt uns Herr bei Deinem Wort*
> *Und steur' des Papsts und Türken Mord.*"

The Emperor stood by the Pope and the Edict of Worms, but was more moderate than his fanatical surroundings, and treated the Lutherans during the Diet with courteous consideration, while he refused to give the Zwinglians even a hearing. The Lutherans on their part praised him beyond his merits, and were deceived into false hopes; while they would have nothing to do with the Swiss and Strassburgers, although they agreed with them in fourteen out of fifteen articles of faith.[1]

The Saxon Elector, as soon as he received the summons to the Diet, ordered the Wittenberg theologians, at the advice of Chancellor Brück, to draw up a confession of faith for possible use at Augsburg, and to meet him at Torgau. He started on the 3d of April with his son, several noblemen, Luther, Melanchthon, Jonas, Spalatin, and Agricola, stopped a few days at Coburg on the Saxon frontier, where Luther was left behind, and entered Augsburg on the 2d of May.

The Emperor was delayed on the journey through the Tyrol, and did not arrive till the 15th of June. On the following day he took a devout part in the celebration of the Corpus Christi festival. He walked in solemn procession under the most scorching heat, with uncovered head, heavy purple cloak, and a burning wax-candle. The Protestant princes absented themselves from what they regarded an idolatrous ceremony. They also declined to obey the Emperor's prohibition of evangelical preaching during the Diet.

---

[1] Luther wrote to Hausmann, July 6, 1530: "*Mirum est quam omnes ardeant amore et favore Cœsaris.*" In De Wette-Seidemann, VI. 116. Melanchthon praised the virtues of the Emperor extravagantly, even after the Diet. "Corp. Ref." II. 430 sq., 361; Virck, *l.c.*, 338 sq.

Margrave George of Brandenburg declared that he would rather lose his head than deny God. The Emperor replied: "Dear prince, not head off, not head off." [1] He imposed silence upon the preachers of both parties, except those whom he should select. The Protestant princes held service in private houses.

The Diet was opened on Monday, June 20, with high mass by the Cardinal Archbishop of Mainz, and a long sermon by Archbishop Pimpinelli of Rossano, the papal nuncio at the court of Ferdinand. He described, in elegant Latin, the tyranny of the Turks, reproved the Germans for their sleepiness and divisions, and commended the heathen Romans and Mohammedans for their religious unity, obedience, and devotion to the past. A few days afterwards (June 24) the papal nuncio at the Diet, Laurentius Campegius (Campeggi) warned the Estates not to separate from the holy Catholic church, but to follow the example of other Christian kings and powers.

The Emperor desired first to secure help against the Turks, but the Protestants insisted on the priority of the church question. He accordingly commanded them to have their confession ready within four days, and to hand it to him in writing. He did not wish it to be read before the Diet, but the Protestants insisted upon this. He then granted the reading in Latin, but the Elector of Saxony pressed the rights of the German vernacular. "We are on German soil," said he, "and therefore I hope your Majesty will allow the German language." The Emperor yielded this point, but refused the request to have the Confession read in the city hall where the Diet met.

---

[1] "*Lieber Fürst, nicht Kopf abhauen, nicht Kopf ab.*" Andreas Osiander understood him to say, "*mehr Kopf abhauen*," and so reported to Luther, June 21, 1530; adding, "*neque enim recte Germanice aut Latine novit.*" Krafft, *Briefe und Documente*, 67; Janssen, III. 166. Charles usually spoke in French; but he declared that he would sacrifice any other language, even Spanish or French, yea, one of his states, for a better knowledge of German.

On the twenty-fifth day of June — the most memorable day in the history of Lutheranism, next to the 31st of October — the Augsburg Confession was read, with a loud and firm voice, by Dr. Baier, vice-chancellor of Electoral Saxony, in the German language, before the Diet in the private chapel of the episcopal palace. The reading occupied nearly two hours. The Emperor, who knew little German and less theology, soon fell asleep.[1] But the majority listened atten tively. The Papists were surprised at the moderation of the Confession, and would have wished it more polemical and anti-catholic. The bishop of Augsburg, Christoph von Stadion, is reported to have remarked privately that it contained the pure truth. Duke William of Bavaria censured Eck for misrepresenting to him the Lutheran opinions; and when the doctor said he could refute them, not with the Scriptures, but with the fathers, he replied: " I am to understand, then, that the Lutherans are within the Scriptures, and we Catholics on the outside ?"

Dr. Brück, the Saxon chancellor who composed the preface and epilogue, handed to the Emperor a German and a Latin copy of the Confession. The Emperor kept the former, and gave the latter to the Elector of Mainz for safe-keeping. The Latin copy (in Melanchthon's own handwriting) was deposited in the archives of Brussels, and disappeared under the reign of Duke Alba. The German original, as read before the Diet, was sent, with the acts of the Diet, to the Council of Trent, and never returned. But unauthorized editions soon appeared in different places (six German, one Latin) during the Diet; and Melanchthon himself issued the Confession in both languages at Wittenberg, 1531.

Both documents were signed by seven princes; namely, the Elector John of Saxony, Landgrave Philip of Hesse,

---

[1] Brentius: " cum confessio legeretur, obdormivit." The Emperor was equally sleepy on the 3d of August during the reading of the papal confutation.

Margrave George of Brandenburg, Duke Ernest of Lüneburg, Duke John Frederick of Saxony, Duke Francis of
Lüneburg, Prince Wolfgang of Anhalt ; and by two representatives of free cities, Nürnberg and Reutlingen.

The signing required considerable courage, for it involved
the risk of the crown. When warned by Melanchthon of
the possible consequences, the Saxon Elector nobly replied :
" I will do what is right, unconcerned about my Electoral
dignity. I will confess my Lord, whose cross I esteem more
highly than all the power on earth."

This act and testimony gave great significance to the
Diet of Augsburg, and immortal glory to the confessors.
Luther gave eloquent expression to his joy, when he wrote to
Melanchthon, Sept. 15, 1530 : [1] " You have confessed Christ,
you have offered peace, you have obeyed the Emperor, you
have endured injuries, you have been drenched in their revil-
ings, you have not returned evil for evil. In brief, you have
worthily done God's holy work as becometh saints. Be glad,
then, in the Lord, and exult, ye righteous. Long enough
have ye been mourning in the world ; look up, and lift up
your heads, for your redemption draweth nigh. I will can-
onize you as a faithful member of Christ. And what greater
glory can you desire ? Is it a small thing to have yielded
Christ faithful service, and shown yourself a member worthy
of Him ? "

The only blot on the fame of the Lutheran confessors of
Augsburg is their intolerant conduct towards the Reformed,
which weakened their own cause. The four German cities
which sympathized with the Zwinglian view on the Lord's
Supper wished to sign the Confession, with the exception
of the tenth article, which rejects their view; but they were
excluded, and forced to hand in a separate confession of
faith.

[1] In De Wette, IV. 165.

§ 118. *The Negotiations, the Recess, the Peace of Nürnberg.*

The remaining transactions during this Diet were discouraging and unfruitful, and the result was a complete, but short-lived, victory of the Roman Catholic party.

Melanchthon during all this time was in a state of nervous trepidation and despondency.[1] Before the delivery of the Confession he thought it too mild and pacific; after the delivery, he thought it too severe and polemic. So far was he carried away by his desire for reunion, and fears of the disastrous results of a split, that he made a most humiliating approach to the papal legate, Campeggi, who had advised the Emperor to crush the Protestant heresy by fire and sword, to put Wittenberg under the ban, and to introduce the Spanish Inquisition into Germany. Two weeks after the delivery of the Confession, he assured him that the Lutherans did not differ in any doctrine from the Roman Church, and were willing to obey her if she only would charitably overlook a few minor changes of discipline and ceremonies, which they could not undo.[2] And, to conciliate such a power, Melanchthon kept aloof as far as possible from the Zwinglians and Strassburgers. On the 8th of July he had

---

[1] He spent his time " *in lacrymis ac luctu,*" was exhausted and emaciated. See his letters, and those of Jonas and Osiander, in " Corp. Ref.," II. 125 sq., 157, 163.

[2] He wrote two letters to Campeggi, July 6, and two to his secretary, July 7 and Aug. 5. See " Corp. Reform.," II. 168-174, and 240. In the first letter, after a quotation from Plato and some words of flattery, he makes this astounding concession (fol. 170): " *Dogma nullum habemus diversum ab ecclesia Romana. . . . Parati sumus obedire ecclesiæ Romanæ, modo ut illa pro sua clementia, qua semper erga omnes gentes usa est, pauca quædam vel dissimulet, vel relaxet quæ jam mutare nequidem si velimus queamus. . . . Ad hæc Romani pontificis auctoritatem et universam politiam ecclesiasticam reverenter colimus, modo nos non abjiciat Rom. pontifex. . . . Nullam ob rem aliam plus odii sustinemus in Germania, quam quia ecclesiæ Romanæ dogmata summa constantia defendimus. Hanc fidem Christo et Romanæ ecclesiæ ad extremum spiritum, Deo volente, præstabimus. Levis quædam dissimilitudo rituum est quæ videtur obstare concordiæ.*" Of similar import are the propositions he sent to Campeggi, Aug. 4 (fol. 246).

a personal interview with Campeggi, and Aug. 4 he submitted to him a few mild conditions of peace. The cardinal expressed his great satisfaction at these concessions, but prudently reserved his answer till he should hear from Rome.

All these approaches failed. Rome would listen to nothing but absolute submission.

Melanchthon soon found out that the papal divines, especially Eck, were full of pharisaical pride and malice. He was severely censured by the Nürnbergers and by Philip of Hesse for his weakness, and even charged by some with treason to the evangelical cause. His conduct must be judged in the light of the fact that the Roman Church allowed a certain freedom on the controverted points of anthropology and soteriology, and did not formally condemn the evangelical doctrines till several years afterwards, in the Council of Trent. The Augsburg Confession itself takes this view of the matter, by declaring at the close of the doctrinal articles: " This is the sum of doctrine among us, in which can be seen nothing which is discrepant with Scripture, *nor with the Catholic or even with the Roman Church*, so far as that Church is known from the writings of the Fathers." Melanchthon may be charged with moral weakness and mistake of judgment, but not with unfaithfulness. Luther remained true to his invaluable friend, who was indispensable to the evangelical cause, and did it the greatest service at Augsburg. He comforted him in his letters from Coburg.[1]

The Lutheran Confession was referred for answer, i.e., for refutation, to a commission of twenty Roman theologians, who were present at the Diet, including Eck, Faber, Cochlæus, Wimpina, and Dittenberger. Their answer was ready July 13, but declined by the Emperor on account of its length and bitter tone. After undergoing five revisions, it was approved and publicly read on the 3d of August before

[1] See letter of Sept. 11, 1530, in De Wette, IV. 163.

the Diet, in the same chapel in which the Protestant Confession had been read. The Emperor pronounced the answer " Christian and well-considered." He was willing to hand a copy to the Protestants, on condition to keep it private ; but Melanchthon prepared a refutation, at the request of the Lutheran princes.

The Emperor, in his desire for a peaceful result, arranged a conference between the theological leaders of the two parties. Eck, Wimpina, and Cochlæus represented the Roman Catholics ; Melanchthon, Brenz, and Schnepf, the Lutherans. The discussion began Aug. 16, but proved a failure. A smaller committee conferred from the 24th to the 29th of August, but with no better result. Melanchthon hoped against hope, and made concession after concession, to conciliate the bishops and the Emperor. But the Roman divines insisted on a recognition of an infallible church, a perpetual sacrifice, and a true priesthood. They would not even give up clerical celibacy, and the withdrawal of the cup from the laity ; and demanded a restoration of the episcopal jurisdiction, of church property, and of the convents.

Luther, writing from Coburg, urged the hesitating theologians and princes to stand by their colors. He, too, was willing to restore innocent ceremonies, and even to consent to the restoration of episcopacy, but only on condition of the free preaching of the gospel. He deemed a reconciliation in doctrine impossible, unless the Pope gave up popery.[1]

On the 22d of September the Emperor announced the Recess of the Diet ; that, after having heard and refuted the Confession of the Protestants, and vainly conferred with them, another term for consideration till April 15, 1531, be granted to them, as a special favor, and that in the mean time they should make no new innovations, nor disturb the

---

[1] *Summa, mihi in totum displicet tractatus de doctrinæ concordia, ut quæ plane sit impossibilis, nisi papa velit papatum suum aboleri."* Letter to Melanchthon, Aug. 26, in De Wette, IV. 147.

Catholics in their faith and worship, and assist the Emperor
in the suppression of the Anabaptists and those who despised
the holy sacrament. The Emperor promised to bring about
a general council within a year for the removal of ecclesiastical grievances.

The signers of the Augsburg Confession, the cities of
Frankfurt, Ulm, Schwäbisch Hall, Strassburg, Memmingen,
Constance, Lindau, refused the recess. The Lutherans protested that their Confession had never been refuted, and
offered Melanchthon's Apology of the same, which was rejected. They accepted the proposed term for consideration.

The day after the announcement of the Recess, the Elect-
or of Saxony returned home with his theologians. The
Emperor took leave of him with these words: " Uncle, uncle,
I did not look for this from you." The Elector with tears in
his eyes went away in silence. He stopped on the journey
at Nürnberg and Coburg, and reached Torgau the 9th of
October. The Landgrave of Hesse had left Augsburg in
disgust several weeks earlier (Aug. 6), without permission,
and created fears of an open revolt.

Luther was very indignant at the Recess, which was in
fact a re-affirmation of the Edict of Worms. To stop the
progress of the gospel, he declared, is to crucify the Lord
afresh; the Augsburg Confession must remain as the pure
word of God to the judgment day; the mass cannot be tolerated, as it is the greatest abomination ; nor can it be left
optional to commune in one or both kinds. Let peace be
condemned to the lowest hell, if it hinder and injure the gospel and faith. They say, if popery falls, Germany will go to
ruin. It is terrible, but I cannot help it. It is the fault of
the papists.[1] He published early in 1531 a book against the
Edict of Augsburg, which he ascribes to Pope Clement " the
arch-villain," and Campeggi, rather than to the Emperor, and
closes with the wish that " blasphemous popery may perish

---

[1] See his Exposition of chs. 6–8 of John (1530–32), Erl. ed. XLVIII. 342
sq.

in hell as John prophesies in Revelation (14:8; 18:2; 22: 20); let every Christian say, Amen."[1] In the same year he warned the Germans to be ready for defense, although it did not become him as a minister to stir up war.[2]

The Recess of the Diet was finally published Nov. 19; but its execution threatened to bring on civil war, and to give victory to the Turks. The Emperor shrank from such consequences and was seriously embarrassed. Only two of the secular princes, Elector Joachim of Brandenburg and Duke George of Saxony, were ready to assist him in severe measures. The Duke of Bavaria was dissatisfied with the Emperor's efforts to have his brother Ferdinand elected Roman king. The archbishops of Mayence and Cologne, and the bishop of Augsburg, half sympathized with the Protestants.[3] But the Emperor had promised the Pope to use all his power for the suppression of heresy, and was bound to execute as best he could the edict of the Diet after the expiration of the term of grace, April 15, 1531.

The Lutheran princes therefore formed in December, 1530, at Smalcald, a defensive alliance under the name of the Smalcaldian League. The immediate object was to protect themselves against the lawsuits of the imperial chamber of justice for the recovery of church property and the restoration of the episcopal jurisdiction. Opinions were divided on the question whether the allies in case of necessity should take up arms against the Emperor; the theologians were

---

[1] "*Glossen auf das vermeintliche kaiserliche Edict*," in Walch, XVI. 2017 sqq.; Erl. ed. XXV. 51–88.

[2] *Warnung an seine lieben Deutschen*, Erl. ed. XXV. 1–51. The Romanists regarded this as an incendiary call to open rebellion. He defended himself against this charge, in *Wider den Meuchler in Dresden*, 1531 (Erl. ed. 89–109).

[3] Albrecht accepted from Melanchthon the dedication of his commentary on the Romans and sent him a cup with thirty gold guilders (1532). He also sent to Luther's wife a present of twenty guilders, which Luther declined. Köstlin, II. 427; Janssen, III. 203. Hermann of Cologne afterwards professed Protestantism, and made an abortive attempt to reform his diocese with the aid of Bucer and Melanchthon.

opposed to it, but the lawyers triumphed over the theological scruples, and the Elector of Saxony pledged the members for defensive measures against any and every aggressor, even the Emperor. At a new convent at Smalcald in March, 1531, the League was concluded in due form for six years. It embraced Electoral Saxony, Hesse, Lüneburg, Anhalt, Mansfeld, and eleven cities. Out of this League ultimately arose the Smalcaldian war, which ended so disastrously for the Protestant princes, especially the Elector of Saxony and the Landgrave of Hesse (1547).

But for the present, war was prevented by the peace at Nürnberg, 1532. A renewed invasion of Sultan Suleiman with an army of three hundred thousand, in April, 1532, made conciliation a political and patriotic duty. The Emperor convened a Diet at Regensburg, April 17, which was transferred to Nürnberg; and there, on July 23, 1532, a temporary truce was concluded, and vigorous measures taken against the Turks, who were defeated by land and sea, and forced to retreat. The victorious Emperor went to Italy, and urged the Pope to convene the council; but the Pope was not yet ready, and found excuses for indefinite postponement.[1]

John the Constant died in the same year, of a stroke of apoplexy (Aug. 16, 1532), and was followed by his son John Frederick the Magnanimous, who in the Smalcaldian war lost his electoral dignity, but saved his evangelical faith.

§ 119. *The Augsburg Confession.*

I. Editions of the Augsb. Conf.: The best critical edition in the 26th vol. of the "Corpus Reformatorum," ed. BRETSCHNEIDER und BINDSEIL (1858), 776 pages. It gives the Invariata and the Variata, in Latin and German, with critical apparatus, list of MSS. and early editions, and the preceding documents: viz., the Articles of Visitation, the Marburg, the Schwabach, and the Torgau Articles.

---

[1] Luther chastised the Pope with all his power of irony and sarcasm for his conduct in regard to a council, in his book *Von den Conciliis und Kirchen*, 1539 (Erl. ed. XXV. 219-388).

The Confession in Latin or German, or both, is embodied in all the collections of Lutheran symbols by RECHENBERG, WALCH, WEBER, HASE, MEYER, FRANCKE, MÜLLER.

Separate modern editions by TWESTEN, TITTMANN, WEBER, WIGGERS, FÖRSTEMANN, HARTER, etc.

English translation, with Latin text, in SCHAFF, *Creeds*, III. 3–73; in English alone, in HENKEL, *Book of Concord*, 1854, and JACOBS, *Book of Concord*, Philad., 1882. The first English translation was made by RICHARD TAVERNER, London, 1536, the last, on the basis of this, by CHARLES P. KRAUTH. (See B. M. SCHMUCKER: *English Translations of the Augsb. Conf.*, Philad., 1887, 34 pp.)

On the literature compare KÖLLNER: *Symbolik der Lutherischen Kirche*, Hamburg, 1837, pp. 150–152, with a full history of the Conf., pp. 153–396.

II. Histories and monographs: the works of CHYTRÆUS, CŒLESTIN, CYPRIAN, SALIG, PFAFF, FICKENSCHER, FORSTEMANN, etc., quoted in § 117. Recent works: KÖLLNER, 1837 (see above). RUDELBACH: *Die Augsb. Conf. nach den Quellen*, Dresden, 1841. G. PLITT: *Einleitung in die Augustana*, Erlangen, 1867–68, 2 Parts; *Die Apologie der Augustana*, Erl., 1873. W. J. MANN: *A Plea for the Augsburg Confession*, Philadelphia, 1856. STUCKENBERG: *The History of the Augsb. Confession*, Philad., 1869. ZÖCKLER: *Die Augsb. Conf.*, Frkf.-a.-M., 1870. VILMAR: *Die Augsb. Confession erklärt*, Gütersloh, 1870. A brief account in SCHAFF: *Creeds* (4th ed. 1884), I. 225–242. On the Roman Catholic side see JANSSEN, III. 165–211, and L. PASTOR: *Die kirchlichen Reunionsbestrebungen während der Regierung Karls V.*, Freiburg, 1879, 22 sqq.

III. On special points: Luther's relation to the Augsb. Conf. is discussed by RÜCKERT, Jena, 1854; CALINICH, Leipz., 1861; KNAAKE, Berlin, 1863. The relation of the A. C. to the Marburg, Schwabach, and Torgau Articles is treated by ED. ENGELHARDT in the " Zeitschrift für hist. Theol.," 1865, pp. 515–529; and by TH. BRIEGER in "Kirchengesch. Studien," Leipzig, 1888, pp. 265–320.

The Augsburg Confession is the first and the most famous of evangelical confessions. It gave clear, full, systematic expression to the chief articles of faith for which Luther and his friends had been contending for thirteen years, since he raised his protest against the traffic in indulgences. By its intrinsic merits and historic connections, it has become the chief doctrinal standard of the Lutheran Church, which also bears the name of the " Church of the Augsburg Confession."

It retains this position to this day, notwithstanding the theological and ecclesiastical dissensions in that communion. It furnished the keynote to similar public testimonies of faith, and strengthened the cause of the Reformation everywhere. It had a marked influence upon the Thirty-nine Articles of the Church of England.[1] In the final revision by the author, and with the necessary change in the tenth article, it has also been frequently adopted by Reformed divines and congregations. But it was never intended, least of all by Melanchthon, who mended it to the last moment and even after its adoption, as an infallible and ultimate standard, even of the Lutheran Church. It was at first modestly called an "Apology," after the manner of the Christian Apologies in the ante-Nicene age, and meant to be simply a dispassionate statement in vindication of the Lutheran faith before the Roman Catholic world.

It is purely apologetic, and much more irenic than polemic. It aims to be, if possible, a Formula of Concord, instead of Discord. It is animated by a desire for reconciliation with Rome. Hence it is remarkably mild in tone, adheres closely to the historic faith, and avoids all that could justly offend the Catholics. It passes by, in silence, the supremacy of the Scriptures as the only rule of faith and practice, and some of the most objectionable features in the Roman system, — as indulgences, purgatory, and the papal primacy (which Melanchthon was willing to tolerate on an impossible condition). In short, it is the most churchly, the most catholic, the most conservative creed of Protestantism. It failed to conciliate Rome, but became the strongest bond of union among Lutherans.

The Confession is the ripe fruit of a gradual growth. It is based chiefly upon three previous confessional documents — the fifteen Articles of MARBURG, Oct. 4, 1529, the seventeen Articles of SCHWABACH (a modification and expansion

---

[1] See the proof in Schaff, *Creeds of Christendom*, I. 624 sqq.

of the former by Luther, with the insertion of his view of
the real presence), adopted by the Lutheran princes in a con-
vent at Schwabach, near Nürnberg, Oct. 16, 1529, and several
Articles of TORGAU against certain abuses of the Roman
Church, drawn up by Luther, Melanchthon, Jonas, and
Bugenhagen, by order of the Elector, at his residence in
Torgau, March 20, 1530.[1] The first two documents fur-
nished the material for the first or positive part of the
Augsburg Confession ; the last, for its second or polemical
part.

Melanchthon used this material in a free way, and made a
new and far better work, which bears the stamp of his scholarship and moderation, his power of condensation, and felicity
of expression. He began the preparation at Coburg, with
the aid of Luther, in April, and finished it at Augsburg,
June 24. He labored on it day and night, so that Luther
had to warn him against over-exertion. " I command you,"
he wrote to him May 12, " and all your company that they
compel you, under pain of excommunication, to take care
of your poor body, and not to kill yourself from imaginary
obedience to God. We serve God also by taking holiday
and rest."

If we look at the contents, Luther is the primary, Melanchthon the secondary, author; but the form, the method,
style, and temper are altogether Melanchthon's. Nobody else
could produce such a work. Luther would have made it
more aggressive and polemic, but less effective for the occasion. He himself was conscious of the superior qualification
of his friend for the task, and expressed his entire satisfaction
with the execution. " It pleases me very well," he wrote of
the Confession, " and I could not change or improve it ; nor
would it be becoming to do so, since I cannot tread so softly

---

[1] The *Articuli Torgavienses* were formerly confounded with the *Articuli
Suobacences* till Förstemann discovered the former in the archives at Weimar
(1833).

and gently."[1]   He would have made the tenth article on the real presence still stronger than it is; would have inserted his *sola* in the doctrine of justification by faith, as he did in his German Bible; and rejected purgatory, and the tyranny of popery, among the abuses in the second part. He would have changed the whole tone, and made the document a trumpet of war.

The Augsburg Confession proper (exclusive of preface and epilogue) consists of two parts, — one positive and dogmatic, the other negative and mildly polemic or rather apologetic. The first refers chiefly to doctrines, the second to ceremonies and institutions. The order of subjects is not strictly systematic, though considerably improved upon the arrangement of the Schwabach and Torgau Articles. In the manuscript copies and oldest editions, the articles are only numbered; the titles were subsequently added.

I.   The first part presents in twenty-one articles — beginning with the Triune God, and ending with the worship of saints — a clear, calm, and condensed statement of the doctrines held by the evangelical Lutherans: (1) in common with the Roman Church; (2) in common with the Augustinian school in that church; (3) in opposition to Rome; and (4) in distinction from Zwinglians and Anabaptists.

(1) In theology and Christology, i.e., the doctrines of God's unity and trinity (Art. I.), and of Christ's divine-human personality (III.), the Confession strongly re-affirms the ancient catholic faith as laid down in the œcumenical creeds, and condemns (*damnamus*) the old and new forms of Unitarianism and Arianism as heresies.

(2) In anthropology, i.e., in the articles on the fall and original sin (II.), the slavery of the natural will and necessity of divine grace (XVIII.), the cause and nature of sin (XIX.),

---

[1] "*Denn ich so sanft und leise nicht treten kann.*" Letter to Elector John, May 15, 1530. In De Wette, IV. 17. He calls the Augustana *die Leisetreterin*, the softly stepping Confession. Letter to Jonas, July 21, 1530.

the Confession is substantially Augustinian, in opposition
to the Pelagian and semi-Pelagian heresies. The Donatists are
also condemned (*damnant*, VIII.) for denying the objective
virtue of the ministry and the sacraments, which Augustin
defended against them.

(3) The general evangelical views more or less distinct
from those of Rome appear in the articles on justification by
faith (IV.), the Gospel ministry (V.), new obedience (VI.),
the Church (VII., VIII.), repentance (XII.), ordination
(XIV.), ecclesiastical rites (XV.), civil government (XVI.),
good works (XIX.), the worship of saints, and the exclusive
mediatorship of Christ (XX.).

These articles are so guardedly and skillfully worded as
to disarm the papal opponents. Even the doctrine of justification by faith (Art. IV.), which Luther declared to be
the article of the standing or falling church, is briefly and
mildly stated, without the *sola* so strongly insisted on by
Luther, and so objectionable to the Catholics, who charged
him with willful perversion of the Scriptures, for inserting
it in the Epistle to the Romans (3: 28).[1]

(4) The distinctively Lutheran views — mostly retained
from prevailing catholic tradition, and differing in part from
those of other Protestant churches — are contained in the
articles on the sacraments (IX., X., XIII.), on confession and
absolution (XI.), and the millennium (XVII.). The tenth
article plainly asserts the doctrine of a real bodily presence
and distribution of Christ in the eucharist to all communicants, and disapproves (*improbant*) of those who teach dif-

---

[1] In a letter to Brenz, May, 1531 (Corp. Ref., II. 502), Melanchthon
remarks that he did not speak more plainly on this point, "*propter adver-
sariorum calumnias.*" In the Apology of the Confession (Art. IV.), he is
more explicit, and declares this doctrine incidentally to be " the chief point of
Christian doctrine (*præcipuus locus doctrinæ Christianæ*) in this controversy." Müller, *Symb. Bücher*, p. 87. Döllinger charges Melanchthon, in his
varying statements of this doctrine, with sophistry, *Die Reformation*, III.
279 sqq. The revisers of the Luther Bible retained the insertion *allein* in
Rom. 3:28.

ferently (the Zwinglians).[1] The Anabaptists are not only disapproved, but condemned (*damnamus*) as heretics three times: for their views on infant baptism and infant salvation (IX.),[2] civil offices (XVI.), the millennium and final restoration (XVII.).

These anti-Zwinglian and anti-Baptist articles, however, have long since lost their force in the Lutheran Church. Melanchthon himself changed the wording of the tenth Article in the edition of 1540, and omitted the clause of disapproval. The damnation of unbaptized infants dying in infancy, which is indirectly indorsed by condemning the opposite, is a fossil relic of a barbarous orthodoxy, and was justly denied by the Baptists, as also by Zwingli and Bullinger, who on this point were ahead of their age. The first official deliverance against this dogma was raised by the Reformed Church of Scotland, in the Second Scotch Confession (1581), which condemns among the errors of "the Roman Antichrist" "his cruel judgment against infants departing without the sacrament, and his absolute necessity of baptism."[3]

The doctrine of the second advent and millennium (rejected in Art. XVII.), if we except the dreams of the radical wing of the Anabaptists, has found advocates among sound and orthodox Lutherans, especially of the school of Bengel, and must be regarded as an open question.

The last Article of the doctrinal part expresses the assurance that the Lutherans hold no doctrine which is contrary

---

[1] That the Zwinglians are meant by the *secus docentes* (in the German ed., *Gegenlehr*), must be inferred from the preceding Conference at Marburg, and the whole conduct of the Lutherans during the Diet. The omission of Zwingli's name was due, probably, to respect for his friend the Landgrave of Hesse, one of the signers of the Confession.

[2] "They condemn the Anabaptists, who disallow the baptism of children, and *affirm that children are saved without baptism.*" The edition of 1540 adds after "*sine baptismo*" the words "*et extra ecclesiam Christi.*" The Romish Confutation fully approves of the condemnation of the Anabaptists, and calls them "*hominum genus seditiosissimum, procul a finibus Romani imperii eliminandum.*" Corp. Reform., XXVII. 105.

[3] Schaff, *Creeds*, i. 687, iii. 482.

to the Scriptures, or to the Catholic or even the Roman Church, as far as known from the fathers, and differ from her only on certain traditions and ceremonies. Luther knew better, and so did the Romanists. Only Melanchthon, in his desire for union and peace, could have thus deceived himself; but he was undeceived before he left Augsburg, and in the Apology of the Confession he assumed a very different tone.

II. The second part of the Confession rejects, in seven articles, those abuses of Rome which were deemed most objectionable, and had been actually corrected in the Lutheran churches; namely, the withdrawal of the communion cup from the laity (I.), the celibacy of the clergy (II.), the sacrifice of the mass (III.), obligatory auricular confession (IV.), ceremonial feasts and fasts (V.), monastic vows (VI.), and the secular power of the bishops as far as it interferes with the purity and spirituality of the church (VII.). This last Article is virtually a protest against the principle of Erastianism or Cæsaropapacy, and would favor in its legitimate consequences a separation of church and state. "The ecclesiastical and civil powers," says the Confession, "are not to be confounded. The ecclesiastical power has its own commandment to preach the gospel and administer the sacraments. Let it not by force enter into the office of another, let it not transfer worldly kingdoms," etc. And as to the civil power, it is occupied only with worldly matters, not with the gospel, and "defends not the minds, but the bodies and bodily things, against manifest injuries." This protest has been utterly disregarded by the Protestant rulers in Germany. The same Article favors the restoration of the episcopal jurisdiction with purely spiritual and ecclesiastical authority. This also was wholly disregarded by the signers, who were unwilling to give up their summepiscopate which they had claimed and exercised since 1526 with the consent of the Reformers.

The Confession concludes with these words: "Peter forbids bishops to be lords, and to be imperious over the churches (1 Pet. v. 3). Now, our meaning is not to take the rule from the bishops, but this one thing only is requested at their hands, that they would suffer the gospel to be purely taught, and that they would relax a few observances which cannot be held without sin. But if they will remit none, let them look how they will give account to God for this, that by their obstinacy they afford cause of division and schism." [1] Thus the responsibility of schism in the Latin Church was thrown upon Rome. But even if Rome and the Diet had accepted the Augsburg Confession, the schism would still have occurred by the further progress of the Protestant spirit, which no power on earth, not even Luther and Melanchthon, could arrest.

The style of the Latin edition is such as may be expected from the rare classic culture and good taste of Melanchthon; while the order and arrangement might be considerably improved.

The diplomatic preface to the Emperor, from the pen of a lawyer, Chancellor Brück, is clumsy, tortuous, dragging, extremely obsequious, and has no other merit than to introduce the reader into the historical situation. The brief conclusion (Epilogus) is from the same source, and is followed by the signatures of seven princes and two magistrates. Several manuscript copies omit both preface and epilogue, as not properly belonging to the Confession.

Space forbids us to discuss the questions of the text, and the important variations of the Unaltered Confession of 1530,

---

[1] It was Melanchthon's wish (which Köllner chose as motto for his *Symb. d. luth. Kirche*) : "*Utinam utinam possim non quidem dominationem confirmare, sed administrationem restituere episcoporum. Video enim, qualem habituri simus ecclesiam, dissoluta πολιτεία ecclesiastica.*" Occasionally lonely voices are heard for the restoration of episcopacy in the Lutheran Church, but without effect. See F. Haupt, *Der Episcopat der deutschen Reformation, oder Artikel 28 der Augsburg Conf.*, Frankf., 1866; *Luther und der Episcopat*, 1866.

and the Altered Confession of 1540, which embodies the last improvements of its author, but has only a semi-official character and weight within the Lutheran Church.[1]

§ 120. *The Roman Confutation and the Protestant Apology.*

I. *Corpus Reformatorum* (MELANCHTHONIS *Opera*), ed. by *Bretschneider* and *Bindseil*, vol. XXVII. (1859), 646 columns, and vol. XXVIII. 1–326. These volumes contain the *Confutatio Confessionis Augustanæ*, and the two editions of Melanchthon's *Apologia Conf. Aug.*, in Latin and German, with Prolegomena and critical apparatus. The best and most complete edition. There are few separate editions of the *Apology*, but it is incorporated in all editions of the Lutheran Symbols; see Lit. in § 119. The Latin text of the *Confutatio* was first published by A. Fabricius Leodius in *Harmonia Confess. Augustanæ*, 1573; the German, by C. G. Müller, 1808, from a copy of the original in the archives of Mainz, which Weber had previously inspected (*Krit. gesch. der Augsb. Conf.*, II. 439 sqq.).

II. K. KIESER (R. Cath.). *Die Augsburger Confession und ihre Widerlegung*, Regensburg, 1845. HUGO LÄMMER: *Die vor-tridentinisch-katholische Theologie des Reformations-Zeitalters*, Berlin, 1858, pp. 33–46. By the same: *De Confessionis Augustanæ Confutatione Pontificia*, in Niedner's "Zeitschrift für hist. Theol.," 1858. (Lämmer, a Lutheran, soon afterwards joined the Roman Church, and was ordained a priest, 1859, and appointed *missionarius apostolicus*, 1861.) G. PLITT (Luth.): *Die Apologie der Augustana geschichtlich erklärt*, Erlangen, 1873. SCHAFF: *Creeds*, etc., I. 243. The history and literature of the *Apology* are usually combined with that of the *Confession*, as in J. G. WALCH, FEUERLIN-RIEDERER, and KÖLLNER.

The Roman "Catholic Confutation," so called, of the Augsburg Confession, was prepared in Augsburg by order of the Emperor Charles, by most eminent Roman divines of Germany, and bitterest opponents of Luther, especially Drs. Eck, Faber, Cochlæus, in Latin and German.[2] The final

---

[1] See on these questions Schaff, *Creeds*, I. 237 sqq., and especially Köllner, *Symbolik der luth. Kirche*, p. 236 sqq. and 267 sqq.

[2] The full title is *Catholica et quasi-extemporanea Responsio Pontificia seu Confutatio Augustanæ Confessionis*. The first draught was verbose and bitter ("*verbosior et acrior*"); the second, third, fourth, and fifth were briefer and milder.

revision, as translated into German, was publicly read before
the Emperor and the Diet, in the chapel of the episcopal
palace, Aug. 3, and adopted as the expression of the views
of the majority. The document follows the order of the Augsburg Confession. It approves eighteen doctrinal articles of the first part,
either in full or with some restrictions and qualifications.
Even the fourth article, on justification, escapes censure, and
Pelagianism is strongly condemned.[1] The tenth article, on
the Lord's Supper, is likewise approved as far as it goes, provided only that the presence of the whole Christ in either
of the substances be admitted.[2] But Article VII., on the
Church, is rejected;[3] also Art. XX., on faith and good works,
and Art. XXI., on the worship of saints.[4]

The second part of the Confession, on abuses, is wholly
rejected; but at the close, the existence of various abuses,
especially among the clergy, is acknowledged, and a reformation of discipline is promised and expected from a general
council.[5]

The tone of the Confutation is moderate, owing to the
express direction of the Emperor; but it makes no concession

---

[1] The first draught, however, had a lengthy attack upon Luther's *sola fide*.

[2] "*Decimus articulus in verbis nihil offendit si modo credant [principes,*
the Lutheran signers] *sub qualibet specie integrum Christum adesse.*"

[3] Because it is defined as a *congregatio sanctorum*, without including *mali
et peccatores*.

[4] Because it rejects the invocation of saints. "*Hic articulus confessionis
toties damnatus penitus rejiciendus est et cum tota universali ecclesia repro-
bandus.*"

[5] "*Quod autem de abusibus adstruxerunt, haud dubie norunt Principes
omnes et status imperii, neque a Cœs. Maiestate, neque ullis a Principibus
et christiano aliquo homine vel minimum abusum probari, sed optare tum
Principes, tum status imperii, ut communi consilio ac consensu adnitantur,
ut, sublatis abusibus et emendatis, utriusque status excessus aut penitus
aboleantur, aut in melius reformentur, ac tandem ecclesiasticus status multis
modis labefactatus, ac christiana religio, quæ in nonnullis refriguit et
remissa est, ad pristinum decus et ornamentum restituatur et redintegretur.
Qua in re Cœs. Maiestas, ut omnibus constat, hactenus plurimum et laboris
et curæ insumsit, et in reliquum ad hoc negotii omnem suam operam ac
studium serio collocaturam benigne pollicetur.*" Corp. Ref., XXVII. 182 sq.

on the points under dispute. It abounds in biblical and patristic quotations crudely selected. As to talent and style, it is far inferior to the work of Melanchthon. The Roman Church was not yet prepared to cope with the Protestant divines.

The publication of the Confutation as well as the Confession was prohibited, and it did not appear in print till many years afterwards; but its chief contents became known from notes taken by hearers and from manuscript copies.

The Lutheran members of the Diet urged Melanchthon to prepare at once a Protestant refutation of the Roman refutation, and offered the first draught of it to the Diet, Sept. 22, through Chancellor Brück; but it was refused.

On the following day Melanchthon left Augsburg in company with the Elector of Saxony, re-wrote the Apology on the journey,[1] and completed it leisurely at Wittenberg, with the help of a manuscript copy of the Confutation, in April, 1531.

The Apology of the Augsburg Confession is a scholarly vindication of the Confession. It far excels the Confutation in theological and literary merit. It differs from the apologetic Confession by its polemic and protestant tone. It is written with equal learning and ability, but with less moderation and more boldness. It even uses some harsh terms against the papal opponents, and calls them liars and hypocrites (especially in the German edition). It is the most learned of the Lutheran symbols, and seven times larger than the Confession, but for this very reason not adapted to be a symbolical book. It contains many antiquated arguments, and errors in exegesis and patristic quotations. But in its day it greatly strengthened the confidence of scholars in the cause of Protestantism. Its chief and permanent value is historical, and consists in its being the oldest and most authentic

---

[1] He worked so hard at it at Altenburg, even on Sunday, that Luther reminded him to observe the Fourth Commandment.

interpretation of the Augsburg Confession, by the author himself.

The Apology, though not signed by the Lutheran princes at Augsburg, was recognized first in 1532, at a convent in Schweinfurt, as a public confession ; it was signed by Lutheran divines at Smalcald, 1537 ; it was used at the religious conference at Worms, 1540, and embodied in the various editions of the Confession, and at last in the Book of Concord, 1580.

The text of the Apology has, like that of the Confession, gone through various transformations, which are used by Bossuet and other Romanists as proofs of the changeableness of Protestantism. The original draught made at Augsburg has no authority, as it was based on fragmentary notes of Camerarius and others who heard the Confutation read on the 3d of August.[1] The first Latin edition was much enlarged and improved; the German translation was prepared by Justus Jonas, assisted by Melanchthon, but differs widely from the Latin.[2] Both were published together with the Augsburg Confession in October, 1531. Changes were made in subsequent editions, both of the Latin original and the German translation, especially in the edition of 1540. Hence there is an *Apologia invariata* and an *Apologia variata*, as well as a *Confessio invariata* and a *Confessio variata*. The Book of Concord took both texts from the first edition.[3]

§ 121. *The Tetrapolitan Confession.*

I. Editions. The Latin text was first printed at Strassburg (Argentoratum), A.D. 1531, Sept. (21 leaves); then in the *Corpus et Syntagma Confess.* (1612 and 1654); in Augusti's *Corpus libr. symb.* (1827), p. 327 sqq.; and in Niemeyer's *Collect. Confess.* (1840), p. 740–770; comp. Proleg., p. LXXXIII.

---

[1] Corp. Ref., XXVII. 267 sqq. Melanchthon himself did not hear it.
[2] Ibid., 379 sqq.; XXVIII. 1 sqq.
[3] See on the different editions the "Corp. Ref.," XXVI. 697 sqq. and XXVII. 379 sqq.; the Latin text of 1531, p. 419 sqq.; the German translation with the variations of ed. II. (1533), ed. III. and IV. (1540), ed. V. (1550), ed. VI. (1556), in vol. XXVIII. 37–326.

The German text appeared first at Strassburg, Aug. 1531 (together with the Apology, 72 leaves); then again, 1579, ed. by JOHN STURM, but was suppressed by the magistrate, 1580; at Zweibrücken, 1604; in BECK'S *Symbol. Bücher*, vol. I., p. 401 sq.; in BÖCKEL'S *Bekenntniss-Schriften der evang. reform. Kirche* (1847), p. 363 sq. II. GOTTL. WERNSDORFF: *Historia Confessionis Tetrapolitanœ*, Wittenb. 1694, ed. IV. 1721. SCHELHORN: *Amœnitates litter.*, Tom. VI., Francf. 1727. J. H. FELS: *Dissert. de varia Confess. Tetrapolitanœ fortuna prœsertim in civitate Lindaviensi*, Götting. 1755. PLANCK: *Geschichte des protest. Lehrbegriffs*, vol. III., Part I. (second ed. 1796), pp. 68–94. J. W. RÖHRICH: *Geschichte der evangel. Kirche des Elsasses.* Strassburg, 1855, 3 vols. J. W. BAUM: *Capito und Butzer* (Elberf. 1860), p. 466 sqq. and 595. SCHAFF: *Creeds*, I. 524–529.

The Tetrapolitan Confession, also called the Strassburg and the Swabian Confession, is the oldest confession of the Reformed Church in Germany, and represented the faith of four imperial cities, Strassburg, Constance, Memmingen, and Lindau, which at that time sympathized with Zwingli and the Swiss, rather than Luther, on the doctrine of the sacraments.

It was prepared in great haste, during the sessions of the Diet of Augsburg, by Bucer, with the aid of Capito and Hedio, in the name of those four cities (hence the name) which were excluded by the Lutherans from their political and theological conferences, and from the Protestant League. They would greatly have preferred to unite with them, and to sign the Augsburg Confession, with the exception of the tenth article on the eucharist, but were forbidden. The Landgrave Philip of Hesse was the only one who, from a broad, statesmanlike view of the critical situation, favored a solid union of the Protestants against the common foe, but in vain.

Hence, after the Lutherans had presented their Confession June 25, and Zwingli his own July 8, the four cities handed theirs, July 11, to the Emperor in German and Latin. It was received very ungraciously, and not allowed to be read before the Diet; but a confutation full of misrepresentations was prepared by Faber, Eck, and Cochlæus, and read Oct. 24

(or 17).   The Strassburg divines were not even favored with
a copy of this confutation, but procured one secretly, and
answered it by a " Vindication and Defense " in the autumn
of 1531.

The Tetrapolitan Confession consists of twenty-three chapters, besides preface and conclusion.   It is in doctrine and
arrangement closely conformed to the Lutheran Confession,
and breathes the same spirit of moderation, but is more distinctly Protestant.   This appears at once in the first chapter
(On the Matter of Preaching), in the declaration that nothing should be taught in the pulpit but what was either expressly contained in the Holy Scriptures, or fairly deduced
therefrom.   (The Lutheran Confession is silent on the supreme authority of the Scriptures.)   The evangelical doctrine of justification is stated in the third and fourth chapters
more clearly than by Melanchthon; namely, that we are justified not by works of our own, but solely by the grace of
God and the merits of Christ, through a living faith, which is
active in love, and productive of good works.   Images are
rejected in Chap. XXII.

The doctrine of the Lord's Supper (Chap. XVIII.) is
couched in dubious language, which was intended to comprehend in substance the Lutheran and the Zwinglian theories,
and accords with the union tendency of Bucer.   But it contains the germ of the Calvinistic view.   In this ordinance, it
is said, Christ offers to his followers, as truly now as at the
institution, his very body and blood as spiritual food and
drink, whereby their souls are nourished to everlasting life.
Nothing is said of the oral manducation and the participation
of unbelievers, which are the distinctive features of the
Lutheran view.   Bucer, who had attended the Conference at
Marburg in 1529, labored with great zeal afterwards to bring
about a doctrinal compromise between the contending theories, but without effect.

The Tetrapolitan Confession was soon superseded by the

clearer and more logical confessions of the Calvinistic type. The four cities afterwards signed the Lutheran Confession to join the Smalcald League. But Bucer himself remained true to his union creed, and reconfessed it in his last will and testament (1548) and on his death-bed.

§ 122. *Zwingli's Confession to the Emperor Charles.*

Ad Carolum Rom. Imperatorem, Germaniæ comitia Augustæ celebrantem Fidei HULDRYCHI ZWINGLII *Ratio (Rechenschaft). Anno MDXXX. Mense Julio. Vincat veritas.* In the same year a German translation appeared in Zürich, and in 1543 an English translation. See Niemeyer, *Collect. Conf.*, p. XXVI. and 16 sqq. BÖCKEL : *Bekenntnissschriften der reform. Kirche*, p. 40 sqq. MÖRIKOFER : *U. Zwingli*, vol. II. p. 297 sqq. CHRISTOFFEL : *U. Z.*, vol. II. p. 237 sqq. SCHAFF : *Creeds*, I. 366 sqq.

Zwingli took advantage of the meeting of the Diet of Augsburg, to send a confession of his faith, addressed to the German Emperor, Charles V., shortly after the Lutheran princes had presented theirs. It is dated Zürich, July 3, 1530, and was delivered by his messenger at Augsburg on the 8th of the same month; but it shared the same fate as the "Tetrapolitan Confession." It was treated with contempt, and never laid before the Diet. Dr. Eck wrote in three days a refutation, charging Zwingli that for ten years he had labored to root out from the people of Switzerland all faith and all religion, and to stir them up against the magistrate; that he had caused greater devastation among them than the Turks, Tartars, and Huns ; that he had turned the churches and convents founded by the Habsburgers (the Emperor's ancestors) into temples of Venus and Bacchus; and that he now completed his criminal career by daring to appear before the Emperor with such an impudent piece of writing.

The Lutherans (with the exception of Philip of Hesse) were scarcely less indignant, and much more anxious to conciliate the Catholics than to appear in league with Zwinglians and Anabaptists. They felt especially offended that the Swiss Reformer took strong ground against the corporal presence, and incidentally alluded to them as persons who " were looking back to the flesh-pots of Egypt." Melanchthon judged him insane.

Zwingli, having had no time to consult with his confederates, offered the Confession in his own name, and submitted it to the judgment of the whole church of Christ, under the guidance of the Word of God and the Holy Spirit.

In the first sections he declares, as clearly as and even more explicitly than the Lutheran Confession, his faith in the orthodox doctrines of the Trinity and the Person of Christ, as laid down in the Nicene and Athanasian Creeds (which are expressly named). He teaches the election by free grace, the sole and sufficient satisfaction by Christ, and justification by faith, in opposition to all human mediators and meritorious works. He distinguishes between the internal or invisible, and the external or visible, church. The former is the company of the elect believers and their children, and is the bride of Christ; the latter embraces all nominal Christians and their children, and is beautifully described in the parable of the ten virgins, of whom five were foolish. The word " church " may also designate a single congregation, as the church in Rome, in Augsburg, in Leyden. The true church can never err in the foundation of faith. Purgatory he rejects as an injurious fiction, which sets Christ's merits at naught. On original sin, the salvation of unbaptized infants, and the sacraments, he departs much farther from the traditional theology than the Lutherans. He goes into a lengthy argument against the corporal presence in the eucharist. On the other hand, however, he protests against being confounded with the Anabaptists, and rejects their views on infant baptism, civil offices, the sleep of the soul, and universal salvation.

The document is frank and bold, yet dignified and courteous, and concludes thus: " Hinder not, ye children of men, the spread and growth of the Word of God. Ye can not forbid the grass to grow. Ye must see that this plant is richly blessed from heaven. Consider not your own wishes, but the demands of the age concerning the free course of the gospel. Take these words kindly, and show by your deeds that you are children of God."

§ 123. *Luther at the Coburg.*

LUTHER'S Letters from Coburg, April 18 to Oct. 4, 1530, in De Wette, IV. 1–182. MELANCHTHON'S Letters to Luther from Augsburg, in the second volume of the " Corpus Reform."
ZITZLAFF (Archidiaconus in Wittenberg): *Luther auf der Koburg*, Wittenberg, 1882 (175 pages). KÖSTLIN, *M. L.*, II. 198 sqq.

During the Diet of Augsburg, from April till October, 1530, Luther was an honorable prisoner in the electoral castle of Coburg.[1] From that watch-tower on the frontier of Saxony and Bavaria, he exerted a powerful influence, by his letters, upon Melanchthon and the Lutheran confessors at the Diet. His sojourn there is a striking parallel to his ten months' sojourn at the Wartburg, and forms the last romantic chapter in his eventful life. He was still under the anathema of the Pope and the ban of the empire, and could not safely appear at Augsburg. Moreover, his prince had reason to fear that by his uncompromising attitude he might hinder rather than promote the work of reconciliation and peace. But he wished to keep him near enough for consultation and advice. A message from Augsburg reached Coburg in about four days.

[1] Coburg is the residence, alternately with Gotha, of the Duke, and capital of the duchy, of Saxe-Coburg-Gotha, 185 m. S.S.W. of Berlin, nearly midway between Wittenberg and Augsburg, and has now (1888) about sixteen thousand inhabitants. The castle is situated on an eminence overhanging the town, and has been in part converted into a prison and house of correction; but some chambers remain in their original condition, chiefly those occupied by Luther, with his bedstead and pulpit.

Luther arrived at Coburg, with the Elector and the Wittenberg divines, on April 15, 1530. In the night of the 22d he was conveyed to the fortified castle on the hill, and ordered to remain there for an indefinite time. No reason was given, but he could easily suspect it. He spent the first day in enjoying the prospect of the country, and examining the prince's building (*Fürstenbau*) which was assigned him. His sitting-room is still shown. " I have the largest apartment, which overlooks the whole fortress, and I have the keys to all the rooms." He had with him his amanuensis Veit Dietrich, a favorite student, and his nephew Cyriac Kaufmann, a young student from Mansfeld. He let his beard grow again, as he had done on the Wartburg. He was well taken care of at the expense of the Elector, and enjoyed the vacation as well as he could with a heavy load of work and care on his mind. He received more visitors than he liked. About thirty persons were stationed in the castle.

" Dearest Philip," he wrote to Melanchthon, April 23, "we have at last reached our Sinai; but we shall make a Sion of this Sinai, and here I shall build three tabernacles, — one to the Psalms, one to the Prophets, and one to Æsop. . . . It is a very attractive place, and just made for study; only your absence grieves me. My whole heart and soul are stirred and incensed against the Turks and Mohammed, when I see this intolerable raging of the Devil. Therefore I shall pray and cry to God, nor rest until I know that my cry is heard in heaven. The sad condition of our German empire distresses you more." Then he describes to him his residence in the "empire of birds." In other letters he humorously speaks of the cries of the ravens and jackdaws in the forest, and compares them to a troop of kings and grandees, schoolmen and sophists, holding Diet, sending their mandates through the air, and arranging a crusade against the fields of wheat and barley, hoping for heroic deeds and grand victories. He could hear all the sophists and papists chattering around him from early morning, and was delighted to see how valiantly these knights of the Diet strutted about and wiped their bills, but he hoped that before long they would be spitted on a hedge-stake. He was glad to hear the first nightingale, even as early as April. With such innocent sports of his fancy he tried to chase away the anxious cares which weighed upon him. It is from this retreat that he wrote that charming letter to his boy Hans, describing a beautiful garden full of goodly apples, pears, and plums, and merry children on little horses with golden bridles and silver saddles, and promising him and his play-mates a fine fairing if he prayed, and learned his lessons.[1]

Joy and grief, life and death, are closely joined in this changing world. On the 5th of June, Luther received the sad news of the pious death of his father, which occurred at Mansfeld, May 29. When he first heard of his sickness, he wrote to him from Wittenberg, Feb. 15, 1530: "It would be a great joy to me if only you and my mother could come to us. My Kate, and all, pray for it with tears. We would do our best to make you comfortable." At the report of his end he said to Dietrich, "So my father, too, is dead," took his Psalter, and retired to his room. On the same day he wrote to Melanchthon that all he was, or possessed, he had received from God through his beloved father.

He suffered much from "buzzing and dizziness" in his head, and a tendency to fainting, so as to be prevented for several weeks from reading and writing. He did not know whether to attribute the illness to the Coburg hospitality, or to his old enemy. He had the same experience at the Wartburg. Dietrich traced it to Satan, since Luther was very careful of his diet.

Nevertheless, he accomplished a great deal of work. As soon as his box of books arrived, he resumed his translation

[1] See above, p. 464.

of the Bible, begun on the Wartburg, hoping to finish the Prophets, and dictated to Dietrich a commentary on the first twenty-five Psalms. He also explained his favorite 118th Psalm, and wrote ver. 17 on the wall of his room, with the tune for chanting, —

"*Non moriar, sed vivam, et narrabo opera Domini.*"

By way of mental recreation he translated thirteen of Æsop's fables, to adapt them for youth and common people, since "they set forth in pleasing colors of fiction excellent lessons of wise and peaceful living among bad people in this wicked world." He rendered them in the simplest language, and expressed the morals in apt German proverbs.[1]

The Diet at Augsburg occupied his constant attention. He was the power behind the throne. He wrote in May a public "Admonition to the Clergy assembled at the Diet," reminding them of the chief scandals, warning them against severe measures, lest they provoke a new rebellion, and promising the quiet possession of all their worldly possessions and dignities, if they would only leave the gospel free. He published a series of tracts, as so many rounds of musketry, against Romish errors and abuses.

He kept up a lively correspondence with Melanchthon, Jonas, Spalatin, Link, Hausmann, Brenz, Agricola, Weller, Chancellor Brück, Cardinal Albrecht, the Elector John, the Landgrave Philip, and others, not forgetting his "liebe Kethe, Herr Frau Katherin Lutherin zu Wittenberg." He dated his letters "from the region of the birds" (*ex volucrum regno*), "from the Diet of the jackdaws" (*ex comitiis Monedularum seu Monedulanensibus*), or "from the desert" (*ex eremo, aus der Einöde*). Melanchthon and the Elector kept him informed of the proceedings at Augsburg, asked his advice about every important step, and submitted to him the draught

---

[1] The MS. of his translation and adaptation of these fables has recently been re-discovered in the Vatican Library by Dr. Reitzenstein, and published, with an interesting facsimile, by E. Thiele: "*Luthers Fabeln nach seiner wiedergefundenen Handschrift*," etc. Halle (M. Niemeyer), 1888 (19 pages).

of the Confession. He approved of it, though he would have liked it much stronger.   He opposed every compromise in doctrine, and exhorted the confessors to stand by the gospel, without fear of consequences.

His heroic faith, the moving power and crowning glory of his life, shines with wonderful luster in these letters. The greater the danger, the stronger his courage.   He devoted his best hours to prayer.   His "Ein feste Burg ist unser Gott," was written before this time,[1] but fitly expresses his fearless trust in God at this important crisis, when Melanchthon trembled.   "Let the matter be ever so great," he wrote to him (June 27), "great also is He who has begun and who conducts it; for it is not our work. . . . 'Cast thy burthen upon the Lord; the Lord is nigh unto all them that call upon Him.'   Does He say that to the wind, or does He throw his words before beasts? . . . It is your worldly wisdom that torments you, and not theology.   As if you, with your useless cares, could accomplish any thing!   What more can the Devil do than strangle us?   I conjure you, who in all other matters are so ready to fight, to fight against yourself as your greatest enemy."   In another letter he well describes the difference between himself and his friend in regard to cares and temptations.   "In private affairs I am the weaker, you the stronger combatant; but in public affairs it is just the reverse (if, indeed, any contest can be called private which is waged between me and Satan): for you take but small account of your life, while you tremble for the public cause; whereas I am easy and hopeful about the latter, knowing as I do for certain that it is just and true, and the cause of Christ and God Himself.   Hence I am as a careless spectator, and unmindful of these threatening and furious papists.   If we fall, Christ falls with us, the Ruler of the world.   I would rather fall with Christ than stand with the Emperor.   Therefore I exhort you, in the name of

[1] See above, 468, 502 sq., 741 sq.

Christ, not to despise the promises and the comfort of God, who says, 'Cast all your cares upon the Lord. Be of good cheer, I have overcome the world.' I know the weakness of our faith; but all the more let us pray, 'Lord, increase our faith.'"

In a remarkable letter to Chancellor Brück (Aug. 5), he expresses his confidence that God can not and will not forsake the cause of the evangelicals, since it is His own cause. "It is His doctrine, it is His Word. Therefore it is certain that He will hear our prayers, yea, He has already prepared His help, for he says, 'Can a woman forget her sucking child, that she should not have compassion on the son of her womb? Yea, these may forget, yet will not I forget thee " (Isa. 49 : 15). In the same letter he says, "I have lately seen two wonders: the first, when looking out of the window, I saw the stars of heaven and the whole beautiful vault of God, but no pillars, and yet the heavens did not collapse, and the vault still stands fast. The second wonder: I saw great thick clouds hanging over us, so heavy as to be like unto a great lake, but no ground on which they rested; yet they did not fall on us, but, after greeting us with a gloomy countenance, they passed away, and over them appeared the luminous rainbow. . . . Comfort Master Philip and all the rest. May Christ comfort and sustain our gracious Elector. To Christ be all the praise and thanks forever. Amen."

Urbanus Rhegius, the Reformer of Braunschweig-Lüneburg, on his way from Augsburg to Celle, called on Luther, for the first and last time, and spent a day with him at Coburg. It was "the happiest day" of his life, and made a lasting impression on him, which he thus expressed in a letter: "I judge, no one can hate Luther who knows him. His books reveal his genius; but if you would see him face to face, and hear him speak on divine things with apostolic spirit, you would say, the living reality surpasses the fame. Luther is too great to be judged by every wiseacre. I, too, have written

books, but compared with him I am a mere pupil. He is
an elect instrument of the Holy Ghost. He is a theologus
for the whole world."

Bucer also paid him a visit at Coburg (Sept.
25), and sought to induce him, if possible, to a more friendly attitude
towards the Zwinglians and Strassburgers. He succeeded at
least so far as to make him hopeful of a future reconciliation.
It was the beginning of those union efforts which resulted
in the Wittenburg Concordia, but failed at last. Bucer
received the impression from this visit, that Luther was a
man "who truly feared God, and sought sincerely the glory
of God."

There can be no doubt about this. Luther feared God,
and nothing else. He sought the glory of Christ, and cared
nothing for the riches and pleasures of the world. At
Coburg, Luther was in the full vigor of manhood, — forty-six
years of age, — and at the height of his fame and power.
With the Augsburg Confession his work was substantially
completed. His followers were now an organized church
with a confession of faith, a form of worship and government, and no longer dependent upon his personal efforts.
He lived and labored fifteen years longer, completing the
translation of the Bible, — the greatest work of his life, —
preaching, teaching, and writing ; but his physical strength
began to decline, his infirmities increased, he often complained of lassitude and uselessness, and longed for rest after
his herculean labors. Some of his later acts, as the unfortunate complicity with the bigamy affair of Philip of Hesse,
and his furious attacks upon Papists and Sacramentarians,
obscured his fame, and only remind us of the imperfections
which adhere to the greatest and best of men.

Here, therefore, is the proper place to attempt an estimate
of his public character, and services to the church and the
world.

§ 124.   *Luther's Public Character, and Position in History.*

In 1883 the four hundredth anniversary of Luther's birth was celebrated with enthusiasm throughout Protestant Christendom by innumerable addresses and sermons setting forth his various merits as a man and a German, as a husband and father, as a preacher, catechist, and hymnist, as a Bible translator and expositor, as a reformer and founder of a church, as a champion of the sacred rights of conscience, and originator of a mighty movement of religious and civil liberty which spread over Europe and across the Atlantic to the shores of the Pacific.   The story of his life was repeated in learned and popular biographies, in different tongues, and enacted on the stage in the principal cities of Germany.[1] Not only Lutherans, but Presbyterians, Congregationalists, Episcopalians, Methodists, Baptists, Unitarians, united in these tributes to the Reformer.   The Academy of Music in New York could not hold the thousands who crowded the building to attend the Luther-celebration arranged by the Evangelical Alliance in behalf of the leading Protestant denominations of America.[2]

Such testimony has never been borne to a mortal man. The Zwingli-celebration of the year 1884 had a similar char-

---

[1] See the Lit. on p. 104.   The martyr-Emperor, Frederick III., as crown prince, representing his venerable father, Emperor William I. of Germany, was the leading figure in the celebration at Wittenberg, Sept. 12–14, 1883, and gave it a national significance.   The Luther-celebration produced several Luther-dramas, by Henzen (1883), Devrient (7th ed. 1888), Herrig (9th ed. 1888), and Trümpelmann (2nd ed. 1888).   Comp. G. A. Erdmann, *Die Lutherfestspiele*, Wittenberg, 1889.

[2] The meeting of the Evangelical Alliance of the U.S., then under the management of Drs. Prime and Schaff (Presbyterians), was the most representative and impressive Luther celebration in America; it was addressed by Hon. John Jay (Episcopalian), Dr. Phillips Brooks (Episcopalian), Dr. Wm. M. Taylor (Congregationalist), Bishop Simpson (Methodist), Dr. Krotel (Lutheran), Dr. Crosby (Presbyterian).   The music was furnished by the New York Oratorio Society.   The Evangelical Alliance issued also an invitation to the Protestant churches in the United States to celebrate Luther's birthday by sermons on the Reformation.

acter, and extended over many countries in both hemispheres, but would probably not have been thought of without the preceding Luther-celebration.

And indeed Luther has exerted, and still exerts, a spiritual power inferior only to that of the sacred writers. St. Augustin's influence extends wider, embracing the Roman Catholic church as well as the Protestant; but he never reached the heart of the common people. Luther is the only one among the Reformers whose name was adopted, though against his protest, as the designation and watchword by the church which he founded. He gave to his people, in their own vernacular, what no man did before or since, three fundamental books of religion, — the Bible, a hymn-book, and a catechism. He forced even his German enemies to imitate his language in poetry and prose. So strong is the hold which his Bible version has upon the church of his name, that it is next to impossible to change and adapt it to modern learning and taste, although he himself kept revising and improving it as long as he lived.[1]

Luther was the German of the Germans, and the most vigorous type of the faults as well as the virtues of his nation.[2] He is the apostle of Protestant Germany, fully as much as Boniface is the apostle of Roman Catholic Germany, and surpasses him vastly in genius and learning. Boniface, though an Anglo-Saxon by birth, was more a Roman than a German; while in Luther the Christian and the German were one, and joined in opposition to papal Rome. All schools of Lutheran divines appeal to his authority: the extreme orthodox, who out-Luther Luther in devotion to the letter; the moderate or middle party, who adhere only to

[1] The *Probebibel*, so-called, of 1883, though prepared by a company of able scholars appointed by various German States, is a timidly conservative revision, does not touch the Erasmian text, and allows innumerable inaccuracies to stand from respect to Luther's memory; and yet even this revision revises too much for the Lutherans of strict orthodoxy. His popularity is a hinderance to progress.

[2] See H. v. Treitschke's eloquent address, *Luther und die deutsche Nation*, Berlin, 1883 (29 pages).

the substance of his teaching; and the rationalists, who reject his creed, but regard him as the standard-bearer of the freedom of private judgment and dissent from all authority.[1]

His real strength lies in his German writings, which created the modern High-German book-language, and went right to the heart of the people. His greatest production is a translation, — the German Bible. Italians, Spaniards, and Frenchmen, who knew him only from his Latin books, received a very feeble idea of his power, and could not understand the secret of his influence.[2] The contemptuous judgments of Pope Leo, Cardinal Cajetan, Aleander, and Emperor Charles, echo the sentiments of their nations, and re-appear again and again among modern writers of the Latin races and the Romish faith.

Nevertheless, Martin Luther's influence extends far beyond the limits of his native land. He belongs to the church and the world.

Luther has written his own biography, as well as the early history of the German Reformation, in his numerous letters, without a thought of their publication. He lays himself open before the world without reservation. He was the frankest and most outspoken of men, and swayed by the impulse of the moment, without regard to logical consistency or fear of consequences. His faults as well as his virtues lay on the surface of his German works. He infused into them his intense personality to a degree which

---

[1] Professor Ad. Harnack (*Martin Luther*, Giessen, 1883, p. 4) well says: "*Fast jede Partei unter uns hat ihren Luther und meint den wahren zu haben. Die Verehrung für Luther vereinigt mehr als die Hälfte unserer Nation und die Auffassung Luther's trennt sie. Von Luther's Namen lässt so leicht kein Deutscher. Ein unvergleichlicher Mann ist er Allen, ob man ihm nun aufpasst, um ihn anzugreifen, oder ob man ihn rühmt und hoch preist.*" The Germans, if we may say so, worship Luther, Frederick the Great, Goethe, and Bismarck. Of these, Luther is most worthy, and was least desirous, of praise.

[2] Hallam also, ignoring Luther's German writings, calls his polemical books "bellowing in bad Latin," "scandalous," and "disgusting." (*Literature of Europe in the 15th, 16th, and 17th centuries*, II. 306, N.Y. ed.)

hardly finds a parallel except in the Epistles of the Apostle
Paul.

He knew himself very well. A high sense of his calling
and a deep sense of personal unworthiness are inseparably
combined in his self-estimate. He was conscious of his prophetic and apostolic mission in republishing the primitive
gospel for the German people; and yet he wrote to his wife
not to be concerned about him, for God could make a dozen
Luthers at any time. In his last will and testament (Jan. 6,
1542) he calls himself "a man well known in heaven, on
earth, and in hell," but also "a poor, miserable, unworthy
sinner," to whom "God, the Father of all mercies, has intrusted the gospel of His dear Son, and made him a teacher
of His truth in spite of the Pope, the Emperor, and the
Devil." He signs himself, in that characteristic document,
"God's notary and witness in His gospel." One of his
last words was, "We are beggars." And in the preface of
the first collected edition of his works, he expresses a wish
that they might all perish, and God's Word alone be
read.

Luther was a genuine man of the people, rooted and
grounded in rustic soil, but looking boldly and trustingly to
heaven with the everlasting gospel in his hand. He was a
plebeian, without a drop of patrician blood, and never
ashamed of his lowly origin. But what king or emperor
or pope of his age could compare with him in intellectual
and moral force? He was endowed with an overwhelming
genius and indomitable energy, with fiery temper and strong
passions, with irresistible eloquence, native wit, and harmless
humor, absolutely honest and disinterested, strong in faith,
fervent in prayer, and wholly devoted to Christ and His gospel. Many of his wise, quaint, and witty sayings have passed
into popular proverbs; and no German writer is more
frequently named and quoted than Luther.

Like all great men, he harbored in his mind colossal contrasts, and burst through the trammels of logic. He was a giant in public, and a child in his family; the boldest reformer, yet a conservative churchman; the eulogist of reason as the handmaid of religion, and the abuser of reason as the mistress of the Devil; the champion of the freedom of the spirit, and yet a slave of the letter; an intense hater of popery to the last, and yet an admirer of the Catholic Church, and himself a pope within his own church.[1] Yet there was a unity in this apparent contradiction. He was a seeker of the righteousness of works and peace of conscience as a Catholic monk, and he was a finder of the righteousness of faith as an evangelical reformer; just as the idea and pursuit of righteousness is the connecting link between the Jewish Saul and the Christian Paul. It was the same engine, but reversed. In separating from papal catholicism, Luther remained attached to Christian catholicism; and his churchly instincts were never suppressed, but only suspended to re-assert themselves with new and greater force after the revolutionary excesses of the Reformation.

His history naturally divides itself into three periods: the Roman-Catholic and monastic period, till 1517; the Protestant and progressive period, till 1525; the churchly, conservative, and re-actionary period, till 1546. But he never gave up his devotion to the free gospel, and his hatred of the Pope as the veritable Antichrist.[2]

---

[1] Comp. the admirable description of Luther by Hase in his *Kirchengesch.* (11th ed., p. 400), and at the close of his *Prot. Polemik.* The Roman Catholic Möhler (*Kirchengesch.*, III. 148) thinks that out of Luther's writings might be drawn "the most glorious apology of the Catholic Church." Harnack (*l. c.*, p. 5) calls him "a sage without prudence; a statesman without politics; an artist without art; a man free from the world, in the midst of the world; of vigorous sensuality, yet pure; obstinately unjust (*rechthaberisch ungerecht*), yet concerned for the cause; defying authority, yet bound by authority; at once blaspheming and emancipating.reason."

[2] An interesting parallel in this and other respects may be drawn by some future historian, between Luther and Bismarck, whose political influence upon Germany in the nineteenth century is as powerful as Luther's ecclesiastical influence was in the sixteenth. Bismarck was originally an intense

Luther's greatness is not that of a polished work of art, but of an Alpine mountain with towering peaks, rough granite blocks, bracing air, fresh fountains, and green meadows. His polemical books rush along like thunderstorms or turbid mountain torrents. He knew his violent temper, but never took the trouble to restrain it; and his last books against the Papists, the Zwinglians, and the Jews, are his worst, and exceed any thing that is known in the history of theological polemics. In his little tract against the Romish Duke Henry of Brunswick,[1] the word Devil occurs no less than a hundred and forty-six times.[2] At last he could not pray without cursing, as he confessed himself.[3] He calls his mastery of the vocabulary of abuse his rhetoric. " Do not think," he wrote to Spalatin, " that the gospel can be advanced without tumult, trouble, and uproar. You cannot make a pen of a sword. The Word of God is a sword; it is war, overthrow, trouble, destruction, poison; it meets the children of Ephraim, as Amos says, like a bear on the road, or like a lioness in the wood."[4] We may admit that the club and sledge-hammer of this Protestant Hercules were necessary for the semi-barbarous Germans of his day. Providence used his violent temper as an instrument for the destruction of the greatest spiritual tyranny which the world ever saw. Yet his best friends were shocked and grieved at his rude personalities, and condem-

aristocrat, but became the boldest liberal, and ended as a conservative statesman, though without surrendering the creations of his genius. He defeated Catholic Austria and France, and protested that he would never go to Canossa; yet he met Pope Leo XIII. half way, and repealed the unjust May-laws in the interest of patriotism, without surrendering any religious principle. With all his faults, he is the greatest statesman and diplomatist of the century, and the chief founder of the Protestant German Empire.

[1] He calls him *Hanswurst*, Jack Sausage.

[2] So says Döllinger (*Die Reform.*, III. 265, note), who counted the number. He adds, that in Luther's book on the Councils, the devils are mentioned fifteen times in four lines.

[3] See the passages above, p. 657 sq., note 3.

[4] Comp. the comparison between Luther and Melanchthon, p. 193 sq.

natory judgments of such men as Erasmus, Zwingli, and Œcolampadius, not to speak of his Romish adversaries. Nothing shows more clearly the great distance which separates him from the apostles and evangelists.

But, with all his faults, he is the greatest man that Germany produced, and one of the very greatest in history. Melanchthon, who knew him best, and suffered most from his imperious temper, called him the Elijah of Protestantism, and compared him to the Apostle Paul.[1] And indeed, in his religious experience and theological standpoint, he strongly resembles the Apostle of the Gentiles, — though at a considerable distance, — more strongly than any schoolman or father. He roused by his trumpet voice the church from her slumber; he broke the yoke of papal tyranny; he reconquered Christian freedom; he re-opened the fountain of God's holy Word to all the people, and directed the Christians to Christ, their only Master.

This is his crowning merit and his enduring monument.

Augustin, Luther, Calvin.

The men who, next to the Apostles, have exerted and still exert through their writings the greatest influence in the Christian Church, as leaders of theological thought, are St. Augustin, Martin Luther, and John Calvin: all pupils of Paul, inspired by his doctrines of sin and grace, filled with the idea that God alone is great, equally eminent for purity of character, abundance in labors, and whole-souled consecration to the service of Christ, their common Lord and Saviour; and yet as different from each other as an African, a German, and a Frenchman can be. Next to them I would place an Englishman, John Wesley, who, as to abundance of

---

[1] He announced the death of Luther to his students with the words: "*Ah! obiit auriga et currus Israel, qui rexit ecclesiam in hac ultima senecta mundi. . . . Amemus igitur hujus viri memoriam.*"

useful labor in winning souls to Christ, is the most apostolic man that Great Britain has produced.

Augustin commands the respect and gratitude of the Catholic as well as the Protestant world. He is, among the three, the profoundest in thought, and the sweetest in spirit; free from bitterness and coarseness, even in his severest polemics; yet advocating a system of exclusiveness which justifies coercion and persecution of heretics and schismatics. He identified the visible catholic church of his day with the kingdom of God on earth, and furnished the program of mediæval Catholicism, though he has little to say about the papacy, and protested, in the Pelagian controversy, against the position of one Pope, while he accepted the decision of another. All three were fighters, but against different foes and with different weapons. Augustin contended for the catholic church against heretical sects, and for authority against false freedom; Luther and Calvin fought for evangelical dissent from the overwhelming power of Rome, and for rational freedom against tyrannical authority. Luther was the fiercest and roughest fighter of the three; but he alone had the Teutonic gift of humor which is always associated with a kindly nature, and extracts the sting out of his irony and sarcasm. His bark was far worse than his bite. He advised to drown the Pope and his cardinals in the Tiber; and yet he would have helped to save their lives after the destruction of their office. He wrote a letter of comfort to Tetzel on his death-bed, and protested against the burning of heretics.

Luther and Calvin learned much from Augustin, and esteemed him higher than any human teacher since the Apostles; but they had a different mission, and assumed a polemic attitude towards the traditional church. Augustin struggled from the Manichæan heresy into catholic orthodoxy, from the freedom of error into the authority of truth; the Reformers came out of the corruptions and tyranny of the papacy into the freedom of the gospel. Augustin put the church above the Word, and established the principle of catholic tradition; the Reformers put the Word above the church, and secured a progressive understanding of the Scriptures by the right of free investigation.

Luther and Calvin are confined in their influence to Protestantism, and can never be appreciated by the Roman Church; yet, by the law of re-action, they forced the papacy into a moral reform, which enabled it to recover its strength, and to enter upon a new career of conquest. Romanism has far more vitality and strength in Protestant than in papal countries, and owes a great debt of gratitude to the Reformation.

Of the two Reformers, Luther is the more original, forcible, genial, and popular; Calvin, the more theological, logical, and systematic, besides being an organizer and disciplinarian. Luther controls the Protestant churches of Germany and Scandinavia; Calvin's genius shaped the confessions and constitutions of the Reformed churches in Switzerland, France, Holland, and Great Britain; he had a marked influence upon the development of civil liberty, and is still the chief molder of theological opinion in the Presbyterian and Congregational churches of Scotland and North America. Luther inspires by his genius, and attracts by his personality; Calvin commands admiration by his intellect and the force of moral self-government, which is the secret of true freedom in church and state.

Great and enduring are the merits of the three; but neither Augustin, nor Luther, nor Calvin has spoken the last word in Christendom. The best is yet to come.

NOTES.

REMARKABLE JUDGMENTS ON LUTHER.

Luther, like other great men, has been the subject of extravagant praise and equally extravagant censure.

We select a few impartial and weighty testimonies from four distinguished writers of very different character and position, — an Anglican divine, two secular poets, and a Catholic historian.

I. Archdeacon CHARLES JULIUS HARE (1795–1855) has written the best work in the English language in vindication of Luther. It appeared first as a note of 222 pages in the second volume of his *The Mission of the Comforter*, 1846 (3d ed. 1876), and afterwards as a separate book shortly before his death, 2d ed. 1855.

Luther has been assailed by English writers on literary, theological, and moral grounds: 1, for violence and coarseness in polemics (by Henry Hallam, the historian); 2, for unsoundness in the doctrine of justification, and disregard of church authority (by the Oxford Tractarians and Anglo-Catholics); 3, for lax views on monogamy in conniving at the bigamy of Philip of Hesse (by the same, and by Sir William Hamilton).

These charges are discussed, refuted, or reduced to a minimum, by Hare (who had the largest Luther library and the fullest Luther knowledge in England), with ample learning, marked ability, and in the best Christian spirit. He concludes his vindication with these words: —

"To some readers it may seem that I have spoken with exaggerated admiration of Luther. No man ever lived whose whole heart and soul and life have been laid bare as his have been to the eyes of mankind. Open as the sky, bold and fearless as the storm, he gave utterance to all his feelings, all his thoughts. He knew nothing of reserve; and the impression he produced on his hearers and friends was such, that they were anxious to treasure up every word that dropped from his pen or from his lips. No man, therefore, has ever been exposed to so severe a trial; perhaps no man was ever placed in such difficult circumstances, or assailed by such manifold temptations. And how has he come out of the trial? Through the power of faith, under the guardian care of his Heavenly Master, he was enabled to stand through life; and still he stands, and will continue tc stand, firmly rooted in the love of all who really know him."

II. GOETHE, the greatest poet and literary genius of Germany, when he was eighty-two years of age, March 11, 1832 (a few days before his death), paid this tribute to Luther and the Reformation, as reported by Eckermann, in the third or supplemental volume of the *Conversations* of that extraordinary man: —

"We scarcely know what we owe to Luther, and the Reformation in general. We are freed from the fetters of spiritual narrow-mindedness; we have, in consequence of our increasing culture, become capable of turning back to the fountain-head, and of comprehending Christianity in its purity. We have again the courage to stand with firm feet upon God's earth, and to feel ourselves in our divinely endowed human nature. Let mental culture go on advancing, let the natural sciences go on gaining in depth and breadth, and the human mind expand as it may, it will never go beyond the elevation and moral culture of Christianity, as it glistens and shines forth in the Gospels.

" But the better we Protestants advance in our noble development, so much the more rapidly will the Catholics follow us. As soon as they feel themselves caught up by the ever-extending enlightenment of the time, they must go on, do what they will, till at last the point is reached where all is but one."

III. HEINRICH HEINE, of Jewish descent, poet, critic, and humorist, the Franco-German Voltaire, who, like Voltaire, ridiculed with irreverent audacity the most sacred things, and yet, unlike him, could pass from smiles to tears, and appreciate the grandeur of Moses and the beauty of the Bible, pays this striking tribute to the Reformer: —

" Luther was not only the greatest, but also the most German man of our history; and in his character all the virtues and vices of the Germans are united in the grandest manner. He had also attributes which are rarely found together, and are usually regarded as hostile contradictions. He was at once a dreamy mystic, and a practical man of action. His thoughts had not only wings, but also hands; he spoke and he acted. He was not only the tongue, but also the sword of his age. He was both a cold scholastic stickler for words, and an inspired, divinely intoxicated prophet. After working his mind weary with his dogmatic distinctions during the day, he took his flute in the evening, looked up to the stars, and melted into melody and devotion. The same man who would scold like a fishwoman could also be as soft as a tender virgin. He was at times wild as the storm which uproots the oaks, and again as gentle as the zephyr which kisses the violets. He was full of the most awful fear of God, full of consecration to the Holy Spirit; he would be all absorbed in pure spirituality, and yet he knew very well the glories of the earth, and appreciated them, and from his mouth blossomed the famous motto: ' Who does not love wine, wife, and song, remains a fool his whole life long.' [1] He was a complete man, — I might say, an absolute man, — in whom spirit and matter are not separated. . . .

" Honor to Luther ! Eternal honor to the dear man, to whom we owe the recovery of our dearest rights, and by whose benefit we live to-day ! It becomes us little to complain about the narrowness of his views. The dwarf who stands on the shoulders of the giant can indeed see farther than the giant himself, especially if he puts on spectacles; but for that lofty point of intuition we want the lofty feeling, the giant heart, which we cannot make our own. It becomes us still less to pass a harsh judg-

[1] This is a mistake; see p. 465 sq.

ment upon his failings: these failings have been of more use to us than
the virtues of a thousand others.   The polish of Erasmus, the gentleness
of Melanchthon, would never have brought us so far as the divine brutality
of Brother Martin. From the imperial Diet, where Luther denied the
authority of the Pope, and openly declared 'that his doctrine must be
refuted by the authority of the Bible, or by the arguments of reason,' a
new age has begun in Germany. The chain wherewith the holy Boniface
bound the German church to Rome has been hewn asunder. . . . Through
Luther we attained the greatest freedom of thought; but this Martin
Luther gave us not only liberty to move, but also the means of moving,
for to the spirit he gave also a body. He created the word for the thought,
— he created the German language. He did this by his translation of the
Bible. The Divine author of this book himself chose him his translator,
and gave him the marvellous power to translate from a dead language
which was already buried into another language which did not yet live.
How Luther came to the language into which he translated the Bible I
cannot conceive to this day. . . . This old book is a perennial fountain
for the renewal of the German language." — *Zur Geschichte der Religion
und Philosophie in Deutschland*, 2nd ed. 1852, in Heine's *Sämmtl. Werke*,
vol. III. 29 sqq.

IV. J. DÖLLINGER, the most learned Catholic historian of the nineteenth
century, in his *Lectures on the Reunion of Christendom* (*Ueber die Wieder-
vereinigung der christlichen Kirchen*, Nördlingen, 1888, p. 53), makes the
following incidental remark on Luther and the Reformation : —
"The force and strength of the Reformation was only in part due to the
personality of the man who was its author and spokesman in Germany. It
was indeed Luther's overpowering mental greatness and wonderful many-
sidedness (*überwältigende Geistesgrösse und wunderbare Vielseitigkeit*) that
made him the man of his age and his people. Nor was there ever a German
who had such an intuitive knowledge of his countrymen, and was again so
completely possessed, not to say absorbed, by the national sentiment, as the
Augustinian monk of Wittenberg. The mind and spirit of the Germans was
in his hand as the lyre is in the hand of a skillful musician. He had given
them more than any man in Christian days ever gave his people, — language.
Bible, church hymn. All his opponents could offer in place of it, and all
the reply they could make to him, was insipid, colorless, and feeble, by the
side of his transporting eloquence. They stammered, he spoke. He alone
has impressed the indelible stamp of his mind on the German language and
the German intellect; and even those among us who hold him in religious
detestation, as the great heresiarch and seducer of the nation, are con-
strained, in spite of themselves, to speak with his words and think with his
thoughts.

"And yet still more powerful than this Titan of the world of mind was
the yearning of the German people for deliverance from the bonds of a
corrupted church system. Had no Luther arisen, a reformation would still
have come, and Germany would not have remained Catholic."

Dr. Döllinger delivered the lectures from which this extract is taken, after his quarrel with Vatican Romanism, in the museum at Munich, February, 1872. They were stenographically reported in the "Köllner-Zeitung," translated into English by Oxenham (London, 1872), and from English into French by Madame Hyacinthe-Loyson (*La réunion des églises*, Paris, 1880), and at last published by the author (1888).

This testimony is of special importance, owing to the acknowledged learning and ability of Döllinger as a Roman Catholic historian, and author of an elaborate work against the Reformation (1848, 3 vols.), consisting mostly of contemporaneous testimonies. He is thoroughly at home in the writings of the Reformers, and prepared a biographical sketch of Luther,[1] in which he severely criticises him for his opinions and conduct towards the Catholic Church, but does full justice to his intellectual greatness. He says, p. 51, " If we justly call him a great man, who, endowed with mighty powers and gifts, accomplishes great things, who, as a bold legislator in the realm of mind, makes millions subservient to his system, then the peasant's son of Möhra must be counted among the great, yea, the greatest men. This also is true, that he was a sympathizing friend, free of avarice and love of money, and ready to help others."

Döllinger was excommunicated for his opposition to the Vatican decree of infallibility (1870), but still remains a Catholic, and could not become a Protestant without retracting his work on the Reformation. He would, however, write a very different work now, and present the Reformation as a blessing rather than a calamity to Germany, in the light of the events which have passed since 1870. In one of his *Akademische Vorträge*, the first volume of which has just reached me (Nördlingen, 1888, p. 76), he makes the significant confession, that for many years the events in Germany from 1517 to 1552 were to him an unsolved riddle, and an object of sorrow and grief, seeing then only the result of division of the church and the nation into hostile camps; but that a closer study of the mediæval history of Rome and Germany, and the events of the last years, have given him a better understanding and more hopeful view of the renewed and reunited German nation as a noble instrument in the hands of Providence. This is as far as he can go from his standpoint.

§ 125. *Ein feste Burg ist unser Gott.*

I conclude this volume with Luther's immortal hymn, which is the best expression of his character, and reveals

---

[1] *Luther, eine Skizze*, Freiburg-i.-B., 1851. I have a copy with notes, which the old Catholic Bishop Reinkens, a pupil of Döllinger, kindly gave me in Bonn, 1886. It appeared in the first edition of Wetzer and Welte's *Kirchen-Lexikon*, vol. VI. 651 spp.

the secret of his strength as well as the moving power of the Reformation.[1]

A tower of strength[2] our God is still,
A good defense[3] and weapon;
He helps us free from all the ill
That us hath overtaken.
Our old, mortal foe[4]
Now aims his fell blow,
Great might and deep guile
His horrid coat-of-mail;[5]
On earth is no one like him.[6]

Ein' feste Burg ist unser Gott,
Ein' gute Wehr' und Waffen.
Er hilft uns frei aus aller Noth,
Die uns jetzt hat betroffen.
Der alt' böse Feind,
Mit Ernst er's jetzt meint;
Gross' Macht und viel List,
Sein grausam Rüstung ist,
Auf Erd' ist nicht sein's Gleichen.

By might of ours can naught be done:[7]
Our fate were soon decided.
But for us fights the champion,[8]
By God himself provided.
Who is this, ask ye?
Jesus Christ! 'Tis he!
Lord of Sabaoth,
True God and Saviour both,
Omnipotent in battle.[9]

Mit unsrer Macht ist nichts gethan,
Wir sind gar bald verloren:
Es streit't für uns der rechte Mann,
Den Gott hat selbst erkoren.
Fragst du, wer Der ist?
Er heisst Jesus Christ,
Der Herr Zebaoth,
Und ist kein andrer Gott;
Das Feld muss Er behalten.

Did devils fill the earth and air,[10]
All eager to devour us,
Our steadfast hearts need feel no care,
Lest they should overpower us.
The grim Prince of hell,
With rage though he swell,
Hurts us not a whit,
Because his doom is writ:
A little word can rout[11] him.

Und wenn die Welt voll Teufel wär'
Und wollt uns gar verschlingen,
So fürchten wir uns nicht zu sehr,
Es soll uns doch gelingen.
Der Fürst dieser Welt,
Wie sau'r er sich stellt,
Thut er uns doch nichts!
Das macht, er ist gericht't;
Ein Wörtlein kann ihn fällen.

[1] The translation was made by my esteemed friend, Professor Thomas Conrad Porter, D.D., of Easton, Penn., several years ago, but finished in February, 1888, and is almost equal to that of Thomas Carlyle in its reproduction of the rugged force of the original, and surpasses it in rhythmic accuracy. Comp. 468, 502, sq.

[2] Carlyle: "A safe stronghold."　　　　[3] "A trusty shield."—C.
[4] "The ancient prince of hell."—C.
[5] "Strong mail of craft and power He weareth in this hour."—C.
　　　　"In grim armor dight,
　　　　Much guile and great might."—Longfellow.
[6] "On earth is not his fellow."—C.
[7] "By force of arms we nothing can."—C.
[8] "The proper man."—C.　　　　[9] "Shall conquer in the battle."—C.
[10] "And were this world all devils over."—C.　　　　[11] "slay."—C.

The word of God will never yield
To any creature living;
He stands with us upon the field,
His grace and Spirit giving.
Take they child and wife,
Goods, name, fame, and life,
Though all this be done,
Yet have they nothing won:
The kingdom still remaineth.

[1] *stehen.*

Das Wort sie sollen lassen stan[1]
Und kein'n Dank dazu haben.
Er ist bei uns wohl auf dem Plan[2]
Mit seinem Geist und Gaben.
Nehmen sie den Leib,
Gut, Ehr', Kind und Weib;
Lass fahren dahin,
Sie haben's kein'n Gewinn;
Das Reich muss uns doch bleiben.

[2] *Kampfplatz.*

Facsimile of a Letter of Martin Luther, 1543.

1 Co 15

Absorpta est Mors in Victoriam

Esaia 25

בלע המות לנצח

praecipitavit Mortem in aeternum

weil Adam lebt (das ist sundiget) verschlinget
den Tod das leben. Wenn aber Christus stirbt
(das ist gerecht wird) verschlinget das leben den T[od]

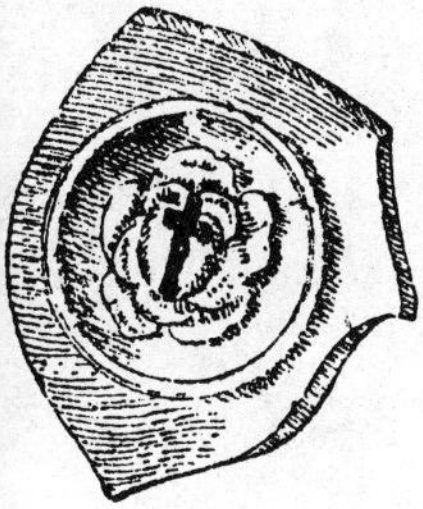

Das sey Gott gelobt das Christus
stirbt und recht

lebet

Martinus Luther.
1543.

ALPHABETICAL INDEX OF NAMES AND TOPICS

Adrian VI., Pope, 11, 392 sq.

Alber, Erasmus, 507.

Alber, Matthæus, 578, 620.

Albrecht (Albert), archbishop of Mainz, 9; intrusted with the sale of indulgences, 150 sq.; his character, 150; exposes a collection of relics, and is rebuked by Luther, 339; makes an apology, 340; sends a wedding present to Luther, 459.

Albrecht of Brandenburg, 508.

Albrecht, Duke of Prussia, 588, 590 sqq.

Aleander, papal legate, 287, 289, 293, 299, 301 sq., 306, 307.

Alexander VI., prohibits the printing of heretical books, 564.

Alexander, James W., 511.

Amandus, 591.

Amsdorf, 143; ordained bishop of Naumburg by Luther, 540; his later life, 542.

Anabaptists, 60, 65, 529, 545, 578, 602, 606 sqq.

Andreæ, John V., 666.

Anglican Church, its liturgy, 486.

Antichrist, views of the Reformers on, 529 sqq.

Apology of the Augsburg Confession, 715 sqq.

Aquinas, Thomas, on persecution, 50 sqq.; Luther's judgment of, 536.

Articles of Smalcald, 672.

Audin, 101 sq.

Augustin, St., on church authority, 39; on persecution, 54; views on the church (distinction of pure church and mixed church), 522; how appreciated by Luther, 534; catechetical works, 551; compared with Luther and Calvin, 736 sq.

Augsburg, Confession of, on the church, 529; on the Lord's Supper, 671; prepared by Melanchthon, and read before the Diet of Augsburg, 706 sqq.

Augsburg, Diet of, 1530, 696 sqq.

Augsburg, Reformation in, 577.

Augsburg, Treaty of Peace of, 686.

Babylonian captivity of the church, 213 sqq.

Baird, H. M., 56, 57.

Balan, 287.

Baptism, Luther's views on, 218 sq., 605 sqq.

Baptism of infants, 607 sqq.

Baur, F. C., 15.

Baxter, R., 80, 651 sq.

Beard, Charles, 12, 91.

Benedict XIV., on Bible-reading, 19.

Bergius, 652.

Bertheau, Karl, 653.

Berthold of Mainz, 564.

Beza defends the burning of Servetus, 70.

Bible translated by Luther, 340 sqq.

Bindseil, 363.

Bismarck, 600; compared with Luther, 734.

Bismarck and Leo XIII., 257.

Bohemian Brethren, 181, 508, 538.

Bora, Catharina von, Luther's wife, 456 sqq., 460, 645.

Bordier, H., 56.

Borthwick, Miss Jane, translator of German hymns, 511.

Bossuet, 92; on Luther, 491.

Brandenburg Confession, 598.

Braunschweig-Lüneburg, 576.

Bremen, Reformation of, 574.

Brenz (Brentius), 579; on the real presence, 622: at Marburg, 629.
Breslau, Reformation of, 573 sq.
Brieger, 94, 287, 288.
Briesmann, Joh., 591.
Briggs, Charles A., 651 sq., 653.
Browne, Robert, on church and state, 76, 545.
Bucer, Martin, 479, 481, 571 sqq.; 619; 623; at Marburg, 636 sq.; B. and the Tetrapolitan Confession, 719; visits Luther on the Coburg, 729.
Bugenhagen, 347, 467, 567, 575, 621 sq.
Bull of Excommunication, 227, 235 sqq.
Burkhardt, 100; on Luther's testimony at Worms, 309.
Burning of books, 563 sq.

Cædmon, 497.
Cajetan, Cardinal, his interview with Luther, 172 sqq.
Calvin, John, on reason and revelation, 32; on the canon, 38; on church union, 46; on persecution, 65 sqq.; defends the burning of Servetus, 70; his marriage, 478; on the Church, 532; relation to Luther, 659; tribute to Luther, 661; compared with Luther and Zwingli, 669; his doctrine on the Lord's Supper, 678 sqq.; compared with St. Augustin and Luther, 736 sq.
Camerarius, Joachim, 568, 570.
Candlish, 520.
Canstein, 349.
Capito, 571.
Caracciolo, 289.
Carlstadt, on the canon, 35; in sympathy with Luther, 143; at the Leipzig Disputation, 179; in the disturbances at Wittenberg, 379 sqq.; his end, 390 sq.; connection with the Peasants' War, 441; view on the Lord's Supper, 618 sq.; 639.
Catechetical instruction, 551.
Catechisms of Luther, 550 sqq.
Catechisms, Lutheran, Heidelberg, Anglican, and Westminster, compared, 555 sqq.
Catharinus, Luther's book against, 295.
Catholic, origin of the term, 522.
Catholic Church, see Church.
Celibacy, clerical, 474 sqq.

Censorship of books, 564 sqq.
Charles II., 80.
Charles V., his election as German emperor, and public and private character, 262 sqq.; his ecclesiastical polity, 272 sqq.; relation to Luther, 275; abdication and cloister-life, 276 sqq.; his intolerance, 283; his death, 284; opens the Diet of Worms, 288; hesitates between religion and politics, 290; cites Luther to Worms, 293; his judgment of Luther, 306; decides against Luther, but respects his safe-conduct, 314 sqq.; and the Pope, 687 sqq.; crowning of, 693: at the Diet of Augsburg, 696 sqq.
Christoffel, 630.
Church, different views of the, 520 sqq.; in the Bible, 521; in the creeds, 522: according to Augustin, 522; Wiclif, 524; Hus, 525; among the Reformers, 526 sqq.
Church and State, 518, 542 sqq.
Church festivals, 493.
Church government and discipline, 515; Episcopal, 516; Lutheran, 517; Presbyterian, 518; Congregational, 518.
Clerical marriages and family life, 473 sqq.
Clement VII., 395, 396, 687, 693 sq.
Cochlæus, 287, 293, 350, 562, 702.
Coleridge, S. T., on the burning of Servetus, 69.
Collin, 629.
Confutation, papal, of the Augsburg Confession, 715 sqq.
Congregational church polity, 518, 538.
Conscience, liberty of, 311.
Consubstantiation, 671.
Cordus, Euricius, 636.
Covenanters, 80.
Cox, Miss or Mrs. Frances Elizabeth, translator of German hymns, 511.
Cranmer, Archbishop, 480, 570.
Crato von Crafftheim, 574.
Cromwell on toleration, 78.
Crotus, Rubeanus, 296, 377.

Dalton, Hermann, 64.
Decius, Nicolaus, 508.
Denominationalism and Protestantism, 43 sqq.

Dévay, 655.
Devil, described by Luther, 335.
De Wette, his edition of Luther's letters, 100, very often quoted.
Dexter, H. M., 75, 76, 78.
Didymus, 380.
Dietenberger, 350, 364.
Dietrich, Veit, 507, 542.
Diets, of Worms, 287; Nürnberg, 392 ; Speier, 683, 690 sq.; Augsburg, 696 sqq.
Dorner, 95 ; on the defects of Lutheran ethics, 667 ; on the words of institution, 674 sq.
Dort, Synod of, expels the Arminians, 71, 87.
Döllinger, his work on the Reformation, 23, 96 ; his judgment of Melanchthon, 187; his protest against papal infallibility, 313; his judgment on Luther's Bible version, 361; on Luther's doctrine of the slavery of the will, 430 ; on Erasmus, 433 ; on the humanists, 435 ; his tribute to Luther, 740 sq.
Drews, on Pirkheimer, 439.
Drummond, on Erasmus, 401, 402, etc.
Dury, John, 657.

Ebert, Paul, 507.
Eck, of Ingolstadt, writes against the Theses of Luther, 168 ; at the Disputation in Leipzig, 178 sqq., 180 sq.; instigating the bull of excommunication, 227; his German version of the Bible, 364; at the Diet of Augsburg, 702.
Eck, of Trier, puts the questions to Luther at Worms, 301, 303 sqq.
Edward VI., 72.
Edwards, Thomas, against toleration, 77.
Egelhaaf, 96.
Ein feste Burg, 468, 502 sq., 742 sq.
Elizabeth, Queen, 73.
Emser, 294, 350, 360, 363, 398.
England, Reformation of, 87 sq.; Church of, 516.
Eoban, 296, 377, 408.
Episcopacy, retained, 516 sq.; Luther's views of, 517.

Epistolæ obscurorum Virorum, 197, 201.
Erasmus, 18, 356 ; his judgment on Melanchthon, 186 ; his position, 401 ; sketch of his life, 404 ; his religious opinions, 411 ; his works, 415 ; his relation to the Reformation, 421 ; his relation to Luther, 422 ; doctrine on free-will, 428 ; final alienation from Luther and the Reformation, 433 ; on Luther's marriage, 459 ; on the marriage of Œcolampadius, 479 ; complains of the rapid sale of Luther's works, 561 ; on the eucharist, 621.
Erfurt, Luther at, 109 ; passing through, 296.
Erichson, 630.
Erik, Duke of Brunswick, 307.
Esch, John, 601.
Eucharistic controversies, 612 sqq.; ethics of, 662 sqq.; theories of, compared, 669 sqq., 612 sqq., 662 sqq.
Evangelical, meaning of, 692.
Evangelical Union, 599 ; motto of, 650 sq.

Feige, John, 640.
Ferdinand and Isabella, 272.
Findlater, Mrs. Eric, 511.
Fisher, G. P., 12, 91.
Flacius, 573.
Flysteden, Peter, 601.
Foster, F. H., 630.
Formula Concordiæ, on the doctrine of the Lord's Supper, 670, 672 sq.
Frank, Gregor, 652.
Frederick the Wise, Elector of Saxony, founds the University of Wittenberg, 132 sqq.; calls Luther, 135 ; his dream, 167 ; calls Melanchthon to Wittenberg, 188 ; consults Erasmus about Luther, 232 ; declines the German crown, and nominates King Charles of Spain, 268 ; is pleased with Luther's speech at Worms, 307; protects him on the Wartburg, 332 ; his cautious policy, 381 ; forbids Luther to return to Wittenberg, yet allows him to remain, 383 ; Luther's letter to him, 383 ; his death and character, 450.

Frederick I., 597.

Frederick II., 598.

Frederick III., 453.

Frederick William, Elector, 596, 598 sq.

Frederick William III., of Prussia, 599.

Frederick William IV., of Prussia, 156, 599.

Freedom and Toleration, 686 sq.

Freedom, Christian, Luther's tract on, 220 sqq.

French Protestantism, 87.

Friedberg, E., 515, 520.

Froben, John, 399, 408; see Erasmus.

Frundsberg, Georg von, his words of encouragement to Luther at Worms, 302.

Gebhardt, O. von, 357.

Geiler of Kaisersberg, 9.

Georg, Duke of Saxony, at Leipzig, 178, 181; at Worms, 292 ; hinders the Reformation, 567.

Georg von Polenz, bishop of Samland, 539.

German Nobility, Luther's Address to the, 206 sqq.

Germany and the Reformation, 97 sqq.

Gillespie, on toleration, 75.

Gillett, C. R., 651.

Glapio, John, confers with Brück at Worms, 291; with Bucer and Sickingen at the Ebernburg, 299.

Glareanus, on Erasmus, 427.

Goethe, quoted, 311, 335; on Protestant pastors, 482; on Luther, 739.

Goldsmith, Oliver, his "Vicar of Wakefield," 482.

Goodwin, Dr., on religious liberty, 78.

Gottschick, 520.

Gregory VII., 475.

Grimm, Jacob, on Luther's merit for the German language, 359.

Grimm, Wilibald, 340, 359.

Hagen, 321.

Hallam, on Luther, 732.

Hamburg, Reformation of, 575.

Hamilton, Patrick, 587.

Hardwick, 90.

Hare, Archdeacon, on Luther, 738.

Harms, Claus, 604.

Harnack, Adolf, 104, 261.

Harnack, Theod., 103.

Hassencamp, 579 sqq., 630.

Haupt, Hermann, 353.

Häusser, 90 and passim.

Hedio, 571, 629 sqq., 633, 636, 719.

Hefele, Bishop, on Hus and Sigismund, 312.

Hegel, on Luther's Bible version, 341.

Heidelberg Catechism, 555 sqq.; teaching on the Lord's Supper, 681.

Heine, on Luther, 739.

Heinrich, Duke of Saxony, 568.

Heinrich von Zütphen, 574, 601.

Heliand, 497.

Henry VIII., 72; his controversy with Luther, 396 sqq.

Heppe, 95, 579, 629.

Herder, 482.

Hergenröther, 89, 91 and passim.

Herrgott, 567, 602.

Hering, 143.

Hess, John, 573.

Hesse, Reformation of, 579 sqq.

Holland, Reformation of, 87.

Homberg, Synod of, 581 sq.

Hooper, Bishop, on separation of church and state, 76, 545.

Hospinian, 630.

Hübmaier, 578, 606 sqq.

Huguenots persecuted, 56 sq.; 596.

Hus, 181, 209 ; his views on the Church, 525, 527.

Hutten, Ulrich von, his relation to Luther and the Reformation, 196 sqq.; his attacks on Rome, 198 sqq.; his character, 200 ; during the Diet of Worms, 292, 308 sq., 323 ; controversy with Erasmus, 427.

Hyacinthe, Père, 476.

Hymnody, evangelical, 494 sqq.

Index librorum prohibitorum, 566.

Indulgences, 146 sqq.

In necessariis unitas, 650 sqq.

Innocent III., 18, 56.

Irenics, 650 sqq.

Janssen, Joh., 96 sq., 151, 487, and very often quoted in Literature.

Jews, Luther's views on, 61.

John a Lasco, 64.
John Frederick the Magnanimous, elector of Saxony, 132, 452 sq.; 706.
John the Constant, elector of Saxony, 132, 452; institutes church visitation, 547; his stand at the Diet of Speier, 691; at the Diet of Augsburg, 697 sqq.; 700; his death, 706.
Jonas, Justus, 296, 458, 507, 552, 567, 639.
Jostes, 353.
Julius II., 128, 149.
Jürgens, 101, 137, 157, 158, and passim.
Justification by faith, 20 sqq., 122 sqq.; 667.
Juterbog, 154.

Kahnis, 16, 96, 674 sq., and passim.
Kaiser (or Käser), 602.
Kampschulte, 110, 297, 375, 377.
Kapp, quoted, 559, 561, 565 sq.
Kawerau, 100, 139.
Kehrein, 340.
Keller, Ludwig, 91, 118, 353, 578.
Klarenbach, Adolph, 601.
Klimesch, 342.
Knaake, 100, 156.
Knox, John, 88, 480, 666.
Koch, 494.
Kohler, 516.
Kolde, 103, 104, 340 and passim.
Köstlin, Julius, Life of Luther, etc., 103; judgment on Luther, 468; judgment on Luther and Zwingli, 668 sq.; very often quoted in the sections on Luther (see Luther).
Kradolfer, 629.
Krafft, W., 340, 344, 352.
Krauss, Alfred, 520.
Krauth, Ch. P., 95, 613, 664.

Lambert of Avignon, 518, 579, 582 sqq., 586 sq., 639, 649.
Lange, John, 143.
Lauterbach, 468, 519, 542.
Lecky, 26, 80.
Leipzig Disputation, 178 sqq.
Lenz, Max, 579, 581, 629.
Leo X., 8, 149, 169, 170, 175, 226; excommunicates Luther, 227 sqq.; prohibits the printing of heretical books, 565.

Leo XIII., on Thomas Aquinas and religious liberty, 57 sq.; makes peace with Bismarck, 257.
Liberty, religious, 50 sqq., 311 sq., 544.
Link, Wenzeslaus, 143, 206, 570.
Lord's Supper, the, restored, 492; controversies on the, 612 sqq.; views of Luther, Zwingli, and Calvin on the, 663 sqq.
Löscher, V. E., 94, and often quoted.
Loserth, Joh., 524 sq.
Louis XIV., 57.
Louisa Henrietta of Brandenburg, 596.
Lücke, 651.
Luther, on the Scriptures, 16 sqq., 34 sqq.; on justification, 20 sqq., 122 sqq.; on the priesthood of the laity, 24; on reason and revelation, 30 sq.; on James, Hebrews, etc., 35, 42; on inspiration, 36; on religious liberty, 59 sqq.; on the Jews, 61 sq.; literature on, 99 sqq.; his youth and training, 105 sqq.; at Erfurt, 109; his conversion, 112 sqq.; his monastic life, 113 sqq.; relation to Staupitz, 117 sqq.; religious experience, 122 sqq.; ordination to the priesthood, 125; journey to Rome, 126 sqq.; professor in Wittenberg, 132, 135 sqq.; relation to mysticism, 141 sqq.; penitential psalms, 143; opposition to Tetzel, 148 sqq.; publication of the 95 Theses, 155 sqq.; his last judgment on Tetzel, 169; against Prierias, 170; conference with Cajetan, 172 sqq.; with Miltitz, 175 sqq.; at the Leipzig Disputation, 178 sqq.; relation to Melanchthon, 190 sqq.; relation to Ulrich von Hutten, 196 sqq.; crusade against popery, 203 sqq.; Address to the German Nobility, 206 sqq.; Babylonian captivity of the church, 213 sqq.; Christian freedom, 220 sqq.; last letter to Leo X., 226; his excommunication, 227 sqq.; burns the Pope's bull, 247 sqq.; journey to Worms, 294 sqq.; his testimony before the Diet of Worms, 300 sqq; reflections on his testimony, 311; private conferences with, after the Diet, 314 sqq.; as a popular writer, 321 sq.; on the Wartburg, 330 sqq.; his

conflicts with the Devil, 334 sqq.; his translation of the Bible, 340 sqq.; revision of his translation, 366; his judgment of Melanchthon's theology, 373 sq.; his return to Wittenberg, 382 sqq.; restores order, 387 sqq.; controversy with Henry VIII., 396 sqq.; relation to Erasmus, 422, 429; on the slavery of the human will, 430; advocates, and then abandons, the cause of the peasants, 445; urges the suppression of the rebellion, 446; his views on the three Saxon electors, 453; his marriage, 454 sqq.; his home-life, 460 sqq.; letter to his son Hans, 464; his temperance, 465; his hospitality, 467; on astronomy and astrology, 469 sq.; his income and property, 471; his personal appearance, 472; reforms public worship, 486 sqq.; as a preacher, 490 sq.; as a hymnist, 502 sq.; on common schools, 512 sqq.; on church government and discipline, 516, 518 sqq.; views of the catholic church, 527 sqq.; on the Pope and the Roman church, 529 sq.; on the value of tradition, 531; judgments concerning the church fathers, 534 sqq.; his views of the ministry and episcopal succession, 537; asserts the right of a congregation to self-government, 538; ordains a deacon, 539; consecrates a bishop, 540; and defends the daring act, 541; advocates separation of church and state, 543 sq.; unfavorable view of princes, 544; transfers to them the supervision of the churches, 545; but complains of them, 546; urges church-visitation in Saxony, 547 sqq.; his catechisms, 550 sqq.; rapid spread of his publications, 561 sqq.; preaches in Leipzig, 568; relation to Lambert of Avignon, 582 sq., 585; relation to Albrecht and the Reformation in Prussia, 590 sqq.; on Protestant martyrs, 601; against the Anabaptists, 606 sqq.; against Carlstadt, 617 sqq.; on John Wessel, 618; against Zwingli, 620 sqq., 654; teaches the ubiquity of Christ's body, 626, 628; his conduct at Marburg, 632 sqq.; letter to his wife from Marburg,

645; his last attack upon the Sacramentarians, 654; on praying and cursing, 657; his relation to Calvin, 659 sq.; praised by Calvin, 661; view on the Lord's Supper, 663; compared with Zwingli, 669; his eucharistic doctrine, 669 sqq.; his influence on the Augsburg Confession, 723; sojourn on the Coburg, 723 sqq.; his last labors, 729; his public character and place in history, 730 sqq.; compared with St. Augustin and Calvin, 736 sqq.; Ein feste Burg, German and English, 741.

Lutheran Church, 517; present views on eucharist, 663, 674. See Luther, Melanchthon, and other titles.

Lyra, Nicolaus, 356, 536.

Macaulay on Catholicism and Protestantism, 261 sq.

Magdeburg, Reformation of, 573.

Maimbourg, 92.

Manuel, Nicolaus, 327.

Marburg Colloquy, 629; facsimile of signatures, 631; the fifteen Articles of, 646; close and effect, 647 sqq.

Marburg, University of, 586.

Marheinecke, 95 and passim.

Martensen, Bishop, 663, 667.

Martin, Henri, on Calvin, 678 (note).

Mary, in mediæval poetry, 500 sq.

Mass, 485–487, 490, 492.

Mathesius, 101, 152, 468, 508, 542 and passim.

Matrimony, Luther's views of, 219.

Maurenbrecher, 96 and passim.

Melanchthon, on church union, 46; approves the execution of Servetus, 62; literature on, 183; his training, 185 sqq.; early labors, 189 sqq.; relation to Luther, 191 sqq.; his theology, 368 sqq.; dedicates his Loci to Henry VIII., and declines call to England, 399; on Luther's marriage, 460: on astrology, 470; his marriage, 478: on the mass, 485, 489; on Luther as a preacher, 491; on episcopacy, 517; on the church, 529 sq.; on the Pope and the Roman church, 530 sq.; on the ministry, 537, 540; justifies the transfer of episcopal power to the civil magistrate as a matter of temporary necessity, 545 ; complains of abuses, 546 sq.; his instructions to church visitors, 548 ; his conduct at Marburg, 632 sqq., 637 sq.; his part in the sacramental conflict, 654 sqq.; at the Diet of Augsburg, 695 sqq.; 701 sqq.; 706 sqq. See Augsburg Confession.

Meistersänger, 500.

Meldenius, Rupertus, 650 sqq.

Merle d'Aubigné, 90, 95, 288, 333 and *passim*.

Meurer, 101 and *passim*.

Meyer, Joh. Friedrich von, 349.

Michael Angelo, 128.

Michelet, 101 sq., 335.

Mills, Henry, 512.

Miltitz, Carl von, conference with Luther, 175 sqq.; censures Tetzel, 152.

Milton, on persecution, 57.

Minnesänger, 500.

Mitchell, Alex. F., 76, 79.

Möhler, quoted, 530, 533.

Moltke, 600.

Moore, on the Reformers, 475.

Moravians, 598.

Mörikofer, 630.

Moritz, Duke of Saxony, 132, 568.

Mosellanus, 179; on Luther's personal appearance at Leipzig, 180.

Motley, 273.

Müller, Julius, 520, 613.

Münchmeyer, 520.

Münzer, Thomas, 381, 442.

Murner, Thomas, 327 sq.

Mysticism, Luther's relation to, 141 sq.

Neander, 598.

Nevin, J. W., 613.

Nürnberg, Diets of, 392, 395.

Nürnberg, Peace of, 706.

Nürnberg, Reformation of, 569 sqq.

Œcolampadius, 409 ; on Erasmus, 412 ; controversy with Pirkheimer, 437; his marriage, 479 ; his views on the Lord's Supper, 620 sqq.; at Marburg, 637 sqq.; contending with Luther, 642 sq.

Osiander, Andreas, 570, 595.

Owen, Dr., on toleration, 79.

Pack, Otto von, 689 sq.

Panzer, 340.

Papacy and the Reformation, historical view of, 252 sqq.

Peasants' War, 434 sqq.

Persecution of heretics, defended by Augustin and Thomas Aquinas, 54 sqq.; in the Netherlands, 56 ; in St. Bartholomew's Night, 56 ; under Louis XIV., 57 ; of the Waldenses, 57; never condemned by the Pope, but indirectly approved by the papal Syllabus of 1864, 57 sq.

Peucer, Caspar, 64.

Philip, Landgrave of Hesse, visits Luther at Worms, 308 ; his bigamy, 481, 581 (note); introduces the Reformation in Hesse, 579; his character, 580 sq.; founds the University of Marburg, 586 ; convenes the Conference at Marburg, 630 ; his political aspiration and relation to Zwingli, 633 sq.; intercedes for peace, 642, 646; at the Diet of Augsburg, 699, 704.

Pierre d'Ailly, on the Lord's Supper, 615.

Pirkheimer, Wilibald, 181, 434 sqq.

Pius IV., 11, 18.

Pius IX., condemns Bible societies, 19.

Planck, 95.

Polenz, Georg von, 592 sqq.

Poliander, 591.

Pollich, 134.

Popery. See Papacy.

Popular literature in favor of the Reformation, 321 sqq., 560 sqq.

Presbyterian church polity, 518, 583, 585.

Presbyterians in Scotland, persecuted, 80.

Prierias, Sylvester, 171.

Priesthood of the laity, 24.

Printing-press and the Reformation, 560 sqq.

Protest, the, at Speier, 690 sq.

Protestants, origin and meaning of the name of, 692.

Protestantism and Romanism, 3 sqq.; and Rationalism, 26 sqq.; and Denominationalism, 43 sqq.; and religious liberty, 50 sq.; propagation of, 558 sqq.; persecution of, 600 sqq.

Prussia, Reformation of, 588 sqq.

Prussian Union, 598 sqq.

Psalms, Luther's commentary on, 138 sq.; Penitential Psalms, 143.

Puritanism, 74, 88.

Queis, Erhard von, bishop of Pomesania, 539, 593.

Rachel, 343.

Ranke, Leopold von, 91, 96 ; on the papacy, 260; on Luther's Little Catechism, 551; on the spread of the Reformation, 558 ; on Luther as an author, 559 ; very often referred to in Literature.

Rationalism and Protestantism, 26 sqq.

Reformation, necessity of, 8 sqq.; preparation for, 12 sqq.; genius of, 14 sqq.; principles of, 16 sqq.; literature, 89 sqq., 94 sqq.; Reformation and the Papacy, 252 sqq.

Reinkens, Old Catholic Bishop, 476.

Religious liberty and Protestantism, 50 sqq., 543 sq.

Reuchlin, 187.

Reusch, 121, 566.

Reuss, Edw., 340, 356.

Revision of Luther's Bible, and of the English version, 366 sqq.

Revival of letters, 13. (See Erasmus.)

Rhegius, Urbanus, 576, 577, 728.

Richter, A. L., 515.

Ritschl, 118, 520.

Rome, sacking of, 687 sq.

Rommel, 630.

Rörer (Rorarius), 347, 348; ordained deacon by Luther, 539.

Rosenblatt, Wilibrandis, 479.

Rothe, R., against the distinction between the visible and the invisible church, 520, 526.

Russell, Arthur Tozer, 511.

Rutherford, Samuel, against toleration, 76.

Sachs, Hans, writes for the Reformation, 324, 506, 507, 569.

Sacerdotalism, 603.

Sacrament of the Lord's Supper, 215; controversies on the, 612 sqq.; contest at Marburg, 632 sqq.; Luther's Short Conf., 654 sqq.; theories of, 663 sqq.

Saxony, Reformation of, 567 sqq.

St. Bartholomew, Massacre of, 56.

St. Peter's Church in Rome, 149.

Scandinavia, Lutheran Church of, 516.

Schaff, Philip, quoted, 14, 19, 46, 50, 358, 368, 512, 523, 528.

Schenkel, 14, 90, 287.

Scheurl, 120, 143.

Schleiermacher, 598.

Schools, common, 512 sqq.

Schneesing, 508.

Schneider, 137, 494, 503.

Schwenkfeld, Caspar, 574, 654, 656.

Scotland, Reformation of, 88.

Scriptures and tradition, 16 sqq.

Seckendorf, 95 and passim.

Seidemann, 100,178.

Sermon in Protestant worship, 490.

Servetus, 62, 65 sqq., 70.

Sickingen, Franz von, 201 sqq.

Sigismund, John, Elector of Brandenburg, 596 sq.; his Confession, 598.

Sleidan, 89.

Smalcaldian League, 706.

Spalatin, 89, 94, 144, 287, 298, 304, 306, 310, 346, 452, 460, 582.

Spalding, M. J., 92, 473, 475, 480.

Speier, Diet of (1526), 683.

Speier, Diet of (1529), 690.

Spener, 665.

Spengler, Lazarus, 570.

Speratus, Paul, 508, 591.

Stahl, 515.

Staupitz, 117 sqq., 174.

Steitz, 287.

Stevens, Henry, 351, 354.

Stier, Rud., 349.

Strassburg, Reformation of, 571 sqq.

Strauss, D. F., on Ulrich von Hutten, 196, 200 ; on Erasmus, 421 ; on Pirkheimer, 434.

Sturm, Jacob, 633, 644.

Sunday, observance of, 493 sq.

Superintendents, 517.

Swiss Reformation, 87.

Syllabus, Papal, 27.

Teplensis, Codex, of the German New Testament, 342 sq.

Territorial system, beginning of, 684.

Tetrapolitan Confession, 718 sqq.

Tetzel, John, 148, 151 sqq., 169.

Teutonic Knights in Prussia, 589 sq.
Theologia Germanica, 142.
Theses, Ninety-five, 155 sqq.; the full text of, 160 sqq.
Theses controversy, 167 sqq.
Thuanus (De Thou), 92
Toleration and intolerance, 50 sqq., 71 sqq.; and freedom, 686.
Toleration, Act of, 81.
Tollin, H., on Servetus, 69.
Transubstantiation, rejected by Luther, 215.
Tschackert, 588, 593.
Tyndale, William, 587.

Ubiquity of Christ's body, 625, 628.
Ullmann, 12.
Ulrich of Württemberg, 579, 639.
United States, Constitution of, guarantees religious liberty, 81 sq.
Ursinus, 574.
Usteri, 629, 646.

Voes, Henry, 601.

Wackernagel, 495, 496, etc.
Waddington, 90.
Walch, ed. of Luther's Works, 99; and very often quoted in the sections on Luther.
Waldis, Burkhard, 507.
Walther, 99.
War panic, occasioned by Pack, 689.
Wartburg, 332 sq.
Weisse, Michael, 508.
Weller, 542.
Wesley, John, translator of German hymns, 510; followed the example of Luther in ordaining a superintendent, 540; his importance, 736.
Wessel, John, 617 sq.
Westminster Confession, on religious liberty, 77, 543; on the Pope, 533; on the Lord's Supper, 681 sq.

White, Andrew D., 470.
Wiclif, his views on the church, 524 sq.
William I., Emperor of Germany, 600.
Williams, Roger, on toleration, 75, 84.
William and Mary, 81, 88.
Wimpina, Conrad, 168.
Winkler, George, 601.
Wittenberg Concordia, 654.
Wittenberg, University of, 132 sqq; city of, 134.
Wolsey, Cardinal, 9.
Worms, Diet of, 287 sqq.; Edict of, 318 sqq., and often alluded to.
Wordsworth, William, on Protestant pastor, 483.
Worship, public, reform of, 484 sqq.
Wulfila, Gothic version of the Bible, 342.

Ximenes, 18.

Yuste, 278.

Zell, Catharine, 633.
Zwickau Prophets, 380 sq.
Zwilling, Gabriel, 380.
Zwingli, Ulrich, on reason and revelation, 32; on the canon, 37; on persecution, 65 sq.; his death, 87; his marriage, 479; on the visible and invisible church, 525; his influence in South Germany, 578; his controversy with Luther, 620 sqq.; relation to Anabaptists, 609; his view on the Lord's Supper, 604 sq., 612, 620 sqq.; writes against Luther, 623 sqq.; at Marburg, 632 sqq.; prayer before conference, 636; his character misunderstood by Luther, 664; his tribute to Luther, 667 sq.; his theory of the Lord's Supper, 676 sq.; his Confession to Charles V. at the Diet of Augsburg, 721 sq.